LEGACY OF A DIVIDED NATION

DATE DUE

~~MY 17 '99~~			

DEMCO 38-296

To the memory of Anwar Jamal Kidwai

and for Ravinder Kumar

MUSHIRUL HASAN

Legacy of a Divided Nation

India's Muslims
since Independence

WestviewPress

A Division of HarperCollins*Publishers*

Published in the United States of America by
Westview Press, Inc.,
5500 Central Avenue, Boulder, Colorado 80301-2877

h or by
ng
torage
iting

le from

ISBN 0-8133-3339-3 (HC), 0-8133-3340-7 (pbk.)

Typeset by Print Line, New Delhi
Printed in India by Thomson Press (India) Ltd

CONTENTS

PREFACE AND ACKNOWLEDGEMENTS

This book is a historian's journey into India's agonising past and its postcolonial predicaments. I hope it will stimulate discussion on the country's partition and contribute to the debates in which scholars of South Asia are currently engaged about the future direction of Indian society. At a time when India celebrates its fiftieth anniversary of independence, the legacy of that historic and momentous event would surely be an important subject of scholarly engagement.

It has not been easy for a historian to traverse the rough terrain of Indian politics in the post-independence decades. Many contemporary themes and issues were unfamiliar to me. Then, I found to my dismay, that government sources were not accessible and that primary data on the Muslim communities on the post-independence period were inadequate; yet a number of ill-founded theories were reflected in the growing volume of literature on Islam and India's Muslims. If I have overcome some of these hazards, it is owing to the unflagging support of several institutions and scholars. It is hard to list them all, but I am especially grateful to Aijaz Ahmad, Ramchandra Guha, Claudia Liebeskind, Ritu Menon, Joane Nagel and Achin Vanaik who scrutinised the manuscript at different stages and made invaluable suggestions. Francis Robinson offered me many constructive comments which have helped clarify and improve the presentation. I have also received much encouragement from V.N. Datta who read the final draft meticulously and made substantial stylistic changes. So did the publisher Christopher Hurst and his colleague Michael Dwyer. I thank them for preparing the groundwork for the publication of this book and for their patience and understanding.

Many of the chapters of this book were presented in conferences or seminars at the Universities in Aurangabad, Calcutta, Chandigarh and Kurukshetra, and at the following institutions: Sahitya Akademy and Max Mueller Bhavan, Delhi; the Institute of Advanced Study, Berlin; the Rockefeller Foundation, Bellagio; the British Association for South Asian Studies, Cambridge; and the Asian History Congress held in Hong Kong. In December 1993 I lectured at Amherst College, Columbia University, the University of Michigan and the University of Pennsylvania. In February 1995, I was invited as an Associate Professor to lecture at the Centre d'Etudes de l'Inde et de l'Asie du Sud in Paris. As the 'South Asia Lecturer' for 1996 in Australia, I shared my work with colleagues in Perth,

Adelaide and Sydney, and at the Australian Asian Studies Conference in Melbourne. I have had many fruitful discussions at these places, though sadly not in my own University which I cannot enter for fear of violence and intimidation. That this can happen in the heart of India's capital does not seem to worry many people.

Shauq tha jo yaar ke kuche hame layaa tha Mir
Paon me taqat kahan itni ke ab ghar jaiye

This brings me to my harrowing experiences since 21 April 1992 and to the enormous debt I owe to a number of colleagues and friends who have contributed to the making of this book. They rallied to my side when I was vilified, assaulted and eventually hounded out of the Jamia Millia Islamia because of my comment on the banning of the *Satanic Verses*. Some colleagues at the University faced the fundamentalist onslaught at great personal risk and were exemplary in their courage and tenacity. I appreciate the warm friendship and camaraderie of many others who have been concerned about me and my future in Jamia. I take this opportunity to express my gratitude and thanks to Rukun Advani, Aijaz Ahmad, Muzaffar Alam, Aziz Al-Azmeh, Rajendra Bajpai, Chris Bayly, Bharati Bhargava, Rajeev and Tani Bhargava, Sudeep Banerji, Amrita Basu, Arun Chacko, Kunal and Shubhra Chakrabarty, Raj Chandavarkar, Sudhir Chandra, Suranjan Das, Asghar Ali Engineer, Francine Frankel, Satish Jacob, Habeeb and Atiya Kidwai, Rajni Kothari, Dharma Kumar, D.A. Low, David Ludden, Barbara Metcalf, Gail Minault, Ranjit Nair, Ashis Nandy, A.G. Noorani, R.M. Pal, K.N. Panikkar, Prabhat and Utsa Patnaik, Imrana Qadeer, S.K. Rao, Rajat Ray, Kumkum Sangari, D.L. Sheth, Suresh Shukla, Amrik Singh, Sumit and Tanika Sarkar, Romila Thapar, Hari Vasudevan and Achin Vanaik. Organisations like *Sehmat* in Delhi, the Communist Party of India, and the Communist Party of India (Marxist) were consistently supportive; just a handful of political leaders, among them a scion of a once dominant family in Jamia, endorsed, organised and sustained the student protest. Fellow-historians throughout the country expressed solidarity, though my former teachers in the department of History at Aligarh's Muslim University, including some with radical pretensions, were not among them. It is fortunate that there were so few like them in the academic world.

Saeed Naqvi and Aruna Naqvi were kind, generous and indulgent. Saeed Bhai, with his characteristic enthusiasm, took up the cudgels on my behalf in his column and alienated many tall poppies in the establishment. I am specially grateful to Anuradha and Kamal Mitra Chenoy, Prabhat Patnaik, Praful Bidwai and Seema Mustafa for sharing my anxieties and mobilising opinion in my support. I greatly value their warm friendship. I appreciate the sympathy and understanding of South Asian scholars overseas, including Hamza Alavi, Milton Israel, Francis Robinson and

Ashutosh Varshney, who expressed their views in writings. Hamza Alavi, for one, shared his anguish with two Marxist historians, one in Aligarh and the other in Calcutta. 'From what I know', he wrote on 26 April 1995, 'the Jamia authorities seem to have proved incapable of taking a stand against the fundamentalists. ... Rather they seem to have surrendered to them. ... It is extraordinary that this should be happening in India which has taken such pride in its secularism.' He continued: 'I am inclined to think that this issue has gone far beyond that of a single individual academic having to sort out his problems privately with his own institution. ... it has now become a wider issue, one of principle that should concern the entire Indian academic community and indeed Indian society. What kind of society are you trying to build? Surely this is a test. As a Pakistani who has a long record of respect and friendship for his Indian colleagues I feel that I must personally do something to draw your attention to this outrageous situation.'

Newspaper editors—Mohan Chiraghi, Vinod Mehta and Dileep Padgaonkar—allowed the 'Jamia affair' to be covered extensively and underlined the climate of intolerance on the campus. 'The issue', as one of them pointed out, 'is no longer personal. The question today is much larger. What kind of society do we want to live in? A society where the individual's thought-process is controlled by a handful of self-appointed guardians of public morality, or a genuinely democratic society which guarantees every individual the right to free speech?' Many others commented on the unedifying spectacle of a leading Congress Muslim politician using the *Satanic Verses* issue, and the forces of religious intolerance it was bound to release, as a means both to regain leverage in the affairs of the Jamia and to bring to heel, perhaps to bring down, somebody like me who was expected to sweep away old lines of patronage and old cosy (corrupt) habits and endeavour to modernise the University. As my innings on the unfriendly Jamia turf comes to a close, I wish to acknowledge their solidarity which has been a great source of strength and acted as a stimulus to writing this book.

My greatest debt, personally and intellectually, is to Zoya, who has been an active partner in my intellectual life for nearly two decades. She worked her way through the Jamia crisis with poise and dignity. Her energy and optimism fortified my confidence and enabled me to withstand an ill-advised campaign. My situation in Jamia may not change, but we are comforted by the electorate's better judgement in not electing them to parliament in the recent elections, including a Congress Muslim politician who was caught with dirty hands in the agitation.

This book is dedicated to the late Anwar Jamal Kidwai, a man committed to liberal and secular values and imbued with the zeal to reform, change and modernise Muslim society and education, and to Ravinder Kumar, Director of the Nehru Memorial Museum and Library in New

change and modernise Muslim society and education, and to Ravinder Kumar, Director of the Nehru Memorial Museum and Library in New Delhi, for his interest in this work and for his advice and support on many personal and scholarly matters. It would embarrass him if I were to detail his numerous acts of kindness and generosity towards me.

Likhte rahe junoon ki hikayaat-i khun chekaan
Harchand is mein haath hamare qalam hue

It would be intellectually satisfying if, in some ways, this book is regarded as a personal manifesto, a statement through the history of partition and its aftermath, of the values which India's Muslims should cherish, of the national priorities they should promote.

Aye dil tamaam nafa hai sauda-i ishq me
Ek jaan ka ziyaan hai so aisa ziyaan nahin

September 1996   M.H.

Publisher's Note

On 31 October 1996, while this book was in print, the unexpected happened. Amid heavy police deployment and protests from a section among the students, Professor Hasan entered his University for the first time in four-and-a-half years. Delhi's *Indian Express* commented the next day: 'It was the end of a long journey for Mushirul Hasan – a journey that traversed an almost surreal landscape of slander, physical attack, misrepresentation, and relentless politicking. [. . .] For Hasan, four valuable years have been lost in a non-controversy. But it may just have been worth it if the message that emanates from the Jamia Millia Islamia episode is that scholarship cannot march to the beat of the mullah, just as art cannot dance to the music of the Bajrang Dal [a right-wing Hindu organisation].'

TABLES

GLOSSARY

ahl-i Hadith	refers to a group preferring the authority of Prophetic tradition over that of a ruling by one of the schools of the Islamic jurisprudence.
alim (plural *ulama*)	scholars, learned men, particularly in the religious sciences.
anjuman	an association, usually of Muslims.
ashraf	term usually used to describe those Muslims descended from immigrants in India; the Syeds (descendants of the Prophet) and Shaikhs (descendants of his Companions).
auqaf	see *waqf* (singular).
azan	the call to prayers.
biddat (*bidah*)	lit. 'innovation'; accretion to religious purity.
biradari	community.
crore	ten million, written 10,00,00,00.
dar al-harb	'the abode of war'; territory not under Islamic law.
dar al-Islam	'the abode of Islam', territory where Islamic law prevails.
dar al-ulum	lit. 'the abode of Sciences', a Muslim theological seminary such as Firangi Mahal and Deoband.
dargah	Muslim shrine or tomb of a holy person and an object of pilgrimage, e.g., Dargah-i Gharib Nawaz Muinuddin Chishti at Ajmer in Rajasthan.
fatwa	generally a written opinion on a point of Islamic law (see *shariat*) given by a *mufti* or an *alim* of standing.
ghazal	one of the three most important poetic forms, besides the *qasida* and *masnavi*.
hadith	account of what the Prophet said or did, or of his tacit approval of something said or done in his presence.
haramzadgi	behaving like a *haramzada*, bastard.
hazrat	a title of extreme respect; expression of veneration, e.g., Hazrat Ali.
hijrat	act of migration from persecution to safety; especially of the Prophet Mohammad from Mecca to Medina in AD 622, the starting point of the Islamic era; used frequently during the Pakistan movement.
Hindutva	a contemporary right-wing movement of Hindu self-assertion, for Hindu rights and Hindu nationhood.
ijma	'agreement', 'consensus'; one of the bases (*usul*) of the Islamic religious law.

ijtehad	lit. 'exerting oneself'; technical term in Islamic law, first for the use of individual reasoning in general, and later, in a restricted meaning, for the use of the method of reasoning by analogy (*qiyas*).
ilm	'knowledge'.
imam	'leader', especially prayer-leader in the mosque; used by the Shias (see Shia) for the twelve 'successors' of Prophet Mohammad starting from Ali, cousin and son-in-law of the Prophet.
imambara	lit. 'house of the Imam'; place where *tazias* are kept to mourn the martyrdom of Hazrat Imam Husain, e.g., the great Asaf-ud Daulah's *Imambara* in Lucknow.
jamaat	body, group, e.g., Jamaat-i Islami; a congregation for prayers.
jehad (jihad)	'an effort' or 'a striving', a religious war undertaken by Muslims against the unbelievers.
kafir	a non-Muslim; one who practices *kufr*, infidelity.
kalima	Muslim attestation of faith in the Unity of God and the finality of Mohammad's Prophethood.
Karbala	the site in Iraq where Husain was martyred.
karkhandar	artisan.
khalifa	a successor; a lieutenant; a viceregent or deputy.
khatib	the preacher, or reader of the sermon in congregational prayers.
khutba	the sermon or oration delivered at the time of congregational prayers.
lakh	unit of one hundred thousand, written 10,00,00.
madarsa (madrasah)	a secondary school or college for Muslims (plural *madaris*).
majlis	assembly, organisation, e.g., *Majlis-i Mushawarat;* a body, e.g., *Majlis-i Ittehadul-Muslimeen.*
maktab	school for teaching children the elements of reading, writing and Quranic recitation. (plural *makatib*)
masjid	a mosque, a place of worship (*namaz*).
maulana	term generally used for a Muslim doctor of law; a professor; a learned man.
maulvi (maulavi)	from *maula*, a lord or master; generally used for a learned man.
millat	religious community, especially community of Islam (*millat-i Islamia*).
mlecchas	unclean, applied to non-Hindus by the Hindus.
mohalla	quarter of a city.
Muharram	first month of the Muslim lunar calendar, the month in which Husain was assassinated.
mulla	theologian, scholar; usually denotes a person attached to a mosque.

pir	a Sufi master on the mystical path; also known as *murshid*.
qasbah	town, e.g., Rudauli in Barabanki district.
qaum	used in Urdu to mean community or nation, according to context.
rais	an Indian of respectable position.
rath yatra	a chariot procession led by the BJP leader, L.K. Advani, in September-October 1990 traversing several states.
sajjada-nashin	successor to the leadership of a *pir* and custodian of a sufi shrine.
sangathan	a movement aimed at unity and the knowledge of self-defence among Hindus.
sangh parivar	the term, 'the RSS family', is its own coinage.
shariat	the Islamic Law, including both the teachings of the Quran and of the traditional sayings of Prophet Mohammad.
Shia	'followers', the followers of Ali, the first cousin of the Prophet and the husband of his daughter Fatima.
shuddhi	'purification', reconversion to Hinduism of those who embraced other faiths.
silsilah	literally 'a chain', chain of spiritual descent, a Sufi order.
Sunni	'one who follows the trodden path'; applied to the largest sect of Muslims who acknowledge the first four Khalifa (*Khulafa*) as the rightful successors to the Prophet.
Syed (saiyid)	descendant of Prophet Mohammad, especially a descendant of Imam Husain.
tabligh	the Muslim conversion movement, e.g., Tablighi Jamaat.
taqlid	lit. "winding round" in the sense of blind acceptance of the *shariat*.
tazia	lath and paper models of the tombs of Imam Husain and his family carried in procession during Muharram.
ulama (singular *alim*)	commonly applied to Muslim doctors in Islamic law and theology.
ummat	community, people, nation, i.e., *Ummat-i Islamia* or *Ummat-i Mohammadi*.
urs	'wedding', term frequently used in India for the festival commemorating the death of a saint.
waqf	term signifying the appropriation or dedication of property to charitable uses and the service of God.

1

INTRODUCTION

At a party held during the United Nations session in 1949, the Turkish representative looked at the name card of Mohammad Mujeeb, the vice-chancellor of Delhi's Jamia Millia Islamia, saw he was a Muslim, and at once asked: 'Are there still any Muslims in India?'[1]

Readers in the mid-1990s need no reminding that India has one of the largest Muslim populations in the world, 110 million, smaller only than that of Indonesia (Table 1.1).[2] The landscape from Kashmir to Kanyakumari is dotted with mosques, sufi shrines, *makatib* and *madaris*. The call for prayer goes out not just in Delhi, Agra, Lucknow, Jaunpur, Bhopal and Hyderabad, the traditional centres of Muslim power in medieval India, but also in remote towns and villages. In Kerala alone there are at least 5,350 mosques, representing approximately one mosque for every 500 Muslims.[3] *Tabligh* work, conducted under the aegis of the Tablighi Jamaat, goes on unhampered as the inspired activists move from place to place spreading the message of Allah and extolling the virtues of *namaz*, or daily prayers. Huge gatherings, like that at Tonk (Rajasthan) in 1992, are organised each year.[4] The flow of pilgrims to Mecca and Medina – 24,227 in 1990 – continues unabated. They come from all parts of the country – from the heights of Leh in Ladakh to the predominantly Muslim islands in the Indian Ocean (Table 1.2).

It is also not necessary to remind our readers that Muslim rituals, symbols and institutions remain intact despite India's partition and the inter-

---

[1] Mohammad Mujeeb, *Islamic Influence on Indian Society* (Meerut: Meenaskshi Prakashan, 1972), p. 193.

[2] For the all-India spread of the Muslim population, see Rasheeduddin Khan, *Bewildered India: Identity, Pluralism, Discord* (Delhi: Har-Anand, 1994), pp. 93-5. For city and some districtwise figures, see Aijazuddin Ahmad, *Muslims in India, 1990-93*, vol. 1: *Bihar*, vol. 2: *Rajasthan*, vol. 3: *Delhi* (Delhi: Inter-India Publications, in process of publication).

[3] Ronald E. Miller, *Mapilla Muslims of Kerala* (Hyderabad: Orient Longman, 1992 rev. edn), p. 232. For Bengal see Richard M. Eaton, *The Rise of Islam and the Bengal Frontier 1204-1760* (Berkeley, CA: University of California Press, 1993), chapter 9.

[4] Shail Mayaram, 'The Indian National Congress and the Ulama', Iqbal Narain (ed.), *Secularism in India* (Jaipur: Classic Publishing House, 1995), p. 136.

Table 1.1. RELIGIONS OF INDIA (1991 CENSUS)

	Total population	Hindus	Muslims	Christians	Sikhs	Buddhists	Jains	Other	Religion not stated
India	*838,583,988*	*82.41*	*11.67*	*2.32*	*1.99*	*0.77*	*0.41*	*0.38*	*0.05*
Andhra Pradesh	66,508,008	89.14	8.91	1.83	0.03	0.03	0.04	n.a.	0.02
Andaman & Nicobar Islands	280,661	67.53	7.61	23.95	0.48	0.11	0.01	0.09	0.22
Arunachal Pradesh	864,558	37.04	1.38	10.29	0.14	12.88	0.01	36.22	2.04
Assam	22,414,322	67.13	28.43	3.32	.07	.29	.09	.62	0.4
Bihar	86,374,465	82.42	14.8	–	0.98	0.09	–	0.03	1.67
Chandigarh	642,015	75.84	2.72	0.99	20.29	0.11	0.24	0.01	0.01
Dadra & Nagar Haveli	138,477	95.48	2.41	1.51	0.01	0.15	0.38	20.59	–
Delhi	9,420,644	83.67	9.44	0.88	4.84	0.15	1.00	0.01	0.01
Goa, Daman & Diu	1,169,793	64.68	5.25	29.86	0.09	0.02	0.04	1.67	–
Gujarat	41,309,582	89.48	8.73	0.44	0.08	0.03	1.19	0.03	0.02
Haryana	16,463,648	89.21	4.64	0.10	5.81	0.01	0.21	–	0.02
Himachal Pradesh	5,170,877	95.90	1.72	0.09	1.01	1.24	0.20	–	0.02
Karnataka	44,977,201	85.45	11.64	1.91	0.02	0.16	0.73	0.01	0.08
Kerala	29,098,518	57.28	23.33	19.32	0.01	–	0.01	0.01	0.04
Lakshadweep	51,707	4.52	94.31	1.16	–	–	–	–	0.01
Madhya Pradesh	66,181,170	92.80	4.96	0.65	0.24	0.33	0.74	0.09	0.19
Maharashtra	78,937,187	81.12	9.67	1.12	0.21	6.39	1.22	0.13	0.14

Manipur	1,837,149	57.67	7.27	34.11	0.07	0.04	0.07	0.77	–
Meghalaya	1,774,778	14.67	3.46	64.58	0.15	0.16	0.02	16.82	0.14
Mizoram	689,756	5.05	0.66	85.73	0.04	7.83	–	0.27	0.42
Nagaland	1,209,546	10.12	1.71	87.47	0.06	0.05	0.10	0.48	0.01
Orissa	31,659,736	94.67	1.83	2.10	0.05	0.03	0.02	1.26	0.04
Pondicherry	807,785	86.16	6.54	7.23	–	0.01	0.06	–	–
Punjab	20,281,969	34.46	1.18	1.11	62.95	0.12	0.10	0.01	0.07
Rajasthan	44,005,990	89.08	8.01	0.11	1.48	0.01	1.28	–	0.03
Sikkim	406,457	68.37	0.95	3.30	0.09	27.15	0.01	0.09	0.04
Tamil Nadu	55,858,946	88.67	5.47	5.69	0.01	–	0.12	0.01	0.03
Tripura	2,757,205	86.50	7.13	1.68	0.03	4.67	0.01	0.01	–
Uttar Pradesh	139,112,287	81.74	17.33	0.14	0.48	0.16	0.13	0.01	0.01
West Bengal	68,077,965	74.72	23.61	0.56	0.08	0.30	0.05	0.67	0.01

Source: Census of India 1991, series – 1, India, paper 1 of 1995: *Religion*, pp. xii-xxiii.

community rift that followed it. Muharram is observed with much the same solemnity and élan in Lucknow, Jaunpur, Bombay, Calcutta, and Hyderabad as in Tehran, Shiraz, Isphahan and Qum. The processions get bigger as more and more Shias, along with the Sunnis and Hindus, mourn the martyrs of Karbala who were brutally killed on the banks of Euphrates in 680 AD.[5] Likewise Sufi shrines and the countless variations in celebrating the local saints lend a truly Indian colour to the Muslim practice in the subcontinent.[6] Sufi Islam is usually eclectic and tolerant towards other faiths. Orthodox Sunni Islam, on the other hand, seeks to build up an ideological edifice on the foundation of 'pure, true Islam'; it rejects 'external' cultural influences, and imposes a uniformity of belief and practice through the extensive network of traditional schools and colleges.

Table 1.2. DISTRIBUTION OF HAJ PILGRIMS BY STATE

	By air	By sea	Total
Andhra Pradesh	686	250	936
Assam	401	263	664
Bihar	232	539	771
Gujarat	1254	166	1420
Delhi	415	26	441
Jammu & Kashmir	1259	202	1461
Karnataka	922	239	1161
Kerala	2008	297	2305
Madhya Pradesh	917	160	1077
Maharashtra	2480	357	2837
Rajasthan	1064	145	1209
Tamil Nadu	996	135	1131
Uttar Pradesh	5925	1088	7013
West Bengal	515	647	1162
Haryana	220	32	252
Other states	308	79	387
Total	19,602	4,625	24,227

Source: *Muslim India*, August 1991, p. 356.

[5] The Shias, according to one estimate, are 10-15 per cent of the total Muslim population of India. Nadeem Hasnain and Sheikh Abrar Husain, *Shias and Shia Islam in India* (Delhi: Harnam Publications, 1988), p. 14. See also Paul Jackson (ed.), *The Muslims of India: Beliefs and Practices* (Bangalore: Theological Publications in India, 1985), p. 40; Mushirul Hasan, 'Traditional Rites and Contested Meanings: Sectarian Strife in Colonial Lucknow' in *Economic and Political Weekly* (hereafter *EPW*), 2 March 1996; and the excellent background study by J.R.I. Cole, *Roots of North Indian Shi'sm in Iran and Iraq: Religion and State in Awadh, 1722-1959* (Delhi: Oxford University Press [hereafter OUP], 1989); John L. Esposito (ed.), *The Oxford Encyclopedia of the Modern Islamic World* (New York: OUP, 1995), vol. 4, pp. 55-69.

[6] Christian W. Troll (ed.), *Muslim Shrines in India: Their Character, History and Significance* (Delhi: OUP, 1989); P.M. Curie, *The Shrine and Cult of Muin al-Din Chishti of Ajmer* (Delhi: OUP, 1989); Desiderio Pinto, *Piri-Muridi Relationship: A study of the Nizamuddin Dargah* (Delhi: Manohar, 1995).

In 1990, 6,285 Sunni *madaris* in Kerala employed more than 42,575 teachers and served 911,460 students.[7] In Calicut and Mallapuram, a district formed in 1969 by merging the contiguous backward regions of the erstwhile Palghat and Kozhikode districts in Kerala, twenty Arabic-medium colleges are supported by some Arab countries and by rich Muslims who made their fortunes in the Gulf.[8] In 1994, the Dar al-ulum at Deoband in Saharanpur district of Uttar Pradesh (hereafter UP) had nearly 3,000 students enrolled, of whom about 500 hailed from fifteen other countries.[9] The Mazahir al-ulum, not far from Deoband, and the Nadwat al-ulama in Lucknow are the other major centres.[10] On the stretch of road from Deoband to the foothills of Mussoorie, there are probably more *makatib* and *madaris* than in the capitals of some Muslim countries. 'Today', comments one of Nadwa's most eminent scholars, 'no Muslim or even Arab country can boast of the high standard of the *hadith* traditions found in some of the Indian institutions.'[11] Scores of Dini Talimi (religious education) schools – more than 2,000 with an enrolment of more than 600,000 pupils – function in UP.[12]

No doubt some of Islam's manifestations kindle memories of temple destruction and forcible conversions,[13] nurture ill-will, and – as in the case of the Babri Masjid at Ayodhya, the Shahi Idgah at Mathura and the

---

[7] Miller, op. cit., p. 234.

[8] For a background study see K.T. Mohammad Ali, *The Development of Education Among the Mapillas of Malabar 1800 to 1965* (Delhi: Mines Publishers, 1990).

[9] For an authentic history of the seminary at Deoband see Barbara Daly Metcalf, *Islamic Revival in British India: Deoband, 1860-1900* (Princeton University Press, 1982). Marc Gaborieau has traced the influence of the Dar al-ulum and the Mazahir al-ulum, founded in 1868 at Saharanpur, on the migrant labourers, especially the bangle-makers in parts of Nepal in the Himalayan foothills. 'The Transmission of Islamic Reformist Teachings to Rural South Asia', *Modes de transmission de la culture religieuse en Islam* (Paris: Institut Français d'Archéologie Orientale du Caire, 1993).

[10] For the history of Nadwat al-ulama, see Mohammad Ishaq Jalis Nadwi, *Tarikh Nadwat al-ulama*, vol. 1 (Lucknow: Nadwat al-ulama, 1983), and Shams Tibriz Khan, *Tarikh Nadwat al-ulama*, vol. 2 (Lucknow: Nadwat al-ulama, 1984); and Syed Abul Hasan Ali Nadwi, *Karawan-i Zindagi* (Lucknow: Maktaba Islamia, 1983); S. Jamal Malik, 'The Making of a Council: The Nadwat al-ulama', *Islamic Culture* (Hyderabad), January 1994. For the Mazahir al-ulum, see Mohammad Zakariya Kandhalwi, *Aap Beeti: Autobiography* (Delhi: Idara Ishaat-i Diniyat, 1993).

[11] Syed Abul Hasan Ali Nadwi, *The Musalman* (Lucknow: Academy of Islamic Research and Publications, 1977 edn.), p. 118.

[12] For syllabi, see *Khaka Nisab-i Taleem*, Proceedings of the Executive of the Dini Talim Board, 19 April 1970 (Delhi, n.d.). For state-wise listing of *madaris* see Kuldip Kaur, *Madrasa Education in Rural India* (Chandigarh: Centre for Research in Rural and Industrial Development, 1990), pp. 310-53; *Directory of Muslim Institutions and Organisations in Uttar Pradesh* (Aligarh: UP Rabita Committee, 1993).

[13] M.R. Malkani, *The Politics of Ayodhya and Hindu-Muslim Relations* (Delhi: Har-Anand, 1993), pp. 112-13.

Gyanvapi mosque in Varanasi – ignite the flames of violence.[14] Yet the spread and variety of Muslim religious sites and their co-existence with Hindu, Buddhist, Jain and Christian religious places of worship provide living testimony to the fusion of ideas and beliefs and 'the transmission of cultural effects and impulses'.[15] No doubt stray and *orchestrated* instances of religious frenzy, stirred by religious revivalists and manipulated by vested interests, including power-hungry politicians, cause friction, deepen prejudices and lead to the symbolic representation of Muslims as the 'alien'.[16] Still, the 'clash of civilisations' theory or the supposed historic enmities dating back to the early Arab or Turkish conquests is refuted by the weight of historical and contemporary evidence. 'Discounting the riots which are temporary and not general', commented the Turkish visitor, Halide Edib, 'the Muslim masses, both rural and city dwellers, were nearer to the Hindu than they are to any outside Muslims.'[17]

An inspiring legitimation of the more mundane expressions of peaceful co-existence comes daily in the sounds of Muslim *shahnai* (a reeded, clarinet-like instrument) mingling in the *arti* of Hindu temples in Banaras, including that of the most sacred Vishvanath temple;[18] or in some villages near Ajmer, close to the shrine of the Chishti saint Muinuddin Chishti, where Muslims celebrate the Hindu festival, *Diwali*, with a full-fledged Lakshmi (goddess of wealth) *puja*.[19]

The birth of Pakistan on 14-15 August 1947 undermined, from the liberal and left perspective, the values of religious tolerance and cultural pluralism. The ideological foundations of secular nationalism, the main plank of the Indian National Congress in its mobilisation campaigns, also weakened. For the Muslim communities that remained in India, partition was a nightmare. The demographic picture changed drastically in Punjab and Bengal, two of the provinces which had their largest concentration in South Asia. Large numbers of Muslims – about 6 to 7 million – from the

[14] 'The Hindu has for decades stored within his unconscious rages against the Muslims for humiliating memories they evoke, for their conquering role in Indian history, for their role in dividing the subcontinent, for their special status today as a political pawn during elections, and the pseudo-privileges which these generate, such as the retention of their personal laws.' Ratna Naidu, quoted in James Warner Bjorkman (ed.), *Fundamentalism, Revivalists and Violence in South Asia* (Delhi: Manohar, 1988), p. 18.

[15] Nadwi, *The Musalman*, p. 76.

[16] Sudhir Kakar, *Shamans, Mystics and Doctors: A Psychological Enquiry into India and its Healing Traditions* (Delhi: OUP, 1982), pp. 60, 63, 87.

[17] Halide Edib, *Inside India* (London: Geo. Allen and Unwin, 1937), p. 315.

[18] Judy F. Pugh, 'Divination and Ideology in the Banaras Hindu Community', in Katherine P. Ewing (ed.), *Shariat and Ambiguity in South Asian Islam* (Delhi: OUP, 1988), p. 289. *Arti* is a worship ceremony in which lighted lamps are moved in a circle before the image of the diety.

[19] *Times of India*, 10 September 1995.

'minority provinces' emigrated to Pakistan.[20] Lawyers, doctors, engineers, teachers and civil servants were comfortably ensconced in Lahore or Karachi either in response to Mohammad Ali Jinnah's clarion call or to bolster their career prospects. On the other hand, the so-called Islamic community in India, which had no place in Jinnah's Pakistan, was 'fragmented', 'weakened', and left vulnerable to right-wing Hindu onslaughts.

The areas most affected were Kashmir, Punjab, UP, Bihar and Bengal and the princely states of Rampur, Bhopal and Hyderabad. Fewer Muslims in southern and western parts joined the exodus to Pakistan, hence these regions did not experience major social upheaval or economic dislocation. This fact reflects the profound differences in the way most Muslims in the north and the south perceive and relate themselves to the world they live in. An important concern of this book is to discover the nature and variety of their experiences after partition.

Islam in India, past and present, unfolds a bewildering diversity of Muslim communities.[21] No statistical data are required to establish their location in multiple streams of thought and interactions with them. Their histories, along with social habits, cultural traits and occupational patterns, vary from class to class, from place to place, and from region to region.[22] They speak numerous dialects and languages and observe wide-ranging regional customs and local rites despite the intervention of the

---

[20] Papiya Ghosh, 'Reinvoking the Pakistan of the 1940s: Bihar's "Stranded Pakistanis" ', *Studies in Humanities and Social Sciences* (Shimla), 1, 1, 1995, pp. 131-46; D.A. Low (ed.), *The Political Inheritance of Pakistan* (London: Macmillan, 1991); Ansar Hussain Khan, *The Rediscovery of India: A New Subcontinent*, (Hyderabad: Orient Longman, 1995) p. 185. The Calcutta-born author was educated at the Government College, Lahore, migrated to Pakistan as a child on 6 August 1947, joined the United Nations, and reverted to Indian nationality in 1986.

[21] See, for example, Satish C. Misra, *Muslim Communities in Gujarat: Preliminary Studies in their History and Social Organisation* (Bombay: Asia Publishing House, 1964); T.N. Madan (ed.), *Muslim Communities of South Asia: Culture, Society and Power* (Delhi: Manohar, 1995, rev. and enlarged edn); Mohammad Mujeeb, *The Indian Muslims* (London: Geo. Allen and Unwin, 1967); Asghar Ali Engineer, *The Bohras* (Delhi: Vikas, 1980), and his *The Muslim Communities of Gujarat: An Exploratory study of Bohras, Khojas and Memons* (Delhi: Ajanta, 1989).

[22] According to Nadwi, 'the social life of the Indian Muslims, the pattern of their family life in particular, does not present any marked divergence from the surrounding culture of the people among whom they happen to reside. In a country so vast as India is ... the culture of the Indian Muslims too is marked by distinctive features, customs and manners, like that of their compatriots.' Nadwi, *The Musalman*, p. 41. See also Imtiaz Ahmad (ed.), *Family, Kinship and Marriage among Muslims in India* (Delhi: Manohar, 1976), and his *Ritual and Religion among Muslims in India* (Delhi: Manohar, 1980). For a contrary view, notice the comment that 'it is not their [Muslim] regional, linguistic, cultural, class and sectarian hetrogeneity but their comparative homogeneity, based on the basic tenets of the Muslim faith and creed, that is more striking.' Iqbal A. Ansari (ed.), *The Muslim Situation in India* (Delhi: Sterling, 1989), p. 1.

Islamists. Caste exists as a basis of social relations, although it differs from the Hindu caste system in details.[23] In several domains Muslims make up an integral part of the larger socio-cultural complex dominated by values and ideologies of the Hindu caste tradition.[24]

The economic profile of Muslims, too, is varied. Traders, businessmen, merchants and industrialists are no doubt comfortably placed, but the vast majority of Muslims, including the impoverished peasants and landless labourers, are the bulk of the rural poor and the industrial proletariat.[25] The fortunes of Muslim professionals dwindled and their influence waned after partition, yet some of them have prospered during the recent decades owing to the expansion of trade, commerce, industry and the service sectors in medium-sized urban centres, and some have benefited from powerful social and class factors, and family and political ties. This study examines the nature of such changes, along with the causes and implications of 'Muslim backwardness'.

Socio-economic divisions are compounded by doctrinal and sectarian schisms. In Lucknow conflict is more common between Shias and Sunnis than between Hindus and Muslims.[26] Here, as elsewhere in the subcontinent, Shias and Sunnis pray separately, each under their own prayer leaders. School children are sometimes enrolled in denominational schools. Shias and Sunnis eschew intermarriage, and they even bury their dead in separate graveyards. Sunni Islam is itself deeply fissured: the ideologues of the Deobandi and the Barelwi 'schools', who do not identify with each other's socio-religious codes, have been involved in ceaseless doctrinal controversies, regularly sensitising their followers through lectures, religious sermons and published literature to their mutual differences. In sum, whether for economic or doctrinal reasons, most Muslims take their commitment to Islam not only as one among other values, but

[23] Imtiaz Ahmad (ed.), *Caste and Social Stratification among Muslims in India* (Delhi: Manohar, 1978).

[24] C. G. Hussain Khan, *Marriage and Kinship among Muslims in South India* (Jaipur: Rawat Publications, 1994), p. 170.

[25] For two recent statements on the subject of Muslim 'backwardness', see Rafiq Zakaria, *The Widening Divide: An Insight into Hindu-Muslim Relations* (Delhi: Viking, 1995); Omar Khalidi, *Indian Muslims since Independence* (Delhi: Vikas, 1995). Primary literature on the economic status of the Muslims is thin; so one relies on stray and inconclusive evidence based on field surveys, personal accounts and newspaper reports. Many such 'sources' shed no light on the success stories. Again, while a good deal more has appeared on the educational profile of the Muslims, much of it is analytically poor. For example, Salamatullah, *Education of Muslims in secular India* (Chandigarh, 1994); Akbar Rahman, *Aqliat ke Taalimi Huqooq aur Masail* (Jalgaon: Educational Academy, 1990); M.K.A. Siddiqi, *Educating a Backward Minority* (Calcutta: Abadi Publications, 1984); and Mumtaz Ali Khan, *Muslims in the Process of Rural Development* (Delhi: Uppal, 1984). *Muslim India*, published by Syed Shahabuddin from Delhi, is useful and the data provided is generally reliable.

[26] Theodore P. Wright, 'The Politics of Muslim sectarian conflict in India , *Journal of South Asian and Middle Eastern Studies*, 3, 1980, pp. 67-73.

also as something which is itself differentiated internally into a number of detailed commitments.[27] The nature and implications of these internal differentiations and the negotiated commitments flowing from them will be spelt out later.

It needs to be emphasised that Islam did not come to the subcontinent in a single time-span, but over a succession of periods of unequal length; consequently, its diffusion took place in a variety of forms from class to class and from one area to another. The difference in the phases in which people 'experienced' Islam brought with it variations in the nature of challenges facing Muslims in different regions, a potentially rich but hitherto neglected area of study. In its local and regional specificity, therefore, Islam cannot be portrayed as a social entity whose 'essential' core is immune to change by historical influences. Consider Kashmir. In the valley, where most Muslims live, Islam absorbed many social and cultural practices of pre-Islamic origin, which are today attacked by the Ahl-i Hadith and the Jamaat-i Islami.[28] And in the neighbouring Punjab, a territory divided into two unequal halves in 1947, it provided a repertoire of concepts and styles of authority which served to encompass potentially competing values, including the values of tribal kinship, within a common Islamic idiom.[29] In Bengal, an area far removed from the centre of imperial power, Islam took many forms and assimilated values and symbols which were not always in conformity with the Quranic ideals and precepts. The religio-cultural idioms underwent a rapid change, giving birth to a set of popular beliefs and practices which in essence represented the popular culture of rural Bengal rooted in the pre-Islamic past. The local syncretic beliefs and practices, predating the advent of Islam in the region, thus formed the popular culture in Bengali Islam from the begin-ning.[30]

We should consider too the evolution of what was once proudly proclaimed but is now pooh-poohed in some circles: a syncretic and composite culture in the Indo-Gangetic belt. The historical literature on the subject, mostly produced at the universities in Allahabad, Aligarh and Lucknow, is of great value. Scores of writers have described the corporate identity of the towns and the largely cordial interaction of the mixed Hindu

[27] Aqeel Bilgrami, 'What is a Muslim? Fundamental Commitment and Cultural Identity', *EPW*, 16-23 May 1992, p. 1071. Reprinted in Gyanendra Pandey (ed.), *Hindus and Others: The Question of Identity in India* (Delhi: Viking, 1993).

[28] Mohammad Ishaq Khan, *Kashmir's Transition to Islam: The Role of Muslim Rishis* (Delhi: Manohar, 1994).

[29] David Gilmartin, 'Customary Law and Shariat in Punjab' in Ewing (ed.), op. cit., p. 44.

[30] Rafiuddin Ahmed, 'Conflicts and Contradictions in Bengali Islam: Problems of Change and Adjustment' in ibid., pp. 115, 119. See also Tazeen M. Murshid, *The Sacred and the Secular: Bengal Muslim Discourses, 1871-1977* (Calcutta: OUP, 1995).

and Muslim populations. In Ahmed Ali's Delhi,[31] Rahi Masoom Reza's village Gangauli,[32] Attia Hosain's Hasanpur,[33] or Intizar Husain's Husnpur (Beautiful Town), the parallel worlds of, say, Bhagatji and Abba Jan in the novel *Basti*, of Hindu mythology and Muslim legend and lore, could exist in reality and not only in the writer's fancy.[34]

Similarly, Islam south of the Vindhyas evolved a tradition of worship marked by a striking capacity to accommodate itself to indigenous patterns of faith and worship. It gained a foothold because of its capacity to forge links with the religions and peoples of the wider society, and to offer a form of access to the divine which could be grasped and built upon through means already present within these societies. This interpenetration was neither 'degenerate' nor a product of superficial accretions from Hinduism. The sharing of beliefs and practices was built up into a dynamic and expansive religious system.[35]

'If I were an eighteenth or early nineteenth century Muslim', commented Mohammad Mujeeb, 'I could easily have become that public nuisance called a "reformer". I could have said: "Islam is deep beneath Hindu influences, let us dig it out, clean it and see what it really looks like."'[36] Hence Maulana Abul Kalam Azad, who knew his Islam and his

[31] First published in 1940 by the Hogarth Press on the initiative of E.M. Forster, *Twilight in Delhi* by Ahmed Ali (1910-94) depicts 'a phase of our national life and the decay of a whole culture, a particular mode of thought and living, now dead and gone already right before our eyes'. Ahmed Ali, introduction, *Twilight in Delhi* (Delhi: OUP, Golden Jubilee edn, 1991), p. viii.

[32] Rahi Masoom Reza (1927-92) was born in a Shia family of Ghazipur district in Uttar Pradesh. In his own words: 'The Jana Sangh says that Muslims are outsiders. How can I presume to say they are lying? But, I must say I belong to Ghazipur. My bonds with Gangauli are unbreakable. It's not just a village, it's my home ...'. His novel *Adha Gaon* [Half-a-Village] is a tale about the passing time in Gangauli village, about the dreams and aspirations of young people caught up in the communal crossfire of the 1940s. It 'is a tale of those ruins which were once houses, and it is a tale of those houses which have been built upon those ruins'. The novel is in parts also a political commentary with insights into the Muslim League's mobilisation campaigns.

[33] Attia Hosain (b. 1913) came from a *taluqdari* family of Awadh. She was educated at the La Martiniere School for Girls and the Isabela Thoburn College in Lucknow. She was greatly influenced in the 1930s by the left-wing activists and attended the first Progressive Writers' Conference. Her own ideal of womanhood was embodied in Sarojini Naidu, who 'overcome my shyness' to attend the All India Womens' Conference in Calcutta in 1933. She settled in London in 1947. 'Events during and after Partition are to this day very painful to me. And now, in my old age, the strength of my roots is strong; it also causes pain, because it makes one a "stranger" everywhere in the deeper area of one's mind and spirit *except where one was born and brought up*.' Quoted in *Phoenix Fled*, introduction by Anita Desai (Calcutta: Rupa, 1993), p. xiii.

[34] Intizar Husain, *Basti*, transl. Frances W. Pritchett (Delhi: Indus, 1995), p. x.

[35] Susan Bayly, *Saints, Goddesses and Kings: Muslims and Christians in South Indian Society, 1700-1900* (Cambridge University Press [hereafter *CUP*], 1990), pp. 13-14.

[36] Mujeeb, *Islamic Influence*, p. 11.

history better than most, spoke of 'a notable event in history', the fusion of the Islamic and Hindu cultural currents, and 'eleven hundred years of common history'. This joint wealth, according to him, was the heritage of common nationality. In one of his most eloquent speeches, he declared:

I am proud of being an Indian. I am a part of the indivisible unity that is Indian nationality. I am indispensable to this noble edifice and without me this splendid structure of India is incomplete. I am an essential element which has gone to build India. I can never surrender this claim.[37]

Azad, who bore the brunt of religious animus with dignity and fortitude, was overwhelmed by partition.[38] Yet he could envisage an Islam not of sectarian belligerence but of confident partnership with other cultural and religious entities.[39] He 'saw much, suffered much and changed much.'[40] If old memories were revived for him, he would simply say: 'Why expose the scar on one's heart? No one is to blame. I alone am to blame. I was so incompetent that I could not succeed in keeping back the Muslims of India from committing deliberate suicide.'[41]

Many followed in the footsteps of the Maulana, though several scholars, theologians and political leaders also contested his reading of the past and his vision of the future. Maulana Abul Ala Maududi, an erudite scholar and founder of the Jamaat-i Islami, and a section of Deobandi, Barelwi and Firangi Mahal *ulama* argued within the framework of 'Islamic conscientisation', presented Islam as an alternative to the 'degenerating world ideologies', tried to bolster solidarity among Muslims, and equipped them to resist 'the threat of secular influence'. Jinnah, the chief architect of Pakistan, also had a different agenda. It was he who represented Islam and Hinduism as different and distinct social orders, and who insisted, contrary to his earlier conviction, that their followers belonged to two entirely different and distinct civilisations based on conflicting ideas and conceptions.

Who, then, is a Muslim? What, if any, specific identity is associated with the Muslims generally and with India's Muslims in particular? Is it divinely ordained or related to features that have always been characteristic of the so-called *Islamic* governments and societies? How important is the community's own self-image which is subtly moulded by a combination of 'internal' factors and external interventions? Is it the

---

[37] *Presidential Address, Indian National Congress, Fifty-third session, Ramgarh, March 1940. Translated from the Original Hindustani* (no date or place).

[38] Ian Henderson Douglas, *Abul Kalam Azad: An Intellectual and Religious Biography,* edited by Gail Minault and Christian W. Troll (Delhi: OUP, 1988), pp. 237-8, and V.N. Datta, *Maulana Azad* (Delhi: Manohar, 1990), for a sensitive portrayal of Azad's career.

[39] Kenneth Cragg, *The Pen and the Faith* (Delhi: ISPCK, 1986), p. 29.

[40] S.M. Ikram, *Modern Muslim India and the Birth of Pakistan,* quoted in ibid., p. 32.

[41] Quoted in Cragg, op. cit., pp. 29-30.

outcome of colonial images, of treating Muslims as an undifferentiated religious and political category? Finally, to what extent has the post-colonial state, too, viewed Muslims as a religious collectivity, who are also presumed to represent a separate political entity?

Justice Mohammad Munir, the chairman of a committee to inquire into the anti-Ahmadiya (Qadiani) riots in Pakistan, asked the *ulama* to define a Muslim. Significantly, no two learned divines agreed. The committee's own dilemma was summed up succintly: 'If we attempt our own definition as each learned divine has done and that definition differs from that given by all others, we unanimously go out of the fold of Islam. And if we adopt the definition given by any one of the *ulama*, we remain Muslims according to the view of that *alim* but *kafirs* according to the definition of everyone else.'[42] In fact the enquiry was 'anything but satisfactory'. The report concluded on a wary note: 'If considerable opinion exists in the minds of our *ulama* on such a simple matter, one can easily imagine what the difference on more complicated matters will be.'[43]

Who, then, is a Muslim? The variety of meanings attached to defining a Muslim are illustrated by an *alim* of Lucknow's Nadwat al-ulama, by an erudite liberal scholar who guided the affairs of the Jamia Millia Islamia for decades, and by a socialist writer, journalist and filmmaker.

A distinguishing feature of the entire Muslim community, including Indian Muslims, is that the fundamental basis of their existence as a religious community [*millat*] is a well-defined, distinct and immutable faith and a divinely ordained canon [*shariat*].[44] (Syed Abul Hasan Ali Nadwi, 1974)

... If we have to define the Indian Muslims, we can only say that they are Indians who call themselves Muslims, who believe in the unity and fraternity of the Muslims as a religious and social community, and are capable of showing in practice that they act in accordance with this belief, however they might differ in doctrine and observances.[45] (Mohammad Mujeeb, 1967)

Maula Bakhsh, a peasant, lives in Tamil Nadu and speaks Tamil. In Andhra Pradesh he speaks Telegu. In Bengal his language is Bengali. Do we think of such a Muslim for whom I have invented the name Maula Bakhsh? ... Jinnah, Khaliquzzaman, Maulana Azad, the Aga Khan, M.C. Chagla and the Raja of Mahmudabad .... were Muslims. So was Hakku, the elderly grandmother of our locality. She was a weaver. She prayed five times a day. She was so deeply moved by one of Gandhi's speeches that after Allah and his Prophet she would repeat the name of the Mahatma. At the age of seventy she stitched her own *khadi* coffin, because she did not want her body to be wrapped and

---

[42] *Report of the Court of Inquiry constituted under the Punjab Act II of 1954 to enquire into the Punjab Disturbances of 1953* (Lahore: Government Printing Press, 1954), p. 218.

[43] Ibid., p. 215.

[44] Nadwi, The Musalman, p. 105.

[45] Mujeeb, *Indian Muslims*, p. 23.

then buried in a foreign cloth.

So when people discuss India's Muslims I wonder who are they talking about. Maula Bakhsh? Jinnah and Co.? Or Hakku?[46] (Khwaja Ahmad Abbas, 1975)

Such historical and sociological descriptions, which are adequately reflected in this work, make it clear that boundaries are multiple, and at no time is one boundary the sole definer of an identity. Yet at different times and for different reasons there is a 'relevant boundary' that gains prominence and defines the us/them divide. It tends to reject the 'other' and frequently reinforces itself by defining the 'us', not by its members' specific positive attributes but by the elements in opposition to the 'other'. This mode stresses the negative, expands elements of separation, and sometimes makes it harder to identify the broader groupings that always exist, albeit in weaker form.[47]

Much the same process took place in the early 1940s, changing the complexion of politics and society. The secular political platform – eroded by colonial policies, caste and communitarian politics and Hindu and Muslim revivalism – narrowed. The areas of contestation were enlarged as the British, responding to nationalist aspirations, grudgingly shared some of their powers with Indians and introduced some form of self-government. The 'us' and 'them' divide sharpened in the urban areas and the vast rural hinterland when the sectarian passions were stirred to gain short-term political advantages. Cross-community networks weakened and age-old ties were broken for the time being. It happened too soon, too suddenly, and on a scale beyond anybody's imagination. Many were dumbfounded by the turn of events. Many more were tormented by the disturbance to their quiet and peaceful world.

The post-independence generations in the subcontinent are, however, largely unfamiliar with the events that traumatised families and friends not so long ago, or detached from them. Most ignore the epic human tragedy that took place in and soon after August 1947. Most wish to erase the memory of a painful and brutal past. Much of the information or 'analyses' that filters to them through hearsay accounts, fiction, cinema and the print and television media is lamentably impressionistic, lop-sided and coloured by majoritarian bias. Although films like *Garam Hawa* and *Mammo* in India depict and drive home the poignancy and tragedy of nationally contrived divisions and borders,[48] most others lack depth,

---

[46] Khwaja Ahmad Abbas, 'Maula Bakhsh bhi ek Hindustani Mussalman hai', *Gagan*, in Urdu (Bombay: Mussalman Number, 1975), pp. 96-7.

[47] The idea and the text is based on Ismail Serageldin, 'Mirage and Windows: Redefining the Boundaries of the Mind', *The American Journal of Islamic Social Sciences*, 2, 1, spring 1994. For a sensitive autobiographical reflection see Azra Razzack, 'Growing Up Muslim', *Seminar* (387), November 1991, pp. 30-3.

[48] *Mammo*, directed by Shyam Benegal, was the opening film at the 26th International Film

sympathy, poise and sensitivity.

Partition literature in the subcontinent is also inadequate and lacking in scholarly rigour. The frameworks are generally flawed, for they preclude serious examination of the impact of colonial policies, the rise and impact of Hindu and Muslim revivalist movements, the creation of religious identities, and the intra-class competition for a greater share in the emerging power structures. Most authors are concerned to fault the Other.[49] Some act as spokesmen and advocates for the Congress or Muslim League creed. Apologists claim that partition has allowed the fulfilment of legitimate aspirations. Critics condemn it for mutilating historic national entities.[50] Hence mutually hostile camps are pitched in the arena of historiography. The strong reactions provoked by the publication of Maulana Azad's 'Complete Version' of *India Wins Freedom* reveals, moreover, that the focus on all-India politicians and on party statements and resolutions has reduced many discussions to mutual accusations and recriminations.[51] Finally, most conclusions are tailored to suit preconceived notions and suppositions – so much so that several writers in their wisdom trace the Pakistan 'idea' to Turkish rule in the thirteenth century, to Shah Waliullah of Delhi in the eighteenth, and to Syed Ahmad Khan, founder of the M.A.O. College at Aligarh.

This book, far from being a detailed or a 'complete' and 'objective' account of the Partition movement, seeks to build on the insights of regional and local studies.[52] The specific questions it addresses are why and how the two-nation theory emerged, why and how different forms of

---

Festival held in Bombay on 10-20 January 1995, a city racked by Hindu-Muslim violence. The script of the film is based on the true story of an aunt of Khalid Mohammad, the film critic of the *Times of India*. It portrays how a person like Mammo is trapped by borders which are not of her making.

[49] Arun Shourie, *Religion in Politics* (Delhi: Roli Books, 1987), pp. 195, 213. And the view of the late Girilal Jain, an influential editor of the *Times of India*: 'In the final analysis, they [Muslims] decided in the 1940s that the country would be partitioned; no attempt at re-writing history can cover up the truth', *Sunday Mail* (Delhi), 12 November 1989. See Zakaria, op. cit., for a different perspective, and Moin Shakir, *Khilafat to Partition* (Delhi: Kalamkar Prakashan, 1970).

[50] See T.J. Fraser, *Partition in Ireland, India and Palestine* (London: Macmillan Press, 1984), for a comparative study of the histories of partition in three countries.

[51] Rajmohan Gandhi, *India Wins Errors: A Scrutiny of Maulana Azad's India Wins Freedom* (Delhi: Radiant Publishers, 1989); Riazur Rahman Sherwani, *India Wins Freedom: Ek Mutala*, in Urdu (Aligarh: Academy Books, 1990).

[52] For example, of two recent studies on Bengal that by Joya Chatterji, *Bengal Divided: Hindu Communalism and Partition, 1932-1947* (CUP, 1995), is one of the best accounts of the partition movement in a region, and Tazeen M. Murshid, *The Sacred and the Secular: Bengal Muslim Discourses, 1871-1977* (Calcutta: OUP, 1995) is a major advance on most existing works. With the monographs of Ayesha Jalal, David Gilmartin, Ian Talbot, Sarah Ansari and Suranjan Das, we now have a fairly good idea of the regional 'roots' of the Pakistan movement.

identities and consciousness were translated into a powerful campaign for a Muslim state, and why, how and when the Muslim League enlarged its constituency. I touch on the neglected terrain of what Partition symbolised to its supporters and detractors alike, and the meanings attached to the two-nation theory and its off-spring, the Islamic Republic of Pakistan. I examine the complex nature of the Muslim League campaign, question its representation as a unified, cohesive entity tied to shared religious goals, and assess its ideology and mobilisation within different perspectives. In this way I hope to provide the reference-point for understanding Partition and its legacy.

Sections of the book also unfold the 'Other Face of Freedom', the tremendous human cost, the dispossession and anguish of millions, and the violence and brutalities, captured by Jawaharlal Nehru, India's first prime minister, in an impromptu radio broadcast on 9 September 1947:

It is an extraordinary thing that I have seen. I have seen horror enough and I have seen many people die. [...] Death is bad and painful, but one gets used to death. But there are some things much worse than death that have taken place. I am ashamed of the acts that my people have done and I fear the disgrace and the consequences of evil deeds will remain with us for a long time. [...] This morning, our leader, our master, Mahatma Gandhi, came to Delhi, and I went to see him, and I sat by him for- a while wondering how low we have fallen from the great ideals that he had placed before us. [53]

The author's journey through the riot-torn cities is painful and hazardous. So also is its description and interpretation, as the unseemly furore over *Tamas*[54] and *Bombay* illustrated.[55] Yet I tread the delicate path of recording and analysing the woes of divided families, the plight of migrants, the pain, trauma and sufferings of those who had to part from their kin, friends and neighbours. Their testimonies neither resolve major controversies nor satisfy everybody's curiosity, but they lend authenticity to historical narrations, shed light on how partition affected millions, and

---

[53] Sarvepalli Gopal (ed.), *Selected Works of Jawaharlal Nehru* (Delhi: OUP, 1986), vol. 4, pp. 54, 55, 56.

[54] A television film, based on the Hindi novel *Tamas* (Darkness) by Bhisham Sahni (b. 1915), caused a stir in 1988 among right-wing Hindu groups, leading to protests and a demand for its telecast to be suspended. But the Bombay High Court and the Supreme Court rejected the plea. The court verdict was that *Tamas* 'takes us to a historic past - unpleasant times, when a human tragedy of great dimension took place in the subcontinent. [...] Naked truth in all times will not be beneficial but truth in its proper light indicating the evils and the consequences of those evils is constructive and that message is there in *Tamas*.'

[55] *Bombay* is a riveting film about a Hindu-Muslim marriage with the bloody background of frenzied rioting in late 1992 and early 1993. Some Muslim groups strongly objected to several scenes so that the screening of the Tamil and Telugu versions was stopped in many areas. In Hyderabad, Muslim youths attacked theatres in protest. Many took exception to the director, Mani Ratnam, yielding to the request by the Shiv Sena chief, Bal Thackeray, for several cuts that would improve the way he is portrayed in the film.

reveal much more about 'colonialism', 'nationalism' and 'communalism' than private papers, official records and newspaper editorials.

For these reasons I have pressed into service some creative writers – mostly those who reject, implicitly or explicitly, religion ('communal', in common parlance) as the prime explanatory category, who invoke symbols of unity rather than disunity, and who are wedded to composite and syncretic pan-Indian values. The locale of their stories, the carefully woven themes around innocent and sometimes gullible individuals, and the subtle delineation of their characters, such as the inmates of a mental hospital in Saadat Hasan Manto's short story *Toba Tek Singh*, communicate a strong message.[56] Scores of writers such as Manto, Krishan Chander, Rajinder Singh Bedi, Khushwant Singh, Bhisham Sahni, Qurratulain Hyder, Ismat Chughtai and Intizar Husain would say that whatever the cause and whosoever's the responsibility, the country's vivisection was a colossal tragedy, a man-made catastrophe brought about by politicians who lacked the will, imagination and foresight to resolve their disputes over power-sharing and who failed to grasp the grave implications of division along religious lines.[57]

Not surprisingly, Partition cast its shadow over many aspects of state and society after independence.[58] It raised serious and contentious matters

[56] Saadat Hasan Manto, *Kingdom's End and Other Stories,* transl. from the Urdu by Khalid Hasan (Delhi: Penguin Books India, 1989).

[57] See the collection of stories in Mushirul Hasan (ed.), *India Partitioned: The Other Face of Freedom,* 2 vols (Delhi: Roli, 1995); Alok Bhalla (ed.), *Stories About the Partition of India,* in 3 vols (Delhi: Indus Publishers, 1994); 'Memories of Partition', *Seminar* (420), August 1994; Veena Das, *Critical Events: Moments in the Life of the Nation* (Delhi: OUP, 1994); Urvashi Butalia, 'Community, State and Gender: On Women's Agency during Partition', *EPW,* 24 April 1993; Ritu Menon and Kamla Bhasin, 'Recovery, Rupture, Resistance: Indian State and Abduction of Women during Partition', *EPW,* 24 April 1993. For a recent critique of their writings, see Anne Hardgrave, 'South Asian Women's Communal Identities', *EPW,* 30 September 1995. See also Ian Talbot, *Freedom's City: The Popular Dimension in the Pakistan Movement and Partition Experience in North-West India* (Karachi: OUP, 1995).

[58] A study on social tensions, commissioned by the Education Ministry in 1949-50 and directed by Gardner Murphy, was the first to explore the problems of India's Muslims after independence and partition. It was carried out in seven cities, with three teams concentrating on Lucknow, Aligarh and Bombay. Gopal Krishna prepared a similar study for the Ministry of Home Affairs, Government of India, at the Centre for the Study of Developing Societies in Delhi. For their findings, see Gardner Murphy, *In the Minds of Men: The Study of Human Behaviour and Social Tensions in India* (New York: Basic Books, 1953), and Gopal Krishna, 'Problems of Integration in the Indian Political Community: Muslims and the Political Process' in Dilip K. Basu and Richard Sisson (eds), *Social and Economic Development in India: A Reassessment* (Delhi: Sage, 1986). For recent literature covering different aspects of the post-partition developments, Ayesha Jalal, *Democracy and Authoritarianism in South Asia* (CUPress, 1995); T.V. Satyamurthy (ed.), *State and Nation in the Context of Social Change,* vol. 1 (Delhi: OUP, 1994), and his *Region, Religion, Caste, Gender and Culture in Contemporary India,* vol. 3 (Delhi: OUP, 1996); Achin Vanaik, *India's Painful Transition: Bourgeois Democracy in India* (London: Verso, 1990); Atul Kohli, *The State and Poverty*

about the relationship of religion and politics, the efficacy of secularism in a riot-torn society, the place of religious minorities in the new political arrangements. Influential Muslims had to negotiate the dialectics of pluralism and secularism, devise ways and means of carving out their place in society, and establish their niche in the post-colonial democratic structures. By focussing on institutions such as the Aligarh Muslim University and the Jamia Millia Islamia and organisations like the Jamaat-i Islami, the Jamiyat al-ulama and Tablighi Jamaat, I try to examine their understanding, conclusions and answers to their post-imperial predicaments, trace their responses to the transformative processes and the attendant challenges thrown up after independence, explore liberal and reformist ideas among Muslim publicists, intellectuals and journalists and their articulation after partition, and the right-wing Hindu assault on the Babri Masjid.

There exists much 'conventional wisdom' on the Muslim *communities* in South Asia. Many stereotypical images are associated with them.[59] Some academic exchanges have taken place,[60] but on balance the engagement with the Muslims during the post-independence period is distinctly more polemical than scholarly.[61] Just a handful of liberal and Marxist scholars,

---

in India (CUniversityP, 1987); Sarvepalli Gopal, *Jawaharlal Nehru: A Biography, 1947-1956*, vol. 2 (Delhi: OUP, 1979); Paul R. Brass, *Language, Religion and Politics in North India* (CUP, 1974).

[59] M.S. Golwalkar, *Bunch of Thoughts* (Bangalore: Jagarana Prakashana, 1980 edn), chapter 16. And the opinion of a medieval Indian historian: 'The insistence of the Muslims on their Personal Law, their reluctance to Family Planning, their pacts of privileges with political parties at the time of elections in particular and their receiving millions of dollars to help in proselytising endeavours all point to their desire and determination to grow in numbers and Islamise Hindustan.' K.S. Lal, *Indian Muslims: Who are they* (Delhi: Voice of India, 1990), p. 39.

[60] Francis Robinson, 'Nation Formation: The Brass Thesis and Muslim Separatism', and reply by Paul R. Brass, *Journal of Commonwealth and Comparative Politics*, 15, 3, November 1977, pp. 215-34. Francis Robinson is also part of a debate conducted in *Contributions to Indian Sociology* between sociologists and a historian. See Charles Lindholm, 'Caste in Islam and the Problem of Deviant Systems: A Critique of Recent Theory' in Madan (ed.), *Muslim Communities of South Asia: Culture, Society and Power*, pp. 449-68.

[61] P.C. Joshi, 'The economic background of communalism in India' in B.R. Nanda (ed.), *Essays in Modern Indian History* (Delhi: OUP, 1980), p. 168. On the paucity of literature on social change taking place among Muslims, see Imtiaz Ahmad (ed.), *Modernization and Social Change Among Muslims in India* (Delhi: Manohar, 1983), pp. xviii-xxix, and T.N. Madan's comment: 'While historians have for long regarded South Asia as an area of immense if not unique interest from the Muslim point of view, and many approaches and schools of historiography flourish, high-quality sociological studies of these Muslim communities are rather rare.' Madan (ed.), *Muslim Communities of South Asia*, introduction, p. xi. A number of studies in the West, which are preoccupied with 'Muslim Fundamentalism' and equate Islam with West Asia or Iran (not even South-East Asia) take little or no notice of the presence of India's Muslims.

often derided as 'pseudo-secularists' by right-wing Hindus and Muslims, have produced worthwhile studies.[62] As a result, the field has remained

[62] It is impossible to list all of them, but I have in mind, among others, the writings of Mohammad Mujeeb, Abid Husain, Mushirul Haq and A.R. Saiyed, all connected with the Jamia Millia Islamia; Alam Khundmiri, Moin Shakir, Imtiaz Ahmad, Asghar Ali Engineer, A.G. Noorani, Rafiq Zakaria and M.R.A. Baig. For a bibliographical survey see Mohammad Haroon, *Muslims of India* (Delhi: Indian Bibliographic Bureau, 1989), and Harsh Kapoor, *Resources Against Communalism and Religious Fundamentalism in India* (Paris: Women Living under Muslim Laws, April 1995). Christian W. Troll, former professor at the Jesuit Institute of Religious Studies, Delhi, published several volumes on religious and educational institutions. The painstaking researches of Theodore W. Wright are considerable. Regional and local studies are mostly thinly researched. Electoral studies by Gopal Krishna, Myron Weiner, Harold A. Gould, Paul R. Brass and Imtiaz Ahmad challenged many commonly-held assumptions about the pattern of Muslim voting, though such writings are scarce nowadays. There is no book on the Muslim organisations after independence, though essays on the Jamaat-i Islami and the Tablighi Jamaat have recently appeared in journals and books, e.g., Mumtaz Ahmad, 'Islamic Fundamentalism in South Asia: The Jamaat-i Islami and the Tablighi Jamaat', in Martin E. Marty and R. Scott Appleby (eds), *Fundamentalism and the State: Remaking Polities, Economies and Militance* (Chicago, University Press, 1993); Seyyed Vali Reza Nasr, The *Vanguard of the Islamic Revolution: The Jama'at-i Islami of Pakistan* (Berkeley, CA: University of California Press and London: I.B. Tauris, 1994), and his *Mawdudi and the Making of Islamic Revivalism* (OUP, 1995).

Hindu-Muslim riots (mostly referred to in India as communal riots) have been reported and analysed, especially in Bombay's *Economic and Political Weekly*. See also Veena Das (ed.), *Communities, Riots and Survivors in South Asia* (Delhi: OUP, 1990); M.J. Akbar, *Riot after Riot* (Delhi: Penguin Books India, 1991, rev. and updated edn), and the volumes edited by A.A. Engineer. Gender issues among Muslims received scholarly notice after the Shah Bano affair in 1983 and the Babri Masjid controversy. See, e.g., Shahida Latif, *Muslim Women in India: Political and Private Realities, 1890s-1980s* (Delhi: Kali for Women, 1990); Zoya Hasan (ed.), *Forging Identities: Gender, Communities and the State* (Delhi: Kali for Women, 1994); Tanika Sarkar and Urvashi Butalia (eds), *Women and the Hindu Right* (Delhi: Kali for Women,1995). For surveys and general accounts on aspects of 'Muslim politics', law, religion, education and institutions in various collections, see W.C. Smith, *Islam in Modern History* (Princeton University Press, 1957); D.E. Smith (ed.), *South Asian Politics and Religion* (Princeton University Press, 1966); S.T. Lokhandwala (ed.), *India and Contemporary Islam* (Simla: Indian Institute of Advanced Study, 1971); Zafar Imam (ed.), *Muslims in India* (Delhi: Orient Longman, 1975); *Muslim Communities in non-Muslim States* (London: Islamic Council of Europe, 1980); Ratna Naidu, *The Communal Edge to Plural Societies: India and Malaysia* (Delhi: Vikas, 1980); M. Ali Kettani, *Muslim Minorities in the World Today* (London, New York, 1986); Jim Masselos (ed.), *India: Creating a Modern Nation* (Delhi: Sterling, 1990); Ramashray Roy and Richard Sisson (eds), *Diversity and Dominance in Indian Politics*, vol. 2 (Delhi: Sage, 1990); K.N. Panikkar (ed.), *Communalism in India: History, Politics and Culture* (Delhi: Manohar, 1991); Robert D. Baird (ed.), *Religion and Law in Independent India* (Delhi: Manohar, 1993); Tahir Mahmood, *Statute-Law Relating to Muslims in India: A Study in Constitutional Perspectives* (Delhi: Institute of Objective Studies, 1995); A.R. Saiyed, *Religion and Ethnicity Among Muslims* (Jaipur: Rawat Publications, 1995); 'Islam', *Seminar* (416), April 1994; 'Communalism Divides', *Seminar* (374), October 1990.

For the Babri Masjid-Ramjanmabhumi and its violent aftermath, see Praful Bidwai *et al.* (eds), *Religion, Religiosity and Communalism* (Delhi: Manohar, 1996); Ashis Nandy *et al.*, *Creating a Nationality: The Ramjanmabhumi Movement and the Fear of the Self* (Delhi: OUP, 1993); Nilanjan Mukhopadhyay, *The Demolition: India at the Crossroad* (Delhi:

wide open for the polemical writings of A.B. Shah, a self-professed follower of M.N. Roy and founder of the 'Indian Secular Society', his friends Hamid Dalwai and M.A. Karandikar, the late Girilal Jain, also a 'Royist' and former editor of the *Times of India*, and Arun Shourie, an author-journalist whose essays on 'Islam' and 'Muslims' inflame rather than soothe religious passions.[63]

The standard tenet for such authors has been that 'Islam' as such provides a complete identity, explanation and moral code for Muslims, and the mere fact of people being Islamic in some general sense is conflated with that of their adherence to beliefs and policies that are strictly described as 'Islamist' or 'fundamentalist'. Orthodox Islam, according to them, promotes political quietism, discourages secular formations, and rules out 'the rise of a movement that may question in any radical sense the ideological basis of a Muslim society'.[64] That is why India's Muslims, supposedly loyal to the dictates of the *ulama* and theologians, resist democracy and secularism. In the terms of a typical Orientalist cliché, Islam was not just a religion but a complete way of life. The totalitarian character of the faith seemed to imply that only a totalitarian state could put its dogmas into practice.[65] Thus the highly pernicious and crude observation:

Another important factor contributing to Indian Muslims' backwardness has been their rigid adherence to outdated ideological/theological doctrines. There has been virtually no worthwhile renaissance in Muslim society. The Muslims continue to be fanatically devoted to religion at the cost of nationalism and modernization. The Muslim. masses, in spite of their secularized rulers and environment, have turned deaf ears to the message of secularism and democracy, and have remained constant in their belief in God, the Prophet, and the Quran.

Indus, 1994); D. Mandal, *Ayodhya: Archaelogy after Demolition* (Delhi: Orient Longman, 1993); *Citizens Tribunal on Ayodhya: Report of the Inquiry Commission* (Delhi: July 1993); *India Briefing, 1993* (Boulder, CO: Westview Press, 1993); Sarvepalli Gopal (ed.), *Anatomy of a Confrontation: The Babri Masjid-Ramjanmabhumi Issue* (Delhi: Viking, 1991); Sushil Srivastava, *The Disputed Mosque: A historical inquiry* (Delhi: Vistaar Publications, 1991). For articles in journals and magazines, see *South Asia*, special issue, 17, 1994; 'South Asia responses to the Ayodhya crisis', *Asian Survey*, 33, 7, July 1993; 'Ayodhya', *Seminar* (402), February 1993. For the rioting in Bombay, see Dilip Padgaonkar (ed.), *When Bombay Burned* (Delhi: UBS, 1993).

[63] A.B. Shah, *Religion and Society in India* (Bombay: Somaiya, 1981), and his *Challenges to Secularism* (Bombay: Nachiketa, 1968); M.A. Karandikar, *Islam in India's Transition to Modernity* (Delhi: Orient Longman, 1968); Arun Shourie, *Indian Controversies: Essays on Religion and Politics* (Delhi: ASA, 1989), and his *A Secular Agenda* (Delhi: ASA, 1993); S.E. Hasnain, *Indian Muslims: Challenge and Opportunity* (Bombay: Lalvani, 1968). Shourie is a regular columnist. In September 1995, some of his articles on Muslims published in a Hindi newspaper led to protests in the town of Bareilly in UP, and to the imposition of curfew by the district authorities. *Statesman* (Delhi), 25 September 1995.

[64] A.B. Shah, introduction, Hasnain, op. cit., p. 5.

[65] For an elaboration of this point, see Gudrun Kramer, 'Islamic Notions of Democracy', *Middle East Report*, July-August 1993, and the recent writings of Fred Halliday.

They abide by the values and religious advice of the *mullahs* and refuse to come to terms with sweeping changes taking place around them.[66]

There is also the following Hindu propagandist view put forward by one of its most consistent exponents:

There is plenty of evidence to show that the muslim behaviour pattern has remained true to type in the years after 1947. We have witnessed an increasing incidence of street riots staged by the same sorts of muslim hooligans, on the same sort of petty pretexts as in the years preceding Partition...Meanwhile, muslim majorities can be manipulated in many more districts by mass conversion of the weaker sections of Hindu society with the help of petro-dollars, by mass infiltration from Bangladesh and Pakistan, and by mass breeding under divine command from the quran and the *hadis*. The contours of the controversy can be seen by all those who have not become blinded by secularist slogans or have not been demoralised by a vote-hungry politics.[67]

In an article published in 1981 which has not received the attention it deserves, Peter B. Mayer identified three major approaches arising from the broader traditions of 'Oriental' studies, and found each one of them 'reductionist' in character, based on false assumptions, and irremediably flawed methodologically. According to him, the 'reification' of Islam in the realm of political ideas results in the postulation of a 'Quranic Political Culture' based on the formal ideology of the religion. Instead of considering what political ideas any particular group of Muslims holds, and the relations between these and their social conditions and practice, the reification of Islam leads to essentially circular suggestions that both practice and ideas are identical with the Quranic Political Culture. In Mayer's own study of two towns (Tiruchirapalli in Tamil Nadu and Jabalpur in Madhya Pradesh) 'ordinary Muslims emerge...not as one would have been led to expect as members of a monolithic community sitting sullenly apart, but as active participants in regional cultures whose perspective they share'. He concluded:

The views of contemporary Indian Muslims have been found to be more diverse, more complex, and better integrated with those of Indians of other religious beliefs than the statements found within the corpus of received opinions on the subject suggest. The obstinacy of resistance to this simple truth is in itself a matter of more than passing significance; until the ghosts of the political struggles of the past century are put to rest, and with them the reproduction

[66] Dhirendra Vajpeyi, 'Muslim Fundamentalism in India: A Crisis of Identity in a Secular State' in Dhirendra Vajpeyi and Yogendra K. Malik (eds), *Religious and Ethnic Minority Politics in South Asia* (Delhi: Manohar, 1989), p. 62.

[67] It is noteworthy that 'Muslim', 'Quran' and 'Hadis' are spelt with small letters whereas 'Hindu' is spelt with a capital 'H'. Sita Ram Goel, *Muslim Separation: Causes and Consequences* (Delhi: Voice of India, 1983), pp. 4, 5-6. See also J.A. Naik, *Death or Resurrection: A Story of the Hindus* (Delhi: Ajanta, 1994); B.N. Jog, *Threat of Islam: Indian Dimensions* (Bombay: Unnati Prakashan, 1995).

of fallacious conceptions of Indian Muslims, the true complexity, diversity and integration of Muslims in India will remain obscured.[68]

I seek to disentangle some of these issues, question the essentialist view of Indian Islam, evaluate whether or not Muslims have been rethinking traditional Islamic tenets in terms of the contemporary situation, and show in what senses there is not, and in what sense there is, a conflict between the 'traditional' and the modern, democratic and secular forces. That is why I spell out the issues underlying past and present, Islamist and modernist movements, discuss the contested terrain of who represents Muslims in state and society, the nature of the political and religious leadership, and the ability of that leadership to connect with the different political, economic, cultural, linguistic and educational experiences of most Muslims.

Consistent with my earlier works, I treat the religious-constituted blocs, from whichever side they come, with utmost caution. I regard the followers of Islam not as a religious collectivity, homogenous and structured, but as a disparate, differentiated and stratified segment of society. I locate their histories and contemporary experiences in the 'Indian environment' (to borrow Aziz Ahmad's phrase) and not in relation to the so-called world of Islam, which is far removed from the imagination of most Muslims. I therefore examine the dynamics of living in a broadly democratic and secular ethos, and highlight an emerging pattern of pragmatic engagement with the social, political and economic processes. My concern is with the matter-of-fact narration of those forces that promote or retard this process rather than with discovering mysterious 'essences' that prevent 'Indianisation' or 'integration' into the 'national mainstream'.

At a time when some in the West talk too readily of a 'green menace', and others are prepared to go along with Samuel P. Huntingdon's vision of the future in terms of a 'clash of civilisations', it is important to take a fresh look at Hindu-Muslim relations in contemporary India. At a time when the Islamists and the Hindu Sangh-combine (RSS, BJP, VHP and other affiliated organisations) are busy disseminating their world view, it is necessary to explore the 'modernist' understanding of Islam, the enthusiastic participation of Muslims in democratic processes and their support, whatever the reasons, for a secular state and society. At a time when secularism as a concept and as a state policy is under critical scrutiny,[69] it is worth examining not just the theory but the strength and

---

[68] Peter B. Mayer, 'Tombs and Dark Houses: Ideology, Intellectuals, and Proletarians in the Study of Contemporary Indian Islam', *Journal of Asian Studies*, 25, 3, May 1981, pp. 484, 497. Reprinted in Ahmad (ed.), *Modernisation and Social Change*, op. cit. See also, S.A.K. Haqqi, 'Muslims in India: A Behavioural Introduction', in Ansari (ed.), op. cit., p. 58.

[69] Prakash Chandra Upadhya, 'The Politics of Indian Secularism', *Modern Asian Studies*,

fragility of the secular experiment over the last four decades. At a time when some regard Hindutva as the new mode of civil society, it is imperative to ask how and why this is so.[70]

Few would deny that such issues have serious implications for democracy and secularism, for 110 million Muslims, and for the future of Islam in the subcontinent. They need to be studied afresh as, fifty years after independence, India carries the burden of the past in grappling with regional conflicts, religious antipathies and sectarian strife. This work evaluates the impact of the processes of political, economic and cultural fusions and fissions on Muslims, and thus tries to restore a perspective on the contemporary predicaments of Indian society.

In general, the sequence of events followed in this work is chronological, although I sometimes turn back and forth to discern elements of continuity, change and disjunctions in the flow of ideas and the trajectory of movements. Secondly, I hope that my understanding of 'nation', 'community', 'communalism' and 'secular nationalism' is embedded in my approach, methodology and arguments.

Legacy of a Divided Nation begins with Partition and concludes with the demolition of the Babri Masjid at Ayodhya on the fateful afternoon of 6 December 1992. Both are momentous events, symbolising heightened religious consciousness, the renewed salience of Hindu-Muslim schisms, and the weakness and ultimate retreat of the state in dealing with Hindu and Muslim extremism. My main engagement is with their *legacy* and, in a more general sense, with the current debate about the possible direction of Indian society, the future of secularism, and the fate of religious minorities.

For these reasons the themes underlined in this work concern the nation as a whole and not just a region or a community. Yet the main story revolves around UP, India's most populous state in the heart of the Hindi-speaking belt.[71] Although it has fewer Muslims than Jammu and

---

26, 4, 1992, pp. 815-53; Mark Juergensmeyer, *The New Cold War?: Religious Nationalism Confronts the Secular State* (Delhi: OUP, 1993); Katherine K. Young, 'The Indian Secular State under Hindu Attack: A New Perspective on the crisis of Legitimation', in Ninian Smart (ed.), *Ethnic and Political Dilemmas of Modern India* (London: Macmillan Press, 1993), pp. 194-234; 'Revivalism and Identity', *Seminar* (411), November 1993; 'Secularism in Crisis', *India International Centre Quarterly* (Delhi), 26, 1, spring 1993.

[70] 'Simply stated, Hindutva is the character or quality of being Hindu. [...] Basically, Hindutva is India's agenda for coming into its own after centuries of vicissitudes.' Malkani, op. cit., p. 147. See also Walter K. Anderson and Shridhar D. Damle, *The Brotherhood in Saffron: The Rashtriya Swayamsevak Sangh and Hindu Revivalism* (Delhi: Vistaar, 1987); Bruce Graham, *Hindu Nationalism and Indian Politics: The Origins and Development of the Bharatiya Jana Sangh* (CUP, 1990); Tapan Basu et al., *Khaki Shorts and Saffron Flags* (Delhi: Orient Longman, 1993).

[71] UP's population, according to the 1991 census, was 140 million. See Brass, *Language, Religion and Politics*, op. cit.; Harold A. Gould, *Grass Roots Politics in India: A Century of Political Evolution in Faizabad District* (Delhi: Oxford and IBH Publishing Co., 1995); Zoya Hasan, 'Pattern of Resilience and Change in Uttar Pradesh Politics', in Francine R.

Kashmir, Assam, Bengal and Kerala, this has not diminished UP's importance in politics and in several sectors of the economy. Some among them, chiefly in certain central and western districts, are rich peasants, wealthy artisans, entrepreneurs, traders and exporters. They command wealth, political power and patronage. They are involved in state and national politics, and tied to all-India, regional and local parties. Their bonds with the 'community' – a constituency they assiduously nurse – are strong. They fund local schools and colleges, contribute to the building and upkeep of mosques, and take up the 'Muslim causes'. The additional leverage is gained by tying up with the intricate caste-based alliances and combinations.[72] As a result, a new set of leaders with a different social background has replaced the *taluqdars*, petty landlords or urban-based professionals who dominated the Muslim League before independence. They have rewritten the pre-Partition agenda by accommodating both community and caste- and class-based interests, and picked up support from a much broader constituency.

UP has remained the home of several Muslim political organisations and prestigious educational centres, such as Aligarh's Muslim University, Deoband's Dar al-ulum and Lucknow's Nadwat al-ulama. Some of the key debates have been conducted in these institutions. Some of the major movements such as the Hindi-Urdu controversy,[73] the agitation for banning cow-slaughter, the clamour for a separate Muslim nation and the Hindutva campaigns can be traced to UP. Some of the most violent Hindu-Muslim riots after independence have erupted there.[74]

UP is supposed to be the land of Aryavarta. The birthplace of Ram and Krishna and the numerous pilgrimage centres are located here. Muslims, too, cherish their historic and contemporary associations with some of its towns, and take pride in its mosques, shrines, *imambaras* and educational centres. Lucknow, Rampur, Faizabad and Jaunpur were the home of great musicians, dancers, Urdu writers and poets, and the focus of much creative and intellectual activities. The Awadh court was, wrote Abul Halim Sharar (1860-1926), the essayist-novelist,

... the final example of oriental refinement and culture in India. There are several other courts to remind us of former times, but the one in which old culture and

---

Frankel and M.S.A. Rao (eds), *Dominance and State Power in Modern India: Decline of a Social Order*, vol. 1 (Delhi: OUP, 1989).

[72] Zoya Hasan, 'Shifting Ground: Hindutva Politics and the Farmers' Movement in Uttar Pradesh' in Tom Brass (ed.), *New Farmers' Movement in India* (London: Frank Cass, 1995).

[73] Brass, *Language, Religion and Politics*, chapter 4; Ather Farouqi, 'Urdu Education in India: Four Representative States', *EPW*, 2 April 1994. See also, *The Annual of Urdu Studies* (University of Wisconsin-Madison: Centre for South Asia) no. 10, 1995.

[74] Asghar Ali Engineer (ed.), *Communal Riots in Independence India* (Delhi: Sangam, 1984); Akbar, op. cit.; Pramod Kumar, *Polluted Sacred Faith: A Study on Communalism and Violence* (Delhi: Ajanta, 1992).

social life reached its zenith was this court of Awadh which was established not long ago and, after making astonishing advances, came to an abrupt end.[75]

In present-day India UP takes pride not in the values cherished by Sharar or Attia Hosain, but in its demographic weight and its consequent political clout. The future of the Congress, as also of various caste-based alliances, rests in UP. The fate of the Hindutva campaign, triggered off in its most recent incarnation by the Babri Masjid-Ramjanmabhumi issue, is likely to be decided by the UP electorate. In other words, UP 'matters' a great deal more in the post-Ayodhya period because of the way in which the 'politics of difference', the cultural heterogeneity and the intellectual diversities will be played out.[76] Ultimately, the electorate in UP and its legislators would tilt the balance in deciding whether India remains 'secular' or not.[77]

[75] Abdul Halim Sharar, *Lucknow: The Last Phase of an Oriental Culture*, transl. and edited by E.S. Harcourt and Fakhir Hussain (London: Paul Elek, 1975).

[76] Alok Rai, in *Seminar* (432), August 1995, p. 13.

[77] The total strength of the Assembly (Vidhan Sabha) in Lucknow was 422 in 1993. The state elects 85 members of parliament to the Lok Sabha in Delhi.

2

THE MYTH OF MUSLIM UNITY: COLONIAL AND NATIONAL NARRATIVES

'Of all the great religions ... Islam alone was borne forth into the world on a great wave of forceful conquest.... There was seldom a pause in the consolidation of Mahomedan power, seldom a break in the long-drawn tale of plunder and carnage, cruelty and lust, unfolded in the history of the earlier dynasties that ruled India.'

Valentine Chirol (1852-1929)[*]

'You never ceased proclaiming that Islam spread by the sword: You have not deigned to tell us what it is the gun has spread.'

Akbar Allahabadi (1846-1921)[†]

'Hinduism, with its love of images and symbols, and its polytheism, and Islam with its strict Unitarian faith and its strong iconoclastic principles, are at opposite poles.'

Reginald Craddock (1868-1937)[‡]

I

A disquieting feature of the Hindutva wave was the demolition of the Babri Masjid at Ayodhya; equally, the way Hindu propagandists conjured up the image of a community outside the 'national mainstream'. The familiar representation of Indian Muslims was as aggressive fundamentalists, the descendants of the depraved and tyrannical medieval rulers who demolished temples and forcibly converted Hindus to Islam. They were also portrayed as 'fifth columnists', tied to Muslim countries through the common Islamic bond. They were, moreover, demonised as 'separatists' and indicted for partitioning the country in August 1947.

Some of these images and impressions gained currency during the

---

[*] *India Old and New* (London: Macmillan, 1921), pp. 46-7.
[†] Ralph Russell, *The Pursuit of Urdu Literature: A Select History* (Delhi: OUP, 1992), p. 131.
[‡] *The Dilemma in India* (London: Constable, 1929), p. 10.

second half of the nineteenth century. Why has the image of the Other not altered or modified over time? And why have secular and modernist ideologies failed to mediate effectively and communicate an alternative world view? Is it because of the Muslim intelligentsia's own assertion of a unity of interest and ideal and their conviction that they were part of an indivisible community with one way of thinking? Or were they logical victims of their own myth-making, claiming for themselves an alien culture (if not origin) and being so regarded by others? What weight does one attach to the representation of Muslims in colonial and national narratives and its significance in the evolution of a *Muslim* personality in the subcontinent? The colonial government's role is largely familiar. Much less known is how the 'nationalist' images and stereotypes were just as important as the colonial framework that was evolved to define and categorise Muslims.

Any number of scholarly studies, Edward Said's *Orientalism* included, are replete with instances of Islam being represented as a hostile and aggressive force, and of Muslim societies being caricatured as rigid, authoritarian and uncreative.[1] Several British writers on India, some occupying high government positions, perpetuated a repertoire of such images, construing Islam as an emblem of repellent otherness, 'the faith of a body of savage marauders and conquerors, who swept over the land ... in a series of cruel raids, bringing rapine and destruction in their train.'[2] The Sultans of Delhi, like their Ottoman counterparts in Constantinople, were projected as great iconoclasts and considered tokens of evil and scapegoats for acts with which they had no connection. Bishop Heber, a fervent missionary who stayed in India from 1823 to 1826, wanted Hindus to be reminded 'that we did not conquer them, but found them conquered, that their previous rulers were as much strangers to their blood and to their religion as we are, and that they were notoriously far more oppressive masters than we have ever shown ourselves.'[3]

For most travellers, missionaries, administrators and ethnographers[4]

---

[1] Edward W. Said, *Orientalism* (London: Routledge & Kegan Paul, 1978); Normal Daniel, *Islam and the West: The Making of an Image* (Edinburgh University Press, 1960); Aziz Al-Azmeh, *Islams and Modernities* (London: Verso, 1993).

[2] W. Crooke, *The North-Western Provinces of India: Their History, Ethnology, and Administration* (1897, Delhi: 1975 reprint), pp. 258-9.

[3] M.A. Laird (ed.), *Bishop Heber in Northern India: Selection from Heber's Journal* (CUP, 1971), p. 64. 'With the monumental wreckage of those early Mahomedan dynasties, steeped in treachery and bloodshed', commented Valentine Chirol (1852-1929), journalist and in charge of the foreign department of *The Times* (1908-12), 'the plain of Delhi is still strewn.' *India Old and New*, p. 3.

[4] The literature on the subject is vast, though its fuller analysis is awaited. For clues and insights see Daniel, *Islam and the West*, op. cit., pp. 266-85; A.J. Greenberger, *The British Image of India: A Study on the Literature of Imperialism 1880-1960* (London: OUP, 1969); Peter Hardy, *The Muslims of British India* (CUP, 1972), pp. 1-2, 62-91; Francis Robinson,

Islam was static and dogmatic. Its adherents were conservative, rigid, haughtily contemptuous of things 'modern' and influenced by an obsolete system of education.[5] Major-General Stockley Warren was upset that a Muslim 'coolie' was not persuaded to take brandy for medicinal purposes: 'These men I presume we shall ultimately civilise, make them Christians and drunkards, and lead them to liberty.'[6] The civil servant E.C. Bayley told the viceroy Northbrook in 1864 that the standard of 'Muslim morality' was appallingly low. The 'corruptions' in Muslim manners and social habits, he added, had taken place long before they came into contact with the Europeans.[7]

A 'community' so steeped in religious obscurantism was prone to be hostile to the British government. Arthur Owen, veteran of the 1857 days, referred to the 'wily Mahratta' and the 'crafty Brahman'. But he was more concerned with the 'sensual Mohammadan' and his belief that 'if one of their creed falls in battle against the infidels, Christians in particular, he is immediately translated to the garden of paradise.'[8] Writing nearly half a century later, Bampfylde Fuller, first lieutenant-governor of the new province of East Bengal and Assam, discovered an 'undertone of [Muslim] hostility to their Christian rulers'. 'Of such men

---

Separatism Among Indian Muslims: The Politics of the United Provinces' Muslims, 1860-1923 (CUP, 1974), pp. 164-73; David Lelyveld, *Aligarh's First Generation: Muslim Solidarity in British India* (Princeton University Press, 1978); Gyanendra Pandey, *The Construction of Communalism in Colonial India* (Delhi: OUP, 1990); Clinton Bennet, *Victorian Images of Islam* (London: Grey Seal, 1992); Carol A. Breckenridge and Peter van der Veer (eds), *Orientalism and the Postcolonial Predicament* (Delhi: OUP, 1994); David Ludden (ed.), *Contesting the Nation: Religion, Community and the Politics of Democracy in India* (Philadelphia: University of Pennsylvania Press, 1996); Michael R. Anderson, 'Islamic Law and the Colonial Encounter in British India' in Chibli Mallat and Jane Connors (eds), *Islamic Family Law* (London: Graham and Trotman, 1990); Avril Powell, *Muslims and Missionaries in Pre-Mutiny India* (London: Curzon Press, 1993); Lucy Carrol, 'Colonial Perceptions of Indian Society and the Emergence of Caste(s) Associations', *Journal of Asian Studies*, 27, 2, February 1978, pp. 223-50; and Kenneth Jones, 'Religious Identity and the Census' in N.G. Barrier (ed.), *The Census in British India* (Delhi: Manohar, 1981), pp. 83-5.

[5] Sidney Low, *A Vision of India* (London: Smith, Elder, 1911), p. 281. Low was an eminent journalist and writer. His book was well received by *The Times* in London, and by Curzon and Morley. And the comment of the Earl of Ronaldshay, Bengal governor (1917-22): 'A candid Muhammadan would probably admit that the most powerful factors in keeping the majority of Moslems aloof from the educational movement of the day were pride of race, a memory of bygone superiority, religious fears, and a not unnatural attachment to the learning of Islam.' *India: A Bird's-Eye View* (London: Constable, 1924), p. 235.

[6] Reminiscences [typescript], Mss. Eur. C-607, India Office Library and Oriental Collection, London [IOL]. The Major retired from service in 1885.

[7] E.C. Bayley to Northbrook, 10 July 1874, Northbrook papers, Mss. Eur. C-144/17, IOL.

[8] Arthur Owen, 'Recollections of a Veteran of the Days of the Great Indian Mutiny of 1857' (Lahore, 1915, 2nd edn), Mss. Eur. 239/120, IOL.

it may be truly said that at heart they are disloyal, and probably await their opportunity for manifesting their feelings in hostile acts.'[9]

Owen, Fuller and others, though by no means all British functionaries, assumed that Islam in the subcontinent was indelibly stamped by its early history, particularly by its original social carriers, and that Islamic values, inherently hostile to the West, caused and led to Muslim antipathies towards the government. In fact, the call to wreak a special vengeance upon Muslims, in the wake of the 'Wahabi' movement[10] and the 1857 revolt,[11] demonstrated how things 'Islamic' were construed, located, categorised and connected.

Another common belief was that the British presence irked Muslims because they identified themselves with the fortunes of the erstwhile ruling classes, preserved in their blood the pride of a conquering race,[12] and 'cherished in their hearts some memory of the days when their fathers were the masters of India, and they believe, rightly or wrongly, that if ever the English power were shaken they would regain their old dominance.'[13] Harcourt Butler, governor of the United Provinces in 1918-20 during the heyday of British imperialism, raised the spectre of a Muslim 'conspiracy' to overthrow the British with the aid of their 'virile' co-religionists in India and overseas.[14]

Evidence in support of such contentions was thin. The fact that a Shah Waliullah or a Mirza Ghalib bemoaned the decline of the Mughal empire should not be treated lightly, but it should also not be construed as a generalised or undifferentiated 'Muslim response'. Most Muslims had no cause to be lyrical on the glory of the Mughals or mourn its fall. Doubtless, the élite or their interlocutors sought an external Muslim imperium for help in reconsolidating their local or regional authority. Thus Shah

---

[9] Bampfylde Fuller, *India The Land and Its People*, pp. 41 and 124, and his *The Empire of India* (London: Pitman, 1913). And the view that 'the Mahomedan star is not in the ascendant, and his position wars with his religion. That enjoins conversion by the sword if need be, and an almost fierce intolerance of the idolater. His whole entourage therefore is galling.' Low, *Vision of India*, p. 281; also, Flora Annie Steel, *India* (London: A. & C. Black, 1905), p. 180.

[10] Qeyamuddin Ahmad, *The Wahhabi Movement in India* (Delhi: Manohar, 1994 revised edn).

[11] Thomas R. Metcalf, *The Aftermath of Revolt: India, 1857-1880* (Delhi: Manohar, 1990 reprint), pp. 298-302.

[12] Harcourt Butler, 'The Country, Peoples, Language and Creeds' in John Cumming (ed.), *Modern India: A Co-operative Survey* (Delhi: OUP, 1932), p. 15; G.T. Garrat, *An Indian Commentary* (London: Cape, 1929), p. 172, basing his assessment on the dubious testimony of the Khoja spiritual leader, the Aga Khan.

[13] Low, *Vision of India*, p. 281.

[14] *Speeches, by Harcourt Butler delivered at the M.A.O. College, Aligarh, on 25 November 1919* (Allahabad: Pioneer Press, 1921), pp. 140-1, and his *India Insistent* (London: Heinemann, 1931), p. 38; and Lelyveld, op. cit., pp. 9-10.

Waliullah turned to an Ahmad Shah Abdali or a Najib al-daula to rescue India for Islam; Syed Ahmad of Rae Bareli corresponded with Central Asian rulers to recognise his *Khilafat*.[15] But British officials would have known from their own interactions and administrative experience that most Muslims were prepared to make the colonial government work, and seek adjustments within, and gain benefits from, administrative and bureaucratic structures. Yet most of them stuck to their inherited frameworks and legitimised those policies that were designed to tame and humble the supposedly recalcitrant Muslims. 'The world is full of groups relying on their connection with some dominant "race" elsewhere,' commented the historian G.T. Garrat. 'The claim is natural enough, but the English, in accepting this picture of the Moslems as a race apart, seem to have been misled by a writer of genius [Rudyard Kipling], who had, however, a journalist's flair for the picturesque, and who always saw the Peninsula in terms of the Punjab.'[16]

The generalities extended, especially after 1857, to an appraisal of Indian Islam, of Muslims and their relationship with other religious groups, especially the 'Hindus'. Some British officials found it easy to get on with the Muslims at a social level.[17] They could understand the essentials of their faith, 'built on Jewish foundations and devoid of the crudities and subtleties of Brahminism.'[18] But most came to India with their pre-conceived notions about the strong bonds that tied Indian Islam with the Arabian peninsula, about Muslims forming a well-knit religious entity, acting as a monolith and keeping the desert faith pure in the land of idol-worshippers.[19] There were some saner voices, but most came to the conclusion that Muslims were endowed with 'cultural coherence', a real sense of unity transcending considerations of race, class, language and region, and 'an essential community of thought' and view point which was authoritatively voiced through their representative bodies.[20] 'The solidarity of Islam was a hard fact against which it was futile to run one's head.'[21]

---

[15] Hardy, *Muslims of British India*, pp. 54, 58.

[16] Garrat, *Indian Commentary*, p. 173.

[17] As opposed to 'the Hindu, with his glib tongue, his pliant brain and back, his fantastic social rites, and his incomprehensible religion....' Low, *Vision of India*, p. 281.

[18] George Lumley to Linlithgow, 14 December 1939, L/P&J/8/645, IOL.

[19] The unifying force of Islam, commented Fuller, 'has checked schism, and religious divisions are few in number.' Bampfylde Fuller, *Studies of Indian Life and Sentiments* (London: John Murray, 1910), p. 125. See also W.W. Titus, 'The Reaction of Muslim India to Western Islam' in John R. Mott (ed.), *The Muslim World Today* (London: Hodder and Stoughton, 1925), p. 93; Claude H. Hill, 'Religion and Caste in India' in *India and the Durbar* (London: Macmillan, 1911), p. 210. He was editor of *The Times*.

[20] Henry Whitehead, *Indian Problems in Religion, Education, Politics* (London: Constable, 1924). He was Bishop of Madras before becoming a Fellow of Trinity College, Cambridge; Garrat, *Indian Commentary*, p. 172.

[21] Lawrence, second Marquess of Zetland, *Essays* (London: Constable, 1956), p. 119. See

The governor of Bengal, who administered a province largely populated by Muslims, illustrated the strength of the call of Islam – 'a call which rings insistently in the ears of the devout Muslims, whether of India or elsewhere, drowning the call of country and all else.' He put forward the official view, unchanged for nearly a century, that the

....ethnic pageant which passes across one's vision as one travels over India is made up of many tableaux. There is one such tableau which at once arrests attention because of the many points of contrast which it provides with the rest of the procession .... It is a tableau in which we see represented a religion, a civilization and culture, and an outlook differing profoundly in all material respects from those of Hinduism.[22]

Such impressions were based on patently hollow theories, mostly divorced from realities on the ground. Islam in its Perso-Arabic attire failed to make much sense in India. Hence, the attempt by its 'cultural mediators' to marry Islamic traditions with syncretic and symbolic forms.[23] In the process, the pristine purity of dogmas and tenets was tailored to suit local customs and heterodox traditions which found a place in the corpus of beliefs and religio-cultural practices. Medieval sultans may have wanted to erect a uniform religio-cultural system and impose religious authority from 'great' or 'middle' traditions, but long distances and syncretic beliefs and practices inhibited them from doing so. In the end the 'Islamic Little Tradition' – i.e., Islam as it was practised in everyday life – with its roots firmly anchored in Indian soil, developed autonomously from centralised political control.[24] The Faraizis in Bengal, the *mujahidins* in the north-west, and other itinerant preachers imposed their will sporadically in certain areas, but their impact was transient.

British civil servants – from William Crooke to Malcolm Darling – knew this well enough. From Unnao, close to Lucknow in UP, Charles Alfred Elliot reported the strong tendency among Muslims to assimilate with their Hindu neighbours. He found them wearing *dhotis* and using '*Ram-Ram*' as the mode of salutation.[25] Fuller wrote on Hindu influences among Muslims: in purely agricultural districts the people 'not only understand each other's systems, but the systems often seem to overlap.' Hindus and Muslims attended each other's festivals, and sang each other's songs.[26] Both in urban and rural areas, most Hindus venerated Husain, the

---

also T.W. Holderness, *Peoples and Problems of India* (London: Constable, 1911), p. 127.

[22] Ronaldshay, *India: A Bird's-Eye View*, p. 214.

[23] Asim Roy, *The Islamic Syncretistic Tradition in Bengal* (Princeton University Press, 1983), p. 249.

[24] The argument is based on Frank C. Darling, *The Westernization of Asia: A Comparative Political Analysis* (Boston: G.K. Hall, 1939), pp. 21-9.

[25] C.A. Elliot, *Laborious Days* (Calcutta: J.Larkins, 1892), p. 28.

[26] Fuller, *Studies*, pp. 130-1; Edward Thompson, *The Reconstruction of India* (London:

grandson of the Prophet Mohammad, and incorporated his cult into their ritual calendar as yet one more divinity in the pantheon. His trials and tribulations at Karbala, now in Iraq, and his courage and tenacity inspired unbounded faith in a universal nemesis ensuring justice for oppressed souls.

W.H. Sleeman found Hindu princes in central and southern India, 'even of the brahmin caste', commemorating Muharram. The historian Ameer Ali was told by his father that during his youth in the 1860s he had many Hindu friends and that 'in those days there was no bitterness between Hindus and Muslims. They both lived and worked together in complete amity.' Lytton, Bengal's governor in the 1920s, noticed how well the rank and file of the communities got on with each other in all the daily business of life.[27] O.M. Martin, having served in the province from 1915 to 1926, was emphatic that their mutual dependence and friendship was not a temporary occurrence but part of an old and cherished tradition.[28]

Colonial knowledge created and perpetuated myths and conjured up stereotypical images of peoples and countries as part of an imperial design of fortifying the ideological edifice of the Empire. Therefore, much of the knowledge and understanding derived from experience in the field was not reflected in concrete political decisions or translated into constitutional decrees. In the constitutional plans, which broadly reflected the colonial assumptions about Indian society, the Mapilla Muslim appeared indistinguishable from Kipling's sturdy Pathan; the Urdu-speaking landed élite of Awadh were no different from the Tamil-speaking merchant brethren; E.M. Forster's Cambridge friend Syed Ross Masood was cast in the same mould as a *karkhandar* (artisan) in Delhi's old city; Shias and Sunnis, Bohras and Khojas, the Barelwis, the Deobandis and the Ahl-i Hadith were all considered part of pan-Indian Islam.[29]

Faber and Faber, 1930), p. 234.

[27] Ameer Ali, *Echoes of British India* (privately published in England in 1979 by Lady Ameer Ali), p. 137, MSS. EUR. C 336/2, Ameer Ali Collection. For accounts of Muharram observances, see P.D. Reeves (ed.), *Sleeman in Oudh: An Abridgement of W.H. Sleeman's 'A Journey Through the Kingdom of Oude in 1849-50 '* (CUP, 1971); W.S. Blunt, *India under Ripon: A Private Diary* (London, 1909), p. 72; Walter Roper Lawrence, *The India We Served* (London: Cassell, 1928), pp. 292- 3. For Bengal, see Earl of Lytton, *Pundits and Elephants: Being the Experiences of Five Years as Governor of an Indian Province* (London, 1942), p. 172; Garrat, *Indian Commentary*, pp. 175-6, 181.

[28] Memoirs of O.M. Martin (typescript), Centre for South Asian Studies, Cambridge [CSAS].

[29] Bishop Heber first came in contact with the Bohras – 'by far the wealthier and more industrious party' – in Rajasthan. He found them to be 'peaceable and orderly merchants and tradesmen' with considerable 'influence and privileges' in Central India. His other interesting observation was that the Bohras were 'agreeing far better with both Jains and Rajpoots than their Sunnite rivals'. *Bishop Heber in Northern India*, p. 282.

It is true that the conventional wisdom about Muslims and their role in the 1857 revolt was questioned by, among others, George Campbell, second-in-command to James Outram after the capture of Lucknow;[30] W.W. Hunter, Bengal civilian and India's first Director-General of Statistics;[31] and W.S. Blunt, an old-fashioned patriot shocked by the vulgarity of the new imperialism.[32] But there was no significant appraisal of existing theories, no substantial change in thinking or attitudes. Muslims were no more than 'a nation of 50 million, with their monotheism, their iconoclastic fanaticism, their animal sacrifices, their social equality and their remembrance of the days when, enthroned at Delhi, they reigned supreme from the Himalayas to Cape Cormorin.'[33]

This was the viceroy Dufferin writing in 1888. Just a decade later, Anthony Macdonnell, UP's lieutenant-governor (1895-1901), treated Muslims with the same degree of suspicion and ill-will. He believed that theological seminaries, such as the Nadwat al-ulama, promoted disaffection and sedition. Adding credence to wild and exaggerated notions about pan-Islamism, he expressed the belief that Muslims were loyal to the Ottoman Khalifa.[34] This was a false assumption; there was no pan-Islamic ferment in UP or anywhere else in the country. Scores of influential Muslims denied the Turkish Sultan's claim to be a Khalifa. If others did not do so, it was because the British themselves encouraged pan-Islamic sensibilities in order to bolster their imperialist concerns in the Balkans.

Political rights, Syed Ahmad Khan said, 'were more important than religious traditions, and so long as the Muslims lived freely under British rule they would remain good subjects.'[35] Maulvi Zakaullah (1832-1910), eminent historian and professor of Arabic and Persian at Muir Central

---

[30] He emphatically denied that there was a Muslim insurrection or that Muslims were a formidable danger to the government. He was unhappy at their 'exclusion' and 'degradation'. He insisted that 'each section of people in each district must be judged by their acts, and not otherwise; and that they should be fairly judged – not by a foregone prejudice, but with an equal mind'. James Outram, *Memoirs of my Indian Career* (London: Macmillan, 1893), p. 397.

[31] W.W. Hunter, *Indian Mussalman: Are they Bound in Conscience to Rebel against the Queen* ? (Calcutta, 1945 edn), p. 123. For an analysis of Hunter's work, see Lelyveld, op. cit., pp. 10-14.

[32] Unlike the great majority of his compatriots, Blunt studied Islam and followed the fortunes of Muslim societies with an open mind. Of his book *The Future of Islam*, he wrote: 'In it I committed myself without reserve to the Cause of Islam as essentially the "Cause of God" over an immense portion of the world, and to be encouraged, not repressed, by all who cared for the welfare of mankind.' His sympathy for Islam eventually led him to champion the Arab cause against European intervention and Ottoman injustices. Rana Kabbani, *Europe's Myths of Oriental Devise and Rule* (London, 1986), pp. 96-7.

[33] Dufferin's Minute of November 1988, quoted in Hardy, op.cit., p. 1.

[34] Mushirul Hasan, *Nationalism and Communal Politics in India, 1885-1930* (Delhi: Manohar, 1991), pp. 53-4; Robinson, *Separatism*, pp. 133-4.

[35] Robinson, op.cit., p. 112; Hardy, op.cit., p. 178.

College in Allahabad, agreed that his co-religionists should not look to foreign countries for guidance, since 'for a thousand years, our own religion of Islam had been intimately bound up with India; and in India, Islam had won some of its greatest triumphs, for its own popular form of civilization.'[36] Syed Mehdi Ali (Nawab Mohsinul Mulk), Syed Ahmad's close friend and secretary of the Aligarh College (1898-1907), made clear that Turkey's Sultan could not exercise any of the powers and prerogatives of the Khilafa over India's Muslims, who were not bound by their religion to obey him.[37]

Overseas writers visiting India, including Halide Edib, insisted that Muslim allegiance to England during the First World War 'demolished a strong historical myth – it showed that political Pan-Islamism was a mere bogey. The attachment of the Indian Muslim to the interests of his country was a greater reality than his solidarity with Muslims outside India. *It may be useful for Western powers with Muslim colonies to realize that there is a distinct sense of nationhood separate from their religious life.* The Indian Muslim would resent an Afghan-Muslim domination and fight it; the Arab-Muslim would resent a Muslim-Turkish domination and fight it as much as he would any non-Muslim domination, if he ever got his independence.'[38]

The direction and flow of 'Muslim Politics', guided first by Syed Ahmad and later by the Muslim League, was towards compromise and accommodation with the government. New generations grew up for whom foreign rule was an unchanging fact of life, whether they liked it or not. Most modern and traditionally-educated Muslims, for whom the Faraizi or the Barelvi adventures were faint memories, sensed that they could no longer live in a stable and self-sufficient system of inherited culture. They recognised the need to generate the strength to survive in a world dominated by colonialism.[39] The *ulama*, many of whom had been harshly treated as arch-enemies of the British, made it clear after 1857 that their main plank was adjustment to the raj rather than repudiation of it. Abdul Hay (1848-86), a prominent *alim* of Lucknow's prestigious theological seminary in Firangi Mahal, considered the acceptance of British presence and the learning of English to be lawful as long as no harm to Islam resulted.[40] Deoband's Dar al-ulum, established in 1867, originated in a reconciliatory spirit and not in defiance of *Pax Britannica.*

[36] Annemarie Schimmel, *Islam in the Indian Subcontinent* (Leiden: E.J. Brill, 1980), p. 197.

[37] *Eminent Mussalmans* (Madras: G.A.Natesan, n.d.), p. 91.

[38] Halide Edib, *Inside India* (London, 1937), pp. 317-18. Emphasis added.

[39] Mushirul Hasan, 'Resistance and Acquiescence in North India', in Mushirul Hasan and Narayani Gupta (eds), *India's Colonial Encounter: Essays in Memory of Eric Stokes* (Delhi: Manohar, 1993); Hardy, op.cit., pp. 94-115.

[40] Barbara Daly Metcalf, *Islamic Revival in British India: Deoband, 1860-1900* (Princeton University Press, 1982), p. 279; Hardy, op. cit., p. 14.

In 1870 Maulana Ahmad Riza Khan (1856-1921), founder of the Barelwi school and the Ahl-i Sunnat wa Jamaat, declared British India a *dar al-Islam* (land of Islam).[41]

Macdonnell not only ignored these trends but also demonstrated lack of appreciation of the official line, which had grudgingly veered round to two sets of views: one based on the bizarre belief that the Muslims had to be won over because they were so terrible and fear-inspiring,[42] and the other on pragmatic imperial considerations. How could so many Muslims, some wielding local power and influence, be alienated for so long? They had to be enlisted 'as allies and auxillaries',[43] courted to thwart nationalist aspirations and to counter rabble-rousers in the Congress. They had to be quietened by a judicious mixture of buffets and boons. Mayo's note of 26 June 1871 on Muslim education indicated a change in course.[44] His successor, Northbrook, gained kudos for 'doing great good in directing attention to the long and grievously neglected subject of Mussalman education'.[45] Mayo had begun to fill the cup of reconciliation, Northbrook held it out.[46]

Charged with clearing up the political rubble created by Curzon's ill-advised decision in 1905 to partition Bengal, Minto probably extended his brief in according legitimacy to a deputation of thirty-five Muslims who met him at Simla on 1 October 1906. He did not ask them to establish their credentials or ascertain whether they were self-appointed leaders of the community and had a political constituency of their own. He merely assumed that the deputation had a 'representative character' and expressed the 'views and aspirations of the enlightened Muslim community of India'.

The crucial issue is not whether the Simla deputation was a 'command

[41] Quoted in Mujeeb Ahmad, *Jamiyyat Ulama-i Pakistan 1949-1979* (Islamabad: National Institute of Historical Research, 1993), p. xv. For a detailed analysis, see Usha Sanyal, *Devotional Islam and Politics in British India: Ahmad Riza Khan Barelwi and his Movement, 1870-1920* (Delhi: OUP, 1996).

[42] Edward Thompson to Wedgewood Benn, 31 December 1930, L/PO/6/74 (ii), IOL.

[43] Alfred Lyall to Morley, 4 February 1909, quoted in Robinson, op.cit., p. 170. This view could sometimes get mixed up with the articulation of world-wide imperial interests. For example, in the 1870s, the viceroy was told by the colonial office to remove any 'just cause of [Muslim] complaint, because, in the event of any action against Russia, our allies must be the Mahometans of Central Asia, Afghanistan, and of Russia'. To Northbrook, 21 February 1873, Northbrook papers, MSS. Eur. C-144/21 (1) IOL. Similar views were expressed during the First World War.

[44] Hardy, op. cit., p. 90; and Lelyveld, op. cit., p. 12.

[45] Rev. J. Long to Northbrook, 19 July 1873, Northbrook papers, Mss. Eur. C-144/21 (1). The secretary of state told the viceroy on 23 October 1882: 'If there be any real special grievances which affect the Muslim population which we can fairly remove, by all means let it be done.'

[46] Hardy, op. cit., p. 91.

performance' – a charge levelled against Minto's government but laboriously refuted by a number of historians – but the political conse-quences of acknowledging and encouraging a separate Muslim per-sonality. The stark reality is that whether it was masterminded by the Aligarh College principal W.A.J Archbold, or the viceroy and the Liberal secretary of state John Morley, the Simla deputation paved the way for establishing the first pan-Indian Muslim organisation with a political manifesto designed by the Muslims and for the Muslims. For this reason the Muslim League, founded in December 1906, symbolised, from a strictly official angle, a major and decisive break with 'the silent policy of the earlier decades'.

The Act of 1909, introduced to defuse the Congress demand for a greater share in administration and decision-making, was a calculated master-stroke. Separate electorates, along with reservations and weightages, gave birth to a sense of Muslims being a religio-political entity in the colonial image – of being unified, cohesive and segregated from the Hindus. They were homogenised like 'castes' and 'tribes' and suitably accommodated within political schemes and bureaucratic designs. Self-styled leaders were emboldened to represent an 'objectively' defined community and contend with others for patronage, employment and political assignments. In this way separate electorates created space for reinforcing religious identities, a process which was, both in conception and articulation, profoundly divisive. In effect the Morley-Minto Reforms ingeniously challenged those assumptions which guided many nationalists to cultivate a pan-Indian identity, and through a judicious mixture of concessions and guarantees undermined the broad-ly secular foundations of Indian nationalism. The ideological contours of the future Pakistan were thus delineated by British opinion and policy-makers long before Jinnah burst upon the political scene with his insis-tence on having a Muslim nation.

This argument extends to the emergence of caste-cluster conscious-ness. By viewing caste categories as units of patronage and proscription, the government forced a predictable response: those seeking patronage or protesting proscription had to speak in the name of the bureaucratically recognised category. In these circumstances the emergence of 'caste' publicists, spokesmen and associations says more about the way in which the foreign rulers viewed Indian society and sought to come to terms with it, and about the agility of the Indian response, than it does about the ubiquity of 'caste' sentiment.[47]

---

[47] Lucy Carroll, 'Colonial Perceptions of Indian Society', op. cit., p. 249. For the implications of separate electorates and the claims of Muslims as 'an objectively-defined Muslim community', see Farzana Shaikh, *Community and Consensus in Islam*, pp. 90, 157-9, and David Gilmartin, 'Democracy, Nationalism and the Public: A Speculation on Colonial Muslim Politics', *South Asia*, 14, 1, 1991, p. 125.

The Montagu-Chelmsford Reforms (1919) mirrored the same colonial assumptions. The Act of 1935 held out the prospect of a divided country and implicitly endorsed the hitherto hazy notion of an incipient Muslim country. Indeed, if the British were to lean too much towards the Muslim League in the early 1940s, it was partly because their own political and institutional frameworks left them with little choice but to depend on its leaders. After 1909 the structures of governance offered the Muslim League much greater space for articulating communitarian interests.

The Congress Muslims, on the other hand, were awkwardly placed. They were constrained, because their conception of nationhood had no place in the constitutional blueprint. The overall thrust of British policies led to their political isolation. A man of Dr M.A. Ansari's stature was virtually prevented from attending the Round Table Conferences in London (1930-3), convened by the British Prime Minister Ramsay Mac-Donald to resolve the political deadlock in India. Rank communalists, on the other hand, were welcomed with open arms and fêted.[48] Congress Muslims like Azad were 'the wrecking horse', just because Jinnah, whose own status was far from assured, insisted on their exclusion from the Simla Conference held on 25 June 1945.[49] Jinnah's plea, not unheeded in official quarters, was that no one but a Muslim Leaguer could represent the Muslims. This moment in history must have been relished by the surviving architects of the 1909, 1919 and 1935 constitutions.

In the final analysis, the British bequeathed to the Indian Republic a truncated nation, distorted perspectives, blurred images and a number of vague and undifferentiated categories. If the history of inter-community relations is to be rewritten, it has to steer clear of colonial paradigms and be freed from the stranglehold of an intellectual tradition, Orientalism or otherwise. The individual and collective experiences of Muslims need to be located in the subcontinent's history and viewed afresh, in the light not of abstract and arbitrary categories but of irrefutable evidence of their complex but long-standing day-to-day interactions with various groups and communities.

---

[48] Mushirul Hasan, *A Nationalist Conscience: M.A. Ansari, the Congress and the Raj* (Delhi: Manohar, 1987).

[49] Pethick-Lawrence to Cripps, 30 September 1939, in Nicholas Mansergh (ed.), *The Transfer of Power, 1942-7* (London: Her Majesty's Stationery Office, 1969), vol. 1, p. 629. See also my edited volume *Islam and Indian Nationalism: Reflections on Abul Kalam Azad* (Delhi: Manohar, 1992), pp. 93-4. The Simla Conference was convened by the viceroy, Wavell, to resolve the political issues at the end of the war in Europe, but it broke down. 'So my efforts to bring better understanding between the parties have failed and have shown how wide is the gulf,' noted the viceroy.

II

Some enlightened Muslims in the last quarter of the nineteenth century longed for an 'objective' assessment of their history and sociology and a rigorously argued repudiation of certain popular notions about themselves. To whom could they turn? Some theologians and publicists were no doubt trained to debate and defend matters of faith but because of their narrow world-view, traditional training and religious dogmatism were ill-equipped to match Orientalist scholarship. The intervention of scholars at Aligarh, Delhi, Patna and Calcutta was far more impressive and in tune with Western intellectual pursuits. Aligarh College, for one, was the visible embodiment of the victory of the forces of progress. New schools of research, interpretation and reconstruction of 'Muslim thought' developed in this sleepy town of western UP. It was here that movements of reform were consummated. A typical Aligarh version of reform Islam, based on nineteenth-century liberalism and humanism, grew up in opposition both to the orthodox stream and to the popular syncretism of the masses. But the intellectual energy released by the pioneering endeavours of Syed Ahmad, Shibli Nomani, Altaf Husain Hali, Maulvi Zakaullah and the 'First Generation' of students lost momentum once the reformist trends started to become ever more intertwined with political controversies. The ambition of an average student, drawn from the landed class and the upper bourgeoisie, was to enter government service. His pride was soothed, thanks to early pan-Islamic stirrings, by being reminded that he was a unit in the great democracy of Islam, and in witness of this brotherhood he jauntily wore the Turkish *fez* on his head. The traditional curricula at the college, emphasis on fidelity to the raj, and the social origins of its students bred a 'sectarian' milieu. Hence, while the Hindus took to liberal ideas, the Muslims 'took comfort from time-honoured aristocratic values'. Thus, despite the apparent similarity in curricula, not only was education 'much less broad-based' for the Muslims but it did not favour the growth of liberal ideas.[50] Aligarh produced, for the most part, cautious pedagogues instead of a few thinkers of surpassing boldness. There appeared a cloud, to borrow Clifford Geertz's expression, of not very distinguished and usually rather unoriginal academics.[51] This

---

[50] Jawaharlal Nehru, *An Autobiography* (London: Geo. Allen and Unwin, 1936), p. 464; Hardy, op. cit., pp. 103-4. Rafiq Zakaria, *Rise of the Muslims in Indian Politics: An Analysis of Developments from 1885 to 1906* (Bombay: Somaiya, 1970), p. 351, quoted in Asma Barlas, *Democracy, Nationalism and Communalism: The Colonial Legacy in South Asia* (Boulder, CO: Westview, 1995), p. 148.

[51] Nehru and M.N. Roy were in substantial agreement over Aligarh's role after the death of Syed Ahmad Khan. I am fascinated by M.N. Roy's reflections, the more so because he arrived at certain important conclusions without any close contact with the university or its scholars. The communist leader pointed out that Aligarh failed to produce youthful elements holding social and political ideas similar to the Hindu intellectuals who conceived of a

was true also of other centres of learning. Once the newly-emerging Muslim bourgeoisie developed a vested interest in the power structures, the initial thrust to reformist ideas was considerably diluted.

The few who stayed out of the charmed circle of government servants and addressed themselves to issues of reform and innovation were unable to correct colonial stereotypes or stir a discussion comparable in depth and vigour to the debates outlined in Albert Hourani's incisive book *Arabic Thought in the Liberal Age*.[52] Part of the reason was their self-image as part of a community – a monolithic *umma* – that remained, or was normatively expected to remain, the same across divisions in space and time. This theme was often powerfully expressed across a number of élite scholastic factions, especially of Sunni Islam, for whom Sufi and syncretic practices and Shia beliefs in general, were just so many deviations from the norm.[53] Time and again the theme of eternal and unmitigated Hindu-Muslim hostility was echoed. So also the view that 'internal' differences among groups of Hindus and/or Muslims were secondary and irrelevant to the more fundamental religious cleavage.

Muslim intellectuals did not examine such convictions in the light of their normal way of living. Had they done so, they would have discovered ample evidence of great 'internal' political, moral and social tensions and their disruptive effects. In this way they would have understood themselves better and made their conduct and behaviour intelligible to others. Instead, a number of historical works produced during the last-quarter of the nineteenth century emphasised, as did Ameer Ali and Shibli Nomani, the history of Islam rather than that of Indian Islam. Most were unconcerned with social and economic issues. This tendency was most pronounced in Bengal. Muslim writers, including creative poets and novelists, were not only preoccupied with the purity of their racial pedigree to the exclusion of other issues (most belonged to the *ashraf* or élite as opposed to the *ajlaf*, or local 'low-borns'), but they refused to accept Bengali as their mother-tongue, viewing it as a 'Hindu' language.[54]

Did nationalist writers, historians, social reformers and political activists conceptualise the social reality differently, or question the Muslim

---

political nationalism as expressed in the Congress. While the early generation of the Hindu intelligentsia imbibed progressive social and political views, the Aligarh alumni belonged to the landed aristocracy with social and political tendencies that were predominantly feudal. M.N. Roy concluded that 'the absence of a class cohesion was responsible for the political divergence between the Hindus and Muslims .... Elements so diverse socially could not unite in a national movement.' M.N. Roy, *India in Transition* (Bombay: Nachiketa Publications, 1971 reprint), p. 222.

[52] Albert Hourani, *Arabic Thought in the Liberal Age, 1798-1939* (London: OUP, 1970).

[53] Metcalf, op. cit., pp. 40-2, 57-9, 291-2, 307-8.

[54] Mujeeb, *Islamic Influence*, p. 68. Barlas, op. cit., pp. 147-53; Rafiuddin Ahmed, *The Bengal Muslims, 1871-1906: A Quest for Identity* (Delhi: OUP, 1974); Sufia Ahmad, *Muslim Community in Bengal, 1884-1914* (Dacca: OUP, 1974), pp. 336-7.

élite's highly exaggerated and romanticised assessment of its historic role and destiny? Did they attempt to refute colonial stereotypes and rectify the image of a static 'community' sunk in torpid medievalism, insulated from the winds of change, influenced by the diktat of the *mullahs*, tied to the Islamic community, susceptible to pan-Islamic influences, and organised – despite internal differentiations – on a pan-Indian or a transnational basis?

There was no getting away from this exercise. Sections of the intelligentsia – creatively engaged in generating political awakening across the caste, community and region divide – had to set the agenda within the parameters of a pan-Indian framework. They also had to redefine the terms of the debate, not so much on Muslims or on Indian Islam but on inter-community relations. It made sense to harness their intellectual resources to demonstrate that Muslims, in both their historical and contemporary settings, were part of and not separate from the 'Indian reality' and that colonial stereotypes, often reinforced by Muslim élite perceptions, were based on false premises. This was a necessary pre-condition for establishing their all-India credentials, as also to hasten the process of nation-building with Muslims as co-partners. Moreover, they had to contend with a problem summed up by Gulshan and Chandra, the two fictional characters in Firoz Khan Noon's novel, published in 1941, and bridge the gulf separating the followers of Islam and Hinduism. Gulshan told Chandra:

'Do not carry away the idea that I think ill of you for your ignorance, because there are thousands of us Hindus, men and women, who are as ignorant of the great Muslim religion and its philosophy as you are of ours. You will meet millions amongst us, who know no more about Islam than that it introduced into India loose trousers and a spouted pot for ablutions. There are also millions amongst us who know no more about the Hindu culture than what is represented by *langoti* [jackystrap dress] and *dal-roti* [lentil and bread/vegetarian diet]. It is only the irascible, fiery and short-tempered who speak evil of other people's religion.'[55]

III

There are numerous tracts and treatises on Hindu-Muslim intermingling, on social and cultural fusion and on the commonality of inter-community interests. They reveal an enlightened conception of state and society grounded in traditions of religious tolerance, syncretism and fraternal

---

[55] Firoz Khan Noon, *Scented Dust* (Lahore, R.S.M. Gulab Singh, 1941), p. 293. This novel was written at the request of an English friend to anquaint him with some of the contemporary themes in Indian politics and society. A leading landlord of Punjab, the author played a key part in the Muslim League.

living. From Raja Rammohun Roy to Jawaharlal Nehru, liberal, eclectic and radical ideas and movements held their ground. Some were creatively expressed in the poetry of Rabindranath Tagore and the young Mohammad Iqbal, others in a series of religio-reformist trends and institutions. Serious political initiatives, such as that taken by C.R. Das in Bengal, aimed to resolve the communal deadlock to create a joint Hindu-Muslim front.[56]

Yet a more rounded view of the vast and amorphous 'nationalist' literature reveals, first of all, the uncritical acceptance of colonial constructions, their political legitimation through pacts, accords and 'unity' conferences; and, secondly, the inner religio-cultural tensions within the nationalist paradigm. In tangible terms, this meant that subcontinental themes on communal amity and understanding, shorn of their rhetorical value, were not quite a major reference-point in creating or articulating a truly national consciousness. This requires elaboration.

First and foremost, the intellectual probings, as well as being sketchy and superficial, were marred by a majoritarian perspective. The upper castes, convinced of their own superiority in the realm of ideas and thought, regarded Islam as a rather crude approach to the problems of philosophy and metaphysics.[57] There were consequently no serious interpreters of Islam, no counterparts of Al-Beruni, Amir Khusro, Malik Mohammad Jaisi, Abul Fazl, Raskhan, Rahim or Dara Shikoh.[58] Some left-wing intellectuals were disturbed by this: M.N. Roy, for example, was surprised that Hindus and Muslims, having lived together for so long, did not appreciate each other's culture and religion; that the Muslims were 'generally considered to be an extraneous element'; and that educated Hindus were unaware of 'the immense revolutionary significance of Islam'. He concluded that a radical change in mutual attitudes 'would shock the Hindus out of their arrogant self-satisfaction, and cure the narrow-mindedness of the Muslims of our day by bringing them face to face with the true spirit of the faith they profess'.[59]

---

[56] For an appreciation of the role of C.R. Das, see Begum Shaista Ikramullah, *Huseyn Shaheed Suhrawardy* (Karachi: OUP, 1991), pp. 23-4.

[57] Jawaharlal Nehru, *The Discovery of India* (Calcutta: The Signet Press, 1946 reprint), p. 225.

[58] Wilhelm Halbfass, *India and Europe: An Essay in Understanding* (Albany: State University of New York Press, 1988), chapter 2.

[59] M.N. Roy, *The Historical Role of Islam* (Delhi: Indian Renaissance Institute, 1981 reprint). This book was first published in 1939 but written in jail in the early 1930s. It was translated into Hindi as *Islam ki etihasik bhoomika* by Chandrodaya Dixit (Bikaner: Vagdevi Prakashan, 1988). A devout follower of Jainism wrote: 'To ascertain the truth about the teaching of Islam, and to separate its valuable gems from valueless stones as also from glittering pebbles, so that its beauty may be brought in the limelight of public notice.' Champat Rai Jain, *The Lifting of the Veil or the Gems of Islam* (Bijnor: Jaina Parishad Publishing House, 1931).

Nineteenth-century writers and reformers, many of whom grudgingly came to terms with the Muslim presence, accepted the knowledge derived from medieval chroniclers, selectively translated by British historians. Thus the Muslim intrusion was treated as an aberration or a break in the continuity of Brahmanical traditions; Indian culture was equated with Vedic culture, Indian philosophy with Vedanta, Puranas and the Upanishads, and Indian religions with Hinduism.[60] Most accounts, with their focus on the Muslim ruling élite, their military exploits and their glittering durbars, ignored the subtle fusion of 'Little Traditions' at the Sufi shrines particularly and in the rural hinterland generally. Islam had no Max Mueller (1823-1900) to detail how its dogmas and tenets were gradually incorporated into regional and local belief structures and rituals; how Muslims, converted to Mohammad's religion at different times and for different reasons, were integrated with the rest of the population through an identifiable historical process. Islam was mistakenly viewed as part of the 'Great Tradition' – codified, rigid, unchanging, insular and closed to external influences. Its followers, whether converted or not, were cast in a specifically Muslim/Islamic mould. Regardless of economic status, caste, language or regional affinity, their identity was understood, defined and described in strictly doctrinaire terms.

K.M. Panikkar, who was otherwise identified with the liberal stream, commented that 'the organisation of Islam in India was ... frankly communal, and its outlook was governed by the single fact of ensuring to the Islamic nation in India its independence and authority'. Muslims constituted a society everywhere and were much more than a religious minority. Their culture and way of life were different from those of the Hindus and other communities around them: 'Unlike the Christians who, though they profess a different religion, are not in their way of life different from the Hindus, the Muslims, whether in the South of Kerala

---

[60] Such views were endorsed by quite a number of liberal and secular scholars as well as politicians before and after independence – for example, the contention that 'the great principles of Islam did not affect Hinduism as a whole' or that the 'social structure of Hinduism remained almost unaffected by 700 years of association with Islam'. K.M. Panikkar, *The Foundations of New India* (London: Geo. Allen & Unwin, 1963), p. 56. In fact, '700 years of Islamic authority over the Indo-Gangetic plain ... had left Hinduism in a state of depression. It was the religion of a subject race, looked down upon with contempt by the Muslims as idolatry'. K.M. Panikkar, *Asia and Western Dominance* (London: Geo. Allen & Unwin, 1953), p. 240. Likewise, it was common to identify India with Hinduism and with 'Hindu culture' and 'Hindu civilization'. This was a classic British theory reinforced by Indoligists of different intellectual pedigrees. 'To me', wrote Walter Roper Lawrence, 'India is Hindu, and whatever the picture of "India Reformed" may have been in the minds of the imaginative men who made the rough sketch, in the finished work the Brahman will be the central and the striking figure.' *The India We Served*, p. 127, and the Earl of Ronaldshay, *The Heart of Aryavarta: A Study of the Psychology of Indian Unrest* (London: Constable, 1925), p. 2.

or in Kashmir, represent a culture of their own.'[61] Such views stand refuted in a large number of serious sociological and historical studies, though Hindu polemic against Muslims is still constructed on the notion of a standardised and canonical view of Islam.

Islam's militancy and inflexible doctrinal structure were major concerns for Swami Dayanand Saraswati, founder of the Arya Samaj; he was a relentess critic, and his celebrated text, *Satyarth Prakash*, was the basis of anti-Islamic polemics in Punjab.[62] Pandit Lekh Ram, Swami Sharaddhanand and Lala Lajpat Rai, his ideological successors, subjected the Quran to severe criticism; they depicted Mohammad as a man of dubious sexual ethics and interpreted Islam as a religion sanctifying war and the slaughter of non-believers.[63] 'When I consider how devoted a Muslim is to his religion', wrote Lajpat Rai, whose father turned Muslim for a while, 'how he regards the propagation of Islam as a bounden duty and how he believes that the highest reward is attached to converting a man to Islam, I can well imagine what great pressure must my father's Muslim friends have brought to bear upon him ... and how often they must have tried to induce him to become a Mussalman openly.'[64] Such views corresponded to the oft-repeated colonial axiom that Muslims were so deeply committed to fulfilling their Islamic obligations that they were prone to being swayed by orthodox rather than heterodox ideas. They were relentless crusaders, intolerant of other religious beliefs and imbued with a missionary zeal.

Invoking the past lent credence to such a reconstruction. Major literary writers, though by no means all, contrasted the glory of pre-medieval India with the oppressive character of 'Muslim' dynasties, and commented on the overall degradation of Hindus and the pernicious influence of Islam on their social customs. Gopal Ganesh Agarkar (1856-95), Gopal Hari Deshmukh (1823-92) and Vishnushastri Chilunkar (1850-82), leading Marathi writers, portrayed Muslims as bullies and fanatics, since they believed violence and aggression to be the essence of their civilisation.[65]

---

[61] Panikkar, op. cit., pp. 55, 60; see S. Radhakrishnan, *Eastern Religions and Western Thought* (London, 1940 edn.), p. 339; and the comment of a senior Congress leader: 'The Muslims are an all-India community. Whether organised in one overall organisation or not, it often feels the identity of the interests of its members and acts unitedly where its minority rights are concerned.' J.B. Kripalani, *Minorities in India* (Calcutta, n.d.), p. 40.

[62] 'The Quoran, the Quoranic God and the Muslims', according to Dayanand, 'are full of bigotry and ignorance'. J.T.F. Jordens, *Dayananda Saraswati: His Life and Ideas* (Delhi: OUP, 1978), p. 268.

[63] K.W. Jones, *Arya Dharm: Hindu Consciousness in 19th-Century Punjab* (Berkeley, CA: University of California Press, 1976), pp. 145, 150; J.E. Llwellyn, *The Arya Samaj as a Fundamentalist Movement: A Study in Comparative Fundamentalism* (Delhi: Manohar, 1993), pp. 104-8.

[64] V.C. Joshi (ed.), *Lajpat Rai: Autobiographical Writings* (Delhi: University Publishers, 1965), p. 14.

[65] B.G. Gokhale, 'Hindu Responses to the Muslim Presence in Maharashtra' in Yohanan

Bal Gangadhar Tilak, the fiery politician-writer, sought to build a Maratha identity through a conscious choice of historical figures and symbols that evoked memories of Muslim oppression and exploitation. His essentialist endeavours to define Muslims through constant references to Mahmud of Ghazna, Alauddin Khalji, Timur, Aurangzeb and Ahmad Shah Abdali created a major religious divide in Maharashtra society and provided ideological coherence to the Hindu Mahasabha and the Rashtriya Swayamsewak Sangh (RSS), two of the most militant Hindu organisations in the 1930s and '40s.

Noted Hindi writers like Bharatendu Harishchandra (1850-85), Pratap Narain Misra (1856-94), Radha Charan Goswami (1859-1923) and Kisorilal Goswami (1866-1932) represented the pre-colonial era as a chronicle of rape and abduction of Hindu women, the slaughter of sacred cows and the defilement of temples. Bharatendu referred to the 'wounds in the heart' kept green by the sight of Aurangzeb's mosque beside the sacred Vishwanath temple in Varanasi.[66] Two closely-related themes figure in his work: the down-trodden, long-suffering Hindu and the dominant, oppressive Muslim. In his play *Nildevi*, Muslim characters are cruel, cowardly, treacherous, bigoted and debauched, while Hindus, though sometimes portrayed as meek and submissive, demonstrate courage, honour and fidelity.[67]

Kisorilal, following some notable British historians, described in his novel *Tara* (1902) the depraved conditions at the court of Shahjahan in Agra: intrigues, scenes of illicit love, murder among Muslims.[68] Misra and Radha Charan chastised Muslims as the 'abominably impure *mlechchas*' and damned them as rank outsiders. They denounced the medieval rulers – 'those mad elephants' – who 'trampled to destruction the flourishing lotus-garden of India' and lamented that Muslims slaughtered cows with impunity and prevented or obstructed Hindu religious processions.[69]

Friedmann (ed.), *Islam in Asia*, vol. 1: *South Asia* (Jerusalem: The Hague Press, 1984), pp. 162-7.

[66] Sudhir Chandra, 'Communal Consciousness in Late 19th Century Hindi Literature', in Mushirul Hasan (ed.), *Communal and Pan-Islamic Trends in Colonial India* (Delhi: Manohar, 1987), pp. 180-95.

[67] Christopher R. King, 'Hindu Nationalism in the Nineteenth Century U.P.' in Dhirendra K. Vajpeyi (ed.), *Boeings and Bullock-Carts: Essays in Honour of K. Ishwaran* (Delhi: Chanakya Publication, 1990), pp. 187, 191; see also Yogendra Malik, 'Reflections of Inter-Communal Relations through Hindi Fiction' in Vajpeyi (ed.), *Boeings and Bullock-Carts*, chapter 9; R.S. McGregor, 'A Hindu Writer's Views of Social, Political and Language Issues of his Time: Attitude of Harischandra of Banaras (1850-1885)', *Modern Asian Studies*, 25, 1, 1991, pp. 91-100.

[68] P. Gaeffke, *Hindi Literature in the Twentieth Century* (Wiesbaden: Harrassowitz, 1978), p. 27.

[69] Sudhir Chandra, *The Oppressive Present: Literature and Social Consciousness in*

Bankim Chandra Chatterjee (1838-94), who saw medieval India as a period of bondage, interpreted the Hindu chieftain's resistance to the Mughals as a form of national resistance. Muslim rule, according to him, brought neither material nor spiritual improvement to India. He saw in Islam a quest for power and glory, devoid of spiritual and ethical qualities, irrational, bigoted, devious, sensual and immoral, and a complete antithesis of his 'ideal' religion.[70]

Bhudev Mukhopadhyay (1827-94), for one, questioned this version as a mischievous fabrication of British historians. In his view, the Sultans of Delhi aided the process of unification and contributed significantly to the emergence of an inchoate consciousness of community among Indians. He emphasised the common ties that bound Muslims with the rest of the population, pointing out that Islam in the subcontinent was quite different from Islam elsewhere both in doctrine and in internal social practices.[71] Romesh Chandra Dutt (1848-1909), who wrote a major exposé of British economic policies and the inspiration behind the rise of 'economic nationalism', avoided the familiar portrayal of Muslims as innately wicked and bloodthirsty. *The Lake of Palms*, an English translation of the Bengali text, generally avoided the more or less brazen confrontation of Hindus and Muslims and the attendant display of anti-Muslim bias that provided a staple for his historical novels.[72] Nevertheless, the picture of Muslims as alien emerges just as strongly in his novels and fictions; they were not quite 'like us'; they were enemies of 'our' country and religion.[73]

The Bengali intelligentsia of Nirad C. Chaudhuri's generation read and absorbed the spirit of such writings. 'Nothing was more natural for us', commented Chaudhuri, 'than to feel about the Muslims in the way we did.' They were told, even before they could read, that the Muslims

---

Colonial India (Delhi: OUP, 1992), p. 120.

[70] Partha Chatterjee, *Nationalist Thought and the Colonial World: A Derivative Discourse* (Delhi: OUP, 1980), p. 77; Tapan Raychaudhuri, *Europe Reconsidered: Perceptions of the West in the Nineteenth Century World* (Delhi: OUP, 1988), pp. 188-9; Tanika Sarkar, 'Imagining Hindurashtra: The Hindu and the Muslim in Bankim Chandra's Writings' in Ludden (ed.), *Contesting the Nation*, op. cit., pp. 162-84. For a different interpretation, see Sisir Kumar Das, *The Artist in Chains: The Life of Bankim Chandra Chatterjee* (Delhi: New Statesman Publishing House, 1984), appendix C: 'A Muslim Baiter?'

[71] Sudipta Kaviraj, 'The Reversal of Orientalism: Bhudev Mukhopadhyay and the Project of Indigenist Social Theory'. Vasudha Dalmia and H. von Stietencron (eds), *Representing Hinduism: The Construction of Religious Traditions and National Identity* (Delhi: Sage, 1995) pp. 253-82; Raychaudhuri, op. cit., pp. 41-3.

[72] Sudhir Chandra,'Towards an Integrated Understanding of early Indian Nationalism' in Alok Bhalla and Sudhir Chandra (eds), *Indian Responses to Colonialism in the 19th Century* (Delhi: Sterling, 1993), p. 18.

[73] Sudhir Chandra, 'The Lengthening Shadow: Secular and Communal Consciousness' in Bidyut Chakrabarty (ed.), *Secularism and Indian Polity* (Delhi, 1990).

had ruled and oppressed the Hindus, spread their religion with the Quran in one hand and the sword in the other, abducted Hindu women, destroyed temples, and polluted sacred places. 'As we grew older we read about the wars of the Rajputs, the Marathas, and the Sikhs against the Muslims, and of the intolerance and oppressions of Aurangzeb.'[74]

Bengali thinkers and reformers, according to Nirad Chaudhuri, based their life-work on the formula of a synthesis of Hindu and European currents. Islamic trends and 'Muslim sensitivities' did not touch the arc of their consciousness. They stood outside as an 'external proletariat'.[75] If they wanted to enter the Bengali cultural world they could do so 'only after giving up all their Islamic values and traditions'. In this way the new Indian/Bengali culture of the nineteenth century built a perimeter of its own and put specifically Muslim influences and aspirations beyond the pale.[76]

Nirad Chaudhuri is no different. Though a self-proclaimed liberal humanist, he nursed contempt and deep-seated hostility towards the Muslims in Calcutta, a city where he spent most of his life.[77] It was just the same in Kishorganj, now in Bangladesh. 'We became conscious of a new kind of hatred for the Muslims' during the *swadeshi* movement. A cold dislike for them 'settled down in our heart, putting an end to all real intimacy of relationship.'[78] He rejoiced at Italy's attack on Tripoli in 1911, also when Turkey joined the German side at the end of 1914 'so that the Muslims would be taught a lesson'.[79] 'Strongly anti-Muslim in 1920' owing to the Khilafat upsurge, he was uneasy with the 'menacing assertiveness' of the Bengali Muslims. He was 'repelled' by the thought of living in a province where Muslims would be a dominant social and cultural entity.[80] His clear-cut verdict was that Muslims constituted a *society* of their own with a distinctive culture. They could not be absorbed

---

[74] Nirad C. Chaudhuri, *The Autobiography of an Unknown Indian* (New York: Macmillan, 1951), p. 227.

[75] It has been noted that the peasants, most of whom were Muslims, never entered Bankim's fictional mind. While commenting on the present in polemical prose, Bankim could see the Hindus and the Muslims both as sections of the oppressed masses but in his historical novels the Muslim was always perceived as the alien. Meenakshi Mukherji, 'Rhetoric Identity: History and Fiction in Nineteenth Century India', in Bhalla and Chandra (eds), op. cit., p. 35. See also Pradip Kumar Datta, 'Dying Hindus: Production of Hindu communal common sense in early 20th century Bengal', *EPW*, 19 June 1993, pp. 1305-25, and Tanika Sarkar, 'Imagining Hindu Rashtra', op. cit.

[76] Chaudhuri, op.cit., pp. 226-7.

[77] Ibid., p. 228.

[78] Ibid., p. 232.

[79] Nirad C. Chaudhuri, *Thy Hand, Great Anarch! India, 1921-1952* (Delhi: Times Book International, 1987), p. 37.

[80] Ibid., p. 466.

into a unified nation. For this reason the arguments trotted out to contest the demand of the Indian Muslims to have their own way of life were 'false' and 'foolish'.[81] 'When I see the gigantic catastrophe of Hindu-Muslim discord of these days I am not surprised, because we as children held the tiny mustard in our hands and sowed it very diligently. In fact, this conflict was implicit in the very unfolding of our history, and could hardly be avoided.'[82]

The following description, which must not be conveniently dismissed as an illustration of Nirad Chaudhuri's 'eccentricity', sharply reflects the images of Muslims and the contempt with which they were referred to by sections of the haughty English-educated Bengalis:

One day I saw a procession of Muslim divines trooping into Sarat Babu's [Sarat Chandra Bose, 1889-1989] house. I was quite familiar with the modern Muslim dress, but had no idea that these learned Muslims wore different clothes. They did, for they had green gowns on and big turbans on their heads.[...] We, the educated and urban Bengalis,... did not even imagine that such persons existed in Bengal. I with my knowledge of Islamic painting could only assume when I saw them that they were crude incarnations of the Muslim divines I had seen portrayed in Persian or Mughal miniatures.[...] Their faces were grave, and even stern. One face struck me very forcibly. It was pinched and peevish, but of an incredible ferocity. The eyes were large, black, and burning, and in that emaciated face they looked even blacker and larger.[...] He looked like an ill-dressed Robespierre, the sea-green Incorruptible. Sarat Babu's house was not only crowded for the occasion with these survivals of Islam, but even reeked of them.[83]

Such representations of Muslims did not augur well for the nationalist agenda of welding various communities into a unified nation. The Congress movement, in particular, imposed serious demands on its leaders to define the contours of multi-culturalism and religious pluralism in order to preserve the fragile social fabric that was being steadily undermined by British policies as well as by Hindu-Muslim revitalisation campaigns. Otherwise the laudable Congress goal of a composite nationality was bound to run into serious difficulties. Nehru rightly emphasised that 'only by thinking in terms of a different political framework – and even more so a different social framework – can we build up a stable foundation for joint action'.[84]

---

[81] Chaudhuri, *Thy Hand, Great Anarch*, p. 39.

[82] Chaudhuri, *Autobiography*, p. 225.

[83] Chaudhuri, *Thy Hand, Great Anarch !* p. 469.

[84] Nehru, *Autobiography*, p. 137.

IV

Nehru's perspective was influenced by his cosmopolitan family background, his education in England, his social and cultural ambience in Allahabad, and his long-standing friendship and political camaraderie with influential Congress Muslims, including Ansari, Azad, Syed Mahmud, Khaliquzzaman, Tassaduq Ahmad Khan Sherwani and Abdul Majid Khwaja. He was a product of the cultural norms and intellectual background of the Urdu-speaking élites of the Indo-Gangetic belt and his sensibilities were influenced by them. He went to Harrow School and read history at Trinity College, Cambridge, and interacted with Fabian socialists in London. Such interactions widened his intellectual horizon and enriched his appreciation of political and social transformative processes around the globe. He could thus locate in perspective the rapid changes, some of a revolutionary nature, taking place in countries like Egypt, Turkey and Iran. Discussions with Azad and other Muslim scholars gave him a better understanding of Indian Islam and medieval Indian history. In *The Discovery of India* he analysed late nineteenth-century reformist currents, commended Syed Ahmad Khan's bold initiatives, commented on the nationalist stir among the young Muslim intelligentsia of north India, noted the 'sensation' created by Azad, 'this very youthful writer and journalist', and assessed Iqbal's impact on the younger generation of Muslims.[85]

More than anything else, Nehru attributed the social, educational and economic backwardness of most Muslims – not, like his political comrades, to any innate failing but to concrete historical and sociological factors.[86] He knew, so he said, more about their hunger and poverty than those who talked in terms of percentages and seats in councils. He claimed to be in closer touch with them than most of their self-styled leaders. He had vast Muslim audiences in different parts of the country. They did not ask him about the communal problem or percentages or separate electorates. They were more interested in land revenue or rent, debt, water rates, unemployment, and their many other burdens. How, then, could he accept the Muslim League's pretentious claims, and recognise him as the 'sole spokesman'? The League leadership deliberately exploited religion in order to avoid discussing problems of the common man.

A simple fact that eluded most of Nehru's comrades was that India was not at any stage structured around religious solidarities or polarised along 'communal' lines. Nehru's exceptionally eclectic mind grasped this reality. He believed that inter-community conflicts, as and when they occurred, were counterposed to the quiet, commonplace routines in which communities intermingled. Cross-community linkages rather than

---

[85] Nehru, *Discovery of India*, pp. 297-305.
[86] Ibid., p. 340.

religious ties influenced the direction in which patronage, authority and economic relations flowed into everyday life. Consequently it was both possible and desirable to reinforce traditional linkages through 'mass contact' and a radical socio-economic blueprint. Moreover, it was feasible to blunt the impact of communal slogans by reducing class disparities, creating opportunities for upward mobility, and making the masses aware of their mutual interdependence, their shared historical experiences and their common concerns, interests and destiny.

This was the impulse behind Nehru's brainchild, the Muslim Mass Contact Campaign, launched in March 1937.[87] The idea was to approach the Muslims not as a collective fraternity but as a segment of an im- poverished population. The principal motivation was to convince them that they did not constitute a 'nation', and that their fortunes were not tied to their Muslim brethren *per se* but to fellow-artisans, peasants and workers in other communities. Nehru conducted dialogue with Jinnah on these lines, questioned the rationale of 'Muslim nationalism' in a society traditionally anchored in cultural and religious pluralism, and criticised the creation of a 'Muslim Identity' in the garb of Islam. He tried in vain to delink issues of proportion and percentages of seats from the more basic contradictions between nationalism and colonialism. He expected Jinnah to draw his constituency into this just and legitimate struggle as co-citizens and not as a preferential religio-political collectivity.

To Nehru the two-nation idea was anathema and no more than a reversion to some medieval theory. 'Why only two I do not know, for if nationality was based on religion, then there were many nations in India. Of two brothers one may be a Hindu, another a Moslem; they would belong to two different nations. These two nations existed in varying proportions in most of the villages in India. They were nations which had no boundaries; they overlapped. A Bengali Moslem and a Bengali Hindu, living together, speaking the same language and having much the same traditions and customs, belonged to different nations.'[88]

There was much ambiguity and fuzziness in nationalist thinking about the corporate identity of Muslims. Nehru removed some of it: 'There can be and should be religious or cultural solidarity. But when we enter the political plane, the solidarity is national, not communal; when we enter the economic plane the solidarity is economic.'[89] In what way, he asked, were the interests of the Muslim peasant different from those of the Hindu

[87] Mushirul Hasan, 'The Muslim Mass Contacts Campaign: Analysis of a Strategy of Political Mobilization' in Richard Sisson and Stanley Wolpert (eds), *Congress and Indian Nationalism: The Pre-Independence Phase* (Berkeley, CA: University of California Press, 1988).

[88] Nehru, *Discovery of India*, pp. 341-2

[89] To Mohammad Ismail Khan, 26 December 1927, S. Gopal (ed.), *Selected Works of Jawaharlal Nehru* (Delhi: Jawaharlal Nehru Memorial Fund, 1976), vol. 8, p. 203.

peasant, or those of a Muslim labourer, artisan, merchant, landlord or manufacturer different from those of his Hindu counterparts? The ties that bound people were common economic interests and, in the case of a subject country especially, a common national interest.[90] If the country began to think and act on these lines, the 'myth' of communalism would disappear along with the pseudo-religious mentality.[91] Communalism was not, after all, the power it was made out to be; it was a creation of educated classes in search of office and employment. The problem was essentially one of protection of interests, and religion was merely a useful stalking-horse for this purpose.[92] The 'real conflict had nothing to do with religion, though religion often masked the issue, but was essentially between those who stood for a nationalist/democratic/socially revolutionary policy and those concerned with preserving the relics of a feudal regime. In a crisis the latter depended on foreign support which is interested in preserving the *status quo*.'[93]

The basic premise of Nehru's argument was valid. There was nothing wrong in arguing that religious solidarity should not be the basis for political activism, or that religious symbols of disunity be shunned in public life. The alternative strategy, worked out by Tilak in Maharashtra or the *swadeshi* leaders in Bengal, had created fissures in the liberation struggle, offended Muslims in those regions, and enfeebled the intellectual underpinnings of secular goals set by the Congress.

Nehru was not the sole champion of secular nationalism; yet he, more than anyone else, enriched its content. He provided depth to debates on secularism within the Congress, as also in left circles, by introducing complex but relevant historical and contemporary themes drawn from India and other societies. He did so not on the basis of abstract principles of Western democracy – a charge commonly levelled against him by his detractors – but because of his own acute understanding of the wider social and political processes in history. There is no reason to believe that his perceptions were flawed, or to doubt his motives or intentions.

In sum, Nehru's ideas ran contrary to Jinnah's two-nation theory and to the thinking of some of his own Congress colleagues who decried his 'pro-Muslim' proclivities. They were a mixed bag – 'Hindu nationalists', 'traditionalists' and, in Nehru's own view, 'Hindu communalists' masquerading as Congressmen. Whatever the fine distinctions in their world-view, they paid lip-service to the Congress ideals but quietly nursed the vision of a Hindu nation. Most were haunted by the spectre of

---

[90] Statement to the press, 10 January 1937, ibid., vol. 8, p. 12.
[91] Presidential Address at Punjab National Conference, Amritsar, 11 April 1928, ibid., vol. 3, pp. 225-6.
[92] Ibid., vol. 8, p. 120.
[93] Nehru, *Discovery of India*, p. 343.

pan-Islamism, even though the rallying symbol – the Khilafat – had disappeared in 1922. Some insisted that the fortunes of the Islamic world counted far more with Muslims than their own country's political regeneration; others harped on their aggressive instincts and the militancy of their faith.

While a distinction needs to be made between the self-professed Hindu publicists and the secular wing within the Congress party and organisation, the political consequences of some of their judgements and perceptions were much the same. Both endorsed the Lucknow Pact (December 1916) and similar accords on the mistaken belief that Muslims constituted a separate religious and political entity.[94] In this way both groups legitimised – each in its own independent perspective – the gradual evolution of a *Muslim* personality in Indian politics. In so doing they not only aided a potentially divisive trend but also jettisoned their own moral authority to challenge the assumptions outlined in the Acts of 1919 and 1935. Moreover, they created the space for certain strident sectional claims to be accommodated in the political agenda – some unwittingly or perhaps in good faith, others for more devious reasons. In each case the end-result was the same.

Both the political language within which the Congress sought accommodation with Muslim political activists, and the basis on which Mohandas Karamchand Gandhi established an *entente* with pan-Islamic leaders during the Khilafat movement in the early 1920s, had far-reaching consequences. The energy derived from recognising Muslims as a distinct religious and political unit implied that the basic terms of reference precluded any lasting solution of the communal tangle.

The Congress was sensitised to this reality after the Muslim outcry over certain policies adopted by its ministries (formed under the 1935 Act during 1937-9) in UP, Bihar and Bombay.[95] But it was too late to retrace its steps. Various political currents, which could be managed earlier and harnessed for nationalist goals, developed their own independent energy and flowed in several different directions. The Congress agenda could no longer be written afresh in the post-war years without the Muslim League, the RSS and the Hindu Mahasabha, both votaries of a Hindu nation, and the British who still held the scales despite the erosion of their political and moral authority in the aftermath of the Quit India movement in 1942. There were not just 'two parties', as Nehru haughtily announced in 1937, but as many as *four* parties in the fray. Nehru and his socialist comrades swallowed this bitter pill when they helplessly witnessed the collapse of the Muslim Mass Contact Campaign.

[94] Mushirul Hasan, *Nationalism and Communal Politics*, pp. 102-3.
[95] Mushirul Hasan (ed.), *India's Partition: Process, Strategy and Mobilization* (Delhi: OUP, 1993), pp. 16-26.

It is not the intention here to present an image of an always-liberal, enlightened, largely innocent Muslim community – 'sinned against' but hardly ever 'sinning'; nor to suggest that its fortunes or misfortunes can be explained solely in terms of unremitting, overwhelming power and prejudice of the British and the 'Hindu' intelligentsia. Aijaz Ahmad, whose writings have clarified several methodological issues, correctly maintains that sections of the Muslim intelligentsia have made their own history at least as much as others have made it for them – and the reality that they have not made it very well must engage social scientists.[96]

It is therefore important to examine the depth, vigour and variety of Muslim revivalism, consider why the ideas of a singular community appear in Muslim writings, and why Islamic symbols of disunity were sometimes preferred to Indian historical symbols of unity, and explore how Islamic ideas moulded élite perceptions.[97] We need to become more fully acquainted with the Muslim educational system – 'the master institution', in the words of Clifford Geertz – in perpetuating an Islamic tradition and in creating an Islamic vision.[98] In this context the part played by the itinerant preachers and the *ulama* requires detailed investigation, not just as models of 'Islamic conduct' or as interpreters of the *Shariat* but also as leaders of a political 'community' in the making. We need to delineate, just as Syed Ahmad, Hali, Iqbal and Azad did, the implications of their social conservatism in a society that was rapidly changing under colonial rule, as also the ill-effects of their resistance to innovation and change and their suppression of dissent and interpretation (*ijtehad*). These issues, which sometimes escape the attention of Western scholarship, are critically important to the citizens of South Asia generally and to Muslim communities in particular.

Finally, it is necessary to deconstruct the language of minorityism and uncover the motives of those practitioners of modern-day politics who purported to represent the *millat*, or the 'community' as a whole, but were actually exploiting Islam and communitarian solidarity as a shield to cover their political designs. The general implication of this idea was summed

---

[96] I am grateful to Aijaz Ahmad for his thoughtful written comments on the first draft of this chapter. Many of his suggestions have been incorporated in this revised version. His main argument is that the British Orientalists invented rather little and in fact took over several themes that were powerfully expressed by the Muslim intelligentsia. This interface between certain kinds of British writing and certain kinds of Islamic ones, and their subsequent re-surfacing in various forms of subsequent articulations, is something that neither 'Saidian diktat' nor the idea of 'colonial discourse' can ever accommodate. See his *In Theory: Classes, Nations, Literatures* (London: Verso, 1992), and the rather uncharitable denunciatory critique of his book in *Public Culture*, 6, 1, Fall 1993.

[97] Brass, *Language, Religion and Politics.*

[98] Clifford Geertz, 'Modernization in a Muslim Society: The Indonesian Case', Robert N. Bellah (ed.), *Religion and Progress in Modern Asia* (New York: The Free Press, 1965), p. 95; Metcalf, *Islamic Revival*, op. cit.

up by Chandra in her conversation with her life-long friend Gulshan. 'You see, my dear', she said, 'a man will use any old argument to achieve his object in all walks of life, and this communal discord is a very useful and good stick with which our men-folk can beat the old India goat – her political progress.' Troubled by the communal cleavage, she remarked angrily: 'This Hindu-Muslim discord only exists because it pays our men-folk to keep it going.'[99]

What we ideally need is a triangular narrative in which the Muslim is not a privileged victim but as much an actor as the others, a theme pursued in this book. The main thrust of this discussion is to identify points of convergence between the colonial and nationalist discourses and to argue that, despite different sorts of constraints, it was still possible for fervent advocates of Indian nationhood to thwart Hindu majoritarianism and Muslim nationalism. Among the available options was to evolve, in the spirit of Ghalib's quintessential message, an independent/autonomous discourse, discard communal categories, the mainstay of religious mobilisation, and ignore the Muslim élite's self-image and perceptions of its role and destiny in history. There were, objectively, profound historical and sociological reasons for doing so. The fact that this was not done concertedly and systematically weakened the cause of, and the case for, multi-culturalism, religious pluralism and secular nationalism.

My creed is oneness, my belief abandonment of rituals
Let all communities dissolve and constitute a faith.[100]

Mirza Asadullah Khan Ghalib (1797-1869)

99   Noon, *Scented Dust*, p. 282.
100   Russell, *Pursuit of Urdu Literature*, p. 71.

3

MAKING A SEPARATE NATION

'Pakistan was founded because the Muslims of the subcontinent wanted to build up their lives in accordance with the teachings and traditions of Islam, because they wanted to demonstrate to the world that Islam provides a panacea to the many diseases which have crept into the life of humanity today.'

Liaquat Ali Khan*

'It is one of the greatest frauds on the people to suggest that religious affinity can unite areas that are geographically, economically, linguistically and culturally different.'

Abul Kalam Azad†

India's partition in August 1947 is supposedly 'the most eloquent and compelling witness to the Muslim sense of separate identity and of the validity of Islamic nationalism as the contemporary force of its expression'.[1] The rhetoric of Muslim solidarity which preceded that cataclysmic event reinforces the impression that Muslims are susceptible to religious appeals, act as a cohesive entity, and further their interests through religious and political networks.[2]

Theories associated with the partition keep such images alive and define, in large measure, the terms of post-independence arguments on

* Constituent Assembly of Pakistan, *Debates*, 7 March 1949, vol. 5, p. 3.
† *India Wins Freedom: An Autobiographical Narrative* (Delhi: Longmans, 1959), p. 227.

[1] Kenneth Cragg, *The Call of the Minaret* (New York: OUP, 1966), pp. 4-5. And the view: 'The recasting of Pakistan history is an attempt to redefine Pakistan and Pakistani society and to endow the nation with a historic destiny....Viewed from this angle, it becomes essential to project the movement for Pakistan as the movement for an Islamic State, the creation of which became a historic inevitability with the first Muslim invasion of the subcontinent'. Pervez Amirali Hoodbhoy and A.H. Nayyar, 'Rewriting the History of Pakistan' in Mohammad Asghar Khan (ed.), *Islam, Politics and the State: The Pakistan Experience* (London: Zed Books, 1985), p. 176; Chaudhri Muhammad Ali, *The Emergence of Pakistan* (New York: Columbia University Press, 1967).

[2] Francis Robinson, 'Islam and Separatism' in Mushirul Hasan (ed.), *Communal and Pan-Islamic Trends*, pp. 344-81.

Muslims and on what is described in the subcontinent as the 'communal problem'. During the massive upsurge over Ayodhya's Babri Masjid in 1989-92, it was widely argued that Muslims, having divided the country, should migrate to Pakistan or live in India on terms laid down by the Hindu parties. The slogan 'Pakistan or *Qabristan*' (graveyard) was commonly raised in predominantly Muslim localities to intimidate an already beleaguered minority. Images created during such campaigns will recur indefinitely unless the partition story is unfolded and its complexity unravelled. Social scientists in search of scapegoats or taking cover behind fanciful theories can hardly grasp a phenomenon that has so profoundly influenced the destiny of millions in the subcontinent.

Archival materials, including the invaluable 'Transfer of Power' documents published in England, have exploded several myths, raised fresh doubts and opened up significant areas of research. Historians, some with great sophistication, have enriched the discussion on the circumstances leading to partition and their analysis. Yet a considerable number of unexplored themes need to be brought to the forefront in the historical narrative. Mistaken assumptions and theories, which constitute the staple diet of generalists and professional social scientists alike, require critical evaluation and probing.

I reflect on just a few aspects of Pakistan's story from the perspective outlined in an introductory essay to an earlier work.[3] I have neither written an episodic history nor presented facts in chronological sequence. My purpose is to delineate the ideology of 'separatism' and its modes of expression and assertion, and unfold the character, orientation and social roots of the Muslim League movement. I also assess how contemporaries reacted to the two-nation idea, its legitimation and impact on the lives of millions who had no say in the actual transfer of power to two sovereign nations. I discuss the enormity of their tragedy, vividly described by historians, journalists, civil servants, creative writers and poets, as also the pain, suffering and trauma of many others for whom 1947 continues to be 'a year of our shame, not a year of our achievement'.[4]

It is no longer useful to argue, as is commonly done in popular and scholarly interchanges, over the question of whether Jinnah bargained for a separate nation or not. What is relevant in the present state of our knowledge is his forceful articulation of the two-nation theory and his success in mobilising people in such large numbers and to such great effect. For those confronted with and troubled by partition's bitter legacy, the critical and unresolved issue is how the *Quaid* (leader) and his

---

[3] Mushirul Hasan (ed.), *India's Partition*, introduction, pp. 1-43.

[4] Rajmohan Gandhi, *Understanding the Muslim Mind* (Delhi: Penguin India, 1986), p. 1; Kamaladevi Chattopadhyaya, *Inner Recesses Outer Spaces* (Delhi: Navrang, 1986), pp. 306-7; Aruna Asaf Ali, *Fragments From the Past* (Delhi: Patriot Publishers, 1989); D.P. Karaka, *Betrayal in India* (London: Gollancz, 1950).

lieutenants came up with and effectively deployed a powerful symbol to galvanize Muslims and create in them the urge to join the crusade for a separate homeland. How their goals were achieved in so short a time requires examination.

Was there intrinsic merit in religious/Islamic appeals? Does one search for clues in UP society, the citadel of Muslim orthodoxy? – in the changing political alignments in Muslim-majority provinces? – in the evolution of 'separatist' ideas, reinforced by colonial policies, from Syed Ahmad Khan to Mohammad Iqbal whose populism provided a grand ideology, a phantasmogoria in which some Muslims could find their image? – in the ensuing clash between Hindu and Muslim resurgence? – in violent contests over religious symbols, a dispute recently played out around the Babri Masjid at Ayodhya? – in a community's perception of being different from 'others' and its élites' fears of being eased out from power structures? – in the exploitation of religious and cultural symbols and their manipulation by competing élites to secure a vantage-point in government, business and the professions? – or in the peculiar class formation and class contradictions which attended the evolution of the Indian bourgeoisie?[5]

I

As a general proposition, it is necessary to repudiate suggestions implying the 'inevitability' of partition on the basis of Hindu-Muslim feuds that took place before and after the advent of British rule. Also, it is not helpful to trace the evolution of those ideas, many of which were fostered by the British or popularised by sections of the Muslim élite, which saw the followers of Islam as an exclusive entity separate from others, made them aware of the ideal of Muslim brotherhood and sensitised them to the historical necessity of living under Muslim governments. Although some people believed in such notions and loudly proclaimed them, it is doubtful whether they contributed to the actual *creation* of an over-arching 'Muslim identity'. Even if they did, there remains the key question that eludes most historical explanations: how were nebulous concepts of an Islamic state or a Muslim government, floated by diverse groups for mixed reasons, so quickly and effectively transformed into a powerful movement for separation?

The ultimate success of the League's project needs to be located not so much in the realm of ideas but in the context of the performance and

[5] Y.V. Gankovsky and L.R. Gordon-Polonskaya, *A History of Pakistan 1947-58* (Moscow: Nauka, 1964); Syed Nesar Ahmad, *Origins of Muslim Consciousness in India: A World-System Perspective* (New York: Greenwood Press, 1991).

subsequent resignation of Congress ministries in 1939, the fluid political climate on the eve of and during the war, the Congress decision to launch the 'Quit India' movement (1942), and the government's readiness to modify its political strategy towards the League. During these years, Jinnah emerged as a key political player and made the British relent to his assured status as the sole spokesman for the Muslims.[6] Those were also the years when his two-nation theory, first floated in March 1940, offered a rallying symbol to disgruntled elements who now had a cause to fight for.

In other words, the idea of two separate states itself, though talked about in muted fashion after the Khilafat and Non-Co-operation days, came to be formally mooted in a specific context when tangible material considerations, especially those relating to power-sharing, figured prominently on the political agenda. In fact, the swiftness with which the idea succeeded in becoming actualised and the intensity of emotions involved had more to do with the political and economic anxieties of various social classes than with a profound urge to create an Islamic/Muslim state. Both in its conception and articulation the Muslim League's demands summed up the fears and aspirations of the newly-emergent professional groups, especially in UP and Bihar, the powerful landed classes in Punjab, Sind and UP, and the industrial magnates of western and eastern India.

A prominent Leaguer from Bengal commented: 'The great yearning for office which is still uppermost in the minds and hearts of the majority of the Muslim politicians today is really heart-rending.'[7] He should have added that such politicians were not tied down to any political shibboleths but moved by a lively regard for their own material benefits. By following Jinnah's lead they made a calculated decision to throw their full weight behind the government, take advantage of the resignation of Congress

---

[6] The general outline of political history is discussed in the works of: Ayesha Jalal, *The Sole Spokesman: Jinnah, the Muslim League and the Demand for Pakistan* (CUP, 1982); Khalid b. Sayeed, *Pakistan: The Formative Phase, 1857-1948*, (London: OUP, 1968); Gowher Rizvi, *Linlithgow and India: A Study of British Policy and the Political Impasse in India, 1936-1943* (London: Royal Historical Society, 1978), pp. 106-7; Farzana Shaikh, *Community and Consensus in Islam*, pp. 212-13; Stanley Wolpert, *Jinnah of Pakistan* (New York: OUP, 1984); Anita Inder Singh, *The Origins of the Partition of India, 1936-1947* (Delhi: OUP, 1987); the collection of essays in C.H. Philips and M.D. Wainwright (eds), *The Partition of India: Policies and Perspectives* (London: Geo. Allen & Unwin, 1970); Chatterji, *Bengal Divided*; and Murshid, *The Sacred and the Secular*. See also Asim Roy, 'The High Politics of India's Partition: The Revisionist Perspective', *Modern Asian Studies*, 24, 2, 1990; Gyanendra Pandey, 'The Prose of Otherness', in David Arnold and David Hardiman (eds), *Subaltern Studies VIII: Essays in Honour of Ranajit Guha* (Delhi: OUP, 1994); Ayesha Jalal, 'Secularists, subalterns and the Stigma of "Communalism": Partition historiography revisited', *Indian Economic and Social History Review*, 31, 1, 1996, pp. 93-103.

[7] Hassan to Jinnah, 9 April 1943, Z.H. Zaidi (ed.), *M.A. Jinnah-Ispahani Correspondence, 1936-1948* (Karachi: Forward Publications Trust, 1976), p. 347.

ministries, and pre-empt the possibility of their returning to power. E.J. Benthall, finance member of the viceroy's council, commented on his meeting with Jinnah on 4 March 1940: 'An unsatisfactory and inconclusive talk. His main interest is to keep Congress out while he builds up power and influence.'[8]

Pirs, sajjada-nashins and sections of the Deobandi and Barelwi *ulama* discovered an opening in the rapidly-changing political scene. While the going was good for the League, they jumped into the political arena to advance their material well-being, protect their vital landed interests in Punjab and Sind, safeguard religious establishments under their vigil and control, and defend their status as guardians, custodians and interpreters of the *Shariat*. They found themselves, after nearly two decades, busy re-enacting the critical role they had performed during the Khilafat activity in the early 1920s.

Some *ulama* were of course not as cynical as the others. They nursed an 'Islamic vision', championed 'Islamic nationalism' and sympathised with religio-political fundamentalism. Maulana Jamal Mian of Lucknow's Firangi Mahal, son of the renowned *alim* Abdul Bari, was one of them,[9] as were the venerable Deobandi *ulama*, Ashraf Ali Thanwi and Shabbir Ahmad Usmani. Out of conviction too, Mohammad Amir Ahmad Khan, the Raja of Mahmudabad, fervently advocated an Islamic state: 'When we talk of democracy in Islam', he wrote to the historian Mohib-bul Hasan, 'it is not democracy in the government but in the cultural and social aspects of life. Islam is totalitarian – there is no denying about it. It is the Quran that we should turn to. It is the dictatorship of the Koranic laws that we want – and that we will have – but not through non-violence

---

[8] Diary, box no. xii, Benthall papers, CSAS. This is confirmed by strong reactions to several proposals mooted at the time to break the deadlock, including the recommendations of a conference chaired by the Liberal leader Tej Bahadur Sapru in February 1942. Prompted by urgent telegrams from Liaquat Ali Khan, more than 165 resolutions were passed by League branches against transferring power and authority to a central government to be set up 'on the basis of India being a single national unit and enjoying dominion status in action, thereby establishing Congress or Hindu Raj'. It was made clear that 'Muslim India will never accept such a position which is sought to be secured by Hindu leaders who are virtually hand in glove with the Congress and other allied Hindu organisations in the country.' The Non-Party or Sapru Conference, 1942, vol. 334, part 1, Freedom Movement Archives (FMA), University of Karachi.

[9] Maulana Jamal Mian was a key figure in mobilising the *ulama* at Lucknow's Firangi Mahal. He invited Jinnah to inaugurate the Pakistan Club 'to further the cause of Pakistan', revived the daily newspaper *Hamdam* 'to serve the cause of the Muslims and the Muslim League ideals', and attended most of the *ulama* conferences. He had close contacts with M.A.H. Ispahani, the industrialist, and with Mohammad Amir Ahmad Khan, the Raja of Mahmudabad. On the Pakistan issue, the Firangi Mahal was split. Jamal Mian went to Pakistan, though many of his kinsmen stayed behind. For Jamal Mian's correspondence with Jinnah, see Correspondence of Jinnah, United Provinces (UP), vol. iv, Shamsul Hasan Collection (SHC), Karachi.

and Gandhian truth.' 'The creation of an Islamic state–mark my words gentlemen, I say Islamic and not Muslim', he said during the Bombay Muslim League conference on 24-26 May 1940, 'is our ideal.[...] The state will conform to the laws as laid down in Islam.[...] The unchangeable law of Islam will *ipso facto* be applied and enforced.'[10] But not everybody endorsed such a utopian view, and that included the Raja's lawyer-brother. Most desired Pakistan's future constitution to be modelled on 'the latest and most up-to-date experiences of the practical working of Democracy' rather than on vague slogans of *Hukumat-i Ilahiya* (Government of God).[11]

Mohammad Mujeeb, Jamia Millia Islamia's vice-chancellor, recalled how prominent Leaguers took to praying in public when their critics pointed out the inconsistency of representing Islam and neglecting even the elementary religious obligations.[12] 'We used religion, and the real danger of extinction that it faced, to gain our freedom,' commented Firoz Khan Noon. When Sher Ali Khan, brother of the Nawab of Pataudi (Iftikhar Ali Khan), returned to Punjab in early 1946, he found that 'religious fervour was definitely the pace-setter'. 'Whenever I heard of Pakistan, I heard of religion,' he wrote in his memoirs. He found 'the political atmosphere charged with a communal approach' in Lahore and Multan.[13] The ability of Muslim League spokesmen to communicate their Muslimness and their Islamic convictions lies at the heart of their extraordinary success in creating a separate state.

II

Historians of Pakistan must dig in vain to unearth the two-nation theory in most of Jinnah's pre-March 1940 writings and speeches. However, they are sure to find repeated exhortations on Hindu-Muslim amity, cultural pluralism and secularity. Of course he sharply denounced the Congress leaders, accusing them of responsibility for alienating Muslims through 'Hindu' policies, and of creating class bitterness and communal war, and

[10] The Raja of Mahmudabad, 'Some Memories', in Philips and Wainwright (eds), *The Partition of India*, p. 388. The Raja of Mahmudabad to Mohibbul Hasan, 28 October 1939, personal collection.

[11] Maharajkumar Amir Hyder Khan (Nabbu Mian) to Jinnah, 3 December 1945, UP, vol. iv, SHC.

[12] Mohammad Mujeeb, 'The Partition of India in Retrospect', in Philips and Wainwright (eds), op. cit., p. 408.

[13] Firoz Khan Noon, *From Memory* (Lahore, 1966), p. 216; Major General Sher Ali Khan, *The Story: Soldiering and Politics in India and Pakistan* (Lahore: Jamal Mahmud Press, 1988, 3rd edn), p. 110.

strengthening the imperialistic hold.[14] His speech at the Sind Muslim League Conference in October 1938 was a stinging attack on Congress; he stigmatised its High Command as the greatest enemy of India's progress, and with Catonian vehemence and repetition questioned its claim to represent the Muslims. The presence of a few 'misguided' and 'misled' Muslims made no difference to him. The worst 'toady' on earth, he stated, 'the most wicked communalist toady amongst Muslims, when he surrenders unconditionally to the Congress and abuses his own community, becomes the nationalist of nationalists tomorrow.'[15]

Jinnah's stance was belligerent, yet he was inclined to negotiate with the Congress. His major public pronouncements in 1938, including the famous *Id* speech at Lahore which the Sandhurst-educated M.R.A. Baig is said to have helped him draft, was 'a model of communal moderation'.[16] In an article published on 19 January 1940 he did not refer to Hindus and Muslims carving out their separate destinies, or talk of separation, but commented somewhat ambiguously on two nations 'who both must share the governance of their common motherland'. But he did not rule out co-operation with the Congress 'so that the present enmities may cease and India may take its place amongst the great countries of the world'.[17]

Jinnah changed course, something he did with greater alacrity on the eve of the transfer of power when he realised that the Congress, constrained by its own political compulsions and the mounting pressure from Hindu parties, was not strongly placed to accommodate his claims or conduct an open-ended dialogue with him. On the other hand, a beleaguered war-time government, busy picking up support from all quarters to maintain its credibility, was ready to give him a patient hearing. So the Quaid, always eager to move centre-stage and be one up on Gandhi and Nehru, occupied a vantage-point for the first time in his public life. He raised his stakes by demanding equality with the Congress, and insisted, as he did at the Simla Conference in 1945, that Congress Muslims be left in the cold and excluded from negotiations. He was no longer obliged to play second-fiddle to the Congress. He did not need to plead for concessions, as he did at the National Convention in December 1928 or at the Round Table Conference in London, but was powerfully placed to talk the British officials into recognising the weight of his demands.

---

[14] Sharifuddin Pirzada (ed.), *Foundations of Pakistan*, (Karachi: National Publishing House, 1970), vol. 2, p. 268.

[15] *Quarterly Review*, 1 May-31 July 1938, p. 35; Mudie Papers, Mss. Eur. file no. 125/143, IOL; speech at Lucknow, 15-18 October 1937, Pirzada (ed.), *Foundations*, vol. 2, pp. 270, 304.

[16] Tara Ali Baig, *Portraits of an Era* (Delhi: Roli Books, 1988), p. 64; see also Saad R. Khairi, *Jinnah Reinterpreted: The Journey from Indian Nationalism to Muslim Statehood* (Karachi: OUP, 1995), pp. 361-2.

[17] *India's Problem of Her Future Constitution* (Bombay: Saxon Press, 1940), p. 28.

To proclaim his individuality and assert his newly-acquired status, Jinnah resolved to re-write the nationalist agenda he himself had outlined at the League's Lucknow session in December 1916, the year of the Lucknow Pact. Although he did not mention 'Pakistan', his Lahore speech in March 1940 was a watershed, symbolising a decisive shift in his ideology.[18] He no longer championed secular nationalism, nor was he Sarojini Naidu's 'ambassador of Hindu-Muslim unity'. He cultivated instead the image of a twentieth-century Muslim messiah with the mission of liberateing a 'community' from the shackles of 'Hindu tyranny'. He talked of divergent nationalities incapable of being transformed or fused into one nation. Islam and Hinduism represented two of the nationalities. They were not religions in the strict sense of the word but distinct social orders. Their adherents belonged to two different civilisations, based on ideas and world-views that were at variance with each other. For this reason India was always divided into 'Hindu' and 'Muslim' segments. To yoke together two such nations in a single state was a recipe for disaster. The Muslims formed a 'nation' by any standard definition; they must secure their homelands, their territories and their state. A great responsibilty rested on the educated Muslims to transform this idea into reality. 'Unless you get this into your blood', they were told emphatically, 'unless you are prepared to take off your coats and are willing to sacrifice all that you can and work selflessly, earnestly and sincerely for your people, you will never realize your aim.'[19]

Mumtaz Shah Nawaz (1912-48), a young writer born into one of the most prominent landowning families of Lahore, looked at the faces around her in the *pandal*.[20] She saw in their eyes the fading of her dream of Hindu-Muslim unity in a free India. But she also saw in those very eyes the dawn of a new ideal that had already gripped their hearts. It was as if someone had said to them 'You should be free! – and this and this alone is the way .... And they had lifted up their eyes to gaze at new horizons and their minds had raced ahead of them down fresh vistas of thought.'[21]

---

[18] Ayesha Jalal interprets the resolution as a spectacular demonstration of Jinnah's skills in harnessing the diverse interests of the Muslims with the intention of establishing the League's credentials as the authoritative spokesman of Muslim interests. Farzana Shaikh, on the other hand, has argued that the resolution was more than just a spectacular *tour de force*. It became a part of a more profound and persistent concern to restore to the religious community its significance as a political order where power, as an instrument of righteousness, would be a Muslim prerogative. Jalal, *The Sole Spokesman*, pp. 54-5; Shaikh, *Community and Consensus*, p. 207; see also Asim Roy, 'The High Politics of India's Partition: The Revisionist Perspective', pp. 385-415.

[19] Pirzada (ed.), *Foundations*, vol. 2, pp. 338, 339.

[20] Mumtaz, or 'Tazi' as she was called by her family, died in a plane crash in Ireland on 15 April 1948.

[21] Mumtaz Shah Nawaz, *The Heart Divided* (Lahore: ASR Publications, 1990, 2nd edn), p. 411. See David Willmer, 'The Islamic State as *telos*: Mumtaz Shah Nawaz's Narrative of

A fervent nationalist with socialist leanings, Mumtaz returned from Lahore, the venue of the Muslim League session in March 1940, to Amritsar 'with anguish in her heart'. Her early adulthood had been strongly influenced by the civil disobedience movement in 1930-2. Her mother Jahan Ara Shah Nawaz, daughter of Mian Mohammad Shafi, an influential Punjab politician, recalls that she donated to the Congress the proceeds of a poem published in the *Spectator* around the time when her grandfather was representing the Muslim League at the Round Table Conference in 1930. She loved and idolised her country as the motherland. But suddenly she was face to face with a demand for its partition, a demand that came from her own people, the ones she loved and cherished, from those whose integrity she could not doubt, from her father and uncle.[22] Like so many educated Muslims in her generation, who had otherwise no place for religio-political fundamentalism in their cultural and intellectual milieu, Mumtaz was confused and bewildered by the turn of events. Her conscience was stirred by the League call, a transition reflected in the character of Zohra in her novel *The Heart Divided*, while secular nationalism, the mainstay of a generation of Punjab leaders from the days of the Rowlatt *Satyagraha* (1919), ceased to be attractive.

In the highly charged political and communalised climate, sensitive minds asked new questions and searched for outlets to express their dilemmas and anxieties. In fact, the potential of the emerging 'Muslim nationalism' to cause conflict within families is a central theme of *The Heart Divided*, written in 1943, the year following the conversion of Mumtaz Shah Nawaz to the Muslim League, and published in 1948, the year after Pakistan was born. By undertaking to write a narrative of Pakistan, she tried to come to terms with the conflicts present in the narrative of her own life.[23]

Much the same conflict is revealed in the following description by Attia Hosain in her novel *Sunlight on a Broken Column*, first published in 1961:

No one seemed to talk any more; everyone argued, and not in the graceful tradition of our city where conversation was treated as a fine art, words were loved as mediums of artistic expression, and verbal battles were enjoyed as much as any delicate, scintillating, sparkling display of pyrotechnic skill. It was if someone had sneaked in live ammunition among the fireworks. In the thrust and parry there was a desire to inflict wounds. Even visitors argued. A new type of person now frequented the house. Fanatic, bearded men and young zealots...; rough country-dwelling landlords and their 'courtiers' ... Every

---

Pakistan and Modernity' in *The Indian Economic and Social History Review* 32, 4, October-December 1995.

[22] Nawaz, op. cit., , pp. 412, 413. See also Mehr Nigar Masroor, *Shadow of Time*, ed. Lala Chatterji and Ranjanha Ash (Lahore: ASR, 1995).

[23] Willmer, op. cit., pp. 426-7.

meal at home had become an ordeal as peaceful as a volcanic eruption.[24]

These narratives are seemingly 'fictional', but are in fact fairly accurate representations of the political ferment which split middle class and landowning families along ideological lines, and poignant autobiographical reflections on them. They are historical texts in so far as they illuminate certain aspects of the liberation struggle which are only dimly covered in records and private papers. They bring out the tensions, conflicts and contradictions in movements perceived as monolithic, autonomous and linear. They introduce a nuanced discourse in an area of research dominated by highly magisterial generalisations.

III

Jinnah boasted in May 1940 that he headed an all-India organisation which had a 'flag, a platform, a policy and a well-considered programme'.[25] In reality, his League was dominated, as it had always been since its inception in December 1906, by people from the Muslim-minority provinces. Out of a total membership of 503 in the 1942 council, 245 belonged to those areas; of twenty-three working committee members in 1945-7, only ten came from the Muslim-majority provinces.[26]

The Bengali and Punjabi Muslims had no reason to change course. As Fazlul Haq conceded, the League's strategies endangered their authority and the cross-communal alliances they had so assiduously built since the mid-1920s.[27] In some circles, the two-nation idea had an emotive appeal, but it made no sense to the rank and file of Punjab's Unionist Party – or, for that matter, to the Bengal's Krishak Proja Party, which was 'non-communal in conception and approach' though 'dominantly Muslim in composition and leadership'.[28] Thus Sikander Hyat Khan, Fazlul Haq and Allah Bakhsh of Sind unfurled the banner of revolt by accepting the War Council's membership. They defied the League's mandate, making clear that they led non-communal parties, representing the whole Province and did not speak on behalf of any denominational group.[29] Although the

[24] Attia Hosain, *Sunlight on a Broken Column* (Delhi: Penguin Books, 1992), p. 230.

[25] Message sent to the Bombay Presidency Provincial Muslim League Conference, *India's Problem*, op. cit., p. 18.

[26] Sayeed, *Pakistan: The Formative Phase*, p. 206.

[27] Fazlul Haq's case against People's War, in *Jinnah-Ispahani Correspondence*, appendix xviii, p. 692.

[28] Humayun Kabir, *Muslim Politics, 1906-1942* (Calcutta: Gupta Rahman and Gupta, 1944), p. 10.

[29] Extract from the fortnightly report [FR] on the political situation in Bengal, in governor-general to secretary of state, 28 August 1941, Home Political, file no. 18/1, 1941, National Archives of India NAI.

Punjab Premier wavered and eventually capitulated to save his skin, Fazlul Haq protested, just as he had done during the Congress-League parleys in November-December 1916, against the way in which the interests of Bengali and Punjabi Muslims were being imperilled by the self-styled Muslim leaders of UP and Bihar.[30] Allah Bakhsh, the man who stoutly resisted Jinnah's intrusion into Sind, also did not comply with the League's mandate: 'My position as Premier imposes distinct obligation that in all public matters I should be solely guided by interests of the whole Province and not by any partisan communal or sectional considerations whatsoever.'[31]

The Quaid was unsettled. He knew that while other Muslim leaders were unwilling to put a brake on his lead because it suited their interests, his mission could only be accomplished in the long run by taming the recalcitrant Bengali and Punjabi Muslims. He pleaded with the Punjab delegates to 'substitute love for Islam and your nation, in place of sectional interests, jealousy, tribal notions and selfishness'.[32] E.J. Benthall sensed that if Punjab and Bengal backed out, 'Jinnah's position might rapidly be undermined and jealousies are no less extant in the Moslem camp than elsewhere. Congress are well aware of these.'[33] In any case nobody, not even Jinnah, had an inkling about the shape and form of the future Pakistan. Sher Ali Khan's discussions with the Nawab of Bhopal and his brother Iftikhar Ali Khan, the well-known cricketer and ruler of the Pataudi state (now in the state of Haryana, bordering Delhi), led him to conclude: 'It was quite clear that Pakistan was coming, but when, and finally in what form, was not clear.'[34] 'Pakistan, let us frankly admit, is not practical politics today', was the verdict of another League sympathiser.[35]

The underlying ambivalence in certain quarters was compounded by the cool reception to the Pakistan idea itself. Fazlul Haq faced a dilemma: he had stirred up a hornets' nest at Lahore, where he moved the 'Pakistan resolution' for tactical reasons, but he spent sleepless nights thereafter when the League machinery virtually wrecked his own power-base among the Muslim peasantry. Only a month later he talked of working for a united India.[36] Sikander Hyat Khan, averse to Jinnah's overtures in Punjab, was 'disturbed'. He had no doubt drafted the resolution at Lahore, but provided for definite links with the Centre so as to preserve national

[30] 12 September 1941, ibid.
[31] 30 August 1941, ibid.
[32] Quoted in Sayeed, op. cit., p. 198.
[33] Benthall Papers, CSAS.
[34] Sher Ali Khan, *The Story*, p. 110.
[35] Quoted in *India's Problem of her Future Constitution*, p. 105.
[36] *Tribune*, 29 April 1940, quoted in Inder Singh, *Origins of the Partition*, p. 58.

unity.[37] The offshoot of the Lahore meeting was not what he had bargained for. It was dangerous playing the communal game in Punjab; the price for the keeping Jinnah in good humour was too high. This realisation led Sikander to distance himself from the Pakistan demand:[38] 'We do not ask for freedom, that there may be a Muslim Raj that and a Hindu Raj elsewhere.' He added:

If you want real freedom for the Punjab ... then that Punjab will not be Pakistan, but just Punjab, the land of the five rivers: Punjab is Punjab and will always remain Punjab whatever anybody may say. This then, briefly, is the political future which I visualise for my province and for my country under the new Constitution.[39]

The picture was much the same in other provinces. No Muslim minister in Sind endorsed the Lahore resolution; Allah Bakhsh, erstwhile premier, described it as 'harmful and fantastic'.[40] Political pundits in western India were unimpressed.[41] S.A. Brelvi (editor of the *Bombay Chronicle*), M.C. Chagla (lawyer and a former associate of Jinnah) and Mohammad Yasin Nurie (former minister (1937-9) in the Bombay government) considered Jinnah's scheme 'disastrous'. They were uneasy at the prospect of becoming 'aliens in our own lands so that a great Muslim state should spring up in the North. Are we going to sell our birthright for a mess of communal pottage?' Millions of Hindus and Muslims lived all over the country in perfect amity and concord, 'happily oblivious of the fact that the League had decreed overnight that they are no longer citizens of the same country, that they must look upon each other as foreigners and that they must evolve a separate and distinct culture.'[42]

In UP the Pakistan idea was widely regarded as a bargaining move, 'a counter demand to that of the Congress'.[43] Educated Muslims in the province, as also in Bihar, feared that Pakistan would provide a homeland for those living in majority areas but not in other parts. Such apprehensions haunted the Nawab of Chattari, leader of the UP Agriculturists' Party. He was unsure how Muslim interests in 'Hindu-majority provinces' would be safeguarded.[44] Syed Wazir Hasan, architect of the 1916 Luck-

[37] Malcolm Darling to Linlithgow, 25 April 1940, L/P&J/8/506, part b, IOL.

[38] Gilmartin, *Empire and Islam*, pp. 184-5.

[39] Quoted in Ian Talbot, *Punjab and the Raj, 1849-1947* (Delhi: Manohar, 1988), pp. 190-1, and his *Provincial Politics and the Pakistan Movement: The Growth of the Muslim League in North-West and North-East India, 1937-1947* (Delhi, 1988).

[40] Inder Singh, op. cit., p. 58.

[41] Governor of Bombay to Linlithgow, 30 March 1940, L/P&J/8/512, part 2, IOL.

[42] Draft of the statement in M.C. Chagla papers, Nehru Memorial Museum and Library (NMML), New Delhi.

[43] Enclosure 2 in: UP governor to governor-general (telegram), 31 March 1940, Linlithgow papers (125/108), IOL.

[44] To Jinnah, n.d. (probably written in early January 1940), L/P&J/8/507, IOL.

now Pact, rejected the notion of Hindus and Muslims constituting two different nations. The assumption, he wrote, was as ill-founded as the conclusion.[45] Maulana Husain Ahmad Madani, *alim* from Deoband's theological seminary, characterised the Pakistan movement as the 'death-knell' for the Muslims in 'Muslim-minority provinces'. His colleague and co-founder of the Jamiyat al-ulama, Maulana Anwar Sajjad, dismissed the suggestion that the numerical strength of the Muslims in such areas would in itself safeguard their interests elsewhere.[46] Mahmudabad's Raja, who had set out to study at the feet of Tagore in Shantiniketan but was hijacked by some League enthusiasts, considered withdrawing from active politics because of his differences with Jinnah. But his industrialist friend, M.A.H. Ispahani, would not let go. It was not at all desirable for the Raja, he said, to change over to a full-time concentration of religion within the four walls of the Mahmudabad fort.[47]

At the beginning of 1942, the viceroy Linlithgow himself could find no genuine enthusiasm for Pakistan among the Muslim Leaguers he had met. He believed that most Muslims viewed Pakistan as a symbol of a vague resolve against 'Hindu domination', which rarely implied a positive commitment to creating a sovereign state. He concluded that they would be content with Pakistan within some sort of a federation.[48]

The viceroy should also have referred to Muslim organisations doggedly opposed to Jinnah's Pakistan demand; to the Jamiyat al-ulama, founded during the Khilafat ferment and closely allied with the liberal and secular-minded Muslims of Ansari's and Azad's generation;[49] the All-

---

[45] Wazir Hasan, 'The Theory of Two Nations', *Twentieth Century*, April 1940, p. 635; *Hindustan or Pakistan: Partition or Unity* (Lahore: Ilami Markaz, n.d.). Its author Abdul Majid was professor at Forman college, Lahore. There is extensive literature, much of it either unexplored or considered unimportant, refuting the two-nation idea and endorsing theories on composite and plural nationhod. I believe an analysis of such writings would illuminate both the presence of a powerful liberal and secular intelligentsia as well as the wide spectrum of opinion among Muslims. There are biographies of Ajmal Khan, Azad, Mohamed Ali, Ansari, Mazharul Haq, Ghaffar Khan, Rafi Ahmad Kidwai, Yusuf Meharally and Zakir Husain. There are useful autobiographical accounts as well. Notable among them are Khwaja Ahmad Abbas, *I am not an Island: An Experiment in Autobiography* (Delhi: Vikas Publishing House, 1987) and his *Bombay My Bombay* (Delhi: Ajanta Publications, 1987); M.R.A. Baig, *In Different Saddles* (Bombay: Asia Publishing House, 1967); and M.C. Chagla, *Roses in December: An Autobiography* (Bombay: Bharatiya Vidya Bhavan, 1973).

[46] Quoted in Ziya-ul-Hasan Faruqi, *The Deoband School and the Demand for Pakistan* (Bombay: Asia Publishing House, 1963), pp. 111-2.

[47] Hassan to Jinnah, 17 December 1942, *Jinnah-Ispahani Correspondence*, p. 312.

[48] Inder Singh, op. cit., p. 239.

[49] I.H. Douglas, *Abul Kalam Azad: An Intellectual and Religious Biography*, eds Gail Minault and C.W. Troll (Delhi: OUP, 1988); V.N. Datta, *Maulana Azad* (Delhi: Manohar, 1990); Mushirul Hasan (ed.), *Islam and Indian Nationalism*; and my *A Nationalist Conscience*; V.N. Datta and B.E. Cleghorn (eds.), *A Nationalist Muslim and Indian Politics* (Delhi: Macmillan, 1974); Mushir U. Haq, *Muslim Politics in Modern India* (Meerut:

India Momin conference of Muslim weavers of eastern UP and Bihar, secular-oriented and tied to the Congress;[50] and the Khudai Khidmatgars in the North-West Frontier Province (NWFP), led by the charismatic figure of Khan Abdul Ghaffar Khan, who spurned religious slogans, rebuffed Jinnah's initiatives and fought valiantly for a united India. Here the League failed to rally support on the Pakistan issue in the 1945-6 elections, because to the average Pakhtun the suggestion of Hindu domination was 'laughable'. A plebiscite on the limited choice of joining India or Pakistan was forced on them. Those who decided in favour of Pakistan were a mere 9.52 per cent of the population; the rest had not spoken their minds. Ironically, a Congress ministry under Khan Saheb, brother of Ghaffar Khan and personal friend of Jawaharlal Nehru, was in power in the NWFP when Pakistan came into being.[51]

The Ahrars, the Khaksars[52] and leaders of the Shia Political Conference[53] endeavoured to break the Hindu-Muslim impasse and spurned the Pakistan demand.[54] In general, however, their initiatives were weakened by internal strife, sectarian allegiances, regional loyalties, and a highly utopian notion of Islamic nationalism. Senior leaders succumbed to communal pressures. In May 1943 the All-India Ahrar Working Committee adopted '*Hukumat-i Ilahi*' as its goal, and retreated from the decision taken just a year later to launch civil disobedience against the government. Syed Ataullah Shah Bukhari, the charismatic leader, yielded to religious exigencies.[55] Some of his staunch supporters, active during the civil disobedience movement (1930-2), drifted apart. Abdul Qayum of Kanpur, member of the Majlis-i Ahrar Working Committee, 'accepted the ideal of Pakistan'.[56] Maulana Abdul Hakim Qasuri, Ahrari and Con-

Meenakshi Prakashan, 1970); and Mohammad Muzaffar Imam, *Role of Muslims in the National Movement* (Delhi: Mittal Publication, 1987).

[50] For their deliberations and activities, as also of the All-India Azad Muslim Board and the Hindu-Muslim Unity Conference in June 1942, see *Indian Annual Register IAR*, 1942, vol. 6, pp. 329-36; Smith, *Modern Islam*, pp. 241-68.

[51] The League won 17 of the 36 Muslim seats in the 1945-6 elections; the Congress won 19. The Congress also won 11 non-Muslim seats for a total of 30 seats in a house of 50 members. K.B. Sayeed, *Politics in Pakistan: The Nature and Direction of Change* (New York: Praeger, 1980), p. 21.

[52] Kabir, *Muslim Politics*, pp. 40-4.

[53] Mushirul Hasan, 'Sectarianism in Indian Islam: The Shia-Sunni Divide in the United Provinces' *Indian Economic and Social History Review*, 27, 2, 1990.

[54] For Azad Muslim Conference, see *IAR*, 1944, vol. 1, pp. 241-2; Smith, *Modern Islam*, pp. 268-9.

[55] See Jaan Baaz Mirza, *Amir-i Shariat* (Lahore: Maktaba Tabsara, n.d.); Shorish Kashmiri, *Boo-i gul Nala-i dil Dud-i Chiragh-i Mehfil* (Lahore: Chattan, 1972), and his *Tehrik-i Khatm-i Nabuat* (Lahore: Chattan, 1980 edn.).

[56] To Jinnah, 6 April 1943, UP, correspondence-general, vol. 1, SHC, and Malik Ahmad to Jinnah, 15 August 1945, inviting the Quaid to join the Khaksars for 'the cause of Musalmans

gress worker, went over to the League.[57] Inayatullah Khan, Khaksar 'officer' for eight years, told Jinnah that 'in case you fail to achieve Pakistan by negotiation, then only bloodshed and war will be the choice. In case this becomes inevitable, every man of the nation is duty bound to fight by your side. I am one of the crores.'[58] The Khaksars demanded in their last public appearance in India, 'an undivided Pakistan stretching from Karachi to Calcutta'. Its leader, Allama Mashriqi, migrated to Pakistan, founded the Islam League, and died in 1963 in Lahore.

Organised formations, such as the Ahrar party, were prone to divisions and ideological hair-splitting. But student bodies, literary societies, city and district clubs and associations, mostly not even footnoted in histories of nationalism, kept up their good work unobtrusively. Anwar Jamal Kidwai (died 1996), activist of the Lucknow university union and follower of the Allahabad-born communist leader, Shafiq Naqvi (died 1992), described the League as 'socially reactionary', and he marshalled histori- cal, economic and cultural arguments to defend secularism.[59] Scholars at the Jamia Millia Islamia, tucked away in a remote part of South Delhi, emphasised that India's Muslims had deep roots in Indian society and were natural inhabitants of an *Indian* world. They had much in common with other communities 'in fundamental, religious and moral conscious- ness, social structure, family life and the general way of living that can easily fit into any rational pattern of National Culture'.[60]'In name Jamia was also a university ... but in fact it was a camp of the satyagraha volunteers,' recalled K.M. Ashraf who left Aligarh's Muslim University to join the Jamia.[61]

The liberal-socialist combine resisted attempts to transform the Aligarh Muslim University into an 'arsenal of Muslim India'.[62] Khwaja Ahmad Abbas, Ansar Harvani, Asrarul Haq 'Majaaz' and Ali Sardar Jafri spearheaded the All-India Students' Federation (AISF) and later the Progressive Writers' Movement. Urdu poets and writers, especially those

---

and Islam' and assuring him that 'they in their turn would extend every help to the Muslim League'.

[57] To Nawab Iftikhar Husain of Mamdot, n.d., FMA, box no. 56. The Maulana was a disciple of Abdul Hakim Qasuri and belonged to the Ahl-i Hadith school.

[58] Inayatullah Khan to Jinnah, 29 March 1946, General Correspondence, Delhi, SHC; Shan Muhammad, *Khaksar Movement in India* (Meerut: Meenakshi Prakashan, 1972), p. 140.

[59] A.J. Kidwai, 'Pathology of Pakistan', *Twentieth Century'*, November 1940, p. 139.

[60] Syed Abid Husain, *The National Culture of India* (Delhi: Asia Publishing House, 1956), p. 176, and *The Destiny of Indian Muslims* (Bombay: Asia Publishing House, 1965); Mujeeb, *The Indian Muslims*; 'A Note on the Jamiyah Milliyah Islamia', in Smith, *Modern Islam*, pp. 147-54.

[61] K.M. Ashraf on Himself, in Horst Kruger (ed.), *Kunwar Mohammad Ashraf: An Indian Scholar and Revolutionary, 1903-1962* (Berlin [East]: Akademie-Verlag, 1966), p. 391.

[62] See Mushirul Hasan, 'Nationalist and Separatist Trends in Aligarh, 1915-1947', in A.K. Gupta (ed.), *Myth and Reality: The Struggle for Freedom in India* (Delhi: Manohar, 1987).

tutored in Marxism-Leninism and connected with the Progressive Writers' Movement, denounced sectarianism and religious obscurantism. Partition along religious and cultural lines was the greatest barrier in realising their dream of a free and socialist India based pre-eminently on communal harmony.[63]

The 'Jinnah legend' disconcerted the influential Muslim professionals in Bombay, such as Nurie, Brelvi, Chagla, Moinuddin Harris, M.R.A. Baig and the socialist Yusuf Meharally. They were alarmed that Dadabhai Naoroji's disciple was leading Muslims towards a dangerous precipice. 'I have heard much indignation expressed against the attitude of Mr Jinnah', commented J.H. Taleyarkhan, 'but never had I heard him indicted so severely as he was by Nurie – an ardent but a right-thinking and far-seeing Muslim who, because he has the interest of his community at heart, bleeds to see them sacrificed on the altar of Mr Jinnah's policy.'[64] Chagla, having parted company with Jinnah on the Nehru Committee Report (August 1928), considered it a 'grievous fallacy' to mistake religion for culture and confuse a community with a nation. India's modern history had evolved on the one great assumption of the oneness of the Indian people. And because Hindu-Muslim relations were sometimes marred by sectarain violence, there was no reason to scrap the whole of India's political past. 'A political faith should be something lasting – and I never thought Mr Jinnah belonged to the category of men who foreswore their faith because of temporary irritation or momentary anger and indignation'.[65]

Even by conventional standards of 'success' and 'failure' it is still not easy to write off the progressive Muslim intelligentsia or heap scorn on their framework of analysis, their intervention in the partition debate and their passionate defence of India's unity and secular identity. Their perspective, combined with the activism of the Jamiyat al-ulama, the Momin conference and the Khudai Khidmatgars, enriched the secular discourse. And their activities disproved the widely accepted notion that the Pakistan movement was unified and ideologically cohesive, or that its progress was unimpeded because of the overwhelming enthusiasm of the masses and the intelligentsia alike. Its supposed unity is proved to be hollow when its more glaring contradictions are brought to light. There is no better way of doing so than to analyse why some Muslims hitched their fortunes to the League bandwagon.

---

[63] Muhammad Sadiq, *Twentieth Century Urdu Literature* (Karachi: Royal Book Co., 1983), pp. 192-3; Ali Jawad Zaidi, *A History of Urdu Literature* (Delhi: Sahitya Akademi, 1993), pp. 360-1; Russell, *Pursuit of Urdu Literature*, chapters 13-4.

[64] J.H. Taleyarkhan, *They Told Me So* (Bombay: Thacker, 1947), p. 120.

[65] Statement, n.d., Chagla papers, NMML.

IV

A common assumption in several historical writings is that the League's support structure remained unchanged throughout the 1930s and '40s. It is also taken for granted that everyone who rallied round the green flag was uniformly wedded to, and inspired by, a shared ideal of creating an egalitarian society based on the Islamic model. Both assumptions are questionable. For one, the entry of individuals and collective formations into the League happened at different points of time and for altogether different reasons. Take the Jamaat-i-Islami, founded in August 1941. Its *amir*, Abul Ala Maududi, rejected nationalism and democracy because in his view both would lead to the predominance of Indian and/or non-Islamic forces and influences. Even a cursory glance at the meaning and essence of nationalism, he wrote, was enough to reveal that Islam and nationalism were poles apart, and that the Muslim's loyalty, which is religious, cannot be given to an entity such as the nation. For these reasons, Muslims should become better Muslims, and cast off any Indian, Western or secularist influences.[66]

Maududi was convinced that the League was ill-suited to carry out a revolution that would bring about a truly Islamic order. He believed that those trained in running the affairs of the secular state were unfit for an Islamic state which required human beings of a very different character for its citizens, voters, councillors, office-bearers. A truly Islamic socio-political system required selfless, God-fearing men accountable to Allah, who preferred the next life to the present, and who had no interest in worldly success or failure. So 'why should we foolishly waste our time in expediting the so-called Muslim national state and fritter away our energies in setting it up, when we know that it will not only be useless for our purpose but will rather prove an obstacle in our path?'[67]

By 1945, however, Maududi had put many such ideas in cold storage. He accepted the reality of Pakistan, opting for a gradualist approach towards the Islamisation of its law and constitution, although he had condemned the League for taking a similar line. The Jamaat i-Islami, having sensed victory for the protagonists of Pakistan, was pushed into spearheading a fundamentalist movement to transform the new country from a Muslim homeland into an Islamic state.[68]

---

[66] A.A. Maududi, *Nationalism and India* (Lahore: Maktaba-i Jamaat-i Islami, 1947, new edn), p. 10.

[67] A.A. Maududi, *The Process of Islamic Revolution* (Lahore, 1955, 2nd edn), p. 37.

[68] For details, see Malise Ruthven, *Islam in the World* (New York: OUP, 1984), pp. 326-31; Leonard Binder, *Religion and Politics in Pakistan* (Berkeley: CA, University of California Press, 1963); Charles J. Adams, 'The Ideology of Mawlana Mawdudi' in Smith (ed.), *South Asian Politics and Religion*, pp. 371-97.

The entry of Muslim traders, merchants and businessmen was likewise a belated affair. They were not much concerned with the righteousness of the cause, since they had participated in major commercial bodies with their Hindu, Jain and Parsi counterparts well until the mid-1930s.[69] The direction of the Bombay cotton mills in an industrial centre where Indians rather than Europeans control led the enterprises reflected 'a high degree of inter-communal co-operation'.[70] In other parts of western India the Khojas, Bohras and Memons shared social and cultural traits with the Hindus and seemed indifferent to the intrusion of religion in the world of business. The Muslim Chamber of Commerce (MCC), founded in 1932 in Calcutta, did raised no specific Muslim issue till 1942; it acted in unison with the Federation of Indian Chambers of Commerce and Industry (FICCI) and endorsed its policies.[71] In fact, a separate Muslim Chamber of Commerce did not find favour in Peshawar, where Hindu and Muslim merchants happily ran their combined Association.[72]

Ispahani, Adamji Haji Dawood, G.A. Dossani and Sultan Chinoy energised the MCC in the early-1940s. Plans were laid in September 1943 to launch a Federation of Muslim Chambers of Commerce and Industry as a counterpart to FICCI.[73] A year later, Ispahani proudly announced that the Federation had grown into a robust and representative body of Muslim merchants and industrialists.[74] Jinnah was sceptical of the venture, and talked of the 'paper scheme', the delay in holding the first meeting and the loss of valuable time and opportunity. 'Every week that passes', he told Ispahani, 'is now not only creating a sense of frustration and despair amongst those who have worked and are willing and ready to work, but in the rapid developments that are taking place, Muslim India will unfortunately find itself as usual with the motto "Too Late".'[75]

The first meeting, held in Delhi on 19 April 1945, was poorly managed, thinly attended and ignored by the press.[76] But some months later the MCC appeared more visible with more and more Muslim capitalists, traders, merchants and businessmen of Sind, Bombay and Bengal backing the League with their money-bags. Muslim capitalists in Bombay did so

---

[69] Claude Markovits, 'Businessmen and the Partition of India', in Dwijendra Tripathi (ed.), *Business and Politics in India: A Historical Perspective* (Delhi: Manohar, 1991), p. 288, and his *Indian Business and Nationalist Politics 1931-39: The Indigenous Capitalist Class and the Rise of the Congress Party* (CUP, 1985).

[70] A.D.D. Gordon, *Businessmen and Politics: Rising Nationalism and a Modernising Economy in Bombay, 1918-1933* (Delhi: Manohar, 1978), p. 64.

[71] Markovits, 'Businessmen and the Partition', p. 289.

[72] To Jinnah, 18 March 1944, *Jinnah-Ispahani Correspondence*, p. 409.

[73] To Jinnah, 3 September 1944, ibid., p. 369.

[74] To Jinnah, 24 October 1944, ibid., p. 433.

[75] Jinnah to Hassan, 15 April 1945, ibid., p. 444.

[76] Jinnah to Hassan, 6 May 1945, ibid., p. 449.

because of the steady decline of their political influence and economic fortunes.[77] In UP there were no major Muslim industrialists, bankers or financial companies, and petty small traders, merchants and shopkeepers used the cover of the Muslim League to resist various government regulations that came into effect after the end of the war in Europe. The Tobacco Merchants' Association in Lucknow, Barabanki and Rae Bareli sought the League's intervention against the imposition of a higher excise duty on tobacco, because it 'affects the industry, the public and the Muslim businessmen'.[78] The emphasis on 'Muslim businessmen' was not without meaning or purpose.

The League seized the opportunity to act as an arbiter to project itself as the champion and defender of 'Muslim rights'. In 1943 the city branch in Budaun espoused the grievances of Muslim retailers in the textile industry and of well-placed grain merchants, who were upset by newly-introduced grain control regulations.[79] I.I. Chundrigar, minister for trade and industries, was asked to appoint 'Muslim Importers' in districts with a large Muslim population, 'as non-Muslim importers take no interest in importing varieties of cloth which are needed for use by Muslims.'[80] In Gorakhpur the Muslim Defence Committee, founded in 1942, obtained licenses for Muslim dealers in salt, kerosene, cooking oil, grain and standard cloth because 'Hindu officers are giving trouble as usual'.[81] Traders and shopkeepers in Agra had their own complaints; they promptly started a Muslim bank, whose directors and shareholders were staunch Leaguers.[82] Kargha stores were set up in Gorakhpur, Lucknow, Allahabad, Mirzapur, Banaras and Sandila to 'popularise the use of Muslim-made articles'.[83] Muslim Merchants' Associations mushroomed in at least six towns of Sind. Everyday the secretary received applications for licences to control shops.[84]

Nevertheless, the reasons for trading, merchant and business groups to split along religious lines were not strong enough. The divide was the result of political uncertainties, growing economic strains during the post-War years and Hindu-Muslim acerbities accompanied by extensive violence. The British stood idly by, lacking the will to check the drift, the

---

[77] Ahmed, *Origins of Muslim Consciousness*, pp. 224, 226-7.

[78] Telegram from secretary, Tobacco Merchants Association, Lucknow; from Nazirullah Husain of Rae Bareli and Hafiz Munnay, Nawabganj, Barabanki, FMA (335).

[79] FR, 4 June 1945, Frampton Papers, CSAS. He was chief secretary in UP government.

[80] Resolution passed at the public meeting held under the auspices of the Budaun city League on 1 May 1943, vol. 355, FMA. Abdus Samad Muqtadari to Chundrigar, 25 April 1947, vol. 360, FMA.

[81] Muslim League Civil Defence Committee, vol. 315, FMA.

[82] Faiyaz Khan to Liaquat Ali Khan, 26 May 1941, box no. 12, FMA.

[83] Rizwanullah Khan to Liaquat Ali Khan, 8 December 1941, vol. 326, part 2, FMA.

[84] To Liaquat Ali Khan, 6 November 1943, box no. 31, FMA.

political void and the senseless killings. The Congress record, marred by indecision, instransigence and factionalism, was caught up in the communal cauldron. The League's fervour and zeal was matched by the militancy of the RSS and the Hindu Mahasabha. 'There is no sign as yet', reported Burdwan's district commissioner, 'that political events are being considered in other than a communal spirit and all problems – whether in the provincial or all-India sphere – not directly related to the tense communal situation in the province have evoked little interest.'[85]

The extreme communalism of the Suhrawardy ministry (1945-6) in Bengal and the unhappy experience of the interim ministry, which the Congress and the Hindu Mahasabha exploited to the full, ended the lingering doubts and lurking fears about the outcome of partition. The Birlas and the Dalmias, whose communal proclivities were not hidden from anyone, concluded that partition was the only way to end the communal deadlock.[86] Muslim business magnates – not so numerous or influential as their Marwari, Sindhi and Parsi counterparts but beginning to play a part in Muslim League politics – entertained serious apprehensions over their future in undivided India.[87] They were wary of big business, as well as of Congress politicians. Nehru's statement of 10 July 1946, defending a strong centre capable of deploying 'central authority to restrict the freedom of action of Muslim-majority provinces in their provincial domains', caused a flutter. It was read as implying the supremacy of the Tatas, the Birlas and the Dalmias in the competitive wilds of an independent India.[88] For Muslim industrialists this was a dreadful prospect, and they began to pack their bags and move to new frontiers to establish their stronghold in areas where they would enjoy undisputed political and economic hegemony.

Pakistan was a way out of their predicament: it guaranteed to the MCC heavyweights a bright future.[89] Thus the Ispahani and Haroon families held key leadership positions in the provincial and League structures and provided financial support. So did the Memons – the Adamjees, Haroons,

---

[85] FR, for the second half of September 1946, file no. 2, J.M.G. Bell papers, CSAS.

[86] Bell observed that Suhrawardy's performance not only ruled out prospects of an independent Bengal, but also convinced the Bengali Hindus that they could not expect a fair deal from a government with a slight Muslim majority. 'India: Which got the best of the deal?', file no. 3, Bell papers. For the role of the industrialists, see Medha Malik Kudaisya, 'The Public Career of G.D. Birla' (unpubl. Ph.D. thesis, University of Cambridge, 1992), pp. 246-51.

[87] Some of the reasons are explained in Stanley A. Kochanek, *Interest Groups and Development: Business and Politics in Pakistan* (Delhi: OUP, 1993), pp. 19-21.

[88] Quoted in Jalal, *Sole Spokesman*, p. 210, n. 34.

[89] See Shahid Javed Burki, *Pakistan under Bhutto, 1971-1977* (London: Macmillan Press, 1980), pp. 16-20.

B.M. Abu Bekr and others.[90] The Adamjees, known as the 'jute-kings', played a Birla-like role in financing and mobilising Calcutta Memons for the League's activities. The Habib, Shaikh and Wazir Ali families were strong converts to the Pakistan idea.[91]

Hamza Alavi has emphatically argued that the salariat of northern India – not the predominantly Gujarati Muslim trading communities – played the key role in the Pakistan movement.[92] However, Yuri Gankovsky, Gordon-Polonskya and Stanley Kochanek present a somewhat different picture. Evidence is thin, yet it is possible to assign an equally important role to the salariat class and the trading communities, each in their own spheres of influence. When Sher Ali Khan returned to India in 1946, he found a number of 'non-political' friends, along with industrialists and commercial magnates, actively working for the Muslim League.[93]

The Muslim landowning group was a class apart. Thanks to active British patronage, they had laid down the terms of organised communitarian politics, set up the Simla Deputation in October 1906 and lent moral and material sanction to the League. Their political fortunes dwindled during the Khilafat movement, but they quickly recovered some of their prestige in the legislative councils created by the Montagu-Chelmsford Reforms. In Punjab, UP and Bengal they worked smoothly with other groups till the 1930s, when rapid political changes, especially in UP, led to their slow but steady eclipse. Malcolm Hailey, their mentor in UP, recorded their 'tale of defeats' and lamented that they 'proved themselves a broken reed'.[94] It was not the same in Punjab, where Sikander Hyat Khan and Khizr Hyat kept the Unionist Party flag flying until it was lowered against the background of increasing political uncertainty following the abortive Gandhi-Jinnah talks (1944), the Simla Conference (1945), and the progressive escalation of Hindu-Muslim violence. In 1936 'very few of us had believed in Partition or in the Muslim League or in Jinnah', wrote Firoz Khan Noon.[95] By 1945 his family, along with the Hyat and the Daulatana families from whom the Unionist Party had

---

[90] Sergey Levin, 'The Upper Bourgeoisie from the Muslim commercial community of Memons in Pakistan, 1947 to 1971' in Yuri V. Gankovsky (ed.), *Soviet Scholars View South Asia* (Lahore: People's Publishing House, 1975).

[91] Kochanek, op. cit., p. 21.

[92] Hamza Alavi, 'Pakistan and Islam: Ethnicity and Ideology' in Fred Halliday and Hamza Alavi (eds), *State and Ideology in the Middle East and Pakistan* (New York: Monthly Review Press, 1987), p. 65.

[93] *A History of Pakistan*, op. cit.; and M. T. Stepanyants, *Pakistan: Philosophy and Sociology* (Moscow: Nauka, 1971).

[94] Hailey to Harry Haig, 27 November 1934, Hailey papers, Mss. Eur. file no. E 220/28 a, IOL.

[95] Noon, *From Memory*, p. 188.

traditionally drawn its leaders, had switched their allegiance to the League.[96]

In UP, the landlord party was humbled by the Congress in the February 1937 elections. Its leaders, known for their internal rivalries and petty squabbles, went their separate ways; communal antipathies, otherwise dormant, had broken their back. Several Hindu *taluqdars*, active in 1935 refurbishing the communally-oriented Oudh Liberal League, crossed over to the Hindu Mahasabha. Important Muslim *taluqdars* held office in the All-Parties Conference and the Unity Board in the early 1930s and then assisted in the League's revival.[97] Raja Rampal Singh noted how many landlords 'kept two arrows to the string of their bows'. 'Their one foot', he continued, 'is in the Hindu Mahasabha, the Muslim League, the Muslim Conference or similar sectional institutions and the other in the National Agriculturists' Party.'[98] The Nawab of Chattari, who broke away from the League Parliamentary Board in April-May 1936 to revive a mixed party in preference to a Muslim one, was targeted by the Hindu Sabha. 'Their aim', he complained, 'is only to destroy the Agriculturists' Party and to divide the Hindus and Muslims in two separate camps.' His dilemma was real: he could not return to the League fold, yet his adversaries projected him as a Muslim and not as an agriculturist or a *zamindar*. If the 'aggressive Hindu mentality' remained unchanged, he told Hailey, 'perhaps I will have to say publicly that I was wrong in thinking that a mixed party could succeed in these provinces and that I have failed.'[99]

Religious division was not uncommon in the ranks of landlords in UP and elsewhere. Hindu and Muslim revitalisation activity towards the end of the nineteenth century, chiefly in North India, had quite a grip on them. Some saw themselves as the defenders of the faith, and in that role patronised *dargahs* and *madaris, gaurakshini sabhas* (cow-protection societies), religious fairs and Hindi propagation and proselytising societies. But there was still a silver lining. Points of contact and inter-cultural cohesion, a legacy of composite *mores* created by the Mughal emperors, did not disappear overnight. Urdu, spoken by Hindus and Muslims alike, still served as a powerful symbol of inter-community unity. Festivals were commonly celebrated. Muharram was solemnly observed by Hindus and Muslims alike. Quite a number of Muslim landlords, especially in western UP, were late converts to Islam, and their natural inclination was to go along with members of their caste rather than pay heed to the communal claptrap.

---

[96] Talbot, *Punjab and the Raj*, pp. 197-201.
[97] Peter Reeves, 'Landlords and Party Politics' in D.A. Low (ed.), *Soundings in South Asian History* (Berkeley: University of California Press, 1968), p. 273.
[98] Peter Reeves, *Landlords and Government in Uttar Pradesh* (Delhi: OUP, 1991), p. 217.
[99] 28 October 1936, Hailey papers, file no. E 220/28 c, IOL.

In other words, the communal breach need not have taken place despite the involvement of some individuals in sectarian activities. There was, above all else, still some space for class-based politics within and outside the institutional domain. The landlords had a common benefactor in the British government. Men with socialist and communist leanings were, on the other hand, their chief adversaries out to destroy their source of livelihood – so much so that Nawab Muhammad Yusuf of Jaunpur was willing to negotiate with the Hindu Mahasabha but not with the Congress. 'The community of interest between the League and the Mahasabha', he told Jinnah, 'can be created by the zamindars through their full weight in favour of such an understanding.'[100]

To begin with, the Congress agrarian agenda produced varying tactical responses. A number of 'Hindu' landlords, having discovered during the UP Tenancy Bill debate (1937-9) that they had friends and powerful allies in the Congress, started playing a different tune altogether and were overnight visible on Congress party platforms.[101] Their instinct for survival in an otherwise turbulent political world led them to be on the 'right side', cultivate party leaders and pay lip-service to their political creed. In the process they ignored the words of wisdom they had intermittently received from Harcourt Butler, Malcolm Hailey and Harry Haig, three of their most consistent friends heading the UP government.[102] On the other hand, 'Hindu' landlords suspicious of Congress intentions and with broad communal inclinations turned to the Hindu Mahasabha; their Muslim counterparts courted Jinnah. In August 1936 the Raja of Jahangirabad, a ruler with vast estates, met Jinnah and decided to contest the Assembly election as an independent and not as a member of the National Agriculturists' Party; in return the League agreed not to put up a candidate.[103] Soon afterwards leading *rais*, *zamindars* and *taluqdars* became more closely identified with the League.[104] Some did so lazily and unthinkingly, but others were more aware of what they were doing. They were chiefly those who dominated landlord politics from the mid-1920s, adorned the council benches, and used coercive methods as well as their connections to counter peasant movements.

Landlords formed the largest single group in the League council. Of 503 members, there were as many as 163 landlords, with Punjab contributing the largest share of 51, followed by UP and Bengal.[105] Some in UP spearheaded the League offensive, including Nawab Jamshed Ali Khan

[100] Nawab Muhammad Yusuf to Jinnah, 4 October 1942, UP, vol. vi, SHC.

[101] Reeves, *Landlords and Government*, pp. 269-70.

[102] Harry Haig to Linlithgow, 7 October 1937, Haig papers, file no. 115/17 b.

[103] Haig to Linlithgow, 23 August 1936, Haig Papers, file no. 125/11 b.

[104] For their correspondence with Jinnah, see UP, vol. vi, SHC.

[105] Sayeed, *Pakistan: The Formative Phase*, p. 207.

of Baghpat, president of the UP Zamindars' Association, Muzaffarnnagar, Nawab Mohammad Ismail Khan of Meerut, Nawab Muhammad Yusuf of Jaunpur, the Raja of Pirpur with his estate in Faizabad, Azamgarh and Sultanpur districts, and Jinnah's close lieutenant, Nawabzada Liaquat Ali Khan. Equally energetic were the Rajas of Mahmudabad, Jahangirabad and Nanpara, all Awadh *taluqdars*. The Raja of Nanpara wrote to Jinnah:

The solid stand taken by you at the Simla Conference has made me firm in the conviction that the Muslim League is the only organisation that is fearlessly and honestly championing the Muslim cause.[...] Overwhelmed by your states-manship and overjoyed by the thought that it is being utilised for the purpose of bringing gain to the Musalmans of India I have decided to work for the League in my Province and to do my utmost in winning the elections.[106]

The Raja of Mahmudabad, having broken away from his father's nationalist legacy, was the most prominent and energetic League stalwart in Awadh. He was an organiser, a fund-raiser and an ideologue. Jinnah was like an 'uncle' to him, 'the only one person in this world who is as interested in me as my father could be'.[107] Aligarh and Bulandshahar districts had a fairly substantial concentration of Muslim landlords. There the League had staunch patrons in the Nawab of Chhatari and Nawab Mohammad Ismail Khan and among the successors of Nawab Muzam-milullah Khan of Bhikampur (1865-1938), Habibur Rahman Khan Sher-wani and Nawab Faiyaz Ali Khan (1851-1922) of Bulandshahr.[108] They were men of power and wealth in their localities. Some were influential in the Aligarh Muslim University, which they used to tilt campus politics in favour of the League.[109]

These landlords were by no means a unified or cohesive collectivity, yet their overriding concern was to safeguard their future in a Congress-dominated government, which they thought was inspired by Bolshevik ideas. Such anxieties, reinforced by the administration's paranoia of socialist stirrings in the colonies, were echoed time and again in response to peasant movements in some parts of UP and Bihar.[110] The spread of Bolshevism, Syed Raza Ali had warned Hailey, was fraught with dreadful consequences. It meant that 'the whole society would have to be reconstructed on lines most repugnant to the people.'[111] Nawab Muhammad Yusuf of Jaunpur was wary of 'Marxian philosophy which derives its life blood by

106 To Jinnah, 21 September 1945, correspondence-general, UP, vol. iv, SHC.

107 To Jinnah, n.d., correspondence-general, UP, vol. iv, SHC.

108 Zoya Hasan, *Dominance and Mobilisation: Rural Politics in Western Uttar Pradesh 1930-1980* (Delhi: Sage, 1989), pp. 93-6.

109 Mushirul Hasan, 'Nationalist and Separatist Trends in Aligarh', op. cit.

110 Kapil Kumar, *Peasants in Revolt: The Landlords and the Raj in Oudh* (Delhi: Manohar, 1984); Reeves, *Landlords and Government*, chapters 2-3.

111 12 May 1930, Hailey papers, file no. E 220/18 b.

economic struggle and strife between Nation and Nation and Classes and Masses on the foundations of hatred and economic struggle.'[112]

The agrarian programme, embodied in the UP Tenancy Bill, was the last straw. It set off the alarm bells and stiffened the resolve to fight it tooth and nail. 'We taluqdars have ancient rights and privileges, given by a special charter,' thundered Uncle Hamid in Attia Hosain's *Sunlight on a Broken Column*. 'Who are these leaders, in fact? Men without responsibility who can make wild promises. I tell you, not only the landlord but the State is endangered by them.' 'I am a part of feudalism, and proud to be', Uncle Hamid told his son. 'I shall fight for it. It is my heritage – and yours.'

The Tenancy Bill was construed, quite wrongly of course, as a conspiracy against the Muslim landlords in particular, and 'destructive of the culture of the minority community, sustained by the patronage of the Muslim landed aristocracy'.[113] Consequently, they rushed to the League to thwart the 'Bolshevik menace'. 'I and Moslem zemindars look up to you', implored Yusuf, 'to protect our fundamental rights and save them from economic ruination or elimination in U.P.'[114]

Though not positioned to fulfil such expectations, Jinnah harnessed the landlord support to extend the social base of his movement. In a province where the Muslim League had been in disarray since 1937, the year of its ignominious defeat in elections, the entry of influential sections of the landed aristocracy signified a major breakthrough. It was a windfall, a vital asset and a morale-booster to the organisation and the cause. The Quaid, who could not have expected a better deal, felt elated. Things were steadily working his way up. His trump card was UP, a province where the ideological contours of Pakistan were delineated with some degree of precision.

V

Standard accounts of the 'Freedom Movement in Pakistan' portray a unified, harmonious and selfless leadership, inspired by high ideals of service to the Muslim community and motivated by the fervour to create a state and society in conformity with Islamic law.[115] This interpretation

[112] To Jinnah, 3 August 1945, UP, vol. vi., SHC.

[113] Quoted in Lance Brenann, 'The Illusion of Security: The Background to Muslim Separatism in the United Provinces', *Modern Asian Studies*, 18, 2, 1984, p. 352. The point is substantiated in the discussion between Uncle Hamid and his son Saleem. References to Uncle Hamid are drawn from Attia Hossain, *Sunlight on a Broken Column*, pp. 231, 232, 234.

[114] To Jinnah, 14 January 1946, UP, vol. vi., SHC.

[115] Notice, for example, the works of K.K. Aziz, I.H. Qureshi, Hafeez Malik and Chaudhri Muhammad Ali. See also Sharif al-Mujahid, *Quaid-e-Azam Jinnah: Studies in Interpretation*

is falsified by the Muslim League records, along with Jinnah's correspondence in the Shamsul Hasan collection in Karachi. These papers point to
the presence of groups who were either pushed into taking religious/Is-
lamic positions or for whose material concerns the time was ripe at this
particular historical juncture. They also indicate that the League was
moulded into a powerful force by 'a coterie of politicians who do not
brook opposition and who are determined to have everything in their own
autocratic fashion'. Above all, the papers shed light on the Quaid's
unassailable power and authority, 'the will of one man [who] is more
haughty and arrogant than the proudest of the Pharaohs'.[116]

The depth and intensity of jealousies and internal discord,[117] reflected
in such statements, are not commensurate with the 'pure' intentions
attributed to the League and its following or the romanticised image
associated with it. To put such impressions in perspective and grasp the
internal dynamics of the power-politics involved, it is pertinent to comment on the nature of individual/group antipathies and probe those critical
areas where the 'faithful' themselves were so hopelessly split. The aim is
not to reduce the reputations of historic figures or belittle the Pakistan
movement but to enlarge our knowledge and understanding of them.

In July 1941 Jinnah was told about 'the influx of undesirable and
dubious persons', including those who had just a few years ago treated
the League's workers with 'amused contempt'. 'Self-seekers' had suddenly thrust themselves into committees by 'crooked and unscrupulous
means' when they realized that the League's star was in the ascerdant.[118]
In August 1944 the Raja of Mahmudabad warned his 'dearest uncle':

Since 1937 whenever there was any danger to the Muslim League I always
apprised you of the situation and you had never found the facts untrue or
mutilated. Today I visualise a similar occasion when our political existence
and your 7 years of labour is in serious danger of disintegration and dissolution.

The Raja described the power struggle between Khaliquzzaman and the
'Lucknow group' on the one hand, and Nawab Mohammad Ismail Khan
and the 'anti-Lucknow' faction on the other. He wrote at length, just as
Ismail had done earlier,[119] about the misdeeds of Rizwanullah, UP
League's provincial secretary, whom he charged with investing 'all his
loose capital of time & money' to create his own clique. A meeting at

---

(Karachi: Quaid-e-Azam Academy, 1981).

[116] 'Fazlul Haq for a new progressive All India Muslim League', 21 June 1942,
Jinnah-Ispahani Correspondence, appendix, viii, p. 667.

[117] These extended to student bodies as well, forcing the president of the Punjab Students'
Federation to resign. Hameed Nizami to Jinnah, 13 December 1942, *The Quaid-e-Azam
Papers, 1941-42* (Karachi: East and West Publishing Co., 1976), p. 253.

[118] Jamiluddin Ahmad to Jinnah, 11 July 1941, ibid., pp. 25-6.

[119] Ismail Khan to Jinnah, 7 July 1944, UP, vol. iv, SHC.

Allahabad 'opened new avenues of open transactions. God alone knows how much money was collected.' Even after two years of bickering, accounts were not submitted. By that time 'the thieves fell out amongst each other.'[120] Rizwanullah was accused of misappropriating funds, although the League's working committee turned a blind eye to his misdeamenour. The Raja, for whom this was like a 'thunderbolt', sharply dissented, and on 10 December 1944 the provincial League working committee, 'a body comprises [sic] mostly of aristocrats [sic] of Lucknow and their obedients' led by Khaliquzzaman, set up a parallel committee to weaken Ismail's hold over the parliamentary board.[121] In the end, two bodies were formed. One derived its power from the working committee and the other from the provincial parliamentary board.[122]

The election and nomination of office-bearers to elective posts and to city and district Leagues caused endless wranglings and resulted in resentment and bitter feuds. Thus the UP League's decision to contest municipal elections in 1944, which the Congress boycotted, led to a spate of protests over the choice of candidates by party bosses, most of whom used the occasion to extend their power-base in the districts on the strength of caste and sectarian and factional allegiances. The contentious issue, according to the president of the Bulandshahar district League, was whether people sitting in Lucknow had the last word in adopting candidates or whether local leaders like himself had a say or not. Obviously he preferred the district League's autonomy, an anathema to the political heavyweights in Delhi and Lucknow.[123] Badrul Hasan resigned, and·was not alone in so doing. Uneasiness prevailed elsewhere; resignations poured forth almost daily from district and city Leagues in protest against the parliamentary board's 'prejudice [sic] and short-sighted policy'.[124]

Petitions and complaints from Lucknow, Kanpur, Aligarh, Budaun, Moradabad, Bareilly, Allahabad and Banaras innundated the parliamentary board's office. Syed Zakir Ali's selection from the Agra-Etawah-Farrukhabad seat led to objections. Sahibzada Amir Hamza, a *rais* of the area, warned: 'I think that if the masses are, in certain respects, an immoveable mass they are, in other respects, an irresistible force.'[125] Aggrieved candidates in Allahabad lampooned their president, Zahur Ahmad, and

---

[120] The Raja of Mahmudabad to Jinnah, 11 August 1944, and Maulana Jamal Mian to Jinnah, 12 July 1944, UP, vol. iv, SHC.

[121] Mohammad Yaqub, president Kanpur Muslim League, to Jinnah, n.d., correspondence-general, UP, vol. i, SHC.

[122] *Pioneer*, 13 December 1944.

[123] Syed Badrul Hasan to Liaquat Ali Khan, 13 February 1940, UP Provincial Muslim League, 1939-41: Bulandshahr League affairs, part xviii, FMA.

[124] For example, Mahmud Hashmi of Bareilly to Jinnah, 1 November 1944, UP, correspondence-general, vol. i, SHC.

[125] Sahibzada Amir Hamza to Jinnah, 14 January 1946, ibid.

other stalwarts for playing second-fiddle to Nawabs, Khan Bahadurs and other vested interests.[126] The Anjuman-i Tanzim al-Muslimeen in Banaras objected to the choice of Mohammad Shakoor Ansari, a wrestler.[127] Syed Mustafa Raza, general secretary of the Shia Political Conference, was upset at being overlooked in Bahraich rural constituency.[128] A.B.A. Haleem, professor at Aligarh's University, harboured ill-feeling towards his vice-chancellor, Dr Ziauddin, for using his political clout to exclude him from the hustings in the Aligarh-Hathras-Mathura constituency.[129] More than 100 representations questioned the wisdom of putting up M.M. Bashir, general secretary of the Jamiyat al-Quresh who belonged 'to the camp of our enemy' and had put on the League mask for the time being.[130] His *bête noire*, Khan Bahadur Abdul Moquit Khan Sherwani, staked his claim on the grounds that as many as eighty-three voters belonged to the Sherwani clan, whereas a mere twenty were Lal Khanis, the clan of Bashir.[131]

Shia-Sunni schisms marred the League's image in Budaun, with Maulana Abdul Hamid, a prominent figure in the All-India Muslim League, and Mohammad Iqtidaruddin Hasan accusing each other of inflaming sectarian passions.[132] The latter was disgusted by the vitiated atmosphere and disappointed with the leadership's apathy. He resigned from the League's district council and its working and defence committees.[133] The Shia-Sunni issue also loomed large in Meerut. Taqi Hadi, selected from the Meerut-Muzaffarnagar rural constituency to the UP legislative council, was attacked because he was a rank 'outsider' from Amroha; the 'appellant' was 'doubly qualified', because as well as being a Shia he had many of his relatives on the voter's list.[134]

Such acerbities were not confined to the League. The Congress was no less faction-ridden, and personal ties, caste considerations and regional

---

[126] To Jinnah, 28 October 1944, ibid; Zahid Ali Khan to L.A. Khan, 10 March 1942, vol. 354, FMA.

[127] To Jinnah, 15 January 1946, correspondence-general, UP, vol. i, SHC.

[128] To Jinnah, 15 January 1945, ibid.

[129] 'Abba' Haleem was able to secure the active backing of various localities in the old city, as also from the Muslim Mazdoor Association, the Muslim Tailoring Association and the local parliamentary board. A.B.A. Haleem to L.A. Khan, n.d. box no. 148, FMA.

[130] Box no. 148, FMA. Bashir's strength lay in the fact that he was general secretary of the All India Jamiyat al-Quresh, an organisation that controlled, regulated and was responsible for the slaughter of animals for sale and for producing dairy products.

[131] To president, Muslim League parliamentary board, 22 January 1946, box no. 150, FMA.

[132] To M.A. Jinnah, 21 July 1942, *Quaid-e-Azam Papers*, p. 221.

[133] Abdul Waheed Khan to chairman, central parliamentary board, 21 February 1946, box no. 150, FMA.

[134] Representation of Syed Ahmad of Diwan Khana-Valley bazaar, Meerut, 22 February 1946, box no. 150, FMA.

loyalties were equally important there. The All India Congress Committee and the Congress Working Committee often acted in an authoritarian way, and would tolerate no opposition; village and district Congress committees were brushed aside. At the same time, some of the Congress factions and units were also committed to specific social and economic programmes and identified with them. They were able to operate effectively and act independently in pursuit of their objectives, and for this reason they had a place in the party as well as the organisation. This was less so with the groupings in the League. Part of the reason was Jinnah's unassailable position and the constant fear of his authority being undermined. As a result, independent initiatives were treated with suspicion or as acts of defiance. New ideas breaking out among fiery young idealists, in spite of being confined to only a few, were promptly nipped in the bud. Criticism of landowners and industrial magnates was also discouraged; it could not have been otherwise for a party so heavily dependent on their patronage. Thus Jinnah came out strongly against the left-wing and radical elements who proposed democratic reforms and economic policies to reflect the aspirations of the Muslim masses.[135] He directed his ire against Z. H. Lari and the 'progressive group' in Lucknow[136] and against G. M. Sayed (d. 1995) of Sind whose unforgivable sin was to criticise Sind's landowning politicians and the central high command. Sayed was expelled.[137] In a nutshell the leadership's broad strategy, one that paid off for the time being but was counter-productive in the long run, was to take cognisance of the sensibilities of powerful and influential social classes, stifle internal debate and gloss over class contradictions. Anyone who standing on the League ticket no matter who was backed 'even if it be a lamp-post'.[138] The more the merrier (*Log ate raye aur caravan banta gaya*).

Jinnah preferred not to be bogged down by innumerable petitions and representations; he simply directed petitioners to the Committee of Action, set up in December 1943, or the central parliamentary board.[139] He wrote to Maulana Akram Khan in Calcutta, 'I have worked hard and put our people on a clear road. This has taken seven years of very hard work. I expect now that those who are in charge of the provincial organisations

---

[135] Sayeed, *Pakistan: The Formative Phase*, p. 153.

[136] FR, first half of September 1945, Frampton papers. The resolution moved by Lari at the December 1943 session of the League proposed the appointment of a committee to formulate a five-year plan for the economic and social uplift of the Muslims. He also demanded that 'landlordism ... should be abolished and peasants should be free'. Sajjad Zaheer, *People's War*, 9 January 1944, in *A Case for Congress-League Unity*, p. 35.

[137] Sayeed, op.cit., p. 210.

[138] Ibid., p. 212.

[139] To Mahmud Hashmi, 14 November 1944; to Mohammad Yaqub, president Kanpur city League, 5 January 1945, Correspondence-general, UP, vol. i, SHC.

and those who desire to lead our people should work in a team in an organised manner and systematically carry on their work.'[140]

VI

So, why did the Pakistan idea cause such excitement? How could so many disparate groups strive for and eventually accomplish their goal of partition? How could a highly stratified community, united only by religious ties, act unitedly to secure its Pakistan? What factors bridged local, regional, class and sectional dissimilarities to create an overriding interest in an Islamic/Muslim nation? In other words, how and why did Jinnah's mobilisation campaign succeed and not the forces of secular nationalism?

Part of the explanation lies in the sustained and carefully-orchestrated campaign from 1937 onwards. The initial impetus was provided by the Congress-led Muslim Mass Contact programme.[141] The League, abandoning its quaint constitutionalist image in favour of populism, counter-attacked with its own mass contact, led by the Raja of Mahmudabad.[142] This populism drew heavily on Muslim/Islamic values, on memories of renowned Muslim generals and warriors, chiefly those who had humbled Rajput and Maratha chieftains. Wild promises were made of restoring Islam's glory in the future Muslim state, of liberating the Muslim peasantry from the tutelage of the Hindu moneylender and the bondage of the Hindu *zamindar*. According to the Raja of Mahmudabad, Islam believes in an 'unhampered despotism', a 'despotism for the benefit of the oppressed and not the oppressor. It does not glorify poverty, neither does it look down upon it. It is contemptuous towards the few rich and that is right.' Hoping that class differences 'will be swept out – not by a broomstick but by force', he urged his historian friend, Mohibbul Hasan, 'to love Islam'. 'Freedom, liberty, equality (as they are used) are Western prejudices. Sir Sikanders and Haqs harp on them. They will be out of tune soon.'

Mohammad Iqbal, *Shair-i Mashriq* (poet of the east), offered a romantic egalitarian vision to nurture, a vision shimmering with an idealised recall of the heroic past. He inspired faith, pride and confidence in the

---

[140] 27 August 1945, Bengal, vol. iv, SHC.

[141] See Mushirul Hasan, 'The Muslim Mass Contacts Campaign' in Sisson and Wolpert (eds), *Congress and Indian Nationalism*, pp. 198-222.

[142] See my introduction to *India's Partition*, pp. 15-26. In addition, care was taken to reorganise the League, amend its constitution and set up provincial and district branches. In November 1941 the Honorary Secretary, Liaquat Ali Khan, directed provincial organisations to hold district conferences, organise tours of prominent leaders, recruit new members and impart religious training to them. 'The training in each province of a sufficient number of propagandists', he wrote, 'is an indispensable necessity.' Committee for Action, 1944, vol. 159, part 2, FMA.

Islamic heritage. Instead of the dry ritualised dogma of the *ulama*, he emphasised Islam's social dynamism, an Islam which had created equality between the rich and the poor, Arab and non-Arab. In a situation where the Indian 'middle class' lived in colonial subjection and in competition with their 'Hindu' counterparts, Iqbal's eloquent poetry inspired a new sense of dignity and importance. Muslims from the modest middle-class stratum, having once been mobilised by Azad, the Ali brothers and other pan-Islamists around the Khilafat issue, were greatly moved by his powerful Islamic images.[143]

The Pirpur and Shareef Reports detailed the 'wrongs' of the Congress ministries, highlighted the 'injustices' and 'atrocities' committed against the Muslims.[144] Jinnah's call to observe 'deliverance day' was designed to revive real or imaginary memories of the 'Hindu Raj' and instill in Muslims the fear of another round of Congress rule.[145] The plan was crudely conceived, although it brought forth immediate political gains. Soon enough, the Muslim masses were misled into thinking that the Congress ministries were busy establishing a 'Hindu Raj'.[146] The Congress, according to the Raja of Mahmudabad, was 'ardently insincere about a united India'. He wrote to Mohibbul Hasan:

After all what has a majority to fear from a minority? She can give the smaller nationalities a blank cheque and then even remain quite safe. Nehru even now cannot see the grievances and the rights of the minorities with a microscope. He is mad. Bose talks exactly like the viceroy – he talks only of the present

---

[143] Ishtiaq Ahmad, *The Concept of an Islamic State* (London: Pinter, 1987), pp. 66-7; Khairi, *Jinnah Reinterpreted*, pp. 345-6; Nehru, *Discovery of India*, p. 303.

[144] These reports were compiled by the Raja of Pirpur, Syed Mohammad Mehdi, and S.M. Shareef as a catalogue of 'Hindu oppression' during the Congress ministries in 1937-9. Although the evidence collected was thin and mostly unsubstantiated, both the reports had much propaganda value. See, for example, the pamphlets written by one Maulvi Anis Ahmad, a research student in the theology department of Aligarh's Muslim University, Box no. 151, FMA. See my introduction to *India's Partition*, pp. 15-26.

[145] On 2 December 1939, Jinnah announced 22 December as a 'Day of Deliverance and thanksgiving as a mark of relief that the Congress regime at last ceased to function'. His resolution stated that 'the Congress Ministry has conclusively demonstrated and proved the falsehood of the Congress claim that it represents all interests justly and fairly, by its decidedly anti-Muslim policy.'

[146] The *Inqilab* of Lahore was edited by Ghulam Rasool Mehr and Abdul Majid Salik. It was in the forefront of a virulent campaign in Punjab, accusing the Congress ministries for ushering in 'Hindu Raj', (31 March 1939), condemning Nehru for starting the Muslim mass contact campaign to create internal strife (*khaana-jangi*) among Muslims (30 April 1937), and criticising Gandhi for championing 'Hindu causes' and for being indifferent to the plight of Muslims (11 January 1939). The Jamiyat al-ulama, the Ahrars and the Congress Muslims followed the 'wrong path' (*ghalath-rawish*), adhered to a 'false ideology' (*ghalath-maslak*) and pursued a 'mistaken strategy' (*ghalath-tariqa-i kar*) (18 April, 22 May, 25 July 1937; 19 May, 10 June 1938). The League's voice was, on the other hand, in defence of the *millat* (1 January 1939), as also its demand for Pakistan. Editorial entitled *Hindustan ki Taqseem ke siwa koi chara nahi hai* (There is no alternative to Pakistan), 6 September 1949.

and keeps mum about the future. Gandhi, the beneficent, sees no light. He still is prone to wander in the wilderness. The Viceroy knows well his own game. He cares a brass button about the minorities. As the true representative of a merchant nation he knows well his buyers and sellers. So what is to be done? If the Congress were sincere they could have passed a simple resolution of a few lines asking the Muslim League to cooperate for the cause of independence and assuring them of their most loyal and cordial relations.

'For the Pakistani mind', wrote a League spokesman,

the Congress cult is associated with hypocritical whining about non-violence, scraggy chocolate-coloured longevity-seekers sitting in loin-cloth and weaving metaphysical hocus pocus with subtle schemes of economic pressure, five-foot four-inch processionists with flat noses and bulging cheeks shouting outlandish slogans in shrill voices – all this smelling strongly of usury, untouchability and an inordinate hatred and fear of the Muslims.[147]

Another League sympathiser from Saharanpur commented in April 1940 that 'a soldier without arms and a political party without an organ are doomed to failure'.[148] By 1944-5 he would have had no cause to complain; the League's publicity and information department was energised, English- and Urdu-language newspapers were pressed into service,[149] and books and pamphlets endorsing Jinnah's blueprint for a Muslim state, including some written by left-wing activists, circulated widely. Danial Latifi, an Oxford graduate and author of the Punjab Muslim League manifesto, wrote *Why I have joined Muslim League* in 1945. He also compiled *Statistics of Pakistan* so that every Muslim might 'be a conscious architect of his own destiny and thereby assist the Quaid-i Azam in his historic mission of winning Pakistan for us'.[150] Sajjad Zaheer, co-founder of the Progressive Writers' Movement and a communist, regarded the Pakistan demand as the 'logical expression of the development of political consciousness among the Muslim peoples of India'. He described the League as an effective 'anti-imperialist, liberationist' force and its demand as 'a just, progressive and national demand, and [a]

---

[147] El Hamza, *Pakistan: A Nation* (Lahore: Sh. Muhammad Ashraf, 1942, 2nd edn), p. 127.

[148] Syed Ali Mahdi to Liaquat Ali Khan, 11 April 1940, vol. 352, FMA.

[149] *Dawn* was a 'stepping stone for a first-class English daily': *Manshoor*, the League's official organ, was compulsory reading for members of the provincial council and the district and primary Leagues. Committee for Action, 1944, vol. 159, part 2, FMA. But not everybody was impressed with these newspapers. The *Dawn* weekly was thought to be 'much below standard' in UP. *Manshoor* was found wanting in coverage of the League activities in UP, 'for which Bareilly and Bulandshahr have registered their complaints'. S.M. Rizwanullah to Liaquat Ali Khan, 5 December 1941, vol. 326, part 2, FMA. The Imam of Delhi's Juma Masjid was among the few who welcomed the *Dawn* 'as the sole champion of Muslim rights'. To Jinnah, 12 October 1942, *Quaid-e-Azam Papers*, p. 245.

[150] Secretary, Publicity and Information Department, to Danial Latifi, 26 December 1945, box no. 49, FMA.

positive expression of the very freedom and democracy for which Congressmen have striven and undergone so much suffering all these years'.[151]

Other men with communist/socialist leanings, including Mian Iftikharuddin of Punjab, G.M. Sayed, president of the Sind provincial League, and Abdul Hashim, secretary of the Bengal provincial League, were influenced by the Communist Party view that the Pakistan stir was a movement of the (weak) Muslim national bourgeoisie and therefore a legitimate anti-imperialist campaign, deserving of communist support, in line with the stand taken by Lenin at the Second Congress of the Communist International in 1921.

In retrospect K.M. Ashraf believed that India's Communist Party was 'misled by the slogan of self-determination and mistook Muslim communalism for something representing the organised expression of the Rerhi-Pak-Pathan Nationalities for self-determination'. It was certainly a distortion, 'because we conveniently forgot the whole history of British imperialism and communal politics.' Likewise, Khwaja Ahmad Abbas commented: 'India was killed by the Communist Party of India which provided the Muslim separatists with an ideological basis for the irrational and anti-national demand for Pakistan. Phrases like "homeland", "nationalities", "self-determination" etc. were all ammunition supplied by the Communists to the legions of Pakistan.'[152]

Ishtiaq Husain Qureshi, historian at Delhi university, argued that India's Muslims constituted a nation held together by a common allegiance to Islam.[153] Abdus Sattar Kheri, whose pro-Nazi activities had led to his arrest but who was released on the intervention of Jinnah, claimed 'the inalienable right of nationhood'.[154] So did Jamiluddin Ahmad and Qazi Said-ud-din, both lecturers at Aligarh.[155] The Bengal provincial League published 50,000 copies of a pamphlet entitled *How Much is the Difference?* to counter 'the malicious propaganda being carried out by some of the so-called Nationalist Muslims'. It was written by Humayun Akhtar, managing director of the Orient Gold Industries on

[151] Sajjad Zaheer, *A Case for Congress-League Unity* (Bombay: (People's Publishing House, 1944).

[152] Interview with K.M. Ashraf, 27 October 1960, in Kruger (ed.), *Kunwar Mohammad Ashraf*, p. 413; Abbas, *I am not an Island*, p. 281; Hamza Alavi, 'Pakistan and Ideology', op. cit., p. 65; Shri Prakash, 'CPI and the Pakistan Movement', *Studies in History* (Delhi), 3, 1-2, January-December 1981.

[153] I.H. Qureshi, *The Future Development of Islamic Polity*, Pakistan Literature Series (PLS) 8 (Lahore, 1946); *National States and National Minorities*, PLS 1 (Lahore, 1945). These tracts were published at Sh. Muhammad Ashraf in Lahore.

[154] Jamiluddin Ahmad, *Some Aspects of Pakistan* (1946), PLS 3.

[155] Kazi Saiduddin Ahmad, *The Communal Patterns of India* (1945), PLS: 2; and his *Politico-Regional Division of India* (1945), PLS: 4 and *Is India Geographically One?* (1945), PLS: 6; Ali Ahmad Faziel, *Power Resources of Pakistan* (1946), PLS: 10.

45 Dharamtalla Street, and it is reproduced here to indicate the League's religious rhetoric.

Orthodox Islam	Orthodox Hinduism
Salutation: As-Salammo' alaikum.	Ram Ram.
Acclamation: Allah-o-Akbar.	Banda Mataram.
Religious Book: Quran Majeed.	Vedas, Puranas, Upanishads, Bhagavad Gita, etc.
Belief in the Unity of God. Islam stands for unity and brotherhood.	Belief in numerous inanimate and animate representations of God incarnating on earth.
Islam stands for fraternity and universal brotherhood.	Hinduism perpetuates social distinctions and upholds the caste system.
Muslims: Abolishers of Idolatory	Hindus build and worship idols.
Discrimination between truth and falsehood considered the prime object of Creation.	Belief in the doctrine of 'Ram-Lila'; i.e., all things were created by God for sport.
Man responsible and accountable for all his actions and deeds in this world.	Man's actions in this world considered to be designed and prompted by God.
In Islam any Muslim can qualify to become a religious leader.	In Hinduism only a Brahman is eligible.
Muslim law of Inheritance provides for an equitable distribution of the deceased property to the heirs and successors.	By the Hindu Law of succession, property is inherited by the sons only, mostly by the eldest son.
Circumcision: an initiatory rite among Muslims.	Not approved.
Tattooing or colour-marking the body not permissible.	Religious symbols are marked on forehead and pig-tails kept.
Lusty music and dancing prohibited among Muslims.	Distinctive cultural virtue.
Obscenity in art explicitly prohibited.	Cave-idols representing nude bodies and phallic symbols considered as relics [*sic*] of praise and charm.
Fishes and all sea animals considered the normal creations of God.	Evolved by the sperm emitted by their God.
Growth of trees are of no religious significance in Islam.	'Pipal', 'Tulsi' and the 'Plantain' considered sacred.
Snake considered a venomous reptile, thus generally killed.	Considered a divine creature.
Muslims believe eclipse to be a geographical phenomenon.	Hindus observe the moment as an evil-ridden occasion.
Muslim bury the corpse.	Hindus cremate the dead.
Muslims purify by ablution.	Hindus consider cow's urine to be a sanctifying fluid.
Muslims eat beef.	Majority worship cow.
Majority are meat-eaters.	Majority vegetarian.
Muslims generally dine in company in common dishes.	Hindus commonly dine on leaves.

General dress: *Pyjama* and *Teh-mad*.	General dress: *Saree* and *dhoti*.
Urdu script (Arabic character).	Hindi script (Devanagri character).
Muslims perform the *Haj* at the Kaaba.	Hindus go for their *tirath* to Banaras, Gaya and Mathura.
Muslims have no belief in palmistry, magic and superstitions.	Most Hindus harbour such beliefs.
Muslims believe in the existence of Paradise and Hell.	Hindus believe in life after death, and that the human soul, after achieving *mukti*, will be absorbed into their God.

A good many Urdu poets and writers endowed the new nation with a historic destiny and projected the Pakistan project as a crusade for an Islamic state. They catalogued the social and cultural divide between Hindus and Muslims, described at length their unique and distinctive features, boasted of their glorious past in India and elsewhere, and took pride in pan-Islamism and their worldwide Islamic culture and civilisation. They idolised Jinnah and eulogised him as the custodian (*pasban*) of the community, its leader (*Mir-i Karawan*) and the symbol of Islam (*Nishan-i Islam*).[156]

Notions of 'Islamic identity' and romanticised visions of a Muslim/Islamic nation that run through poems exemplify a form of religious awareness that was deliberately heightened through a systematic campaign. This was because specifically Islamic slogans, some with divisive overtones, were the basis of Muslim togetherness. The legislators were consequently required to sign a skillfully drafted affidavit: its language and its content were explicitly Islamic. This document, like a number of other manifestos, was designed to underscore the Islamic dimensions of the Pakistan movement. The Raja of Mahmudabad conceded that appeals in the name of Islam heightened Muslim consciousness. He found the leadership at the top to be generally secular-minded and trained in modern political methods. But at the 'lower levels', especially among fieldworkers, it was common to conduct propaganda along religious lines.[157] The Pakistan idea was thus embedded in the popular imagination as a religious crusade led by Muslims in defence of Muslims and Islam.

The All-India Muslim National Guards, headed by Nawab Siddique Ali Khan, central legislative assembly member, popularised such an idea with great effect. Conceived on much the same lines as the RSS, with a *Salar-i Aala* (supreme commander), the National Guards wore uniforms and received preliminary military training. Pledged to strive for the

---

[156] Mahmud-ur-Rahman, *Jang-i Azadi ke Urdu Shuara* [Urdu Poets in the freedom struggle] (Islamabad, 1968), p. 37; and the poem read at the Muslim League session on 26 December 1943, quoted in Abida Riasat Rizvi, *The Leaves of Gold* (Karachi: Anjuman Press. 1976), p. 340. See also Mushirul Hasan (ed.), *India Partitioned*.

[157] 'Some Memories', op. cit., p. 389.

'freedom and glory of the Muslim nation', they led a 'simple and rigorous life worthy of a *mujahid*'. They worked for the League's 'consolidation and progress' and 'in true Islamic spirit for the uplift of the social, educational and economic standard of the Muslims'.[158] In practice the National Guards were the ideological stormtroopers of the League. They were pressed into service to distribute the ever-increasing League literature, organise public meetings, canvass for votes at election time, disrupt anti-League or pro-Congress gatherings and intimidate their political rivals. In 1947-48 some were accused of instigating riots.[159]

The Muslim Defence Committees in UP, established in 1942, did much the same. Their chief area of operation was in Gorakhpur and Azamgarh, as well as some other towns in central and eastern UP.[160] In both these two towns they relied on certain local *maktabs* and *madarsas* connected with the Barelwis, who had a vast following in the artisan and weaving communities of the region. In 1946 they acted in concert with the Aligarh students who thronged the cities of eastern UP to spread the League's gospel.

By 1945-6 the National Guards and Defence Committees worked effectively in UP and in other states (Tables 3.1–3.3). In Aligarh district 29,000 National Guards were active and in Sitapur 10,000.[161] The Civil Defence Committee in Gorakhpur district had eighty-four branches, each branch covering ten villages, 7,881 'defence volunteers' and 106 *akharas*. The one in Azamgarh had over 600 'defence volunteers', along with *akharas* 'for their physical development'.[162] Sure enough, such networks helped the League in UP to achieve impressive victories in the municipal elections held in 1944. Their Congress Muslim rivals suffered defeat in all the districts except Lucknow, Bareilly and Meerut.[163]

The Committee for Action was similarly an instrument to tighten control over provincial and district Leagues and instire discipline,[164] and

---

[158] Box no. 204, FMA. See also, Talbot, *Freedom's City*, chapter 2. Attia Hosain, *Sunlight on a Broken Column*, p. 158.

[159] Thus when Shah Nawaz, a comrade of Subhas Bose, rose to speak in Calcutta, he was roughly handled by the National Guards. He was reminded 'of the attitude of his own community to his activities'. Secret Report on the political situatioon in Bengal for the 2nd half of January 1946, J.M.G. Bell papers, CSAS.

[160] Syed Zakir Ali to Rizwanullah, 5 April 1943, vol. 315, FMA. Zakir Ali was member of the Muslim League Council and the UP Muslim League Parliamentary Board, and vice-president of the Agra Muslim League Council.

[161] FR, 4 June 1945, Frampton papers, CSAS.

[162] UP Muslim League Civil Defence Committee; vol. 315, FMA.

[163] Statement showing the result of municipal elections in UP, 1944, vol. 336, FMA.

[164] The Committee for Action appointed Nawab Siddique Ali Khan on 13 May 1944. Its powers and authority were enhanced when the League's Working Committee dissolved the Civil Defence Committees transferring its functions to the Committee of Action. Committee for Action, 1944, vol. 155, part 1, FMA. See Sayeed, *Pakistan: The Formative Phase*, pp. 190-2.

Table 3.1. PRIMARY MEMBERS, PRIMARY LEAGUES AND
NATIONAL GUARDS IN PUNJAB, 1941

District	Primary members	Primary Leagues	National Guards
Montgomery city	227	–	25
Amritsar dist.	765	22	–
Batala city	300	1	–
Montgomery city	3,200	20	–
Sheikhupura dist.	500	36	–
Sialkot dist.	1,500	15	–
Rawalpindi city	1,200	8	25
Attock dist.	491	6	–
Ferozepur city	255	6	–
Rohtak city	250	3	–
Ferozepur dist.	3,515	15	–
Rewari city	620	1	40
Lahore city	2,000	5	80
Total	14,823	138	170

Note: There were 41 branches affiliated to the Punjab Provincial Muslim League.
Source: Freedom Movement Archives, University of Karachi, Karachi.

to mobilise students, the *ulama*, the *pirs* and the *mashaikh*. In early September 1944 prominent *ulama* of Nadwat al-ulama, Deoband, Saharanpur and Thana Bhawan were invited to meet some of its members, including G.M. Sayed, Maulanas Jamal Mian and Abdul Hamid Budauni, and the Raja of Mahmudabad.[165] In October 1946 they re-assembled at the Committee's behest to ponder over the future of Muslims and of Islam in India.[166] Some required little persuasion: Maulana Mohammad Ibrahim, *fazil* of Deoband and editor of *Ansar Gazette* published from Bijnor, was won over through financial inducements.[167]

[165] Secretary Committee for Action to G.M. Sayed, 2 September 1944, Committee for Action file, 1944, vol. 2, part 2, FMA.

[166] Box no. 56, FMA.

[167] Latifur Rahman to Liaquat Ali Khan, 8 September, 11 October 1945, vol. 148, FMA.

Table 3.2. PRIMARY MEMBERS, PRIMARY LEAGUES
AND NATIONAL GUARDS IN U.P., 1941

District	Primary Leagues	Primary members	National Guards
Meerut	9	2,160	150
Saharanpur	5	1,852	51
Muzaffarnagar	6	6,000	107
Agra	18	5,938	300
Etah	5	1,000	25
Aligarh	27	10,309	600
Bareilly	16	4,681	200
Bijnor	14	2,432	150
Budaun	11	3,563	200
Moradabad	20	4,200	300
Shahjahanpur	1	5,528	110
Pilibhit	8	2,971	100
Allahabad	16	7,000	300
Kanpur	18	11,051	600
Firozabad	7	1,595	50
Etawah	4	1,019	53
Mirzapur	7	1,348	59
Banaras	13	4,100	200
Ballia	–	900	5
Jaunpur	6	4,000	50
Gorakhpur	26	4,002	300
Basti	7	1,472	50
Azamgarh	–	640	10
Nainital	5	1,000	75
Lucknow	13	12,789	200
Unnao	10	1,024	10
Rae Bareli	4	1,132	10
Hardoi	5	2,000	40
Sitapur	6	1,000	20
Kheri	5	1,000	5
Gonda	5	1,000	25
Bahraich	6	3,547	100
Sultanpur	32	5,187	200
Partabgarh	–	4,000	–
Bulandshahr	7	n.a.	–
Total	98	121,440	4,685

Source: Freedom Movement Archives, University of Karachi, Karachi.

Table 3.3. PRIMARY MEMBERS, PRIMARY LEAGUES AND
NATIONAL GUARDS IN BIHAR, 1941

District	Primary Leagues	Primary members	National Guards
Patna	27	8,500	250
Gaya	49	20,000	500
Arrah	11	4,000	125
Saran	25	7,000	800
Champaran	28	5,000	300
Muzaffarpur	18	10,000	350
Darbhanga	19	10,000	600
Bhagalpur	13	8,000	500
Monghyr	29	7,993	1,100
Purnea	20	25,000	700
Santhal Parganas	11	1,551	55
Hazaribagh	33	10,000	250
Ranchi	10	3,000	100
Palamau	6	4,020	24
Manbhum	15	10,000	25
Singbhum	9	5,000	30
Total	323	139,064	5,709

Note: Thana Muslim Leagues 323
Sub-division Muslim Leagues 52
District Muslim Leagues 16
Mohalla and village Muslim Leagues, not counted as primary Muslim Leagues 670
Source: Freedom Movement Archives, University of Karachi, Karachi.

VII

Wo mutrab aur wo saaz wo gaana badal gaya
neendain badal gain wo fasana badal gaya
rang-i rukh-i bahaar ki zeenat hui nai
gulshan me bulbulon ka tarana badal gaya

[The minstrel, the music and the melody have all changed.
Our very sleep has changed; the tale we used to hear is no longer told;
the nightingales in the garden sing a different song.]

Akbar Allahabadi

In 1938 Jinnah congratulated himself for removing the 'unwholesome
influence' of *maulanas* and *maulvis*.[168] Just a few years later, he did
the exact opposite by courting Muslim divines. During the Khilafat

movement, he had opposed the mixing of religion and politics, but in February 1939 he concurred with a deputation of the *ulama*, led by Ashraf Ali Thanwi, that religion could not be divorced from politics in Islam.[169] In 1945 he helped the League to formulate a full-fledged scheme for approaching the *sajjada-nashins* in UP, and for holding *ulama* conferences throughout the province.[170]

Sustained efforts, with generous financial backing, bore fruit. A highly impressive meeting, chaired by the Deobandi *alim* Maulana Shabbir Ahmad Usmani, took place in late December 1945 – it cost the League rupees 4,000.[171] The same year, Jinnah persuaded Shabbir Ahmad Usmani to mobilise the *ulama* in support of the Pakistan cause. Accordingly Calcutta was the venue of a conference held on 28-31 October 1945, convened under the aegis of the newly-founded Jamiyat-i Ulama-i Islam (Appendix C). More than 5000 *ulama*, along with their sympathisers, attended. The organisers were thrilled. Their prized trophy was Maulana Mohammad Zahir Qasimi, grandson of Mohammad Qasim Nanotawi, the revered co-founder of Deoband's Dar al-ulum.[172]

The meeting at Lahore in January 1946, attended by leading *ulama* from the Firangi Mahal, Deobandi, Barelwi and Ahl-i Hadith schools, was a milestone. No such gathering had taken place since the Khilafat movement, and never before had so many divines assembled in one congregation. It was the only occasion, after the heady Khilafat days, when so many *ulama* spoke and acted in unison; their speeches, interspersed with Quranic verses, were full of passion and fervour.

A committee of eminent *pirs* and *maskaikh* was hurriedly formed in 1946. In October and November of that year sufis and *sajjada-nashins*, especially in Punjab, lent their weight to the clarion call for a Muslim state.[173] To Pir Sahib Manki Sharif of the frontier region Jinnah wrote: 'It

---

[168] *IAR*, 1938, vol. 1, p. 382, quoted in Sayeed, op. cit., p. 205.

[169] Abdur Rahman, *Maimaran-i Pakistan* (Architects of Pakistan) (Lahore, 1976).

[170] Ahsanul Haq to Z.A. Ansari, n.d., box 56, FMA.

[171] S.A. Ashraf to Liaquat Ali Khan, 14 January 1946, box 46, FMA.

[172] His statement was: 'At this critical juncture when the *millat* is involved in a life and death struggle, when enemies of Islam have challenged the integrity of the millat, are openly denying the very existence of Mussalmans as a separate nation, are trying to wipe out all the fundamental principles that go to distinguish Islam from heresy, are making nefarious designs to enslave the Muslim nation and are out to destroy the very idea of establishing an independent Muslim State ... it is the duty of the *Ulemas* [*sic*] of Islam to centralise their efforts and mobilise all their forces to meet the situation and give practical effect to the Quranic injunctions. The right to rule rests with Allah alone.' Printed Material, box no. 1, FMA. The English translation, from which the above is reproduced, is in box 56, FMA.

[173] Among the sufis and *mashaikh* who publicly supported the League were: Mian Muhammad Ali Mohammad, Sajjada-Nashin Dargah Mian Muhammad Shah, Hoshirapur district; Maulana (*Mujtahid*) Mohammad Bashir Khizraji, a Shia Imam; Diwan Syed Ale Rasool Ali Khan, Sajjada-Nashin Dargah Ajmer Sharif; Makhdoom Syed Khizr Hyat Khan,

is needless to emphasise that the Constituent Assembly which would be predominantly Muslim in its composition would be able to enact laws for Muslims, not inconsistent with the _Shariat_ laws and the Muslims will no longer be obliged to abide by un-Islamic laws.'[174] The _sajjada-nashins_ of some prestigious shrines in the western districts of Punjab linked some of the local issues with the broader concept of Islamic community embodied in the Pakistan idea,[175] and their charisma and appeal was such that some city-dwelling and landowning élite members of the Lahore Gymkhana Club were presented to the public as _pirs_ and _sajjada-nashins._[176] Aided by the _mullahs_ in Punjab, these people in turn exerted all kinds of pressure on Muslim voters; there was even talk of excluding the League's detractors from burial in Muslim cemeteries, and of their being consigned to hell after death.[177] The _pirs_ of Sind acted as interpreters for the League, translating its policies into a language which had considerable appeal to the Muslims in the countryside – most did so after the resounding success of the Karachi session of the League in 1943, where they turned up with a large contingent of followers. The same year they contributed to the League's victory in the by-election to the Shikarpur constituency,[178] leaflets bearing messages from Ashraf Ali, Shabbir Ahmad Usmani and Zafar Ahmad Ansari being were widely circulated in UP.[179]

Sajjada-Nashin Darbar Hazrat Shah Jeona, Jhung district; Syed Munawwar Ali Shah Husaini Al-Kazmi Al-Mashhadi, Sajjada-Nashin Syed Mathwi Sam Lahori; Pir Badruddin Chishti, Sajjada-Nashin Rupana Sharif, Muktsar tahsil; Pir Syed Shah Gilani, Sajjada- Nashin Hazrat Miyamir, Lahore; Makhdoom Imam Bakhsh, Sajjada-Nashin Khanqah Mubarak Hazrat Deen-Panah, Muzaffargarh district; Syed Mohammad Husain Shah Qadiri Al-Kirmani, Sajjada-Nashin Darbar Shergarh, Montgomery district; Pir Syed Hafiz Jamaat Ali Shah, Alipur, Sialkot district; Syed Amir Shah Gilani, Sajjada-Nashin Dargah Sakhi Saidan Sain; Anwar Ali Shah Gilani, Sajjada-Nashin Dargah Hazrat Syed Nau Bahaar Shah; Hafiz Mohammad Zahur Ali Shah Naqshbandi, Darbar Naqshbandi, Dargah Chaura Sharif; Pir Ladle Husain, Sajjada-Nashin Gulbarga Sharif; Maulana Ghulam Sadiduddin, Sajjada-Nashin Tausa Sharif; Maulana Syed Fazal Shah, Amir Hazbullah Jalalpur Sharif; Sajjada-Nashin Paktpan Sharif; Syed Ghulam Mohiuddin, Sajjada-Nashin Goltra Sharif; Maulana Mohammad Qamaruddin, Sajjada-Nashin Siyal Sharif. _Pakistan Hamara Qaumi Nasb-ul Ain Hai_ [Pakistan is our nation's ideal] and leaflet entitled _Hazrat Sufia-i Karaam ka Elaan-i Haq: Sirf Muslim League ki Himayat Karen_ (Declaration of Truth by the venerable Sufis: Reserve support for the Muslim League) (Publicity and Information Department: Punjab Muslim League), box 151, FMA.

[174] Sayeed, _Pakistan: The Formative Phase,_ p. 198.

[175] Gilmartin, _Islam and Empire,_ p. 215.

[176] Quoted in Sayeed, _Politics in Pakistan,_ p. 15.

[177] Pir Jamaat Ali Shah said in Sialkot: 'If anyone who was standing under the flag of the _kufr_ [apostate] died, will you bury him in the Muslim graveyard? Will you pray at his funeral?' (The crowd shouted; 'No, No']. _Khutbat-i All-India Sunni Conference: 1925-1947_ (Gujrat, 1978), p. 39.

[178] Ansari, _Sufi Saints and State Power,_ pp. 125-6.

[179] For example, _Irshad-i Aliya Janab Hakim al-Millat Maulana Shah Ashraf Ali Thanwi_

In effect, the strategy was to isolate the pro-Congress *ulama* and to target Mufti Kifayatullah and Maulanas Ahmad Said, Hifzur Rahman, Habibur Rahman and Husain Ahmad Madani, all of whom had been founders of the pro-Congress Jamiyat al-ulama. The Urdu paper *Inqilab* way harsh in its critism, calling them them 'Hindu stooges'.[180] The more serious-minded took pains to refute Madani's thesis on composite nationalism, citing Iqbal's verse – *Mulla ko jo hai Hind me sajda ki ijazat: Nadan samajhta hai ke Islam hai Azad* (The mullah is allowed to perform his prayers in Hindustan; such is his naivety that he thinks that Islam is free of danger).[181] Madani and his colleagues were ridiculed, physically assaulted and persecuted by their detractors.[182] A relentless vilification campaign was mounted in the name of Islam.

Efforts were underway to curb Madani's 'anti-Muslim' activities in Deoband. The Nawab of Chattari, firmly ensconced in Hyderabad, was urged to use his influence with the Nizam, 'the biggest donor to the institution', and to 'put an end to the practice of the teaching staff taking part in political activities particularly of the type with which Maulana Husain Ahmad Saheb is associated'. The Maulana's attitude 'has exasperated the Muslim community and if he is allowed to continue his political activities, I am afraid it may affect the institution which has rendered good service to the Muslim community'.[183]

In December 1945 Zafar Ansari, member of the Jamiyat-Ulama-i-Islam, and other *ulama* informed Deoband's *Majlis-i Shura* (syndicate) that some students and teachers were engaged in anti-Muslim activities.

Kalimat al-Haq (Statement of Ashraf Ali Thanwi, the *alim* who guides and speaks the Word of God); *Maulana Zafar Ahmad Saheb Thanwi, Khalifa-i Azam wa Janashin Hazrat Maulana Ashraf Ali Thanwi ka Paigham Musalmanan-i Meerut division ke Nam* (Message of Zafar Ahmad, Khalifa and successor of Ashraf Ali Thanwi to the Muslims of Meerut Division). Printed Material, box. 1, FMA. For the Barelwi *ulama*, see Sanyal, *Devotional Islam and · Politics in British India*, 'Epilogue'.

[180] The *Inqilab* (Lahore) targeted the Jamiyat leaders as 'Congress Maulvis'. Their chief *bête noire* was the *Shaikhul Hadith*, Husain Ahmad Madani. The columnists regreted that he, the venerable Maulana Mahmud Hasan's favourite disciple, did not understand the 'intricacies' of modern politics and was misled by the Congress. See *Inqilab*, 11 September 1937, 15 March 1938, 19 May 1938, 6 January 1939.

[181] Ghulam Mohiuddin, *Hindu Congress ka Dawa-i Qaum-parasti aur Qaum-parast Mussalman* (Nationalist Claims of the Hindu Congress and the Nationalist Muslims) (Publicity and Information Department: Muslim League, n.d.).

[182] An otherwise diehard League supporter in Meerut district was deeply upset that venerable Islamic scholars like Madani and Maulvi Kifayatullah were ridiculed and insulted in public. He reported how the polling agents of the Jamiyat al-ulama were roughed up by League workers in Anchaul village. So was the local *qazi* and imam of the mosque. Rafiq Ahmad [a B.A. final student] to Liaquat Ali Khan, 10 June 1945, box 151, FMA, and Asir Adradi, *Tarikh Jamiyat al-ulama-i Hind* (Delhi, 1403 A.H.), pp. 157-62. For a differrent view, see Khairi, *Jinnah Reinterpreted*, op. cit.

[183] 10 December 1945. The correspondent's name is not given. Box 56, FMA.

The *Majlis-i Shura*, chaired by Kifayatullah, ignored the protest,[184] but an 'Open Letter' denounced the Deoband management, headed by the *Mohtamim* (Principal) Qari Mohammad Tayyab, for turning the *Bayt al-Islam* (House of Islam), founded by Qasim Nanotawi, into 'Gandhi's Ashram'.[185]

The League's prized trophies in UP were Ashraf Ali Thanwi and Shabbir Ahmad Usmani, two of Deoband's most revered scholars. Both were committed to a state with Islamic courts, a *Bayt-al Mal* (welfare treasury) and the *Shariat* laws in force. Ashraf had aired these ideas as long before as June 1928, and corresponded with Jinnah on the subject a decade later. He organised two successful deputations, first in December 1938 and later in February 1939, to secure assurances that the *Shariat* would not be tampered with, and then tried to set aside misgivings about the *la-dini* (irreligious) character of a future Pakistan. He wanted the *ulama* to swell the ranks of the League to make sure that it was run by true Muslims and not by ungodly men. Any conciliation with the Congress was ruled out, its policies and programmes were equated with Bolshevism. He detailed the *sakhti* (harshness) and *tashadud* (oppression) of the Congress ministries, the destruction of the Muslim educational system and the treatment of Urdu as an orphan language. Urdu's defence, he announced in a *fatwa*, 'is a defence of Islam'. He described Gandhi as a *bad-din* (faithless), *ado-i Islam* (enemy of Islam), *makkar* (deceitful), *bad-fahm* (ignorant and naive), *taghut* (a demon), and *dajjal* (imposter).[186]

Ashraf Ali died on 20 July 1943, long before his cherished dream could be fulfilled. But his mission was carried on by Maulana Zafar Ahmad Thanwi and by Mahmud Hasan's disciple, Shabbir Ahmad Usmani, who quitted Deoband with sixty students and some colleagues.[187] Thanwi declared in a statement published in the Bombay *Khilafat* of 6 October 1945 that it was sinful to rally around the flag of the *mushrikeen* (religious opponents), and went on to address the Muslim League conference at Meerut on 2 December 1945. He and his contingent were present in full strength at the Jamiyat-Ulama-i Islam conference at Calcutta, where some

---

[184] Box 56, FMA. Haji Mohammad Husain and Syed Muslehuddin of Bengal and Maulana Mohammad Yaqub and Zafar Ahmad Ansari of UP were amomg those who met the *Majlis-i Shura* on 25 December 1945. They explained that the 'present *anti-millat* activities ... of the Dar al-ulum were not only against its declared constitution but caused deep resentment among the Musalmans of India, who desire and demand that the Dar al-ulum should either refrain from taking active part in politics or at least not side with a political party which is playing into the hands of the Hindu Congress.'

[185] Open Letter, n.d., Printed Material, box 1, FMA.

[186] Rahman, *Maimaran-i Pakistan*, pp. 205-6, 208; Ahmad Saeed, *Maulana Ashraf Ali Saheb Thanwi aur Tehrik-i Azadi* (Rawalpindi, 1972), pp. 29, 36-7, 53, 70.

[187] Syed Mahboob Rizvi, *History of the Dar al-ulum Deoband* (Allahabad: Sahitya Mudranalaya, 1980), p. 240.

of his writings, including the pamphlet entitled *'Maujooda siyasi Kash-makash me Mussalman kiya karen?'* (What is the way out for Muslims in the present political crisis?), were distributed. It was clear that

....the 10 crore Mussalmans in India are definitely a nation. It is imperative that this nation should have a permanent centre in the subcontinent of India so that it may give shape to its own ideals and its development may take place according to Islamic principles. This can be realized only if a Muslim state, in other words Pakistan, is established in those parts of India where the Mussalmans are in majority.[188]

Deoband's Mufti Mohammad Shafi, another venerable *alim*, echoed similar views, claiming that the political and religious rights of the Muslims were being 'trampled' by the 'Hindu' Congress. He argued in his *fatwa* that only an organised body like the Muslim League could counter the forces inimical to Islam. He talked of two centres – a 'Muslim centre', where the *Shariat* would be enforced, and a 'Hindu centre', where the rights of the Muslim minority would be protected through a contract. The 'Islamic centre' would guarantee their safety and wellbeing. He concluded:

India, once a *dar al-Islam* for centuries, is now under the political hegemony of the non-Muslims. [For this reason] many anti-*Shariat* laws were being enforced and the rights of the Muslims are being trampled. [Under these circumstances] it is obligatory to either do away with this system or to reduce its pernicious impact. They must do so in every part of the country and through all possible means. This is necessary for the liberation [*istikhlaas*] of the *dar al-Islam*. In other parts of the country [where such efforts are not likely to be undertaken] the Muslims must continue their struggle for safeguarding the rights of their co-religionists, because this is how the weak can be helped.[189]

Such views were contested. Leading Jamiyat al-ulama spokesmen, who suffered years of imprisonment and made sacrifices for freedom, saw India as a future confederation of two religious and political communities, the Muslim and the Hindu, which would have co-operated successfully against their common enemy, the British. Madani, in particular, defended full and individual Muslim participation in the freedom struggle by advancing a theory of territorial nationhood for India. This theory was sharply rebutted by Iqbal.[190] In his exchanges with the poet,

[188] *Asr-i Jadid* (Calcutta), 21 November 1945, quoted in *Why I Joined Muslim League* (Delhi: Dept. of Publicity and Information, All-India Muslim League, 1945). For the role of Shabbir Ahmad Usmani, Zafar Ahmad Ansari and Mufti Mohammad Shafi, see I.H. Qureshi, *Ulema in Politics* (Karachi: Maarif, 1974 edn), pp. 360-2. For Ashraf Ali Thanwi's role, see Abdul Majid Daryabadi, *Maasireen* [Contemporaries] (Karachi, n.d.), pp. 15-21.

[189] *Congress aur Muslim League ke mutaliq Sharai Faisla* [The Verdict of the *Shariat* on the Congress and the Muslim League] (Deoband: Kutub-Khana-i Idara-i Ishaat, n.d.).

[190] For Iqbal, see Annemarie Schimmel, *Gabriel's Wing: A Study into the Religious Ideas*

as with other public figures, Madani rejected Jinnah's two-nation idea, arguing that just as men's differences in appearances and traits do not come between them and their common humanity, so differences of faith and culture do not come between the inhabitants of India and their association and partnership in their homeland. Solidarity of religious sentiment is not to be expected – indeed Madani said that the Congress itself recognised that the different religions and cultures in India would need protection from each other after the British withdrawal from India.[191]

A widely shared belief among a number of theologians, especially at Deoband and Nadwat al-ulama in Lucknow, was that Pakistan divided and weakened the community of Islam in the subcontinent and destroyed the dream, cherished by thinkers from Shah Waliullah to Maududi, of preserving its unity, inner strength and dynamism. Pakistan symbolised, within their framework, an ill-conceived retreat, fraught with serious consequences for the future of Indian Islam.[192] Thus the *Burhan*, an organ of the reformist *ulama* from Deoband, indicted the Muslim League for its 'collosal blunder', which had no parallel in the history of Islam. 'The verdict of history will go against a leadership which brought ruin and destruction to the community.'[193]

Azad had echoed similar sentiments some months before, on 23 October 1947, when he told the Delhi Muslims: 'The debacle of Indian Muslims is the result of the colossal blunders committed by the Muslim

---

of Sir Muhammad Iqbal (Leiden: E.J. Brill, 1963), p. 198; Shaikh, *Community and Consensus*, pp. 200-2, 203-5; and the essays in C.M. Naim (ed.), Iqbal, *Jinnah and Pakistan: The Vision and the Reality* (South Asian series no. 5, Syracuse University, 1979). For Madani, see Peter Hardy, *Partners in Freedom--and True Muslims: The Political Thought of Muslim Scholars in British India 1912-1947* (Lund: Studentlitteratur, 1971), pp. 38- 9, and his *Muslims of British India*, pp. 243-6; Faruqi, *Deoband School*, pp. 103-4.

[191] For a refutation of Madani's thesis, see Maulana Razi, *Mutahida Qaumiyat aur Islam* (Lahore, 1967 edn.); Asrarul Haq Siddiqi, *Congress Ulama ki Siyasi Karwatain* (Delhi, n.d.), an 'Open Letter' criticising Madani's speech in Saharanpur at the Jamiyat al-ulama session. Akbar Illahabadi's verse – *Congress ke maulvi ko kiya puchte ho kiya hai; Gandhi ki policy ka Arabi me tarjuma hai* – (What is there to know about the Congress-*maulvi*; he reflects Gandhi's policy in Arabic) was in wide usage to malign Madani.

[192] See, for example, Maulana Abul Hasan Ali Nadwi, *Karawan-i Zindagi* (Lucknow: Maktaba-i Islam, 1983), p. 342; Faruqi, *Deoband School*, pp. 126-7. 'Pakistan was a deviation from the Islamic ideal of a universal state'. Its creation divided the 'Muslim nation of India into two separate entities'. Ishtiaq Ahmad, *The Concept of an Islamic State*, p. 81. And the comment: 'For the Muslims of the new Dominion of India, Pakistan was even a Pyrrhic victory. It was a victory which turned into defeat at the moment of being gained. They had, by their votes in 1945-6, proclaimed that Islam and Muslims must, in the twentieth-century, have their own state in order to be fulfilled. But after 1947 the Muslims of India have been obliged to live a version of Islam and of Muslim life in which that fulfillment is denied to them.' Hardy, *Muslims of British India*, pp. 254-5.

[193] *Burhan* (Delhi), April 1948, p. 133. See also Abdul Majid Daryabadi, *Ap Biti* (Lucknow: Maktaba Firdaus, 1989, 2nd edn), pp. 263-4.

League's misguided leadership.'[194] He reflected on the same subject in *India Wins Freedom*.

The only result of the creation of Pakistan was to weaken the position of the Muslims in the sub-continent of India. The 45 million Muslims who have remained in India have been weakened.[...] If we had remained steadfast and refused to accept partition, I am confident that a safer and more glorious future would have awaited us.[...] History alone will decide whether we have acted wisely and correctly in accepting partition.[195]

The judgement of historians, as also the 'verdict of history' that Azad or the *Burhan* talked of, will differ once the Pakistan story is demythologised and its complexities are unravelled. But what is clear from the narrative so far is that the colonial government *created* a community in its own image and allowed its war-time ally, the League, to transform a segmented population into a 'nation' or a 'juridical entity'.[196] With the benefit of hindsight, it is equally clear that neither the 'community' nor the 'nation' was firmly anchored in its respective setting. The 'community' was battered, bruised and fragmented. The Muslim nation, on the other hand, was beset with difficulties and saddled with serious problems from the day of its birth. This was hinted at in September 1947 by H.S. Suhrawardy, whose dream of a united Bengal was shattered before the actual transfer of power. 'I think', he wrote, 'Pakistan has provided a homeland for the Muslims living in those majority areas, but not a homeland for the Muslims of India. The Muslims in the Indian Union have been left high and dry.'[197]

Choudhry Khaliquzzaman was wiser after the event. He agreed that the two-nation theory '*never paid any dividends to us*', (emphasis added) and that 'it proved positively injurious to the Muslims of India, and on a long-term basis for Muslims everywhere.'[198] With an air of desperation, he commented on how 'our erstwhile comrades in arms [in Muslim-

---

[194] Quoted in Syeda Saiyidain Hameed (ed.), *India's Maulana: Abul Kalam Azad* (Delhi: Indian Council of Cultural Relations, 1990), pp. 170-1.

[195] Azad, *India Wins Freedom*, p. 22.

[196] 'In the realistic sense, there was no such thing as a "Muslim nation" because it had no territory to call its own: there was, at best, only a disembodied National ego that was clamouring for a place to call its own.' A.K. Brohi, *An Adventure in Self-Expression* (Lahore: Publishers United, 3rd edn.), p. 411.

[197] Quoted in Choudhry Khaliquzzaman, *Pathway to Pakistan* (Lahore: Longmans, 1964), p. 398. See also Shorish Kashmiri, *Boo-i gul Nala-i dil Dud-i Chiragh-i Mehfil*, chapter entitled' Hum Azad ho gaye' (We are Free) in which Suhrawardy and Khaliquzzaman are cited extensively.

[198] Khaliquzzaman, op. cit., p. 400; Burki, *Pakistan under Bhutto*, chapter 2 entitled 'Insiders and Outsiders'; and the comment of Begum Ikramullah: 'It was the Muslim minority in India who had led the movement for Pakistan, but when Pakistan came into being they were left behind.' Ikramullah, *Huseyn Shaheed Suhrawardy*, p. 59.

majority areas in the fight for Pakistan' were too busy thinking of their own future in the expected new set-up. He talked of a 'natural barrier' between them and those living, say, in UP and Bihar.[199] If so, why did they not give serious thought to the fate of Muslims who were going to be left in India? There was no explanation. Just evasive answers and jutifications after the fact.[200]

Whether they knew the answers or not, the fact is that millions were indifferent to the colonial and League definitions of a 'community' or a 'nation'. In Khori Gali, a mountain pass over the Thanedar range of Naushera near the 'Line of Control', lived Khori Baba: in 1949 he was asked by Pakistani soldiers to cross over to their side, but he had no reason to do to and refused. India was his ancestral land where he and his forebears had lived in perfect amity with the Hindus.[201] In the case of Kemal, one of the central characters in Attia Hosain's novel *Sunlight on a Broken Column*. his voice quivered with suppressed emotion as he said: 'I see my future in the past. I was born here, and generations of my ancestors before me. I am content to die here and be buried with them.'[202] The Khori Babas, the Kemals and the Zohras expose the myth of 'Muslim Unity' just as they poignantly illustrate how the Pakistan movement conveyed very different meanings to different people.

---

[199] Khaliquzzaman, op. cit., p. 390.

[200] When asked why he had not given any thought to the fate of Muslims left in India, Suhrawardy replied: 'I was not an all-India leader. I was the leader of the Muslims of Bengal today, and in the Pakistan I had envisaged, Bengal would have remained an entity and the Muslims would have been in a majority there. They alone were my concern.' Ikramullah, op. cit., pp. 59-60.

[201] *Communalism Combat* (Bombay), 4 October 1993.

[202] Attia Hosain, *Sunlight on a Broken Column*, p. 288.

4

INDIA PARTITIONED: THE OTHER FACE OF FREEDOM

'Farhan kissed her hands and dropped them and went towards the window. "Sarla how often have I risen in this room, in this Delhi and seen the minarets nestling near the domes. It's always been a picture of love. Hodgson dragging Bahadur Shah and then ordering the killing of the Emperor's sons and displaying those royal bodies in the *bazaars* of Delhi could not dim the glow of love that Delhi evokes. Not Nadir Shah's cruel sacking of Delhi but Mir's poetry remains. Yet today, having seen the lacerated bodies of Muslims, Sikhs and Hindus, I feel this city has become a vestibule of hate. History, it appears, is an invitation to revenge. Religion, it seems the licence to kill, the greater savagery denoting greater dedication. Oh my Rajput princes, we were both wrong, you and I, not for loving each other, but for becoming part of political forces which could not bear to live together, nor negotiate with their own people in mind, which made plans for India's freedom but forgot the future." '

Mehr Nigar Masroor*

'Partition came and we accepted it because we thought that perhaps that way, however painful it was, we might have some peace to work along our own lines. Perhaps we acted wrongly. It is difficult to judge now. And yet the consequences of that partition have been so terrible that one is inclined to think that anything else would have been preferable. That partition has come, and it brought in its train other vast changes. There is no going back now to India as it was before the partition.'

Nehru to the Nawab of Bhopal, 9 July 1948†

We have examined both the political and religious drive behind the Muslim League movement as well as its wide-ranging implications. This chapter offers a slightly different historical agenda, though it must be read

* *Shadow of Time* (Lahore, 1995), pp. 212–13
† *SWJN*, second series, vol. 7, p. 6.

with and as a sequence to the previous one. It aims to rescue, at least partly, the current debates on partition from the votaries of secular nationalism and their unrelenting critics, and to create space for other voices to be heard. The engagement is not with high politics or with the so-called guilty men of the 1940s, but with creative writers and poets. It tries to illustrate, with the aid of memoirs, eye-witness accounts, poems and short stories, what the Pakistan *movement* symbolised at various historical moments and in local situations, such as the Aligarh Muslim University, and the variety of meanings that were frequently attached to nation, nationalism and communitarian identity.

Predictably, the principal characters in this discussion speak in different voices, underline diverse concerns, invoke their own selective symbols and memories, and marshal their specific individual and collective intellectual resources. At another level, however, there is a noticeable convergence of ideas and shared experiences. That is why scores of writers of all kinds communicate to us the trauma and anguish of a generation that was caught up in the crossfire of religious sectarianism on the eve of partition and in its aftermath. To label them as 'Hindus', 'Muslims' or 'Sikhs' is unjust, and to locate them within narrow territorial boundaries, such as 'India', 'Pakistan' or 'Bangladesh', is equally erroneous. Their writings encompass a wide range of human feelings, emotions and sensitivities and make sense only as an indivisible component of the subcontinent's shared and composite social, cultural and literary heritage. It is necessary to keep such a vibrant legacy intact against fundamentalist onslaughts if the country's political division is not to be allowed to cast its lengthy shadows on present-day South Asian politics and society.

Those speaking through this account do not occupy centre-stage in national or provincial arenas of formal and institutional politics. Some are no doubt high-profile writers and poets, involved in literary movements imbued with socialist and Marxist ideas. But most are not 'major' actors in public life; by conventional political standards, they are not even 'minor' players. Yet their voice, subtle but effective, must be heard loud and clear to reveal the other face of freedom. Their portrayal of a fragmented and wounded society, engulfed in widespread violence, must command greater attention even if cynical and self-seeking politicians, impervious to human suffering and to the consequences of their ill-conceived and reckless designs, ignored their timely warnings and signed united India's death-warrant.

There can be no doubt that many writers and poets in English, Punjabi, Hindi, Urdu and Bengali – more than political commentators and analysts – encapsulate the mood and sensitivity of those aggrieved and tormented men and women, rich and poor, Hindu, Muslim or Sikh, who had no say in the actual transfer of power to two countries. They do so with great effect and poignancy. In a sense, therefore, their powerful images and nuanced descriptions expose the inadequacy of numerous political narratives on independence and partition and compel us to consider new themes and approaches that have so far eluded the grasp of most historians of South Asia.

Writers like Saadat Hasan Manto, Rajinder Singh Bedi, Ahmed Ali, Attia Hosain, Rahi Masoom Reza and Intizar Husain provide a foundation for developing an alternative to current expositions of a general theory on inter-community relations in modern India. Their representation of a contemporary reality, grim and sordid in its manifestations, may stir the individual and collective imagination of sensitive readers – in Lahore, Delhi and Dacca; in Pyongyang and Seoul; in Berlin and Bonn before 1989; and in the war-torn cities of Bosnia-Hercegovina.

I

'A huge procession which took almost an hour and a quarter to pass through the gaily decorated streets of Karachi, 1500 *khaki* and grey-clad Muslim National Guards drawn from all over the country, Muslim students and Muslim children's squads, Muslim League leaders and Ministers in a train of one hundred motor cars – picture all this, and then think of the handful of individuals who àttended the ... session of the Muslim League which was also held at Karachi 36 years ago in the year 1907. "This procession", said Jinnah while unfurling the flag of the League, "is the symbol of the unity and strength of the Muslims." '

> *People's War* (newspaper), 9 January 1944, quoted in Zaheer,
> *A Case for Congress-League Unity*, p. 32

Rehmat Ali's 'Pakistan scheme', published in Cambridge in January 1933, caused political embarrassment back home and was summarily dismissed as 'chimerical' and 'impracticable'.[1] For nearly a decade thereafter Pakistan remained a pipe-dream and the League a paper body. But when the dust settled after the Lahore meeting in March 1940, Pakistan was no longer an elusive goal, and the League no longer a benign organisation. Having refurbished its image, reorganised its structure at various levels and formulated a strategy to deepen its popular base, the League picked up seats in by-elections, increased its membership, secured a firm foothold in Muslim-majority provinces, and commanded widespread endorsement from various groups and social classes. In the

---

[1] Abdullah Yusuf Ali and Zafarullah Khan, quoted in *Minutes of Evidence given before the Joint Committee on Indian Constitutional Reforms*, quoted in K.K. Aziz, *Rehmat Ali: A Biography* (Lahore: Vanguard, 1987), pp. 93-4.

sixty-one by-elections held for Muslim constituencies during 1937-43, the League bagged forty-seven seats. The Congress managed to secure only four. The League polled about 4.5 million or 75 per cent of the Muslim votes in 1945-6 and won 460 out of 533 Muslim seats in the central and provincial elections.

The Canadian scholar W.C. Smith, then researching in India, estimated that the League had conquered the bulk of the middle as well as the lower middle classes.[2] By 1942 Jinnah 'actually assumed a position like Gandhiji so far as Muslims were concerned'.[3] He was 'a sword of Islam resting in a secular scabbard'.[4] His Pakistan idea 'appeared a thing to laugh at five years ago: now, though I think it is impracticable, it has become the slogan and watchword of the Muslim masses.'[5] Jinnah, commented R.W. Sorensen, was the incarnation of one idea, 'but the idea can be fertile once it has succeeded.' Muslim Leaguers earnestly believed that Pakistan was

...the inviolable prelude to their communal well-being and prosperity. They may or may not be deluded in this, other elements may adulterate their zeal, but in the emotional fervour of the two thousand or so students who greeted us with green flags chanting 'Pakistan' in unison at Lahore; in the frenzied cries that met Jinnah when he spoke to thousands in the same town when we were there; in the long elaborate exposition I heard at a Moslem tea gathering at Allahabad; in the somewhat confused utterances of three opulent and corpulent Muslim spokesmen at Peshawar; in the persistence of those who pursued me at the last Indian gathering; and in a score of other instances, *I perceived that Pakistan had 'caught on' with large numbers of Moslems and had become an intense political-religious faith* [emphasis added].[6]

The evidence to substantiate these impressions is irrefutable. The League's prospects in Punjab, always a matter of concern to Jinnah and his lieutenants, improved vastly after the collapse of the Jinnah-Sikander Pact in April 1944. Its political strategies, coupled with an intensive publicity *blitzkrieg*, paid off. Two influential groups in Punjab society – landlords and *pirs*, whose directives were widely disseminated by means of leaflets and wall-posters – deserted the Unionist Party for reasons that

[2] Smith, *Modern Islam*, p. 312. And the following comment of another contemporary towards the end of 1942: 'From a highly respectable and somewhat sedate body of aristocratic and well connected gentlemen for whom politics was a polite diversion from the urgencies of official or professional life, the League has changed into a proletarian gathering of impassioned and fervent men who throw balance and moderation to the winds for what they regard to be a righteous cause.' Kabir, *Muslim Politics*, pp. 26-7.

[3] Ashraf in Kruger (ed.), *Kunwar Ali Ashraf: An Indian Scholar and Revolutionary*, p. 414.

[4] R.W. Sorenson, *My Impression of India* (London: Meridian Books, 1946), p. 109.

[5] J.D. Tyson to Folk, 17 November 1946, Mss. Eur., file no. E 341/41, J.D. Tyson papers, IOL.

[6] Sorenson, op. cit., p. 111.

are now known through the scholarly researches of David Gilmartin, Ian Talbot, Ayesha Jalal and Imran Ali. Their conversion to the League's creed enabled Jinnah to raise his party's flag in the 'cornerstone' of Pakistan.[7] Before the war, Hindus, Muslims and Sikhs had mostly lived as neighbours in rural Punjab. With the intensive propaganda produced during the 1945-6 elections, communal politics burst into the village, setting Muslim against non-Muslim and giving both communities a new and exciting word – freedom.[8] M.A.H. Qadiri, professor of zoology at Aligarh Muslim University, found 'a great change in the mentality of ... the Muslim masses' in rural Punjab; they were 'aroused and inspired by the message of Pakistan'.[9] Although some areas remained untouched, 'responsible' and 'influential' League managers toured the province, familiarised people with their agenda, established League branches and recruited primary members.[10] Malcolm Darling had this to say during his tour of the Punjab:

If only propaganda had not poisoned the air with hatred and distrust, Hindu, Muslim and Sikh could have continued to live happily together in the village, as they had done for over a hundred years.[...] We met Muslims who for generations had their genealogies kept and horoscopes cast by Brahmins, and passed villages owned by Muslim and Sikh, or by Hindu and Muslim, sprung from a common ancestor, and we even came across one village where Hindu, Muslim and Sikh were of the same tribe. Without neighbourliness there can be no comfort in village life, but, alas, propaganda with its ghastly brood – mutilation, massacre and rape – has turned Jinnah's two-nation creed in the village from a theory into a bloody fact.[11]

Similar processes were at work in Sind. The League successfully projected its image as the defender of Islam, exploited the Shahidganj mosque affair which resulted in religious strife and violence,[12] and toppled Allah Bakhsh's pro-Congress ministry, replacing it by one headed

---

[7] Ian Talbot, 'The Growth of the Muslim League in the Punjab, 1937-1946', *The Journal of Commonwealth and Comparative Politics*, 1, 1, March 1982, and his 'Deserted Collaborators: The Political Background of the Punjab Unionist Party, 1923-1947', *Journal of Imperial and Commonwealth History*, 11, 1, October 1982; Gilmartin, *Empire and Islam*, chapter 6, and his 'Religious Leadership and the Pakistan Movement', *Modern Asian Studies*, 13, 3, 1979, pp. 485-517; Craig Baxter, 'Union or Partition: Some Aspects of Politics in the Punjab, 1936-1945', in Lawrence Ziring, Ralph Braibanti and Howard Wriggins (eds), *The Long View* (Durham, NC: Duke University Press, 1977).

[8] Malcolm Lyall Darling, *At Freedom's Dawn* (London: OUP, 1949), p. 299.

[9] To Jinnah, 8 February 1946, UP, vol. v, SHC.

[10] Inspection report, 26 February 1945, Committee for Action, 1945, vol. 201, part 1, FMA.

[11] Darling, op. cit., pp. 302-3.

[12] The Shahidganj mosque was a religious site in dispute between Muslims and Sikhs, but it was awarded to the Sikhs by a special government tribunal in the early 1930s. For Jinnah's role, see Shorish Kashmiri, *Paas-i Diwar-i Zindan* (Lahore: Chattan Press, 1971), p. 59.

by a League sympathiser, Mir Bandeh Ali Khan Talpur.[13] This was not enough! 'In every mosque', reported an activist,

....the principle underlying the 'Buy from Muslim' campaign was explained and the pulpits [*sic*] were asked to exhort the congregationists to take to trade. [...] A day was fixed as the 'Muslim Trade Day' and an appeal was issued to the Muslims ... to observe the day. As many as 200 places in the province observed and celebrated the day.[14]

The involvement of the *pirs* and other religious men was an additional bonus. They were reassured that their interests would be firmly secured under a League-led government, and offered thousands of rupees in offerings to persuade them to take part in canvassing.[15] By 31 May 1945, the Sind provincial League had developed a high profile (Table 4.1). In a province where political activity had been sporadic on the Khilafat issue, the League had 450 branches comprising, at least on paper, well over 126,484 members.[16] Membership rose by 1944 to 550,000.[17]

Table 4.1. SIND PROVINCIAL LEAGUE, 1945

Districts	Total population	Muslim population	%	Primary Leagues	Primary members	%
Karachi	327,195	284,588	87	21	3,701	1.3
Hyderabad Sind	758,748	507,620	67	15	4,100	0.8
Tharparkar	581,004	292,025	50	72	9,539	3.3
Nawabshah	584,177	436,414	75	45	10,033	2.3
Dadu	389,380	329,991	85	26	2,318	0.7
Larkana	511,208	418,543	82	18	3,329	0.8
Upper Sind Frontier	304,034	275,063	90	24	2,898	1.0
Sukkur	692,558	491,634	71	14	4,198	0.9
Karachi city	388,655	162,447	42	32	11,534	7.1

Source: Box no. 31, Freedom Movement Archives, University of Karachi, Karachi.

[13] Sarah Ansari, *Sufi Saints and State Power*, pp. 118-20, 121; Rizvi, *Linlithgow and India*, p. 124; Sayeed, *Nature and Direction of Change*, pp. 8-16.

[14] Honorary secretary, Sind provincial League, to Liaquat Ali Khan, 6 November 1943, box no. 31, FMA.

[15] In one contest the local *pir*, with a fine impartiality, preached in favour of the League at one end of the constituency and for the Unionist Party at the other. Darling, op. cit., p. 85.

[16] Box no. 31, FMA.

[17] Ansari, op. cit.

The League bandwagon also rolled on in the Central Provinces and Berar, Bombay and Madras (Tables 4.2-4.3). Towards the end of 1941 Madras claimed to have 112,078 members (Table 4.4). By 1944-5 Bengal had branches in eighteen out of twenty-eight districts; primary membership rose to 550,000.[18] These figures 'exceeded the number ever scored by any organisation in the province not excluding the Congress'.[19]

The League started off unsteadily in UP only to gain substantially after March 1940 (Table 4.5). The province chief secretary thought that 'the Pakistan scheme now seems to be an accepted part of the tenets of the League.'[20] The provincial conference at Allahabad on 23-24 December in 1940 attracted over 10,000 people.[21] So did the drive to enrol members; nearly 20,939 people were recruited in Allahabad and 27,600 in Muzaffarnagar district.[22] 'Everyday we eagerly wait for *Dawn*', the president of the Muzaffarnagar branch informed Jinnah, 'to see if you have issued any fresh statement or instruction. How glorious it is to be in communion with you ....'[23] In Deoria the League gained a foothold because of estrangement between Hindus and Muslims. Patrick Biggie, a police officer, commented: 'Any district in the west of the Province will seem like child's play after the many complex problems of Deoria – its dacoities, its communal trouble, murders and political activity.'[24]

Kanpur was much the same during 1939-41. Worker unrest was rampant. Christians were agitated over the sale of church land, and the Shias over police firing on their brethren in neighbouring Lucknow.[25] Hindu-Muslim strife was heightened by disputes over the ownership of parade grounds and the Ramnarain bazaar, the kidnapping of a young boy by Shahid Ali, and the outbreak of riots in June 1939. Tension mounted when the Hindu Sangh observed 'Anti-Pakistan Day' and 'Hyderabad Day' to express solidarity with the Arya Samaj movement in the princely state of Hyderabad. Jinnah provided the healing touch to the beleaguered Muslims. He travelled to Kanpur, hobnobbed with local Muslims, and addressed a public meeting: nearly 25,000 people assembled to listen to

---

[18] Inspection report, 29 March 1949, Committee for Action, 1945, vol. 201, part 1, FMA.

[19] Z.H. Zaidi, 'Aspects of the Development of Muslim League Policy', in Philips and Wainwright (eds), *Partition of India*, p. 268.

[20] FR, first half of September 1940, Mss. Eur., file no. 164/6, R.F. Mudie papers, IOL.

[21] FR, first half of December 1940, ibid.

[22] FR, first half of July 1945, H.J. Frampton papers.

[23] M. Saleem Jan to Jinnah, 21 August 1945, correspondence-general, UP., vol. 1, SHC.

[24] Patrick Biggie papers, CSAS.

[25] Diaries, 10 June 1939, Mss. Eur., file no. E.255/14 Harold Charles Mitchell papers, IOL. He was superintendent of police in Kanpur, 1938-9. The file contains a clipping from the *Pioneer* (24 August 1939) reporting the observance of *hartal* in Kanpur by the Shias, who wore black badges on their arms and put up black flags on their homes.

Table 4.2 PROGRESS OF MUSLIM LEAGUE IN CENTRAL PROVINCES AND BERAR, 1938-43

	1938		1939		1940		1941		1942		1943	
	Primary Leagues	Members on annual rolls	Primary Leagues	Annual members	Primary Leagues	Annual members	Primary Leagues	Annual members	Primary Leagues	Annual members	Primary Leagues	Annual members
Nagpur	6	2,695	4	3,485	1	2,012	1	2,570	3	1,283	–	–
Wardha	2	388	3	400	5	1,050	3	996	4	912	5	770
Chanda	–	–	–	–	–	–	4	565	6	709	5	770
Bilaspur	–	–	–	–	3	390	–	–	–	–	–	–
Raipur	4	501	6	705	4	902	4	701	3	827	3	900
Drug	–	–	–	–	–	–	3	514	2	238	–	–
Bhandara	3	120	–	–	5	243	1	208	–	–	–	–
Balaghat	2	350	1	192	3	350	1	156	2	128	–	–
Seoni	3	374	7	462	6	629	4	506	3	553	–	–
Chhindwara	1	156	3	150	4	260	4	500	4	500	4	500
Betul	5	544	5	796	5	543	5	538	5	561	5	647
Hoshangabad	–	–	4	649	4	350	–	–	1	278	–	–
Nimar	–	–	2	1,950	2	1,866	3	1,677	3	1,500	–	–
Harsingpur	4	1,152	4	1,305	4	1,149	4	798	4	1,243	4	724
Jabalpur	4	6,161	7	10,344	8	8,837	5	6,420	8	10,729	6	6,778
Mandla	–	–	1	100	1	300	2	325	–	–	–	–
Sauger	5	1,730	5	1,120	5	1,582	1	338	5	2,294	–	–
Damoh	–	–	–	–	–	–	–	–	1	640	–	–
Yeotmal	63	4,289	32	2,574	37	3,742	31	3,525	31	3,500	37	3,599
Amraoti	16	1,105	14	1,455	15	1,807	10	1,068	11	1,891	12	1,249
Akola	11	2,025	12	2,287	35	4,053	41	4,750	38	3,357	–	–
Buldana	21	2,411	7	878	14	3,629	16	3,329	19	3,547	–	–
Total	150	24,001	117	28,852	161	33,394	141	29,484	153	34,690	76	15,167

Note: The Provincial Muslim League was affiliated to the All-India Muslim League on 26 November 1938. There was no primary or district League in the Central Provinces in 1937.

Source: Freedom Movement Archives, University of Karachi, Karachi.

Table 4.3. PRIMARY MEMBERS AND MUSLIM LEAGUES IN
BOMBAY PROVINCE, 1941

District	Primary Leagues	Primary members
Ahmedabad	– †	
Kaira	2	2,393
Broach	3	1,569
Surat	– †	
Thana	– †	
Poona	3	598
East Khandesh	5	1,337
Nasik	7	2,477
·Ahmednagar	3	420
Belgaum	– †	
Dharwar	3	1,340
North Canara*	2	515
A. Ward district	Muslim League	1,004
B. Ward	3	4,285
C. Ward	6	1,000
D. Ward	1	1,000
E. Ward	1	3,625
F. Ward	5	1,100
Suburban district	3	1,901
Total	48	24,564

* Includes Wards A to F and the suburban district.
† Report not received.
Source: vol. 357, Freedom Movement Archives, University of Karachi, Karachi.

this rising star in the political firmament.[26]

Aligarh's Muslim University was, as Jinnah once said, 'the arsenal of Muslim India', but this was not so till the late 1930s, when the liberal-socialist combine controlled campus politics. The mood changed with the founding of the All-India Muslim Students' Federation (AIMSF), as indeed with the Student's Union adopting the Lahore resolution as its 'official creed'. The AIMSF launched a quarterly journal in English and

[26] Scrapbook (Kanpur), Mitchell papers; *Pioneer*, 21 May 1939; FR, 2nd half of April 1941, Mudie papers, IOL.

Table 4.4. MUSLIM LEAGUE MEMBERS IN
MADRAS PRESIDENCY, 1938-41

District	Membership in the districts			
	1938	*1939*	*1940*	*1941*
Vizagapatam	–	200	–	–
East Godavari	300	300	1,344	–
West Godavari	130	332	1,003	250
Kistna	518	551	2,286	–
Guntur	736	692	1,706	112
Nellore	–	716	2,942	2,324
Cuddapah	2,410	1,466	1,306	9,059
Kurnool	396	400	4,100	15,599
Bellary	300	950	2,873	4,060
Anantapur	878	5,995	1,576	500
Chittoor	260	576	163	–
Chingleput	550	–	1,600	400
South Arcot	2,939	1,524	2,800	3,759
Madras	5,375	3,655	11,300	15,599
North Arcot	3,096	940	4,202	806
Tanjore	7,202	4,727	6,370	9,751
Trichinopoly	622	1,026	2,560	4,557
Madurai	2,616	1,581	2,751	1,300
Tinnevelly	3,761	6,148	6,482	9,216
Ramnad	3,932	6,948	7,239	15,470
Salem	344	–	3,029	3,058
Coimbatore	898	1,243	4,734	980
The Nilgiris	672	100	–	455
Malabar	5,786	2,741	11,830	7,952
South Kanara	–	–	4,637	7,469
Total	43,721	42,811	88,833	1,12,676

Source: Box no. 31, Freedom Movement Archives, University of Karachi, Karachi.

Table 4.5. MUSLIM LEAGUE MEMBERSHIP
IN U.P., 1940-1/1943-4

	Actual membership			
	1940-1	*1941-2*	*1942-3*	*1943-4*
Meerut dist.	3,000	1,520	1,000	3,000
Meerut city	1,738	1,000	1,400	1,021
Saharanpur dist.	6,078	1,852	2,240	–
Muzaffarnagar dist.	6,050	6,000	6,432	3,688
Muzaffarnagar city	–	–	1,644	2,575
Bulandshahr dist.	–	1,500	2,785	2,215
Agra dist.	1,064	1,373	1,963	1,000
Agra city	2,500	4,565	4,670	2,450
Etah dist.	1,000	1,000	1,280	1,023
Aligarh dist.	4,200	9,223	7,000	6,245
Aligarh city	4,100	1,146	3,328	6,693
Bareilly dist.	3,000	2,342	3,672	1,718
Bareilly city	2,400	2,339	2,444	1,956
Bijnor dist.	–	2,432	2,897	1,500
Budaun dist.	3,708	2,134	2,687	4,809
Budaun city	1,026	1,429	2,117	2,944
Moradabad dist.	1,080	1,000	1,216	1,575
Moradabad city	1,991	1,200	1,494	5,472
Amroha city	1,100	1,000	1,026	5,415
Sambhal city	1,069	1,000	–	–
Shahjahanpur city	1,583	5,538	3,162	1,309
Pilibhit dist.	1,775	Not legible	1,325	1,000
Allahabad dist.	8,560	3,000	–	1,000
Allahabad city	11,009	4,000	1,000	2,000
Kanpur city	16,000	5,932	9,023	11,264
Fatehpur dist.	16,000	1,559	–	–
Etawah dist.	2,025	1,019	–	–
Mirzapur dist.	1,449	1,348	1,022	2,372
Mirzapur city	–	–	1,011	1,002
Banaras dist.	4,000	1,136	–	1,100
Banaras city	4,000	3,000	–	–
Ghazipur dist.	1,000	–	2,054	–
Ballia dist.	1,900	3,498	1,001	2,200
Gorakhpur dist.	2,700	3,000	4,000	16,000
Gorakhpur city	1,156	1,002	1,288	1,200
Basti dist.	2,133	1,472	1,250	–
Azamgarh dist.	1,100	1,000	–	2,000
Nainital dist.	2,000	1,666	1,000	–

Lucknow dist.	5,000	2,287	1,841	2,214
Lucknow city	4,000	10,502	19,068	31,180
Unnao dist.	2,500	1,024	3,083	2,300
Rae Bareli dist.	1,122	1,132	1,214	1,298
Hardoi dist.	1,300	2,000	2,224	2,086
Sitapur dist.	7,000	1,000	1,155	1,471
Kheri dist.	–	1,000	2,417	2,643
Faizabad dist.	1,666	–	–	1,100
Gonda dist.	2,840	1,000	–	–
Barabanki dist.	2,400	–	2,003	2,620
Bahraich dist.	1,315	2,330	1,229	–
Bahraich city	1,312	1,217	1,308	–
Sultanpur dist.	6,055	–	3,705	1,536
Partabgarh dist.	4,000	2,400	–	–
Total	164,004	108,117	117,678	146,194

Source: vol. 357, Freedom Movement Archives, University of Karachi, Karachi.

Urdu; students and teachers churned out pamphlets on Pakistan, such as 'The Nature of Islamic Political Theory' by Jamiluddin Ahmad; 'Industrial Pakistan' by Mohammad Yunus and 'The Herculean Task' by Farzand-i Raza. League stalwarts visited Aligarh periodically. The citadel of Syed Ahmad Khan, who had urged his co-religionists to stay clear of politics, was breached. 'The walls of the Strachey Hall', wrote an AIMSF activist,

....had echoed with the voices of great men right from the days of Sir Syed. These voices are now silent. A new voice had begun to be heard in the later nineteen-thirties, and during the last decade before independence it was the only political voice that mattered in Aligarh: it was the voice of Mohammad Ali Jinnah.[27]

In September 1942, members of the Muslim University Duty Society toured some princely states, carrying 'the torch of League ideals' and discovering 'signs of life and awakening' in the Muslim masses.[28] Jinnah's stirring speech at the University's Strachey Hall on 2 November 1942 must have disturbed Syed Ahmad Khan lying in his grave in the nearby mosque. It certainly caused panic in pro-Congress circles. Aligarh's grand old man, steeped in the feudal traditions of a passing era but keeping pace with the changing world around him, had not been by any means the architect of Muslim nationalism. He was a moderniser, a reformer and an educationist who tried bridging the gulf that separated the colonial government from the remnants of the Muslim élites of north India. His efforts were not wasted, although his death in 1898 brought profound changes. For one, the legacy of compromise and accommodation with the Raj was repudiated by the radicals at Aligarh during the first decade of the twentieth century. The University, modelled on Oxbridge and designed to produce loyalists serving the government, turned into a storm-centre of nationalist activities during the Khilafat and Non-Co-operation enthusiasm. But in the early 1940s the clock was turned back. Memories of the Khilafat excitement faded away. The political message of Shibli, Ajmal Khan, Mohamed Ali, Ansari, Hasrat Mohani, Syed Mahmud, Azad and Maulana Mahmud Hasan, which had once stirred the imagination of students and teachers alike, was lost. Aligarh discovered a new set of heroes, created new symbols to embrace and pinned their hopes not on secular nationalism but on the evolution of a

---

[27] Mukhtar Zaman, *Students' Role in the Pakistan Movement* (Karachi: Quaid-i Azam Academy, 1978), p. 48. Jinnah paid much attention to the mobilisation of students all over the country. He addressed their meetings and conferences and complimented them on various occasions. The students of Bengal, for example, 'were like a rock when the Muslim League was having a very stormy and serious time'. Jinnah to the Raja of Mahmudabad, 27 July 1943, SHC. For the role of Dacca University, see Mahmud Hasan, 'Dacca University and the Pakistan Movement', in Philips and Wainwright (eds), *Partition of India*, pp. 369-73.

[28] Mohammad Mukhtar Anas to Liaquat Ali Khan, 23 September 1942, vol. 237, FMA.

specifically Muslim nationhood. The University was caught up in the communal cauldron and called upon to endorse the Muslim League's demand for a Muslim state.

The broad direction and course of politics at Aligarh was influenced in the early 1940s by the decision of the Communist Party (CPI) to extend its tacit support to the demand for a separate homeland.[29] It was a time when the Germans were pounding the gates of Stalingrad and the Japanese were pushing their way through the forests of Imphal and Kohima to India's eastern border. It was feared that if India were to fall into the hands of the Axis powers the result would be a global disaster for the anti-fascist allies. Thus it had to be prevented at all cost. In India itself there was a political deadlock. There was therefore a desperate search for a solution to the 'Indian problem' – which, according to the new CPI line, lay in 'Congress-League Unity' to be realised through talks between Gandhi and Jinnah. This became the new CPI slogan and was echoed in Sajjad Zaheer's articles in *People's War*. To provide theoretical justification for this new turn in politics, the Comintern and the CPI argued that there was not a single 'National Bourgeoisie' in India; there were two – the 'Indian National Bourgeoisie' and the 'Indian Muslim Bourgeoisie'. The Muslim League was characterised, in accordance with Lenin's famous 'Thesis' at the second Congress of the Comintern, as the party of the Indian Muslim bourgeoisie and not as a 'stooge' of the British, which was how it had been described a short time before.[30] The way was thus opened ideologically for the formula of Congress-League unity and a settlement with the British on the basis of a deal between the two parties that were the supposed bearers of the 'National Democratic Revolution'.

As a sequel to this new policy, the CPI instructed the 'Muslim' communists to join the League. Thus Danial Latifi, having just been called to the Bar, was asked to become office-secretary of the Punjab Muslim League – the 'feudals' in the person of Mian Mumtaz Daulatana kept the secretaryship in their own hands. The change was also apparent on the Aligarh University campus, where, as Hamza Alavi revealed recently, an 'order' came 'from above' instructing them to disband the All India Student's Federation (AISF) branch at Aligarh. Every member was required to join the AIMSF individually. Hamza Alavi was 'outraged by the undemocratic manner in which it was imposed on us without the slightest attempt to engage us in a discussion. I was quite appalled by that dictatorial method. But for that, who knows, I might have even joined the CPI.'

---

[29] Hamza Alavi has recently drawn my attention to the significance of the CPI's intervention. I have quoted at length from his detailed letter to me in July 1994.

[30] P.C. Joshi in his policy statement of February 1942 referred to the League as an emerging 'mass party'. Quoted in Gene Overstreet and Marshall Windmiller, *Communism in India* (Berkeley, CA: University of California Press, 1960), p. 201.

Most fell in line with the 'Adhikari thesis'.[31] 'The communists have openly come out in the field', reported Jamiluddin Ahmad from Aligarh in early 1943, 'preaching communist doctrines, distributing communist literature and their organ of the People's War, and enrolling members of the League. They have established a regular centre at the house of a professor and some other professors are secretly supporting them.'[32] Jinnah could not figure out why this was so. He expressed his disdain for the communists and exhorted the correspondent to 'face any attempts to disrupt the Aligarh solidarity'. 'I should have thought', he continued, 'Aligarh is now strong, well-knit and organised enough to resist any mischief that may be created against us.'[33]

Jinnah's speech in early November 1942, followed by the League's mobilisation drive, sealed the fate of the liberal-left combination on the campus. In October 1944, the Raja of Mahmudabad set up a 'League camp' at Aligarh, and a year later the *Aligarh Magazine* published a 'Pakistan Number'. The seventh AIMSF conference was held on 1-3 March 1945.[34] An atmosphere of 'mystic frenzy' prevailed.[35] An American student recalled how his fellow-students perceived Pakistan 'as a bright dream, a passionate goal, the vision of a Muslim paradise on earth'. A great many – though not all – shared their fancy.[36]

The eagerly awaited 1945-6 elections were 'a matter of life and death'.[37] Most students therefore poured their 'idealistic zeal into the emotionalism of Pakistan'.[38] They were organised into a cohesive force by the vice-chancellor, Ziauddin, a Wrangler from Cambridge; his deputy A.B.A. (Abba) Haleem; Qadiri, a Cambridge graduate who had earned a reputation for his doctoral work at the Cavendish Laboratory; and Manzar-i-Alam, president of the University Muslim League. By 15 November 1945, 650 students were sent to coaching centres – a memorable experience for them: for the first time they received lessons on Islam and in Islamic history, became acquainted with the Pakistan movement's

---

[31] There were some notable exceptions. Hamza Alavi, then a student at the Aligarh University, has written to me that Moonis Raza (d. 1994), former vice-chancellor of the University of Delhi, and a handful of his CPI comrades at Aligarh refused to fall in line with this new thesis. 'But this rump AISF was clearly no longer of any significance for we did not even know of its continued existence. It evidently operated in a clandestine manner.'

[32] Jamiluddin Ahmad to Jinnah, 1 January 1943, Aligarh file, SHC.

[33] Jinnah to Jamiluddin Ahmad, 9 January 1943, ibid.

[34] Mushirul Hasan, 'Nationalist and Separatist Trends in Aligarh', op. cit., p. 124.

[35] Smith, *Modern Islam*, pp. 181-2.

[36] Phillips Talbot, 'I am a Pakistani', 28 November 1956, Ian Stephens Papers, CSAS.

[37] Iqbal Masud to Jinnah, 24 September 1945; M.A. Humayun to Jinnah, 16 August 1945, SHC.

[38] Smith, *Modern Islam*, pp. 181-2.

religious background, and realised what set the Congress and the League apart.[39]

By November 1945 more than 450 students were soliciting support in the North-West Frontier Province, Punjab, UP and Bengal. At least 100 camped in Meerut, Muzaffarnagar, Saharanpur and Dehra Dun in Liaquat Ali Khan's constituency. 'Imagine', wrote the University League's president, 'this large number of educated young men celebrating their *Id* festival in the unfamiliar villages and away from their friends and relatives.'[40] In early 1946, an additional 250 students campaigned in Assam, Sind and Punjab.[41] An ebullient M.B. Mirza, dean of the science faculty, president of the student's union and chairman of the Aligarh election committee, proclaimed: 'So far all the students [are] united and working under one Leader, one Party and one Flag.'[42]

Kalim Siddiqui (died 1996), then living in his ancestral village in north India and once dubbed 'Britain's Angry Ayatollah', happily remembered how three young men from the University planted the League flag in the square and within an hour his quiet village had been turned into a 'Pakistan village'. His mother made League flags out of every piece of green material. A few months later his parents and others walked to the polling booth 4 miles away to vote for Pakistan. 'This was repeated all over India. Seldom in history have so few inspired so many with so little effort.'[43] Siddiqui could well have added that never before in South Asian history did so few divide so many in so short a time. Indeed, never before had so few decided the fate of so many.

Much of what the students said during their tours was not specific to Siddiqui's village but in tune with the religio-fundamentalist tenor of League activity throughout the country. League activists detailed the 'wrongs' done by the Congress ministries. They talked of Muslim children being made to sing the *Bande Mataram*, a poem identified with Hindu nationalism and revivalism. They lamented the exaltation of Hindi and the accompanying attack on Urdu, complained of Muslims being excluded from local bodies and government service, and made much of communal riots and the heavy casualties suffered by Muslims. They referred to the Wardha and the Vidya Mandir schemes and the concomitant danger to Islamic practices and the traditional system of Muslim education.

---

[39] Ziauddin Ahmad to Jinnah, 29/31 October 1945, vol. 5, SHC; Manzar-i Alam to Q.M. Isa, 15 November 1945, vol. 237, FMA; Mushirul Hasan, 'Nationalist and Separatist Trends in Aligarh', op.cit., p. 131, and fn. 93-4, p. 140.

[40] Manzar-i Alam to Q.M. Isa, 19 November 1945, vol. 237, FMA.

[41] Mushirul Hasan, op. cit., p. 131.

[42] Babar Mirza to Jinnah, 8 February 1946, vol. iv, SHC.

[43] Kalim Siddiqui, *Conflict and War in Pakistan* (London, 1972), pp. 50-1.

For some, the chief spur was the fear of Hindu domination: Jinnah's 'Two Nation' expressed the 'ideology' of the weaker Muslim salariat *vis-à-vis* the dominant high-caste Hindu salariat groups.[44] For others such as Omar Ali Siddiqi, who led the Aligarh contingent in Punjab, the battle-lines were drawn between Islam and Hinduism. Raising the spectre of a bloody civil war, he called on his audiences to save the imminent destruction of the Muslim nation.[45]

The martyrdom of Imam Husain was invoked to draw a parallel between the endangered position of Islam in 680 AD and its status in contemporary India. This was the refrain of speeches made during the annual Muharram observances. The Muslim brethren were asked, as at Allahabad in 1945, to defend Islam just as Husain and his seventy-two companions did at Karbala on the banks of the river Euphrates. 'We are Indians not Hindus. Our religion, history, traditions, civilization are separate from the Hindus. [...] This is the moment to be inspired by the life of and emulate the example set by Imam Husain. This is the moment to vote for the Muslim League candidates in the provincial elections. The need of the hour is to rescue the community from the clutches of our enemies.'[46]

The entire campaign was coloured and sustained by religious images and their representation. Shias were tempted to draw on the symbols of martyrdom associated with Ali, cousin and son-in-law of the Prophet, and his son Husain. Sunnis turned to the more fundamental tenets of Islam for legitimation and rationalisation. But their common concern was to picture a besieged and beleaguered community fighting for survival in a world dominated by unfriendly and hostile elements. Their arguments rested on the notion of two warring communities, one using its brute majority to suppress the other. 'Islam in Danger' was their war-cry. Those who agreed were men of faith. Those who dissented were threatened with hell and damnation and even with exclusion from burial in a Muslim cemetery.[47]

The dominant strain of the League campaigns is vividly described in Rahi Masoom Reza's novel *Aadha Gaon* (Half-a-Village). Gangauli village in eastern UP was a microcosm: what was said there by the fiery Aligarh students was repeated all over India, and the themes being emphasised were echoed in areas far removed from Aligarh or Gangauli. For this and other reasons, their dialogue with the rural folk, parts of which are reproduced here, is most illuminating.[48]

---

[44] Hamza Alavi, 'Pakistan and Islam: Ethnicity and Ideology', op. cit., pp. 68-60.

[45] *Dawn*, 19 December 1945.

[46] Dr Najamuddin Jafri, *Suniye Hazrat Imam Husain kya dars dete hai* (Pay heed to Imam Husain's Message), box 151, FMA.

[47] Darling, op. cit., p. 86.

[48] See Ravindra K. Jain, 'Muslim Identity in North India: A Perspective from the Hindi

'If Pakistan is not created the eighty million Muslims here will be made, and made to remain, untouchables', said the other [student]...

One of the young men proceeded to deliver a complete speech which Kammo didn't understand in the least because the young man was mentioning matters not one of which had any connection with him or with Gangauli.

'I can't believe all that, *sahib*', said Kammo after listening to the whole speech. 'Why should this Gaya Ahir, this Chikuriya or Lakhna Chamar or this Hariya Barhai become our enemies, for no reason, after Hindustan gets free? Is that what you people learn over there [Aligarh]?

'At this moment you may not be able to comprehend this fact, but that is indeed what is going to happen. Cows will be tethered in our mosques.'

'*Eh, sahib*, if all the Muslims go to Pakistan, what difference does it make if horses are tied in them or cows? It's not as if Hindus are going to say prayers there. It's a fine old bit of nonsense that we all go to Pakistan and then expect the Hindus to look after our mosques.'

At first the young men tried to persuade the peasant in front of them, but then gradually they became angry--and rightfully so ... One of them said hotly, 'Very well, but don't you complain when the Hindus come and carry off your mothers and sisters'....[49]

'You must all be aware that at the present time, throughout the country, the Muslims are engaged in a life and death struggle for existence. We live in a country where our position is no more than equivalent to that of salt in *dal* [lentils]. Once the protective shadow of the British is removed, these Hindus will devour us. That is the reason that Indian Muslims require a place where they will be able to live with honour....'

It was a very rousing speech. The brothers in Islam even interrupted from time to time to cry out 'Allah-o-Akbar' [God is great]. As a result, a large section of the traders and weavers decided that they should vote for the League as a religious duty. Haji Ghafoor tried to speak several times but the young men wouldn't allow him the opportunity.

'So you people go ahead and fuck your mother!', he fumed. In his rage he even forgot that he was in a mosque. The visitors from Aligarh took full advantage of this foul language. Even the men who were wavering became absolutely solid in their conviction.

The Haji Saheb stormed out of the mosque. The speech had been quite beyond his comprehension. He didn't even understand why all of a sudden Muslims needed a place of refuge. And where was the protective shadow of the British that these boys had made such a song and dance about? No Englishman had ever been seen in Gangauli. And why then hadn't the Hindus killed the Muslims before the British came to India? And what about the fundamental question – was life and death in the hands of God or the British and Jinnah Sahib?

Regional Novel', *Studies in Humanities and Social Sciences*, 1 November 1994, pp. 19-30.

[49] Rahi Masoom Reza, *The Feuding Families of Village Gangauli*, translated from the Hindi by Gillian Wright (Delhi: Viking, 1994), p. 236. I am grateful to the translator and the publisher for permission to reproduce excerpts from the book.

'And we'll still be just weavers. Will the Saiyids start marrying their children to weavers in Pakistan?'[50]

What emerges from this discussion is conflicting perceptions, a sense of impatience and urgency on the part of those who tried to impose their codes on Gangauli and the stout resistance to a discourse that conveyed no real meaning to, say, the Haji Saheb. There were many Gangaulis in India, with their Ghafoors and Hajis, where people did not quite understand the logic behind Muslim nationalism. Hindus and Muslims living in harmony and goodwill could not understand the ill-will and hostility that was conveyed through speeches and pamphlets. That is why one can spot so many Gangaulis on India's map where the League's message reached but failed to impress. Indeed, there were many Gangaulis where the enthusiasts from Aligarh encountered bitter opposition in their bid to win over a following.

Gangauli was a bitter pill to swallow. Yet the scale and depth of intervention from Aligarh tilted the balance in the League's favour in a few constituencies. More than 500 students 'saved the honour' of the party in Meerut and 'won laurels' for its candidate, Liaquat Ali Khan, in 'the already lost battles of his constituency'.[51] They also thwarted, so they claimed, 'the Congress-cum-Nationalist intrigues' at various polling stations in rural areas,[52] and surpassed, as the *Dawn* of 1 December 1945 commented, 'all expectations by their tireless energy and unflinching courage.' 'I have been following the wonderful work that the Aligarh boys have done', Jinnah wrote. 'You have proved what I said, that Aligarh is the arsenal of Muslim India.'[53]

[50] Rahi Masoom Reza, op. cit., p. 241.

[51] Ahmad Faziel to Jinnah, 2 December 1945, SHC; Ikramullah, *Huseyn Shaheed Suhrawardy*, pp. 46-7.

[52] Manzar-i Alam to Qazi Isa, 4 December 1945, vol. 237, FMA.

[53] Jinnah to Zahid Husain, 5 December 1945, SHC. The following details, based on the *Dawn* newspaper of November-December 1945, illustrate the extent of Aligarh's involvement in the elections:

1 December: Jinnah met two leading Aligarh students to discuss the election strategy;
3 December: Aligarh students reached Hardoi on 29 November;
9 December: reported decision to send students to 9 districts in UP;
9 December: Mufti Mohammad Idris, who accompanied the deputation to Bareilly, gave a Quranic interpretation of the Pakistan movement;
11 December: First batch of students reached Delhi *en route* to Lahore;
16 December: Addressed public meetings in Rohtak, Sargodha and Karnal;
25 December: Reported the arrival of 50 students in 3 batches;
26 December: Group led by Qadiri reached Chandausi in Moradabad district;
29 December: Members of the University League reached Lahore, addressed meetings and set up offices at Mamdot, Ferozepur, Mardan; Qadiri, Moinul Haq, the historian, and other teaching members reached Budaun.

Some on the Aligarh campus challenged the underpinnings of the League ideology and tried in vain to counter its activities. Their protests were drowned by the thunderous applause with which Jinnah was greeted during his frequent forays into Aligarh. Their criticism was blunted by the more vociferous League spokesmen in the teaching faculty. In effect, Aligarh pronounced in favour of political separatism and an independent 'Muslim personality', divorced from its history, culture, and traditions. Most voted for a traditionalist-fundamentalist theocracy, an imaginary haven for Muslims.

The decision was fraught with serious consequences for a premier educational institution, as also for the future of Indian Islam. But then, who could explain to the students and teachers that their fears were exaggerated and that their fanciful theories rested on questionable assumptions? There was a time when liberal, socialist and anti-colonial sentiments gripped the campus. Photographs of Mustafa Kemal, hero of the Turkish revolution, Jawaharlal Nehru, Marx and Lenin formed a part of the ideological furniture of hostel rooms. There had been a time when people had turned to an Ajmal Khan or Ansari for political inspiration, but no longer. Public life lacked men of such charisma, stature and political sagacity. How, then, were the Aligarh students to know that religious fervour was blurring their vision – that for the millions who would need to stay behind in India, Pakistan would divide families and friends and destroy the socio-cultural fabric built over centuries of close relationships?[54]

Some League activists in Aligarh and elsewhere discovered, belatedly, that all that glitters is not gold, that the architects of Pakistan had different ideas and that a modern nation-state could not be modelled on medieval theocracies or run on strictly religious lines.[55] Confronted with Hindu-Muslim rioting and the appalling misery of innocent people, they sought to argue that religio-political conflicts, howsoever endemic they might have appeared in the India of the 1940s, should be resolved through means other than secession, separation or partition. But it was too late to change the course of events. Great numbers of people had already set out on the dangerously long trek to the imagined *dar al-Islam*. Many had already lost their lives before reaching their destination.

Kammo, Haji Ghafoor Ansari and Phunnan Miyan in Gangauli village had sensed the impending danger long before. The Haji had exhorted the Aligarh boys: 'No Miyan, I'm an illiterate peasant. But I think that there's

---

According to Khalid bin Sayeed, 'in one critical two-week period some 1,500 students addressed an estimated 7,000,000 Punjabis.' *Politics in Pakistan*, p. 13.

[54] Jameel Jalibi, *Pakistan: The Identity of Culture* (Delhi: Alpha & Alpha, reprint, n.d.).

[55] Jahan Ara Shahnawaz, *Father and Daughter: A Political Biography* (Lahore: Nigarishaat, 1971), pp. 301-2.

not the slightest need to make Pakistan-*Akistan* for the sake of our prayers. Lord God Almighty said quite clearly, "*Eh*, my Prophet. Tell these people that I am with people of the Faith." And someone was saying that this Jinnah of yours doesn't say his prayers.'[56] Phunnan Miyan shared these words of wisdom, adding:

'Is there true Islam anywhere that you can have an Islamic government? *Eh, bhai* [brother], our forefathers' graves are here, our *tazia* platforms are here, our fields and homes are here. I'm not an idiot to be taken in by your "Long live Pakistan".[...]

'You're talking as if all the Hindus were murderers waiting to slaughter us. *Arre*, Thakur Kunwarpal Singh was a Hindu. Jhinguriya is a Hindu. *Eh, bhai*, and isn't that Parusaram-*va* a Hindu? When the Sunnis in the town started doing *haramzadgi* [behaving like a bastard], saying that we won't let the bier of Hazrat Ali be carried in procession because the Shias curse our Caliphs, didn't Parusaram-*va* come and raise such hell that the bier was carried? Your Jinnah Sahib didn't come to help us lift our bier.'[57]

II

At a conference in London in 1967, M.A.H. Ispahani boasted how after achieving their homeland Muslims received 'all the encouragement and opportunity to pull themselves up by the bootstraps and they did.' Listing their achievements in industry, banking and insurance, he concluded:

The Hindu *bania* and the foreigner are no longer in a position to monopolise our economic life, and this is the fruit of the freedom which we won in the form of our separate state. Muslims, having been afforded the opportunity, have fully availed themselves of it and proved their worth. They have also given the lie to the notion that had been spread by hostile elements that Pakistan would not prove to be economically viable. Need I say anything more?[58]

Yes, Mr Ispahani, those directly affected by partition had a lot more to say. It is no doubt true that tangible material benefits accrued to some of the migrants, chiefly from among the 2 million Urdu-speaking refugees (still categorised as *muhajirs*) from UP and Bihar, many of whom monopolised the army, civil service and the professions.[59] The grand bourgeoisie

[56] Rahi Masoom Reza, op. cit., p. 240.

[57] Ibid., p. 149.

[58] M.A.H. Ispahani, 'Factors Leading to the Partition of India', in Philips and Wainwright (eds), *Partition of India*, p. 359; see also Firoz Khan Noon, *From Memory*, p. 216.

[59] There are, of course, varying estimates. According to the 1951 *Census of Pakistan*, the number of refugees by that year exceeded 7.2 million; 6.5 million flowed into West Pakistan and 0.7 million to East Pakistan. The refugees made up 26.1 per cent of the population in West Punjab, 55 per cent in Karachi, 49 per cent in Multan, and 43 per cent in Lahore. Quoted in Gankovsky and Gordon-Polonskaya, *History of Pakistan*, p. 107.

of West Pakistan, originally from Gujarat and Maharashtra, reaped the rewards of supporting the Pakistan demand. People like Habib Ibrahim Rahimtoola, president of the Bombay provincial Muslim Chamber of Commerce, and Ispahani himself, director of his own and other companies, held key diplomatic positions in London and Washington. The great landlords of Punjab and Sind also flourished. Their jealously guarded estates remained intact; in fact, in accordance with the 1950 Act passed in West Punjab, a tenant could be evicted if found guilty of reading out at a public or private meeting the Punjab Muslim League Manifesto of 1944, drafted by Danial Latifi and others. The draft was blasphemous because it advocated land reforms.[60] The nexus of the landowners with the bureaucratic and military establishment enabled them to retain their hegemony in the countryside.

It would be simple enough if the Pakistan story began or ended with the improved fortunes of certain individuals and groups. But that is not so. One must record the immediate and long-term impact on the silent majority, uprooted from home and field and driven by sheer fear of death to seek safety across a line they had neither drawn nor desired. They speak loud and clear through Saadat Hasan Manto's characters.[61] They convey to us how blissfully unaware they were of the deals taking place in Delhi, of Mountbatten's ultimatum that if he did not hear from Jinnah by midnight the Partition Plan would come into effect *in any case*. Fourteen hours to decide the destiny of a nation!

There must also be a place for the harrowing experiences of countless Zahids who boarded the train that would take them to the realisation of their dreams, but of whom not a man, woman or child survived the journey.[62] The narrative must also incorporate the symbolic significance of the crumbling houses in Hasanpur or Gangauli. *Havelis* collapsed and occupants went away, but memories lingered – as also did the sense of loss and deprivation. Those who left were part of the *biradari*; their absence was bemoaned not by one or the other denominational group but by the whole community. The passing of an era did not change everything everywhere. Take Hasanpur: the shadow of litigation to abolish landlordism hung over the estate, yet it did not dampen the enthusiasm of the rural people to welcome those who chose to return to their villages after partition. 'It seemed time had not really moved towards the inevitable end.'[63]

---

[60] Ibid., chapter 7; Kochanek, *Interest Group and Development: Business and Politics in Pakistan*, op. cit.

[61] *Another Lonely Voice: The Life and Works of Saadat Hasan Manto*. Introduction by Leslie A. Fleming (Lahore: Vanguard, 1985), pp. 77-86.

[62] Attia Hosain, *Sunlight on a Broken Column*.

[63] Ibid., p. 299.

The Pakistan story has many facets, but it is surely incomplete without the anguish of those devotees who thought that destiny was taking them far away from the shrines of Nizamuddin Auliya or Muinuddin Chishti – important symbols of a specifically Indian Muslim culture – the *dargahs* of Rudauli, Kakori, Bansa Sharif and Dewa Sharif, the great *imambaras* of Lucknow, Jaunpur and Matiya Burj, and the sites of pilgrimage dotted on India's map.[64] Pakistan would no doubt have its share of mosques, *imambaras* and *dargahs*, but there was no shrine more sacred than that of *Gharib-Nawaz* in Ajmer, no counterparts to the splendid *imambaras* of Lucknow, symbolising the high noon of Nawabi rule in Awadh. The pilgrims knew this; year after year they approached the Indian and Pakistani governments for permission to attend the annual congregation (*urs*) at the shrines of venerable Chishti saints buried in Delhi, Fatehpur Sikri and Ajmer. Between 1955 and February 1959, at least 3,973 'officially-sponsored' individuals performed pilgrimage. Many more came on their own, including 3,925 devotees who travelled to the shrine at Ajmer in 1958-9.[65] Pakistan's existence had not lessened their devotion.

One of Rahi Masoom Reza's characters is Saddan, who migrated to Pakistan. But he still claimed to be the same Syed Saadatul Hasnain Zaidi of Gangauli. How could Gangauli be another country! 'All these faces, plants and trees, these ponds and this indigo godown, these *imambaras* and *tazias* [replicas of Husain's tomb] ... and this Karbala, and these bundles of *marsiyas* [elegies] wrapped in red cloth, lying on pulpits ... all these things could only belong to his own village.' In Pakistan he would miss the *majalis* [Shia congregations during the month of Muharram] of Abbu Miyan and Maulvi Bedar in Gangauli, remember Husain Haidar Miyan's *soz* (dirge) recitations and Masshu-bhai's *nauhas* (a short chanted lament accompanied by breast-beating). 'These memories were of no particular importance, they were extremely foolish memories, but still Saddan embraced each one of them again and again and wept. He yearned for Gangauli ....'[66]

One must also not consciously neglect, like most standard histories of partition, the woes of divided families, the deepening nostalgia for places people lived in for generations and forcibly abandoned, the misery of

[64] Claudia Liebeskind, 'Sufi leadership and "Modernization" in South Asia since 1800', unpubl. Ph.D. thesis, University of London, 1995. See Ziyaud-Din A. Desai, *Centres of Learning in India* (Delhi: Publications Division, 1968), and the scholarly study edited by Christian W. Troll, *Muslim Shrines in India* (Delhi: OUP, 1992).

[65] Jawaharlal Nehru informed the Lok Sabha on 1 September 1955 that 634 devotees (excluding individuals) from Pakistan visited India from 1 January to 15 August 1955. *Lok Sabha Debates*, vol. 5, part 1, 1955, pp. 4320-1. 18 December 1957, 3 March 1959, *Lok Sabha Debates*, vols. 10 and 69, pp. 6076, 3932. It was important too that the number of Hindu and Sikh pilgrims from India to Pakistan from 1955 to 1957 was 2,506.

[66] Rahi Masoom Reza, op. cit., pp. 321, 322.

parting from friends and neighbours. Abdul Qaiyum, who quit the Congress to join the League in 1945, was touched by the sight of friends departing with their families and their moveable property, from a land where they had lived for generations and to which they were devoted. He was distressed to bid farewell to friends with whom he worked for years.[67]

Tears began to flow, wrote a distraught eye-witness of the killings in East Bengal during 1946-7, when she realised that

....the part of Bengal which had been my home was no longer my home. It was a foreign land and I was not very safe in those difficult days.[...] I was more angry than sorry and vowed never to enter the country and see the people who tore me away from my home. The underlying feeling was that we were being driven from our own country. Bengalis are first and foremost Bengalis – then Indian. We were angry with both Nehru and Jinnah for not handling the situation properly.[68]

Mussarat Husain Zuberi, senior civil servant in the communications ministry, was not angry but deeply anguished:

As I was leaving Delhi with its centuries-old hallowed memories of Muslim triumphs, its agonised shameless defeats and dishonour and the phoenix-like birth from its ashes of a new Muslim dominion...I decided to pay a farewell visit to the monuments which enshrined the souls and bodies of those who had marched under their own banner to make us at least a shadow of theirs. They were part of me, my inherited leanings, my history, my culture, part of being known and unknown, conscious and visible.[69]

Manto went to Pakistan in January 1948. He was filled with sorrow when he left Bombay, where he had spent much of his working life. He was not tied to the city for historical, cultural or intellectual reasons, but deeply attached to it because it 'had asked me no questions. It had taken me to its generous bosom, me, a man rejected by his family, a gypsy by temperament.' His Hindu and Muslim friends lived in Bombay and encouraged his creative genius. He earned from a few hundred to several thousand rupees – and spent it all. He married in Bombay. His first two children were born there. 'I was in love with Bombay. I still am.'[70] Manto's agony or *karb* and sense of loss troubled the family of Dwarkada Prashad, uncle of Prakash Tandon:

---

[67] Abdul Qaiyum Khan, 'Reflections on some of the causes of the Partition of the Indo-Pakistan subcontinent', in Philips and Wainwright (eds), *Partition of India*, p. 380.

[68] 'The Memsahib I could never be', H. Ghoshal papers, CSAS.

[69] Mussarat Husain Zuberi, *Voyage Through History*, vol. 1 (Karachi: Hamdard Foundation Press, 1984), p. 103.

[70] Saadat Hasan Manto, 'Not of Blessed Memory', *Annual of Urdu Studies*, 4, 1984, pp. 88-9.

As dawn was breaking, they caught the last view of Gujrat through the shisham trees by the road; a view they had so often seen when going to the river Chenab at *Besakhi.* They looked at the weathered dark brown mass of the city rising as a flat-top cone. My aunt's ancestral house was in the highest *mohalla* inside the fortress, and she could see almost the spot where twenty-seven years ago her palanquin had descended the narrow lanes to our old house inside the Kalri Gate. She wondered what would happen to her house, to her cupboards and trunks full of clothes, linen and utensils, and above all to the buffalo and its calf that she had left tied in the yard.[...] As the truck passed the barrier into 'India', they looked back at Pakistan, their homeland which did not want them.

Today we have no one left in Gujrat. All the Hindus came away at partition. It is strange to think that in all the land between Ravi and Chenab, from Chenab to Jhelum, from Jhelum to Indus, in the foothills and in the plain down to Punjab, where the five rivers eventually merge, land which had been the home of our *biradaris* since the dawn of history, there is no one left of our kind.[71]

The first generation of Urdu poets and writers, many of whom performed the *hijrat* from UP and Bihar, raised a wide range of issues.[72] To which country did they belong? Where did their cultural roots lie? Was their newly-acquired nationality more vital than their larger identity as a civilisation? What would be the cultural symbols of their new identity? Should they take pride in their language, their religion or their regional identity? How would they strike a symbiotic balance between contending identities in a society where religious sensitivity was so greatly heightened by the Pakistan movement? What were their links with their erstwhile homeland? Were these to be severed or renewed after the Indian and Pakistani governments had resolved their differences?

There were no straightforward answers. There were just a few preliminary explorations. Compare the poet Josh Malihabadi's autobiographical reflections with some other contemporary writings. He lived in Lucknow, edited the Urdu journal *Ajkal* (1948-55) in Delhi, and left for Pakistan in 1956 against the advice of his numerous friends and admirers, including

[71] Prakash Tandon, *Punjab Century, 1857-1947* (London: Chatto and Windus, 1961), pp. 246-7, 249; Darling, op.cit.; G.D. Khosla, *Stern Reckoning: A survey of the events leading up to and following the partition of India* (Delhi: OUP, 1989); S.K. Kirpalani, *Fifty years with the British* (Hyderabad: Orient Longman, 1993); M.S. Randhawa, *Out of the Ashes: An account of the rehabilitation of refugees from West Pakistan in rural areas of Punjab* (Bombay, n.d.), pp. 219-20; Sri Prakasa, *Pakistan: Birth and Early Days* (Meerut: Meenakshi Prakashan, 1965); D.F. Karaka, *Betrayal in India,* op. cit., chapters 1-2; Khushwant Singh, *Train to Pakistan* (Delhi: Ravi Dayal, 1990 reprint); J. Nanda, *Pakistan Uprooted: A Survey of the Punjab Riots and rehabilitation Problems* (Bombay: Hindi Kitab, 1948); and the essays of Alok Rai, Tapati Chakravarty, S.S. Hans and N.K. Jain in Gupta (ed.), *Myth and Reality,* op. cit.

[72] Aijaz Ahmad has hinted at some of these themes in *In the Mirror of Urdu* (Shimla: Indian Institute of Advanced Study, 1993). For a detailed discussion, see Talbot, *Freedom's City,* op.cit., for the 'emotional and psychological impact of Partition'.

Jawaharlal Nehru and Abul Kalam Azad.[73] Compare, too, Qurratulain Hyder's short novel *Housing Society* with Mohammad Ahsan Faruqi's *Sangam* (Confluence).[74] Or her first novel *Mere bhi Sanam Khane* with the works of Intizar Husain, perhaps one of the most perceptive creative writers of Pakistan.[75]

Mere bhi Sanam Khane, published in 1947, portrays how the sparks of partition blew up the pathways of a composite culture, leaving behind a yawning gap of burning dust. Intizar Husain's story *Ek bin-likhi Razmiya* (An Unwritten Epic), on the other hand, succeeds in gathering a whole era within its fold by presenting partition and Hindu-Muslim violence against a 'fair-sized social and political backdrop.'[76] Some of his other works reflect the way an ongoing cultural process was stalled in 'a very unnatural way' by a few Muslims and Hindus who, with their puritan frame of mind, contributed to the tragedy that afflicted the subcontinent.

What, according to Intizar Husain, was the cultural process all about? For one, it was not denominational. The 'Indian-Muslim culture' did not bear a religious stamp. It had its own unique history and individuality, and was, above all, distinctively *Indian* and refreshingly different from the cultural mores and paradigms of Muslim countries. Intizar Husain is proud of being a product of such a cultural tradition, one 'which has shaped the history of which I am a part'. Muslims came to Hindustan and formed close and indissoluble ties with its soil. 'Indian Muslim culture is that creative amalgam which came about in response to the intellectual and emotional climate that was here ... the feel of its seasons ... these ties with the land. Much in it is Indian and much was brought from outside.'[77]

Cultural alienation, combined with nostalgia, also struck 'A Muslim' from Delhi who migrated to Dacca, 'a strange land'. He wrote to a

---

[73] Josh Malihabadi,*Yadon ki Barat* (Delhi: Shaan-i Hind Publishers, 1992 enlarged edition). Shabbir Hasan Khan 'Josh' (1898-1982) was one of the leading revolutionary poets. It is interesting that in May 1948 Josh asked for a raise in his salary mentioning, among other things, his contribution to 'progressive tendencies in Indian literarure'. Moreover, he wrote, 'I have been a fearless soldier in the field of India's freedom. I need not quote many names to bear testimony to this statement but will refer to some of my friends and admirers like Pandit Jawaharlal Nehru, Maulana Abul Kalam Azad, Sir Tej Bahadur Sapru, Mrs Sarojini Naidu and Mr Asaf Ali.' Quoted in Jagan Nath Azad, 'Josh Sahib', *Ajkal* (Delhi: Publications Division), April 1995, p. 28.

[74] *Pathjhar ki Aawaz* (Delhi: Maktaba-i Jamia, 1965). She is the daughter of Sajjad Hyder Yaldaram, an Aligarh 'Old Boy', newspaper editor and a leading short story writer. For a short time Qurratulain Hyder (b. 1927) went over to Pakistan but returned to India in 1960.

[75] Muhammad Umar Memon, 'Partition Literature: A Study of Intizar Husain', *Modern Asian Studies*, 14, 3, 1990, p. 377.

[76] Ibid., pp. 402-3; and his 'A Letter from India' in Bhalla (ed.), *Stories About the Partition of India*, vol. 1. For Qurratulain Hyder, see Ali Jawad Zaidi, *History of Urdu Literature*, p. 408.

[77] Interview, *Journal of South Asian Literature*, 18, 2, summer/fall 1983, p. 167.

Lucknawi friend that he joined the Pakistan civil service not because of religio-communal considerations but because of Hindu-Muslim rioting in his locality. But he wondered, in retrospect, if it made sense to live in Dacca amid people with whom he had so little in common and whose manners, customs, language, culture, diet and dress were 'totally different from ours'. He was perturbed that non-Bengalis were shabbily treated by their own co-religionists as intruders and exploiters. Most Bengalis believed that the Punjabi had 'stepped into the shoes of the outgoing masters.'[78]

Living in Karachi, Mohammad Ahsan Faruqi captures the same mood and sums up the dilemma of those *muhajirin* who migrated to Pakistan from northern, central and western parts of India. He wonders how a country created for the Muslims could be so hostile to the *muhajirin*. Ibn Muslim, the central character in the novel *Sangam*, is attracted to Pakistan by the dream of Islamic brotherhood which he sees in Iqbal's poetry and in the actions of Jinnah. But his enthusiasm is dampened when he and others like him are treated as intruders, as aliens, whom 'everyone is bent upon swallowing'. 'The Quaid-i-Azam died and so did his party. And now there is a dispute between the English and Islamic concepts of the nation, and it is we who are the sufferers.'[79]

The *muhajirin* were drawn from diverse socio-economic back-grounds. Their experiences in Pakistan were mixed. Some achieved high levels of affluence – the fortunes of others did not change so dramatically – yet they all had a common refrain in their daily conversations, in mosques, *dargahs* and *imambaras*, the undying memories of their homeland and the consequent nostalgia. This was true of the troubled correspondent from Dacca, the bureaucrat in the communications ministry, the writer Faruqi and the novelist Ahmed Ali,[80] who made this poignant comment:

---

[78] *Hindustan Times*, 19 September 1947.

[79] Munibur Rahman, 'Political Novels in India', *Contributions to Asian Studies*, 6, p. 150.

[80] Perhaps, on reaching the land designated 'Pakistan', people like Ahmed Ali would have discreetly recited the following lament of Mir Taqi Mir, the great Urdu poet, who could not bear to be away from Delhi even for a short while:

> Why do you mock at me and ask yourselves
> Where in the world I come from, easterners?
> There was a city, famed throughout the world,
> Where dwelt the chosen spirits of the age:
> Delhi its name, fairest among the fair.
> Fate looted it and laid it desolate,
> And to that ravaged city I belong.

Ralph Russell and Khurshidul Islam, *Three Mughal Poets: Mir, Mir Sauda, Mir Hasan* (London: Geo. Allen and Unwin, 1969), p. 260.

Seldom is one allowed to see a pageant of history whirl past, and partake in it too. Ever since becoming the capital in the early thirteenth century, imbibing knowledge and ideas and imparting cultures, becoming homogeneous and cosmopolitan in spite of the origins and ethnicity of its rulers and inhabitants, it [Delhi] had remained the embodiment of a whole culture, free of the creedal ghosts and apparitions that haunt some of modern India's critics and bibliographers chased by the dead souls of biased historians of yesterday.[81]

Ahmed Ali could not return to Delhi from Nanking where he was on a deputation from the government of undivided India. He thus concluded an interview on a highly melancholy note. The poet he cited was the irrepressible Mir Taqi Mir (1772-1849), one of the great love poets of world literature:

> What matters it, O breeze,
> If now has come the spring
> When I have lost them both
> The garden and my nest?[82]

Ahmed Ali did not return to the land he loved, and died in 1994.

For the gentlemen living in Dacca or Karachi the cultural journey from Delhi was disconcerting. But for the millions in India and Pakistan the professed ideology of the nation-state itself had no great relevance or immediacy. Take the Muslim weavers of Panipat. They were not fascinated by Pakistan, which they neither understood nor approved of, except as a remote place where Muslims would go, as on a pilgrimage. On the other hand, the few white-collar government employees left for Pakistan hoping to secure rapid promotions but not to set up permanent homes there.[83] Did it really matter to the Mymensingh peasants and the Kanpur mill-workers whether they were to be physically located in 'India' or in 'Pakistan'? What of the employees of the East India Railway in Kanpur who, having opted for Pakistan, subsequently changed their minds?[84] Or the 8,000 government servants who, after provisionally opting for Pakistan, finally returned to their homes in India in March 1948?[85] Or Yaqub Ali, an assistant-engineer in Nadia district? He would not have left but for the fact that his family was 'eyed in silent menace' by his Hindu neighbours. So when politicians in Lutyens's Delhi resolved to partition India and Bengal, Yaqub collected 300 rupees, boarded the

---

[81] *Twilight in Delhi* (Delhi: OUP, 1991), p. viii, and Ahmad Sohail, 'Urdu Afsane ka Nostalgia', *Zehn-i Jadid* (Delhi: Urdu Quarterly), 1994.

[82] William Dalrymple, *City of Djinns: A Year in Delhi* (Delhi: Harper Collins, 1993), p. 65.

[83] Abbas, *I am not an Island*, p. 295.

[84] *Hindustan Times*, 8 October 1947.

[85] Nehru's note to Minister of Home Affairs, 16 March 1948, Gopal (ed.), *SWJN*, second series, vol. 5 p. 458.

train to Calcutta to buy air tickets, and returned to Dacca to fetch his family and his possessions.[86]

Most people, Hindus, Muslims and Sikhs alike, were largely unconcerned with the newly-created geographical entities or indifferent to them. They were needlessly caught up in the cross-fire of religious hatred. Some were driven out of their homes; others drifted from one place to another out of fear, panic and a sense of hopelessness. Most were hapless victims of a triangular game plan, worked out by the British, the Congress and the League without care or consideration for a vast number of people who were committed neither to a Hindu homeland nor to an imaginary *dar-al Islam*. They had no destination to reach, no mirage to pursue. They were unclear whether Lahore or Gurdaspur would be in India or Pakistan. This was the unmistakable message in Bhisham Sahni's story.[87] They did not know whether Gangauli or Hasanpur would be in Gandhi's India or Jinnah's Pakistan.

In fact, 'India' and 'Pakistan' were mere territorial abstractions to people who had no sense of the newly-demarcated frontiers, and little or no knowledge of how Mountbatten's Plan or the Radcliffe Award would change the destinies of millions and tear them apart from their familiar social and cultural moorings. 'The English have flung away their Raj like a bundle of old straw', an angry peasant told Malcolm Darling, 'and we have been chopped in pieces like butcher's meat.'[88] This was a telling comment by a 'subaltern' on the meaning attached to the Pakistan movement.

Imagine the plight of Hindus and Muslims in Malda district. Between 12 and 15 August 1947 it was unclear where it would finally go, to East Pakistan or to India. Up till 14 August the Pakistan flag fluttered over the collectorate, but three days later the district, now reduced to ten pre-partition *thanas*, went to India. It pleased Asok Mitra, the newly-

---

[86] Diary, p. 2, Mss. Eur. file no. C/188/8, A.J. Dash papers, IOL.

[87] 'The decision about the creation of Pakistan had just been announced and people were indulging in all kinds of surmises about the pattern of life that would emerge. But no one's imagination could go very far. The Sardarji sitting in front of me repeatedly asked me whether I thought Mr Jinnah would continue to live in Bombay after the creation of Pakistan or whether he would resettle in Pakistan. Each time my answer would be the same, "Why should he leave Bombay? I think he'll continue to live in Bombay and continue visiting Pakistan." Similar guesses were being made about the towns of Lahore and Gurdaspur too, and no one knew which town would fall to the share of India and which to Pakistan. People gossiped and laughed in much the same way as before. Some were abandoning their homes for good, while others made fun of them. No one knew which step would prove to be the right one. Some people deplored the creation of Pakistan, others rejoiced over the achievement of independence. Some places were being torn by riots, others were busy celebrating Independence ...' Bhisham Sahni, 'We Have Arrived in Amritsar' in Stephen Alter and Vimal Dissanayake (eds), *The Penguin Book of Modern Indian Short Stories* (Delhi: Penguin Books India, 1989), pp. 180-7.

[88] Darling, op. cit., p. 307; see also Kirpalani, op.cit.

appointed district magistrate, to discover that very few of the Muslim staff in the collectorate had opted for Pakistan.[89]

We are told that in those days of inglorious uncertainties the rank and file of the League hoped against hope for a last-minute confederation or a Congress-League agreement that would rule out the division of the country.[90] Whether this is true or not, expectations of what partition would bring were curiously mixed. Some longed for Lahore's inclusion in India; others wished that the partition line in Punjab would be drawn below Delhi. 'For millions of people like myself', wrote Begum Shaista Ikramullah, 'to whom Delhi was synonomous with Muslim culture, a Pakistan without Delhi was a body without heart.'[91] She 'never even dreamt' that she would have to leave the city which she loved in its every mood. The frontiers of Pakistan had not been defined and it never occurred to her that Delhi would not be included within it:

How sure we were that Delhi was ours and would come to us can best be illustrated by this incident. We were having a picnic on the terrace at Humayun's tomb when my sister-in-law remarked: 'Do you think you will get Delhi if Pakistan is established?' My husband replied pointing to the domed and turreted skyline of Delhi: 'Look at it – whom do you think it seems to belong to?' and Dina could not deny that the essentially Muslim character of its architecture seemed to proclaim that Delhi belonged to the Muslims. And so it did, in every way, except population. No, that is not true, even by counting the heads it would have been ours, had the dividing line come below and not above Delhi. But by dividing Punjab, our overall majority was lost, so we lost Delhi. And today its mosques and minarets join the mosques and minarets of Cordova and Grenada in saying: The descendants of Arabs, they were, those who created me. I stand here, a memorial to their vanished glory.[92]

Pakistan was won, but people on both sides of the fence were tormented by gruesome killings, by the irreparable loss of friends and families and by the scale and magnitude of an epic tragedy. There were memories on both sides of living in close proximity with friends and neighbours, of a shared cultural and intellectual heritage, and of fighting together for independence and raising the banner of revolt against colonial rule. The birth of Pakistan, a prized trophy for some, destroyed Iqbal's melodious lyric of syncretic nationalism – *Naya Shivala* (New Temple) – once the ideal of patriots and freedom-fighters. It severed or fragmented

[89] Asok Mitra, *The New India, 1948-1955: Memoirs of an Indian Civil Servant* (Bombay: Popular Prakashan, 1991), p. 2.

[90] Ikramullah, *Huseyn Shaheed Suhrawardy*, p. 51.

[91] Ibid., p. 59. For a different perspective, see Kirpalani, op.cit., p. 307.

[92] Begum Shaista S. Ikramullah, *From Purdah to Parliament* (London: The Crescent Press, 1963), pp. 135-6. For Ahmed Ali's swimming 'through great oceans of nostalgia before finally coming ashore on a strand of melancholy', see Dalrymple, op. cit., p. 64; Masroor, *Shadow of Time*, pp. 213-14.

cultural ties and undermined a vibrant, composite intellectual tradition. The birth of freedom on that elevated day – 14 August for Pakistan and 15 August for India – 'did not bring India any such ennobling benediction. On the contrary, the country was shaken by a volcanic eruption.'[93] There was not much to celebrate at the fateful midnight hour or at the dawn of independence.

> This is not that long-looked-for break of day
> Not that clear dawn in quest of which those comrades
> Set out, believing that in heaven's wide void
> Somewhere must be the star's last halting place
> Somewhere the verge of night's slow-washing tide,
> Somewhere an anchorage for the ship of heartache.[94]

The Raja of Mahmudabad, who had devoted many years fighting for his 'Islamic state', was an unhappy man. He recalled 'the general sense of gloom and despondency that pervaded the two newly-created nation states. Instead of the joy and expectancy which should have been ours after these years of struggle there were only premonitions of impending conflicts and a promise of future struggle.'[95] The Raja hurried to Pakistan, leaving behind vast estates, his wife the Rani of Billehra, his young son, and his dear brother Maharajkumar Mohammad Amir Hyder Khan. The Baradari in Qaiser Bagh, where his father had hosted the Lucknow Congress in December 1916, was still there to remind citizens of its nationalist associations. But the Mahmudabad House nearby, with dusty portraits of Motilal Nehru, Tej Bahadur Sapru and Sarojini Naidu, looked desolate. The beautiful but crumbling fort and *imambaras* at Mahmudabad in Sitapur district were mostly abandoned. They came alive only during the ten days of Muharram, when the Raja's son, brother and his family travelled to Mahmudabad to mourn the martyrdom of Imam Husain.

For Intizar Husain partition was 'a complex and convoluted human tragedy'. He tried to comprehend, in the light of India's rich ancient and medieval history, how the 'new man' – cruel, violent and ruthless – appeared on the scene in 1947. 'How and why did this occur? What historical process gave rise to it? And what has happened to that history which, for example, had produced the Buddha? What new era of history had been ushered in? Or is it that mankind is such a creature who can build a movement over centuries, can construct diverse philosophies, but when the crisis comes, when some critical moment occurs, his animal emerges

---

[93] Chattopadhyaya, *Inner Recesses Outer Spaces*, p. 306.

[94] V.G. Kiernan (ed.), *Poems by Faiz* (London, 1971), p. 123.

[95] The Raja of Mahmudabad, 'Some Memories', in Philips and Wainwright (eds), *Partition of India*, p. 389.

from within to overwhelm him?'[96] Many of his stories reflect isolation, uncertainty, deprivation, grief, and a sense of being cut off from a better and richer past – just the kind of experience, in short, that partition might be expected to create.[97]

Jameel Jalibi, a former vice-chancellor of Karachi University, lamented how the Indo-Muslim cultural heritage, the pride of the *muhajirin*, had ended at the Wagah border and how access to it was controlled by passports and visas. 'This is where our national tragedy begins.' He argued: 'We cannot afford to commit the error of excluding from our cultural history the cultural heritage that has accrued to us as the accumulation of a thousand years of Indo-Muslim culture. Can we be daring enough to begin our new history with 1947 as a turning point where we turned our back on this heritage because of geographical demarcation and a new-born sense of statehood?'[98] Ahmed Ali, who 'never opted for Pakistan', identified himself with the civilisation of Delhi that came into being through the mingling of two different cultures, Hindu and Muslim. 'That civilization flourished for one thousand years undisturbed until certain people came along and denied that great mingling had taken place.'[99] His poignant introductory comment in his novel, which was edited out because it was based in Delhi, the 'forbidden' city across the border, sums up the predicament of a generation which was decidedly unsure of its cultural and intellectual moorings.[100]

So which country did Ahmed Ali, Attia Hosain, Faiz Ahmad Faiz, Josh Malihabadi, Sajjad Zaheer or Manto belong to? India or Pakistan? Manto for one tried in vain to 'separate India from Pakistan and Pakistan from India.' He asked himself: 'Will Pakistani literature be different – and

[96] Intizar Husain, op.cit., p. 161; see also the comment of N.S. Khan, a Lahore-based publisher: 'The history we read in school', he observed in his introductory note to the novel *The Heart Divided* by Mumtaz Shah Nawaz, 'had a broader canvas. It did not start for instance with the invasion of India by the Muslims, and definitely not just with the movement for Pakistan, and in that we were a fortunate generation with a sense of our own history that included the time span, the colour, the dynamism, and the tolerance that was also India. We were products of a variety of cultures, religions, and histories, and we were taught to be proud of it. I was also fortunate that I came from a house where, even though the family was from what is now India, India as a separate country, and Hindus as a separate people, was never mentioned. Delhi was just another city (like Karachi was), a city in which my grandmother lived, and from where she came to see us every year.' *The Heart Divided*, p. vi.

[97] Francis W. Pritchett, 'Narrative Modes in Intizar Husain's Short Stories', op. cit., p. 192.

[98] Jameel Jalibi, op. cit., p. 8. And the comment of A.K. Brohi: 'Literature in Pakistan is merely the product of influences which are unconnected with Pakistan, in the sense that they are, regarded historically, older than the Pakistan-idea itself. Sanskrit, Hindi, Arabic, Persian appear to have moulded the intellectual thought-currents as even the poetry of a purely lyrical type in India .... There is no originality of any kind which may be regarded as *our literature* [emphasis added].' Brohi, *An Adventure in Self-Expression*, p. 427.

[99] Dalrymple, op. cit., p. 63.

[100] *Twilight in Delhi*, op. cit.

if so, how? To whom will now belong what had been written in undivided India? Will that be partitioned too?' He continued:

What my mind could not resolve was the question: what country we belong to now, India or Pakistan? And whose blood was it that was being so mercilessly shed every day? And the bones of the dead, stripped of the flesh of religion, were they being burned or buried?[...]

Everyone seemed to be regressing. Only death and carnage seemed to be proceeding ahead. A terrible chapter of blood and tears was being added to history, a chapter without precedent.

India was free. Pakistan was free from the moment of its birth, but in both states man's enslavement continued: by prejudice, by religious fanaticism, by savagery.

The uppermost question in Manto's mind was: 'Were we really free?' Both Hindus and Muslims were being slaughtered. Why? There were different answers: the Indian answer, the Pakistani answer, the British answer. Surely 'every question had an answer, but when you tried to unravel the truth, you were left groping.'[101] And there was no answer.

Manto's postscript on a colossal human tragedy must not be overlooked by social scientists attempting to appreciate and analyse the partition movement. His anguish and dilemma were not of an individual alone, but were shared by the silent majority on both sides of the fence, including those 1,000 persons who, after eighteen months of separation, met at the Husainiwala customs barrier in February 1949. They did not pull out daggers and swords but 'affectionately greeted and embraced one another with tears rolling down their cheeks'.[102] Their sentiments can neither be reflected in the elegant exchanges between the viceroy and secretary of state nor in the unlovely confabulations between the Congress and the League managers.

III

'Aaj Shabbir pe kya alam-i tanhai hai '

Mir Anis (1802-75)

'What a world of loneliness lies upon Shabbir [Imam Husain] this day!' Everyone who heard these words in Gangauli started crying and lamenting. They did so to mourn Imam Husain's martyrdom in Karbala centuries

---

[101] *Annual of Urdu Studies*, op. cit., pp. 89-90; see also *Saadat Hasan Manto: Kingdom's End and Other Stories*. Translated from the Urdu by Khalid Hasan (Delhi: Penguin Books India, 1989), pp. 5-7.

[102] *Hindustan Times*, 28 February 1949.

ago, but also because 'the cut umbilical cord of Pakistan was around their necks like a noose, and they were all suffocating.'[103] Now they knew what 'a world of loneliness' meant! Life was not the same any more with friends and relatives across the border. People were worried about their kith and kin.[104] They were alone and depressed throughout the day. And the nights became intolerable. 'There was a desire to dream, but what was there safe to dream about?'[105] The atmosphere was foul and murky all around. It was such that 'the blood of one's veins was wandering hopelessly in Pakistan, and the relationships and mutual affections and friendships ... were breaking, and in place of confidence, a fear and deep suspicion was growing in people's heart.'[106]

In short independence and partition brought varied moods of loneliness. Every individual in Gangauli 'had found himself suddenly alone'.[107] All of them turned, just as they did every day of their existence, to Husain and his seventy-two companions for strength, confidence and spiritual comfort.

[103] Rahi Masoom Reza, op. cit., p. 292.
[104] Ibid., p. 293.
[105] Ibid.
[106] Ibid.
[107] Ibid., p. 292.

5

SECULARISM: THE POST-COLONIAL PREDICAMENT

'The principal question ... is not whether Indian society will eventually become secularized as Nehru believed it would, but rather whether it is desirable that it should.'

T.N. Madan, *Journal of Asian Studies*, 27, 3, November 1987,
. pp. 747-60.

'Modern India has a lot to answer for so have the cosmopolitan intellectuals in this part of the world. They have failed to be respectful to the traditions of tolerance in Indian society. These traditions may have become creaky but so is, it is nor pretty clear, the ideology of secularism itself.'

Ashis Nandy, in Veena Das (ed.), *Mirrors of Violence*, pp. 68, 73.

Debates connected with secularism are not new.[1] Turn to the *Journal of Asian Studies*, *Modern Asian Studies*, *Economic and Political Weekly*, *Seminar* and newspaper columns in India and you will find detailed reflections on the strength and failings of the secular experiment. The sociologist T.N. Madan generated a controversy when he told the American Association for Asian Studies in 1987 that 'at present secularism in South Asia as a general shared credo of life is impossible,

---

[1] Various meanings are attached to secularism, and we follow here the following standard textbook definition: 'The secular state is a state which guarantees individual and corporate freedom of religion, deals with the individual as a citizen irrespective of his religion, is not constitutionally connected to a particular religion nor does it seek either to promote or interfere with religion.' Smith, *India as a Secular State*, p. 4. The use of 'secular idea', 'secular agenda' and 'secular project' in this and other chapters flows from this definition. For reflections on secularism from different perspectives, see S. Khan, 'Towards a Marxist understanding of *Secularism*', *EPW*, 7 March 1987; Rajni Kothari, 'Class and Communalism in India' and his 'Cultural Context of Communalism in India', *EPW*, 3 December 1988 and 14 January 1989; *EPW*, 9 July 1994, for a number of seminal essays; André Beteille, 'Secularism and Intellectuals', *EPW*, 5 July 1994; Antony Copley, 'Indian Secularism reconsidered: from Gandhi to Ayodhya', *Contemporary South Asia*, 2, 1, 1993, pp. 47-65.

as a basis for state action impracticable, and as a blueprint for the future impotent.'[2] Likewise Ashis Nandy's 'anti-secular manifesto' is reproduced in scores of journals and magazines. He challenges 'the hegemonic language of secularism popularised by the westernised intellectuals and middle classes exposed to the globally dominant language of the nation state'. He argues, just as Madan did, that both the ideology and the politics of secularism 'have more or less exhausted their possibilities and we may now have to work with a different conceptual frame which is already vaguely visible at the borders of the Indian political system.' A far more serious venture, according to Nandy, would be to explore the philosophy, symbolism and theology of tolerance in the various faiths of the citizens and hope that the state systems in South Asia would learn something from everyday Hinduism, Islam, Buddhism and/or Sikhism, rather than wish that ordinary Hindus, Muslims, Buddhists and Sikhs will learn tolerance from the various fashionable theories of statecraft.[3]

Scores of writers, including some contributors to the *Economic and Political Weekly*, have challenged the arguments of Madan and Nandy.[4] Some are serious; others are largely polemical in content. But most are caught up in a scholastic exercise, vying with each other to come up with nuanced definitions and uncover different sets of meanings which bear little relationship to the concrete realities faced by the political leadership in the aftermath of partition. The context is lost sight of, as are the processes that led to the adoption of a secular regime.

Here both the context and the process are emphasised from the perspective of a historian and a reading of India's liberation struggle lasting more than six decades. There is also an attempt to review the secular experiment in its implications both for other plural societies endeavouring to tackle their ethnic, regional and regional problems in Asia and Africa, and for India's Muslims who in 1981, according to the census of that year, numbered more than 110 million and formed the country's largest minority.

I

On 8 July 1948, Nehru wrote to the Nawab of Bhopal:

I believe in India being a secular state with complete freedom for all religions and cultures and for cooperation between them. I believe that India can only

---

[2] T.N. Madan, 'Whither Secularism?', *Modern Asian Studies*, 27, 3, 1993, pp. 667-97, and 'Religion in India', *Daedulus*, 118, 4, Fall 1989.

[3] Veena Das (ed.), op. cit., p. 86. See his 'Anti-Secular Manifesto', *Seminar* (314), 1985; 'Secularism on the Run', *Manthan*, June 1991, and 'The Political Culture of the Indian State', *Daedalus*, 118, 4, Fall 1989.

[4] For example, Akeel Bilgrami, 'Two concepts of secularism', *EPW*, 9 July 1994; Beteille, 'Secularism and Intellectuals', op. cit., pp. 559-66.

become great if she preserves that composite culture which she had developed through the ages. I confess however that doubts sometimes assail me whether this is going to happen or not. And yet at the back of my mind I feel sure that whatever might happen in the present, sometime or other, India will have to tread that path to self-realisation and greatness. I am anxious therefore that the Muslims in India as well as other religious groups should have the fullest freedom and opportunity to develop themselves. I am entirely hostile to Hindu or any other communalism in India.[5]

Nehru's optimism was finely balanced against the painful recognition that forces of secular nationalism were badly bruised at the dawn of independence and that partition signified the failure of the Congress-liberal-socialist combine to keep the nation's fabric intact. Gandhi was aware of this harsh reality. So were leaders of diverse political backgrounds who, while rejoicing in the freedom that had crowned their efforts, saw their lifelong mission being dissipated in those terible days. The pageantry and ceremony over, free India was confronted with a troubled legacy, as also with the need to devise a strategy to deal with religious minorities, especially the Muslims who stayed put in the country of their birth. Should the constitution being hammered out in the Constituent Assembly reflect the broadly secular language of Indian nationalism or move towards the goal of Hindu *Rashtra*, especially when neighbouring Pakistan was refurbishing its Islamic image? Why, it was asked, should Hindus deny themselves a pre-eminent position merely for the sake of placating Muslims? Why should minority rights be guaranteed in Bharatvarsha and not across the border where non-Muslims were treated as second-class citizens? There was, finally, the highly pernicious theory that the Muslims having led, conducted and supported the clamour for Pakistan should be made to pay a price for their 'betrayal'. M.S. Golwalkar, the RSS chief, firmly believed that the followers of Islam had not 'turned patriots overnight' after 1947. On the contrary, their 'menace' had increased 'a hundredfold'. From Delhi to Rampur and Lucknow they were 'busy hatching a dangerous plot, piling up arms and mobilising their men and probably biding their time to strike from within when Pakistan decides upon an armed conflict with our country'.[6]

The debate between the 'secularists' and the votaries of Hindu *Rashtra* was certainly not conducted in such stark terms. Nor was it articulated around well-defined notions of secularism *versus* communalism. On the contrary, there were points of divergence and convergence between 'secular' and 'communal' discourses and there was ambiguity in these discourses too. There was only a thin dividing line between the present

---

[5] S. Gopal (ed.), *SWJN*, second series, vol. 7, p. 7.

[6] M.S. Golwalkar, *Bunch of Thoughts* (Bangalore: Jagarana Prakashana, 1980 edn.), p. 239.

situation and the days of Tilak, the symbol of Maratha pride, who revived a Hinduised past through the use of religious idioms and symbols. But the critical issue, which eluded the grasp of the Muslim League or was calculatedly ignored by it, was that the rank and file in the Congress did not necessarily endorse overt manifestations of Hindu nationalism. In general, the secular non-secular divide was pushed under the carpet to lend a semblance of unity to nationalist aspirations, just as social and linguistic cleavages were brushed aside to sustain a united front.

The mood and temper changed after independence. It was no longer necessary for the Congress to maintain the facade of unity or cohesion; indeed, the temptation was to carry the unfinished ideological battle to its logical culmination, to isolate the standard-bearers of socialism and secularism, and to wipe out the political legacy of Gandhi and Nehru. The political climate was conducive to this: the country was plagued by bloody violence, and religious passions were inflamed. So a Hindu-centred view, nurtured by revitalisation movements since the 1920s, came to be stridently expressed in both Congress and non-Congress circles. Hindu parties were themselves not immediately catapulted into political prominence, largely because Gandhi's assassination on 30 January 1948 created a mood of revulsion towards them. Yet the cynicism and ill-will generated by partition legitimised their pronounced hostility towards the Muslims, lent weight to the critique of Congress' 'appeasement' policy and emboldened them to demand preferential treatment for their constituency, which was mostly drawn from millions of hapless refugees cruelly displaced from their homes in Pakistan. Hindu Mahasabha and RSS leaders bluntly pointed out that secularism, championed by the Nehru-Azad combine, had lost its justification in August 1947, and that conciliation and compromise with the Muslims had failed to keep India united. 'A fanatic Moslem State ... was not conquered by the sword as the Moghals or the Muslim invaders did centuries ago, but merely handed over by the Congress "Jaichands" by a mere stroke of the pen, in conspiracy with a representative of the British Government.'[7] The Congress 'blunders', another Hindu Mahasabha ideologue commented, had resulted

....in the vivisection of our motherland – this "Pitribhoo" and 'Punyabhoo' of the Hindus. The Hindus ... today stand dispossessed of the frontiers of their motherland. The tragedy does not end here. Even our very *Swadharma* is in danger of being annhilated and effaced, at the hands of our Conscience-keepers – the Congress leaders. When they hate the very word 'Hindu', where is the necessity to think of faith and culture which appears foreign to them.[8]

---

[7] Indra Prakash, *Hindu Mahasabha: Its contribution to India's Politics* (Delhi: Akhil Bharatiya Hindu Mahasabha, 1966), p. 87.

[8] Indra Prakash, *A Tale of Blunders* (Delhi: Dharmarajan Press, 1947), p. 92. In his

Faced with the stark reality of making a decisive choice at a critical historical juncture, the Congress was inevitably drawn into such debates. Hindu traditionalists as well as Hindu nationalist campaigned against the secular project. The large-scale exodus of Hindus from Pakistan, along with reports of their persecution and sufferings, imposed additional strains on the secular agenda. Some in Congress pooh-poohed the idea altogether, others expressed serious reservations. In the end, however, Nehru and his liberal-socialist allies had their way. They viewed pre-independence nationalism and post-independence secularism as segments of the same continuous tradition.[9] Thus, like Gandhi throughout his public life, they invoked powerful historical symbols of unity. 'If India is to survive as a civilized democracy', commented the *Hindustan Times* only a few months after independence, 'the fight against communalism should be waged on all fronts. No quarter should be given to Hindu or Sikh communalism any more than to Muslim communalism. All the fountain-springs of communal poison should be closed.'[10]

Yet no two Congressmen understood the meaning of secularism in the same way. But what was generally agreed among them, without their being able to articulate the point explicitly, was that the state as such should not be identified with any particular faith or controlled by it. Nor should its laws be dictated by the fundamentalism of a particular religion, or religion play any part in state affairs. In the spirit of the Karachi Congress resolutions of 1931, each citizen must have equal rights and obligations.[11] Separate electorates and reservation of seats for Muslims, two major impediments to achieving national integration, had absolutely no place. In sum, a political consensus was arrived at out of the varied experiences of the past.[12] It was a consensus of great significance.

The All-India Congress Committee reaffirmed its commitment to a non-communal, democratic and secular polity in mid-November

---

presidential address delivered on 21 October 1951 at the Jana Sangh session, S.P. Mookerjee launched his tirade against Nehru for having 'sacrificed Indian nationalism at the altar of Muslim communalism.' Rebutting the charge that the Jana Sangh was communal, Mookerjee asked: 'Do you fight against the communal award? Who gave the communal percentages for the purpose of having some pact with the Muslim League? Who agreed to partition the country? [...] But having sold the country at the altar of communalism to come forward and say that we are communalists is a perversion of truth.' Quoted in Balraj Madhok, *Dr Syama Prasad Mookerjee: A Biography* (Delhi: Deepak Prakashan, 1954), pp. 71, 83.

[9] Smith, *India as a Secular State*, p. 145.

[10] *Hindustan Times,* 12 October 1947.

[11] Moin Zaidi (ed.), *Congress and the Minorities: Preserved National Cohesion* (Delhi, 1984); see also resolution drafted by Nehru and passed by the Congress Working Committee on September 1950 and at the plenary session on 21 September 1950, *SWJN,* vol. 15, part 1, p. 127.

[12] Norman D. Palmer, *The Indian Political System* (Boston: Houghton Mifflin, 1961), p. 91.

1947.[13] Gandhi began a fast on 12 January 1948 to draw attention to the need of protecting the Muslims and 'to make the majority community in India search its heart and purge itself of hatred and the desire to retaliate';[14] no such initiative was taken in Pakistan where Hindus were made the victims of religious persecution. Nevertheless Nehru insisted that whatever might happen in Pakistan, the Congress 'must pursue with even greater determination than in the past our efforts at forming a secular State in which men of all communities can walk with their heads high.'[15] The idea of two nations, each based on a religion, was opposed to the secularity on which the Indian state was established:

India is a secular nation which guarantees equality of citizenship to people of all religions. We consider our Muslim population – we have some fifty million of them – as part of our nation, the Indian nation, and not some other Muslim nation. We have Hindus, Muslims, Sikhs, Christians and other religious communities, and we obviously cannot consider them as different nationalities. Such an approach would be absolutely fatal from our point of view. If we consider this two-nation theory which Pakistan is sponsoring, what happens to our Muslim population? Do we have to consider them as a different nation just because they have a different religion? The very concept is fantastic. It might lead to further trouble, division and disruption of the nation.[16]

Debates on fundamental rights and minority rights in the Constituent Assembly proceeded on similar lines.[17] That members had not the skills to nuance and historicise the meanings of the term secularism should not be held against them. What is striking is the political acumen with which they were able to recognise that secularism, a 'progressive' and 'modern' ideal, was preferrable to a theocratic state, whose outlines were being worked out in Karachi and Lahore. A state with a secular face could offer a rallying point for unity, while a Hindu *Rashtra* was sure to lay the seeds of discord and disunity.

Secularism did not find a place in the preamble till 1976 when the 42nd Constitutional Amendment made India a 'Sovereign, Socialist, Secular Democratic Republic'. Yet its broad principles were embodied in

[13] 22 November 1947, G. Parthasarathi (ed.), *Letters to Chief Ministers 1947-1949* (hereafter *Letters*) (Delhi: Jawaharlal Nehru Memorial Fund, 1985), vol. 1, p. 21.

[14] The Mahatma ended his fast on 19 January, five days after it began. His fast, according to the *Hindustan Times* (Delhi) of 18 January 1948, 'may prove a turning point in our history. Let the chapter of revenge close, and the chapter of reconstruction begin.'

[15] 20 February 1948, ibid., p. 67.

[16] Quoted in Robert D. Baird, 'Religion and the Legitimation of Nehru's Concept of the Secular State', in Bardwell L. Smith (ed.), *Religion and the Legitimation of Power in South Asia* (Lieden: E.J. Brill, 1978), pp. 80-1.

[17] See, Ralph H. Retzlaff, 'The Problem of Communal Minorities in the Drafting of the Indian Constitution', R.N. Spate (ed.), *Constitutionalism in Asia* (Bombay, 1963), pp. 55-73; W.H. Morris-Jones, *Parliament in India* (London: Longmans Green, 1957), pp. 83-6.

the constitution, especially in those Articles dealing with fundamental rights.[18] The constitution-makers harnessed their intellectual resources and varied political experiences to prepare a secular blueprint. They differed over matters of detail and emphasis, but their overriding concern was to reconcile the interests and aspirations of profoundly divergent castes, communities, linguistic groups and regions. In so doing they did not give the nation a perfect model, free of ambiguities, contradictions and inconsistencies. But against the background of partition and a riot-torn society they plotted a trajectory for a multi-religious and multi-cultural plural society. They lay bare the outlines of a secularisation process – 'the process by which sectors of society and culture are removed from the domination of religious institutions and symbols.'[19] It was no wonder that the 'founding fathers' were aware that this was a monumental undertaking. 'In our country', said one of them, 'we had to harmonise the interests as well as the proselytising proclivities of some of our own religions – and we have many more religions I am afraid than many other countries – and yet we have struck upon a solution which, I am sure, will be considered not only by constitutionalists but also by sociologists all over the world to be highly progressive.'[20]

Recent debates on secularism, triggered off by the Hindutva upsurge in the mid-1980s, are largely the outcome of the Constituent Assembly discussions and related to it. There was much confusion then, as now, about the scope, relevance and meanings of secularism. In the hallowed precincts of the Assembly there was uncertainty and scepticism, just as doubt hang over academic and university circles today. Secularism was equated then with western liberalism or with minority appeasement, and it still is today. Critics, irrespective of party affiliation, were wary of separating religion and politics. They questioned the conceptual basis of a secular state and society and doubted the efficacy of applying Western notions of state and civil society to a country where 'primordial' loyalties were a powerful binding force. They argued then, just as they do now, that the 'hegemonic language of secularism' of the Westernised intellectuals and middle classes was no more than a Western import grafted onto a traditional social order.

For the constitution-makers, who were in any case setting up the Westminster model of parliamentary democracy, the issue was not the European origin of the secular idea but its appropriateness in a country of diverse faiths, multiple identities and varied cultural and intellectual

---

[18] Smith, *India as a Secular State*, chapter 4.

[19] L. Peter Berger, *The Social Reality of Religion* (London: Allen Lane, 1973), p. 113.

[20] 17 November 1949, *Constituent Assembly Debates* [CAD], vols. 10-12 (Delhi: Lok Sabha Secretariat, 1989, 2nd reprint), p. 628; J.M. Shelat, *Secularism: Principles and Application* (Bombay, 1972), p. 121.

norms. They were not bogged down by finer issues of definition, categorisation and application of secularism. They simply wanted to ensure that the essence of secularism – the impartiality and strict neutrality of the state in its relations with the religious institutions and practices of the different communities – was understood by the people. Their chief aim was to prescribe norms of civil society, without reference to scriptures or religious texts, and to develop what was Nehru's great passion: a scientific temper without the encumbrance of scholasticism and traditionalism. Certainly they did not presuppose the creation of an anti-religious state, but a state wherein people would rise above their narrow emotional orbit 'to integrate into a multi-dimensional harmonious fellow feeling.'[21] Thus a Constituent Assembly member claimed:

When this Constitution comes into law it will be with pride that our nation will be remembered by the nations of the world that in our Constitution we have kept no room for communalism and that we are in the true sense of the word a secular State'.[22]

The framers of the constitution, as indeed those with the burden of implementing its provisions, mostly did not have a common plank or starting-point; they differed among themselves, just as they differed with others, in their analytical framework and in their intellectual ethos, designated as 'Western' in much fashionable social science literature. As a heterogenous group, drawn from mixed social and educational backgrounds, they subscribed to a variety of world views and were susceptible to them. Some could be described as being rooted in the soil and nurtured in the sturdy, long-standing 'indigenous' traditions of Hinduism.[23] Though imbued with the modern concept of secularism and the political symbolism associated with it, they nevertheless held to *Sarva Dharma Sambhava* (Unity of Faiths) as the solid foundation for harmonious living. They claimed that their concept was consistent with the eclectic, reformist trends in Hindu society and approximated with Gandhi's concern to strengthen the moral edifice of the Indian state.[24] 'This Constitution',

---

[21] Kamaladevi Chattopadhyaya, *Inner Recesses Outer Spaces*, p. 306; Panikkar, *Foundations of New India*, pp. 166-7; S. Radhakrishnan, quoted in Smith, *India as a Secular State*, p. 147; K.Subba Rao, *Conflicts in Indian Polity* (Delhi: Lajpat Rai Memorial Lecture, 1970), pp. 38-42; P.N. Bhagwati, 'Religion and Secularism under the Indian Constitution', in Baird (ed.), *Religion and Law*, op. cit.; Amit Sarkar, *Secularism and Constitutionality* (Delhi: Uppal Publishing House, 1988), chapters 2-3.

[22] 26 May 1949, *CAD*, vol. 8, p. 318.

[23] J.P. Suda, *Indian Constitution Development and National Movement*, pp. 520, 521-2, quoted in Palmer, op. cit., fn. 27, p. 103.

[24] Shelat, *Secularism*, p. 88; Sampurnanand, *Memoirs and Reflections* (Delhi: Asia Publishing House, 1962), pp. 164-6.

Krishnamoorthy Rao declared in the Constitutent Assembly, 'is a harmonious blending of the best Indian traditions.'[25]

The liberal-left combination, on the other hand, refrained from invoking sacred traditions. A secular state as a political solution for modern India was based on the contention that it afforded the optimum freedom for the citizens to develop into fully integrated human beings. This was a modern goal, rational and scientific, and in addition a specifically Indian goal. These values should have been apparent to all, and it was because of this that they were for Nehru and his colleagues both ultimate and the final legitimation for the secular state.[26]

The inspiration came from several different sources – from nineteenth-century British liberalism, Fabian socialism and the revolutionary fervour generated by socialism and communism. But the reference point was the Congress-led freedom struggle and its broadly secular goals and secular leadership. *Sarva Dharma Sambhava* as a concept captured the spirit of religious tolerance and equanimity without envisaging a disjunction between the state and religion. What was therefore found suitable, though not without murmuring in certain quarters, was the Western variant of secularism.

Some grasped the significant implications of their action and readily accepted them, but others did not. But most knew well that the secular model alone could contain centrifugal tendencies which threatened after 1947 to undermine an already fractured social structure. No wonder secularism, along with 'democratic socialism', occupied centrality in their public discourse. It remained, at least in public pronouncements and party manifestoes, 'a priceless heritage of our country, ... the foundation on which a progressive modern State can be built for the welfare of the common man'.

If party resolutions can be taken as indicating the thought-process of the upper echelons of the Congress leadership, then the consensus arrived at in Jaipur on 18-19 December 1948 carries some meaning. The resolution, introduced by Pant and seconded by Purshottamdas Tandon, showed how political leaders with uncertain faith in secularism were pushed into taking positions reflecting the political mood and in line with the overall Congress approach and strategy.[27]

---

[25] 22 November 1949, *CAD*, vol. 10-12, p. 812.

[26] Baird, op.cit., p. 86.

[27] 'The long past of India is evidence of the spirit of tolerance which was the basis of life and culture in this country. India has been and is a land of many religions and many races and must remain so. The freedom of India can only be based on a recognition of an overriding unity binding together the richly varied cultural life of the country, which should have full play. The aim of the Congress has therefore been to develop this great country as a democratic secular state which neither favours nor discriminates against any particular religion.' Valmiki Choudhary (ed.), *Dr Rajendra Prasad: Correspondence and Select*

The Congress had large numbers of motivated and faithful secularists. But there were quite a number of soft advocates as well, people who kept their options open and chose to follow the path of caution in the political world. Friction and conflicts between them and the hard-liners were not uncommon, although this did not lead to a showdown or an open breach. The thrust of Congress policies remained broadly secular; the aim was not to 'secularise' every citizen but to ensure that the benefits of its welfare plans and economic measures accrued to the underprivileged and not to any particular denominational group.[28] Political and institutional structures, some inherited from the *raj*, were energised to drive home the message that Congress policies, such as *zamindari* abolition in 1951, served the poor and backward and not the followers of any particular denominational group. This was secularism in practice.

The Congress was, moreover, imbued with a mission to secure India's rightful place in the comity of nations, to lead the non-aligned world, to set an example worthy of emulation by the newly-independent countries of Asia and Africa, and to spread 'spiritual light in Asia, indeed, in the world which, groping in darkness, cries for a deliverer to liberate humanity from the constant threat of war, hunger and disease.'[29] The Congress believed that this mission was achievable, if India kept its own house in order through democracy and secularism.

There was a question-mark on the nature and purpose of such a 'mission'. Awkward and uncomfortable questions were raised – not merely by the Hindu Ideologues – about the ambiguities in the secular model itself. The president, Rajendra Prasad, himself conceded that the 'defects' in the constitution 'are inherent in the situation in the country and the people at large ... We have communal differences, caste differences, language differences, provincial differences and so forth.'[30] It was by no means easy to smother these differences merely through constitutional provisions, a point Rajendra Prasad made with clarity. Was the Congress in a position to do so? Since it had failed to mediate between the warring communities in the 1940s, there were serious doubts about its ability to keep the secular flag flying in the Hindi- Hindu heartland. How were such apprehensions to be dispelled? And how was confidence to be instilled in

---

Documents, vol. 10 (Delhi: Allied, 1988), p. 250. See also, resolution drafted by Nehru and passed by the Congress Working Committee in September 1950 and at the plenary session on 21 September 1950, *SWJN*, vol. 15, part 1, p. 127.

[28] For Assembly debates, see speeches by Sita Ram S. Jajoo and Shibban Lal Saxena, *CAD*, vols 10-12, p. 781.

[29] *Hindustan Times*, 15 August 1948.

[30] 26 November 1949, *CAD*, vols 10-12, pp. 993-4. Shibban Lal Saxena said that the constitution was a compromise and had all the 'defects' of a compromise. He thought that it was a compromise 'between men of various views, both conservatives and radicals, inside the Congress.' 19 November 1949, ibid., p. 705.

the rank and file of the party? The Congress leadership was in a serious predicament.

Ironically the birth of Pakistan 'smoothened', as Ajit Prasad Jain said in the Constitutent Assembly on 22 November 1949, 'our work of con- stitution-making.' In particular 'the question of minorities, which had been our headache and which thwarted all our efforts for the solution of national problems, has ceased to be a live issue.'[31] Furthermore, the end of colonialism, the adoption of a democratic constitution and the political hegemony of the Congress changed the political landscape and created a climate conducive for secular ideas to take root. As years and decades passed, the secular experimentation became an integral part of the democratisation process. Secularism itself acquired new meanings and found new modes of expression – something not to be decried. An inflexi- ble, static and doctrinaire definition would have inhibited newly-emergent social classes and political élites from being closely identified with the values and symbols associated with the changing political culture. In fact, a redeeming feature of the post-Nehru era was that these groups did not – as had been predicted – shun the secular model. Instead they enriched its social content, which is how its appeal went far beyond the charmed circle of the élites. This is probably why what began as a mere experiment in a riot-ravaged and communally-polarised India of 1947-9 acquired legitimation in the political, cultural and intellectual discourses.

II

'If the cry of Hindi, Hindu, Hindustani is boldly faced by the Congress with a constructive mind the party in power has a chance of putting through a 10-year programme of national reconstruction.'

Hindustan Times, 1 January 1949

During the 1950s and '60s, a period which bore the imprint of Nehru's ideas and personality, the problem was not that the secular blueprint was conceptually flawed or that the constitution-makers were proceeding on wrong assumptions. The real challenge was to legitimise, through estab- lished democratic conventions and institutional frameworks, the secular ideology and process. The critical task was to complete the unfinished agenda of Indian nationalism.[32] This is where the party system generally, and the Congress governments, in particular, failed to deliver. Policies and programmes, launched with much aplomb, did not energise secular tendencies. A civil society was modelled, thanks to Nehru's ingenuity,

[31] 22 November 1949, *SWJN*, vol. 8, p. 804.
[32] Speech by Rajendra Prasad, 26 November 1949, op. cit., pp. 993-4.

without the necessary ideological inputs to sustain it over an extended period. Everybody swore by secularism but few tried to harness the country's enormous intellectual resources towards secularisation. The constitution was commendable – as too were the laws, rules and regulations. Minorities enjoyed equal rights. However, translating constitutional guarantees into practice was an awesome task, and Muslims in particular complained of discrimination and lack of opportunity. The leadership, as Nehru told the UP chief minister, was weak and ready to compromise with something that was morally and politically reprehensible. So the rank and file went astray.[33]

Ideological coherence was lacking in the ruling party as well as the opposition. Secular slogans were reiterated *ad nauseam*, only to be discarded openly or in more subtle ways. Parties which waxed eloquent about national integration forged unprincipled electoral alliances and in elections selected candidates with the old communal, caste and linguistic considerations in mind. It was not always, as Nehru thought, a sign of communalism in the selectors themselves: it also reflected the selectors' inclination to seek short-cuts to victory. A political analyst commented:

What has the Congress done to pull up its party organisations in those states which have flagrantly violated the principles of integration of the people which it swears by? Is there any guarantee ... that in selecting candidates for the next election, the Congress will not be guided in its choice by caste or communal considerations? It does not lie in the mouth of a party to say that, when it can form an alliance with a communal organisation for capturing and retaining power in the state government. Wording of a resolution in immortal prose is no way of putting principles into action.[34]

Nothing illustrates the point better than the two by-election campaigns: one in Faizabad, close to the temple city of Ayodhya, in 1948 soon after independence, and the other in Amroha a few months before Nehru's death in 1964.

In 1948 the Faizabad district became the focal point of a political showdown between Acharya Narendra Deva, a socialist leader, and his Congress rival Baba Raghava Das. During the campaign, Pandit Govind Ballabh Pant, a veteran Congress leader from the hill districts of UP, visited Ayodhya and declared that the Acharya (i.e., a man of knowledge) did not believe in the divinity of Lord Ram; this was proved by the fact that he did not wear a *chhot*, or tuft of hair at the back of the head, like all devout, Hindus. Baba Raghava Das, for his part, moved among his followers distributing the sacred *tulsi* leaves to emphasise the spiritual

---

[33] To G.B. Pant, 17 April 1950, *SWJN*, vol. 14, part 2, p. 294.

[34] *Economic Weekly* (Bombay), 14 January 1961.

difference between himself and his socialist adversary. Ayodhya voted for the Baba.[35]

In Amroha, a quiet town in western UP with a history of Hindu-Muslim amity, 'communalism has been blowing through the by-election, leaving a stain on everything.'[36] The spark that ignited trouble was the last-minute inclusion of Hafiz Mohammad Ibrahim, central minister for irrigation and power, as the Congress candidate against Nehru's *bête noire*, Acharya Kripalani.[37] The Congress did so on the strength of the 38 per cent Muslim and 22 per cent Harijan votes in the constituency. But it paid dearly for its miscalculation. The polling was high and Kripalani won because of the consolidation of the 'Hindu vote' and a split in the Muslim ranks. In the process the Congress performed badly, although it masked this with an isolated victory in Jaunpur. The stunning defeats in Amroha, coinciding with those in Farrukhabad and Rajkot, was a reminder that all was not well with the party machinery, 'a cumbersome mass which is weighed down by complacency, its fibre weakened by the love of indolence, drained of the capacity and even the will to fight, as uninspired itself as it is uninspiring for others.'[38]

Nehru himself was not proud of his government's record. With Hindu communalism and militancy finding justification in the massive influx of refugees from west Punjab and east Bengal, he was dismayed to find some of his life-long comrades, including senior ministers and chief ministers, being swayed by right reaction. Before his own parting of the ways, Acharya Kripalani, as Congress president, felt uneasy with Nehru's policy towards Pakistan. He wanted an immediate blockade of Kashmir, a complete break in economic relations with Pakistan, strong measures on evacuee property, and rejection of the standstill agreement with the Nizam of Hyderabad.[39] His successor, Pattabhi Sitaramayya, spoke at the All India Hindu Code Bill Conference chaired by Jagatguru Shankaracharya.[40] The country's president, Rajendra Prasad, presided over a Cow Welfare Workers' Conference, along with the Agriculture minister Jairamdas Doulatram.[41] He insisted against Nehru's advice on inaugurating

---

[35] Harold A. Gould, *Politics and Caste*, vol. 3 (Delhi: Chanakya, 1990), p. 49.

[36] Pran Chopra, 'Contrast in campaigns of Amroha candidates', *Statesman*, 17 May 1963.

[37] Kripalani alleged that priests were brought from shrines and Muslim students from Deoband and Aligarh to canvass for Ibrahim. *Statesman.*, 31 May 1963.

[38] Pran Chora, 'Ominous lessons of the by-elections', Ibid., 31 May 1963; Bashiruddin Ahmed, 'Congress Defeat in Amroha: A Case Study in One Party Dominance', *EPW*, 22 May 1965.

[39] Stanley Kochanek, *The Congress Party of India: The Dynamics of One-Party Dominance* (Princeton University Press, 1968), p. 10.

[40] *Hindustan Times*, 8 March 1949.

[41] Ibid., 7 March 1949.

the rebuilt Somnath temple;[42] he could not refuse the invitation 'when it comes from the Rajpramukh of the State who also happens to be the Chairman of the Board of Trustees and the Board has two members of the Central Cabinet on it and perhaps also the Chief Minister of the State'.[43] When Nehru objected to K.M. Munshi's association with the project, the latter retorted: 'I have laboured in my humble way through literary and social work to shape or integrate some aspects of Hinduism, in the conviction that alone will make India an advanced and vigorous nation under modern conditions.'[44]

The president also came out strongly against the Hindu Code Bill,[45] a cause for which he found powerful support in the Congress. K.N. Katju, a senior Congressmen and governor of Bengal, approved the president's stand that discussion on the bill be postponed until the election of the new legislature:

It may be that the orthodox opinion does not find adequate opportunity for expression in the daily Press, but the mere fact that the newspapers are generally inclined to propagate what they consider progressive views in these matters does not negative (*sic*) the existence of a very substantial volume of opinion to the contrary in the country. In my opinion any drastic change in the structure of Hindu society will cause great resentment and great discontent, and this is not the time to multiply or accentuate differences.[46]

Vallabhbhai Patel, who wielded much influence in the Congress organisation and was the country's first home minister, relapsed into his old attitude of suspecting Muslim loyalty. He removed Muslim officials who had opted to stay in India, resisted Nehru's efforts to reserve certain residential areas in Delhi for Muslims, and opposed his suggestion of employing Muslims to deal with Muslim refugees.[47] To him India's Muslims were hostages to be held in security for the treatment of Hindus

[42] To Nehru, 10 March 1951, *Rajendra Prasad: Correspondence*, vol. 14, p. 155.

[43] Ibid., p. 38.

[44] K.M. Munshi, *Indian Constitutional Documents: Pilgrimages to Freedom (1920-1950)* (Bombay: Bharatiya Vidya Bhavan, 1967), pp. 563-4.

[45] Reba Som, 'Jawaharlal Nehru and the Hindu Code: A Victory of Symbol over Substance', *Modern Asian Studies*, 28, 1, February 1994; Madhu Kishwar, 'Codified Hindu Law: Myth and Reality', *EPW*, 13 August 1994; President's Note on the Hindu Code Bill, *Rajendra Prasad: Correspondence*, vol. 12, pp. 287-8; S. Gopal, *Jawaharlal Nehru: A Biography, 1947-1956*, vol. 2 (Delhi: OUP, 1979), pp. 77-8, 155.

[46] Katju to Rajendra Prasad, 15 August 1948, *Rajendra Prasad: Correspondence*, vol. 10, p. 56.

[47] Gopal, *Jawaharlal Nehru*, vol. 2, pp. 15-6. 'I do not think', Patel wrote to Neogy on 9 December 1947, 'we can accept the principle that persons belonging to one community should be appointed to deal with members of that community nor should it be desirable to concede that a non-Muslim government servant is less friendly disposed to a Muslim evacuee.' Durga Das (ed.), *Sardar Patel's Correspondence 1945-50*, vol. 4 (Ahmedabad: Navajivan Publishing House, 1972), p. 385.

in Pakistan. If they wanted to live in peace they had to prove that their sympathies were not with Pakistan or the secessionists in Kashmir and Hyderabad. Mere declarations of loyalty to the Indian Union, he said at Lucknow on 6 January 1948, were not going to serve any purpose; 'only practical proof' would do so. He told Muslims: 'You cannot ride on two horses. You select one horse, whichever you like best.'[48] A week later, Patel set a test for the Muslims during the by-election campaign for the Lucknow Assembly seat. He warned that 'a Hindu State would become inevitable instead of a secular democratic state' if the Muslims continued to conduct 'communal' politics. He added: 'You do not know what it is costing the government to protect you'.[49]

The UP chief minister Govind Ballabh Pant, B.G. Kher,[50] Acharya Kripalani,[51] and Charan Singh spoke in much the same vein. The real test of Muslim loyalty, according to Pant, was whether Muslims would shed their blood fighting the Pakistani hordes.[52] Charan Singh, Jat leader from Baghpat, felt that the presence of Muslims who had sided with British imperialists and conspired against freedom endangered 'the safety and existence of whatever is left of our beloved country.'[53] Such insinuations hurt Muslim sensitivities. 'It is very painful', said Husain Imam, a liberal lawyer-politician from Bihar,

....to be reminded every day that we are responsible for bringing Pakistan into existence. In its creation the Congress was as much a party as anybody else. In that spirit I request that Muslims should not be regarded as hostages. They should be regarded as citizens of India with as much right to live and enjoy the amenities of India – the land of their birth – as anyone else.[54]

Delhi and UP, the heartland of Aryavarta, showed a poor record in providing the healing touch. First, the Hindi-Urdu controversy heightened insecurity among the Urdu-speaking sections in North India, the arena where religio-cultural symbols had been hotly contested for well over a century. Then followed the agitation to ban cow-slaughter. On both

---

[48] *For a United India: Speeches of Sardar Patel, 1947-50* (Delhi: Publications Division, Government of India, 1989), pp. 64-9.

[49] *Hindustan Times*, 15 January 1948.

[50] He asked Muslims to surrender arms as an 'earnest expression of complete faith in the government to which they owed allegiance.' He wanted them to 'cease to be communally-minded.' 10 October 1947 and his speech at Allahabad, 26 December 1947, ibid.

[51] He was insistent that Muslims should influence public opinion against the Nizam of Hyderabad; otherwise their profession of loyalty would not go down well with 'the man in the street.' Ibid., 14 and 23 April 1948.

[52] Ibid., 9 October 1947.

[53] Ibid., 10, 12 October 1947.

[54] 8 November 1948, *CAD*, vol. 7, p. 305.

counts, the pressure mounted by the cow-protectionists bore fruit. The language issue was settled in Hindi's favour. In October 1947 the UP government, followed by the Central Provinces and Bihar, introduced Hindi as the sole language of administration.[55] Cow-slaughter was also banned in the Congress-ruled states of UP, Bihar, Madhya Pradesh and Rajasthan, though in different phases. These decisions symbolised the inexorable drift towards a greater identification with specifically Hindu causes. The energy released sparked off controversies which reached their climax nearly four decades later when the Babri Masjid issue was pressed into service to assert and test the strength and vitality of Hindutva ideology.

The functioning of the ministry of relief and rehabilitation, headed first by K.C. Neogy and later by Mohanlal Saxena, indicated which way the wind was blowing. Their pronounced antipathy towards the Muslims was talked about in the corridors of power. Neogy, who resigned from the Cabinet along with Shyama Prasad Mookerjee on the agreement with Pakistan, took little trouble over rehabilitation Muslims uprooted from their homes.[56] This was apparent when, despite Gandhi's interventions and Vinoba Bhave's valiant efforts, it took a while to settle the Meos in Gurgaon, Alwar, Bharatpur and Buria.[57] Mohanlal Saxena, who had ordered the scaling of Muslim shops in Delhi and UP, was severely reprimanded for the way in which he implemented the permit system and the provisions of the evacuee property ordinance.[58] Rajendra Prasad was upset when permits were issued to those Muslims who wished to return from Pakistan to India. 'We shall be taking a very heavy responsibility if we allow and encourage this one-way traffic', he warned the prime minister. Many Muslims with distant relatives who had gone to Pakistan were harassed. Freedom-fighters were not spared. Achhru Ram, cus-todian-general of evacuee property, worked in the interests of Hindu refugees eyeing the property of those who had left their homes for Pakistan or had moved to safer areas in India.[59]

Nehru was upset. 'All of us', he wrote with anguish, 'seem to be getting infected with the RSS mentality. This is a curious finale to our careers.[...]

---

[55] Seth Govind Das, 15 November 1948, Shibban Lal Saxena, 16 November 1948, *CAD*, vol. 7, pp. 223, 286. Azad protested against the UP government's decision. 'In the circumstances', the Maulana stated in the Constituent Assembly, 'fact and fair play demanded that Urdu should have been given official recognition at least in its place of birth, namely U.P.'. Quoted in Kerrin Dittmer, 'The Hindi-Urdu Controversy and the Constituent Assembly', *Journal of Politics*, vol. 6, 1972, p. 20. For a perceptive analysis of the Urdu-Hindi controversy, Brass, *Language, Religion and Politics*, chapter 4.

[56] Nehru to Mohanlal Saxena, 29 November 1948, *SWJN*, vol. 8, p. 155.

[57] Gopal, *Jawaharlal Nehru*, vol. 2, pp. 76-7.

[58] 4 October 1951, *Letters*, vol. 2, p. 509.

[59] Nehru to Mohanlal Saxena, 29 November 1948, *SWJN*, vol. 8, p. 155.

If the present Hindu outlook does not change radically, I am quite sure that India is doomed. The Muslim outlook may be and, I think, is often worse. But it does not make very much difference to the future of India.[60] He bemoaned how some of his colleagues had forgotten 'one of the basic principles and planks of the Congress – inter-communal unity', and how those who talked of a secular state 'have understood it least and belied it by their own words and actions.'[61]

The drift was most noticeable in UP, Nehru's home state. It was like a 'foreign land' to him. The Congress did not represent the voice of the party he knew but something he had opposed for the greater part of his life.[62] Some of its stars, including Purshottamdas Tandon, fanned the fires of communal unrest and adopted stridently communal positions. How could the speaker of the state assembly and president of the UP Congress chair a refugee conference in November 1949, which gave expression to excessively intolerant and communal views? The prime minister was indignant. 'You have become to large numbers of people in India some kind of a symbol of this communal and revivalist outlook', he candidly told Tandon. 'Is the Congress going that way also? If so, where do I come into the picture, whether it is the Congress or whether it is the Government run by the Congress? Thus this larger question becomes related to my own activities.'[63]

Pant's secular credentials were seriously in doubt. He made clear to his officials, though there is no documentary evidence to support this charge, that they were not to employ Muslims in government or the police force. Nehru chided his government, especially the local authorities in Lucknow and Banaras, for banning an anti-RSS demonstration. The impression created was that the goverenment was in some way prepared to encourage the RSS.[64] This impression gained ground when the Congress president, Pattabhi Sitaramayya, stated at Kanpur on 10 October 1947 that the RSS was not 'the enemy of the Congress'. Nor was it communal like the Muslim League or the Hindu Mahasabha.[65] Patel, who endorsed this opinion, invited the Hindu Mahasabhites to join the Congress. This was in January 1948. In the same speech, he expressed unhappiness over the fact that some of his colleagues wanted to crush the RSS with a *danda*

---

[60] 12 May 1950, *Letters*, vol. 2, p. 83.

[61] Nehru to Pant, 17 April 1950, *SWJN*, vol. 14, part 2, p. 293; Rajendra Prasad to Nehru, 10 August 1948, *Rajendra Prasad: Correspondence*, vol 12, p. 2.

[62] Ibid.

[63] Nehru to Tandon, 8 August 1950, *Sardar Patel's Correspondence,* vol. 10, p. 198;Nehru to Rajendra Prasad, 8 December 1949, *SWJN,* vol. 14, part 1, p. 429.

[64] Nehru to Pant, 4 September 1949, *SWJN*, vol. 13, p. 183.

[65] Quoted in B.D. Graham, *Hindu Nationalism and Indian Politics: The Origins and Development of the Bharatiya Jana Sangh* (CUP, 1990), p. 20.

[stick]. 'After all', he said, 'RSS men are not thieves and dacoits. They are patriots. They love their country. Only their trend of thought is diverted. They are to be won over by Congressmen with love.'[66]

Sampurnanand, UP's chief minister (1954-60), shared the anti-Muslim bias of his predecessor and the hostility towardsUrdu. In no country, he said, can the language of the bazaar serve as the nation's official language.[67] To give Urdu such a status would be a 'great insult' to the common people. To call that language Hindustani the 'injustice could not be removed, but a fraud would be perpetrated on the people.'[68] Nehru rightly spoke of communalism invading the minds and hearts of those who in the past had been pillars of the Congress.[69]

Nehru's adversaries in the party's higher echelons did not approve of his sledgehammer efforts to change the fabric of Hindu society, his lenient policy towards Pakistan, and his undue tenderness for the Muslims. But Nehru repudiated such criticism, as he had done time and again. 'Whatever the provocation from Pakistan and whatever the indignities and horrors inflicted on non-Muslims there, we have got to deal with this minority in a civilised manner. We must give them security and the rights of citizens in a democratic State. If we fail to do so, we shall have a fastering sore which will eventually poison the whole body politic and probably destroy it.' 'For all of us in India', he told the chief ministers in May 1950, 'the issue of communal unity and a secular state must be made perfectly clear. We have played about with this idea sufficiently long and moved away from it far enough. We must go back and go back not secretly or apologetically, but openly and rather aggressively.'[70] The past was a constant reference point. The prime minister invoked the Congress record to legitimise its secular discourse after partition. In this context he pointedly referred to the Mahatma's message of communal peace and· his exemplary courage in extinguishing the flames of religious hatred. In so doing, Nehru tried to settle the issue of whether the government and the party were going to adhere to 'old Congress principles in regard to communalism' or whether the country as a whole was going to drift away from them.[71]

In his writings and speeches Nehru reinforced his image as an enemy of narrow-mindedness, intolerance and religious bigotry. His exhortations were impressive and his conduct exemplary. He promoted a certain sense of togetherness in an otherwise ramshackle Congress coalition. Yet he

---

[66] *For a United India*, pp. 68-9.

[67] Sampurnanand, *Memoirs and Reflections*, p. 85

[68] *Hindustan Times*, 18 April 1949.

[69] Nehru to Pant, 17 April 1950, *SWJN*, vol. 14, part 2, p. 293.

[70] 15 October 1947, *Letters*, vol. 1, p. 2, and vol. 2, p. 84.

[71] 2, 9 May 1950, ibid., vol. 2, pp. 84. 113.

failed to refurbish its democratic and secular credentials despite his own unassailable authority, stature and charisma. The Congress under his stewardship gradually ceased to be at the head of a democratic and secular movement. Provincial and local leaders, having demonstrated vigour and vitality during the anti-colonial stir, ignored ideological issues. They were part of an unwieldly club, resting on their oars, and embroiled in intrigue factionalism and machinations to control the levers of power. Programmes and manifestoes, laced with radical and populist slogans, were subordinated to cold electoral calculations or made part of them. 'The Congress', Nehru wrote to the president of the republic just over two years after unfurling the national flag at Delhi's Red Fort,

....is simply fading away before our eyes. Even a fading might have been tolerated, but something worse is happening. There is no discipline left, no sense of common efforts, no cooperation, no attempt at constructive effort (apart from a few), and our energies are concentrated in disruption and destruction.[72]

A party which had once captured the imagination of millions ceased to command respect. People voted but not for reasons which had inspired them to rally around the Congress flag since the advent of the Mahatma on the national scene. Travelling through the villages of Saharanpur, Muzaffarnagar and Bijnor districts, Mira Behn, one of Gandhi's disciples, found 'extreme dissatisfaction with the Congress regime.' She told Rajendra Prasad and Nehru,

'I don't think you good people at the helm of affairs fully realise this state of things .... If they [peasants] voted Congress this time it was only because they could not at the moment think of anything better to do, but these elections have started a serious thinking process which is not going to stop ....'[73]

The party's upper hierarchy, having tasted power, were reluctant to relinquish it. Even the lower echelons of the party were fired with dreams of achieving office and who, 'basking in the glow of far-away ministers, strut the party world of rural villages and small district towns like pinchbeck Hampdens ordering local official about and patronising the people.' This, of course, was only till election time, when their tone perceptibly changed.[74]

Secularism, democracy and socialism brought votes; so every *khadi*-clad Congressmen swore by those principles to secure a firm foothold in the shifting sands of politics, but in the end such short-term gains did not bolster their image. Proclamations on unity, integration and secularism bagan to sound hollow. How could the image of Indian unity be sustained

---

[72] Nehru to Rajendra Prasad, *SWJN*, 8 December 1949, vol. 14, part 1, pp. 428-30.

[73] Mira Behn to Rajendra Prasad, 6 April 1952, *Rajendra Prasad: Correspondence*, vol. 15, p. 37.

[74] Frank Moraes, *India Today* (New York: Macmillan, 1960), p. 17.

by eye-catching laces and frills? It had to have 'the supporting stays of harder materials.'[75]

Nehru was sensitive to this: he conceded in May 1950 that 'during the last two and a half years or more we have gradually drifted because of the pressure of circumstances towards a communal reaction to the communal problem.'[76] He was troubled by the lack of social consciousness and homogeneity, the disruptive tendencies in the Congress, the recrudescence of Hindu-Muslim violence and the rise of communalists, 'who function on the mental planes of the fascists and the Nazis.'[77] He was worried by the total disregard of Congress's own legacy and the present aversion to values which had once been the hallmark of the organisation. The drift continued. Nehru, as always, sensed the malady but failed to act decisively or intervene effectively. He did little to revitalise the party machine, which was geared solely to devising electoral strategies and conducting election campaigns. Serious ideological issues, some of which had engaged Congress politicians during the heyday of nationalist euphoria, were virtually pushed away from the Congress agenda. Few heeded Mira Behn's timely admonition that 'the Congress should recognise that it was the ideals that conquered, and it is those ideals alone that can successfully overcome the difficulties and dangers which today surround us on all sides.'[78] What follows is a critique not of Nehru's motives or intentions but of his failure to steer the secular ship through the rough waters of Indian politics. The focus on him is intended to illustrate the problems faced by the Congress party and government in fulfiling its secular obligations.

Consider, for instance, the happenings at the century-old trouble spot in Ayodhya, where on the night of 21-22 December 1949 images of Ram were surreptitiously installed in the Babri Masjid. Nehru knew that the conduct of Faizabad's district officer, K.K.K. Nayar, was not above reproach and that influential UP Congressmen like Baba Raghavdas and Vishambhar Dayal Tripathi had fomented trouble in the area.[79] He was also aware that Pant, having dissuaded him from visiting Ayodhya, 'refrained from taking definite action'.[80] Yet he made no effort to mobilise his enormous political resources to resolve a long-standing controversy which was threateningd to shatter his own secular dream.[81] Forty-two years

[75] *Economic Weekly*, Annual Number, February 1962.

[76] 17 May 1950, *Letters*, vol. 2, p. 97.

[77] 2 November 1950, ibid., p. 13.

[78] Mira Behn to Nehru, 23 January 1952, *Rajendra Prasad: Correpondence*, vol. 15, p. 7.

[79] Nehru to Lal Bahadur Shastri, 9 July 1950, *SWJN*, vol. 14, part 2, p. 6.

[80] Nehru to K.G. Mashruwala, 5 March 1950, ibid., p. 445.

[81] It has been suggested, though in a different context, that Nehru was averse to open expression of conflict, and that he had expressed himself in favour of procrastinating over a

later, when Hindu fanatics demolished the mosque in broad daylight, people turned to Nehru's correspondence in 1950 to discover how he had unwittingly allowed the issue to drag on, leaving a blot on Indian democracy and secularism.

Nehru did not show the same firmness in breaking up the Patel-Pant-Tandon nexus as he did in isolating his natural allies in other radical parties. He sought to evolve a 'consensual' model and create a broad-based 'coalition' of 'progressive' elements. The strategy enabled him to push through some worthwhile social and agrarian programmes, including abolition of *zamindari*, and the limit on urban and rural land and property. In general, however, Nehru was inclined not to combine with secular forces outside the Congress to combat communalism. He distanced himself from the socialists, accused the communist party of following the 'policy of sabotage and terrorism', dismissed the first communist ministry in Kerala, and imprisoned Sheikh Mohammad Abdullah, the charismatic leader of the National Conference in Kashmir. He refrained from banning the communist party because 'the slight balance in favour of banning is rather outweighed by Communists posing as ideological martyrs instead of saboteurs and terrorists.'[82] Surely this consideration could not have weighed with the prime minister in pressing his own initiative for banning the RSS – 'so utterly little-minded and lacking in not only vision but in commonsense or common understanding.'[83] On 15 July 1948 the ban on the RSS was removed, and the next day its leader, M.S. Golwalkar, was released from jail, the *Organiser*, its semi-official organ, resumed its publication on 22 August.

In the matter of a uniform civil code, Muslim members of the Constituent Assembly ruled out interference in Muslim personal law.[84] Hasrat Mohani, who had been associated with the founding of the Communist Party of India in 1928, declared: 'If there is anyone who thinks that he can interfere in the personal law of the Muslims, then I would say to him that the result will be very harmful.[...] They will have to face the iron wall of Muslim determination to oppose them in every way.'[85] The Congress was taken in by such rhetoric. Nehru's failing, which he shared with some other Constituent Assembly members,[86] was that he allowed self-styled

---

divisive issue rather than precipitating it. Kothari, *Politics in India*, p. 157; see also Sudipta Kaviraj, 'On State, Society and Discourse in India' in James Manor (ed.), *Rethinking Third World Politics* (London: Longman, 1991), and Bilgrami, 'Two concepts of secularism', op. cit., for a critique of the Nehruvian vision.

[82] 6 December 1948, *Letters*, vol. 1, p. 243.

[83] Ibid.

[84] Speeches by Z.H. Lari and Husain Imam, 8 November 1948, *CAD*, vol. 7, p. 303.

[85] Quoted in Vasudha Dhagamwar, 'Women, Children and the Constitution: Hostages to Religion, Outcaste by Law' in Baird (ed.), *Religion and Law*, pp. 226-7.

[86] Zoya Hasan, 'Secularism Confounded: Equality Suspended, Debating Legal Reform',

Muslim leaders a voice in whether or not to provide equality before the law for all Indian women, or whether to promulgate a common civil code, thus precluding either. He preferred a uniform civil code, although he often argued in the same breath that the time was not ripe for bringing Muslims within its purview. This stance matched neither his zeal for modernisation nor his concern for the advancement of under-privileged groups, including Muslim women. It dampened immediate prospects for social reforms, precluded the possibility of amending certain socially repugnant family laws which were being dropped or modified in Muslim societies, and gave religious traditionalists a decisive say in thwarting progressive legislation. The timing was a matter of political judgement, but the initiative for doing so should have rested with parliament and not with the defenders of the *status quo*, such as the Jamaat-i Islami, who did not share Nehru's vision of a socially emancipated, forward-looking India.

Sometime in 1961 the Cabinet received suggestions for the review and reform of Muslim personal law. Nehru was enthusiastic, pointedly mentioning changes that had taken place in Tunisia, Egypt and Pakistan. There were lengthy discussions during 1961-2, and the Law ministry was asked to make appropriate recommendations. But the mere hint of an inquiry in the ministry's annual report led to a public outcry. The Jamaat-i Islami and the Jamiyat al-ulama lodged strong protests. More trouble followed when the government-appointed committee held its first meeting. It consisted of the central minister Hafiz Mohammad Ibrahim, Humayun Kabir, the socialist Farid Ansari, Muzaffar Husain of the Republican Party, Jamia's vice-chancellor Mohammad Mujeeb, and the social worker Begum Anis Kidwai. A gathering of Muslim ministers and members of parliament, chaired by the vice-president of the republic Zakir Husain, urged the government 'not to take any initiative' to reform Muslim personal law. They wanted changes in 'administrative and legal matters, consistent with the principles of the Quran and the *Hadith*', to be left to the Muslims.[87]

Nehru's legacy was such that no government after him could contemplate reforms to ensure the equal status of Muslim women in matters of divorce, maintenance and inheritance. Electorally the risk was too great. State intervention was not only desirable but actually possible during the Nehru era, but was virtually ruled out afterwards. And when the state intervened in the Shah Bano case in 1986, it did so with an eye on the 'Muslim vote' and to defend a traditionalist interpretation of the *Shariat*, that was untenable in most Muslim societies. This was the logical consequence of drawing the *ulama* into the debate, accepting the authen-

---

unpublished paper presented at the SSRC conference at Bellagio (Italy), August 1994.
[87] *Statesman*, 9 July 1963.

ticity of their version and legitimising the All-India Muslim Personal Law Board as the sole custodians, interpreters and transmitters of the *Shariat*.

Appropriately enough, India's Supreme Court asked the union government, more than three decades later in July 1995, what it had done to implement Article 44 of the Constitution which enjoins upon it to initiate steps for providing a uniform civil code. The Congress is likely to remain, as it has done for several decades, studiously silent in order to win back the Muslim vote lost in the aftermath of the Ayodhya dispute. Most other parties, too, have not fared any better. They are mostly ambivalent, though individual leaders have taken an unequivocal position. The right-wing Hindu parties, on the other hand, have a straight-forward agenda: the ruling BJP-Shiv Sena coalition in Maharashtra in western India has introduced legislatation in the state assembly to enforce a uniform civil code. The move is both arbitrary and inspired by cynical considerations. The cry for a uniform civil code serves to deepen anti-Muslim sentiments and consolidate the 'Hindu vote'. Meanwhile, sections of the liberal-left intelligentsia, too, argue that different ethnic, religious and linguistic groups are entitled to preserve their traditions, cultures and personal laws. They are beginning to question the common assumption that a uniform civil code would lead to greater harmony and integration. There is talk of 'reform from within'. It is doubtful, however, if the All-India Muslim Personal Law Board or organisations like the Jamaat-i Islami and the Jamiyat al-ulama would pay heed to such a mild plea. They have developed, thanks to the legitimacy endowed to them by the Indian state from the days of Nehru, a vested interest in preserving the status quo.

Nehru's ambivalence is also reflected in his attitude towards Urdu. He knew that Urdu was not spoken by Muslims alone but by millions of non-Muslims in Kashmir, Punjab, UP, Bihar and Bengal. He knew that it was a vital and graceful aspect of a vibrant composite tradition in the Indo-Gangetic belt. He himself read Urdu prose and poetry, and was an admirer and friend of writers and poets like Anand Narain Mulla, Sajjad Zaheer, Josh Malihabadi and Firaq Gorakhpuri and Faiz Ahmad Faiz. He argued, just as Gandhi had done, the case of Hindustani 'to foster a sense of unity among our countrymen' and criticised those who created the Hindi-Urdu controversy. He failed to understand the hostility to the inclusion of simple Urdu words in Hindustani and the concerted attempts to introduce a difficult form of Hindi simply out of hatred of Pakistan. The position of Hindi was assured – Urdu was not its rival – so why were Hindi zealots trying to suppress the language of Mir and Ghalib? Why such narrowness of vision?[88]

---

[88] 1 August 1953, *Letters*, vol. 3, p. 350, and summary of a news item on Urdu, *Hindustan Times*, 9 December 1955.

Nehru posed these questions to Tandon, Pant, Govind Das, Sampurnanand, Kamalapathi Tripathi, Ravi Shankar Shukla and K.M. Munshi, the star performers at the Hindi Sahitya Sammelan. They represented Hindu nationalism within the Congress ranks with no interest in Nehru's cherished projects – fostering a composite heritage and encouraging India's diverse and rich intellectual and cultural traditions. They were instinctively hostile to any trace of 'Muslim'/Islamic inheritance, and hence Hindustani, which they saw as a mask for Urdu, was anathema to them. They depicted it as a Muslim language, which it was not, and identified it with the Pakistan movement. They demanded that Hindi alone, written in the Devanagari script, be made India's official language.[89]

Muslims did not contest this claim – how could they? They merely proposed that more time be allowed for the change-over.[90] What they clamoured for, along with many Hindus, was Urdu's recognition as a second regional language in areas where it was widely spoken by Hindus and Muslims alike. Lala Raj Kanwal from Punjab wanted Urdu to be treated as the second language, and spoke against the politics of 'anger, vengeance or retribution' in the Constituent Assembly. 'I am a Punjabi', he added, 'and like most Punjabis have suffered grievously in a variety of ways on account of the partition, but that should not make me forgetful of our duty towards the country. We should also not forget that the Father of the Nation during his lifetime freely and unreservedly expressed himself in favour of Hindustani.'[91]

Ravi Shankar Shukla, on the other hand, rebutted Nehru's insistence on broadening the conception of the national language to include Urdu and Urdu script, in particular. He wrote:

We have already paid a heavy price for our policy of appeasing communalism. No more quarter can be given to communalism. We must build a strong nation on the solid foundation of a single national language and a single national script. We must know in what way inclusion of Urdu and the Urdu script makes for broadmindedness, culture and scholarship, and advocacy of Hindi and Devanagari smacks of a narrow and perverted nationalism'.[92]

Kamlapathi Tripathi said to Nehru on the eve of the crucial Congress meeting, after which the Constituent Assembly declared Hindi the national language, 'Maharaj, I am for Hindi.'[93] Sampurnanand, in charge of the

---

[89] Jyotirindra Das Gupta, *Language Conflict and National Development: Group Politics and National Language Policy in India* (Berkeley, CA: University of California Press, 1970), pp. 131-2.

[90] Begum Aijaz Rasul, 8 November 1948, *CAD*, vol. 7, p. 306.

[91] 6 November 1948, ibid., p. 281.

[92] Ravi Shankar Shukla, 'Pandit Nehru and National Language', *Hindustan Times,* 18 April 1949.

[93] Kamlapathi Tripathi, *Freedom Movement and Afterwards* (Varanasi: Vishwavidyalaya,

education portfolio in Lucknow, made it clear at the UP Hindi Sahitya Sammelan in 1949 that Urdu could not have the status of a state language. The Urdu style was distinctly 'unnational, if not anti-national', and he claimed that Urdu writers had made a deliberate and painstaking effort to 'effect a break with Indian tradition'.[94] He added:

The Urdu writer does not know that India once produced a Bhima; he has only heard of Rustam. If he has occasion to speak of great kings, he will wax eloquent over Dara, Sikandar, Kaikhusro and Jamshed.[...] Fed on such insidious poison, there is little wonder that the average educated Muslim feels no pride in the land of his birth and all that it stands for.[...] When great Urdu poets give expression to convert, through their language, the streets of Lucknow and Delhi into the streets of Isphahan, there is no cause to be surprised if, to the reader of such stuff, India appears almost to be a land of exile.[95]

The pro-Hindi lobby, which was vocal in the Constituent Assembly, had its way. 'The Hindi-Hindustani controversy has come to an end', stated Seth Govind Das, 'simply because Article 99 of the Constitution refers to 'Hindi or English alone in relation to the transaction of business in our Parliament. Thus the question of Hindustani exists no more.'[96] Hindi was the state language and medium of instruction in the vast territory extending from the eastern border of Bihar to the western boundary of Rajasthan. In accordance with the UP government's administrative order of 8 October 1947 and the UP Official Language Act of 1951, Hindi in the Devanagari script was declared to be the state language.[97] The UP Board of High School and Intermediate Education decided on Hindi as the sole medium for writing the High School examinations from 1953 onwards.[98] In April 1954 the Congress Working Committee recommended that Hindi be made a compulsory subject at various stages in schools and colleges, although it also approved, as a concession to anti-Hindi sentiments in the south, the programme of replacing English by Hindi in stages over a period of fifteen years.

All this while in many places active and aggressive campaigns were

1969), p. 69.

[94] *Hindustan Times*, 18 April 1949.

[95] Sampurnanand, 'Our National Language', ibid., 14 November 1947; and Tandon's speech in June 1948, quoted in Graham, op. cit., p. 114. For K.M. Munshi, see his *Sparks from a Governor's Anvil*, vol. 1 (Lucknow: Publications Bureau, 1956).

[96] 15 November 1948, *CAD*, vol. 7, p. 223.

[97] The Muslim League members, led by Z.H. Lari, walked out of the house when the UP assembly, chaired by Tandon, decided to transact its business in Hindi. Khaliquzzaman used this issue as a pretext to resign from the legislature as well as the Constituent Assembly. *Hindustan Times*, 5 November 1947; Graham, op. cit., pp. 113-4; Jyotirindra Das Gupta, op. cit., p. 141; S. Dwivedi, *Hindi on Trial* (Delhi: Vikas, 1981), pp. 233-5.

[98] *Hindustan Times*, 4 March 1949.

mounted against Urdu 'as if Urdu were some dangerous enemy in our ranks.'[99] UP and Bihar governments suspended aid to Urdu-medium schools. Many children and their parents had no opportunity to learn Urdu. Nehru deprecated these trends in Congress-ruled states, 'because all my cultural standards are affected by it ... [and] the future integration of India appears to me to suffer.'[100] In an implied rebuke to Pant, home minister since 1955, he made clear at a Cabinet meeting that he would face communal disturbances rather than do the Urdu-speaking people a manifest injustice. This, he said was not a personal or a sentimental matter but one of vital significance for the future.[101] But then the gulf between resolution and implementation yawned as wide as ever. Nehru's intentions were clear. At the same time he was resigned to the fact that 'if my colleagues do not agree, I cannot help it.'[102]

The Hindi-Urdu controversy, which began in the 1860s had soured inter-community relations. Though essentially sparked off by wider prospects of public employment, Hindi and Urdu gradually became, each to own more vocal protagonists, a matter of cultural survival, an issue of religio-cultural identity around which communitarian politics could be conducted. Thus Hindu revitalisation movements in Punjab, UP and Bihar, especially those linked with the Arya Samaj, laid stress on Hindi's imperilled future. On the other hand, the urban-based educated Muslims in North India, drawn principally from *ashraf* groups (upper-caste Muslims, i.e., Syeds who claimed to be descendants of the Prophet, and the Shaikhs/Siddiqis), viewed their activities as an organised attack on their cultural identity. The rejection of Urdu, built up as a literary and conversational language by the combined efforts of both Hindus and Muslims, made it appear that the Muslim contribution to India's culture was being rejected, and that the culture of free India would be exclusively Hindu.[103] 'A Muslim', wrote Z.H. Lari from Lucknow,

....has no objection to the prevalence of Hindi, but definitely resents the exclusion of Urdu as it affects not only his self-respect but jeopardises his culture and educational progress. How can a child receive primary education in a language other than his own? This is lost sight of by the majority in their present revengful mood. But to injure a limb is to injure the body.[104]

Urdu's growth and its enormous creative potential were stifled after independence. Having survived lazily in the alleys and by-lanes of

[99] 20 September 1953, *Letters,* vol. 3, p. 379.

[100] Ibid.

[101] Gopal, *Jawaharlal Nehru,* vol. 3, p. 27.

[102] Speech at Madras, 26 July 1948, *SWJN,* vol. 7, pp. 512-3.

[103] Mujeeb, *Islamic Influences,* p. 201.

[104] Z.H. Lari, 'The Muslim Problem in India', *Hindustan Times,* 15 August 1948.

predominantly Muslim localities, the language of Mir, Ghalib, Iqbal, Brij Narain Chakbast, Josh, Faiz and Firaq is gasping for breath in govern- ment-sponsored academies. Except for some districts in UP and Bihar, it is no longer used in administration, the judiciary or the police. Even symbolic attempts by the central or state governments to promote Urdu have led to a violent backlash, as in UP in the 1980s, and later in Karnataka. Widespread riots were triggered off by the UP government's decision in 1989 to make it the state's second official language. A ten-minute Urdu television news bulletin in Bangalore led to rioting in the first week of October 1994, leaving thirty dead. In just a few hours a somnolent city became a hive of tensions, with daggers, petrol-bombs and stones breaking out from gullies and balconies. In most areas, Urdu has thus become the language of Muslims only. An extensive survey by Ather Farouqui of the Jawaharlal Nehru University in Delhi through Bihar, West Bengal, Andhra Pradesh and Maharashtra disclosed that not a single non-Muslim student was enrolled to study Urdu even as an optional subject at the primary or secondary level, or opted for Urdu as the medium for education.

Nawab Mohsinul Mulk, one of the architects of the Urdu agitation in 1900-1, would have bemoaned the language's decline in the verse he wrote in protest against Anthony Macdonnell's 'Hindi resolution':

> *Chal Saath ke Hasrat dil-i mahrum se nikle*
> *Ashiq ka janaza hai badi dhum se nikle*

III

In a Nehruvian perspective, the first decade after independence rekindled hopes of a bright future. Nehru was at his best guiding the country's foreign policy with remarkable alacrity and leading the non-aligned movement along with Nasser, Sukarno and Tito. There were notable achievements on the domestic front. Nehru glowed with satisfaction 'at the sight of our nation on the march, realizing its goals one by one.' Watching the Republic Day parade in 1955, he had a sense of fulfillment 'in the air and of confidence in our future destiny.'[105] Two years later, the chief ministers were told:

If we look around to various countries which have recently attained freedom...India compares very favourably with them, both in regard to our stability and the progress we have made in these last ten years. The record is a creditable one, and this is increasingly recognised by other countries of the world'.[106]

[105] 26 January 1955, quoted in Gopal, *Jawaharlal Nehru,* vol. 2, p. 317.
[106] 5 May 1957, *Letters,* vol. 4, p. 485.

There was a silver lining on the communal front too. Hindu-Muslim clashes did indeed take place in the 1950s – at Lucknow and Bhagalpur in September 1950, at Dhanbad in January 1951 and in Nizamabad, Gulbarga, Aligarh and Mathura in August 1953. Several towns of UP, Madhya Pradesh and West Bengal were afficted with riots in early September 1956 over the reprinting of a book, *Living Biographies of Religious Leaders*, which carried a foreword by K.M. Munshi. During March-April 1959 rioting broke out at Sitamarhi and Akhta in Bihar, Mubarkarpur in UP, and Bhopal in Madhya Pradesh. But compared with the brutal history of Hindu-Muslim feuds, especially the ghastly happenings in 1946-9, the communal temperature in the 1950s remained relatively low. There was a lull after a violent storm, a clear and downward trend in communal incidents from 1954 to 1960, which, according to a report, was 'a remarkably good year with only 26 incidents in the country.'[107]

Communal organisations maintained a low profile. The Muslim League lay dormant after making familiar noises in the Constituent Assembly over separate electorates and reservation of seats, but it was soon disbanded and prominent leaders left for Pakistan in 1948-9. For example, Khaliquzzaman went on a 'peace mission' to Pakistan and stayed there permanently. The Majlis-i Ittehadul-Muslimeen, revived in the 1930s by Nawab Bahadur Ali to safeguard the throne of the Asaf Jah dynasty in Hyderabad, was dissolved in 1949.[108] Stray and isolated efforts to start new organisations, an idea mooted at the Aligarh convention held in October 1953, were foiled by Congress Muslims for fear of a Hindu backlash.

Hindu communal organisations earned respectability, especially among Hindu refugees from Pakistan, and found sympathisers in the Congress. But the intense public feelings aroused by Gandhi's assassination moved the balance of advantage within the Congress towards the liberals, who were strengthened by a profound moral indignation against the social and political views of the Hindu parties. The RSS was widely denounced; its cadres had 'neither the robust commonsense of the masses nor the sober balance of the middle class.'[109] A communal body, organised on semi-militarist lines and working mostly in secret, would impose a 'fascist tyranny'. The RSS had no reason to exist following partition and dissolution of the League in most places. A democratic state could not allow 'private armies' to influence the political process.[110]

The RSS was declared an unlawful association on 4 February 1948,

---

[107] *India Today: being a collection of research papers on burning topics of the day* (Delhi: Research Bureau, United News of India, 1970), p. 41.

[108] *Hindustan Times*, 14 August 1949.

[109] Ibid., 1 January 1949.

[110] Ibid., 11 December 1948.

and by early December more than 2,000 of its activists had been gaoled.[111] The *shakhas* lay low, confining themselves to their 'social function' and group discussions. In August 1948 Guru Golwalkar pleaded with Nehru to let the RSS join the government in combating the communist menace, and assured Patel that 'if·you with government power and we with organised cultural force combine, we can soon eliminate this menace.' Other methods to get the ban removed proved equally abortive, including a campaign of collecting signatures and a brief *satyagraha*. Golwalkar called off the *satyagraha* in January 1949.[112]

In mid-February, the Hindu Mahasabha suspended its political activities 'in order to tide over the immediate crisis' arising out of Gandhi's assassination. The decision was rescinded on 6-7 November at Delhi. In August 1949 B.G. Khare, first premier of the Congress ministry (1937-9) in the Central Provinces, joined the Mahasabha to fill the vacuum caused by the resignation of Shyama Prasad Mookerjee and death of Bhai Parmanand and B.S. Moonje. On a countryside tour in 1951-2, N.C. Chatterjee expounded *Akhand Hindustan* (United India incorporating India, Pakistan and Burma). He condemned the Congress in his speeches for its inability to keep the country's unity intact.[113] 'We believed in Akhand Hindusthan', he declared, 'and firmly hold that the vivisection of the country was a betrayal and the result of an unholy compact between the Congress, the Muslim League and British Imperialism.'[114] In 1954 the Hindu Mahasabha called for a ban on foreign missionaries. 'If the conversion of Hindus to other faiths was not stopped, a day might come when these converts might demand the further break-up of this country on the same basis as the Muslims did.'[115] Around the same time, the movement against cow-slaughter gathered momentum in UP with demonstrations, strikes and *satyagraha*. There were also Some sporadic incidents in Calcutta and Bombay.[116]

Hindu mobilisation campaigns cut little ice. Pant, UP's chief minister, characterised the anti-cow slaughter *satyagraha* as 'blackmail political tactics.'[117] The RSS was put in the dock for its belligerence and pronounced hostility towards the minorities. The Mahasabha's credibility was low: 'The explanation for ex-loyalists suddenly blossoming into

---

[111] *Hindustan Times*, 11 December 1948.

[112] Tapan Basu et al., *Khaki Shorts.* p. 31.

[113] Speech at the Bankura District Conference on 16 June 1951 and presidential address at the 30th session of the Hindu Mahsabha held on 28 December 1952, Hindu Mahasabha Tracts.

[114] Ibid., p. 3.

[115] *Statesman*, 10 May 1954.

[116] Ibid., 19, 21, 24, 25, 29, 30 September 1954.

[117] *Hindustan Times*, 10 May 1949.

super-patriots', commented the *Hindustan Times* 'lies in the fact that to the Hindu Mahasabha leaders any stick is good enough to beat the Congress with.[...] 'One has only to calculate all the consequences of what the Mahasabha wants to discover the spurious nature of its political platform.'[118] Even Vallabhbhai Patel was constrained to ask: does the Mahasabha concede to the Muslims the right to form political parties on the basis of religion? 'If it does not, it has no right to claim to itself a privilege it is not willing to concede to others. For the effective functioning of democracy in the country, we must eschew both communalism and direct action.'[119]

Organised Hindu communalism suffered major reverses. Although the Hindi zealots succeeded in destroying Urdu's future, they were forced, because of the strong anti-Hindi sentiments beyond the Vindhyas, to accept the continuing use of English for official purposes (of the Union) for fifteen years. In September 1954 an anti-cow slaughter bill was defeated in the Delhi Assembly, and three Jana Sangh members walked out.[120] In March 1955 a government-appointed committee on the preservation of cattle did not approve of a complete ban on cow slaughter.[121] Nehru stoutly resisted the Indian Cattle Reservation Bill, introduced by Govind Das in 1955 as a sequel to the Cattle Preservation Bill of 1951, asserting that it was a matter for consideration by the state governments, not parliament. He was prepared to stake his prime ministership on this issue, and the house rejected the bill by a vote of 95 to 12; only two Congressmen, Tandon and Thakur Das Bhargava, ignored the Congress whip and voted for the measure.[122]

Nehru had his way on the Hindu Code Bill[123] and on dual membership of the Congress and the RSS[124] He acted firmly and decisively, a quality that did not come to him naturally, in ensuring the reversal of the Congress Working Committee's decision, which had been backed by Patel and Pattabhi Sitaramayya. Patel's death on 15 December 1950 swung the balance in Nehru's favour. His liberal and socialist followers sensed victory when Tandon, elected to the Congress presidency on the strength of Patel's support, was made to resign. Nehru himself was elected to the

---

[118] Speech at Kanpur, *Statesman*, 1 October 1954.

[119] *Hindustan Times*, 7 December 1948.

[120] *Statesman*, 18 September 1954. In neighbouring UP, however, the Gosamavardhan committee recommended a total ban on cow-slaughter. The governor, K.M. Munshi, announced the ban on 10 March 1955. *Statesman*, 11 February 1955.

[121] Ibid., 10 March 1955, for the recommendations of the committee.

[122] Smith, *India as a Secular State*, pp. 485-6.

[123] Gopal, *Jawaharlal Nehru*, vol. 2, p. 313.

[124] See Graham, op. cit., p. 20.

post at an AICC meeting on 8 September 1951. It was a moment of triumph.

Finally the Jana Sangh, founded on 21 October 1951, failed to attract more than 3.1 per cent of votes in the first parliamentary election; its share of seats in the Lok Sabha was three. In 1957 the Mahasabha's strength in the Lok Sabha dwindled from 4 to 2. Three of its former presidents – N.B. Khare, V.G. Deshpande and N.C. Chatterjee – suffered defeat. Although the Jana Sangh's strength rose from 3 to 5 seats in the Lok Sabha and from 34 to 46 seats in the state assemblies, its overall performance was uninspiring.[125]

It was thus clear that despite bitter memories of partition and ruptured Hindu-Muslim relations, the Jana Sangh-RSS-Mahasabha combination had no immediate prospect of wresting the political initiative from the Congress. The secular fabric was no doubt fragile and vulnerable to their assault, but secular goals and aspirations in the country at large had not lost their appeal. The communist-dominated trade union movements, teachers' associations, student unions and scores of poets and writers in Hindi, Punjabi, Bengali and Urdu invoked and rallied a round secular symbols and slogans. Communal wounds were healed through stories, plays, poems, novels, paintings and the media. The Progressive Writers' Movement had seen better days, yet there were dedicated and committed creative writers who kept it going.[126] The Indian People's Theatre (IPTA) lost much of its initial vigour and momentum, but it continued to make its presence felt in some areas of the country.[127]

In the political domain, to be 'non-secular' still carried a stigma. To adopt 'non-secular' postures was still, as Patel, Tandon and Pant discovered the hard way, an act of political blasphemy, an unforgivable sin. Politicians could build their reputations on the strength of their identification with secular causes. Those who wavered were certain to fall in public esteem and tarnish their image. This was the dominant political culture till the early 1960s.

As Nehru would have watched the Republic Day parade on 26 January 1957, he must have reflected on the passing decade with mixed feelings. He would have derived some satisfaction at the country surging ahead, however

---

[125] Graham, op. cit., pp. 19-21; Craig Baxter, *The Jana Sangh: A Biography of an Indian Political Party* (Philadelphia: University of Pennsylvania Press, 1969)), chapter 5; Walter Anderson and Shridhar D. Damle, *The Brotherhood in Saffron: The Rashtriya Swayamsewak Sangh and Hindu Revivalism* (Boulder, CO: Westview, 1987).

[126] Hafeez Malik, 'The Marxist Literary Movement in India and Pakistan; *Journal of Asian Studies*, 26, 4, 1967; Carlo Coppolla (ed.), *Marxist Influences and South Asian Literature* (Delhi: Chanakya Publications, 1988); Ann Lowry Weir, 'Socialist Realism and South Asian Literature', *Journal of South Asian Literature*, 27, 2 summer/fall 1992.

[127] Sudhir Pradhan (ed.), *Marxist Cultural Movement in India*, vol. 2 (Calcutta, Navana, 1982).

imperfectly, in its quest for secularism state and society, and relieved that neither the relevance nor the utility of the secular experience was in doubt. He could move on to the next decade convinced that a vital component of the massive task of nation-building was to strengthen the secular fabric.

Secular and democratic trends in the 1950s could not conceivably go unnoticed by large numbers of Muslims still reeling under the impact of partition. 'The first year of independence', commented Z.H. Lari, once a key figure in the UP Muslim League, 'is about to run out.[...] Its close has left Muslims sad and gloomy.[...] But they have the satisfaction that India has mastered the forces of violence. A year is of little account in a nation's life.'[128] To have adopted secularism 'was a historic deed of the national leadrship of the country, despite the reactionary example set up by Pakistan and the pulls and pressures of the communal elements in the country.'[129] The constitution had provisions for safeguarding minority rights, while the Congress under Nehru's leadership had created sufficient space for the Muslims to identify and integrate with the larger democratic and secularising processes and to carve out, along with others, a place for themselves in free India. In a speech delivered at the Aligarh Muslim University, an institution which had once rebuffed Nehru and Azad in preference to Jinnah and Liaquat Ali Khan, the prime minister stated on 24 January 1948 with his characteristic eloquence:

Education is meant to free the spirit of a man and not to imprison it in set frames. I do not like this university being called the Muslim University just as I do not like the Banaras University to be called the Hindu University. That does not mean that a university should not specialise in particular cultural subjects and studies. I think it is right that this university should lay special stress on certain aspects of Islamic thought and culture.

I want you to think about these problems and come to your own conclusions. These conclusions cannot be forced upon you except to some extent, of course, by the compulsion of events which none of us can ignore. Do not think that you are outsiders here, for you are as much the flesh and blood of India as anyone else, and you have every right to share in what India has to offer. But those who seek rights must share in the obligations also. Indeed, if the duties and obligations are accepted, then rights automatically flow from them. I invite you as free citizens of free India to play your role in the building of this great country and to be sharers, in common with others, in the triumphs and setbacks alike that may come our way. The present with all its unhappiness and misery will pass. It is the future that counts, more specially for the young, and it is this future that beckons to you. How will you answer that call?[130]

[128] *Hindustan Times*, 15 August 1948.

[129] Maulana Ikhlaq Husain Qasmi, *Jamaat-e-Islami and Secularism* (Delhi: Sampradayikta Virodhi Committee, n.d.), p. 5.

[130] Convocation Address at the Aligarh Muslim University, 24 January 1948, *SWJN*, 2nd series, vol. 5, p. 27.

6

FORGING SECULAR IDENTITIES

Nehru would have noticed quite a number of familiar faces in the sprawling Convocation *pandal*. Next to him on the podium was Nawab Mohammad Ismail Khan, vice-chancellor of Aligarh's Muslim University. Adorning the front row of seats in the audience were members of the Muslim landed gentry, including the Nawab of Rampur, Nawab Muzammilullah Khan, Habibur Rahman Khan Sherwani and the Nawab of Chattari. There were others as well, awed by the occasion and by Nehru's presence. They listened with rapt attention to his eloquent speech, admired his courage, candour and breadth of vision, and felt relieved that the university, having fallen on evil days, would have the place due to it in Nehru's India.[1]

Nehru was in Aligarh on a mission of peace and goodwill, to provide the healing touch, allay the fears of a beleaguered Muslim intelligentsia and assure them of a safe future. His intention was to reach out to all, including his old-time friend Nawab Mohammad Ismail Khan, a key figure in the League's revival in UP. There were other notable League figures in the audience who had decided to stay in India. Most looked out of place, self-conscious and noticeably overwhelmed by the occasion.

Nehru was generous and magnanimous. There were perfectly sound reasons for him to undertake the peace mission to the university, once the storm-centre of the Pakistan movement but now struggling for survival. Partition, the culmination of a man-made catastrophe, had not put an end to murder, rape and mutilation in divided Bengal or Punjab, the two states which had been the scene of killings even before the 'tryst with destiny'.[2]

---

[1] *Leader* (Allahabad), 25, 27 January 1948; 'Premier Prodigal' (editorial), 26 January 1948.

[2] The scale of rioting in 1946 is clear from the following details:
(*a*) In Bengal and the Bombay province 5,094 people were killed between 1 July and 30 October. (L/PJ/8/575)
(*b*) In the Bihar Sharif division, where Muslims constituted 90 per cent of the 750,000 population, 3,000 Muslims were killed in November. (H.B. Martin, additional district magistrate, papers, CSAS).
(*c*) In the same month widespread rioting broke out at Garhmukteswar in Meerut district, and 200 Muslims were killed. Rioting then spread to Moradabad, Kanpur, Allahabad and the Gorakhpur division. (FR, first half of November 1946, H.J. Frampton papers).

Close to three-quarters of a million Punjabis died in mutual massacres during the first days of independence.[3] When August 15 came, this famous province – '*terra antiqua potens armis atque ubere glebae*' – was 'ripped in two like a piece of old cloth and handed over in a day to anarchy, savagery and ruin.'[4]

The unprecedented scale of violence was accompanied by one of the greatest mass migrations this century. Hindus and Sikhs in Pakistan were mercilessly displaced or brutally murdered. Between August 1947 and March 1948, about 4.5 million Hindus and Muslims migrated from West Pakistan to India and about 6 million Muslims moved in the reverse direction. From 1950 to 15 October 1952, over 9,32 lakhs of Hindus came from East Pakistan to India, while nearly 384,000 Muslims went from India to East Pakistan (Table 6.1).[5] A fair number of Hindus continued living in Sind after 1947 but they were gradually squeezed out.[6] Many survived to tell tales of childhoods broken in two, of long journeys on foot,

---

(*d*) The countrywide list of casualties from 18 November 1946 to 18 May 1947 was:

Province	Killed	Injured
Madras	–	13
Bombay	321	1,119
Bengal	186	965
UP	17	53
Punjab	3,024	1,200
Bihar	7	35
CP	2	12
Assam	14	–
NWFP	414	150
Delhi	29	69
Total	4,014	3,616

Source: L/PJ/8/572 (A).

(*e*) According to the under-secretary of state for India, a total of 12,400 people were killed during 1946.

[3] Leonard Mosley, *The Last Days of the British Raj* (London: Weidenfeld and Nicolson, 1961), p. 11; Penderel Moon, *Divide and Quit* (London: Chatto and Windus, 1964), p. 293; Taya Zinkin, *Reporting India* (London: Chatto and Windus, 1962); Ian Stephens, *Pakistan* (London: Ernest Benn, 1964 edn); Suranjan Das, *Communal Riots in Bengal 1904-1947* (Delhi: OUP, 1991).

[4] Darling, *Freedom's Door*, p. 305.

[5] 4 December 1952, *Letters*, vol. 3: *1952-1954*, p. 195; see also *Millions on the Move: The Aftermath of Partition* (Delhi: Publications Division, n.d.), pp. 5-7. By the end of October 1947, 30,000 Muslims moved from Amritsar to the Wagah border; 50,000 from Kartarpur to Beas; 50,000 from Hissar to Ferozepur on their way to Pakistan; 80,000 from the cattle fairground in Amritsar to Wagah. Three trains carrying 12,800 Muslims passed through Amritsar on 28 October (*Hindustan Times*, 31 October 1947).

[6] 4 December 1952, *Letters*, vol. 3, p. 195.

of abandoned homes, of sisters kidnapped or raped – 'the ghastly but familiar litany of partition horrors'.[7]

Life was no less harsh for India's Muslims, especially in areas where the impact of partition was more traumatic. They were gripped with fear and anxiety. Their initial confidence in the Congress leadership, bolstered by Nehru's exemplary role, was shattered. Their faith in age-old tradition-al ties, which influenced the decision of many to stay out in the country of their birth, was shaken. The ugly turn of events in Gurgaon district, close to Delhi and the scene of a virtual 'civil war' after August 1947, was repeated all over the Indo-Gangetic belt.

During his tour in 1946-7 Malcolm Darling found, in the tract between the Beas and Sutlej rivers, much similarity between Hindus and Muslims. He asked how was Pakistan to be fitted into these conditions?[8] He was bothered by the same question while passing through the country between the Chenab and Ravi, and commented:

What a hash politics threatens to make of this tract, where Hindu, Muslim and Sikh are as mixed up as the ingredients of a well made *pilau* [rice cooked with fowl or meat] ... I noted how often in a village Muslim and Sikh had a common ancestor. It is the same here with Hindu and Muslim Rajputs, and today we passed a village of Hindu and Muslim Gujars. A Hindu Rajput ... tells me that where he lives in Karnal to the south there are fifty Muslim villages converted to Islam in the days of Aurangzeb. They belong to the same clan as he does, and fifteen years ago offered to return to the Hindu fold, on the one condition that their Hindus kinsfolk would give them their daughters in marriage. The condition was refused and they are still Muslim. In this area, even where Hindus and Muslims belong to different clans, they still interchange civilities at marriage, inviting *mullah* or Brahmin, as the case may be, to share in the feasting.[9]

If this was so, how did Jinnah's Pakistan destroy such long-standing ties with such ease? Why did *Palbandi* or *pal* loyalty, having traditionally served as a unifying bond for decades in the Palwal, Gurgaon and Ballabhgarh *tahsils*, collapse so quickly? How does one account for the failure of people like Kanwal Khan and Syed Mutlabi Faridabadi who, according to P. Brendon, deputy-commissioner of Gurgaon, worked steadily among the Meos to win them over to a form of 'rural communism'?

Part of the explanation lies in the political decisions taken in Delhi which left their imprint on the provinces and localities and quickened the pace of communal mobilisation. In some ways, the reasons why combined socio-economic networks failed to withstand the communal onslaught

---

[7] Dalrymple, *City of Djinns*, pp. 42-3; *Seminar*, (Delhi) 'Partition', 420, August 1994; Mushirul Hasan (ed.), *India Partitioned*, vol. 2; Talbot, *Freedom's City*, op.cit.

[8] Darling, op. cit., p. 100.

[9] Ibid., p. 109.

were specific to Punjab and bore little resemblance to what occurred in UP or Bengal. In most parts of the region (some form part of the Haryana state), once the restraint of *palbandi* broke down, 'a surge of orthodox feeling came over the Hindu people and they readily accepted the leadership of local *sadhus* and of the RSS.'[10] Muslim Rajputs in Dhulkot village, near the modern Palam airport, bore the brunt of a massive attack, and most hurried to Pakistan. Those living in Rewari *tahsil* did the same for similar reasons and in similar circumstances. The Muslim inhabitants of the region were indistinguishable from their Ahir and Rajput neighbours in social customs and religious rites. They were not swayed by the Muslim League claptrap. They had not heard of a blueprint for an Islamic state or society; instead they attended Congress gatherings, voted for the Unionist Ahir MLA, and founded a high school that was officially recognised in early 1947.[11] Why would such people abandon the homes that had been theirs for generations and the school they had built so recently? The answer is that they were driven out by *trishul*-wielding RSS zealots.

Certain villages of Rohtak[12] and Ambala districts[13] were rocked by similar acts of aggression. So was Delhi's rural hinterland. State forces in the nearby tracts of Alwar and Bharatpur joined with mobs in determined onslaughts against hapless Muslims.[14] The Meos, in particular, were displaced and left high and dry. Their fate hung in the balance, because the arbiters of their destiny in Delhi had little sympathy for their rehabilitation or interest in it. 'My own mind is perfectly clear in these matters', Nehru told Mehr Chand Khanna in early June 1949, 'and I have viewed with dismay and sorrow the narrow and communal outlook that has progressively grown in this country and which shows itself in a variety of ways.'[15] However, by May 1949, 62,000 Meos of Alwar and Bharatpur

[10] P. Brendon papers, CSAS. Brendon was deputy-commissioner of Gurgaon from January 1945 to June 1947.

[11] Ibid. The RSS gained a strong foothold in Punjab in 1938-9 through the efforts of Gokul Chand Narang, Bhai Parmanand and his son-in-law. In 1942 its membership in Punjab was 10,000, including 400 regular volunteers. By January 1947, it was up to 47,000. Golwalkar's tour of the province bolstered the RSS. In June 1947, the RSS had 59,200 members and an income of Rs 104,000 as against Rs 86,700 in the previous month. These details are based on *RSS in the Punjab* (Lahore, 1948), Ian Stephens papers, CSAS.

[12] Trevor Royle, *The Last Days of the Raj* (London: Michael Joseph, 1989), p. 189.

[13] *The Memoirs of Lord Ismay*, p. 437. Muslims were forcibly sent away from the Ambala district at the rate of about 2,000 a fortnight. Nehru to Gopichand Bhargava, 15 June 1948, *SWJN*, vol. 6, p. 128; see also Nehru to Shankar Prasada, 3 October 1948, *SWJN*, vol. 7, p. 128 (the volume numbers of *SWJN* refer to the new series).

[14] The Raja of Alwar had close links with the RSS and the Hindu Mahasabha, and is said to have supervised the killing of Muslims in Alwar and Bharatpur. Nearly 110,000 Muslims were displaced in the region. In Kapurthala state too, there was widespread violence against the Muslims in August-September 1947. Syed Azhar Husain Zaidi, *The New Nazis* (Karachi, n.d.).

[15] Nehru to Mehr Chand Khanna, 6 June 1949, *SWJN*, vol. 11, p. 80.

Table 6.1. MIGRATION BETWEEN EAST BENGAL AND
WEST BENGAL, ASSAM AND TRIPURA

TO INDIA BEFORE THE INDO-PAKISTAN AGREEMENT		
	Hindus	*Muslims*
From East Bengal to West Bengal (7 Feb. – 8 April 1950)	547,049	6,847
From East Bengal to Assam (7 Feb. – 8 April 1950)	190,530	Negligible
From East Bengal to Tripura	120,000	n.a.
Total	857,579	6,847

TO INDIA AFTER THE AGREEMENT		
From East Bengal to West Bengal (9 April – 25 July 1950)	999,290	218,708
From East Bengal to Assam (9 April – 27 July 1950)	191,751	46,617
From East Bengal to Tripura (9 April – 18 July 1950)	93,582	32,083
Total	1,284,623	297,408
Grand total	2,142,202	304,255

FROM INDIA BEFORE THE AGREEMENT		
From West Bengal to East Bengal (7 Feb. – 8 April 1950)	65,537	254,715
From Assam to East Bengal (7 Feb. – 8 April 1950)	Negligible	124,063
From Tripura to East Bengal	Negligible	n.a.
Total	65,537	378,778

FROM INDIA AFTER THE AGREEMENT		
From West Bengal to East Bengal (9 April – 25 July 1950)	503,273	409,741
From Assam to East Bengal (9 April – 25 July 1950)	32,561	37,578
From Tripura to East Bengal (9 April – 18 July 1950)	5,417	2,649
Total	541,251	449,968
Grand total	606,824	828,746

MIGRATION FIGURES

After the Agreement (9 April 1950 – 25 July 1950)

From East Bengal to India	
— Hindus	1,284,623
— Muslims	297,408
Total	1,582,031

Table 6.1 *contd.*

From India to East Bengal		
— Hindus		541,251
— Muslims		449,968
	Total	991,219

Notes

1. The foregoing figures do not take into account those who migrated between East and West Bengal on foot or by country boats, or those who travelled by train between East Bengal and Jalpaiguri. A considerable number crossed the border on foot.

2. About 250,000 Muslims migrated from UP to West Pakistan, of whom 5,000 returned to India.

Source: Appendices to the Parliamentary Debates, July-August 1950, annexure 19, pp. 36-7.

---

had their land and homes restored to them due to non-official efforts, inspired by Gandhi's assurances to the Meos whom he addressed at Gurgaon on 19 December 1947 and by Vinoba Bhave's bold initiatives.[16]

Delhi – the city which the great Urdu poets like Mir Taqi Mir, Sauda (1706-81), Ghalib and Shaikh Mohammad Ibrahim Zauq (1789-1854) refused to abandon even under trying circumstances – turned hostile to its own legacy and inhospitable to its own citizens. The capital was no longer the bulwark of peace and harmony during the last six days of August and the first fortnight of September 1947. A nightly curfew was imposed from 25 August, and another and more rigorous one from 28 August to 1 September. Looting, arson and murder were rampant. The Grand Trunk Express was stopped and almost every Muslim man, woman and child was killed. Ishtiaq Husain Qureshi recalled how Muslims of Timarpur living in close proximity to the University of Delhi bore the brunt of the frenzy and how the campus was targeted forcing him and his family to move to the refugee camp in the Old Fort (*purana qila*). Qureshi, professor of history at the Delhi University, and Zakir Husain, then Jamia Millia's vice-chancellor, met Gandhi the same day. 'We did not have to tell him much because his workers were reporting events fully and truly .... I said to him that only he could stop the carnage. For a moment he grew thoughtful and promised simply, "I will put in my best in the effort." And I think he did keep his promise. Otherwise he would not have been assassinated.'[17]

[16] *Hindustan Times*, 28 May, 7 June 1949; on the rehabilitation of Meos, *SWJN*, vol. 11, pp. 97-111, and *Rajendra Prasad: Correspondence*, vol. 11, pp. 100-1. Likewise, Muslims living in the sixteen villages around Delhi were resettled in their homes. *Hindustan Times*, 13 July 1948. See also Shail Mayaram, 'Speech, Silence and the Making of Partition Violence in Mewat', Working Paper, Institute of Development Studies, Jaipur, no. 54, 1995.

[17] I.H. Qureshi, *From Miraj to Domes* (Karachi: Saad Publication, 1983), pp. 70-1; Ale Ahmad Suroor, *Khwab Baqi Hain* (Aligarh: Educational Book House, 1991), pp. 131-2. Not far from Delhi – on the Grand Trunk (GT) Road – there were many unreported incidents. Thousands of Muslims inhabiting the Jumna belt took refuge in Dankaur, a

Legacy of a Divided Nation

A number of mosques in Delhi and elsewhere were either destroyed or taken over by enraged Hindus and Sikhs who had seen their own places of worship razed to the ground in Pakistan.[18] Khwaja Bakhtiyar Kaki's shrine in Mehrauli, venerated by Hindus and Muslims alike, was damaged: the Mahatma, sensitive to the shrine's symbolism, visited Mehrauli on 27 January 1948 and pledged government's help in repairing the damage.[19] Muslim workers in the Delhi Cloth Mills were locked up in a secure part of the factory and, when the tumult died down, transferred to Bharat Ram's Pakistan factory in Lyallpur.[20] The killing, burning and looting were not confined to the crowded poverty-stricken areas of the walled city; they swept along New Delhi's wide avenues, past the Lutyens/Baker buildings of the recently defunct British government, the arcaded modern shopping centres, and the comfortable bungalows of the officials. In Lodhi colony, Sikh bands burst into the white Lutyens bungalows belonging to senior Muslim civil servants and killed anyone they found at home.[21] The urban artisan and entrepreneurial classes were reduced by riots and migration in the east and south of Delhi. In Ajmeri Gate, close to the famous Delhi College, there was much bloodshed. Most Muslim shoemakers in the old cobblers' bazaar fled to Karachi in 1947. In Sabzi Mandi, Paharganj and Karol Bagh, where the population was equally balanced, Hindus and Sikhs – half out of fear and half out of malice and greed – eliminated the Muslims. Nirad Chaudhuri, then living in old Delhi, was so shocked by what he saw on 7 September that he broke

---

'lamentable sight.' Many were massacred in Aqilpur village on the Bulandshahr road. 36 June and 3 July 1947, Mujtaba Khan papers, FMA, Karachi. Such was the climate that in just five days – 5-10 October 1947 – nearly 40,000 Muslims left Delhi for Pakistan. Many others from the city, as also from Moradabad and Bareilly, sought refuge in Rampur, an area with a large Muslim population. For much the same reason, 200,000 Muslims reached Hyderabad from Bombay, CP and Berar. Rampur and Hyderabad, princely states with Muslim rulers and substantial Muslim populations, offered a sense of security. *Hindustan Times*, 12, 21, 31 October 1947.

[18] 117 mosques were occupied by Hindus and Sikhs, and some were converted into temples. In Buria (Ambala district) twenty mosques remained under non-Muslim control till December 1948. But the main problem was restoring confidence among 12,000 Muslims who were ill-treated by the civil authorities. Aziz Ahmad, 'India and Pakistan' in Ann K.S. Lambton and Bernard Lewis (eds), *The Cambridge History of Islam*, vol. 2A, p. 73 (CUP, 1977), p. 117; Nehru to C.M. Trivedi, 14 December 1948, *SWJN*, vol. 8, pp. 134 (n.2), 135. By the end of January 1948, over fifty mosques were 'vacated'. *Hindustan Times*, 15 January 1948.

[19] Nehru's note to the private secretary, 13 December 1948, *SWJN*, vol. 8, p. 134.

[20] Royle, op. cit., p. 204. Azad to Patel, 27 November 1947, *Sardar Patel's Correspondence*, vol. 4, p. 367.

[21] Dalrymple, op. cit., pp. 42-3; Pervival Spear, 'The Position of the Muslims, before and after Partition' in Philip Mason (ed.), *India and Ceylon: Unity and Diversity* (London: OUP, 1967); Stephens, *Pakistan*, p. 190.

down and cried bitterly.[22] Throughout the weekend he saw Muslims

... waiting for the evacuating lorries with vacant looks in their eyes, disregarding the rain and the storm, as if their only thought were to escape the spectre that was treading at their heels. During the days of British rule their lives, like those of all humble Indians, had only been the lives of working bees and their homes had been far less clean and comfortable than the cells of a beehive. Now even these were being denied to them. They were losing the right of toiling and living even as working bees. Among my co-religionists any expression of sympathy for these men was highly unpopular, sometimes considered even immoral. The ground for this denial of sympathy was the murder and dispossession of the Hindus and Sikhs in the Western Punjab. Throughout the country the theory had gained ground that the oppression of one minority could be counterbalanced only by the oppression of another.[23]

By 1951 nearly 3,29,000 Muslims in Delhi had headed off to Karachi, the city that already contained 200,000 refugees who had fled from the capital to Pakistan in the upheaval of 1947. Delhi's Muslim population was thus reduced from 33.22 per cent in 1941 to 5.71 per cent a decade later.[24] Most fled in terror and sought shelter in refugee camps. Thousands were herded within the walls of the *purana qila* with no proper shelter, no doctor and no sanitary arrangements. 'When we ourselves were uprooted from our house', recalled Badruddin Tyabji (died 1996), then a young civil servant who had to seek shelter with a friend, 'our two Muslim servants – a cook and a bearer – had also to seek shelter there. Merely paying them an occasional visit to see how they were getting on was itself a harrowing duty not devoid of risk. What it must have been like living there, I cannot imagine.'[25]

[22] Chaudhuri, *Thy Hand, Great Anarch!*, p. 841.

[23] Ibid., p. 850.

[24] The corresponding percentage of Hindus and Sikhs rose from 61.80 and 1.76 per cent in 1941 to 84.16 and 7.86 per cent, respectively. *Gazette of India: Delhi* (Delhi: Delhi Administration, 1978), p. 172; V.K.R.V. Rao and P.B. Desai, *Greater Delhi: A Study in Urbanisation 1940-1959* (Bombay: Asia, 1965), p. 56; Asok Mitra, *Delhi: Capital City* (Delhi: Publications Division, 1970), chapter 3.

DELHI'S POPULATION BY RELIGION, 1901-61 (%)			
	1901	*1931*	*1951*	*1961*
Hindus	74.10	62.85	84.16	81.05
Sikhs	0.04	1.01	7.86	7.67
Muslims	24.28	32.53	5.71	5.84
Jains	1.12	0.84	1.16	1.11
Christians	0.46	2.67	1.07	1.10

Source: Gazetteer of India (Delhi: Delhi Administration, 1976), p. 143.

[25] Badruddin Tyabji, 'Chaff and Grain', *India and Foreign Review* (Delhi), 15 June 1964, pp. 21-5, and his *Memoirs of an Egoist*, vol. 1, (Delhi: Orient Longman, 1988); Anis Kidwai, *Azadi ki Chaon Mein* (Delhi: National Book Trust, 1980), and *Memoirs of Lord Ismay*, p. 437.

Brave and courageous men and women all over the country, Mridula Sarabhai and Anis Kidwai being the most prominent in Delhi, provided succour to the unhappy victims of rape, assault and abduction, set up relief camps and offered food and medicines to the weak and vulnerable. Stories of stoicism, courage and generosity were reported from all parts of the country – from Punjab where Muslim *muhajirin*, moving from Beas to Amritsar, received fresh drinking water and milk;[26] from Rasulpur near Agra cantonment, where the Hindus persuaded twenty Muslims waiting at the railway station to return to their village;[27] from village Barhari in Basti district, where Raj Kishore, a Congress leader, saved Muslim lives;[28] from Patna, where the husband of Nayama Khatoon Haider, a Bihar legislator, was rescued from being lynched by an angry mob.[29] Here is a vivid description of such gestures of kindness, warmth and humanity:

Where were you, Zahra, when I sat up through the nights, watching village after village set on fire, each day nearer and nearer? ... Do you know who saved me and my child? Sita, who took us to her house ... And Ranjit, who came from his village, because he had heard of what was happening in the foothills and was afraid of us. He drove us back, pretending we were his family, risking discovery and death ....

Do you know who saved all the others who had no Sitas and Ranjits? Where were all their leaders? Safely across the border. The only people left to save them were those very Hindus against whom they had ranted. Do you know what 'responsibility' and 'duty' meant? To stop the murderous mob at any cost, even if it meant shooting people of their own religion.[30]

In the capital itself Nehru himself took personal risks trying to shame the rioters into submission.[31] For him, as indeed for the Mahatma, violence in Delhi and elsewhere was a personal affront as well as a national catastrophe. Everything for which they had spent their lives fighting seemed to be crumbling before their eyes. Their responses stand in sharp contrast to the attitude of their counterparts in Pakistan where there was no concerted endeavour to contain the orgy of violence against the Hindus and Sikhs.[32] There was not much concern either for the plight of Muslims

26 *Hindustan Times*, 2 October 1947.

27 Ibid., 19 October 1947.

28 Ibid., 30 January 1948.

29 Ibid., 22 September 1947; see also 27 April 1948 and 8 July 1949 for similar reports.

30 Attia Hosain, *Sunlight on a Broken Column*, p. 304.

31 Michael Brecher, *Nehru: A Political Biography* (Delhi: OUP, 1959), p. 366; *Memoirs of Lord Ismay*, p. 437; Badruddin Tyabji, *Chaff and Grain* (Calcutta: Asia Publishing House, 1962), pp. 165-8. And 'A Diary of Partition Days' by Ganda Singh and 'Love is Stronger than Hate', in Mushirul Hasan (ed.), *India Partitioned*, vol. 2, pp. 27-121.

32 There were of course some notable exceptions. For example, H.S. Suhrawardy's first speech in the Pakistan Constituent Assembly quoted in Ikramullah, *Huseyn Shaheed Suhrawardy*, appendix 7, pp. 153-9.

across the border: a few routine statements were promptly denounced by prominent Muslim citizens in Delhi and elsewhere.[33] For the cynics in Karachi and Lahore, and that included senior government servants and bureaucrats, the scale and intensity of the rioting vindicated the two-nation theory and their conviction that the 'gulf separating Hindus and Muslims was unbridgeable.

The Mahatma's fast on the morning of 13 January symbolised his inner grief and personal anguish. Nehru, holding the reins of office, did not give up without a fight, although he made concessions to right-wing sentiments and betrayed signs of weakness and fatigue when it came to pressing his own ideas and policies. But when sanity returned, he emerged as the torch-bearer of secularism and helped to bridge the sectarian divide, consistently championing minority rights and justice. 'We have always to remember India as a composite country', he wrote in September 1953, 'composite in many ways, in religion, in customs, in languages, in ways of life.'[34] If this was mere rhetoric, as we are led to believe, what else was he supposed to say? When for example, he learnt that Muslims were poorly represented in government service, he told his chief ministers:

If we are to be secular, stable, and strong State, our first consideration must be to give absolute fairplay to our minorities, and thus to make them feel completely at home in India. We are apt to preach to them too much as to what they should do and some condemn them. That does not help. We have to deal with the psychological reactions of large numbers of people.[35]

Few in the Congress advocated multiculturalism and composite living with equal vigour and earnestness and few heeded Nehru's plea in neighbouring UP to bridge the Hindu-Muslim divide. Partly for their own reasons but also because of unabated violence against them, nearly 4,000 Muslims a day boarded the train to Pakistan. This was the figure in 1950. It later went down to 2,000 but then rose again to 5,000 and above.[36] The Muslim population in UP had been 15.43 per cent in 1941, and was down to 14.28 per cent ten years later. In towns like Shahjahanpur, almost every Muslim packed up to leave, although most returned in due course.[37] Many

---

[33] For example, Liaquat Ali Khan urged the *Id* congregation at Karachi not to forget 'the three and a half crores of Indian Muslims – our blood brothers – who are not free today and who are not celebrating this Id as free and independent people'. This address was condemned by, among others, Abdul Qaiyum Ansari, president of the All-India Momin Conference (serving the interests of the Muslim weavers in UP and Bihar), and Mir Mushtaq Ahmad, a Delhi socialist leader. *Hindustan Times*, 31 July, 1 August 1949.

[34] 20 September 1953, *Letters*, vol. 3, p. 377.

[35] 15 June 1954, ibid., p. 570. Nehru reiterated these views in his correspondence with chief ministers.

[36] 17 May 1950, ibid., vol. 2, p. 94.

[37] Nehru to G.B. Pant, telegram, 11 April 1950, *SWJN*, vol. 14, part 2, p. 267.

left from the Rohilkhand area and from Meerut and Muzaffarnagar districts in western UP. The number of migrants from central and eastern regions was comparatively small, but the proportion of professional emigrants was relatively high. Educational institutions were overnight depleted of students and teachers. Maulana Jamal Mian's departure from Lucknow was a blow to the Firangi Mahal seminary, as was Syed Sulaiman Nadwi's exit from Nadwat al-Ulama, also in Lucknow. Deoband lost many of its stars. Enrolment figures were down from 1,600 to 1,000 in 1947-8. Income dwindled, because a large number of students and patrons migrated to Pakistan.[38] The Aligarh University was now rudderless without some of its distinguished teachers who had gone to Karachi in search of greener pastures, the eventual homeland of the *muhajirin*. A respondent from Aligarh recalled:

The atmosphere was so bad for Muslims that everybody wanted to migrate from here. Whether he was poor or from a wealthy family, everyone wanted to go. Every Muslim who had the capacity to migrate or who had the wealth to shift to Pakistan migrated like anything. All our nawabs, all our leaders, all our technologists, all our educationists.[39]

In Bihar the emigration began in November-December 1946 as a sequel to rioting in Saran, Patna, Gaya, Monghyr and Bhagalpur, but peace was soon restored and the flow of emigration stopped just before partition. There was fresh migration after August 1947 mainly for economic reasons and because of the acute food shortage in North Bihar, which had a common frontier with East Pakistan. Migrants totalled 4-500,000, although some returned to their homes during 1950-1.

The princely state of Hyderabad had received a continuous migration of Muslims, particularly since 1857, from the rest of India. In 1947 the number of immigrants which at first was in thousands, soon increased to hundreds of thousands. Drawn from both the rural and urban areas, they were of all descriptions – traders, artisans, domestic and government servants, agriculturists and labourers, skilled and unskilled. However, the influx came to an abrupt end on 13 September 1948, the day the armed forces of India moved into the state 'in response to the call of the people'. Almost immediately a reverse movement started: a number of Hyderabadi Muslims left for Pakistan, while others returned to those places in India from where they or their immediate forefathers had come in the recent past. Thus the 1941-52 decade witnessed both an influx of Muslims into Hyderabad state and an exodus from it on a large scale.

Elsewhere, nearly 450 Muslims a day continued their trek across the

---

[38] Rizvi, *History of the Dar al-Ulum*, vol. 1, p. 254.

[39] E.S. Mann, *Boundaries and Identities: Muslims, Work and Status in Aligarh* (Delhi: Sage, 1992), p. 60.

Rajasthan-Sind border. From January to 1 November 1952, 62,467 Muslims went *via* Khokhropar to Sind in West Pakistan. 'Some hundreds go daily and have been going, in varying numbers, for the last three and a half years,' Nehru informed his chief ministers. 'The fact that they go there itself indicates that the conditions they live in are not agreeable to them and the future they envisage for themselves in India is dark.'[40] The fact is that quite a large number of established and prosperous professionals from UP, Bihar and the princely states of Hyderabad, Bhopal and Rampur also left: in Hyderabad the *razakars* from 'middle-class' background formed a major segment of the emigrants. They abandoned the city after Indian troops had seized control and integrated the state into the Union, along with the Urdu-speaking Muslims from UP, many of whom had successful careers in the Nizam's service. Typical of these was Begum Pasha Sufi, the daughter of Mohammad Yar Jung and the first woman graduate of Aligarh Muslim University. She resigned as inspector of schools in June 1951 and followed her children to Lahore. Some others left in guilt fearing retribution, some in panic, some because of a vague fear of an uncertain future, some because their promised land had finally come into being and beckoned to them.[41]

Men in government and the professions from Delhi, UP and Bihar formed the core section of *muhajirin*. The Delhi police, according to the city's *Hindustan Times* of 31 July 1948, was depleted of its rank and file because of 'mass desertion'. All the three subordinate judges in the Delhi court rushed to Pakistan;[42] so did Mohammad Wasim, advocate-general of UP and, in the words of the Turkish visitor Halide Edib, 'a landlord who owns considerable land'.[43] He took up the same assignment in Pakistan, leaving behind his father Mohammad Nasim who died at Lucknow in 1953 after a distinguished career in the Awadh bar, and his Oxford-educated brothers, Mohammad Habib, the Aligarh historian, and Mohammad Mujeeb, Jamia's vice-chancellor. People employed with local and provincial governments also opted for Pakistan,[44] although some changed their minds later and returned to India (Table 6.2). Poets and other writers, Josh Malihabadi being the most prominent, joined the trek at different times. Some landlords, including Jinnah's lieutenant Nawab

[40] 4 December 1952, *Letters*, vol. 3, p. 194; see also 4 October 1953, vol. 2, p. 507, 15 November, 1 December 1953, vol. 3, p. 507.

[41] Begum Pasha Sufi, *Hamari Zindagi: Khudnawisht Sawana-i Umri* (Karachi, 1973), p. 125; Narendra Luther, *Hyderabad: Memories of a City* (Hyderabad: Orient Longman, 1995), p. 389.

[42] *Hindustan Times*, 9 August 1948.

[43] Edib, *Inside India*, p. 169.

[44] Among them were 1,900 Muslims of Meerut employed in the railways, in post and telegraph, and the income tax departments; 400 serving the railways in Jabalpur; 1,880 out of 3,200 policemen in Delhi. *Hindustan Times*, 18 October, 18 and 22 November 1947.

Liaquat Ali Khan, was among the *muhajirin*. The Raja of Mahmudabad left his family behind in the sprawling Mahmudabad House in Qaiser Bagh, Lucknow, to undertake the mission of creating an Islamic state and society in Pakistan.

Table 6.2. EMPLOYMENT OF PERSONS WHO OPTED FOR PAKISTAN
AND LATER APPLIED TO REMAIN IN INDIA

1. (a)	Officers and subordinate staff who opted for Pakistan and applied to be retained in India	23,233
(b)	Persons re-employed	19,676
2. (a)	Muslims who opted for Pakistan, did not join duty and applied to stay on in India	16,090
(b)	Muslims re-employed	13,018

Source: Constituent Assembly of India: Legislative Debates, November-December 1949, p. 10.

Many prominent Muslims stayed, including some of those who had headed the Muslim League campaign. Landlords like Nawab Mohammad Ismail Khan, Nawab Jamshed Ali Khan, the Nawab of Chattari and the Rajas of Salempur, Nanpara, Kotwara, Pirpur and Jahangirabad clung to their small estates. Ismail was elected to the vice-chancellorship of Aligarh Muslim University in September 1947, but relinquished it on 14 November 1948. Several others retained their public positions, although they had lost face with their supporters. Prominent among these was Dr Ziauddin (died December 1947), former vice-chancellor of Aligarh's University; Begum Aijaz Rasul, secretary of the Muslim League in the Constituent Assembly; and Asrar Ahmad, member of the legislative assembly and president of the Budaun Muslim League. They swallowed their pride and accepted the 'inevitable', but they encountered criticism and ridicule, and called upon to prove and demonstrate their loyalty.

Many others felt overwhelmed by the climate of hostility, suspicion and distrust. They had a litany of complaints – recurring riots, discrimination in employment and official neglect of Urdu. Syed Mahmud, Nehru's friend and minister in Bihar, protested that Muslims faced harassment and were treated as 'a body of criminals'. He too was not spared: 'Half of my life', he wrote to the chief minister angrily, 'I had to suffer much humiliation as a Congressman at the hands of the British Government in India. Now it seems for the remaining period I have to suffer all these indignities and insults at the hands of the Congress Government. [...] Am I wrong in this conclusion?'[45]

The reaction and experience of a firewood seller in Lucknow was no different:

---

[45] Syed Mahmud to S.K. Sinha, (?) 1948, Datta and Cleghorn (eds), *A Nationalist Muslim and Indian Politics,* p. 264; and Nehru to Pant, 17 April 1950, *SWJN,* vol. 14, part 2, p. 293.

I worked as a clerk in government department in Lucknow till 1949 when I resigned. The fault was not entirely mine. My brother and his family went to Pakistan and I went to see them off till Delhi, staying back a few days more than the sanctioned leave. When I came back, I found my friends behaving as if Pakistan was my personal demand. My boss, he was a Hindu, told me that if I wanted to continue in service, I should change my Muslim name to a Hindu one. Only then did I realise how wise Jinnah was to give a sense of security and home to Muslims. I resigned my job that day itself and since then I have set up this business. Now it has been thirty-five years.[46]

Thirty-one Muslims were gaoled for 'anti-Indian Union' activities and many more were detained under the Public Safety Act.[47] Chand Khan, municipal commissioner in Allahabad, was gaoled under the Maintenance of Public Order Act,[48] and Nawab Ali of the UP medical service on a charge of disloyalty to the Union.[49] Two engineers of the reconstituted Kanpur Development Board faced suspension on a minor charge.[50] Muslims in Agra were required to register themselves with the district magistrate. Their houses were searched and a respectable member of a locality, Shaikh Badruddin, former legislative assembly member, was arrested for possessing unlicensed arms.[51] Muslims in Kanpur had to obtain a permit before travelling to Hyderabad; their relations in Hyderabad wanting to visit them had to register at a recognised hotel or a police station.[52]

Muslim officials on the railways in Kanpur, some of whom had served for more than ten years, faced dismissal. It was common in UP to suspect Muslim officials and push them out.[53] Aligarh's district magistrate was severe on university students and teachers, who had already incurred the wrath of the RSS and some local and provincial Congress leaders for their involvement in the Pakistan movement.[54] The university, faced with difficult times and threatened with closure, was eventually saved by

[46] Quoted in Nirmala Srinivasan, *Prisoners of Faith: A View From Within* (Delhi: Sage, 1989), p. 100.

[47] *Hindustan Times*, 14 August 1948. On arrests of Muslim officers in Hyderabad after the 'Police Action', see Fareed Mirza, *Pre and Post Police Action Days* (Hyderabad, 1976), pp. 43-4.

[48] *Hindustan Times*, 20 November 1947.

[49] Ibid., 22 December 1947.

[50] Ibid.

[51] Ibid., 30 October, 19 November 1947.

[52] Ibid., 5 June 1948.

[53] Nehru to N. Gopalaswami Ayyangar, 25 May 1949, *SWJN*, vol. 11, p. 237.

[54] There were wild rumours of Pakistani officials recruiting Aligarh University students to the army, of arms and ammunition being stored on the campus, and of bombs being recovered from the hostels. Statement by Alugarai Shastri, acting-president, UP Congress, *Hindustan Times*, 13 October 1947.

Nehru's intervention. Zakir Husain, the newly-appointed vice-chancellor, placed it on a firm footing with the active backing of Azad, free India's first education minister. Liberal and socialist teachers, such as the historian Mohammad Habib, the Urdu writer Rashid Ahmad Siddiqi and the Persian professor, Hadi Hasan, staged a rearguard action to combat the influence of communal tendencies. In general, however, Mohanlal Gautam, leading Congressman touring UP, found 'an all-pervading sense of fear' among the Muslims.[55]

Table 6.3. MIGRATION FROM INDIA TO PAKISTAN, AND VICE VERSA, AND EVACUEES' PROPERTY

	Area of agricultural land left (acres)	*No. of houses/huts left*
Bombay	671	641
Delhi	20,198	10,212 houses/ industrial premises
Madras	129	–
Orissa	–	–
United Provinces	14,221	2,398
Bihar	–	–
Patiala State	338,996	n.a.
Faridkot State	40,978	10,303
Bikaner State	1,052,801	8,272

Source: Constituent Assembly of India: Legislative Debates, November-December 1949, p. 4.

The Evacuee Property Laws (Tables 6.3-4) were most inequitable Muslims could not easily dispose of their property or carry on trade for fear that the long arm of the property law might hold them in its grip. The laws restricted business opportunities and crippled large numbers of Muslims, especially in the north and west of India.[56] A number of old Congressmen continued to send small sums of money to their relations in Pakistan, but they were promptly declared evacuees or intending evacuees.[57] Nehru was personally distressed by all this, as also by the spate of communal violence in UP. 'People die and the fact of killing, though painful, does not upset me. But what does upset one is the complete degradation of human nature and, even more, the attempt to find justification for this.'[58]

[55] Nehru to Patel, 27 May 1950, *SWJN*, vol. 14, part 2, p. 268.
[56] 1 December 1953, *Letters*, vol. 3, p. 462. See also, Attia Hosain, *Sunlight on a Broken Column*, p. 278, for a brilliant account of how the legislation came like a 'death-blow'.
[57] Nehru to Pant, 17 April 1950, *SWJN*, vol. 14, part 2, p. 293.
[58] Ibid., p. 268.

Table 6.4. AGRICULTURAL LAND LEFT BY MUSLIMS IN INDIA AND
ACCEDED STATES (*acres, except where otherwise stated*)

	Area	
West Bengal	500	*bighas*
East Punjab	4,358,784	(*total*)
	3,282,979	(*cultivated*)
Bihar	1,161	
Central Provinces	1,111	*bighas*
Uttar Pradesh	14,221	
Ajmer	7,000	
Delhi	20,388	
Patiala	338,996	
Nabha	53,045	
Jind	36,060	
Kapurthala	194,000	
Faridkot	40,978	
Alwar	419,000	
Bharatpur	117,000	
Bikaner	1,052,801	

Source: Constituent Assembly of India: Legislative Debates, November–December 1949, p. 16.

By contrast, some of Nehru's colleagues were unrepentant. A powerful section, led by Patel and Tandon, retorted in answer to the criticism of its murky conduct in handling the civil strife that the strong anti-Muslim sentiments were generated by bitter and painful memories of partition. They pointed out that any other country, afflicted with the division of its territory and the unprecedented scale of transfer of populations, would have been equally prone to such hostility and antagonism. These indications angered Nehru and his liberal and socialist comrades, and dismayed Muslims. Their anxieties over their position deepened and they were compelled to examine the implications of partition for their lives. In many ways their economic and political future was deeply influenced by that cataclysmic event – a theme we explore in the next section.

II

'Partition was a total catastrophe for Delhi,' observed one of the few surviving members of Delhi's Muslim aristocracy. 'Those who were left behind are in misery. Those who are uprooted are in misery. The peace of Delhi is gone. Now it is all gone.'[59] It was as much a catastrophe for

[59] Quoted in Dalrymple, op. cit., p. 58.

Rashid, Parveen or Amir Mohammad Khan, son of the Raja of Mah-mudabad, as for hundreds of thousands of families 'faced with the necessity of changing habits of mind and living conditioned by centuries, hundreds of thousands of land-owners and the hangers-on who had lived on their largesse, their weaknesses and their follies.'[60] The real pinch was felt in Delhi, UP, Bihar and Hyderabad, the areas most affected by riots, the exodus to Pakistan and the extensive skimming off from the professional classes. In UP and Bihar few Muslims were left in the defence services, the police, the universities, the law courts or the vast Central Secretariat in Delhi.[61] In a highly competitive world, large-scale immigration of mostly educated upper-caste Hindus in Lucknow – 70 per cent of the total immigrants – gradually reduced Muslim influence in government, business, trade and the professions.[62]

In Hyderabad Muslims constituted 10 per cent of the population before 1947-48. Muslim government servants held, as in UP, a much higher percentage of posts. But their fortunes dwindled following Hyderabad's merger with the Indian Union. According to Narendra Luther, administrator of Hyderabad from 1974 to 1977, most Muslim officials of the erstwhile princely state were subjected to quick screening. Some were removed, some reduced in rank, some put in jail. Urdu ceased to be the official language and the medium of instruction. The abolition of *jagirdari* affected over 11 per cent of the Muslim population, three-quarters of whom inhabited about a dozen urban centres. Smaller *jagirdars*, in particular, faced a bleak future due to retrenchment in government departments, recession in industry after 1951, and a sharp fall in agricultural prices. The old nobles, the *jagirdars* and the absentee landlords started selling their remaining land and spacious houses to make ends meet. They were suddenly cast into a new unfamiliar world of struggle and competition where it was necessary to work for a livelihood.[63]

The dissolution of the princely states impoverished a large percentage, if not the majority, of the upper classes and the bourgeoisie. Nearly half

---

[60] Attia Hosain, op. cit., p. 276. V.S. Naipaul, *India: A Million Mutinies Now* (Delhi: Minerva Paperback, 1991), chapter 6: 'The End of the Line'.

[61] 20 November 1953, *Letters*, vol. 3, p. 451; and Gopal, *Jawaharlal Nehru*, vol. 2, p. 92.

[62] Radhakamal Mukerjee and Baljit Singh, *Social Profiles of a Metropolis: Social and Economic Structure of Lucknow, 1954-56* (Bombay: Asia Publishing House, 1961), and their *A District Town in Transition: Social and Economic Survey of Gorakhpur* (Bombay: Asia Publishing House, 1965).

[63] This paragraph is based on Luther, *Hyderabad*, op. cit., pp. 344-5, 389; A.M. Khusro, *Economic and Social Effects of Jagirdari Abolition and Land Reforms in Hyderabad* (Hyderabad, 1958), pp. 47-8; Bilkees Latif, *Her India: The Fragrance of Forgotten Years* (Delhi: Arnold Heinemann, 1984), pp. 200-1; Rajendra Prasad, *The Asif Jahs of Hyderabad: Their Rise and Decline* (Delhi: Vikas, 1984). For a different perspective, see K.M. Munshi, *The End of an Era: Hyderabad Memoirs* (Bombay: Bharatiya Vidya Bhavan, 1957).

the population of Hyderabad city depended on the Nizam for their livelihood, and thus with sources of patronage rapidly drying up this section was worse off.[64] A large number of peasants, artisans and retainers also lost the patronage networks that had provided sustenance for them and their extended families.

The rulers of Hyderabad, Bhopal and Rampur were not turned into paupers overnight; they simply lacked the initiative to convert their wealth into more secure and tangible assets. They squandered their inherited resources to maintain their standard of living and allowed properties to be grabbed by unscrupulous land dealers. Their mango orchards, which yielded vast revenues, were generally converted into uneconomic farm lands. Few ventured into business, trade or industry, or realised which way the wind was blowing. They continued living in their decaying palaces surrounded by a retinue of servants, wives, eunuchs and hangers- on. Wallowing in grief and nostalgic for the bygone era, they cursed the *khadi*-clad politicians who had brought the *angrezi sarkar* (British raj) to and end. Accustomed to framing their own laws, codes and regulations, they were irked by the presence of local bureaucrats – the district magistrate, superintendent of police and revenue officials – who were visible symbols of the change in political power and authority. They were distanced from them, insulated from the populace and blissfully unaware of the changes that were visibly taking place in urban and rural areas. Their public contacts were limited to *Id* celebrations or Muharram observances when the *imambaras* were lit up and the mourners turned up at the Nizam's desolate palaces in Hyderabad or the Khas Bagh in Rampur. The memory of the sufferings of Imam Husain and his companions at Kerbala reminded them of their own trials and tribulations. The lowering of the Imam's standard (*alam*) on the tenth of Muharram symbolised their eclipse, their own *Sham-i Ghariban* (mournful culmination of ten days of Muharram).

The abolition of the *zamindari* in 1951 stripped the large landlords of the bulk of their estates and awarded the land to the cultivators.[65] The rural influence of the former Muslim landlords was reduced, even more than that of their Hindu counterparts, because of the smaller number of Muslim peasants in the north and the greater number of urban rentiers among the Muslim landlords.[66] Many former Hindu rentiers and landowners

---

[64] Arifa Kulsoom Javed, *Muslim Society in Transition* (Delhi: Commonwealth Studies, 1990), pp. 30-48.

[65] Reeves, *Landlords and Government in Uttar Pradesh*, pp. 270-306; Elizabeth Whitcombe, 'Whatever Happened to the Zamindars?' in E.J. Hobsbawm (ed.), *Peasants in History: Essays in Honour of Daniel Thorner* (Delhi: OUP, 1990); Thomas R. Metcalf, 'Landlords without Land: The U.P. Zamindars Today', *Pacific Affairs*, spring/summer, 1978.

[66] Brass, *Language, Religion and Politics*, p. 235; Abid Husain, *Destiny of Indian Muslims*,

migrated to places like Kanpur, Gorakhpur and Lucknow in search of new sources of livelihood. Muslim *zamindars* and *taluqdars* were bereft of such ideas. Muslim immigration was a mere 16.28 per cent between 1947 and 1955 from rural areas as compared to 68 per cent among upper and intermediate Hindu castes.[67] The bigger Muslim *taluqdars* suffered more than their Hindu counterparts also because of families being divided, one branch migrating to Pakistan and the other electing to stay. Such was the fate of the *taluqdari* in Mahmudabad, the second largest in Awadh after Balrampur. The Raja left behind his estates in Barabanki, Sitapur and Bahraich districts to be looked after by his brother. He may have wished to return to his place of birth, but the India-Pakistan war in September 1965 would have thwarted his plans. His huge assets were declared 'enemy property'. The Raja's son was a student at Cambridge, far removed from Lucknow or Mahmudabad.[68] The Jehangirabad estate, mismanaged by its raja and his unscrupulous managers, fragmented. Sadly there was no great inclination or incentive to create something out of the extensive and prime urban property in Lucknow and its satellite towns.

The plight of Syed Mehdi, scion of one of the old *nawabi* families of Patna and related to the Nawab of Rampur, typifies the fate of Muslim aristocrats, especially the absentee landlords wholly dependent on income from land. He told the president of the republic, Rajendra Prasad, that he 'would be actually starving if he had not a house which has been rented out and had not been getting rent thereon from month to month'.[69] Others did not even have the chance to vent their grievances, and sulked.

The Awadh *taluqdars*, accustomed to supporting themselves from the rental income of their estates, were greatly traumatised by *zamindari* abolition. Some left for Pakistan, and others retired to anonymity in their villages. Those who stayed found the going tough when their world fell apart; those dependent on the *taluqdaris* for their living were worst off. 'The abolition of zamindari', according to Rashid 'removed our clientele in one fell swoop. all of a sudden the economy changed. And the English customers left. Our shop was "by appointment" to several governors of the province – it was that respected.' Palaces and great houses soon showed signs of neglect. Shops, surgeries, brothels and courts of law lost their best customers. 'The expanding city with its rash of new buildings,

pp. 129-30; Zafar Imam, 'Some Aspects of the Social Structure of the Muslim Community in India', and Imtiaz Ahmad, 'Economic and Social Change' in Zafar Imam (ed.), *Muslims in India* (Delhi: Orient Longman, 1975), pp. 84-90, 234-41.

[67] Mukerjee and Baljit, op. cit.

[68] Naipaul, *India: A Million Mutinies*, p. 371.

[69] Rajendra Prasad to Jawaharlal Nehru, 14 July 1953, *Rajendra Prasad: Correspondence*, vol. 16, pp. 95-6.

its new citizens had new scars added to those left when the royal era was destroyed.'[70]

Some of the smaller *zamindars* managed to keep their status intact by moving into nearby towns and cities in search of better opportunities. A few families in Barabanki district, living in close proximity to Lucknow, did well; among them were the Kidwais of Masauli, Bare Gaon and Gadia.[71] For the younger men in Masauli their future depended on Rafi Ahmad Kidwai, minister in the UP government and a seasoned politician. Those connected with Bare Gaon benefited from their proximity to Shafiqur Rahman Kidwai, who was quiet and self-effacing and had a distinguished record in social service. Most turned out to be successful. Some reaped the rewards of being close to the Congress. They obtained private and government contracts and licences, and secured ambassadorial posts, legislative assembly seats and plum jobs in both the public and private sectors.[72] The family of Shahid Husain of Gadia was split; the son who remained in India joined the Indian Foreign Service. Mubashir Husain (1898-1959), also of Gadia and son of Mushir Husain Kidwai (born 1878), the pan-Islamic ideologue of the early 1920s, was a judge at the Allahabad High Court till 1948.[73] Begum Aijaz Rasul, the wife of the former *taluqdar* of Sandila in Hardoi district and mother-in-law of the novelist Attia Hosain, did quite well for herself, being elected to the UP assembly and the Rajya Sabha and holding ministerial positions till 1971.[74]

There were other success stories too, although for the small Awadh *taluqdars* the overall scene was discouraging. They were squeezed out in Rudauli, Sandila, Kakori and Bansa Sharif, the home of poets and writers and once the haven of cultural excellence and refinement. They lost much of their land to the tenants who acquired legal rights over the areas they cultivated. For them, as for many other, it is signified not only the loss of land but also the end of a cultural and intellectual ambience they had fashioned meticulously. They were estranged from the 'new men', rustic and entreprenurial, who thronged their bazaar and streets and disturbed their social poise and harmony. The three important *taluqdars* in Rudauli – Choudhry Mohammad Ali, Chaudhry Irshad Husain and Choudhry Mohammad Yunus – felt alienated from their surroundings. Mohammad

---

[70] Attia Hosain, op. cit., p. 277, and Rashid, quoted in Naipaul, op. cit., p. 367.

[71] Zarina Bhatti, 'Status and Power in a Muslim-dominated village of Uttar Pradesh' in Imtiaz Ahmad (ed.), *Caste and Social Stratification Among the Muslims* (Delhi: Manohar, 1973), p. 98.

[72] Ibid., pp. 100-1.

[73] Riazur Rahman Kidwai, *Biographical Sketches of Kidwais of Awadh* (Aligarh: Kitab Ghar, 1987).

[74] N.K. Jain (ed.), *Muslims of India*, vol. 2 (Delhi: Manohar, 1979), p. 65.

Ali saw his eldest son and daughters migrate to Pakistan, and his letters to his family in Karachi reflect the pathos, alienation and deprivation of his class.

Gangauli in eastern UP was much the same. When one night a drum-beat announced that *zamindari* was no more, there was confusion all around. For the *zamindars* their universe had suddenly contracted: they had no 'land left equivalent even to the hub of the great wheels which had once been their *zamindaris.*' In just a few moments they collapsed like the tomb of Nuruddin the Martyr, a familiar landmark in the village. In their prayers (*namaz*) they cursed the Congress party. Orchards and fields spreading over huge distances – that great universe – contracted and were contained in a few documents.The Syeds, who for centuries had made Gangauli their home, realised that they no longer had any links with the village they had called their own. Whether to create Pakistan or not had had no meaning to them, but the abolition of *zamindari* shook them to the very foundations of their being. They left their homes, and once they had gone so it was all the same whether they lived in Ghazipur or in Karachi.[75]

The *zamindars* of western UP, on the other hand, were not too badly off. Many switched allegiance to the Congress, and some enjoyed a measure of local goodwill because they had implemented certain provisions of agrarian legislation. Most moved to Aligarh to educate their children. They built or renovated their mansions, developed an interest in local politics and used the university – which they treated as an extension of their estates – as the political arena to demonstrate their influence. It satisfied their pride to serve on the university court or the executive council, be involved in the selection of chancellors, vice-chancellors and senior office-holders, preside over public gatherings, hobnob with district politicians and turn up dutifully at the railway station to greet visiting dignitaries. But when they retired to the privacy of their homes they recounted the harsh encounters, the brute fact of living in a world that was not their own. It was a frustrating experience trying to adapt to their lowered status in a society that was slipping out of their grasp and to live comfortably out of their dwindling assets in the countryside.

By the early 1960s some smaller *zamindars* were struggling to eke out a living. There were those who had limited resources to live on; others relied on inherited charitable endowments or even pawned their family jewellery to maintain a façade of high living. Their crumbling houses on Aligarh's Marris road and Dodhpur bear testimony to their steady im-

---

[75] This paragraph is based on Rahi Masoom Reza, *Feuding Families*, pp. 293-5; see also Attia Hosain, op. cit., and Choudhry Mohammad Ali, *Goya Dabistan Khul Gaya* (Lahore: Academy Punjab, 1956), for matching descriptions. For details on Mohammad Ali, see *Saughaat* (Bangalore), 9, September 1995, and Anwar Husain, *Choudhry Mohammad Ali, Hayat aur Adbi Khidmaat* (Lucknow, 1992).

poverishment. The Muzammil Manzil, once an elegant building with stately arches and gates, was almost in ruins. Its condition symbolised the virtual disappearance of a class once so powerful, wealthy and influential. The more lucky ones, such as the Chattari clan, moved out of Aligarh in search of professional careers. The *sherwani*-clad Nawab lost the vigour and determination which he displayed during his extended and eventful public life, now that he had to cope with harsh realities.

The following description in *Sunlight on the Broken Column* illustrates the adversities of the landed aristocracy:

He [the Raja of Amirpur] lived in retirement at Amirpur, dignified and aloof, bearing the landslide of adversities with courage. His palace in the city had been requisitioned as a government hospital for legislators, and the huge rambling house at the outskirts, with its ornamental gardens divided into building plots, was the centre of the new colonies for the refugees.

The last occasion on which he appeared in public was four years after independence, when he welcomed the President of the Republic to a reception given in his honour by the *Taluqdars*.

There was no illuminations, no fireworks, no champagne, no glitter of precious gems, orders, silks, brocades and ceremonial uniforms. This last reception of the *Taluqdars* was a staid tea-party given by hosts who were soon to have their 'special class' and 'special privileges' abolished.

Dusty portraits and marble statues of stately ex-Presidents of their Associations, and of Imperial representatives, looked down with anachronistic grandeur on tea-tables bearing tea becoming tepid, cakes tasting stale, and Indian savouries growing cold. Guests in *Khaddar* outnumbered those in more formal attires. [...]

With grace and courtesy Amirpur presided over this swan-song of his order, while those who had habitually bowed before authority hovered round their gentle, dignified guests still hoping for manna from Heaven.[76]

III

How did Muslims respond to their own situation in the post-partition decade? Most accounts portray a *community* whose position was hopeless – irrevocably fragmented, bitter and frustrated, leaderless and with no sense of purpose and direction. In *Islam in Modern History*, W.C. Smith observed: 'The Indo-Muslim community, battered by outward circumstance and gripped inwardly by dismay, has stood disconcerted, inhibited from effective self-recognition and from active vitality.' In the view of Percival Spear, the British historian, it was a misconception to treat Muslims as a monolithic entity with one faith or creed and one political expression. Yet he set out to assess their 'inner life or soul in the

---

[76] Attia Hosain, op. cit., p. 309.

New India'. More recently Francis Robinson and Farzana Shaikh have stressed how the ideal of the Islamic community shapes their apprehension of what is legitimate, desirable and satisfactory political action.[77]

The political and intellectual currents in the 'New India' do not sustain the representation of Muslims as a monolithic entity. To suggest that only specifically Islamic issues were of concern to educated Muslims is to overlook certain major streams of thought that were leading towards a broadly secularised view of politics and society. Although the religio-political leadership had invested heavily in safeguarding the *Shariat*, they were equally concerned to come to terms with the consequences of partition, assess the losses and gains, and work out reasonable arrangements with other social groups and political formations. It was the secular and democratic regime, rather than the Islamic dimension, that provided the overarching framework to build new political networks and electoral coalitions.

The task confronting the leadership was hazardous and complicated. It was not easy to invoke historical precedents from India or other multi-cultural societies, or to draw significant lessons from the post-colonial experiences of Muslim societies in North Africa or West Asia. On the contrary, leaders had to locate problems and find answers to contemporary dilemmas within the context of their own society. They had to seek adjustments not as Muslims *per se* but as members of a larger collectivity. They had to accept state laws enacted by parliament and not insist on the application of Islamic law except where marriage, divorce and inheritance were concerned. The British, their chief benefactors for decades, had left the Indian shores. Now, after independence, the Muslim had to tread warily in a very different world.

Within the emerging national theatre there were many possible choices and casts of characters. Muslim leaders could draw on their Indian Islamic inheritance or the secular legacy of the nationalist movement; or combine elements from a variety of cultural and political entitlements. In other words, if Muslims were to make headway in their quest for a better life, their representative organisations had to be guided by fresh responses to the challenges facing the whole country rather than their community only.[78] They had to come to terms with an untested and unexplored social and political reality, for which they would be accountable to the nation at

---

[77] Smith, *Islam in Modern History*, p. 260; Spear, 'The Position of the Muslims', op. cit., p. 46; Robinson, 'Islam and Muslim Separatism', Mushirul Hasan (ed.), *Communal and Pan-Islamic Trends*, p. 373.
[78] See, for example, the articles in *Burhan* (Delhi), an Urdu monthly: 'Taqseem ke baad Hind ke Mussalmanon ka Rujhaan' (Indian Muslim attitudes in the aftermath of partition), 3 August 1951; 'Hindustan Dar al-Kufr hai aur Pakistan Dar al-Islam? (Is India a land of kufr and Pakistan the home of Islam?), 3 September 1951; 'Mussalmanon ka haal aur mustaqbil' (The present and the future of Indian Muslims), 3 October 1951.

large. They had to demonstrate a new political imagination for adapting their agenda and their strategies to the ground rules being laid down on Indian soil.

The political and ideological trends in the 1950s were by no means uniform or linear. They were disparately represented by the former Muslim Leaguers who were overwhelmed by the consequences of having brought Pakistan into being; by Azad and other Congress leaders who supported and fortified the democratic and secular edifice; and by educationists and scholars like Zakir Husain, A.A.A. Fyzee, Mohammad Mujeeb, Abid Husain, K.M. Ashraf, Mohammad Habib and Humayun Kabir. They drew attention to India's unity as 'one of the fundamental postulates of Indian moral consciousness' and pointed out that 'neither in India nor elsewhere did medieval Islam ever postulate a Muslim State as distinct from the government of Muslim officers.'[79] These voices may appear to say many different things, but they point to a largely liberal and secularised discourse that was beginning to appeal to increasing numbers of educated Muslims.

The first sign of change – expected but still of great symbolic value – was the virtual dissolution of the Muslim League in most places. It happened in UP on 31 May 1948 but much earlier in other places.[80] The Delhi Muslims, led by Mir Mushtaq Ahmad, Sardar Ali Sabri and Aziz Hasan Baqai, observed an 'Anti-Pakistan Day' on 10 October 1947 and a 'Dissolve Muslim League Day' a fortnight later.[81] Resolutions and manifestos were adopted in UP and elsewhere urging Muslims to join the Congress 'because it is, as it has always been, the one political party that can establish a stable, truly democratic government and ensure the prosperity and progress of all citizens without any distinction of caste or creed.'[82] Expressions of loyalty and demonstrations of goodwill followed. In response to the appeal of some UP leaders, Muslims of Bareilly decided not to slaughter cows during *Bakr Id*.[83] A district Muslim conference held there welcomed Hindi as UP's official

---

[79] Professor Mohammad Habib, quoted in *Hindustan Times*, 28 December 1947.

[80] For example, Orissa was the first province where 'we formally wound up the Muslim League and merged ourselves in the great brotherhood of the Indian nation.' Ibid., 17 December 1947.

[81] Ibid., 11 and 23 October 1947. The UP Muslim League Parliamentary Board decided to withdraw from the ensuing elections to the legislature. Z.H. Lari, leader of the UP League in the legislature, decided to remain unattached in the Constituent Assembly. Ibid., 20 January, and *Leader*, 25 January 1948.

[82] Statement of Syed Abdullah Brelvi, M.Y. Nurie, K.A. Hamied, Moinuddin Harris, ibid., 6 October 1947; and H.S. Suhrawardy's appeal: 'The political conflict between the Congress and the Muslim League being at an end, nothing now stands in the way of our joining this national organisation, from which we can expect justice, fairplay and a sympathetic reconsideration of our grievances, guided as it is by Mahatma Gandhi and inspired as it is by the idealism of Jawaharlal Nehru.' *Hindustan Times*, 7 October and 27 December 1947.

[83] Ibid., 23 October 1947.

language.[84] In Mysore Muslims agreed to the singing of *Bande Mataram*.[85] As a result of the pervasive insecurity and fear, central government employees found it necessary to affirm their loyalty to the Indian Union.[86] The All-India Muslim Chamber of Commerce and Industry, having organised Muslim industrialists to back Jinnah's demand for partition, announced its 'unreserved loyalty and allegiance.'[87]

Not everybody reacted in such a conciliatory way. When the Budaun district board turned down a proposal to add a few Muslim holidays to the list of public holidays, a Muslim member promptly resigned and others walked out.[88] In 1951 the Jamiyat al-ulama raised the question of reforming charitable endowments and prevailed on the government to introduce legislation in parliament three years later.[89] Although the right to independent, centralised Muslim administration was readily agreed to by the British and confirmed by the government of India in 1947, a series of measures including the Central Waqfs Act (1954) and the UP Muslim Waqfs Act (1960) were enacted by the central and state legislature to regulate the administration of charitable endowments. On 12 September 1948, the Jamiyat al-ulama organised a convention on religious education, followed by a mammoth Bombay Convention in December 1954.[90] The formation of the All-India Deeni Talimi Board (Education Board) was the outcome of these gatherings. Towards the end of 1959, a Muslim Educational Conference at Basti in eastern UP demanded the revision of such text books in the school syllabuses which portrayed Islam and its followers, Islamic rituals and the medieval Indian rulers in a poor light and created ill-will and prejudice towards the Muslims.[91]

There was, moreover, virtual unanimity in opposing any amendment or modification of Muslim personal law. Following demands in certain quarters of a uniform civil code, Muslim theologians, backed by a section of the liberal intelligentsia, made clear that the *Shariat* was divine and immutable and could not be transgressed by parliament or any other authority. In 1982, Ebraham Sulaiman Sait, the Muslim League leader from Kerala, summed up these views in a volume *Islam: Continuity and Change in the Modern World*, edited by John Obert Voll. He wrote:

---

[84] *Hindustan Times*, 8 December 1947.

[85] A 'national anthem' written by the Bengali writer Bankim Chandra Chatterjee. Ibid., 12, 26 October 1947.

[86] Ibid., 15 June 1949.

[87] Ibid.

[88] Ibid.

[89] *Burhan*, November 1952, p. 262.

[90] Ibid., p. 270; see also *Dawat* (Urdu), 15 October 1961; Mohammad Miyan, *Jamiyat al Ulama-i Hind: Mazhabi Taleem aur Tarbiat* (Delhi: Jamiyat al-Ulama-i Hind, 1962).

[91] Nadwi, *Muslims in India*, p. 130.

Anybody who does not have deep convictions in this code of conduct and unflinching faith in the ideology of life i.e. Islam, and considers Muslim Personal Law as outdated or argues for any change in the same, cannot be considered a Muslim in the true sense of the word. It should be clearly understood that because there is an unequivocal law in the Quran or *Hadith* concerning the family life or personal affairs, a Muslim cannot raise the question of reform without challenging Allah's sovereignty and without relinquishing faith in the Day of Judgement...

Ever since the declaration of India as a secular state, the main concern of the Muslims of India ... has been the preservation of their identity as a Muslim community... The most vital part of this protracted struggle concerns the problem of the preservation intact of their Islamic Family Law ... the family is the nucleus of the social structure of Islam. It is the corner-stone of the social edifice erected by Islam. It is the last line of defence against exotic influences and undermining forces which are working to destroy the Islamic way of life... The very existence of Muslim communities anywhere could be exposed to incalculable hazards if the protective hedge of the Family Law ... is allowed to be removed even partly or made ineffective in one way or the other.

There was a consensus too, at least in UP and Bihar, on the dangers overshadowing Urdu's future, and hence the Jamiyat al-ulama jumped into the fray as its foremost defender. At a conference in Lucknow, Maulana Hifzur Rahman and Syed Mahmud made fiery speeches on this subject.[92] 10,000 parents and guardians, worried over diminishing employment prospects for their wards, petitioned the state education minister. On behalf of the Anjuman-i Taraqqi-i Urdu, 2,050,000 signatories submitted a memorandum in support of urdu drafted by Zakir Husain and others to the president of the republic on 15 February 1954.[93]

The defence of Urdu and of family law offered political delinquents a rationale for reviving the League. For example, Nawab Mohammad Ismail Khan announced: 'Recently we demanded religious training and Urdu as the medium of expression in primary schools for those whose mother tongue is Urdu, but the majority community was against us. How could such of our demands reach the Government through the majority community organisation? It is therefore necessary that the League should revive its political activities.'[94] The Nawab may have taken his cue from Kerala and Madras where the League had survived for altogether different reasons,[95] but he was clearly out of touch with the

---

[92] Nadwi, *Muslims in India*, p. 134.

[93] A deputation led by Zakir Husain submitted a memorandum to the president urging him to direct the UP government to recognise Urdu as one of the regional languages. Uma Nehru, H.N. Kunzru and Maulana Hifzur Rahman were among the signatories. *Hindustan Times*, 16 February 1954.

[94] Ibid., 27 May 1949.

realities of Indian politics and unaware of the countrywide revulsion against the League.[96]

Ismail sought to achieve his aim at a conference held at Aligarh in November 1953. There was talk of the oppression of the minorities and the attacks on Islam which had led to 'economic paralysis, cultural death or disintegration and political helotage for Muslims.' The conference president, Badrudduja and ex-mayor of Calcutta with an eccentric streak, offered the community's cooperation to the state, but begged for a 'square deal as an integral part of the Indian nation.' Angry questions were asked in parliament and some adverse comments were made about the staff and students of the Aligarh Muslim University. The League's philosophy, said me member of parliament, was 'still quite rampant'. Sampurnanand, UP's home minister, commented on the 'sinister features' of the gathering.[97] But after all the 'talk and publicity, nothing further was heard of the conference or its plan of launching a party – or indeed of Badrudduja, who faded into oblivion.

At the other end of the spectrum, a spate of meetings took place at which the 'Muslim Nationalist' viewpoint was promoted. The Delhi meeting on 14 November 1947, a day probably chosen to coincide with Nehru's birthday, was the first of its kind after the Azad conference in 1940. It was attended by the legendary figure of Saifuddin Kitchlew, frail, poverty-stricken and depressed by the happenings in Punjab where he had once been lionised by Hindus, Muslims and the Sikhs. Syed Mahmud, along with Rafi Ahmad Kidwai, Syed Abdullah Brelvi, Abdul Majid Khwaja, Nisar Ahmad Khan Sherwani and Yasin Nurie were among the other luminaries; they had been attached to the late Dr M.A. Ansari and the Muslim Nationalist Party founded in July 1929. Zakir Husain, his reputation enhanced by the dogged determination he had shown to uphold Jamia Millia Islamia's secular traditions, stood quietly by. Maulanas Husain Ahmad Madani, Hifzur Rahman and Ahmad Saeed, all of Deoband, lent added weight to this most important of Muslim assemblies after independence. It was unmistakably Azad who stood out in this distinguished gathering, the man to whom people turned for leadership, inspiration and sober judgement.[98]

The Maulana was said to be insular, self-centred and intellectually

---

[95] Theodore P. Wright, Jr. 'The Muslim League in South India Since Independence: A Case Study in Minority Group Political Strategies', *American Political Science Review*, 60, 3, September 1966, pp. 579-99.

[96] For Azad's criticism, see *Hindustan Times*, 12, 29 June 1948.

[97] 9 December 1953, *Lok Sabha Debates*, vol. 5, 1953, pp. 1023-5; 27 June 1961, *Letters*, vol. 5, pp. 456-7; see also Morris-Jones, *Parliament in India*, p. 83.

[98] There were repeated demands from individuals and groups, such as the All-India Momain Conference, that Azad should assume the community's leadership. *Hindustan Times*, 14, 20, 28 October, 27 December 1947.

arrogant. He had kept aloof from several major political gatherings, but did not disappoint his followers on this occasion. He took command – though, as always, diffidently. 'It was not long ago that I warned you', he reminded Muslims in Delhi on 23 October 1947 'that the two-nation theory was the death-knell to a meaningful dignified life ... I told you that the pillars upon which you were leaning would inevitably crumble.' But it was time to begin again with a clean slate. 'Stars may have plummeted down but the sun is still shining. Borrow a few of its rays and sprinkle them in the dark caverns of your lives.' He wanted Muslims to 'pledge that this country is ours, we belong to it and any fundamental decision about its destiny will remain incomplete without our consent.'[99] The speech was written in exquisite Urdu prose, studded with metaphors and eloquently delivered. In much the same vein, he exhorted the Aligarh graduates, who had once hurled abuse at him, to imbibe the spirit of progressive nationalism, the motto of a secular, democratic society. He spoke with great passion. 'When you first joined the university', he said, 'you were members of a subject nation. Today you are leaving as free citizens of Independent India. [...] As citizens of a free state you enter into new responsibilities. The widening of opportunities which freedom has brought has also necessarily brought with it the need for greater loyalty and devotion to your state. Today, there are no limits to what you can achieve but this very fact imposes upon you the duties which freedom brings.' The Maulana shared his optimism on the occasion of the University's Convocation. He stated:

I am not aware what the state of your minds is today, nor in what colours the future appears to you. Does it bring to you the message of closing doors or of opening gates that introduce you to new vistas of experience? I do not know what visions are before you, but I will tell you what visions I see. You perhaps feel that doors that were open have been closed. Isee that doors that were locked have now opened .... What you and I hear are different. You hear the sound of closing doors but I of doors open.[100]

Taken together, the Delhi and Aligarh speeches were sober, statesman-like, analytically sharp and politically mature. They were major political texts underlining the strength and vitality of composite, secular nationalism, and free of polemics. Muslims were told to lift their spirits and combine with democratic and secular forces. The Congress Muslims, in particular, received a coherent political manifesto. Azad defined and enunciated their priorities and preferences in clear terms.

The Delhi meeting was followed by the Lucknow convention on 27-28 December the same year. Here again the Maulana guided the delibera-

---

[99] 23 October 1947, Hameed (ed.), *India's Maulana*, vol. 2, p. 170.
[100] 20 February 1949, *Speeches of Maulana Azad, 1947-1955*, p. 79, 82.

tions, advising the 70,000 Muslims present to eschew communal politics,[101] wind up the Muslim League and all other communal organisations, and join the Congress which stood for unity, democracy and progress.[102] The political mood was much the same as in Delhi, with the proposal to set up a progressive body on the lines of Turkey's Party of Union and Progress being reiterated. Shaukatullah Ansari, (Dr Ansari's son-in-law); Maulana Hifzur Rahman, the Jamiyat al-ulama leader and later member of parliament; and Humayun Kabir, who had acted as Azad's secretary at the Simla Conference in 1946, were appointed secretaries. But the 'Party', which is not mentioned in Azad's book, *India Wins Freedom*, did not take off, and turned out to be one of the several abortive plans mooted from time to time by the Maulana.

In theory free India offered the Congress Muslims of Azad's generation the space to play a critical role as members of a new political élite. They were politically correct in urging Muslims to rally around the Congress and extolling democracy and secularism, but they were not equal to the task of creating a following around issues of literacy, employment and improving the condition of women. They were ideally placed to do so with their political and organisational experience and their closeness to the ruling establishment. But most turned out to be men of straw, squandered the historic opportunity, and the reservoir of goodwill and faith on which they could have drawn. They settled for a soft option, set their eyes on maximising their gains from their links with government and insulated themselves from their own spheres of influence. Most were tempted into public office or co-opted within bureaucratic and administrative structures: those left out in the scramble for posts and positions assiduously prepared the groundwork for the future success of their family and relations. Some spent their inherited wealth to educate their children in élite schools and colleges and in Indian or British universities; others used their political connections to groom their family members for an active political role. Most defended the *status quo* because, thanks to Nehru's patronage, they were integrated into the vast Congress machinery. In return they received ministerial berths, governorships, diplomatic assignments and membership of state and national commissions. Content with their station in life, they felt no obligation towards anyone except their benefactors. Hence, when scholars or publicists prepared impressive lists of the Muslim candidates elected over a period of years, they may have flattered group pride, but this was no more than a Pyrrhic victory.[103]

Most Congress Muslim legislators avoided public forms of protest,

[101] *Hindustan Times*, 28 December 1947; *Leader*, 4 January 1948.

[102] This was a reiteration of the Delhi resolution. Ibid., 15 November 1947.

[103] R.A. Schermerhorn, *Ethnic Plurality in India* (Tucson: University of Arizona Press, 1987), pp. 177-8, and his *Comparative Ethnic Relations* (New York: Random House, 1970).

rebuffed petitions for help on minority questions and eschewed involvement in issues that were dubbed as 'Muslim'. There were three main
reasons for this. First, the electoral process sometimes favoured those who
were docile and reluctant to raise embarrassing issues for fear of being
denied nomination at the next election;[104] secondly, many elected 'representatives' had no constituency of their own and were no obliged to
redress the grievances of the Muslim segment of the electorate or even
draw attention to them; and finally, they suffered from the complex that
to work exclusively among or for the Muslims was a 'communal' act and
should therefore be avoided.[105] Ruling parties found it convenient to keep
such self-proclaimed leaders in tow.

Undoubtedly a great number of dedicated Muslims were not in the
Congress for the picking, but they were tired, broken and defeated, men
disillusioned with the Congress and estranged from it for having agreed
to the partition plan. Saifuddin Kitchlew set high standards of political
morality in public life, and lived and died in abject poverty. Hasrat
Mohani, an outstanding Urdu poet-politician who stayed away from the
Delhi conference, also died in penury. He was at times reckless and
inconsistent, but the credentials of a man who had joined the *swadeshi*
movement in 1909, introduced the 'Complete Independence' resolution
in 1921 and chaired the reception committee of the first communist
conference held at Kanpur in 1925 were unchallengeable Syed Mahmud,
Nehru's close friend, held ministerial positions, but did not amass a
fortune for himself or his family. Abdul Ghani, general secretary and
president of the district and city Congress in Ludhiana, and Maulana
Habibur Rahman, a leading nationalist also of Ludhiana, were both
hard-pressed to make ends meet. These men, with their impeccable
nationalist past, did not bask in the sunshine of freedom. They lost out to
free India's upcoming and enterprising generation of power brokers
within the ranks of Congress Muslims.

Arguably the principal reason why the Congress Muslims in the 1940s
were marginalised lay in the colonial institutional structures which im-
peded the evolution of a secularised political discourse,[106] but there were
no such constraints in free India. On the contrary, there was ample scope
for an imaginative combination the Congress Muslim discourse with
political, social and educational activism, as had been done by Ajmal
Khan and Ansari a generation earlier. There was also ample space for
enriching the content and raising the level of the contemporary debates
on parliamentary democracy, federalism and secularism. But neither

---

[104] Theodore P Wright, Jr. 'The Effectiveness of Muslim Representation in India', in Smith
(ed.), *South Asian Politics and Religion*, pp. 110-18.

[105] Abid Husain, *Destiny of Indian Muslims*, p. 141.

[106] Mushirul Hasan, *A Nationalist Conscince*, pp. 202-9.

before nor after independence was this the ideal or the agenda of the Congress Muslims. Their chief mentor, Ansari, had held them together for nearly a decade. Azad diligently sustained their activities after Ansari, but the Maulana's death in 1958 created a void; There was no ideological anchorage or any political mentor of standing. The few who survived, including Asaf Ali in Delhi, Syed Mahmud in Bihar, and Abdul Majid Khwaja and Hafiz Mohammad Ibrahim in UP, had no public stature or charisma. Their moments of glory in 1947-8 were short-lived – they had stolen the limelight under Nehru and Azad's patronage, and the early 1960s were a spent force, not much heard of or cared for.

More and more educated Muslims searched for alternatives and began their quest to discover fresh ways of forging individual and corporate relationships. More and more consciously tried, in alliance with a cross-section of groups and classes and not merely with their co-religionists, to make the best of the opportunities available to them. Some pinned their hopes on Nehru's leadership, some turned to the Jamaat-i Islami and the Jamiyat al-ulama, some allied themselves with local and regional or-ganisations, while others shunned political formations and sought spiritual solace in the Tablighi Jamaat. Thus there was sufficient space for competing and sometimes complementary interventions by different groups with different perspectives.

IV

TABLIGHI JAMAAT

'The greatest secret of success of the *Tabligh* mission lies in their exploiting the inherent emotional basis rather than attempting to catch the national phonenix. This procedure may appear non-religious but the success rate is cent per cent.'

– Maulana Wahiduddin Khan, *Tabligh Movement* (Delhi: The Islamic Centre, 1994 reprint), p. 66.

Close to Nizamuddin Auliya's *dargah* in Nizamuddin west is the historic Banglewali *masjid*. It was here that the son of Mohammad Ismail (1781-1831), descendant of Shah Waliullah, piloted an extraordinary proselytis-ing project in the late 1920s, which later assumed the name of Tablighi Jamaat. It was from this mosque that Mohammad Ilyas (1885-1994), a man of piety, asserted the primacy of *namaz* or *salat* (prayers) and disseminated Allah's message in the spirit of the Prophet Mohammad and his Companions (*Ashaab*). It was from this mosque, where thousands throng the narrow alley for prayers, that Maulana Mohammad Yusuf

(1917-65), his son, extended the *tabligh* movement to many parts of the world.[107]

The specific underpinnings of the *tabligh* ideology are rooted in the Waliullahi tradition, articulating goals and modes of representation that are drawn from a variety of religio-revival ideas from the days of Haji Shariatallah (1781-1840) in Bengal. It represents a synthesis of multiple theological strands within the Deobandi tradition and draws on earlier manifestation of revivalism in Indian Islam. Its legitimation was derived largely from the spurt in communalism after the Khilafat and Non-Co-operation campaigns, although Mohammad Ilyas himself reacted with explicitly religious symbols and idioms and not in the current political vocabulary. He believed, without involing the experience of Hindu-Muslim feuds in his own time or commenting on them, that the chief infirmity of the Muslims was that their hearts were devoid of religious fervour and they were not eager to seek the knowledge of faith. What they required was religious cleansing, moral uplift and spiritual regeneration. 'If religious inclination and appreciation of the importance of the Faith is produced in their hearts, Islamism will be revived in no time.'[108] The Maulana's main target, indeed the laboratory for testing his ideas, consisted of the Meos. They were truly different from 'mainstream' Islam; they represented the 'little' tradition, neither speaking nor understanding the language of orthodoxy. They lived in a world of their own, untouched by the orthodoxies of Deoband, Nadwat al-ulama, the Ahl-i Hadith or the Barelwi school, and untutored in religious treatises or the *fatawa* of the Deobandi *ulama*, which did not bind them. They were converted to Islam in different periods but retained many Hindu beliefs and customs. Some had Hindu names, and most celebrated Hindu festivals, performed *puja* before Hindu dieties and worshipped the *salar*, or banner, of one Salar

---

[107] For the history of the *tabligh* movement, see I.S. Marwah, 'Tabligh Movement among the Meos', M.S. Rao (ed.), *Social Movements in India* (Delhi: Manohar, 1979); Mushirul Hasan, *Nationalism and Communal Politics*, pp. 232-6; S. Abul Hasan Ali Nadwi, *Life and Mission of Maulana Mohammad Ilyas* translated from Urdu by Asif Kidwai (Lucknow: Academy of Research and Publication, 1983); 'Five Letters of Maulana Ilyas', C.W. Troll (ed.), *Islam in India: Studies and Commentaries* (Delhi: Vikas, 1985), and his 'Two Conceptions of Dawa in India: Jamaat-i Islami and Tablighi Jamaat', *Arch de Sc. soc. des Rel.*, 1994, July-September, pp. 115-33; Maulana Wahiduddin Khan, *Tabligh Movement*, op. cit; Mumtaz Ahmad, 'Islamic Fundamentalism in South Asia: The Jamaat-i Islami and the Tablighi Jamaat of South Asia', in Martin E. Marty and R. Scott Appleby (eds), *Fundamentalism and the State:* Barbara D. Metcalf, 'Remaking Ourselves: Islamic self-fashioning in a global movement of spritual renewal', and Mohammad Talib, 'Construction and reconstruction of the world in Tablighi ideology', unpublished papers presented at workshop on Tablighi Jamaat, Commonwealth House, London, 7-8 June 1990. References to Maulana Mohammad Manzoor Nomani are drawn from his *Islamic Faith and Practice*, translated from Urdu by Asif Kidwai (Lucknow: Academy of Islamic Research and Publications, 1962).

[108] Quoted in Nadwi, *Life and Mission*, p. 163.

Masud Ghazi, believed to be one of the generals of Sultan Mahmud of Ghazna. They did not marry within the *gotra* and their daughters were not entitled to inherit.[109]

Mohammad Ilyas was repelled by such distortions in Meo society, just as Shah Waliullah and his successors had denounced Hindu and Shia accretions. He stood for a return to the fundamentals of Islam, embodied in the observance of *namaz* and the practice of *tabligh* for which the Quran and the *Hadith* were the essential sources. In his vision *tabligh* was 'a process of self-reformation and a service to Allah by his humble slaves. Its main object was to win the good pleasure of Allah and achieve success through service and obedience.' He believed in creating a 'counter-culture' to equip Muslims to encounter and experience the world differently, and enable the faithful to reject those social and religious codes that were routinely followed but were outside the fold of *din* (religion). He therefore chose to work among the Meos after his return to India from Mecca and Medina in September 1925.

Ilyas was the first Muslim reformer to conceive of an elaborate mass contact programme to spread the meaning of the Quran and highlight the virtues of *salat*. He established charitable institutions and educational centres which spread even during his lifetime. He himself undertook two grand tours of Mewat with a large body of companions, but his most extraordinary contribution was to organise *jamaats* (preaching groups), whose disciplined, trained and learned members, fired with religious fervour and leading lives of piety, simplicity and abstinence, travelled far and wide 'acquiring and imparting Islamic knowledge, inviting the attention of the people towards Islamic practices, spreading the message of Allah, hymning his glory and sanctity and offering prayers and supplication at every step':

Anyone who saw the tabligh parties of Mewat, travelling on foot, with blankets thrown on their shoulders, the *Sparaas* tucked under the arms and parched grain or bread tied in a corner of the mantle, their tongues engaged in *zikr*, eyes showing the signs of nightly vigil and the mark of *sajda* on the foreheads would have been reminded of the martyred Companions of the Bir Moona [cf. *Encyclopeedia of Islam*, 2nd edn, I, p. 1232] who were killed while going on the mission of teaching the Quran and imparting the knowledge of the commandments of the *Shariat* or the orders of the Holy Prophet.[110]

Within only a few years, the Tablighi Jamaat left its imprint on several

[109] Mujeeb, *Indian Muslims*, pp. 10-11; Pratap C. Agarwal, 'Islamic Revival in Modern India – the case of the Meos', *EPW*, 18 October 1969, pp. 1677-80; Marwah, 'Tabligh Movement', op. cit., pp. 82-7; Majid Hayat Siddiqi, 'History and Society in a Popular Rebellion: Mewat, 1920-1930', *Comparative Studies in Society and History*, 28, 3, July 1986, pp. 44-7.

[110] Nadwi, *Life and Mission*, pp. 39-40.

caste and trading communities that had escaped the homogenising impact of the 'Great Tradition'. Such was the effect, Ilyas wrote triumphantly to a disciple in Mewat, 'that people have begun to talk of the Great Revolution in this brief period and the unholy sentiments of the people of your region who were steeped in ignorance have begun to change into the noble sentiments of spreading the faith.'[111] Support came from several quarters; from the *ulama* of Mazahir al-Ulum in Saharanpur, Nadwat al-ulama in Lucknow, and the Dar al-ulum at Deoband; from the poor peasants of Mewat and outlying areas; and from Delhi traders and merchants drawn into *tabligh* activity after the fourth *haj* (pilgrimage) performed by Ilyas in 1938, the last before his death. A conference held at Nuh in Gurgaon on 28-30 November 1941 was attended by nearly 25,000 people, and among those present were Maulanas Husain Ahmad Madani and Kifayatullah. Within a few years, wrote Maulana Syed Abul Hasan Ali of Nadwa, the region emerged 'from darkness into light'; thousands of mosques were built where none had previously existed, innumerable *maktabs* and Arabic *madaris* were established, 'Hindu garments' were given up, beards were grown freely, and polytheistic marriage ceremonies were discarded. 'Religious indifference and innovations and lewd and profane habits and customs started to wither away in the new climate of faith and piety.'[112]

The Jamaat's influence has grown steadily since independence. There is no record of membership, yet its presence can hardly be ignored in mosques and educational centres, and equally in railway stations and airports. More and more professionals have entered the fold in Delhi, Aligarh, Bhopal, Patna, Hyderabad, Madras and Bangalore: the Jawaharlal Nehru University and the Jamia Millia in Delhi and the medical and engineering colleges in Aligarh have numerous activists. Some, like certain Christian missionaries, give up successful careers in order to serve Allah. Some, like the Jesuits, make their expertise available to 'Hazrat Ji', head of the Tablighi Jamaat, who coordinates *tabligh* work from the Banglewali *masjid* in Nizamuddin *basti*.

There is no reliable account of meetings and conferences, although stray reports of huge *ijtimas* (religious congregations) circulate by word of mouth. Nobody knows the source of funding; committed activists insist that they pay for their own travel, food and general living expenses. What takes place at small *ijtimas* held in localities, mosques and Muslim institutions is well known, but this is not the case with huge public congregations such as that held at Gaya on 1-4 October 1993.[113] People

---

[111] Quoted in Nadwi, *Life and Mission*, p. 41.

[112] Ibid., p. 41.

[113] *Frontline* (Bangalore), 5 November 1993.

do not, after all, get together in their thousands for nothing; there is a purpose behind such large assemblies and a message that is meant to be communicated, sometimes subtly but generally stridently. What is the message? The average *tabligh* worker, who is not trained to question, does not know. The more established people in the organisation are not easily accessible, and even if they are, they avoid commenting on political issues.

What they frequently dwell upon and take pride in is their important role in bridging the doctrinal divide between various schools of theology and jurisprudence. What they will not react to is why they keep the Shias outside their fold. Is their silence an avowal that for them the Shias, who despite reciting the *kalima* day in and day out, are beyond the pale of Islam? What about the Jamaat's insistence on staying aloof from politics? Does it not amount to conformism and tacit support for the establishment?[114] If so, why is the Jamaat generally acceptable to ruling élites in India and Pakistan? Ayub Khan, the former president of Pakistan, was hostile to the Jamaat-i Islami but soft towards the Tablighi Jamaat. In India *tabligh* workers obtained exit visas and foreign exchange during the 1975-7 Emergency, while the Jamaat-i Islami activists faced severe restrictions.[115]

Whatever the formal posturing, the fact is that the holy men have not stood aloof from political engagements: this is not an indictment but a transparent reality. They participate in political processes in formal and informal ways, although they are reluctant to concede that this is so. They vote in local, provincial and national elections, and discuss a wide range of political issues and their implications because they have a vital stake in the survival of religious institutions and their own future as servants of Allah. Manzoor Nomani told a *tabligh* conference soon after independence that Muslims should back a political party 'that may be expected to safeguard their religious and other interests more justly and fruitfully than the other contesting parties.' He also wanted them to join government if their interests would thereby be better served.

Although Ilyas forbade his followers to enter into religious controversy and disputes over detail, the Tablighi Jamaat frequently finds itself embroiled in political and doctrinal debates, especially with the Jamaat-i Islami, their main ideological adversary, and the Barelwi *ulama*, who uphold the popular and folk-oriented Islam against the Tablighi Jamaat's

[114] The Tablighi Jamaat is also criticised for the following reason: 'There are people who realise that the *muballighin*, by living in an ártifical environment of self- righteousness, have isolated themselves from the realities of life and have completely closed their eyes to the problems facing the Muslim society. Islam is a religion that teaches to face problems boldly and squarely.' Ziya-ul-Hasan Faruqi, 'The Tablighi Jamaat', S.T. Lokhandwala (ed.), *India and Contemporary Islam* (Simla: Indian Institute of Advanced Study, 1971), p. 68.

[115] Mumtaz Ahmad, op. cit., p. 518.

puritanical and reformist orientation. They have themselves taken positions against the Shias (though not officially), and refrain from observing Muharram. Two of its prominent spiritual guides published critiques of the Iranian revolution, accusing Imam Khomeini of being an 'archsectarian Shia' beyond the pale of Islam. Maulana Wahiduddin Khan, editor of *Al-Risala* and sympathiser of the *tabligh* cause, accused the Iranian leadership of driving the world away from Islam by their 'macabre witlessness and vengeful minds that could only come from sick minds.'[116]

Romanticised versions of the Tablighi Jamaat tend to neglect the political meanings and consequences of its activities. The hue and cry over the Islamisation of the Meos and the violent reactions to the sporadic instances of conversions since 1947 should be noted. The conversion of some Hindus to Islam at Meenakshipuram on 19 February 1981,[117] attributed to *tabligh* activists but firmly denied by them, set off the process of Hindutva consolidation. This need not have been so, although a repetition of the Meenakshipuram saga may lead to ugly effects. Spiritual regeneration, even if conducted under the aegis of a formal body, is an unexceptional activity, but it does not combine well with proselytisation, especially in a society where religious sensitivities are so strong and so easily offended.

The Tablighi Jamaat is likely to gain added support in India owing to the deepening frustration caused by the destruction of the Babri Masjid on 6 December 1992 – it is already expanding rapidly in other parts of the world. But in insulating Muslims from legitimate political processes, isolating them from other social and cultural segments and presenting them with a puritanical version of Islam, as was done in the case of the Meos, its actions are fraught with serious dangers. The Meos can do without the *tablighi* intrusion. They should be allowed to fashion their own lives, carve out their own spiritual world and find ways and means of coping with their situation as local conditions dictate.

Islam in India has survived, without compromising on its essential tenets, not in isolation from other cultural, intellectual and religious currents but in close interaction with them. The spiritual guides of the Tablighi Jamaat are, perhaps unwittingly, engaged in reversing an ongoing and dynamic historical process.

---

[116] Quoted in Mumtaz Ahmad, op. cit., p. 523.

[117] Mumtaz Ali Khan, 'Mass Conversions of Meenakshipuram: A Sociological Inquiry' in G.A. Oddie (ed.), *Religion in South Asia: Religious Conversion and Revival Movements in South Asia in Medieval and Modern Times* (Delhi: Manohar, 1991 edn).

JAMAAT-I ISLAMI

'Secularism as a State policy which implies that there should be no discrimination or partiality on the basis of religious belief can hardly be questioned. The Jamaat has categorically stated that in the present circumstances it wants the secular form of Government to continue. [...] But if beyond this utilitarian expediency some people have the deeper philosophical connotations in mind, we beg to differ. These philosophical connotations are essentially Western in origin, and carry a spirit and a history which are truly foreign to our temper and needs.'

Introducing the Jamaat-e-Islami-Hind (Delhi, 1971, 5th imp.), pp. 31-2

The Indian government has given the nod to the Tablighi Jamaat's religious quietism. It has not done so to the Jamaat-i Islami, the prime representative of fundamentalist revivalism in modern times. In 1953 the Lok Sabha discussed its activities, although K.N. Katju, the minister of home affairs, did not volunteer much information.[118] Meanwhile the president, Rajendra Prasad, was fed with various reports, including one submitted by Katju. He concluded:

In Islam, I believe, they do not make any distinction between religion and politics and its whole tenor is to take the two together or side by side. That appears to be the modus operandi of this organisation [Jamaat-i Islami] also, which aims at establishing Islamic rule in India as that is the rule which can be called God's rule and no Muslim can submit to any rule except God's rule. That being so, it is quite intelligible how it [Jamaat-i Islami] cannot appreciate a secular state.[...] It is, therefore, not quite correct to think that it is a religious body and has not much to do with politics.[119]

Rajendra Prasad called for 'most up-to-date and complete information' on the Jamaat-i Islami. However, the Jamaat, operating under the watchful eyes of the police and intelligence services, was well covered; it was treated with suspicion, met with opposition and criticism from several quarters, and was periodically equated with the Hindu Mahasabha and the RSS. Though not made public, the Jamaat-i Islami's links with Islamic groups outside India were regularly monitored. Its conduct at times of communal rioting often led district authorities to arrest its activists; the organisation was banned during the 1975-7 Emergency and its leaders, including two professors of the Aligarh Muslim University, were put in jail. A similar ban, not strictly enforced except in the state of Kerala, came into effect after the razing of the Babri Masjid. The Jamaat-i Islami did not, likewise, sail smoothly in the unsettled waters of Pakistani politics.

---

[118] 15 August 1953, *Parliamentary Debates*, House of the People, vol. 3, no. 8, p. 594.

[119] Rajendra Prasad to K.N. Katju, 23 September 1953, *Rajendra Prasad: Correspondence*, vol. 12, p. 139.

Its insistence in 1949 on an Islamic constitution, backed by public agitation, led the government to jail Maulana Maududi under the Public Safety Act. He was released after eighteen months only to be imprisoned again in 1953 when the violent anti-Ahmadiya riots were sparked off by his polemical attack against the followers of Mirza Ghulam Ahmad (d. 1908), who did not believe in the finality of Mohammad's Prophethood. The Maulana remained in jail for three years.

Established in 1941 more than two decades after the birth of the Jamiyat al-ulama, the Jamaat was founded and diligently nursed not by a traditional *alim* but by somebody who built up his reputation through his journalistic writings and scholarly exegesis of the Quran and the *Hadith*. Maulana Syed Abul Ala Maududi, the founder, had an extraordinary career. He lived through many dramatic events – the Khilafat euphoria, the triumphal march of the League, the vivisection of India and birth of Pakistan, and the rise and fall of successive regimes in the latter country. Though he was a minor player in the 1920s as a Jamiyat al-ulama enthusiast and contributor to its journal, his erudite scholarship and deep involvement in religio-political controversies enabled him to emerge as a major political actor in the late 1930s. He had many admirers and many chosen disciples who were fanatically attached to him; he also made enemies in theological and political circles.[120]

While Mohammad Ilyas was engaged in de-politicising Muslims and limiting their choices to *salat, tabligh* and the service of Allah, Maududi embarked on a mission to create a righteous group in order to effect a political and social transformation based on the Quran and *Hadith*. On the one hand, he criticised the conservative *ulama* for adding many rules of their own to the clear commands of the Quran and Prophetic traditions; on the other, he rejected modernists like Syed Ahmad Khan for allowing themselves to be seduced by the values of an alien system of life. He put forward the thesis – the centrepiece of the Maududi model – that the supreme purpose of Islam was to establish the sovereignty of God on earth by means of a truly Islamic state.

Maududi left for Pakistan from Pathankot in Gurdaspur district (East Punjab). He moved to Lahore with a mission, accompanied by his spirited band of followers. Addressing the annual session of the Jamaat-i Islami in August 1970, he stated: 'Today some persons taunt me as to why I fled from India to Pakistan. I realize that for some persons my coming over to Pakistan was distressing ... They are perhaps not aware that at that time I was in East Punjab, and in the way the Muslims were compulsorily evicted

[120] Maulana Mohammad Zakariya, *Fitna-i Maududiat* (Deoband: Dar al-Musaffirin, n.d.); Mohammad Akram Basirpuri, *Maududi aur Islam* (Karachi: Tajdar Haram Publishing Company, n.d.); Abdul Quddus Rumi, *Maududiat ke ek Aiyane me do Chehre* (Agra: Suhaib Biradaran, 1979), and his *Maududiat Benaqab* (Agra, 1984); K.M. Ashraf, *Hindustani Muslim Siyasat par ek Nazar* (Delhi, 1963).

... there was no option left with me but to migrate to Pakistan'.[121] His schema for the revival or renewal of Islam in its pristine form contained nine steps:

1. diagnosis of the causes of the current state of ignorance;
2. a general scheme for reformulation;
3. a practical identification of available resources;
4. the successful prosecution of an intellectual revolution;
5. the institution of a practical programme of reform;
6. the application of *ijtehad* throughout these steps;
7. struggle against the enemies of Islam;
8. the revival of the Islamic order; and
9. the organisation of a universal revolution aimed at restoring Islam's rightfully pre-eminent position.[122]

Maulana Abul Lais Islahi inherited Maududi's mantle in India, but could he enforce this schema in its entirety? What was implied by the 'struggle against the enemies of Islam'? Who were the 'enemies' – were they the Hindus, the Sikhs, the Christians in India or the entire Christian/Western world? What were the specific implications of reviving an Islamic order in India? Was it, anyway, a desirable project? Was it attainable? Would the Jamaat reject, as Maududi had done, secularism and democracy? Would the concept of territorial nationalism, shunned by Iqbal and Maududi for different reasons and within different perspectives, continue to haunt the Islamists? If so, how did one reconcile Islamic universalism with composite, secular nationalism?

Vague and inconclusive discussions took place and no definitive conclusions were forthcoming. The leadership in India, heavily dependent on Maududi, felt let down and utterly confused. The organisation had picked up support along with the Muslim League in the mid-1940s but was in total disarray after independence. Its command structures, which were central to the monolithic character of the Jamaat, were fractured, and, even more importantly, its ideological balance and equilibrium was badly disturbed.

The history of the Jamaat soon after 1947 was in some ways similar to the Khilafat Committees of the early 1920s. When the Khilafat was itself abolished by the Turks, its vocal protagonists were left high and dry. They had no cause to fight for; the committees were left without a reason for existing. In consequence the Khilafatists drifted apart, although some found independent avenues of self-expression. Some stayed with the Congress or joined socialist and communist movements. But most took the plunge into the muddy waters of communitarian politics.

---

[121] Quoted in Masudul Hasan (ed.), *Sayyid Abul A'ala Maududi and his Thought*, vol. 1 (Lahore: Islamic Publications, 1970), p. 334.

[122] Patrick Bannerman, *Islam in Perspective: A Guide to Islamic Society, Politics and Law* (London: Routledge, 1988), p. 124.

The pan-Islamists of the mid-1920s had wide-ranging options; the Jamaat had none. Its ideologues were constrained to review their own propositions. To begin with, they resisted change; Maududi's disdain for a secular model, succinctly expressed in May 1947, remained the main plank of their ideology. He opposed the 'secular, national democratic system', and appealed to people's consciences to 'observe and test: (*a*) against secularism was the principle of submission and obedience to God; (*b*) opposed to nationalism was humanism; and (*c*) against democracy or sovereignty was the sovereignty of God and the viceregency [Khilafat] of the people.' Islam is believed to be all-encompassing and all-pervasive, and therefore secularism was incompatible with the tenets of the faith. A secular state rested on the denial of God, 'on the denial of sovereignty of His exclusive title to the obedience of His creatures. To owe allegiance to God is to refuse allegiance to every other authority unless the latter acts as His servant and upholds the authority of His Law.' To be secular was a stigma, a sign of being *ghair-mazhabi* or *la-dini* (irreligious/atheistic). In fact, 'the decay of religious faith and its effectiveness in the practical conduct of collective affairs' was because the political leadership was in the hands of unbelievers who denied God openly and rejected His guidance.[123] In an Islamist perspective, the 'Golden Age' – whether viewed in terms of moral purity, military conquest or technological and cultural advancement – was lived according to a formula that made no effort to separate 'belief' from 'life'. On the other hand, in the Islamic memory the concept of secularism was related only to periods of colonial hegemony, or alternatively to national attempts at experimenting with various Western 'developmental formulas' that appear not to have worked.[124]

The Jamaat distanced itself from political parties and elections in order to legitimise its critique – and for other reasons. First, political engagements would weaken its resolve to preserve the pristine purity of their faith and lead them into 'the mire of moral turpitude'.[125] Secondly,

---

[123] Mohammad Mazharuddin Siddiqi, *After Secularism What?* (Rampur: Maktaba-i Jamaat-i Islami, 1952), p. 38. Such views are widely echoed in those circles which take their cue from the fundamentalism of the Jamaat-i Islami – e.g., the argument that religion and secularism were fundamentally incompatible and that, for this reason, there was no common ground between secularism and Islam: 'Islam will not succeed in re-establishing itself by compromise with, or wholesale grafting of, secular ways and institutions. The inevitable result will be a dilution of Islam in all fields of activity.' Altaf Gauhar (ed.), *The Challenge of Islam* (London: Indian Council of Europe, 1978), pp. 298, 301. For a critique of this perspective, see Rafiq Zakaria, 'Is Islam Secular?', Sir Syed Memorial Lecture, 29 October 1988 (Aligarh: Sir Syed Academy).

[124] N. Ayubi, *Political Islam: Religion and Politics in the Arab World* (London: Routledge, 1991), p. 51.

[125] *Introducing the Jamaat-e Islami-i Hind* (Delhi: Jamaat-i Islami, 1971), p. 4. See also C.W. Troll, 'Two Conceptions of Dawa', op. cit.

Muslims were not strong enough to establish the sovereignty of God in place of the sovereignty of the people, yet they were prone to getting themselves 'irretrievably caught up in the whirl of party politics'.[126] Finally, winning an election or two or securing ministerial berths because of the ruling party's patronage was of no consequence for the objective of *iqamat-i din* (establishment, realisation and pursuit of religion).[127]

Even by the standards of contemporary debates in Muslim societies such as those of Egypt and Indonesia, these were retrograde ideas. For more than two decades the Jamaat's appeal and avowed goals rested on these naive and mistaken assumptions. India was not a *dar-al Islam*, nor could it be turned into one. The mixing of religion with politics, reflected in the Jamaat's ideal of a *Hukumat-i Ilahi* (government based on divine commandments), was fraught with danger in any society, but all the more so in a country already split along religious lines. Muslims were free to fulfill their obligations in accordance with the Quran and *Hadith*, but their future had to be defined not in Islamic paradigms but in relation to democratic and secular structures. The Indian state was prepared to tolerate the Jamaat's existence but not its attempts to disturb the social and political order.

The message was loud and clear. The Jamaat leaders realised, though it took them a while to do so, that their theoretical postulates were out of place in India and out of harmony with the rapid changes taking place throughout the world. They had to take a fresh look at Maududi's ideas and examine his legacy. They had to do what a number of newly-liberated Muslim societies had started doing: examine their problems afresh, to help create a modern state and come up with liberal solutions.

At first there was ambivalence in some quarters and serious misgivings in others. But the final verdict, which the diehards have yet to swallow, was in favour of democracy and secularism. 'In the present circumstances', an official publication in 1970 declared, 'the Jamaat-i Islami Hind wants that in contrast to other totalitarian and fascist modes of government, the ... secular democratic mode of government in India

---

[126] 'Acknowledgement of His Sovereignty ... means refusal to accord the right of legislation, be it in political, economic [or] social affairs, to any legislative body, representative or unrepresentative, to any king, dictator or parliament, unless such legislation is based upon and derived from the divine law. [...] To owe allegiance to God is to refuse allegiance to every other authority unless the latter acts as His servant and upholds the authority of His Law. [...] The decay of religious faith and its effectiveness in the practical conduct of collective affairs is directly attributable to the present leadership of mankind which has fallen into the hands of disbelievers who deny God openly and reject His guidance ....' Quoted in Z.A. Nizami, *Jamaat-e-Islami: spearhead of separation* (Delhi: Ministry of Information and Broadcasting, 1975), pp. 18-19.

[127] *Radiance*, 3 July 1966, quoted in Moin Shakir, *Secularisation of Muslim Behaviour*, p. 101, and his *Muslims in Free India* (Bombay: Kalamkar Prakashan, 1972).

should endure.'[128] The Jamaat has not departed from this position. There is much literature on the secular experimentation, just as there are frequent sermons on cultivating a universal outlook and an attentiveness to the spiritual values of the non-Muslims and to the Indian religious traditions. The Jamaat encourages dialogue on the moral and religious questions that arise in the shared national life, and desires co-operation with socially and economically backward classes. In November 1992, in a 50,000-strong gathering in Hyderabad (the city of Maududi's birth), the Jamaat agreed to join hands with anti-communal forces to defend democracy and secularism, and – a significant departure from its earlier stand – to take part in elections and back candidates with 'principles' and 'good character'. There was also talk of creating a united Muslim political front and bridging the gulf between Muslim groups and parties.[129]

The Hyderabad meeting was important seen against the background of the Babri Masjid-Ramjanmabhumi controversy and the spectre of the Hindutva wave overwhelming the secular forces. However, it did not take its decisions out of the blue, since they were part of a creative but inconclusive debate started in the late 1960s. The formal endorsement of secular democracy in those years was made in the light of several important localised and 'external' factors, including the bloody India-Pakistan war in 1965 and its far-reaching political implications. This requires elaboration.

By the late 1960s the Jamaat, which had started with just 240 members in 1947,[130] had grown in size and stature. In 1953, according to information furnished to Rajendra Prasad, it had 150 branches.[131] Three years later local units had increased to 183 with 1,819 paid members,[132] and in 1981 the Jamaat's strength was officially put at 2,831 members, with 36,243 'sympathisers'.[133] It carried influence in Muslim educational centres, including the Aligarh Muslim University where the administration, in deference to Jamaat sensitivities, banned the appearance of women students and teachers on the stage. More important, the Jamaat's earlier

[128] *Introducing the Jamaat-e Islami-i Hind*, pp. 31-2; and Mushir-ul Haq, *Islam in Secular India* (Simla: Indian Institute of Advanced Study, 1972), pp. 7-12.

[129] *Pioneer* (Delhi), 18 November 1992; see also Mumtaz Ahmad, op. cit., p. 504.

[130] The membership at the time of independence was 625. Out of these 240 were left in India, and 385 members were either in Pakistan already or shifted there after independence. Maududi's address, August 1970, quoted in Masudul Hasan, op. cit., p. 333.

[131] Rajendra Prasad to Katju, 11 September 1953, *Rajendra Prasad: Correspondence*, vol. 16, p. 128.

[132] Mumtaz Ahmad, op. cit., p. 504.

[133] M.S. Agwani, 'God's Government: Jamaat-i-Islami of India', in Husain Mutalib and Taj ul-Islam (eds), *Islam, Muslims and the Modern State* (London: Macmillan Press, 1994), pp. 266-7. It is important to note that the Jamaat did not encourage a large membership so that it did not become 'unwieldly and inchoate'. Shakir, *Muslims in Free India*, p. 52.

quiescence was replaced by an interventionist role in 'Muslim affairs' at the regional and national levels. Official and semi-official organs – *Dawat* in Urdu and *Radiance* in English – commented on a wide range of social, political and religious matters. Jamaat leaders attended the Muslim Convention in June 1961 and co-founded the Lucknow-based Majlis-i Mushawarat in 1964. The student wing also made progress. In 1973 the Students' Islamic Organisation (SIO) in UP invited Muslim youth organisations to its annual conference in Aligarh. The state of Emergency during 1975-7 gave impetus to unity and in 1977 the Students Islamic Movement (SIM) was born when the SIO, the Muslim Students' Association in West Bengal, Bihar and Tamil Nadu, and the Ideal Students' League in South India, merged to form a united platform for Muslim students and youth.[134]

All this could be achieved, the Jamaat leaders admitted in private, because of democracy and secularism. They conceded that the political system itself offered scope for ventilating their unfulfilled demands, and this was because the Congress had not abandoned the secular project of Gandhi, Nehru and Azad. They mentioned other notable gains. There was no interference with Muslim theological seminaries; the Muslim family law remained unchanged; Muslim charitable endowments escaped parliament's critical scrutiny – in fact, the 1954 legislation, introduced at the initiative of the Jamaat and the Jamiyat al-ulama, was appreciated.[135] *Tabligh* workers did their usual rounds, and the Jamaat activists also. They have continued to conduct their activities, publish and distribute literature, hold public meetings and conferences, and receive generous donations from some Islamic countries. Although much of their funding is used to aid neo-fundamentalist activities, the flow of cash has not stopped. By 1981, the Jamaat had 548 libraries, 386 reading rooms and 240 regular study circles. It sponsored the publication of 491 books in Urdu, seventy-one in Hindi and seventy-eight in English on the Quran and *Hadith*. It ran newspapers and journals from Delhi, Rampur, Calcutta, Gauhati, Ahmedabad, Mangalore, Calicut and Madras.[136] Schools and colleges, aided by the Jamaat-i Islami, flourish all over the country, and there is no scrutiny of their curriculum.

They invite comparison between India's 'benevolence' and neighbouring Pakistan, a nation won in the name of Islam but plunged in the cauldron of doctrinal, ethnic and sectarian strife. The Barelwis and the Deobandis, two major schools founded in India, carried their feuds to Karachi,

---

[134] 'Indian Jamaat acts to curb influence of Revolution', in Kalim Siddiqui (ed.), *Issues in the Islamic Movement, 1982-83* (London: The Open Press), pp. 166-8.

[135] For example, *Burhan*, 5 November 1953, p. 260.

[136] Agwani, op. cit., p. 267. In 1989 the 'Institute of Objective Studies' in Delhi launched its *Journal of Objective Studies*. Its chief editor is F.R. Faridi.

established their own mosques and founded their own educational institutions. As a result, they do not intermarry or even visit each other's mosques. The Ahmadiyas are intimidated and live in fear; members of the tiny Hindu minority are relegated to the status of second-class citizens; and the Shias, more numerous in Pakistan than in India, are distrusted and condemned for their *biddat* (heretical) practices during Muharram.

In reappraising its ideology and strategy, the Jamaat-i Islami in India was influenced by the political reverses suffered by its sister organisation (not officially) and the lowering of its public image in Pakistan. Maududi still carried weight, but nowhere more than in Egypt where Syed Qutub shared his conviction that Islam was engaged in a *kulturkampf* with Western imperialism and that the reassertion of Islam implied a rejection of Western dominance, Western culture and the identity which the West sought to impose on Muslims.[137] However, his influence in Pakistan diminished as more and more people realised the uglier aspects of his political message and the inglorious record of his party. The Jamaat turned out to be an establishment-oriented party, articulating unrealistic demands. It entered parliamentary politics, backed the powerful landowning classes in Punjab, endorsed the repression of the liberation movement in east Pakistan, formed a coalition with Ziaul Haq and legitimised his 'mockery of Islamic reaffirmation in Pakistan'.[138]

On the other hand, the Jamaat's future is far more assured in India as a key interventionist force in matters classified under the rubric of 'Muslim identity'. The organisation is flush with money for building mosques, establishing schools, publishing Islamic literature and offering scholarships and grants to students and teachers. Some of their institutions, including the 'Institute of Objective Studies', flourish at Okhla in South Delhi in close proximity to the Jamia Millia Islamia. To earn goodwill, some grants and scholarships also go to non-Muslim students. More important, the Jamaat is constantly trying to refurbish its image by cultivating prominent journalists like Kuldip Nayar, former editor of the *Statesman*, and civil rights groups such as the People's Union of Civil Rights (PUCL). It organises conferences and conventions and attracts university professors to lecture and participate in seemingly 'academic' activities. This is to gain respectability in the eyes of the intelligentsia.

These signs of a shift in the Jamaat's political agenda indicate that the Maududi model has been made more flexible to suit Indian conditions. But this does not mean that it has abandoned its goal in India and elsewhere in South Asia of seizing the commanding heights of the state and Islamising state and society. This is not all. Steeped in religious

[137] Leonard Binder, *Islamic Liberalism: A Critique of Development Ideologies* (Chicago University Press, 1988), p. 175.

[138] Mohammad Ikram, *Maududi aur Islam*, pp. 28-48; Mumtaz Ahmad, op. cit.

conservatism and opposed to the 'modernising' processes in education, social reforms and the emancipation of women, the Jamaat is still a retrograde force. Its world-view militates against liberal, progressive and enlightened ideas because of an inflexible interpretation of Islamic doctrines and stout resistance to the eclectic Sufi and syncretic trends in Indian Islam. The few cosmetic changes have not changed the Jamaat into a reformist or modernist movement. Finally, as a militant expression of orthodox Sunni Islam, its ideology promotes sectarian consciousness, widens the Shia-Sunni rift and creates barriers between communities. After all, at the heart of the Jamaat's campaign is the long-cherished ideal of creating a pan-Indian Islamic/Muslim identity. This is, to say the least, a project of political isolation. The Jamaat leaders would, however, contest this formulation in their search for political legitimacy in the liberal and secular establishment.

JAMIYAT AL-ULAMA-I HIND

'It is no exaggeration to say that the history of Jamiat-Ulema-i-Hind after independence is a history of continuous struggle and persistent effort. The constructive efforts ... embrace all spheres; fight against communal disturbances, economic reconstruction, social uplift, dissemination of religious education, safeguarding Muslim Personal Law, the language issue, protection of *Auqaf.*'

Maulana Asrarul Haque Qasimi, *The Community in Retrospect*
(Delhi, n.d.), pp. 3-4.

The Jamiyat al-ulama traced its origin to the movements of Shah Waliullah, his son Shah Abdul Aziz (1746-1824), Syed Ahmad Barelwi (1786-1831), Haji Imdadullah (1817-99), Maulvi Fazl-i Haq Khairabadi (1797-1861), and the founders of Deoband – Mohammad Qasim Nanotawi (1832-80) and Rashid Ahmad Gangohi (1828-1905). It took credit for harnessing anti-colonial sentiments, for 'introducing Gandhiji as a common leader of the freedom movement' and laying the 'foundation of the concept of Secularism' by establishing the provisional government of free India under the presidentship of Raja Mahendra Pratap.[139]

The Jamiyat was actually founded in 1919 by a group of influential *ulama* from Deoband who were concerned to defend, in alliance with the Congress, the Khilafat and the Holy Places of Islam.[140] In the post-

[139] *Jamiyat Ulama-i Hind: Objects and Activities in Brief*, published by Asrarul Haque Qasimi (Delhi, n.d.), pp. 1-2.

[140] Mushirul Hasan, *Nationalism and Communal Politics*, chapter 5 'Islam, Khilafat and Nationalism-I'.

Khilafat era, the Jamiyat shed its pan-Islamic garb to emerge as a quasi-political body with a paid-up membership of about 200,000.[141] It worked closely with the Congress, appearing in joint mass demonstrations, and during the repressive period of the early 1930s at least 20,000 Jamiyat workers were at one time or another imprisoned for political offences. In the 1940s the Jamiyat opposed the two-nation theory to champion secular, composite nationalism (*mutahida-qaumiyat*). Husain Ahmad Madani, its prime leader, cited historical precedents, such as the Covenant at Medina, as justification for supporting India's nationalist movement. The concept of united nationalism was no different from what the Prophet had set out as a principle among the people of Medina. In other words Indians, regardless of religion, were an indivisible part of one Indian nation with one homeland. 'They will', stated the Deoband *alim*,

...fight against the foreign nation which destroys everything and deprives them of their common national interests in order to achieve their rights, to expel the oppressive and merciless force, and shatter the chains of slavery. No one will interfere in the religious affairs of another, and all the peoples who live in India will be free to adhere to their religion and fulfill its commandments.[142]

The country's partition did not make secular nationalism less relevant, but it raised conflicting views on the Jamiyat's future role. When the Muslim divines first met in Bombay and Delhi in April 1948, they did so 'to chalk out the path traversed by the community for reconstruction, for bringing about prosperity, marching shoulder to shoulder with members of other communities inhabiting the country'.[143] But the much-advertised Delhi meeting on 27-28 April, chaired by Azad, turned out to be a damp squib: the *ulama* had their share of *qorma* (a mutton dish) and *biryani* (flavoured rice with meat) and dispersed after blessing the Constituent Assembly members for framing a democratic and secular constitution.[144] The Bareilly conference of the UP branch on 12-13 March 1948 also turned out to be a tame affair.[145]

The Lucknow meeting a month later was more eventful. Muslim divines, wearing their flowing gowns and *sherwanis* and walking around the venue with followers in tow, were present in full strength. Here the Jamiyat, with 2,500 delegates in attendance, resolved to convert itself into a non-political body, eschew politics and devote itself to the community's

[141] Kata L. Mitchell, *India: An American View* (London: John Lane, The Bodley Head, 1943), p. 72.

[142] Quoted in Yohannan Friedmann, 'The Attitude of the Jamiyyat-i Ulama-i Hind to the Indian National Movement and the Establishment of Pakistan', *Asian and African Studies*, 7, 1971, p. 165.

[143] Qasimi, *Community in Retrospect*, p. 1.

[144] *Hindustan Times*, 29 April 1948.

[145] Ibid., 14 March 1949.

spiritual, moral and educational uplift. Maulana Hifzur Rahman, general secretary, dwelt on the Jamiyat's new role. 'Hitherto it has fought for an undivided free India; now it will strive for the creation of a non-sectarian atmosphere in the country bled white by the communal monster.' But the more important resolution, informally adopted in Bombay and Lucknow, was to convert the Jamiyat into a purely religious body. The Maulana made it clear that the Jamiyat would refrain from pro-Congress activities. The clause compelling its members to be loyal Congressmen was dropped from the constitution.[146]

The precise reasons for such decisions, though acclaimed by the national press and national leaders, were unclear.[147] For the time being, there was much speculation, but gradually, the Jamiyat leaders themselves felt uneasy with the Lucknow resolution. For activists like Madani, Ahmad Saeed and Hifzur Rahman, always in the throes of political movements, it was not easy to be distanced from the humdrum of political life. Both as spiritual and political guides they were called upon by their followers to convey their demands and grievances to the appropriate authorities, provide leadership and strengthen their faith in the ruling Congress. They also had much stake in the political system, in occupying centre stage in local, regional and national affairs, and in settling scores with their main political adversary, the Jamaat-i Islami, and wresting the initiative from it. For these reasons, the Jamiyat al-ulama was quickly drawn into the political arena.

The Jamiyat interpreted India's constitution as a social ·contract (*muhaadih*), similar to that concluded by Prophet Mohammad with the Jewish people in Medina.[148] It laid stress on promoting fraternal links between the two estranged communities and ignored the demand, aired in some quarters, for separate electorates and reservation of seats. Both in theory and in practice, democracy and secularism adequately safeguarded and guaranteed the religio-political interests of Muslims. Madani outlined this view in a detailed reply to a troubled correspondent, who was afflicted with the dilemmas faced by many of his brethren after partition.

---

[146] *Hindustan Times,* 19 April 1949. The aims of the Jamiyat were: (*a*) protection of Islamic virtues, relics of Islam and places of worship; (b) to secure and safeguard the religious, educational cultural and civil rights of Muslims; (*c*) religious, educational and social reform of Muslims; (*d*) establishment of such institutions as may be instrumental in the educational, cultural and social progress and stability of Muslims; (*e*) fostering and strengthening of amity between different communities of India in the light of Islamic teachings; (*f*) revival of Islamic and Arabic studies and promotion of education in tune with the needs of the present age; (*g*) propagation and dissemination of the teachings of Islam; (*h*) administration and protection of Muslim *Auqaf. Jamiat Ulama-i-Hind*, op. cit., p. 3.

[147] See editorial entitled 'The Jamiyat's Decision', and the comments of Nehru and Patel, *Hindustan Times*, 18, 19 April 1949.

[148] Ziya-ul-Hasan Faruqi, 'Indian Muslims and the Ideology of the Secular State in India', Smith (ed.), *South Asian Politics and Religion*, p. 149.

His reflections embody not only the Jamiyat's political manifesto, but vividly capture the mood of large numbers of Muslim theologians after partition.[149] Ziya-ul-Hasan Faruqi, a Jamiyat sympathiser at Delhi's Jamia Millia, pointed out that secularism, based on democratic traditions and liberal thought, did not negate or reject religion; on the contrary, it fortified cultural and religious freedom. It was therefore a sensible policy to welcome and applaud the constitution's secular ideal.[150] It was a sound policy to enter the Congress and influence its decisions.

Generally, Madani and his associates were secure in the belief that an enduring Congress-Muslim alliance was the way out of post-partition conflicts. Their conviction was based on pragmatic considerations. It was important to have access to Congress politicians, who controlled the levers of power and patronage networks, to curry favour with them to build schools, colleges and mosques, to secure employment, licences and permits and exemption from local taxes, and to bargain for personal rewards such as membership of *waqf* boards, Haj Committees (to regulate and organise the flow of pilgrims to Mecca and Medina), minority commissions and the Aligarh Muslim University court (Maulanas Hifzur Rahman, Mahfuzur Rahman and Qari Mohammad Tayyab were nominated). It was a major asset to get elected or secure a nomination to state assemblies and parliament. Thus ten of the twenty-one traditionally trained men were among the twenty legislators who claimed adherence to the Jamiyat al-ulama.[151] There were other handy benefits in the form of government grants to Muslim institutions. The Dar al-Musaniffin in Azamgarh, founded by Shibli Nomani, received Rs 100,000.[152] Deoband's Dar al-ulum also counted on discreet government patronage and kept up its links with politicians in Lucknow, the state capital, and Delhi. By 1960, Deoband had awarded degrees to more than 10,000 students.[153] At the time of its centennial year, 1967, which was celebrated with great fanfare, 8,904 schools were formally or informally affiliated to it.[154]

The Congress-Jamiyat *entente* had stood the test of time, but it began cracking up in the 1970s. Part of the reason was the breakdown of the secular consensus and the spurt in Hindu-Muslim violence across large tracts of the country. This led the Jamiyat to invoke specifically Muslim themes of 'solidarity', 'unity' and 'identity' and to organise Muslims in

[149] For the translation of the text, see Friedmann, op. cit., pp. 177-80.

[150] Faruqi, op. cit; Qasimi, *Community in Retrospect*, pp. 2-3.

[151] Theodore Wright Jr., 'Muslim Legislators in India: Profiles of a Minority Elite', *Journal of Asian Studies*, 23, 4, 1964, p. 259.

[152] Moin Shakir, *Muslims in Free India*, pp. 120-1.

[153] Nadwi, *Muslims in India*, p. 88.

[154] Barbara Metcalf, *Islamic Revival*, p. 136.

pursuit of religio-political goals. The reaction was prompt but not based on mature judgement. Having endorsed the principles and not just the ideal of secularism, its leaders would have done better not to rewrite their own agenda in the alphabet of communitarian politics, because by doing so they narrowed their options and support-base. It also affected their general outlook and perspective which became indistinguishable from the fundamentalism of the Jamaat-i Islami.

In the long run, the prospects for a quasi-political body like the Jamiyat to realise specifically Islamic/religious aspirations were dim. If the Muslims were goaded into conducting their affairs as a religious entity, they were more likely to follow the Tablighi Jamaat or the Jamaat-i Islami. If they were to join the electoral process, they had a powerful incentive to ally their fortunes with political formations, the Congress being the most important. That is why the Jamiyat initiatives to build a Muslim front met with no success. The Aligarh Convention in October 1953 was a disappointment, and the Muslim Conference at Delhi on 10-11 June 1961 also failed to draw much political mileage. Attempts to cobble together a coalition on the eve of the 1962 general elections met a similar fate. The Majlis-i Mushawarat, founded in 1964, petered out after a rousing fanfare. The bubble was pricked by some of its own leaders.

Such setbacks were due partly to the Jamiyat's limited agenda. But there were other important forces at work that weakened the sectional parties and groups. These related to the dynamics of competitive electoral politics, the breakdown of the isolation of Muslim voters from the electoral process, and the undermining of communal solidarity by electoral competition.[155] The British had sharply demarcated communal or religious boundaries under the system of separate electorates. One could then be a legislator without representing a single non-Muslim, but this was no longer the call. Muslims seeking election or forming social and political coalitions after independence had also to count on other groups and classes. Such mutual interdependence surely and steadily facilitated their integration into a broad-based polity.

V

The Majlis-i Mushawarat evoked bitter and unpleasant memories of the old Muslim League. So too did the Muslim Majlis in UP and Bihar. They provided legitimation to Hindu parties and pushed more voters towards

[155] Gopal Krishna, 'Electoral Participation and Political Integration', *EPW*, Annual Number, February 1967, p. 187, and his 'Problems of Integration in the Indian Political Community: Muslims and the Political Process', Dilip Basu and Richard Sisson (eds), *Social and Economic Development in India*, p. 181.

candidates appealing to Hindu sentiment. The message, learned the hard way by the architects of the Majlis-i Mushawarat, was that a community-based mobilisation carried serious risks for the Muslims themselves. By 1969-70 self-righteous Majlis leaders, having triggered off a 'Hindu backlash', were resigned to their own political demise; they coolly presided over defunct organisations, worked out alliances with secular parties, and used the leverage thus acquired to enlarge their shrinking constituencies in UP and Bihar.[156]

For most Muslims, far removed from and indifferent to the quibblings in the Jamiyat al-ulama, Jamaat-i Islami or the Majlis-i Mushawarat, the critical issue was not the fate of the *Shariat*, which was in any case accepted by the state as sacrosanct, or the validity of the Islamic state idea; it was to establish, for their own survival and progress, enduring relationships with fellow-citizens and with established political parties. They had to discover new meanings for their existence not in isolation from other groups but through close interaction with them. They had to find new forms of expression within a secularised idiom and explore fresh avenues to articulate their aspirations, anxieties and misgivings. For peasants and workers, as also for trading and business communities, it was relatively easy to revive cross-community linkages and age-old ties fractured by partition, and to become part of the patron-client networks in urban and rural areas. It was, likewise, easy to vote for and expect favours from the Congress, a party guided by Jawaharlal Nehru and identified with him. The following impressions of a respondent in Moradabad (western UP) have interesting implications:

I have begun with Congress, have stayed with Congress and will end with Congress, because Congress is the first party. The flowers that bloom in the field, the crops that grow in the field – they are there because of Congress. Congress has not taken away our land, or snatched our houses – and no party can say this as long as Congress is here. Congress has ended zamindari and treats all zamindars equally whether big or small. There is no need for the Congress party to promise anything or say anything in an election, for whatever they have said, they have done. Whatever flowers and roses are on our way today, they are laid by Congress. All that we have is due to Congress. People ask me to leave Congress, but why should I leave when Congress has given me so many comforts and advantages.[157]

This is a Muslim voter's perception. He is not concerned with his religion but with what the Congress did to improve the lot of the poor. The image

---

[156] Zaheer Masood Quraishi, 'Electoral Strategy of a minority pressure group: the Muslim Majlis-i Mushawarat', *Asian Survey*, 8, 12, pp. 181-2.

[157] Angela Burger, *Opposition in a Dominant Party System: A Study of the Jana Sangh, Praja Socialists and Socialists Parties in Uttar Pradesh, India* (Bombay: OUP, 1969), p. 181.

etched in his memory is of a party wedded to justice, equality and egalitarianism – an impression, incidentally, widely shared by different social classes. Religious minorities, including Sikhs and Christians, inspired by the conviction that the Congress under Nehru's leadership was committed to minority rights, had additional reasons to be enthusiastic. The Congress, always eager to strengthen such impressions, redoubled efforts to project itself as a friend and saviour of religious minorities.

In the first three general elections Muslims were indissolubly tied to the Congress. Of the total number of Muslim legislators in 1952, 142 were Congressmen; in 1957 the figure was 131 out of the 159.[158] In UP, the country's most populous state, Congress Muslims made up the largest proportion of political activists; and a larger proportion of them were elected than the candidates put up by any other party. In the 1962 assembly elections in UP, the Praja Socialist Party and the Socialist Party put up about the same proportion of Muslims – 4 per cent and 9.7 per cent respectively; however, a greater percentage of Muslims were put up and elected from the Congress than from any other party.[159]

The Congress also did well in the Bihar legislative assembly, especially in eastern Purnea district and in those regions of Champaran, Saran, Darbhanga and Bhagalpur districts where Muslims accounted for more than 20 per cent of the population.[160] In Bengal, twenty out of the twenty-seven Congress Muslim candidates were elected in 1957. Both for the state assembly and the Lok Sabha, the West Bengal Congress put up more Muslim candidates in 1962 than in 1957. In the Congress organisations also, Muslim legislators in UP and Bihar occupied key positions.[161] But their numbers could not have been in proportion to the population they represented, because the more established politicians, such as Khaliquzzaman in UP, had deserted the Congress to join the Muslim League in the 1940s.

In areas where the Congress was pitted against the Muslim League or the Ittehadul-Muslimeen, Muslims tended to favour Nehru's party. The Tamir-i Millat, with its ambitious programme of religious education, welfare and economic rehabilitation in Hyderabad, was closer to the

[158] Imtiaz Ahmad, 'The Muslim Electorate and Election Alternatives in UP', *Religion and Society*, 21, 2, June 1974; S.V. Kogekar and Richard L. Park (eds), *Reports on the Indian General Elections 1951-52* (Bombay: Popular Book Depot, 1956), p. 163.

[159] Ibid.

[160] Harry W. Blair, *Voting, Caste, Community, Society: Explorations in Aggregate Data Analysis in India and Bangladesh* (Delhi: Young India Publications, 1979), pp. 33, 37.

[161] Wright, 'Muslim Legislators in India', op. cit., p. 265. Nehru thought differently. He believed that it was not easy for Muslims to be elected to the assemblies and parliament or to secure elective positions in the Congress party and organisation. 26 April 1954, *Letters*, vol. 3, p. 535. Paul R. Brass, *Caste, Faction and Party in Indian Politics*, vol. 2 (Delhi: Chanakya, 1985), pp. 291-2.

Congress and arrayed against the Ittehadul-Muslimeen. The Bihar unit of the Majlis-i Mushawarat, acting under Syed Mahmud's influence, backed as many as fifty Congress candidates for assembly elections.[162] Faridi, founder of the Majlis, conceded in 1967 that 'there is no political party ... at the moment to replace the Congress and to remove it from its dominant position at Delhi.'[163]

Where the Congress was not electable or its candidate had a dubious secular record, Muslims searched for secular-oriented parties, as in Kanpur. Banerji, a popular communist-backed trade union leader, consistently increased his share of their votes;[164] in Amroha, Maulana Ishaq Sambhali, a Deoband *alim*, was elected to parliament on the communist party ticket; in Faizabad too, Muslims preferred the communist candidate in the 1957 parliamentary election but voted for the socialists in the municipal board contest. The socialist candidate's largest vote came from the city, where Muslims were more than 20 per cent of the population. In general, the parties on the left increased their share of Muslim votes whenever Faizabad was trouble-free, but once the communal temperature rose, they quickly shifted their identification from a proletarian to a religious focus. In the former they were linked to Hindus who shared their economic lot; in the latter these links were severed.[165]

These trends refute popular notions of *communal* consciousness as a strong element in voting behaviour. They reveal the strong inclination to reject communally-oriented parties or groups. That is why some attempts in UP and Bihar – mostly feeble, as it happened – to infuse life into the Muslim League proved unsuccessful. The Indian Union Muslim League in Kerala managed to send only one representative to the Lok Sabha in 1957 and two in 1962. The Ittehadul-Muslimeen, confined to electoral segments in Hyderabad, failed to make much headway in state elections. As against this, Muslim candidates contesting elections on the mandate of national parties improved their share of the total votes polled from 65.41 per cent in 1952 to 75.20 per cent in 1960. Their representation in Bihar went up steadily. The number of those elected to the Vidhan Sabha began at twenty-two or about 7 per cent, increased to almost 8 per cent in 1957, dipped below 6 per cent in 1967 and 1969, then recovered in 1972,

---

[162] Brass, *Language, Religion and Politics*, p. 251.

[163] *Seminar* (95) July 1967, p. 14.

[164] Brass, *Caste, Faction and Party*, pp. 291-2; see also V. Graff, 'Religious Identities and Indian Politics: Elections in Aligarh, 1971-1985' in Andre Wink (ed.), *Islam, Politics and Society in South Asia* (Delhi: Manohar, 1981), pp. 152-65.

[165] Harold Gould, 'Religion and Politics in a Muslim Constituency', in Smith (ed.), *South Asian Politics and Religion*, and 'The Congress System in a District Political Culture: The Case of Faizabad District in Eastern Uttar Pradesh', Paul Brass and Francis Robinson (eds), *Indian National Congress and Indian Society, 1885-1985* (Delhi: Chanakya, 1987).

to its level in the 1957 election.[166] 'The increasing tendency of Muslim candidates to assume national party identifications', concluded Gopal Krishna, 'shows that the integrative process is at work.'[167] W.C. Smith prophesied, just a decade after independence, 'the dawn of a new day for Islam and its community, that might mean a great new freedom and creative adjustment and progress of significance beyond India.'[168] For most educated Muslims the decade following independence was a period of trial and soul-searching. Indian Islam, with its 'Little' and 'Great' traditions, was confronted with knotty problems. Some were perceptively examined by the *Burhan*, an influential journal of the reformist *ulama*, but large sections of the Muslim intelligentsia, still bothered with un-resolved issues and inconclusive debates, were often afraid.

However, at the end of the Nehru era the state of uncertainty was beginning to disperse. Educated Muslims in Aligarh, Jamia Millia Islamia, Nadwat al-ulama and Deoband's Dar-al ulum reflected on the passing decade with satisfaction, and they looked ahead with hope rather than despair. This was typified in the reaction to the happenings in Hyderabad, where there was some resistance to its integration into India.[169]

The message from other quarters was equally loud and clear. Maulana Mohammad Manzoor Nomani exhorted Muslim in 1952 not to bother about their weak numerical strength or political status. They must remain true to their faith, serve their fellow-citizens, co-operate with the state and bring 'enlightened' and 'broadminded sections' into power. By doing so they would carve out a position of honour and trust for themselves, win the respect and admiration of their countrymen and strengthen the foun-dations of their faith.[170]

---

[166] Blair, 'Minority Electoral Politics in a North Indian State', p. 1281.

[167] Gopal Krishna, 'Electoral Participation', op. cit., and his 'Muslim Politics', *Seminar* (153) May 1972. For a different view, see Imtiaz Ahmad, 'Indian Muslims and Electoral Politics', *EPW*, 11 March 1967, p. 523; see also Blair, op. cit., p. 1287.

[168] Smith, *Islam in Modern History*, p. 279.

[169] 'When I heard of the action in Hyderabad, I wept for the Musalmans. Yet in the end, despite all the tragic suffering, Hyderabad was a good thing for the Muslims of India. It meant that the last flicker of hope for that kind of absurd fantasy died down – and convinced them that they must face realities of life as they exist.' Quoted in Smith, *Islam in Modern History*, p. 279. Speakers at a public meeting in Calcutta resented the anti-Indian and pro-Pakistan utterances of Kasim Rizvi, leader of the *razakars*. Professor Mohammad Habib of the Aligarh Muslim University, president of the Indian History Congress, called for a blockade of the Hyderabad state. The Maharajkumar of Mahmudabad, who had resigned from the Muslim League in October 1947, demanded the trial of Rizvi. *Hindustan Times*, 14, 15 April 1948.

[170] Nomani, *Faith and Practice*, p. 165. The works of scholars like Mohammad Mujeeb, Abid Husain, K.M. Ashraf, A.A.A. Fyzee and Professor Mohammad Habib, as also the writings of a large number of traditional scholars at Deoband and Nadwa, reflect the same spirit. A sense of optimism is, notably, reflected in many of the contributions published in *Burhan*.

Of course, there was much that was unpalatable to the religio-political leaders. People eased out of the job market were impoverished. Victims of discriminatory practices and communal riots felt frustrated and estranged from the system. At the same time, they could ill afford not to be aware that a country divided on the basis of religion could not suddenly transform itself into a model of inter-community peace and amity. A society with scarce material resources could not offer equal and easy access to government service or the professions. Doubtless, Muslims experienced intense hostility and prejudice in certain quarters, but it is also true that the democratic and secularisation processes – two redeeming features of India's political culture – offered space to them, along with other relatively backward classes, to become established. It was possible to restrict but not easy completely to deny them the opportunities of growth and progress.

The democratic process had many pitfalls, but it served as an integrative force and offered incentives to claim a share in political and institutional structures. Of course, it was not at all easy to draw immediate benefits from the system, nor was it easy to make the élites share power and resources with the less privileged; yet it was possible to make one's way up the ladder, and this is what astute Muslim political activists began to do. Their representation in central and state legislatures was not in proportion to their population (there was no reason why it should have been), but they were not doing badly by their own standards of counting heads on the basis of religious affiliation. Muslim politicians in UP and Bihar, who had grabbed more than their share under the British dispensation, made the best of the opportunities in free India. They were elected from 'Muslim strongholds', as also from 'non-Muslim' areas. If they were deprived of seats it was for considerations other than their being Muslims. Further, they were not the only ones to 'suffer'; lower-caste Hindu communities in UP and Bihar were much more poorly represented in the Vidhan Sabha than the Muslims.[171]

Muslims were no doubt loosing land in certain parts of UP, but so were high-caste Hindus, who accounted for almost half of the alienated land, followed by backward castes and Sikhs. A study of the land transfers since the abolition of the *zamindari* reveals that backward castes had gained most. Of the total land sold by Muslims in the state, half was sold by the landless, followed by some semi-medium farmers in the highest category. At the same time, semi-medium farmers among Muslims purchased land in certain districts of UP.[172]

---

[171] Harry Blair, 'Ethnicity and Democratic Politics in India: Caste as a Differential Mobilizer in Bihar', *Comparative Politics*, 5, October 1972, pp. 107-27, and his 'Minority Electoral Politics', op. cit.

[172] Kirpa Shankar, 'Land Transfers in Uttar Pradesh', *EPW*, 23 July 1988.

The economic and other social transformative changes had a levelling effect, drawing Muslims from various levels in the formal and informal sectors of the economy.[173] The progress was admittedly slow, yet few could miss the signs of the 'community' coming to its own. This was made clear in the August 1951 issue of *Burhan*, a journal with a great sense of realism and pragmatism.[174] The Meos recovered from the shock of 1947-8. Improvement was reflected in the higher rates of literacy, employment and occupation, and the proliferation of schools, colleges and traditional *madaris*, as also in an enhanced interest in modern education, fuller participation in newer employment opportunities, and efforts to reach out into the wider unknown world outside Mewat. A study carried out in 1969 concluded: 'The Meos now view themselves as a part of the Muslim minority community in the larger Indian society and strongly feel the necessity to forge ahead by their own efforts.'[175]

Muslim artisans, manufacturers and other entrepreneurial groups, disrupted by partition, also began to tie up the loose ends, although their initiatives in the 1950s and '60s only bore fruit a decade later in parts of western UP, Bihar, Gujarat and Maharashtra. In general the urban artisan class east and south of Delhi remained relatively well off, although it was reduced in Delhi itself by riot and migration.[176] Weaving communities in eastern UP and parts of Bihar were back in business, organised under the umbrella of the Momin Conference, a powerful pro-Congress body for more than four decades. The abrogation of the evacuee property laws made trade and business easier. The closely-knit Khojas, Bohras and the Memons expanded their business and commercial enterprises in western India, as also at Udaipur (Rajasthan) and Pondicherry, formerly a French colony. Surat, Baroda and Broach in Gujarat and Bombay and Poona in Maharashtra were some of their major strongholds.

In the south, where the Muslims were a relative minority without ruling status for more than 150 years and where the impact of partition was barely felt, life went on as usual without being disturbed by the great communal debates raging in the Hindi heartland. Muslims held their own in mining in Tamil Nadu, shipbuilding in Kerala and other sectors of the economy. Scarlett Epstein noted the strong presence of Muslim merchants in the village of Wangela, Mysore state, and their ability to react to the economic opportunities of shopkeeping.[177] In Tamil Nadu, Muslims were urban-based; in 1961 more than 55 per cent lived in towns compared to only

---

[173] Ali Ashraf, *The Muslim Elite* (Delhi: Atlantic Publishers, 1982).

[174] 'Taqseem ke bad Hind ke Mussalmanon ka Rujhan', *Burhan*, 3 August 1951.

[175] Agarwal, 'Islamic Revival in Modern India', op. cit., p. 1680.

[176] Spear, 'The Position of the Muslims', op. cit., p. 45.

[177] T.S. Epstein, *Economic Development and Social Change in South Asia* (Delhi: OUP, 1962), p. 32.

26.7 per cent for the state population as a whole. They did not have a large commitment to agriculture, although Muslim farmers did reasonably well in the agriculturally poor districts of Tirunelveli and Ramanadapuram and some locations in Tanjore and Madurai. According to the 1961 Census handbook, Muslims were an important trading and shopkeeping community in nearly every district of Tamil Nadu; they had an almost monopolistic control of the hides and skin industry and were prominent in *bidi* manufacturing.[178] The Muslim Tamils of Pallavaram, according to Mattison Mines, adapted themselves successfully to the bazaar economy: 'The fact that Muslim shopkeepers as a group are relatively prosperous helps to explain their lack of interest in education as well as their strong commitment to business as a desirable occupation. It is rewarding.'[179]

In studying 'The Destiny of Indian Muslims', Abid Husain, the Jamia Millia-based scholar, concluded (in 1961) that about 47 million Muslims gradually settled down to a more or less even tenor of life only disturbed occasionally by communal riots: 'The economic conditions also show, on the whole, some changes for the better.'[180] This was also the judgement of Mohammad Mujeeb, W.C. Smith and Percival Spear, serious and sympathetic contemporary scholars of Indian Islam. The Indian Muslims, commented Spear, were a people of the future rather than the past and their fortunes, though clouded for the time being, were brighter in the long run. Having lived in India for many years and taught history at Delhi's St Stephen's College, he believed that the new Indian Islam would be different from the imperial Islam of the Mughals or the decayed Quranic 'Promised Land' of the nineteenth century. 'With these conditions fulfilled, there is no reason why it should not become a vigorous and integrated body, making a creative contribution to a new India.'[181]

We can conclude by looking at another dimension of the debate. A number of Muslim societies have tried to cope with the presence of non-Muslim groups. Some contemporary writers have produced juridical arguments establishing the status of non-Muslims as full citizens rather than protected subjects. But the main orientation among the 'neo-fundamentalists', following in the path laid down by Maududi and Qutub, has been extremely antagonistic to non-Muslims. The dominant concept implies that they should be treated with 'fairness' but excluded from

---

[178] Mattison Mines, *Muslim Merchants: The Economic Behaviour of an Indian Muslim Community* (Delhi: Shri Ram Centre for Industrial Relations and Human Resources, 1972), pp. 91-2, 99.

[179] Ibid., p. 111.

[180] Abid Husain, *Destiny of Indian Muslims*, p. 134.

[181] Spear, 'The Position of the Muslims', op. cit., pp. 49, 50. For Mujeeb, see *Islamic Influences*, p. 199.

political participation. This view is held in Pakistan and Egypt, where the ultra-orthodox attitude does not condone the appointment of non-Muslims to positions of leadership or high power. This, for example, explains the anxieties of the Copts in Egypt, whose full citizenship, established in the early nineteenth century, has now become threatened by a possible revival of the concept of *ahl al-dhimma* ('protected subjects'), who are tradition-ally exposed to a special tax – *jizya* – and not permitted to govern over Muslims or judge between them.[182]

The strength and vitality of India's experiment, mocked at and derided by a motley group of scholars in the subcontinent, rested on a model guaranteeing full citizenship with equal rights and obligations. This 'formula', certainly superior to the 'Islamic alternative' presented by Maududi and the Jamaat-i Islami, is compatible with the secular and egalitarian thrust of India's nationalist movement. The significance of the Nehru era lies in legitimising this consensus after independence.

---

[182] Ayubi, *Political Islam*, pp. 52-3.

7

REDEFINING BOUNDARIES: MODERNIST INTERPRETATIONS AND THE NEW 'INTELLECTUAL STRUCTURES'

'The event of the independence of India as our native land and the first step of its emancipation from the supremacy and dominance of British imperialism is not such a thing that the Dar al-ulum can remain aloof from. The Dar al-ulum is not only elated over the freedom of the native land but is also taking it as a good augury for the real liberty in future and is anticipating it as a prelude to many future joys.'

Qari Mohammad Tayyab (1947)*

'The time has ... come when the bells must toll for the Muslims, too. Let them shed their independent political entity and come out of their isolationist groove of sect, community and the like ... throw in their lot with the social philosophies which are making a bid for economic emancipation through a gigantic movement of the Indian peasants, working class ... and thus gain for themselves their rightful place with the afflicted millions of this country.'

Mir Mushtaq Ahmad (1952)†

Social science scholarship and historiography since the 1970s has generated new approaches and offered new insights into different aspects of Indian society. Change, variety and differences have been highlighted under Marxist, New history, post-modernism and subaltern approaches, but research on Muslims is still mired within traditional frameworks and dominated by widely accepted stereotypes. The existing categories have been questioned but not changed; consequently, ideas and movements associated with Muslims are classified as revivalist rather than reformist, communal rather than secular, separatist rather than nationalist and, finally, reactionary rather than progressive. In this scheme, for example,

---

* Quoted in Rizvi, *History of Dar al-ulum*, vol. 1, p. 247.
† Mir Mushtaq Ahmad to Asoka Mehta, 19 June 1952, Mushtaq Ahmad papers, NMML; and his *National Unity and Solidarity* (Delhi: Unity Book House, n.d.), p. 33.

Syed Ahmad Khan and his associates are either marginalised or dismissed as 'separatist', a derisive expression used for those not conforming to the accepted view of nationalism. The stereotypical figure of Syed Ahmad as the architect of Muslim separatism, mesmerised by the British, remains unaffected by the knowledge of his contribution to introducing rational thought and English education in the last quarter of the nineteenth century. Similarly, the pioneering role of Hali, Maulvi Nazir Ahmad and Shaikh Abdullah, engaged in a project of 'reforming' Muslim women, finds little mention in conventional or unconventional histories and critiques of nationalism or separatism. The old explanations are presumed to unravel and delineate *their* conduct; it is all too readily assumed that they were imbued with 'reactionary' or 'communal' tendencies. There is still talk of a 'Muslim mind', a 'Muslim outlook' and an inclination to construct a Muslim identity around Islam. A sense of Otherness is conveyed in such images and polarities.

Other widely-held beliefs, reflected in both popular and scholarly writings, are that the *mullah*-dominated priestly class, with its parapher-nalia, represents 'true' Islam, while liberal and modernist currents are either secondary or peripheral to the more dominant 'separatist', 'communal' and 'neo-fundamentalist' paradigms. Most writers therefore still prefer studying the Faraizi or the *mujahidin* movements and the *ulama* of Deoband, Nadwat al-ulama and Firangi Mahal and their ideology, world-view and social conduct. Liberal, secular and modernist discourses have yet to figure on their agenda.

Unchanging scholarly perceptions and attitudes, derived from colonial knowledge and worldwide Islamist assertions, express themselves in different ways. Time and time again one is reminded of the pervasive impact of Islam on its adherents, their enduring transnational links and their obsessive concern to defend Quranic values. Similarly one is led to believe that their sole preoccupation is praying, visiting shrines and observing other religious rituals. One is also told that they, more than any other religious collectivity, attach importance and value to their religio-cultural habits and institutions; hence they are more prone – from North Africa to the Moros in the Phillippines – to be swayed by the religious/Is-lamic rhetoric.

This is a familiar classical Orientalist or neo-Orientalist view, based on the solidarity of the *umma* that was invoked to cultivate specifically Islamic ideas and defend Islamic symbols with vehemence and force. Thus the Kanpur Muslims took to the streets when a portion of a mosque in the city was demolished in 1913.[1] Also, Muslims were decidedly

---

[1] Gail Minault, *The Khilafat Movement: Religious Symbolism and Political Mobilization in India* (New York: Columbia University Press, 1982), pp. 46-8; Robinson, *Separatism*, pp. 12-4; Sandria B. Freitag, 'The Roots of Muslim Separatism in South Asia: Personal Practice

outraged over the Khilafat issue and resisted government interference in Muslim family law. This was exemplified in the opposition to the Sarda Marriage Bill of 1929 and similar legislative enactments.[2]

These are no doubt important facets, but their significance should not be overstated to discern a unified structure of consciousness or a *community* acting in unison. What should not be assumed is a teleology dictating its actions or a general acquiescence in the actions of a few. What, one may ask, is exceptional if some Muslims, falling prey to colonial enumerations and definitions and their own fanciful theories, regarded themselves as an indivisible component of a religious collectivity? Other communities had a similar self-image: how else to explain the presence of the Hindu Mahasabha, the RSS and innumerable caste associations? What of nineteenth-century religio-revivalism in Bengal, Maharashtra and Punjab and their deepening anxieties over the evangelical threat to 'Hindu identity'? The eminent historian Susobhan Sarkar commented on 'the obsession with Hindu traditions which helped to keep the men of our [Bengal] renaissance aloof from the masses'.[3]

At the heart of the Arya Samaj's brand of reconstruction and reform was the restoration of the pristine purity of Vedic culture and civilisation. The 'Tilak school' in Maharashtra was concerned with much the same thing. Some leaders of the 'Bengal renaissance' and the *swadeshi* agitation, including Aurobindo Ghose and B.C. Pal, were constructively rethinking their 'Hindu' heritage and meeting the challenges of modern thought by assimilative-creative processes. The Hindi-Urdu controversy and the cow question were evocative symbols of Hindu resurgence in the land of Aryavarta. Indeed, the crusade for Hindi *in opposition to Urdu* was as much linked to government employment as it was to the defence of a widely perceived symbol of a Hinduised identity. Finally, Romila Thapar has revealed how the emergent national consciousness appropriated the Orientalist construction of Hinduism as well as what it regarded as the heritage of Hindu culture. The need to formulate a Hindu community also became a requirement for political mobilisation when

---

and Public Structures in Kanpur and Bombay', in Edmund Burke III and Ira M. Lapidus (eds), *Islam, Politics and Social Movements* (Berkeley: CA, University of California Press, 1988), pp. 115-68.

[2] Shahida Lateef, *Muslim Women in India: Political and Private Realities 1890s-1980s* (Delhi: Kali for Women, 1990), chapter 4; Mohammad Mujeeb, 'Social Reform Among Indian Muslims' (Evelyn Hersey Memorial Lecture: Delhi School of Social Work, 1968), pp. 25-7.

[3] Susobhan Sarkar, Presidential address to the Indian History Congress, December 1971; Kenneth W. Jones, *Socio-Religious Reform Movements in British India* (CUP, 1993), and his *Arya Dharm*, chapter 2; Charles Heimsath, *Indian Nationalism and Hindu Social Reform* (Princeton University Press, 1964); Sumit Sarkar, *The Swadeshi Movement in Bengal, 1903-1908* (Delhi: People's Publishing House, 1973); J.R. McLane, *Indian Nationalism and the Early Congress* (Princeton University Press, 1987).

representation by religious community gave access to political power and economic resources.[4]

The Muslim élite did much the same, appropriating Islamic elements to legitimise their claim for a greater share in existing power structures. They received abundant support from official quarters. Yet there were limits to what they could achieve or what the colonial government could deliver. There were also limits to what the Congress was prepared to concede in its negotiated deals with the raj. Moreover, it was all very well to make noises about pan-Islamism or to plot the contours of a divinely-ordained community, but in reality mobilisation along such lines failed to obliterate internal differentiations. Religious bonds gave a semblance of unity, but they could not always override other forms of identity. The links binding Muslim groups with other social classes, though occasionally strained, were demonstrably more powerful and enduring. The Hindu-Muslim ill-will of the 1940s lessened but did not destroy traditional cross-communal associations.

A Muslim, like his counterpart in any other religious group, has many acts to perform and roles to play. He identifies in varying degrees with different sets of individuals and groups based on ethnicity, region, religion, profession and so on. At no time is one boundary the sole definer of his identity, although at any one time and for any one issue one boundary may become more prominent and define the us/them divide. A Muslim, like a Hindu or a Sikh, has multiple identities: he is a peasant or a landlord, an agricultural worker or a landless labourer, a worker or an industrialist, a student or a teacher, a litigant or a lawyer, a Shia or a Sunni, a Deobandi or a Barelwi (like the Vaishnavites, the Shaivities or the Kabir *panthis* among Hindus). Should we then harp on his Muslim/Islamic identity and ignore everything else, including the secular terms in which he relates to more immediate and pressing socio-economic needs and his wide-ranging interactions with his class and not just his Muslim brethren? The depth and nature of this interaction is a matter of dispute, but that does not justify a discussion in terms of an absolute Muslim/Islamic consciousness. If, as we are told, centuries of common living and shared experiences could not create composite solidarities, how could a specifi-cally Muslim self-consciousness emerge out of their multiple and diverse experiences?

Mohammad Ali Jinnah believed he had the answers. So did the Jamaat-i Islami. They stressed the element of separation, which made it more difficult to stress the broad groupings that already existed in Indian

---

[4] Romila Thapar, 'Imagined Religious Communities? Ancient History and the Modern Search for a Hindu Society', *Modern Asian Studies*, 23. 1989, pp. 209-32; and Arjun Appadurai, 'Number in the Colonial Imagination', in Breckenridge and Van der Veer (eds), *Orientalism*, pp. 314-41.

society. But there were other serious explanations as well, boldly constructed around secular and pluralist conceptions and counterpoised to an essentialist view of Indian Islam. Scholars, artists and creative writers, in particular, contested the definition of 'Muslim identity' – a hackneyed but still popular expression – in purely religious terms (in the context of imperial institutions) and refuted the popular belief that Islamic values and symbols provide a key to understanding the 'Muslim world-view'. They unfolded the past to discover elements of unity, cohesion and integration. They provided historical legitimation for multi-culturalism and religious plurality.

Prominent among them were scholars with pronounced socialist and Marxist leanings, acting as part of liberal-left formations. Keeping in mind their own context, they carried forward the inconclusive debates of the post-1857 decades, when the *ulama* and liberal intelligentsia, confronted by the external political and religio-cultural threat of colonialism, reflected on internal weaknesses within a religious tradition that had strong revivalist as well as liberal and reformist antecedents. They did so because certain key aspects in those debates had contemporary relevance to how Muslims were situated in a world brutally shattered by partition.

The nature of this engagement in post-independence India is the central theme of this chapter, although it is largely confined to the realm of ideas professed and expressed through the Jamia Millia Islamia and the Aligarh Muslim University. Following an exploration of religio-political formations in an earlier chapter, we pursue the debate from where it was left off, to offer a rounded view of the political as well as the intellectual currents in the evolution of a liberal and secular discourse among Muslims.

The intelligentsia – artists and intellectuals – create *mirrors* through which we see ourselves and *windows* through which we perceive reality. It is these mirrors and windows that define the boundaries of ideas and institutions. The intelligentsia's role – both as creators of a cultural outlook and the product of the milieu – is central to this writer's view of what happened in India generally and among certain Muslim groups in particular.

I

The nineteenth century, commented Maulana Abul Kalam Azad, 'marked a spirit of renaissance for the Indian spirit and Aligarh was one of the centres of such renaissance.'[5] Zakir Husain, the author of the Wardha

---

[5] Convocation Address at the Aligarh Muslim University, 20 February 1949, *Speeches of Maulana Azad*, p. 78.

scheme of education and a long-serving vice-chancellor of Aligarh, said to Nehru on his visit to the campus in November 1955: 'The way Aligarh works, the way Aligarh thinks, the contribution Aligarh makes to Indian life ... will largely determine the place Mussalmans will occupy in the pattern of Indian life.'[6] Such magisterial generalisations do not stand the test of historical scrutiny, but they do offer a clue to the role assigned to the university in the intellectual resurgence that took place in the last quarter of the nineteenth century, a phase dominated by Syed Ahmad Khan and the 'Aligarh movement'.

Colonial rule, combined with what Marshall Hodgson described as 'the great Western Transmutation',[7] triggered off major debates and controversies in Islamic lands. Yet its implications are not yet entirely clear in India, mainly because neither the liberal nor the Marxist social scientists have reflected on the evolution of ideas and institutions with any rigour or consistency.

The post-Mutiny era witnessed two kinds of reaction – a traditionalist backlash, sometimes militant but more often mute and a 'modernist' response represented in the 'Delhi school' and 'Aligarh movement'. First and foremost, the followers of Shah Waliullah attributed the political, social and moral 'decline' to Hindu and Shia accretions, to the Western concept of life which, with its extravagant individualism and materialism, was the antithesis of basic values formulated by the Quran. The message from the *mujahidin* in the north-west frontier region and the Faraizis in rural Bengal, as indeed from their counterparts in Egypt, Sudan and Turkey, was that a programme of religious purification, together with religious education and 'Islamic conscientisation' in the form of publications,[8] was an alternative to the 'degenerating' Western ideologies which had plunged the *umma* into crises.[9]

---

[6] Quoted in Mohammad Mujeeb, *Dr Zakir Husain* (Delhi: National Book Trust, reprint 1991), p. 160; see also Saiyid Hamid, *Aligarh Tehrik* (Aligarh Movement), in Urdu (Patna: Khuda Bakhsh Library, 1989).

[7] Marshall G.S. Hodgson, *The Venture of Islam: The Gunpowder Empires and Modern Times* (Chicago University Press, 1974), p. 176.

[8] Francis Robinson, 'Technology and Social Change: Islam and the Impact of Print', *Modern Asian Studies*, 27, 1, February 1993, pp. 231-45. Barbara Metcalf, *Islamic Revival*, pp. 202-5.

[9] S.A.A. Rizvi, *Shah Abdul Aziz: Puritanism, Sectarian Polemics, and Jehad* (Canberra: Ma'rifat Publishing House, 1982), and his *Shah Wali-Allah and his Times* (Canberra: Ma'rifat Publishing House, 1980); For Faraizis see Moinuddin Ahmad Khan, *History of the Faraidi Movement in Bengal (1818-1906)* (Karachi, 1965), and Mohiuddin Ahmad, *Saiyid Ahmad Shahid* (Lucknow: Academy of Islamic Research and Publications, 1975); Qeyamuddin Ahmad, *The Wahhabi Movement*, op. cit.; Barbara Metcalf, *Islamic Revival*, op. cit.; Ahmed, *The Bengal Muslims*, op. cit.; Asim Roy, *Islamic Syncretistic Tradition*, op. cit; S.F. Dale, *Islamic Society on the South Asian Frontier: The Mapillas of Malabar 1498-1922* (Delhi: OUP, 1980).

Some of their ideas went down well in areas where British rule disturbed the *status quo* most: in rural Punjab and Bengal, in particular, through established networks of mosques, *dargahs* and *madaris*. Yet neither the *mujahidin* nor the Faraizis generated a countrywide stir comparable to, say, the Khilafat campaign in the 1920s. They had little success compared with the movements of Usuman dan Fodio in Sahelian Africa, Mohammad Ahmad al-Mahdi in the Sudan, or Sultan Sulaiman in southwestern China. The social equilibrium was disturbed in some areas, though not everywhere – Islamic revival was an obsession with some but not all. The message from Deoband's Dar al-ulum reached far and wide; yet – as the high priests at this major site of Islamic revival lamented, few lived in accordance with their *fatawa*, or decisions on debatable points of Islamic law. The colonial government after 1857 thwarted the orthodox challenge through conciliation and compromise and a policy of balance between what they conceived as the two great communities, the Hindu and the Muslim.

'The upsurge in 1857 offered a rallying point to disgruntled elements in the ruling and service classes. Yet the banner of revolt was not raised everywhere.[10] In most areas Muslims seemed inclined, from the days of Company rule, to arrive at a workable *modus vivendi* with their new rulers and carve out new channels of aspiration and of spiritual creativity. Having read the writing on the wall, they accepted British rule much more gladly than others. There were no doubt a few hard nuts to crack, but most were not repelled by the West but attracted to it, because they found, as did Mirza Abu Talib and Lutfullah during their stay in England, a stable political system, an industrialised economy, and a civilisation with a strong material and cultural foundation.[11] They slowly but surely shed their inhibition to serve the Company. Maulvi Fazl-i Haq Khairabadi took part in the 1857 revolt, yet his father Fazl-i Imam (d. 1829) was the first Indian to accept the office of *mufti* and *sadr as-sudur*.[12] Mohammad Khan of Bilgram, a *qasbah* that had seen better days under the Nawabs of Awadh, joined the foreign department of the governor-general in the early days of Company rule.[13] Ghalib's uncle commanded a contingent on the Company's side in the Anglo-Maratha war of 1802-3.[14] The father of Nawab Mustafa Khan Shefta, another poet, was rewarded with estates

[10] See E.T. Stokes, *Peasants and the Raj: Studies in Agrarian Society and Peasant Rebellion in Colonial India* (CUP, 1978).

[11] Mushirul Hasan, 'Resistance and Acquiescence in North India: Muslim Responses to the West' in Hasan and Narayani Gupta (eds), *India's Colonial Encounter*, pp. 39-64.

[12] Annemarie Schimmel, *Islam in the Indian Subcontinent* (Leiden: E.J. Brill, 1980), p. 186.

[13] Bayly, *Rulers, Townsmen and Bazaars*, p. 356.

[14] Peter Hardy, 'Ghalib and the British', Ralph Russell (ed.), *Ghalib: the poet and his age* (London: Geo. Allen and Unwin, 1972), p. 56.

for bringing about a settlement between Lake and the Maratha commanders.[15]

In Delhi College, subsidised by the British since 1827 and headed by a British principal, Muslim teachers made strenuous efforts to demonstrate the compatibility of Islam with Western thought and values. In his old age Maulvi Zakaullah (1832-1910) used to tell C.F. Andrews with 'kindling eyes' how the scientific lectures in the college were eagerly followed. The young students were allowed to try 'astonishing experiments' with unknown chemical gases. They were invited to dip into the mysteries of magnetism, which was just then coming to the front as a freshly discovered science.[16] The Madarsa-i Aliyah flourished in Calcutta. Among those who benefitted from being educated there were the writer and historian Syed Ameer Ali (1849-1928) and Abdur Rahim (1867-1947), a judge turned politician. In the presidency town of Bombay the tone was set by the Tyabji family whose head, Tyab Ali, was the first Muslim to send his sons abroad for education, and the ladies of the Tyabji-Fyzee family first left *purdah* in 1894. His son Badruddin Tyabji was the first Indian barrister in Bombay, the first Indian judge on the 'Original' side of the Bombay High Court, and the first Indian to act as Chief Justice of the Bombay High Court.[17]

The rapprochement with the British, the guiding principle of most Muslim reformers, went along with much soul-searching and introspection. Newly-founded organisations like the Anjuman-i Himayat-i Islam in Punjab, the All-India Muslim Educational Conference and the Anjuman-i Islam in Bombay started from a healthy scepticism and subjected various suggested positions and approaches to critical analysis. They wondered why the Muslims were not able to integrate their system of education, family structures, economic enterprises and even political aspirations into the 'national mainstream'. What was 'pure' and unadulterated, and what contaminated Islam? Who decided what to keep and what to throw out – and by what criteria? Why the resistance to Western institutions, standards and concepts? What were the deeper causes of the social malaise? What was the remedy?

Inspired by Muslim scholarship from Al-Farabi to Ibn Khaldun and Mohammad Abduh, a number of writers applied a discriminating critical analysis of the topics they addressed, ranging from the social to the

[15] Russell and Khurshidul Islam, *Ghalib: Life and Letters, 1797-1869* (London: Geo. Allen & Unwin, 1969), p. 67.

[16] Gail Minault, 'Sayyid Ahmad Dehlavi and the Delhi Renaissance' in R.E. Frykenberg (ed.), *Delhi Through the Ages: Essays in Urban History, Culture and Society* (Delhi: OUP, 1986), pp. 289-98; C.F. Andrews, *Zakaullah of Delhi* (Cambridge: Heffer, 1929), p. 42.

[17] Theodore P. Wright, Jr., 'Muslim Kinship and Modernization: The Tyabji Clan of Bombay' in Imtiaz Ahmad (ed.), *Family, Kinship and Marriage in Indian Islam*, pp. 217-38.

theological. Thus Hali devoted his *Majalis an-nisa* to the plight of Muslim women.[18] Syed Mumtaz Ali commented on polygamy, the age of marriage, *purdah* and the empowerment of Muslim women.[19] Nazir Ahmad, a civil servant, set a model for writers in the *Mirat al-urus* (The bride's mirror), detailing the evils of polygamy and the virtues of female education and widow remarriage.[20] Justice Shah Din in Punjab advocated training for Muslim girls, if not in scholarly pursuits then at least in the basic skills of reading, writing, arithmetic, hygiene and home economics. He was the first president of the Muhammadan Educational Conference in 1894, and he and Mohammad Shafi were the first Muslims to send their daughters to study at the Queen Mary College in Lahore.[21] In Bombay, Badruddin Tyabji helped found and then for many years ran an educational foundation. The major focus of his career was liberal education for Muslim boys and girls; he campaigned for the Age of Consent Bill which was adopted in the teeth of both Hindu and Muslim opposition, and at the Muhammadan Educational Conference in 1903 he pleaded for the abandonment of *purdah*.[22] In a nutshell, the activities of an Ameer Ali or a Badruddin Tyabji were spurred by the models of European women and European criticism of the treatment of women in Islam. This influenced the very issues they chose to address as well as their own interpretations.[23]

Reformist ideas in the early twentieth century were stimulated by the social and cultural transition and the intellectual ferment in Turkey, Egypt and Iran. For once, new models of conduct were found worthy of emulatation, new icons replaced old ones in the temple of learning, and fresh ideas were imbibed and adapted to suit the Indian environment. Shibli, who taught at the Aligarh College before establishing the Nadwat al-ulama in Lucknow, met Mohammad Abduh, the Grand Mufti, on his Egyptian tour and was much impressed by him.[24] The office of *Ahsan al-Akhbar* in

---

[18] Gail Minault, 'Hali's Majalis un-Nisa: Purdah and Women Power in Nineteenth Century India' in Milton Israel and N.K. Wagle (eds), *Islamic Society and Culture: Essays in Honour of Professor Aziz Ahmad* (Delhi: Manohar, 1983), pp. 39-50; and Khwaja Altaf Husain Hali, *Voices of Silence*. English translation of *Majalis-un Nisa* by Gail Minault (Delhi: Chanakya Publications, 1986 edn).

[19] Barbara Metcalf, 'Reading and Writing about Muslim women in British India' in Zoya Hasan (ed.), *Forging Identities: Gender, Communities and the State*, pp. 10-11, and Gail Minault, 'Urdu Women's Magazines in the Early Twentieth Century', *Women Living under Muslim Laws* (France), 9/10, 1995.

[20] Mujeeb, *Indian Muslims*, pp. 531-3.

[21] *Eminent Mussalmans*, p. 381, and for Shafi's educational activities, see pp. 229-30.

[22] Ibid., pp. 107, 111.

[23] Barbara Metcalf, 'Reading and Writing about Muslim women', op. cit., p. 8; Faisal Fatehali Devji, 'Gender and the Politics of Space: The Movement for Women's Reform in Muslim India 1857-1900', *South Asia*, 14, 1, 1991.

[24] Shibli Nomani, *Safarnama-i Rum wa Misr-o-Sham* (Azamgarh, 1921); Ahmad, *Islamic Modernism*, p. 129.

Calcutta subscribed to Egyptian and other Arab newspapers. This was where the young Azad read *al-Hilal, al-Muqtataf* and Rashid Rida's *al-Manar* and went through Abduh's refutation of Farah Antun in the last-named. He recalled how his interest in religious discussion was enlivened by the tract. He wrote an article on Abduh in which he mentioned that some passages from his *Risalat al-Tawhid* had been translated in the *Aligarh Institute Gazette*, and made it known that in his commentary published in *al-Manar,* Abduh tried 'to relate the significance of the Holy Quran to modern needs'.[25] This was also at the heart of Azad's concern.

Throughout most of his adult life Hakim Ajmal Khan, a senior and venerable citizen of Delhi, wore the *sherwani* and Turkish *fez*, the former an adaptation of the Western coat and the latter a symbol of admiration for Ottoman social change.[26] His life-long friend and comrade, M.A. Ansari, witnessed the impact of the Young Turk Revolution, led by the Committee of Union and Progress, and was impressed by the strength and vitality of the modernising forces in Turkey.[27] He and others took pride in Turkey's onward march. It gladdened their hearts that a country which had suffered the belligerence of the colonial powers was ready to compete with the West for an equal status in the comity of modern nations. This led Iqbal, one of the few Muslim intellectuals in India to welcome the abolition of the Khilafat, to comment: 'If the renaissance of Islam is a fact, and I believe it is a fact, we too one day, like the Turks, will have to re-evaluate our intellectual inheritance.'[28]

Syed Ahmad was of course the trail-blazer. He alone possessed the intellectual resources to reconcile matters of faith with the more immediate task of rescuing Muslims from their downward spiral. He set high value on the social morality of Islam, and justified the adoption of Western ideas and institutions in Islamic terms as being not the introduction of something new but a return to the true spirit of Islam. The practical implications, which the new ideas from the West justified, were more closely related to Indian circumstances. They were not to live as the British themselves lived, but to carve out a place for themselves within the establishment. It was necessary not to imitate the West but to accept

[25] Douglas, *Abul Kalam Azad*, p. 56.

[26] Barbara Metcalf, 'Nationalist Muslims in British India: The Case of Hakim Ajmal Khan', *Modern Asian Studies*, 19, 1, 1985, p. 15, and her 'Hakim Ajmal Khan: Rais of Delhi and Muslim Leader', in Frykenberg (ed.), op. cit., pp. 299-315.

[27] Mushirul Hasan, *A Nationalist Conscience*, pp. 45-7, 131-3.

[28] See Schimmel, *Gabriel's Wing: A Study into the Religious Ideas of Sir Mohamed Iqbal*, pp. 47-8.

only some of its values as at least a second-best substitute for the vanished Muslim glories.[29]

With his sharp analytical mind and his acute sense of the working of historical forces in the shaping of contemporary societies, the Aligarh reformer recognised change and movement in history. He knew his Islamic history well, but he knew his Islam better. He could thus comprehend the scale and depth of reformist ideas and currents, identify elements of change and innovation, and discover a sound theoretical basis for a constructive dialogue with the West. The conclusions he drew and the message he communicated were directed against the theologian's ill-founded assumptions about the West and ill-informed criticism of his own project. He describes in a letter to Nawab Mohsinul Mulk, an esteemed colleague at Aligarh, how he became concerned after the Mutiny for the reform of his community and its education in the modern sciences and in the English language. Despairing of existing commentaries and their preoccupation with trivia, he 'deliberated on the Quran itself and tried to understand from [it] the principles on which its composition is based.'[30] He found that if Quranic principles were adopted there would remain no incompatibility between modern sciences and Islam. He tried to resolve the difficulties inherent in the four traditional sources of Muslim law by a dialectical rationalist exegesis of the Quran; by scrutinising the classical data of the *Hadith*; by an almost unlimited emphasis on *ijtehad* as the inalienable right of every individual Muslim; and finally by rejecting the principle of *ijma* (consensus) in the classical sense which confined it to the *ulama*.[31]

There was a strong resistance to and criticism of Syed Ahmad from identifiable quarters. But in the long run his modernist agenda was acclaimed and endorsed by a new generation of Muslims – including Ansari, Mohamed Ali, Iqbal, Hasrat Mohani – who were alienated by the formalism of the traditional theologians. They were convinced that pursuing modern education and the raising of intellectual standards would not undermine but vindicate the message of Islam. His reformulation of the doctrine in modern instead of medieval terms, like his eclectic worldview, became part of the mental furniture of educated Muslims. Some were inspired by him to found educational centres modelled on the Aligarh College. Thus a *Madarsatul-Islam* in Sind and the Dacca College were set up; the latter, like Aligarh, gained university status after the First World War.[32] Following the Muhammadam Educational Conference at

---

[29] Hodgson, op. cit., p. 335; C.W. Troll, *Sayyid Ahmad Khan: A Reinterpretation of Muslim Theology* (Delhi: Vikas, 1978).

[30] Ahmad and Grunebaum (eds), *Muslim Self-Statement*, p. 40.

[31] Ahmad, *Islamic Modernism*, p. 54.

[32] Schimmel, *Islam in the Indian Subcontinent*, p. 201.

Madras in 1901, the Muslim Educational Association of South India was founded.

Under Syed Ahmad's influence sections of the intelligentsia broke loose from the shackles of orthodoxy and buttressed the cause of reforms and re-interpretation of orthodox doctrines. Thus the historian Ameer Ali followed him in advancing modern concepts for the reorientation of the structure of Islamic social and religious thought, and in drawing a sharp distinction between the moral precepts and the specifically legal provisions of the Quran.[33] In a moving tribute to his intellectual mentor Hali said: 'The world has seen how one man has aroused a whole land, one man saved a caravan from destruction .... True it is that there is a dearth of men in our nation, and if the fragments of broken vessels are piled high, yet among them lie fragments of jewels concealed. Hidden among the gravel there are pearls to be found; and mingled in the sand are particles of gold.'[34]

In his 'Preparatory Years' Syed Ahmad unveiled to the young Azad the true spirit of the Quran and the teachings of Islam.[35] The Maulana compared him with Raja Rammohun Roy, since both left the stamp of their personality on several spheres of intellectual activity. He emphasised that the Syed, who used the metaphor that Hindus and Muslims were the two eyes in Mother India's face, believed strongly in inter-community harmony, and that as the presiding spirit of the Aligarh College he represented the forces of change by challenging traditional values and outmoded beliefs. 'The battle was fought here in Aligarh and Aligarh is the visible embodiment of the victory of the forces of progress.'[36] Iqbal, too, described Syed Ahmad as 'the first modern Muslim to catch a glimpse of the positive character of the age that was coming'. He was 'the first Indian Muslim who felt the need for a fresh orientation of Islam and worked for it'.[37]

Although Syed Ahmad was by far the most prominent advocate of an Anglo-Muslim rapprochement, he was not the only one. Many of his contemporaries were imbued with a similar reformist zeal, and were not unduly upset over Britain's political hegemony. Their overriding concern, for which Syed Ahmad had little sympathy, was to resist the West's cultural penetration. Some notable thinkers from the traditionalist and modernist persuasions took on the burden of this responsibility within a specifically Islamic framework and, in so doing, relied heavily on the neo-

---

[33] Ahmad, *Islamic Modernism*, p. 87; Fazlur Rahman, *Islam* (New York: Holt, Rinehart and Winston, 1966), p. 231.

[34] Ahmad and Grunebaum (eds), op. cit., p. 99.

[35] Quoted in Douglas, op. cit., p. 52.

[36] *Speeches of Maulana Azad*, pp. 78-9.

[37] Quoted in Schimmel, *Islam in the Indian Subcontinent*, p. 198.

traditionalism of the Waliullahi school. But it was not long before cracks began to appear in this collective endeavour. Serious differences in attitudes and approaches come to the surface and caused an open breach in the ranks of the *ulama* and the liberal intelligentsia. Nothing exemplified this better than the cold and uneasy relationship between Aligarh College, seen as symbolising political and cultural capitulation to the British, and Deoband's Dar al-ulum, embodying the spirit of orthodox resistance to foreign rule. The *ulama*, whatever their theological affiliations, symbolised rigid formalism and conservatism, and for this reason they were often criticised and ridiculed. But they were not the kind to keep quiet. They mounted a fierce, mostly polemical attack on their detractors. The type of questioning from reformative groups among young intellectuals created a backlash in the form of sharp denunciation of its 'heretical nature'.[38]

The tug of war was temporarily halted early in the twentieth century when the political landscape was changing in response to major national and transnational developments. This led to a closing-up of the ideological split and a gradual reassimilation of traditional and Western values. Deoband's Dar al-ulum and Aligarh College were no longer bitter foes; and indeed sections at both places engaged in a serious dialogue to bridge the gulf and narrow differences.[39] This was not due to any basic ideological compatibility or the sudden meeting of minds on matters of faith and dogma but because more and more Muslim divines, especially from Deoband and Nadwa, and the men of 'New Light' discovered the value of co-operation, as over the Mussalman Waqf Validating Act (1913).[40] Yet what engaged them most and spurred the unity efforts were not just legal, educational and religious matters but their place in the political arrangements being hammered out in Delhi and Whitehall. Their main preoccupation was to define the *community* afresh in order to suit their spiritual interests as well as the more attractive temporal ones. Their spirited endeavour, for which they revitalised an otherwise defunct Muslim League, was to locate wider communitarian concerns outside the framework of Congress nationalism.

Once the *ulama* and their erstwhile *bête noire*, the Western-trained professional politicians, put their heads together, they came up with a definition developed in the context of colonial institutions and their own scripturalist rhetoric. They sought to create a corporate identity and set

---

[38] Minault, *The Khilafat Movement*, chapter 1; Barbara Metcalf, *Islamic Revival*, chapter 8; Mushirul Hasan, *Nationalism and Communal Politics*, chapter 6; Robinson, *Separatism*, chapters 7-8.

[39] Rizvi, *History of the Dar al-Ulum*, vol. 1, pp. 234-5.

[40] Gregory C. Kozlowski, *Muslim Endowments and Society in British India* (CUP, 1985), p. 182.

Muslims apart from their own class, region and linguistic units. They thrust an Islamic identity on Muslims, many of whom were not accustomed to living in accordance with the *Shariat* or the diktat of the theologians. This was not all. The coming together of the men of religion and the modern-day publicists was counter-productive in so far as it stifled liberal, reformist and secularising currents. For some this brought great relief, though for others there was little cause to rejoice over this ominous development in 'Indo-Muslim' history. It was disturbing that the contours of a *community* were being delineated in complete disregard of its local, regional, class, caste or linguistic specificities.

What did the enumerators find when the first all-India census was tabulated and analysed in 1881? They found that Muslims made up only 19.7 per cent of the population. They uncovered a geographically-dispersed aggregate of Muslims forming neither a collectivity nor a society that was distinct politically, economically or socially. Out of a total population of about 50 million (or one-fifth of the computed total population of 'British India'), the Muslims in Bengal spoke Bengali and those in Punjab mainly Punjabi. Those living in Tamil Nadu spoke Tamil, and those on the Malabar coast, mostly Mapillas, spoke Malayalam. They found Muslims whose religious rituals were strongly tinged with Hinduism and who retained caste and observed Hindu festivals and ceremonies.[41] In the Bengal countryside especially, pre-Islamic birth, marriage and death ceremonies were widely observed.[42] In fact, the entry of Muslims in South Asia through so many and such separate doorways, their spread over the subcontinent by so many different routes over many centuries, and the diffusion of Islam in different forms from one area to the other, ensured that this religion would present itself in those different forms. Neither to its own adherents nor to non-Muslims did Islam seem monolithic, monochrome or indeed mono-anything.[43] Yet by the close of the nineteenth century the *community*, separate and distinct from the 'Others', had arrived with its accompanying baggage of concepts bearing no relation to realities on the ground.

This is why the Simla deputation of 1 October 1906 and the viceroy's response to the 'command performance' appear to be a significant landmark.[44] From then on the Muslim élite and its spokesmen knew their

---

[41] *Census of India*, 1921, vol. 1, p. 115.

[42] Ahmed, *The Bengal Muslims*, p. 134.

[43] Peter Hardy, 'Islam and Muslims in South Asia' in Raphael Israeli (ed.), *The Crescent in the East: Islam in Asia Minor* (London: Curzon Press, 1988), pp. 39-40; Joachim Heidrich, 'Islam as a Political Factor in India' in Holger Preisler and Martin Robb (eds), *Islamic Studies in the German Democratic Republic: Traditions, Positions, Findings* (Berlin: Akademie Verlag, 1982), pp. 76-7.

[44] Robinson, *Separatism*, pp. 165-7; Matiur Rahman, *From Consultation to Confrontation: A Study of the Muslim League in British Indian Politics, 1906-1912* (London: Luzac, 1970).

priorities. They knew who to turn to for political legitimation. They had a threefold aim: to trace the historical evolution of an imaginary *community* as an antithesis to the Congress theory of 'Unity in Diversity'; to emphasise its distinct identity in order to bargain with the government and extract concessions; and to invoke Islamic symbols to mount a movement that would, in its essential thrust, delink specific 'Muslim aspirations' from the broader concerns of the countrywide nationalist upsurge. This is how 'Muslim nationalism' gained legitimacy in government eyes, and why it appealed to the Muslim landed and urban-based professional classes who were apprehensive about their position in the newly-created power structures. Hence every single step towards the devolution of authority to Indian hands was accompanied by initiatives to cement bonds of religious solidarity on the one hand, and accentuate inter-community differences on the other.

The British government had no reason to challenge the Muslim League so long as it could be pressed into service to counter nationalist aspirations. Having created a Muslim identity in Indian politics through the Acts of 1909 and 1919, they could draw comfort henceforth from Jinnah repeating, at the height of his popularity, much the same arguments that had prompted Morley, Minto, Montagu and Chelmsford to concede to the Muslims separate electorates, weightages and reservation in the councils and public services. During the Second World War, Jinnah could play any tune he liked. Officials in Delhi were prepared to give him a patient and sympathetic hearing and support his Pakistan project. He emerged stronger once the guns were silent on all fronts. The British government felt obliged to reward him for dutifully supporting the war effort.

While these games were being played out on the Indian turf with cynicism and insensitivity, a number of Muslim-dominated organisations and institutions sensed the awful consequences of political solidarity being built on religious ties, questioned the conviction (or myth) in certain Muslim circles that the future of Islam in South Asia was endangered by Hindu nationalism, disputed the notion of a monolithic and homogenised community, and challenged the constitutional arrangements that sowed the seeds of discord and disunity. Many people wrote and spoke along these lines. They were idealistic and worked for inter-community harmony. Their banners and flags did not flutter on housetops, and their audiences and readerships did not run to vast numbers. Yet they pressed their views tenaciously; they were men of conviction, and even when Pakistan's creation seemed imminent, they envisaged a future full of hope for the beleaguered Muslims. Their optimism was summed up in the narrative as well as in the title of Tufail Ahmad Manglori's *Musalmanon ka Raushan Mustaqbil* (A bright future for Muslims) and in the writings of social scientists, creative writers and journalists who renewed their intellectual quest and commented on their history and 'destiny' with poise, dignity and self-confidence.[45]

III

The Jamia Millia Islamia (National Muslim University) in Delhi was, in the words of Nehru, 'a lusty child of the non-cooperation movement.'[46] It encapsulated two dominant trends, each finding several points of covergence in the post-Khilafat era: these were the reformist inclination of some *ulama* who were also profoundly anti-British, and the political radicalism of Aligarh-based students who rejected their institution's pro-British proclivities and gravitated towards Gandhi and Nehru. In 1935 the Turkish author Halide Edib found the Jamia to be much nearer to the Gandhian movement than any other Muslim institution; it seemed, in its political aspect, 'like an attempt to understand the *inalienable democracy* of Islam as it was in the earlier Islamic society.'[47] Sturdy Congressmen could thus mingle with ardent socialists and fiery communists. Hence the League's criticism of the Jamia's nationalist complexion.

Whether others agreed or not, the Jamia *biradari* (community) at Okhla in South Delhi was convinced of its quintessential role as a *national* institution, devoted to the service of the nation and destined to contribute to the shaping of modern India. Though founded by Muslims, it was Muslim only in name. The atmosphere was mixed and cosmopolitan, thanks to the presence of several Hindu and Christian teachers, including a few from Germany, a country where some of the Jamia's founders learned their first lessons about British colonialism and developed their antipathy towards it. The theological disputations between the Barelwis and the Deobandis and the doctrinal differences between the Shias and Sunnis, which had marred the campus life in Aligarh, were alien to the culture of the Jamia where no one wished to serve as an exemplar of religiosity.

The Jamia's social and intellectual manifesto was the outcome of enlightened political and intellectual currents sweeping across the

---

[45] The book was first published in 1937. Its fifth edition appeared in 1945 (Kutub Khana-i Aziziya) with an added section 'Raushan Mustaqbil Kyon hai?' (Why a bright future?). The book was commended by, among others, Azad, Husain Ahmad Madani and Khwaja Hasan Nizami.

[46] Message on the silver jubilee of Jamia Millia, 10 September 1946, *SWJN*, second series, vol. 2, p. 386.

[47] Edib, *Inside India*, p. 322; and 'A Note on the Jamiah Milliyah Islamiyah' in Smith, *Modern Islam*, pp. 147-54. For a collection of essays on Jamia's history, coinciding with its 75th anniversary, see *Jamia* (July-August-September 1995), a journal of the Zakir Institute of Islamic Studies, Jamia Millia Islamia, New Delhi.

country. Its educational programmes, outlined in the Wardha scheme of education, bore the imprint of Gandhi's ideas on primary education and incorporated some of Tagore's innovations at Vishwa Bharati in Shantiniketan. Its liberal orientation owed much to Syed Ahmad Khan who, according to Mohammad Mujeeb, 'had a larger view of life than any of the purely religious leaders, and one must be grateful to him for having given commonsense its rightful place in religious thought.'[48] And its own reconstruction of the Islamic ideal of an active political life was inspired by Azad, whose 'neo-intellectual modernism', religious universalism and commitment to composite Indian nationalism represented the essence of what the Jamia stood for. Zakir Husain, vice-chancellor from 1926 to 1948, recalled:

When I was a boy, I was anxious to light the dusty lamp of my life, and like other people, I too had prepared the cotton wicks and had put them in the oil of my soul, and was roaming about to find out from where I could ignite them. The first wick of that soul, the first wick of the lamp, I lit from the lamp of the Maulana. As a student I used to read *Al-Hilal*, and when I read it in the company of my friends, it was at that time that this wick got the fire. Although I have ignited myself from other sources as well, but I do confess today that the first ignition had taken place only from him.[49]

The Jamia fraternity was dumbfounded by the Muslim League rhetoric. Iqbal's plea for a Muslim state in north-western India was opposed to their cherished ideal that Muslims must live and work with non-Muslims to realise common ideals of citizenship and culture. Mujeeb said so to the poet when he visited the campus early in 1935 to preside over Halide Edib's lecture.[50] The two-nation theory was just as much anathema to an institution whose sole *raison d'être* was to promote cultural integration, foster composite and syncretic values and inter-community ties. As the first *Amir-i Jamia* (chancellor), Hakim Ajmal Khan expected the students to know each other's culture: 'The firm foundation of a united Indian nationhood depends on this mutual understanding.'[51] Ansari, who nursed the Jamia when it was threatened with closure, did not believe in a politically separate Muslim community, and often said that the future India must be a field of co-operation between those of different faiths. People could live according to the moral dictates of a religious creed, but theological subtleties and contrived political distinctions must not disturb

[48] Mujeeb, *Indian Muslims*, pp. 447-52.
[49] Quoted in Sheik Ali, *Zakir Husain: Life and Time* (Delhi: Vikas, 1991), p. 49; and Abid Husain, 'Modern Trends in Islam' in *Islam* (Patiala: Guru Nanak Quicentenary Celebration Series, 1969), p. 98.
[50] Philips and Wainwright (eds), *The Partition of India*, p. 406.
[51] Barbara Metcalf, 'Nationalist Muslims in British India', p. 25.

inter-community peace and harmonious living.[52] Writing to Halide Edib, Ansari, the chancellor, observed:

I consider the brotherhood of man as the only real tie, and partition based on race and colour are, to my mind, artificial and arbitrary, leading to division and factious fights.[53]

Jinnah's political agenda in the 1940s ran contrary to the Ajmal-Ansari or the Gandhi-Nehru project. The Jamia *biradari* lionised Gandhi, their chief benefactor, and admired Nehru's intellect, vision and progressiveness,[54] regarding the two as models of impeccable political conduct. The more devoted, Shafiqur Rahman Kidwai being one of them, took to wearing *Khaddar* and the 'Gandhi topi' (Gandhi cap), and took part in civil disobedience campaigns.[55]

Jinnah and his colleagues, on the other hand, were highly critical of Gandhi and Nehru and averse to the Congress brand of nationalism. Not surprisingly they fired their salvo against Ansari and Zakir Husain, rebuked them for turning the Jamia into a 'Hindu stronghold', and criticised its syllabus for cultivating patriotism to the exclusion of Islamic worship. The Jamia's ethos and orientation, stated a well-publicised letter, was prejudicial to Islam.[56] This is what 'A Muslim' said to Jinnah in 1946:

A large factory for the mass Hinduisation of Muslims has been established in Delhi under the very name of the All-India Muslim leaders ... I am referring to the so-called Jamia Millia. Dr Zakir Husain was selected by Gandhi and Co. for carrying out their plan for Hinduising Muslims in the spirit of the Wardha scheme which was prepared ... under the guidance and supervision of Gandhi, the most astute and cunning hypocrite of all time. The object of the Jamia Millia is to make Muslims as much Hindu in outlook and in every other respect as possible .... For example, [the young children] are taught the slogan 'The Muslim League is dead, the Congress is good'. With grown up Muslim boys, more subtle methods are used. The aim is to make their inside Hindu and let their outside remain Muslim. [...]
If this factory for Hinduising Muslims is allowed to continue its evil work, real Islam will soon disappear from India. The great killings like the one in Bihar grieve us most profoundly, but they do not kill Islam. They rather revive

[52] Edib, *Inside India*, p. 323.

[53] Ibid., p. 223.

[54] See, for example, Abid Husain, *The Way of Gandhi and Nehru* (Bombay: Asia Publishing House, 1959), and his *Gandhiji and Communal Unity* (Bombay: Orient Longmans, 1969). He also translated Gandhi's *The Story of My Experiments with Truth* and Nehru's *Autobiography, The Discovery of India* and *Glimpses of World History*; K.G. Saiyidain, *Andhi me Chiragh* (Delhi: Taraqqi Urdu Bureau, 1982 edn), for his essays on Gandhi and Nehru.

[55] Abid Husain dedicated one of his books to Shafiqur Rahman Kidwai, 'who lived and died following *The Way of Gandhi and Nehru*.'

[56] *Millat-i Islamia aur Jamia Millia Islamia, Delhi* (Calcutta, 1941).

it to some extent. But the slow and secret poison of the Jamia Millia Islamia will soon kill Islam, and will make every Muslim a mere 'show-boy' of the Hindus. This is the cleverest plot so far designed for the destruction of Islam in India.[57]

An institution with a secular and nationalist record could not escape the fury of the angry mobs that struck terror in Delhi during the communal holocaust of August-September 1947. Jamia's property at Karol Bagh in old Delhi, where the institution was first headquartered after its brief and lazy existence in Aligarh in 1920-5, was looted and destroyed. The vice-chancellor Zakir Husain ran for his life and had a miraculous escape. The husband of Anis Kidwai, a friend of Jamia, was killed. There were other tragedies, but Jamia lived through these experiences to provide the healing touch. It was, in Gandhi's opinion, 'like an oasis in the Sahara'.[58] 'Few institutions', commented Nehru, 'succeed in retaining for long the impress of the ideal that gave them birth. They tend to become humdrum affairs, perhaps a little more efficient, but without the enthusiasm that gives life. The Jamia, more I think than any other institution that I can think of, retained some of the old inspiration and enthusiasm.' He assured Zakir Husain:[59]

'Now that Gandhiji has gone a very special responsibility attaches to us to carry on the work he was interested in and the Jamia was an important part of this work. Whatever I can do for Jamia, I shall endeavour to do. The world seems a very dark, dismal and dreary place, full of people with wrong urges or no urge at all, living their lives trivially and without any significance. All the more therefore we seek the few sanctuaries and causes and try to derive sustenance from them. I feel overwhelmed, not so much by the great problems facing us, but rather, by the affection and comradeship of friends who expect so much from me. A sense of utter humility seizes me in the face of this faith and trust.'

In the mid-1920s the total enrolment of the schools and colleges was about eighty, with 25-30 teachers. More than three decades later the Jamia remained small. Shortage of funds was a perennial problem, and independence brought no relief. The total grant from 1949 to 1959 was Rs 35,74,80 as against Rs 68,91,034 and Rs 81,83,718 sanctioned to the Aligarh Muslim University and the Vishwa Bharati in Shantiniketan.[60]

---

[57] To the Editor, *Dawn*, n.d., with a copy marked to Jinnah, Correspondence of Quaid-i Azam Mr M.A. Jinnah, Delhi, SHC.

[58] Speech at prayer meeting, 6 April 1947, *The Collected Works of Mahatma Gandhi*, vol. IXXXVII, p. 218.

[59] Nehru to Zakir Husain, 16 February 1948, *SWJN*, second series, vol. 5, p. 561, and his message on the silver jubilee of Jamia Millia Islamia, 10 September 1946, *SWJN*, second series, vol. 1, pp. 385-6.

[60] 31 August 1959, *Lok Sabha Debates*, 1959, vol. 34, p. 5310. The grant from 1959-60 to

But lack of resources was adequately compensated by the pioneering basic and adult education programmes, mixed (co-educational) schools and colleges, and innovative vocational courses designed to attract students from backward Muslim groups such as the Meos in the Mewat region. There was pride in recruiting students from such backgrounds and not from upper middle-class families who invariably found a safe haven for their offspring in Syed Ahmad's 'Muslim's Oxford' at Aligarh. There was pride in employing motivated and dedicated teachers, who did not have the distinction of being educated at premier colleges or universities in India or overseas. The Jamia community boasted of being the only educational centre in the country which was co-educational at all levels, from elementary grades through to the undergraduate course. 'They [girls] leave their homes with the *burqa* [veil] on, and somewhere along the way they take it off.'[61]

The university, in search of moral and political support after independence, could have turned into a quasi-religious or quasi-communal institution, but Jamia remained secular and nationalist to the core. 'I look on this', claimed Mujeeb proudly, 'as a secular school.'[62] This tradition was exemplified in the writings 6f Mujeeb himself and Syed Abid Husain, who had been connected with Jamia since 1925-6. Both were educated in the West and were familiar with the nuances of British and German philosophical traditions and the Western way of life. Yet their world-view was largely moulded by the cultural inheritance of the Indo-Gangetic plain and the secular traditions of Indian nationalism. In their areas of study and research they applied the genuinely scientific and creative approach to the problem of historical method, and avoided a capricious selection of materials. They stayed clear of Shibli's dogmatic reconstruction of the Islamic past, Hali's romanticised imagination, and the demands of religious emotion and theological dogma. They detailed principles of social justice and equality enunciated in the Quran, but were concerned that Muslim societies had not maintained the high standards of social equality, women's rights, just inheritance and the like which are commanded by the Quran. They argued that it was the duty of those serving the public interest actively to improve the status of women; their em-

---

1961-2 (in lakhs) stood as follows:

	1959-60	1960-1	1961-2
1. Recurring grant to Jamia Millia	475,000	560,000	560,000
Non-recurring grant	140,000	Nil	Nil
2. Recurring grant to Rural Institute	170,000	100,000	125,000
Non-recurring grant	65,000	304,000	100,000

Source: Lok Sabha Debates, vol. 63, pp. 2420-1.

[61] Quoted in Greighton Lacy, *Indian Insights* (Delhi: Orient Longmans, 1972), p. 290.

[62] Ibid., p. 288.

powerment should receive top priority. This was a call not to adopt strident Western feminism but to act in accordance with Muslim precepts of the public good and promote the spirit of the fundamental equality – or equity – argued in the best of the Islamic tradition. After all, the most forceful statement of equality before God comes from the Quran (33:35).

For Muslim men and women, for believing men and women, for devout men and women, for men and women who are patient and constant, for men and women who humble themselves, for men and women who give in charity, for men and women who fast (and deny themselves), for men and women who guard their chastity, and for men and women who engage much in God's praise, for them has God prepared forgiveness and great reward.

Yet the 'Muslim society', Mujeeb conceded, 'does not give [in practice] the rights which the *Shariat* has already given [in theory]. [...] With us, reform meant acting more consistently with the religious law [already laid down].'[63] It made no sense to him that works on theology and jurisprudence compiled outside India could not be changed to suit Indian conditions. What was so sacrosanct about the *Shariat* ? 'A bird's-eye view of the variety of beliefs and practices and customs among Indian Muslims will convince us that it was not the *Shariat* of Islam that they adopted but the manners and customs and to some extent even their beliefs that became the *Shariat* of Islam, of their Islam.'[64]

In his *magnum opus* published in 1966, Mohammad Mujeeb, the Oxford-educated vice-chancellor, identified various constituent elements of Indian Muslim religious, political and social life, and revealed some of its essential qualities. He questioned 'the fallacies and illusions that arise out of an identification of the whole ... community with some element of its belief or practice, with some political figures or military or political achievements, with particular social forms and patterns of behaviour, with some historical tendency.'[65] He brought to light the diversity of beliefs, the variety of social forms, the multiplicity of ideas and movements among Muslims and the palpable imprints of a fundamental structural element of the 'traditional' Indian society with its caste system. The only common factor, he argued, was allegiance to Islam, although it was easy to take the Islamic identity of the Muslims as making them a distinct body politic – a nation – which they never were and never wanted to be. He questioned the ways in which educated Muslims saw themselves, arguing that their judgements were inspired by either self-praise or self-pity, and by an idealisation of themselves as the embodiment of religious truth. He was no less critical of others who saw Muslims in parts

[63] Mujeeb, 'Social Reform Among Indian Muslims', p. 4.

[64] Ibid., p. 5.

[65] Mujeeb, *Indian Muslims*, p. 555.

and failed to consider their total experience throughout the course of their history.[66] Taking his cue perhaps from H.A.R. Gibb, Mujeeb was not tempted to reduce history to a pattern of abstract concepts.[67] As is clear from his essay on the sixteenth-century historian Abdul Qadir Budauni, he believed that concrete facts were always to be viewed in the light of their particular concrete circumstances.[68]

In the spirit of liberal-left historians like D.D. Kosambi, Tara Chand, Beni Prasad, R.P. Tripathi, Mohammad Habib and K.M. Ashraf, Mujeeb underlines the historical weight of composite and syncretic forces. 'If the Indian Muslim state is divested of its pseudo-religious guise,' he observed, 'the spirit of the political system will appear to be in accord with what is recognised as the national interest today.'[69] Through a diligent study of the evolution of those ideas and movements that reinforced bonds of inter-religious unity and understanding, he concluded that there were far more convincing reasons for Hindus and Muslims to stay together than to be divided. His experience of living in Delhi, his extensive travels, and the cultural and intellectual milieu of Awadh, which was the home of his distinguished professional family, certainly lent weight to his views. Even when Hindu-Muslim relations reached their nadir in 1946-7, he noticed in the course of his travels:

I remember that shortly after the orgy of violence in Bihar I visited the grave of a Sufi on the banks of the Ganges. The Muslims living in the *dargah* had fled and the place looked desolate. But soon a group of Hindu women appeared. They performed circumambulations and prostrations, as if nothing had happened that affected their sentiments of veneration for the tomb of a Muslim saint.

Mujeeb's natural intellectual inclination was towards men with an enlightened world-view. He therefore wrote essays on Abu Talib and Syed Ahmad Khan, and biographies of Ghalib and Zakir Husain. He began writing on Ansari but made little progress because of his involvement in Jamia. His admiration for Hakim Ajmal Khan and Azad is evident from *The Indian Muslims*. His sympathies lay with such Congress Muslims, the protagonists of composite nationalism, and not with self-seeking politicians like Mohamed Ali. Men like Ajmal Khan, Ansari and Azad provided both a stimulus and a challenge to the Muslim élite who were forced 'to reconsider their cultural and political function as a community, asked for a new philosophy of life, for personalities who would represent

---

[66] Mujeeb, *Indian Muslims*, pp. 24-5.

[67] H.A.R. Gibb, *Modern Trends in Islam* (Chicago University Press, 1947) p. 128.

[68] M. Mujeeb, 'Badauni' in Mohibbul Hasan (ed.), *Historians of Medieval India* (Meerut: Meenaskshi Prakashan, 1982 reprint), pp. 111-18.

[69] Mujeeb, *Indian Muslims*, p. 557.

not communalism but faith, not numbers but values, not multitudes but effectiveness.'[70] The message for his generation was:

Indian Muslims can serve Islam and themselves best by associating themselves with persons and parties who aim at making democracy as real as possible and at achieving the maximum of social justice and social welfare through the legislative and administrative action of the State.[71]

Abid Husain, a Shia married to Swaliha, who was an eminent Urdu writer and a descendant of Hali, studied in Allahabad, Oxford and Berlin. He taught philosophy and literature in Jamia from 1926 to 1956, wrote a number of books, and translated German, English and French texts into Urdu.[72] His forte lay in analysing and evaluating movements outside the conventional category of religion, for he held that 'the work of integrating the various communities into a nation ... cannot be and should not be done on the religious but on the secular plane.'[73] To combat divisive tendencies, it was necessary to impart practical training in schools and colleges 'in citizenship based on the high ideals of nationalism, secularism and democracy.'[74] *The Destiny of Indian Muslims*, published in 1965, was not a work of profound scholarship but a well-argued statement by a Muslim steeped in the nationalist values and traditions of Ajmal, Ansari and Azad. Its author, Abid Husain, dwelt on a common 'national culture', based on the secularism of the Indian state and on 'religious awakening' and a 'spiritual renaissance' among Muslims.[75] His concern was to .prevent Muslims from 'drifting away from the mainstream of national life.'[76] The agenda he set for himself and for the secular and religious leadership was simple enough: drastic changes in the curriculum of *makatib* and *madaris*, reforming Muslim institutions, and allowing *ijtehad* to cope with the demands of the new age. He observed: 'For the last hundred years things have changed and the modern *ulama* must give a *fatwa* giving a new

---

[70] Mujeeb, *Indian Muslims*, p. 557.

[71] Mujeeb, *Islamic Influences*, p. 176.

[72] See Obaidur Rahman, *Syed Abid Husain*, in Urdu (Delhi: Sahitya Akademi, 1995); *Abid Husain Felicitation Volume* (Delhi, 1974), and Sheila McDonough, 'The Spirit of Jamia Millia Islamia as Exemplified in the Writings of Syed Abid Husain' in Robert D. Baird (ed.), *Religion in Modern India* (Delhi: Manohar, 1981), pp. 287- 93. Commenting on *Hindustani Mussalman aina-i ayyam men*, in Urdu (The Destiny of Indian Muslims), and Mujeeb's *The Indian Muslims*, A.A.A. Fyzee wrote: 'The former is a fresh spring of water: lucid, sane and deep; the latter is an encyclopedia of facts – social, cultural, historical and religious.' A.A.A. Fyzee, 'The Muslim Minority in India', *Quest* (Bombay), 1967, p. 4.

[73] Husain, *Destiny of Indian Muslims*, p. 12.

[74] Ibid., p. 8.

[75] Ibid., p. 7.

[76] Husain, *National Culture*, pp. 63-4; see also Ahmad, *Islamic Modernism*, pp. 257-8.

ijtehad to the provisions of the Muslim law.'[77]

The Destiny of Indian Muslims, along with Abid Husain's other works, illustrates how educated Muslims saw their own role after the turbulent decade of the 1940s.[78] The journal *Islam and the Modern Age* and the Islam and the Modern Age Society underscored his broad intellectual concerns as a synthesiser of ideas and a protagonist of a liberal and secular agenda embodying the values of traditional Islam with ideas and institutions associated with the modern West.[79] His main collaborators in this enterprise were K.G. Saiyidain, an educationist who also happened to be a descendant of Hali's family,[80] Ziya-ul-Hasan Faruqi and Mushirul Haq, both educated at the Institute of Islamic Studies at McGill University in Montreal.[81]

Scholars at the Aligarh Muslim University, especially in the departments of history, geography, Islamic Studies and Urdu, were engaged in constructing the past in secular terms, a task undertaken by the erudite Mohammad Habib, brother of Mujeeb, and some of the social scientists in close contact with him.[82] They also tried hard to disentangle the

---

[77] Interview, *National Herald* (Delhi), 2 June 1970.

[78] For example, *The Way of Gandhi and Nehru* (1959); and *National Culture* (1965); *Gandhiji and Communal Unity* (1969); *Mussalman aur Asri Masail* (Delhi: Maktaba Jamia, 1972).

[79] Thus one of the objectives of publishing a set of volumes on 'World Religions' undertaken by the Islam and the Modern Age Society was to enable the followers of different religions to develop 'a better understanding of their own religion'. Abid Husain, preface to Hasan Askari, *Society and State in Islam: An Introduction* (Delhi: Islam and the Modern Age Society, 1978).

[80] Son of Khwaja Ghulam-us Saqlain, a leading writer and journalist, K.G. Saiyidain (1904-71) taught at the Aligarh Muslim University before joining the education ministry of the government of India. His books include *The Humanist Tradition in Indian Educational Thought* (Bombay: Asia Publishing House, 1966) and *Maulana Azad's Contribution to Education* (Baroda: Maharaja Sayajirao University, 1961). He was a great admirer of Azad, whom he described as the '*mir-i karawan*' (leader of the caravan), a close friend of Zakir Husain, the '*mard-i momin*' (man of deep faith), Humayun Kabir, Mujeeb and Abid Husain. He was informally associated with the Jamia Millia Islamia, lived on the campus towards the end of his career, and is buried in the university graveyard. See Swaliha Abid Husain, *Mujhe Kahna kai kuch apni zabaan me: Khwaja Ghulam-us Saiyidain* (Delhi: Saiyidain Memorial Trust, 1974).

[81] Faruqi (1925-96) is best known for his book 'The Deoband School and the Demand for Pakistan', a master's thesis submitted at McGill University under the supervision of Fazlur Rahman. He was an exponent of secularism from the Jamiyat al-ulama perspective. He is a biographer of Zakir Husain (in Urdu) and has contributed research papers on aspects of Indian Islam. Mushirul Haq studied at the Institute of Islamic Studies at McGill University in 1961-7 and is the author of *Muslim Politics in Modern India* (1972) and *Islam in Secular India* (1972), a work dedicated to W.C. Smith. He was killed by 'militants' in Srinagar in 1996 while serving as vice-chancellor of the Kashmir University.

[82] For his presidential address to the Indian History Congress in 1948, see K.A. Nizami (ed.), *Collected Works of Professor Mohammad Habib: Politics and Society During Early*

institution from its Muslim League past and provide a modernist and radical thrust to their intellectual explorations and creative expressions. The tone was set by Zakir Husain, who left Jamia Millia in 1948 to join the Aligarh Muslim University as vice-chancellor.[83] He attracted a number of young scholars with an enlightened world-view, including the historian Syed Nurul Hasan, Moonis Reza, a geographer, and the scientist A.R. Kidwai. Besides these, he harnessed the intellectual resources of a sizeable group of students, many of whom enriched the debate on nationalism and secularism. Aligarh, when he joined it, had an atmosphere of gloom and uncertainty, because of the university's close identification with the Pakistan movement, but he managed to change it. Imbued with a mission 'of great national significance', he undertook 'to build a united nation in a democratic secular State and the role and status of its forty million Muslim citizens within it', to weld together diverse cultures into a harmonious whole and to promote its growth 'in such a manner that each culture shines and lends beauty and strength to the entire whole'.[84] When he left in 1956 to become Bihar's governor, the Aligarh University was on a sound footing, and it was possible for the mantle to pass to others. Zakir Husain had already won laurels by removing the dust that had gathered on the university during the Muslim League campaigns and revived the dampened spirits of teachers and students alike.

In 1947 Aligarh had four faculties and twenty-one departments; in 1964 there were seven faculties and 5,000 students. Today the number of students has risen to 17,200 with a teaching faculty strength of 1,209, seventy-six departments and four colleges, including those for medicine and engineering. The University's non-plan expenditure is Rs 6,048 lakh.

Other signs of change were evident in the debates on the emotive and contentious issue of reforming Muslim family laws. What is there to reform in the Muslim Personal Law? Is reform possible in Islam? Is the Islamic law a product of human intelligence and adaptation to social needs and therefore amenabale to modifications and changes, or is it of divine inspiration and therefore immutable? If so, what lessons should be drawn from the history of reforms in Muslim countries? Or what weight should be given to the views of Muslim thinkers in India, such as Iqbal who

Medieval India (Delhi: People's Publishing House, 1974). See also Ale Ahmad Suroor, 'Hindustani Mussalman', *Gagan*, in Urdu (Hindustani Mussalman number, 1975), p. 73; and Riazur Rahman Sherwani, *Mussalmanan-i Hind se Waqt ke Mutalibat* (Delhi: Makaba Jamia, 1987).

[83] His appointment was 'a triumph for the ideals for which he then stood (in 1920) and which he and his co-workers later sought to embody in the Jamia Millia Islamia.' Editorial, *Hindustan Times*, 3 December 1948; see also Lacy, op. cit., pp. 39-46.

[84] Quoted in A.G. Noorani, *President Zakir Husain: A Quest for Excellence* (Bombay: Popular Prakashan, 1967).

believed that the Muslim liberals were perfectly justified in reinterpreting the fundamental legal principles 'in the light of their own experience and the altered conditions of modern life'?[85]

There were no simple or straightforward answers, all the more so because the key issues that, for example, figured at the International Congress of Orientalists in Delhi in 1964 and a seminar also held there five years later, related to the divine and sacrosanct character of the *Shariat*, the preservation of 'Muslim identity' and fear of Hinduisation.[86] Traditional or conservative opinion, articulated by the Jamaat-i Islami and the Jamiyat al-ulama, was indignant at the prospect of changes in personal law. Modification of laws based on specific injunctions in the Quran or *Hadith* was 'unimaginable'. Attempts to persuade Muslims to substitute man-made laws for 'the universal and faultless laws given by God is a waste of time.'[87] Quranic regulations were authoritative and final for all occasions and for all epochs between the time of revelation and doomsday. Those wanting to tamper with them were enemies of Islam and its followers. Thus the Jamiyat al-ulama leader, Maulana Asad Madani, viewed the plea for reforms as 'a mask for the Jana Sangh's sinister designs to exterminate the Muslim community from India'.[88]

A section of the reformist *ulama* were not swayed by the rhetoric of their more diehard colleagues. Maulana Said Ahmad Akbarabadi, editor of *Burhan*, was one of them. He was educated at Deoband, served as principal of the Madarsa-i Aliya in Calcutta, and retired as professor of theology at the Aligarh Muslim University. He made a distinction between those Quranic injunctions which were specific to the Arab customary law of the time, and those applicable to Muslim and human societies in other times.[89] Moreover, he insisted that the *ulama* should note the changes taking place around them and formulate their ideas in the light of modern thought and in response to Islam's encounter with a wide variety of forces in different parts of the globe, including, of course, the Indian subcontinent. The fact that they did not do so was largely because they did not heed the admonition of Deoband's illustrious co-founder, Maulana Qasim Nanotawi, that traditional education should always be combined with modern knowledge.[90] Said Ahmad rigorously argued that

---

[85] Mohammad Iqbal, *The Reconstruction of Religious Thought in Islam* (Lahore: Javid Iqbal, 1934), pp. 150-60.

[86] J. Duncan M. Derret, *Religion, Law and the State in India* (Lahore, 1968), p. 532; Robert T. Baird (ed.), 'Uniform Civil Code and the Secularization of Law' in Baird (ed.), *Religion in Modern India*, pp. 414-46.

[87] A.A.K. Soze, 'Emancipation: The Two Extremes', *National Herald*, 3 June 1970.

[88] Ibid., 1 June 1970.

[89] Ahmad, *Islamic Modernism*, pp. 254-5.

[90] Said Ahmad Akbarabadi, 'Zamane ke ilmi taqaze aur afkaar-i-jadida', in Naseem Qureshi (ed.), *Aligarh Tehrik: Aghaaz se Anjaam Tak* (Lucknow: Aligarh Muslim University, 1960),

the concept of *tauhid* (Unity of God) implies the unity of all people and all nations. So also did divine revelation or divine guidance (*Al-Huda*).[91] 'It was not only Universal but one and the same also.' He quoted approvingly from Azad, who had pointed out in the *Tarjuman al-Quran* that 'the greater the emphasis that the Quran lays on this truth [the unity of all peoples], the stronger has been the inclination on the part of the world to relegate it to the background.'[92]

A.A.A. Fyzee, Oxford-educated and a scholar of Islamic jurisprudence, held the view that Islam had ceased to be dynamic, and religious practices had become 'soulless rituals', the spirit of the Prophet's message was throttled by fanaticism, its theology gagged by history and its vitality sapped by totalitarianism. He made a strong case for releasing the 'spirit of joy, compassion, fraternity, tolerance and reasonableness'.[93] More important, he positioned himself against the traditional belief that in Islam law and religion are coterminous. Law is a product of social evolution and must change with time and circumstances. He was convinced that 'gradually all individual and personal laws, based upon ancient principles governing the social life of the community, will either be abolished or so modified as to bring them within a general scheme of laws applicable to all persons, regardless of religious differences.' Such a development, he pointed out, will not destroy 'the essential truth of the faith of Islam'.[94] To some 'it would seem that no one can change the fate of the Muslims of India, except the Muslims themselves', but he told the Maharashtra State Muslim Women Conference in Poona on 27 December 1971 that the Muslim Personal Law as practised under the Shariat Act had brought untold miseries to the community and must be discarded in favour of a uniform civil code.[95]

Some of these ideas were inspired by Azad's *Tarjuman al-Quran* and his emphasis there on the rudiments of religious pluralism, which constitutes the basis of the Maulana's modernism. Fyzee regarded this as the only pragmatic solution for the Indian Muslims, and for the preservation and progress of Islam in a composite society.[96] M.H. Beg, a distinguished

---

p. 238. See also Said Ahmad Akbarabadi, 'Firqawaraana Fasaad aur Mussalman', 'Communal riots and Muslims' in *Gagan*, op. cit., pp. 100-9.

[91] Said Ahmad Akbarabadi, 'Islam and other religions', in *Islam*, op. cit., pp. 103-4.

[92] *Tarjuman al-Quran*, quoted in ibid., p. 105. And Abul Kalam Azad, *Basic Concepts of the Quran*, prepared by Syed Abdul Latif (Hyderabad: Academy of Islamic Studies, 1958).

[93] A.A.A. Fyzee, *A Modern Approach to Islam* (Bombay: Asia Publishing House, 1963), p. 112.

[94] Ibid.

[95] Fyzee, 'The Muslim Minority in India', quoted in M.R.A. Baig, *The Muslim Dilemma in India* (Delhi: Vikas, 1974), p. 20.

[96] Ahmad, *Islamic Modernism*, p. 265; see also Gopal Krishna, 'Piety and Politics in Indian Islam', in Madan (ed.), *Muslim Communities of South Asia*, pp. 165-6.

jurist, boldly suggested that Muslim jurisprudence could contribute valuable ideas in formulating a uniform civil code of personal laws. Muslim jurisprudence 'has acted and could still act as a part of that common stock of juristic ideas which have acted and reacted upon each other to produce a composite culture in this country which sustains the secular state.'[97]

There was, predictably, strong opposition to the liberal and secular credo. Some analysts pointed out that the Muslims after 1947 could neither come to terms with the 'newness' of the situation nor feel at home with the new creative upsurge of Indian construction. W.C. Smith wrote: 'Indian freedom they saw rather as the unchecked opportunities for their enemies to hold them down or indeed to crush them.' He concluded that 'only in very limited numbers did Muslims evaluate with true appreciation the ideals and announced objectives of the nation to which they belonged.'[98]

Evidence marshalled in this and the previous chapter leads to slightly different conclusions. No doubt individual Muslims felt weak, fearful and insecure, and some sections were deeply concerned with their identity and the preservation of their religious and cultural heritage. Yet Islam in India was a living and vital religion, appealing to the hearts, minds and conscience of millions, setting them a standard by which to live honest, sober and God-fearing lives. There was no concerted attempt, despite the stridency of Hindu nationalist forces, to undermine their self-perceived interests as a 'community', although Muslim organisations were inclined to make much of the 'persecution' to which their followers were subjected. Nehru's government, on the contrary, created a climate conducive to the political and economic integration of large numbers of Muslims. As a result, 'the realization is growing that they [Muslims] must sink or swim, and the number of those who find swimming is not too difficult if one decides upon it is gradually increasing.'[99] The mood was aptly summed up in 1960 by Maulana Syed Abul Hasan Ali Nadwi, head of Lucknow's Nadwat al-ulama:

The clouds will disperse, as they are bound to, and there will be sunshine again. The Muslims will regain the position in the country which is justly theirs. All the schemes for national reconstruction will remain incomplete if they are left to rot and decay.[100]

---

[97] M.H. Beg, 'Islamic Jurisprudence and Secularism', in G.S. Sharma (ed.), *Secularism: Its Implications for Law and Life in India* (Delhi: Indian Law Institute, 1966), p. 152.

[98] Smith, *Islam in Modern History*, pp. 260, 265, 266.

[99] Mujeeb, *Indian Muslims*, p. 561; see also Abid Husain, *Destiny of Indian Muslims*, p. 166, and Rafiq Zakaria, 'What have the Muslims done for India and Secularism' in Malik Ram (ed.), *Hakeem Abdul Hameed Felicitation Volume* (Delhi: Hakeem Abdul Hameed Felicitation Committee, 1981), pp. 87-101.

[100] Nadwi, *Muslims in India*, p. 139.

In this frame of mind large numbers of Muslims could look ahead with a degree of hope and optimism. 'We must not despair of the future,' wrote Chagla. 'With more education, with more industrialisation of India, with more social reform, the barriers between the two communities must inevitably break down.'[101] If such hopes were disappointed, the explanations would principally lie in the breakdown of the secular consensus in the post-Nehru era.

However, there is a big question-mark over the viability of the approaches and interpretations of liberal and secular-minded Muslims. Doubts have been expressed over their reading of Indian Islam and their thesis on the nature of Hindu-Muslim interaction in the subcontinent.[102] Such doubts will remain for as long as scholarship on Islam and Muslims in the subcontinent remains speculative and tied to stereotypical images and frameworks. What is needed today, more than ever before, is the discovery of new schools of thought and interpretation among Muslims which will place Indian Islam more firmly in its specific Indian environment. The creative intellectual energy released in the first two decades after independence was surely the outcome of a unique 'Indian Muslim' experience of living in a world that was neither Muslim, Hindu nor specifically Western. Both the richness and variety of this experience needs to be highlighted in our studies. In so doing one is sure to notice the disjunction between the formal ideology of Islam and the actual day-to-day beliefs and practices of Muslims.[103] One will certainly notice that the regional traditions and cultural features of Indian Islam were components of, and contributions to, what the liberal and secular nationalists meant by the concept of a composite culture.[104]

We have offered a synchronic view of a particular strand in the north Indian Muslim intelligenstia, one that has been neglected in important studies of Muslim 'separatism' and 'communalism'. It is not the intention to make any bold claims on their behalf, although the voices of the liberal and secular Muslims, hitherto 'feeble' and some would say ineffectual, need to be heard. There is a preoccupation in the contemporary politics

---

[101] Typescript, 6 January 1962; M.C. Chagla papers, NMML.

[102] Francis Robinson, 'Islam and Muslim Society in South Asia', *Contributions to Indian Sociology*, 17, 2, 1983. Maryam Jameelah, converted from Judaism to Islam in 1961 under Maududi's Influence, summed up the standard anti-modernist stance by castigating Syed Ahmad Khan as 'the leading pioneer of modernist apologetics', denouncing Ameer Ali's *The Spirit of Islam* as 'heretical', and chiding Azad for advocating secular nationalism that led to the community's 'ruin and disaster'. *Islam and Modernism* (Lahore, 1968), pp. 52, 56, 74.

[103] Imtiaz Ahmad, 'Unity and Variety in South Asian Islam' in Dietmar Rothermund (ed.), *Islam in Southern Asia: A Survey of Current Research* (Wiesbaden, 1975), p. 5, and his *Ritual and Religion Among Muslims in India*, p. 7.

[104] Heidrich, op. cit., p. 78.

of India with identities, chauvinistic ideologies and movements of discord and disunity. Some attention needs to be paid to ideologies and movements that have historically and contemporaneously tried to unite Hindus and Muslims and furthered the post-colonial agenda of social transformation. This might better illuminate aspects of 'Orientalism and the Postcolonial Predicament'.

8

EMPOWERING DIFFERENCES: POLITICAL ACTIONS, SECTARIAN VIOLENCE AND THE RETREAT OF SECULARISM

'The rudest shock comes from the manner in which the Government and the country are allowing themselves to be pushed off the edge of secularism into the abyss of communal reaction, falling back to the frightening atavism of stagnant, dark and medieval ethos of the Hindi-speaking areas.'

Economic and Political Weekly, 5 November 1966

'Since its gates were unlocked in 1986, Babri Masjid has become a touchstone to secularism and indeed, to the character of the nation... When (it) was destroyed, so was a symbol of India's secular identity. The structure was a symbol of the sense of security of Indian Muslims and in its destruction a large proportion of Hindus misguidedly saw a vindication of their right to assert their dominance. The result is that the structure and symbol have been reduced to a heap of rubble, but the issue the Babri Masjid represented has been vastly aggravated.'

Aroon Purie in *India Today*, 15 February 1993

The slow but steady integration of Muslims into the secular polity suffered a jolt after Nehru's death in 1964. Cracks appeared in the grand cross-communal *entente* he tried to build, stimulating the revival of the Jamaat-i Islami in north India, the Muslim League in Kerala and the Ittehadul-Muslimeen in Hyderabad.[1] Though located in different regions and often

---

[1] Founded in the early twentieth century, the Majlis was energised by Nawab Bahadur Ali in the 1930s to safeguard the throne of the Asaf Jah dynasty in Hyderabad. Its president in 1947 was the 45-year-old Kasim Rizvi. The Majlis claimed to have 500,000 members with 10,000 militant 'National Guards'. Rasheeduddin Khan, 'Muslim Leadership and Electoral Politics in Hyderabad: A Pattern of Minority Articulation', *EPW*, 10 and 17 April 1971; G. Ram Reddy, 'Language, Religion and Political Identity – the Case of the Majlis-i Ittehadul-Muslimeen' in David Taylor and Malcolm Yapp (eds), *Political Identity in South Asia* (London: Curzon Press, 1979).

pursuing different goals, these organisations were the driving force behind Muslim conservatism and reaction. By taking up the cudgels on behalf of the 'community' and exploiting real or imaginary grievances, they gradually legitimised themselves in specific regional and local settings.

Spurred by nationalist feelings during the war with China (1962) and Pakistan (1965), the Jana Sangh (renamed the BJP or the Bharatiya Janata Party in 1977) made electoral gains in UP, Bihar, Madhya Pradesh and secured a tentative foothold in Kerala. Committed to building a resurgent Hindu nation and reviving Hindi-Hindu culture, its ideology was fuelled by the stereotype of an aggressive Islam on the rampage.[2] The Jana Sangh and its ideological mentor, the RSS, repudiated secularism, denounced the Congress for 'pampering' Muslims under the 'camouflage of secularism',[3] and proposed 'Indianisation' of Muslims as the ideal solution to 'the socio-religious as well as the political aspect of the communal problem'.[4]

The Jana Sangh was the only party that increased its popular vote and share of parliamentary and assembly seats in each successive election from 1952 to 1967,[5] and more than doubled its strength in 1962. Compared to 1951-2, the percentage of votes polled showed nearly a twofold increase in Lok Sabha and about one-and-a-half times increase in assembly elections. In UP and Madhya Pradesh, the Jana Sangh was the largest single party apart from the Congress – 49 seats to Congress's 248 in the UP assembly, and 41 seats to Congress's 142 in Madhya Pradesh. This upward trend continued, notably in UP. The party polled 21.67 per cent of votes and gained 98 seats at the fourth general election. In seven major cities – Agra, Allahabad, Bareilly, Kanpur, Lucknow, Meerut and Varanasi – its share of the vote rose from 14.48 per cent in 1952 to 23.90 per cent in 1967 (Tables 8.1 and 2). 'The Creeping Shadow of the Lamp', Jana Sangh's election symbol, was one of the notable features of the post-Nehru years.[6]

Equally ominous was the mushrooming of Hindu parties of all hues. They had numbered less than a dozen in 1951; but by 1987 there were fifty. Active membership ran into several millions. The RSS claimed to

---

[2] V.D. Savarkar, *Historic Statement*, edited by S.S. Savarkar and G.M. Joshi (Bombay: Popular Prakashan, 1967), and M.V. Seshadari (ed.), *R.S.S: A Vision in Action* (Bangalore: Jagarana Prakshana, 1988).

[3] *Akhand Bharat or Akhand Pakistan?* Exchange of Population Conference, New Delhi, 28-29 March 1964.

[4] Balraj Madhok, *Hindustan on the Crossroads* (Lahore, 1946), p. 101, and his *Indianization* (Delhi, 1980), p. 82.

[5] Graham, *Hindu Nationalism and Indian Politics*, pp. 259-65; Baxter, *The Jana Sangh*, pp. 94-102, for the first general election.

[6] Bashiruddin Ahmed, 'Uttar Pradesh', *Seminar* (95), July 1967, p. 42; V.B. Singh, 'Jana Sangh in Uttar Pradesh', *EPW*, January 1971; Graham, *Hindu Nationalism*, op. cit.

Table 8.1. JANA SANGH/B.J.P. PERFORMANCE IN
LOK SABHA ELECTIONS, 1952-1991

	Seats won	Votes %	Share of non-Congress votes %
1952	3	3.1	5.6
1957	4	5.9	11.3
1962	14	6.4	11.6
1967	35	9.4	15.9
1971	22	7.4	13.1
1977	91	14.0	21.4
1980	15	8.6	15.0
1984	2	7.4	14.2
1989	85	11.4	19.0
1991	120	20.1	31.7

Note: 1952-71: Bharatiya Jana Sangh; 1977-80: Jana Sangh faction in Janata Party; 1984-91: Bharatiya Janata Party.

Source: Seminar (417), May 1994, p. 60.

Table 8.2. LEGISLATIVE ASSEMBLY ELECTIONS:
JANA SANGH VOTE-SHARE IN CONTESTED CONSTITUENCIES:
DISTRIBUTION BY POLITICAL REGIONS, 1951/2 -1967 (%)

Region	1951-2	1957	1962	1967
Punjab	7.10	15.30	15.79	21.19
Haryana	16.19	22.95	21.74	24.58
Kumaon	9.90	17.00	12.39	20.30
Upper Doab	8.54	12.20	14.04	16.04
Rohilkhand	17.83	18.59	20.17	26.19
Lower Doab	11.20	12.94	13.06	18.38
Bundelkhand	8.69	10.87	9.21	34.10
Oudh	13.22	23.18	27.32	27.50
Gorakhpur	9.53	12.10	18.66	22.97
Varanasi	10.43	17.28	20.08	23.13
Gwalior	10.72	11.94	9.70	51.58
Malwa	23.72	31.17	42.98	41.89
Rewa	15.78	17.00	19.33	18.37
Narbada	10.37	18.54	22.50	30.09
Chhattisgarh	7.48	14.45	19.94	25.66
Jaipur	24.82	15.50	15.96	35.17
Kotah	13.36	23.46	32.27	50.84
Udaipur	37.15	20.15	28.59	26.19
Thar	6.68	11.52	7.97	231.19

Source: Bruce Graham, *Hindu Nationalism and Indian Politics*, p. 265.

have 20,000 branches with over a million adherents.[7] The Vishwa Hindu Parishad (World Hindu Council, or VHP), founded in 1964 by Swami Chinmayananda, was on the move. It was sustained by the urban proletariat and the unemployed youth, offering the Hindu parties the legitimacy of connections with large religious groups and the manpower of the celibate *sadhus* (holy men) and other workers. It had 3,000 branches with thousands of dedicated members all over the country, especially in western UP. Thus the largest number of participants at the Virat Hindu Sammelan, a congregation of Hindus, in June 1990 came from the Jat-dominated villages in western UP.[8] The Hindu Manch, drawing followers from the lower middle classes, was activated after the highly-publicised conversion to Islam of a few hundred Harijans in the Tamil Nadu villages of Meenakshipuram. The Hindu Shiv Sena courted the Punjabi Hindu migrants. The Ramjanmabhumi Mukti Yagya Samiti, formed in July 1984, jumped into the fray to 'liberate' the 'Ram temple' at Ayodhya.

A set of dramatic and flamboyant demonstrations of religious worship followed. These included the *Ram Shila Pujan* programmes (bricks emblazoned with the name 'Ram' were consecrated, worshipped and aggressively paraded), launched on 15 September 1989, the *shilanyas* ceremony (the laying of the foundation stone of the Ram temple), and L.K. Advani's *rath yatra* (pilgrimage or large-scale procession starting from Somnath, the site where Mahmud of Ghazna destroyed many temples) in September-October 1990. They were clearly designed to create Hindu militancy, raise the religious consciousness of Hindus and make them aware of a quite specific view of Hinduism.[9] The outcome was predictable. Town after town succumbed to riots, arson, killings and finally curfew (see map).

[7] *Sunday* (Calcutta: weekly), 21-27 June 1987, p. 12. In 1979, the Rashtriya Swayam Sevak Sangh had 10,000 branches and 1,200 *pracharaks* (wholetime organisers). In 1989, these numbers rose to 37,000 and 2,000 respectively. Noticeably, the organisational expansion took place in West Bengal as well, a state run by a left coalition headed by the Communist Party of India (Marxist). The RSS had as many as 2,593 branches and sub-branches in West Bengal with 1003, 799 *swayamsevaks* of different categories. In 1988-89, it worked with a budget of nearly two crores of rupees and, in the following year, this budget doubled. Satyabrata Chakraborty, 'Communalism in India: The Changing Scenario', Rakhahari Chatterji (ed.), *Religion, Politics and Communalism: The South Asian Experience* (Delhi: South Asian Publishers, 1994), pp. 30-1.

[8] Juergensmeyer, *Religious Nationalism Confronts the Secular State*, p. 86; Tapan Basu *et al., Khaki Shorts and Saffron Flags*, chapter 3; Zoya Hasan, 'Shifting Ground: Hindutva Politics and the Farmers' Movement in Uttar Pradesh' in Brass (ed.), *New Farmers' Movements in India*, p. 186.

[9] *Sunday Observer* (Delhi), 7-14 October 1990; for riots in UP, Gujarat, Madhya Pradesh, Rajasthan, Bihar and UP, see *Times of India*, 2 November 1990; and Manini Chatterjee, 'The BJP: Political Mobilization for Hindutva', in Bidwai *et al., Religion, Religiosity and Communalism*, pp. 87-106.

JOURNEY OF FAITH?

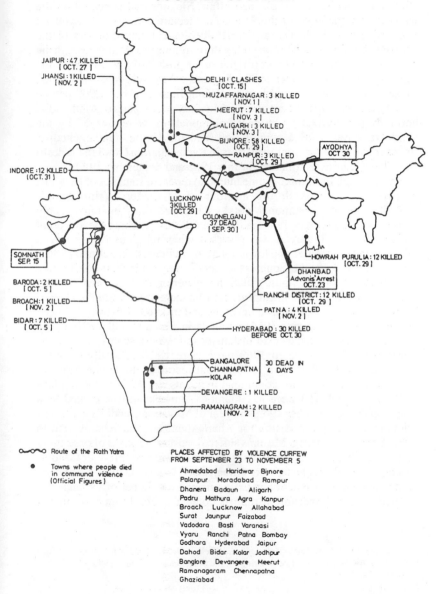

JAIPUR : 47 KILLED
[OCT. 27]

JHANSI : 1 KILLED
[NOV. 2]

DELHI : CLASHES
[OCT. 15]

MUZAFFARNAGAR : 3 KILLED
[NOV. 1]

MEERUT : 7 KILLED
[NOV. 3]

ALIGARH : 3 KILLED
[NOV. 3]

BIJNORE : 58 KILLED
[OCT. 29]

RAMPUR : 3 KILLED
[OCT. 29]

AYODHYA
OCT. 30

INDORE :12 KILLED
[OCT. 31]

LUCKNOW
3 KILLED
[OCT 29]

COLONELGANJ
37 DEAD
[SEP. 30]

SOMNATH
SEP. 15

HOWRAH PURULIA : 12 KILLED
[OCT. 29]

DHANBAD
Advani's Arrest
OCT. 23

BARODA : 2 KILLED
[OCT. 5]

RANCHI DISTRICT : 12 KILLED
[OCT. 29]

BROACH : 1 KILLED
[NOV. 2]

PATNA : 4 KILLED
[NOV. 2]

BIDAR : 7 KILLED
[OCT. 5]

HYDERABAD : 30 KILLED
BEFORE OCT. 30

BANGALORE
CHANNAPATNA   30 DEAD IN
KOLAR   4 DAYS

DEVANGERE : 1 KILLED

RAMANAGRAM : 2 KILLED
[NOV. 2]

○⌒○⌒○   Route of the Rath Yatra

●   Towns where people died
in communal violence
(Official Figures)

PLACES AFFECTED BY VIOLENCE CURFEW
FROM SEPTEMBER 23 TO NOVEMBER 5

Ahmedabad   Haridwar   Bijnore
Palanpur   Moradabad   Rampur
Dhanera   Badaun   Aligarh
Padru   Mathura   Agra   Kanpur
Broach   Lucknow   Allahabad
Surat   Jaunpur   Faizabad
Vadodara   Basti   Varanasi
Vyaru   Ranchi   Patna   Bombay
Godhara   Hyderabad   Jaipur
Dahod   Bidar   Kolar   Jodhpur
Banglore   Devangere   Meerut
Ramanagaram   Chennapatna
Ghaziabad

Source: Times of India; Sunday Observer (Artwork: akm-c s r d.).

The carnage in Bihar's Hazaribagh town and nearby villages in April 1989 was a meticulously planned affair. Slogans had appeared on the walls all over the town, urging Hindus to 'declare with pride that you are Hindus.' The Bajrang Dal and VHP, ideological stormtroopers of the RSS-BJP combine, insisted on taking the religious procession through the Juma Masjid road despite an official order prohibiting it. Likewise the Bhagalpur riots in October 1989, triggered off by the Ayodhya dispute, caused many deaths. According to official figures, about 1,000 people were killed, over 90 per cent of them Muslims. Many parts of south India, normally undisturbed by strident communalism, were swayed by the Hindutva wave. Thus a commission held the Hindu 'fundamentalist' forces responsible for communal riots in Ramanagaram (Andhra Pradesh) and Channapatrna (Karnataka) in July 1988 and September 1990.[10]

Even though India has become inured to repeated statistics of lives lost or property destroyed, the number of 'disorders', 'incidents', 'disturbances' or 'communal riots' – the expressions interchangeably used in official reports – fell steadily in the 1950s, reaching the low point of 26 in 1960. This trend was reversed when religious frenzy seized Jabalpur and other cities and towns of Madhya Pradesh in February 1961: Nehru lamented that the Congress leaders simply sat in their houses, like 'purdah ladies', allowing the situation to deteriorate.[11] Extensive rioting was triggered off by the disappearance of a sacred relic from the Hazrat-bal mosque in Srinagar (Kashmir) at the end of 1963. This was followed by the notorious January 1964 outbursts in Calcutta and 215 villages around the metropolis, as also in Jamshedpur where scores of Muslims were killed. From 1965 to 1969 there were 1,380 officially-recorded 'incidents' (Table 8.3). The 1970 annual report of the Home Minister stated that as against 346 'communal incidents' in 1968, 519 took place in 1969 of which 153 were in Gujarat.[12] Ahmedabad was rocked by a catastrophe in September 1969, the year of Mahatma Gandhi's centenary celebrations and the occasion for Khan Abdul Ghaffar Khan's visit to India. Here, as elsewhere, Muslims suffered most at the hands of rampaging mobs, headed not infrequently by RSS volunteers. The 'Frontier Gandhi' was not amused. His hosts were embarrassed by his outspoken criticism of the government's inaction in extinguishing the flames of violence.

In May 1979 government reports noted a threefold increase in riot

[10] *Frontline*, 13-26 May 1989; *Times of India* (Delhi), 24 July 1993; Amrita Basu, 'When Local Riots Are Not Merely Local: Bringing the State Back in: Bijnor 1988-92', *EPW*, 1 October 1994.

[11] Gopal, *Jawaharlal Nehru*, vol. 3, pp. 171-3; see also B.N. Mullick, *My Years with Nehru 1948-1964* (Delhi: Allied Publishers, 1972), pp. 175-6.

[12] *India Today* (Delhi: Research Bureau, UNI, 1970), p. 56.

Table 8.3. NUMBER OF COMMUNAL INCIDENTS AND PERSONS
KILLED AND INJURED, 1954-1979

	No. of incidents	Killed	Injured
1954	84	34	512
1955	75	24	457
1956	82	35	575
1957	58	12	316
1958	40	7	369
1959	42	41	1344
1960	26	14	262
1961	92	108	593
1962	60	43	348
1963	61	26	489
1964	1070	1919	2053
1965	173	34	758
1966	144	45	467
1967	198	251	880
1968	346	133	1549
1969	519	674	2977
1970	521	298	1723
1971	321	103	1330
1972	240	70	1207
1973	242	72	1550
1974	248	87	1266
1975	205	33	962
1976	169	39	794
1977	188	36	1122
1978	230	110	1853
1979	304	261	2379

Source: Sixth Report of the National Police Commission (Government of India: March 1981),
appendix 2, p. 60.

deaths since 1977, with UP heading the casualty list.[13] The number of
'incidents' reached a new high during 1983-4 and, if the massacre in
Assam is included, an all-time record for lives lost since independence.
The death toll in the 1980s was close to 4,000 – four times that of the
previous decade which saw a relative lull after the Ahmedabad 'disorders'.
In UP alone nearly sixty conflagrations occurred between February 1986
and June 1987, in which more than 200 people mostly Muslims, were
killed and 1,000 injured. Damage to property amounted to 1.5 crores:
Table 8.4 indicates the scale of damage in some 'major' riots. Over the
country as a whole the affected districts rose from sixty-one in 1961 to

[13] *Times of India*, 4 May 1979.

250 in 1986-7 (out of a total of some 350 districts).[14] 'An all-devouring communal fire', a journalist commented in June 1987, 'is raging across the country, threatening the very existence of a multi-religious, multi-cultural and multi-lingual society.'[15] A wounded India with festering communal sores was limping towards the twenty-first century.[16]

Communal riots were not uncommon in the Nehru era, but they were sporadic, localised and controllable. This was not so subsequently: riots at Aligarh, Kanpur, Meerut, Moradabad in UP, Hyderabad in Andhra Pradesh, Bhagalpur in Bihar, and Ahmedabad, Baroda and Surat in Gujarat were bloodier, more widespread and extended over weeks or months. Other ominous signs were their spread to rural areas, the active participation of many more people in looting, arson and killings, and the involvement of the police and para-military forces in stoking the fires of communal unrest.[17] 'I have watched with dismay during the year 1982', observed a senior police officer, 'the conversion of the Uttar Pradesh PAC [Provincial Armed Constabulary] from the model force that I worked with in the fifties to a unit which is feted by the Hindus and hated by the Muslims in the towns of Uttar Pradesh.'[18]

The communalisation of the law and order machinery meant that whenever public authority was compliant to anti-Muslim forces, the administration offered weak or inadequate protection to the targets as well as the principal sufferers. This was a crucial variable in Ahmedabad and the steel township of Jamshedpur. In both places the Congress administration delayed a crackdown on rioters for several days.[19] In UP, on the other hand, the police and the PAC acted as though they were a force expressly organised to beat, loot and kill Muslims.[20] This was so at Aligarh in

---

[14] *Sunday*, 21-27 June 1987, p. 12.

[15] Kuldeep Kumar, in ibid., 21-27 June 1987.

[16] Seema Mustafa, in ibid., 28 December-3 January 1987.

[17] For a seminal essay on the subject, see Stanley J. Tambiah, 'Reflections on Communal Violence in South Asia', *Journal of Asian Studies*, 49, 4, November 1990, pp. 741-60; see also, S.K. Ghosh, *Communal Riots in India: Meeting the Challenge Unitedly* (Delhi: Ashish Publishing House, 1987); Engineer (ed.), *Communal Riots in Post-Independence India* and his *Lifting the Veil: Communal Violence and Communal Harmony in Contemporary India* (Hyderabad: Sangam, 1995); Veena Das (ed.), *Communities, Riots and Survivors in South Asia*; M.J. Akbar, *Riot After Riot: Reports on Caste and Communal Violence in India.*

[18] C.F. Rustamji, 'New Wave of Violence', *Seminar* (281), January 1981, p. 46.

[19] R.A. Schermerhorn, 'The Locale of Hindu-Muslim Riots', *Indian Journal of Politics*, January-June 1971, p. 44; *Times of India*, 22-24 April 1979; *Ranchi Riots: Factual Analysis of the Tragic Happenings in August 1967* (Delhi: Sampradayikta Virodhi Committee, 1968); or earlier in the steel city of Rourkela where police failed to round up the anti-social elements at the first sign of trouble. S.K. Ghosh, *Riots Prevention and Control* (Calcutta: Eastern Law House, 1971), p. 56.

[20] *India Today*, 30 June 1987, pp. 75-6.

Table 8.4. EXTENT OF DAMAGE IN CERTAIN MAJOR RIOTS

Location	No. killed	No. injured	Damage to property (Rs)
Sanchi Hatia	184	n.a.	11,20,000
Ahmedabad	n.a.	1084	4,23,24,069
Bhiwandi	78	n.a.	1,40,10,800
Thana dist.	86	189	n.a.
Jalgaon	43	n.a.	34,74,722
Nahad	nil	15	3,00,063
Delhi	n.a.	n.a.	14,31,651

Source: Sixth Report of the National Police Commission (Government of India, March 1981), Appendix 3, p. 61.

October-November 1978, Moradabad on 13 August 1980, and Meerut in September-October 1982. At Malliana, a township 10 kilometers from Meerut city, a PAC platoon entered the Muslim-majority quarters on the afternoon of 23 May 1987 to kill defenceless people hiding in the courtyards.[21]

I

Indira Gandhi and her refurbished party, created after the 1969 split in Congress, was sympathetic to minority rights and to Nehru's secular legacy. At the same time, she changed course midstream, especially when under pressure from her critics and adversaries. She showed skill in accommodating the centrifugal forces to isolate and deflect the emergence of alternative political currents. For example, when she was unsure of retaining the loyalty of Muslims and the Harijans after the 1977 debacle, she developed an alternative power-base by uniting behind the upper-caste Hindu vote, which on balance had been hostile to her in the past. She grasped the potential of Hindutva and harnessed it to the fortunes of the Congress. She played the communal card in Punjab, Kashmir and the Hindi-Hindu heartland to offset electoral reverses and check the growing disenchantment of the traditional Congress vote-bank. She raised the spectre of a religious war (*dharm yudh*) in Kashmir, reminded minorities of their duties, dwelt on 'our religion and tradition' being under attack, and explained Hindu communalism as 'a reaction to real or imagined threats from communal Muslim organisations'. She engineered Sheikh Abdullah's defeat in Kashmir; allowed Zail Singh, Punjab's chief mini-

---

[21] 'Allegations of extrajudicial killings by the PAC in and around Meerut, 22-23 May 1987' (Amnesty International, November 1987); 'The PAC: Ghost of Meerut', *EPW*, 28 November 1987.

ster in 1972-7, to create fissures in the Akali Dal; and propped up an obscure priest, Sant Jarnail Singh Bhindranwale, to counter anti-Congressism in Punjab.[22] She calculatedly took up the mantle of Hindu protector after the 1975-7 Emergency. Her son Rajiv Gandhi sent out mixed signals. Some saw him as an innovator, a moderniser following in the footsteps of Jawaharlal Nehru, but others construed his moves differently: the RSS cadres voted for him in 1984 and endorsed his policies in 1987.[23]

Shrewd political calculation was reinforced by a personal predilection towards religiosity. Nehru's daughter performed Lakshachandi Path, an elaborate *puja* in a Kali temple at Jhansi. A hundred thousand verses were recited to invoke the primordial power and energy of Chandi, the all-encompassing mother-goddess. The *yagna*, the oblations to fire, and the recitation of the verses was conducted in secret from 1979 to 1983. During the first six weeks after her return to power she worshipped at a dozen shrines, all except one of which were Hindu temples.[24] She swiftly banned the use of beef tallow as soon as the ghee-adulteration scandal broke out, encouraged the invocation of Hindu gods at state functions, and adopted a soft attitude towards Hindu revivalism which expressed itself spectacularly in cross-country marches to 'Save Hinduism'. Far from challenging such a tendency, she decided to ride it as far as it would take her.[25]

The National Integration Council, revived in June 1968 and then again in 1980, gasped for breath; it was reconvened after a gap of three years. The Minorities Commission was denied statutory status, and was used to reward superannuated Congress loyalists who could be given a berth nowhere else. Reports of the Riot Enquiry Commission gathered dust and were eventually discarded. In short, as A.G. Noorani, the author-lawyer, acerbically commented, the prime minister's policy was 'nothing but a cynical exploitation spread over a decade and a half. Its elements were promises galore coupled with administrative cosmetics.'[26]

It was possible to draw important lessons from a constitution that defended and safeguarded India's pluralism and multi-culturalism. Yet separating religion from public life or distancing the party and govern-

---

[22] Moin Shakir, 'Congress and the Minority Vote', in Ramashray Roy and Richard Sisson (eds), *Diversity and Dominance in Indian Politics*, vol. 2, p. 104; for Kashmir, see M.J. Akbar, *India: The Siege Within* (Delhi: Penguin, 1985), pp. 198-200; for Punjab, see Mark Tully and Satish Jacob, *Amritsar: Mrs Gandhi's Last Battle* (London: Cape, 1985).

[23] James Manor, 'Politics: Ambiguity, Disillusionment, and Ferment', in *India Briefing* (Boulder, CO: Westview Press, 1988), p. 7.

[24] Inder Malhotra, *Indira Gandhi: A Personal and Political Biography* (London: Hodder and Stoughton, 1989), p. 231; Pupul Jayakar, *Indira Gandhi: A Biography* (Delhi: Viking, 1992), p. 470; Lloyd and Susanne Rudolph, *In Pursuit of Lakshmi: The Political Economy of the Indian State* (Delhi: Orient Longman, 1987), pp. 42-3.

[25] Akbar, *The Siege Within*, pp. 197-8.

[26] A.G. Noorani, 'Indira Gandhi and Indian Muslims', *EPW*, 3 November 1990, p. 2417.

ment from non-secular causes was not the Congress agenda after Nehru. Hence the feeble secular response to communalism, as also the compulsion to derive political mileage from Hindu symbols, traditions and institutions. Thus it became a routine affair to break coconuts, put vermilion on foreheads and invoke Hindu gods at state functions. Rajiv Gandhi, along with many of his ministerial colleagues, visited the famous Deoraha Baba near Mathura to seek his blessings. At a time when the communal temperature was high, the government television network sponsored a serialised presentation of the great Hindu epics, the Ramayana and the Mahabharata. Both fuelled the revival of religious politics.[27]

Meanwhile, the Congress was busy wooing and pandering to the religious sentiments of Muslim orthodoxy. It did so to ensure that the electoral reverses suffered by the party in by-elections were not repeated nationally. Hence the capitulation over Shah Bano, a housewife from Indore in the central Indian state of Madhya Pradesh, who approached the judicial magistrate in 1978 for a maintenance allowance of Rs 400 a month. Her husband, Ahmad Khan, for his part, said that he had divorced his wife by the irrevocable method of saying *'talaq, talaq, talaq'* and that he was not obliged to provide further maintenance. The magistrate ordered Ahmad Khan to pay Rs 25, later increased to Rs 179 and 20 paise. Ahmad challenged the order in the Supreme Court on the plea that under the *Shariat* the payment of maintenance up to the end of the *iddat* period (three months following the divorce) concluded the responsibilities of the husband. India's highest court did not agree; it upheld the maintenance order under Section 125. All hell broke loose. The judgement led to bitter controversy and the mobilisation of communal forces. The Rajiv Gandhi government succumbed to fundamentalist pressures and passed the infamous Muslim Women (Protection of Rights on Divorce) Act of 1986.[28]

The Act was the child of political opportunism. It was designed neither to empower destitute women nor to keep alive the debate on the overall status of Muslim women. If anything, the unstated aim was to let Muslims, so to speak, stew in their own juice.[29] Arif Mohammad Khan,

---

[27] S.H. Rudolph and L.I. Rudolph, 'Modern Hate', *New Republic*, 22 March 1993; Nicholas Nugent, *Rajiv Gandhi: Son of a Dynasty* (London: BBC Books, 1990), p. 188.

[28] Zoya Hasan, 'Minority Identity: State Policy and the Political Process' in Zoya Hasan (ed.), *Forging Identities*, pp. 64-70; Asghar A. Engineer (ed.), *The Shah Bano Controversy* (Delhi: Orient Longman, 1987).

[29] Ainslie Embree has drawn attention to another theme that ran through the speeches of the government spokesmen: a reference to 'our' law over against 'theirs'. Arun Nehru, Rajiv Gandhi's cousin and minister in his government, spoke of 'our wishes', which included a common legal code, against the 'minority community's wishes', implying that he spoke for India while 'they' spoke for their community, which was separate from India. Ainslie T. Embree, *Imagining India: Essays on Indian History* (Delhi: OUP, 1989), p. 208.

the only minister to defend the Supreme Court judgement, paid dearly for his reasoned position. His voice was stifled. The minister was driven to resign and cast into the political wilderness. Danial Latifi, a veteran Supreme Court lawyer and activist in the 'Committee for the Protection of Muslim Women', wrote indignantly:

All one can say at present is that some Machiavelli seems to have masterminded this entire operation. That master-mind is not a friend of Islam, of the Muslims or the Muslim women. Still less he is a friend of the Republic of India. The Pact that preceded the Bill, of recognition of the so-called Muslim Personal Law Board as a college of cardinals for the Indian Muslims, is not only against Islam but is also the most flagrant exercise of power-drunk autocracy since Caligula installed 'Incitatus', his favourite horse, as Governor of Rome. The Muslim intelligentsia who have opposed this act will continue their struggle against this illegitimate papacy.[30]

Instead of refurbishing its secular image, the Congress establishment heeded the strident clamourings of the Muslim Personal Law Board (MPLB). The immediate consequences were twofold. The BJP received a fresh lease of life, using the Shah Bano episode as a powerful issue for countrywide mobilisation. From 1986 onwards it dominated the ideological agenda with 'minorityism', 'pseudo-secularism' and Hindutva becoming a part of national vocabulary. The defiant posture of the MPLB was, on the other hand, tacitly approved by a weak-kneed Congress establishment. Its leading lights were repeatedly invited for consultations along with Congress ministers, and some of its parliamentary members such as Najma Heptullah, Khurshid Alam Khan and Z.R. Ansari. Khurshid's son, Salman, Oxford-educated and former state minister of external affairs, acted as an unofficial intermediary between the government and the MPLB.

Emboldened by such backing, the MPLB organised a mammoth rally in Lucknow on 8 January 1987. Thousands took to the streets wearing badges saying 'We reject uniform civil code'. The Supreme Court verdict was decried as an assault on the *Shariat*, a sacrilegious trespass into a field it was forbidden to enter. Speaking from the floor of parliament, Z.R. Ansari, minister of state, lambasted the judges for their ignorance of the Quran and *Hadith*. 'If you have a *tamboli* [pan-vendor] doing the work of a *teli* [oil-seller], things are bound to go wrong.'[31]

The 'victory' tasted by the MPLB had an electrifying effect, as is testified by the statements and political manoeuvres of Syed Shahabuddin, editor of *Muslim India*, member of parliament and chief architect of the Babri Masjid Action Committee (BMAC); Sulaiman Sait, whose Muslim League was then a partner in the ruling coalition in Kerala; and

---

[30] Quoted in *Sunday*, 8-14 June 1986.
[31] Ibid., 9-15 March 1986.

Sultan Salahuddin Owaisi, the fiery president of the Ittehadul-Muslimeen, a Congress ally in the Andhra Pradesh municipal elections. Each of them devised his own strategy astutely. Shahabuddin mooted the idea of asking Muslims to stay away from the annual Republic Day celebration in 1987, and he and his BMAC members organised the all-India strike on 1 February, the first anniversary of the day when a district magistrate in Ayodhya threw all caution to the winds and declared the Babri Masjid open for Hindu worship. Yet another huge protest rally followed. For the first time in India's independent history, more than 300,000 Muslims lined New Delhi's stately Rajpath on 30 March 1987 to raise banners and chant slogans demanding an end to discrimination against their brethren.[32] Just a fortnight later, thousands forced their way into several of the protected national monuments in Delhi cared for by the Archaelogical Survey of India, to offer prayers on the occasion of *Shab-i Barat*, a Muslim festival observed to pray for the dead. This was a rare act of defiance, an illustration of how religious passions were inflamed to fever pitch.

In effect the Congress created the space for such assertions by wilfully abandoning its historic role, performed during the freedom struggle, of mediating between different groups in civil society and the state. The sprawling party hierarchy, having once provided a measure of coherence across the vast and diverse subcontinent, allowed the inexorable drift to continue. Nobody criticised the leadership's inaction. Hand-picked professional politicians dominated the All India Congress Committee (AICC) and the Congress Working Committee (CWC). Their survival depended on loyalty to the prime minister, on power-brokers in the market place of Indian politics, and on their ability to manipulate caste and communal loyalties. Just a few grasped the implications of letting the MPLB-BMAC combine seize the political initiative, but they chose to remain silent.

The Congress networks built over many decades collapsed after Nehru. The tendency to centralise power and authority in New Delhi undermined party structures, weakened institutions and created a personalised regime. Rajiv Gandhi in 1985 blasted the 'cliques' that enmeshed 'the living body of the Congress in their net of avarice', and chided their 'self-aggrandizement, their corrupt ways, their linkages with vested interests – and their sanctimonious posturings'.[33] But he was a

---

[32] *India Today*, 15 June 1987, p. 38. In November 1989, over 4,000 people, mostly Muslims, led by the BMAC, courted arrest in Faizabad against the *shilanyas* in Ayodhya.

[33] S.A. Kochanek, 'Mrs. Gandhi's Pyramid: The New Congress' in H.C. Hart (ed.), *Indira Gandhi's India* (Boulder, CO: Westview Press, 1976), pp. 104-5; Sudipta Kaviraj, 'On the crisis of political institutions', *Contributions to Indian Sociology*, 18, 2, 1984, pp. 236-8, and his 'Crisis of the Nation-state in India' in John Dunn (ed.), *Contemporary Crisis of the Nation State* (Oxford: Blackwell, 1995). See also Ashis Nandy, 'The Political Culture of the Indian State', *Daedalus*, 118, Fall 1989. I have taken the quote of Rajiv Gandhi's speech

victim of his own follies. He relied on his hand-picked Doon School (a famed public school at Dehra Dun in UP) friends to run the country, and they did not serve him well. He then turned the AICC and the CWC, tamed and humbled by his mother, into rudderless bodies. Its _khadi_-clad members, acting as courtiers in the Congress durbar which was occasionally held with much fanfare and at great public expense, were out of tune with realities on the ground and indifferent to them. They were clearly ill-equipped to manage mounting social tensions and religious cleavage.

The leadership at the apex, caught up in the arithmetic of electoral politics, sheltered Hindu nationalists and courted Hindu and Muslim communalists. They almost seemed to show a talent for making tactical blunders and pursuing unprincipled policies. How else does one explain a district judge disturbing the _status quo_ over the Babri Masjid and resuscitating a bitter controversy that had lain dormant for nearly four decades after independence? It is unknown who was behind this ill-advised decision. Was it done to create a _Hindu_ constituency, or to mollify enraged feelings over the surrender on Shah Bano? Arun Nehru, Rajiv Gandhi's ministerial colleague whose own conduct in the murky happenings at Ayodhya is not blameless, reported that 'in early 1986 the Muslim Women's Bill was passed to play the Muslim card; and then came the decision on Ayodhya to play the Hindu card. It was supposed to be a package deal. I knew it was a dangerous thing to do and I did not agree.' When asked, Rajiv Gandhi 'merely smiled and observed it was tit for tat for the Muslim Women's Bill.'[34] Thus the secular consensus, the essence of the Nehru era, was conveniently set aside in the relentless quest for political survival.

As if this was not enough, Rajiv Gandhi tacitly supported, in the presence of nearly a million pilgrims who had congregated for a religious _mela_, the VHP's _Ram Shila_ at Ayodhya on 9 November 1989. In retrospect the _Times of India_ commented that the _shilanyas_ ceremony had been 'a dangerous turning point in the history of independent India.' The Congress undoubtedly contributed to the spectacular growth of Hindu chauvinist forces and to the tightening hold of Muslim fundamentalists.[35] Nehru's impetuous grandson unashamedly started his election campaign in November that year from Faizabad close by, by promising to usher in _Ram Rajya_ (the golden rule associated with Ram). His decision to stage

---

from Atul Kohli, _Democracy and Discontent: India's growing crisis of governability_ (CUP, 1990), p. 5.

[34] Arun Nehru, quoted in A.G. Noorani, 'The Babri Masjid-Ramjanmabhumi Question' in Asghar A. Engineer (ed.), _Babri Masjid-Ramjanmabhumi Controversy_ (Delhi: Atlantic, 1990), p. 57.

[35] Editorial, _Times of India_, 27 August 1993.

a *sadbhavana yatra* (march for harmony) some months after his ignominous defeat in the elections was a case of too little, too late.

Likewise, the Narasimha Rao administration imposed bans on the Jamaat-i Islami, the RSS and the VHP, and rushed through flawed legislative enactments, but these could neither heal the deep wounds nor stem the anti-Congress tide.[36] Having failed to protect the Babri Masjid, it searched in vain for ways to placate the Muslims. Apart from the Independence Day promises to rebuild the mosque and set up a finance and development corporation for the minorities, other efforts – spurred by the assembly elections in the four states already ruled by the BJP – were made to recover lost ground.[37] The prime minister had several rounds of talks with the Sunni leader and chairman of the Muslim Personal Law Board, Maulana Syed Abul Hasan Ali Nadwi, popularly known as Ali Mian. In order to soothe ruffled feelings over the Babri Masjid, he agreed to a salary hike for the *imams* of mosques, some of whom had trooped into 7 Race Course Road, the prime minister's house, with a cascade of demands.[38]

Meanwhile the government prepared a blueprint to de-link religion from politics in the form of constitution amendment bills. Much discussion followed in parliament and in the press. In the end, however, the government failed to muster adequate support. An embarrassed minister of parliamentary affairs deferred the adoption of the bills on 24 August 1993.[39] Ironically, while the existential question of whether religion and politics could ever be separated was the talking-point, the prime minister dashed across to Shirdi to pay obeisance to the Sai Baba. He prayed to a specially made silver image of the Baba, sat on a silver stool and bathed the idol in milk. No wonder that no tears were shed over the demise of the constitution amendment bills.

In mid-December 1994 Arjun Singh, a senior minister and formerly a close lieutenant of Indira Gandhi and Rajiv Gandhi in Bhopal as chief minister and in Chandigarh as governor of Punjab, resigned from the cabinet to express his uneasiness over government policies. This was an act of some symbolic importance. It did not stir the secular conscience of his colleagues, but it pressed home the point that the Congress, having shed its secular inhibitions, was no longer in a position to turn the tide in its favour and reap the fruits of using the 'Hindu card' or the 'Muslim

---

[36] For example, reimposing the ban on the VHP in mid-January 1994 was described as a 'meaningless administrative and legalistic exercise' unless backed by a political campaign for secularism. The Congress reimposed a formal ban 'even as it wages a listless battle against the forces of communalism unleashed by the proscribed organisation'. Editorial, *Times of India*, 17 January 1995.

[37] See ibid., 26 August 1993, for the setting up of a cabinet committee for minority affairs.

[38] *Sunday*, 29-August-4 September 1993, pp. 44-5.

[39] Ibid., 25 August 1993, and *Times of India* (editorial), 26 August 1993.

card'.[40] In fact, Arjun Singh and Narayan Dutt Tiwari, the former UP chief minister, both quintessential Congressmen, were the only two important high command stalwarts to stress, albeit belatedly, that religion-based electoral strategies not only divided but also devoured its own protagonists. Others may have agreed but chose not to incur the wrath of the prime minister.

The growing electoral success of the Hindu parties, including the Shiv Sena in Maharashtra, was a pointer to the decline of Congress and the demoralisation in its dwindling cadres. From having only a peripheral presence in the eighth Lok Sabha, the BJP's strength rose to an impressive 86 (not counting the four Shiv Sena members of parliament) in the ninth house. It won comfortably in Madhya Pradesh and Himachal Pradesh in February 1990 and took up the reins in Rajasthan as the leading partner of a coalition. In Gujarat, the BJP came a close second to the Janata Dal and formed a coalition government.

In June 1991, the BJP and not the Congress increased its share of the vote from about 11 to over 20 per cent; indeed the BJP was the only national party to increase its percentage of the popular vote, and it did so all over the country. It swept the 1991 Lok Sabha poll in Gujarat, winning 20 out of 25 seats as against 12 in the 1990 elections. A BJP government was formed in UP for the first time with a clear majority. The BJP also won 50 out of the 82 Lok Sabha seats.[41] Ram scored over Mandal in both the states. 'Secular' India was thus rudely awakened by the loud blowing of conch-shells, and by the growing number of Hindu militants inching their way to the temple of power in New Delhi. Within little more than a decade, the BJP placed Hindutva on the country's political agenda while its precursor, the Jana Sangh, had remained on the fringes of the political system for nearly three decades.[42]

If the BJP's public image was battered in November 1993 and in elections to the Andhra Pradesh and Karnataka assemblies in December 1994, the reason was its lacklustre performance in power. The electorate, hoping to benefit from the promised 'clean' and efficient government, was disillusioned. Having been taken for a ride on the Ram chariot once, they turned to bread and butter issues only to discover that the BJP failed to deliver these as well. The Narasimha Rao government, on its own, did

---

[40] For the text of Arjun Singh's letter, see *Frontline*, 13 January 1995, pp. 10-11. On 25 January Arjun Singh was suspended from the primary membership of the party. This was followed by his expulsion on 7 February.

[41] Yogendra Yadav, 'Electoral Prospects', *Seminar* (417), May 1994, pp. 60-1. For Madhya Pradesh, see Christophe Jaffrelot, 'The BJP in Madhya Pradesh: Networks, Strategies and Power' in Pandey (ed.), *Hindus and Others,* op. cit. For Gujarat, Ghanshyam Shah, 'Tenth Lok Sabha Elections: BJP's victory in Gujarat', *EPW,* 21 December 1991.

[42] Neena Vyas, 'Communal Game: BJP, the Centre Player', *Frontline*, 26, October-8 November 1992, p. 12.

little to dethrone the BJP or to de-communalise the political terrain –
much less to secularise it.

Religious minorities, notably the Christians and the Muslims, were
disenchanted, having lost their faith in a party they had intermittently
backed since independence. That is why in November 1993, December
1994 and February 1995 Muslims virtually voted *en masse* to defeat the
Congress. In Karnataka, now a 'communally-sensitive area' in official
parlance, they went along with the Janata Dal. The Congress, having
managed only 36 of the 224 seats, lost in all the 106 constituencies where
Muslims were above 10 per cent of the population. Of these, Muslims
were over 15 per cent in forty-three constituencies. The Congress was
eased out from those sixty-seven constituencies where the percentage of
Muslims was 5-10.[43] In Gujarat and Maharashtra the anger was frequently
expressed in the refrain that an 'open enemy' was better than a
'treacherous friend' (Congress). In Maharashtra the Muslim population is
around 8.4 per cent with an important voice in 35 out of the 288 assembly
seats. Most felt they were no longer safe under Congress rule. In March
1995 they preferred to vote for the BJP rather than the Congress. The BJP
was thus able to break the Congress stranglehold over the Muslim voters
and form governments in Gujarat and Maharashtra, two of the most
important states in western India.[44]

II

Some of these trends are not new, although they have become much more
closely intertwined with growing communal violence which peaked in
December 1992-January 1993. Doubts were expressed throughout the
1960s over the electoral promises made by the Congress on enlarging
employment opportunities, according Urdu its legitimate status in UP and
Bihar, and upholding the Aligarh Muslim University's denominational
character. Thus speakers at the widely-attended Muslim Convention at
Delhi's Sapru House in June 1961 did not mince words in attacking some
important Congress leaders, their communal proclivities and their links
with Hindu organisations. Syed Mahmud, a prominent Congressman from
Bihar and former minister in Nehru's government, felt that Muslims were

---

[43] Amrose Pinto, 'Karnataka Assembly Elections: An Overview', *EPW*, 31 December 1994,
p. 3309.
[44] Inder Malhotra, 'Hot Pursuit of the Muslim Vote', *Times of India*, 19 January 1995, and
25 January, 3 February for 'Bombay Muslims'. For Gujarat, *Times of India*, 24 January
1995; Asghar A. Engineer, 'Wisdom of Muslim Electoral Behaviour', *Times of India*, 9
January 1995. For insights into other closely-related dimensions, see Zoya Hasan, 'Party
Politics and Communal Mobilization in Uttar Pradesh' and Ghanshyam Shah, 'The BJP and
Backward Castes in Gujarat' in Bidwai *et al.*, op. cit.

reduced to the status of 'second-class citizens'. Maulana Hifzur Rahman of the Jamiyat al-ulama said that aggressive Hindu communalism was vitiating the administrative apparatus.[45] Others gave vent to their anger and frustration in the five-hour concluding session that was open to the press and the public.[46]

The Sapru House Convention and the Jamiyat al-ulama public meeting at Delhi's Urdu Park struck the same note.[47] On both occasions liberal and left-oriented persons dominated the proceedings. Among them were Shah Nawaz Khan, Z.A. Ahmad of the Communist party, M. Harris of the Praja Socialist Party, and G.M. Sadiq of Kashmir. Nehru sent a message endorsing the convention's aim to 'emphasise the fundamental unity of India and to discourage communal and disruptive tendencies.'[48] Syed Mahmud, the chairman, told the audience that Muslims should rally round the prime minister to combat communalism and other divisive forces.[49]

There were concrete reasons for the supreme faith placed in Nehru.[50] But this confidence was slowly eroded by, first, the poor Congress performance in curbing organised communal violence and, secondly, its failure to create and expand educational and promotional avenues for educated Muslims. The 1967 election was an eye-opener. Most Muslims, chiefly in UP, Bihar and Bengal, abandoned the Congress. Political activists, increasingly sceptical of its secularity, debated the future forms of political alignments. Some of these were old campaigners, but a few fresh faces also appeared on the scene, such as Abdul Jalil Faridi, a medical doctor with a high professional reputation. His initial forays into UP's murky political world were tentative, but with the backing of Syed Abul Hasan Ali Nadwi, a scholar-politician and the high priest of Lucknow's Nadwat al-ulama, he eventually succeeded in founding the Majlis-i Mushawarat in August 1964.

The Majlis was a confederation of religio-political groups drawn from the erstwhile Muslim League, the Congress, the Jamaat-i Islami and the Jamiyat al-ulama. Its nine-point *People's Manifesto* offered prosperity, pride and progress to the Muslims generally, but in reality the Majlis demands were tailored to suit the urban-based *ashraf* Muslims of UP and Bihar, most of whom had cornered privileges and grabbed opportunities

---

[45] *Statesman* (Delhi), 12 June 1961. For the text of Syed Mahmud's speech see *Muslim India* (13), January 1984, pp. 64-5.

[46] Ibid., 12 June 1961.

[47] Ibid., 13 June 1961.

[48] Ibid., 11 June 1961.

[49] Ibid., 12 June 1961.

[50] See, for example, Abbas, *I am Not an Island*, p. 293; Badruddin Tyabji, *The Self in Secularism*, p. 126; Baig, *In Different Saddles*, p. 316; Mirza Mohammad Ismail, *My Public Life*, pp. 130-1.

before and after independence. All their less privileged co-religionists were used as pawns on the chessboard of electoral politics: they voted, regardless of party allegiances, for those candidates who subscribed to democratic and secular values and pledged to honour the *People's Manifesto*.[51]

The Majlis started in a high-profile way in north India and obtained some support, but it failed to make much impact in areas where segmented Muslim groups, already integrated into the patron-client network, were strenuously engaged in working out intricate alliances with the Ittehadul-Muslimeen in Hyderabad, the DMK and the Muslim League in Tamil Nadu, the Communist Party of India (Marxist) in Bengal, and the left-wing parties and the Muslim League in Kerala. The Majlis election strategy, devised by amateurs, succeeded briefly in UP and Bihar but not in other regions. The erosion of Congress support among Muslims, especially in 1967, was largely due to the countrywide anti-Congress mood, but the Majlis contributed only marginally to energising this process. Its candidates did not do well at the hustings owing to the small and scattered Muslim votes in most constituencies, although nowadays it is claimed that Muslims make a decisive difference in nearly 150 out of a total of 542 parliamentary constituencies. Those elected on its mandate did an about-turn: most proved indifferent to anxieties over Urdu or the Aligarh Muslim University.[52] In Gujarat the Majlis made an error in backing the Swatantra party of Patidars and Kshatriyas who were traditionally anti-Muslim.[53] In UP the Congress defeat benefitted the Jana Sangh and Charan Singh's Bharatiya Kranti Dal, a party whose secular credentials were dubious.[54]

Syed Mahmud, the only prominent Congressman in the Majlis, quit honourably. Faridi lost his nerve. Running a ramshackle coalition was a far cry from running a medical practice; he was disgusted with internal bickerings between the pro- and anti-Abul Hasan Ali Nadwi's factions and with endemic wrangling between the Jamiyat al-ulama and Jamaat-i Islami ideologues. To extricate himself, he floated the UP Majlis before the mid-term poll in 1969, and two years later reached an electoral understanding with the Congress, now firmly under Indira Gandhi's control. After meeting Faridi on the eve of the 1971 elections, a journalist commented that 'the tiger of Lucknow' had been tamed by Indira

---

[51] Zaheer Masood Qureshi, 'Electoral Strategy of a minority pressure group: The Muslim Majlis-i Mushawarat', *Asian Survey*, 8, 12, December 1968, pp. 981-2; Brass, *Language, Religion and Politics*, pp. 247-55.

[52] See Tyabji, *The Self in Secularism*, p. 128.

[53] Ghanshyam Shah, 'Communal Riots in Gujarat: Report of a Preliminary Investigation', *EPW*, annual number, 1970, pp. 4-7.

[54] Nehru had pulled up Charan Singh for his reported anti-Muslim remarks. See file no. 3, G.B. Pant papers, NMML.

Gandhi.[55] In Bihar, the Majlis was defunct by the time of the 1969 elections; the Congress won fewer seats in the state as a whole, but improved its standing among Muslims.[56]

The collapse of the Majlis was hastened by internal bickering, a divided leadership and limited goals. It was seen across the Vindhya mountains as a quasi-political body with a programme tailored to suit relatively well-to-do *ashraf* Muslims in Delhi, Lucknow and Patna. More important, it was unpopular with liberal and secular as well as right-wing Hindu groups – so much so that the Majlis-backed Subhadra Joshi, a committed secularist previously elected as a Congress parliamentarian, was defeated at the hands of the Jana Sangh. She would have won but for her identification with the Majlis-i Mushawarat. In some other areas, such as Ahmedabad in 1969, the Majlis unwittingly boosted Hindu mobilisation.[57]

The Majlis leaders believed in an undifferentiated 'Muslim vote' waiting to be consolidated and harnessed to create an exclusive Muslim front. But with each election they learnt three important lessons. First, the path of 'contest mobility' was strewn with difficulties;[58] consequently, the Majlis was stigmatised as a sinister, incipient revival of Jinnah's Muslim League, and its demands pushed more votes towards candidates whose appeal was to Hindi and Hindu revivalism. Secondly, democratic institutions, though easy to work with, did not always lend themselves to being effectively used or manipulated by religious collectivities. The bitter controversy over Urdu faced by Congress and non-Congress coalitions in UP and Bihar after 1967 illustrated that parties identified with minority causes ran the risk of eroding their electoral base.[59] Indira Gandhi was aware of this when she talked of a 'Hindu backlash' against any further 'pampering' of the minorities.

Finally, many of the illusions nursed by the Majlis were quickly shattered by the realisation that Muslim activists were not strongly placed to take the political process into their hands as a separate religious entity. They could only wield influence and command allegiance through structured cross-communal linkages and alliances, not community-based ones. Shahabuddin, who tied his fortunes to the socialist wing in the Janata party during the post-Emergency euphoria, conceded years later that Muslim political parties alone, with their limited areas of influence and their small

[55] Anees Chishti, a freelance journalist and biographer of Zakir Husain. Courtesy: Violette Graff.

[56] Blair, 'Minority Electoral Politics in a North Indian State', p. 1286.

[57] Ghanshyam Shah, 'Tenth Lok Sabha Elections', p. 5.

[58] I have borrowed the idea from R.A. Schermerhorn, *Ethnic Plurality in India* (Tucson: University of Arizona Press, 1978), p. 176.

[59] For the controversy over Urdu in UP and Bihar, see Mary C. Carras, *Indira Gandhi: In the Crucible of Leadership* (Boston, MA: Beacon Press, 1979), pp. 124-5.

share of the votes of the 'Muslim Indian community', could not create a 'national consensus'. They could at best serve as faithful and reliable channels to communicate the 'Muslim consensus' and have some of their demands accepted by national parties.[60]

The chorus against the Majlis-i Mushawarat effectively ruined such limited prospects as existed for a Muslim front emerging in UP and Bihar, just as it led to the 'Muslim vote' being split and diversified. More and more Muslims preferred regional parties like the Lok Dal in UP and Bihar, the DMK in Tamil Nadu and the left-wing parties in Bengal and Kerala.[61] The Muslim League in Kerala, which Nehru thought in 1957 was 'a dead horse', was drawn into the Anti-Communist League and prospered as a regional force. The Majlis-i Ittehadul-Muslimeen and the Tamir-i Millat in Hyderabad concentrated on local and regional issues but were open to forging cross-regional linkages.[62] The Ittehadul-Muslimeen, revived in 1957 shortly after the states' reorganisation, contested elections for the first time in 1960 and performed well from 1962 onwards. It sent three members to the Andhra Pradesh assembly in 1969. In 1980, the president, Salahuddin Owaisi, secured 112,000 votes in the parliamentary elections; he won in 1984 by securing 224,000 votes. Clearly, the Majlis and not the secular parties filled up the vacuum created by the state's withdrawal from its role as protector and benefactor of religious minorities.[63]

The 1975-7 Emergency, with the excesses that accompanied it, was the last straw. The pro-Congress coalition of 'traditionalists', 'secularists' and 'repentant Muslim League modernists' was broken up by forced sterilisation, slum removal, police firing on Muslims and suspension of civil liberties, which included the banning of the Jamaat-i Islami.[64] The outcome was a decisive but temporary shift of voters to the Janata party in 1977. But three years later Indira Gandhi could win over major

[60] Editorial, *Muslim India*, August 1984, p. 371.

[61] Gopal Krishna, 'Problems of Integration in the Indian Political Community: Muslims and the Political Process' in Basu and Sisson (eds), *Social and Economic Development in India*, pp. 184-5. For local studies, see Violette Graff, 'Religious Identities and Indian Politics: Elections in Aligarh, 1971-1989' in Wink (ed.), *Islam, Politics and Society in South Asia*; Brass, *Caste, Faction and Party*, op. cit.

[62] Theodore P. Wright, Jr. 'National Integration and Modern Judicial Procedure in India: The Dar-us-Salam Case', *Asian Survey*, 6, 12, December 1966.

[63] Javeed Alam, 'The changing grounds of communal mobilisation: The Majlis-i Ittehadul-Muslimeen and the Muslims of Hyderabad', Pandey (ed.), *Hindus and Others*, pp. 146-76; Omar Khalidi, 'Muslims in the Indian Political Process: Group Goals and Alternative Strategies', *EPW*, 2-9 January 1993, p. 47; G. Ram Reddy, 'The Politics of Accommodation: Caste, Class and Dominance in Andhra Pradesh' in Francine R. Frankel and M.S.A. Rao (eds), *Dominance and State Power in Modern India: Decline of a Social Order* (Delhi: OUP), pp. 285-6.

[64] Theodore P. Wright Jr, 'Muslims and the 1977 elections: a watershed?', *Asian Survey*, 17, 2, December 1977, pp. 1207-20.

segments of the Muslim electorate because of their disillusionment with the Janata party's performance and its ambivalent relationship with the RSS. The Congress vote in constituencies with substantial Muslim populations increased from 29 per cent in 1977 to 38 per cent in 1980. Yet support for the Lok Dal was more pronounced in UP. The Lok Dal won twelve out of the twenty-three seats from the so-called Muslim constituencies and secured 33.3 per cent of the 'Muslim vote' as against 33.4 per cent gained by the Congress. In Bihar, too, the Congress wrested the political initiative from its rivals; but the Lok Dal's percentage of votes in 'Muslim constituencies' was 23.4 per cent higher than its poll (16.6 per cent) in the state as a whole.[65]

Voting patterns in subsequent national or state elections were not uniformly clear, although intense Hindu communal activity, coupled with extended periods of bloody Hindu-Muslim rioting, spurred Muslim organisations to explore alternative means of channelling their discontent. Its most conspicuous expression was the 'Save the Country and Millat Movement', launched on 9 July 1979 by the Jamiyat al-ulama, a pro-Congress body.[66] There were, of course, then and later sharp differences and nuanced variations in perceptions, but Syed Shahabuddin, having quit the benign foreign service to plunge into the volatile world of politics, expressed his feelings much more strongly than others:

Secularism seems to be dying. The spirit of secularism was never weaker; communal fragmentation, never more pronounced; the religious minorities, never more apprehensive. India, never nearer to the Hindu State. Beginning with the Meenakshipuram syndrome ... no Government, since 1947, had come closer to collaboration with the forces of Hindu chauvinism; no Prime Minister had projected such a Hindu face; no ruling party had made such unabashed efforts to win 'Hindu' votes. The communalists of yesterday had become the collaborators of today; the killers of yesterday had become the accomplices of today. India seems to have lost track of the dividing line between Indian and Hindu nationalism, between Gandhi and Savarkar, between Nehru and Golwalkar, between Indianness and Hindutva![67]

---

[65] Myron Weiner, *India at the Polls, 1980: A Study of Parliamentary Elections* (Washington, DC: American Enterprises Institute, 1978), p. 124, and Moin Shakir, 'Congress and the Muslim Vote', in Ray and Sisson (eds), op. cit., p. 103; and for the 1984 parliamentary elections in UP, see Brass, *Caste, Faction and Party*, p. 312.

[66] 'Never before in the history of the country', said the Jamiyat al-ulama, 'have the forces of fascist communalism been so confident and arrogant as today .... The country seems to be falling apart and we stand face to face with a situation in which our freedom and territorial integrity themselves are gravely threatened. In the face of this situation the leaders, the leading workers and sympathisers of the Jamiyat call upon us to come forward and do our duty to the nation. The present movement to "Save the country and the Millat" is an expression of this awareness.' *Save the Country & Millat Movement* (Delhi: Pilot Press, 1979).

[67] *Muslim India*, December 1984, p. 547.

This powerful indictment echoed the hurt pride and indignant mood of the urban-based professional and service communities in north India, the chief arena of religious contestation and communal mobilisation. The spectre of the all-devouring communal monster haunted them more than others, just as it offered overseas Muslim scholars and publicists the opportunity to discredit India's secular pretensions.[68]

III

'Urdu – language of the court in days of royalty – now languishes in the back lanes and gutters of the city. No place for it to live in the style to which it is accustomed, no emperors and nawabs to act as its patrons. Only poor I, in my dingy office, trying to bring out a magazine where it may be kept alive.'

Murad, in Anita Desai, *In Custody*
(Delhi: Penguin Books, 1984), p. 15.

For nearly three decades after independence, the anxieties of the *ashraf* classes in UP and Bihar were mirrored in an important symbol of their hopes and aspirations, the Muslim University at Aligarh. They were deeply interested in preserving its distinct Muslim/minority character and autonomy. The demand was not unusual, because any number of Christian, Sikh and Arya Samaj institutions maintained their denominational character on the strength of constitutional guarantees. But the Aligarh Muslim University was different. It was a spoilt child of the British educational system, an eyesore to the Hindu right because of its role in the Pakistan movement, and an anathema to local colleges in the city which cast envious eyes on the beautifully laid-out campus with manicured gardens, tennis courts, gymnasium and swimming pool. The University was grudgingly tolerated, although its minority status was frequently debated and disputed. Both in the UP Assembly and in Parliament legislators (including Congressmen) raised embarrassing questions over its so-called privileges and continuing links with Pakistan. They insisted that it conform to, and abide by, the norms laid down for other central universities. Nehru, who visited the campus several times, came to the University's defence rebutting ill-founded allegations levelled by some of his own colleagues, including K.M. Munshi, Sampurnanand and Tandon. So did Azad, the country's first education minister. Not surpris-

---

[68] 'Killing Muslims is a Way of Life in India' and 'Muslim blood flows in secular India' in Kalim Siddiqui (ed.), *Issues in the Islamic Movement, 1980-81 and 1982-3* (London: Open Press, n.d.), pp. 103-5, 104-7; M. Ali Kettani, *Muslim Minorities in the World Today* (London, 1986), chapter 5.

ingly, the Medical College is named after Nehru. The only portraits to be found on the sprawling campus are of Syed Ahmad Khan and of Nehru, the University's great benefactor. The library is appropriately named after Azad.

Muslim leaders and educationists agreed that Aligarh should play a pioneering role in promoting modern, scientific education. Zakir Husain and Bashir Husain Zaidi, two of its most distinguished vice-chancellors after independence, piloted such a project with the intention of placing the University on the country's intellectual map, and on a liberal and secular course. In this they were successful: they created new courses, with the infrastructure to sustain them, and did not heed religious considerations in recruitment. Zakir Husain was less of an administrator, but Zaidi, having gained much experience in the erstwhile Rampur state, possessed considerable administrative skills. Both had the advantage of Nehru's firm backing. Zakir Husain had worked closely with the Congress educational programmes and was regarded as the architect of the Wardha scheme of education. Zaidi, on the other hand, played a key part in persuading the Nawab of Rampur to work out the terms of accession with the Indian government.

In the early 1960s, however, the demand for preserving Aligarh's 'minority' character gathered momentum. It was widely argued that the University was founded by a Muslim for the Muslims, and after years of murmuring a showdown became inevitable. In July 1965 the vice-chancellor, Ali Yavar Jung, was gravely assaulted by a group of students who insisted that Syed Ahmad Khan's institution should adequately mirror *Muslim interests* in admission to courses and recruitment to jobs. Professors with liberal-left leanings were roughed up. The government retaliated by ordering the suspension of existing academic and executive bodies. The education minister, M.C. Chagla, dealt firmly with recalcitrant elements on the campus. Muslim politicians, Congress and non-Congress alike, were up in arms: here was a heaven-sent opportunity to champion a *Muslim cause*, carve out a *Muslim constituency* and assume its leadership. It paid to ignite sectarian passions and then curry favour with ministers. Innocent citizens were made to sacrifice even their lives, as in the bangle-producing city of Firozabad in UP, to keep Syed Ahmad Khan's dream alive. Strikes and demonstrations were staged in several parts of UP and Bihar, giving a pan-Indian dimension to a purely local issue. The Aligarh affair was eventually 'settled' in 1981 when Indira Gandhi pushed through the AMU (Amendment) Act to pacify the Muslim publicists. It was by no means a satisfactory resolution. Some of the provisions of the Act struck at the roots of the University's secular and democratic functioning.[69]

[69] For the beginnings of the controversy, see *Burhan*, July 1951, p. 2; Report to the

Debates on the uniform civil code have gone on ceaselessly since independence.[70] Muslim orthodoxy was unequivocally opposed to change, and the liberal view became increasingly blurred because of the unhappy intervention of Hindu ideologues as vocal proponents of reform in Muslim personal law. The Congress stand had been ambivalent from the days of Nehru until Rajiv Gandhi decided to throw his government's weight behind the MPLB in the Shah Bano case. This was a significant and reckless departure from the informal consensus established by Nehru on non-intervention in matters of faith. For the first time since independence the priests and the politicians spearheaded a massive, countrywide fundamentalist upsurge, setting aside party and sectarian allegiances to crusade for a common Muslim/Islamic cause. It was their finest hour. The grand alliance paid off, as it did in the 'triple *talaq*' (divorce) controversy a few years later.[71]

Urdu's uncertain future irked and tormented the north Indian Muslim intelligentsia,[72] yet it was hardly the main plank of any organised or sustained agitation. Public rhetoric was mostly not matched by action. Leading protagonists of Urdu conveniently abandoned the cause – Zakir

---

Government of India regarding the AMU (Amendment) Bill, 1978, annexure 3, in *First Annual Report of the Minorities Commission for the year ending 31 December 1978* (Delhi: Government of India Press, 1979; Violette Graff, 'Aligarh's long quest for "Minority" status AMU (Amendment) Act, 1981', *EPW*, 11 August 1980; Brass, *Language, Religion and Politics*, pp. 223-8.

[70] 'Personal Law ka Masla', *Burhan*, January 1949, p. 3; resolution of the Jamiyat al-ulama in March 1984 and 25-26 November 1985, and editorial in *Muslim India* (14: 16), February and April 1984, pp. 51, 68; Maulana Abul Hasan Ali Nadwi, *Western Civilization – Islam and Muslims* (Lucknow: Academy of Islamic Research and Publication, 1969), for opposition to 'change' and 'reform'; Mushirul Haq, *Islam in Secular India*, chapter 5 and appendices 3-4; and the statement of 338 *ulama* at the Jamiyat al-ulama conference on 11-12 October 1985 against the Supreme Court verdict. *Mussalmanon ka Shakhsi Qanun, Ulama-i Hind, Muftian-i Karan, Mufasirin wa Muhadisin ka Mutaffiqa Faisla* (Delhi: Jamiyat al-ulama, 1985).

[71] The controversy was stirred by Justice Hari Nath Tilhari's judgement in April 1994 declaring 'the unbridled power of divorce by *talaq* through triple announcement' unconstitutional. The judgement was condemned by the Shia theologian, Maulana Kalbe Sadiq, G.M. Banatwala, president of the Indian Union Muslim League, and Zafaryab Jilani, a Lucknow lawyer who came into prominence as a leader of the Babri Masjid Action Committee. For details, see *Sunday*, 1-7 May 1994, pp. 28-33; Furqan Ahmad, *Triple Talaq: An Analytical Study* (Delhi: Regency Publications, 1995).

[72] For early protests against the imposition of Hindi on the Urdu-speaking Muslims, see Ibadat Barelwi in *Burhan*, June 1948 and July 1949; see also the January, May, June, July, September and October 1949 issues of the same journal; Anwar Azeem, 'Urdu – A Victim of Genocide', in Zafar Imam (ed.), *Muslims in India*, pp. 260- 76; Rasheeduddin Khan, 'Minority Segments in Indian Polity; Muslim Situation and Plight of Urdu', *EPW*, 2 September, 1978, p. 1511; memorandum submitted by the Anjuman Taraqqi Urdu, Andhra Pradesh to the Telugu Desam government, 8 February 1983, and the All-India Editors Conference, Patna, 29 May 1984, *Muslim India*, March and December 1984, pp. 127, 567.

Husain did so – after being co-opted by the establishment. Scores of people lamented and shed tears over Urdu's demise. Yet most were comforted by the officially-sponsored Urdu academies, patronage through awards, the popularity of the language in the otherwise 'Hindi'- designated cinema, and a few more or less token concessions to linguistic sensibilities. In the country as a whole, the democratic and secular forces did not have the necessary motivation to defend a language that sym- bolises India's composite heritage. In UP and Bihar the Congress rank and file, the socialists, the Lok Dal and the Janata Dal were either indifferent or hostile to Urdu. The Hindu parties, of course, consistently denied Urdu any official status. Thus when the UP Vidhan Sabha adopted the Official Language (Amendment) Bill in 1989 amid unruly scenes, the BJP's MLAs stormed into the well and raised anti-Urdu slogans like 'Urdu Bill *murdabad*' (Death to the Urdu Bill) and *'Ek Rajya, ek Bhasha, nahi chahiye dusri Bhasha'* (One state, one language, a second language not required).[73]

'Urdu poetry? How can there be Urdu poetry when there is no Urdu language left? It is dead, finished. The defeat of the Moghuls by the British threw a noose over its head, and the defeat of the British by the Hindi- wallahs tightened it. So now you see its corpse lying here, waiting to be buried.' This is not just the anguish of a living Urdu poet in Anita Desai's novel, but a summation of the anger of Urdu-speakers who were appalled by the treatment meted out to the language. The story of a weak, gasping poet in *In Custody* is also the story of Urdu language and literature.

Yet those living in India have to reckon with the stereotypical images propagated by the Hindu 'traditionalists' and 'nationalists' and their myth of a minority pampered by the 'pseudo-secularism' of the Congress governments. 'For too long', thundered Uma Bharati, the saffron-robed member of parliament, 'the government treated Muslims as *ghar-jamai'* (literally, 'favourite son-in-law').[74] The Congress was the principal target for reasons detailed in the *Organiser*, the RSS-BJP mouthpiece, and in the writings of Girilal Jain, Arun Shourie and Swapan Dasgupta.[75] Arun Shourie cited the Congress and Janata Dal election manifestos of 1991 as 'excellent examples' of minority appeasement.[76]

There are more specific charges. First, Muslims, along with Christians, run their own educational institutions without any public accountability.

---

[73] *Times of India*, 3 October 1989.

[74] Quoted in *Sunday Observer*, 14-20 April 1991; see also L.K. Advani's interview in *Sunday*, 29 August-4 September 1983.

[75] Arun Shourie, *Indian Controversies: Essays on Religion in Politics* (Delhi: ASA, 1993), p. 96.

[76] See, for example, the collection of articles in Arun Shourie, *Religion in Politics* (Delhi: Roli Books International, 1987); *Indian Controversies*, op. cit.; Girilal Jain, *The Hindu Phenomenon* (Delhi: UBS Publishers, 1994).

Secondly, they are allowed to marry four wives so that their population, which stood at 2.5 crores in 1947, shot up to nearly 10 crores;[77] their high growth-rate was also due to unwillingness to adopt family planning. The family planning scheme, it is argued, is covertly if not openly forced upon the Hindus while the Muslims and Christians are allowed to procreate without limitation. The government dare not change its strategy for fear of losing Muslim votes.[78] Thirdly, for the same reason, Rajiv Gandhi imposed a ban on Salman Rushdie's *The Satanic Verses*, and his successor V.P. Singh declared the Prophet Mohammad's birthday a national holiday. Finally, Muslims were wilfully appeased by the Muslim Women (Protection of Rights on Divorce) Act, 1986, and through official reluctance to enact a uniform civil code. A leaflet issued by the general secretary of the BJP is appended (Appendixes IV-V); so too its refutation.

Most of the points listed have been convincingly refuted,[79] but some carry conviction. This would not have been so if, instead of making petty concessions to religious fears and sensibilities, the secular establishment had conceived and implemented literacy and poverty alleviation programmes for the poor and impoverished Muslims. It was all very well to push through a retrograde piece of legislation in the Shah Bano case or to rush into banning *The Satanic Verses*, but such 'gestures of goodwill', usually timed to coincide with state or parliamentary elections, proved prejudicial to most Muslims. Religious concessions *per se*, far from making them feel secure or improving their material condition, reinforced the stranglehold of orthodox and conservative clerics. They have also provided the Hindu parties with a stick to beat the Congress with, allowing them to expose

[77] For a refutation of this view, see *Report Minorities*, vol. 2 (Delhi: Ministry of Home Affairs, 14 June 1983) [hereafter *GSC*], p. x. According to the *Report of the Committee on the Status of Women in India (1975)*, during the decades 1931-41, 1941-51 and 1951-61, the percentage of polygamous marriages among Hindus was 6.79, 7.15 and 5.06, respectively. The corresponding percentages for Muslims was 7.29, 7.06 and 4.31. On the basis of the National Sample Survey (1990) it was established that 'the claim of Hindu communal propagandists that Hindus are 'in danger of being swamped by Muslims is a cynical piece of falsehood .... It is short on facts, short on proper understanding of the demographic situation – and short on honesty'. Ashra Krishnakumar, 'Canards on Muslims: Calling the Bluff on Communal Propaganda', *Frontline*, 12-25 October 1991, p. 94.

[78] An incisive essay published in the 1970s refuted this and other arguments which form part of the *sangh parivar* (BJP-RSS-VHP) armoury. Marcus F. Franda, 'Militant Hindu Opposition to Family Planning in India', American Universities Field Staff Report, South Asia Series, vol. 15, no. 2, pp. 1-13; Vasant P. Pethe, 'Hindus, Muslims and the Demographic Balance in India', *EPW*, 13 January 1973. A Muslim author, M.E. Khan, made a strong plea for family planning among Muslims in *Family Planning among Muslims in India* (Delhi: Manohar, 1979).

[79] For example, *Facts against Myths* (Bombay: Vikas Adhyayan Kendra), August 1993; Sitaram Yechury, *Pseudo Hinduism Exposed: Saffron Brigade's Myth and Reality* (Delhi: A CPI [Marxist] Publication, 1993); A.B. Bardhan, *Sangh Parivar's Hindutva versus The Real Hindu Ethos* (Delhi: Communist Party of India, 1992).

the hollowness of a secular polity that rested on pandering to Muslim religious sentiments, invent areas of contestation between 'minority' and 'majority' interests, conjure up the image of the Other, homogenise the segmented Hindu population against the minorities, and create what Romila Thapar has so aptly characterised as 'syndicated, semitised Hinduism'.[80]

The representation of a privileged Muslim community was woven around a palpably false theory of Muslim appeasement, a theory based on the works of Savarkar, Golwalkar and Hedgewar, high priests of the Hindutva philosophy. But there were serious limits to what such representations could achieve electorally. So the evocative symbol of the Ram temple in Ayodhya was added to the BJP-RSS agenda. The strategy worked from 1986 to 1992 because of the attachment to Ram in the land of Aryavarta. It also worked because the Ayodhya symbol simultaneously provided both a rallying counter-ideology against the divisiveness of caste and an all-embracing framework capable of mobilising Hindus as an undifferentiated community. At the same time, the long-awaited miracle at the hustings did not take place. L.K. Advani's chariot came to a standstill. A party riding roughshod over the political process and claiming credit for pulling down the Ayodhya mosque on 6 December 1992 suffered major reverses in state and municipal elections.[81]

IV

On 19-20 December 1964 the *Indian Express* carried two articles describing the position of India's 55 million Muslims as 'sad'. Its author A.G. Noorani commented on Urdu's plight, on the Muslims' unequal treatment in employment, and on the threat to their physical security. 'Add to this a near denial of even the rights to agitate for redress, even to ventilate grievances, and you have the malaise clearly spelt out.' Badruddin Tyabji, a retired diplomat, stressed much the same themes four years later in three articles

---

[80] Romila Thapar, 'Imagined Religious Communities? Asian History and the Modern Search for Hindu Identity', *Modern Asian Studies*, 23, 2, 1989; for a different viewpoint, see Arun Shourie, *A Secular Agenda*, p. 73.

[81] Thus the BJP suffered major setbacks in the elections to the civic bodies in Rajasthan and Madhya Pradesh. In Madhya Pradesh this was the third successive defeat for the BJP following the earlier reverses in the assembly and *panchayat* elections. 'For a party', commented a newspaper editorial, 'which boasted not too long ago that it was within sight of power in Delhi, it must be embarrassing not to be able even to scrape through the local elections in two crucial seats in the Hindi belt. Mr L.K. Advani, acutely conscious of the sorry figure he cut last year when the BJP's exaggerated claims about capturing five states boomeranged, has already all but written off the southern elections also.' *Times of India*, 2 December 1994; see also Amulya Ganguli, 'The Muslim Response: Two years after the Demolition', *Times of India*, 12 December 1994.

published in the *Statesman*.[82] So have others, with elaborate documenta-
tion.[83] The Gopal Singh Committee (*GSC*) submitted its report to the
central government in June 1983.[84] *Radiance*, the Delhi-based English
weekly; *Muslim India*, edited by Syed Shahabuddin; and Aijazuddin
Ahmad's studies reveal how most Muslims, chiefly in UP, Bihar, Madhya
Pradesh, Rajasthan and Bengal, remain on the lowest rung of the ladder
according to the basic indicators of socio-economic development.[85]

The picture emerging from such writings is familiar. A large majority
of the Muslims – nearly 71 per cent – live in rural areas, and are mostly
landless labourers, small and marginal farmers, artisans, craftsmen and
shopkeepers. Their social stratification and class interests are more or less
the same as those of other people in the countryside. More than half of the
Muslim urban population live below the poverty line, compared to about
35 per cent of Hindus. Out of nearly 76 million, more than 35 million live
below the poverty line. The rest are self-employed. Many fewer urban
Muslims work for a regular wage or salary than members of other religious
groups (Table 8.5). In most areas the Muslim share in public and private
employment is small (Tables 8.6 and 8.7). In Kerala, Muslims had a
comparatively higher literacy rate, yet they were far behind others, sharing
the endemic problem of their co-religionists as a whole. The Mappilas, for
example, held only between a quarter and half of the percentage of positions
in government departments, proportionate to their share of the population.[86]

The government machinery has been either hostile or lackadaisical in
responding to individual and collective efforts to redress the inequities
and imbalances in private and public sectors. In May 1983 Indira Gandhi
emphasised her commitment to the secular ideal. 'The India of our
dreams', she wrote, 'can survive only if Muslims and other minorities can
live in absolute safety and confidence.' Acting at the behest of some Muslim
members of parliament and the Jamiyat al-ulama, she issued guidelines

[82] Badruddin Tyabji, 'Participation of Minorities in all Walks of Life', 'Minorities are an
Asset not Properly Utilised', 'Minorities as Contributors to National Life', *Statesman*, 30
April, 7 May, 30 August 1968.

[83] Abad Ahmad, 'Economic Participation', *Seminar* (125), January 1970, p. 26; K.L. Gauba,
Passive Voices (Delhi: Sterling, 1973); N.C. Saxena, 'Public Employment and Educational
Backwardness Among Muslims in India', *Political Science Review*, 2, 2-3,
April-September 1983, p. 157; M. Aslam, 'The UP Muslims – 1947, 1967, 1987', in
Masselos (ed.), *India: Creating a Modern Nation*, pp. 139-41; Asghar A. Engineer, 'Muslims
in a Multi-Religious Society', *EPW*, 3 November 1990, p. 2422; V. Sridhar, 'Fiction and
Fact: The Real Plight of the Minorities', *Frontline*, 12-25 October 1991, pp. 99-100.

[84] The Government of India constituted a panel on 10 May 1980 which submitted its interim
report on 31 January 1981. The second report on minorities, which was largely drafted by
Gopal Singh, was submitted on 14 June 1983.

[85] Aijazuddin Ahmad, *Muslims in India: Bihar*, vol. 1, and his *Muslims in India: Rajasthan*,
vol. 2, and *Muslims in India: Delhi*, vol: 3.

[86] Miller, *Mapilla Muslims of Kerala*, p. 325.

Table 8.5. DISTRIBUTION OF PERSONS BY HOUSEHOLD TYPE
(URBAN) AND HOUSEHOLD RELIGION (× *1,000*)

Household religion	Type of household			
	Self-employed	Regular/wage/ salaried	Casual labour	Others
Hindu	359	467	121	53
Muslim	534	289	134	42
All religious groups	389	436	121	52

Note: Totals for each religion will not add up to 1,000 because of 'non-reporting'.
Source: 'Sarvekshana', September 1990, quoted in *Frontline*, 12-25, October, 1991, p. 101.

Table 8.6. MUSLIM SHARE OF PUBLIC EMPLOYMENT

Name of service	Years/no. of establishments	Total	Muslims	%
A. ALL-INDIA AND CENTRAL SERVICES				
Indian Administrative Service	Total in 1981	3,883	116	2.99
Indian Public Service, Income Tax I	Total in 1981	1,753	50	2.85
Railway Traffic and Account Services	Intake during 1971-80	881	27	3.06
B. RANDOM SURVEY OF PUBLIC EMPLOYMENT				
Central government offices	105 offices in 13 states	75,951	3,346	4.41
State government offices	876 offices in 13 states	826,669	49,718	6.01
Nationalised banks	1,317 branches	113,772	2,479	2.18
Public sector undertakings (central and state)	168 undertakings in 13 states	476,972	51,755	10.85
Total		1,499,881	107,491	6.60

Source: Muslim India, June 1983, pp. 261-63.

Empowering Differences 283

Table 8.7. MUSLIM SHARE OF PRIVATE SECTOR EMPLOYMENT

Corporation	Executive cadre (%)	Supervisory cadre (%)	Worker cadre (%)
TISCO	4.1	5.60	10.30
Texmaco	nil	0.30	4.40
Mafatlal	nil	1.72	3.53
Calico	0.68	n.a.	10.20
Mahindra and Mahindra	1.48	2.25	5.02
Orkay	3.30	3.00	11.90
J.K. Industries	2.63	2.28	5.41
Indian Explosives	nil	2.73	7.09

Source: *Muslim India*, from Minorities Commission, January 1984, p. 17.

on better job opportunities for Muslims,[87] but the central and state governments ignored her directive. Individual appeals to industrialists to recruit Muslim graduates fell on deaf ears. Such was Badruddin Tyabji's experience as Aligarh University's vice-chancellor.[88] He discovered, as have others since, the small proportion of Muslims in large-scale industry or business. Not a single Muslim figured among the 50 industrial houses up till 1985. Muslim industrialists owned only 4 units in a group of 2,832 industrial enterprises, each with sales of Rs 50 million and above. In the smaller industrial sector, they owned about 14,000 units out of a total of 600,000 of which 2,000 belonged to the 'small' category with a limited capital outlay.[89]

In general, Muslim access to government-sponsored welfare projects was limited. For example, up till 1985 Muslims in the lower and middle income groups received 2.86 per cent of houses allotted by the state governments and only 6.9 per cent of licenses for 'Fair Price' shops. Muslim artisans received only 9.15 per cent of the benefits extended by the Khadi and Village Industries Commission (KVIC). Only 301 out of the 10,450 units under the KVIC programme belonged to Muslims; and only 45 million out of 5,846 artisans who gained subsidies for purchasing

[87] Quoted in *GSC*, vol. 1, p. 5.

[88] *Statesman*, 12 April 1968; *Hindustan Times*, 29 April 1968.

[89] *Muslim India* (82), February 1985, p. 82; Vir Sanghvi, 'Coming to Terms with the Hindu Backlash', *Imprint* (Bombay), July 1984, p. 28. As to participation in fresh growth of industries, the situation of industrial licenses issued for units between Rs 3 crores and Rs 20 crores during 1979 and 1980 is as follows:

	Approved	Muslims	Sikhs	Christians	Parsis	Others
1979	260	5	5	–	3	247
		(1.9%)	(1.9%)		(1.2%)	(95.0%)
1980	386	6	14	4	1	361
		(1.5%)	(3.4%)	(1.0%)	(0.30%)	(93.6%)

Source: *Facts Against Myths* (Delhi: Vikas Adhyan Kendra, August 1993).

tools and equipments were Muslims; as were only 99 out of 7,400 who secured other financial benefits. Muslims accounted for 3 per cent of the sums advanced and 3.4 per cent of the recipients of loans for small industry and agriculture in the range of Rs 50,000 to 1 lakh, and less than 6 per cent in the Rs 1 lakh-2 lakhs category. They accounted for 3 per cent of recipients and 1 per cent of sums advanced in the higher bracket of Rs 2-10 lakhs. The *GSC* thought that the poorer Muslims should have benefited most from the Differential Rate of Interest and Composite Loan Schemes, which were meant for lower income groups,[90] but this did not happen.

Many writers emphatically believe that discriminatory practices contributed to Muslims being 'the hewers of wood and drawers of water'.[91] 'Equality of opportunity guaranteed by the constitution', Shahabuddin commented, 'has largely proved to be a mirage in practice. Muslim India suffers from discrimination in access to public employment, to higher education or to career promotion opportunities, to public credit, to industrial and trade licensing.'[92]

Maulana Wahiduddin Khan, a Delhi-based scholar, blames the Muslims' 'own backwardness, which they misguidedly wish to blame on others'.[93] Most Muslim scholars and social and political activists have no sympathy for this view or, for that matter, for the argument that Muslim backwardness is linked to the nature of economic growth, the uneven distribution of material wealth and the slow and tardy progress of the economy as a whole. They likewise do not subscribe to the view that their problems could be solved in the same way as the chronic poverty of the other rural and urban poor.[94] They insist that opportunities for economic advance are specifically blocked for Muslims because of official neglect and discrimination. Hence the clamour for a larger share of the national wealth.

---

[90] *GSC*, vol. 1, p. 89.

[91] Ansar Harvani, a former Congress parliamentarian, quoted in Imtiaz Ahmad, 'Secular State, Communal Society', *Communalism: The Razor's Edge* (Bombay, n.d.), p. 25.

[92] *Muslim India* (26), February 1985, p. 82. And, more recently, the following comment at the Ittehad-i Millat Conference at Bombay in May 1992: 'Economically, the continually declining condition of Muslims and their unemployment in various parts of the country, their poverty, lack of education and deprivation from dignity in life have pushed them down lower than other minorities. The economic condition of our *millat* is so much run-down that there is hardly room for them as class four servants in the government, industrial and private institutions and even on the road as rickshaw pullers. It appears *jhuggi, jhonpris* [temporary shelters as part of urban slums] are the only shelters for them from the inclemency of weather.' *All India Milli Council: Perspective, Significance, Aims and Objectives* (Delhi: All India Milli Council, n.d.), p. 5.

[93] Wahiduddin Khan, *Indian Muslims: The Need for a Positive Outlook* (Delhi: Al-Risala Books, 1994), p. 43.

[94] See, for example, V.K.R.V. Rao's preface to S.N. Faridi, *Economic Welfare of Indian Moslems* (Agra: Ram Prasad, 1965).

'We must demand our due from the system', wrote Shahabuddin at the beginning of 1984. 'We do not cry for favours or preferences but we assert our right to equality.'[95] The All-India Milli Council, formed in 1992, has undertaken to draw attention to 'the continually declining condition of Muslims and their unemployment in various parts of the country'.[96]

Suggestions by some Western scholars that the Muslims, unrestricted by caste considerations, are better placed than most Hindus to grab new economic opportunities are not confirmed by the experience in many places. Those areas which Muslims tend to dominate, such as the lock industry in Aligarh or the bangle industry in Firozabad, are now accessible to others without any sense of caste restrictions.[97] Moreover, scheduled castes and tribes have compensatory programmes; there are none for the Muslims in most states. The backward castes, too, had no access to compensatory schemes until the Mandal Commission report was implemented. Yet they had neutralised their weakness much earlier by the use of political mobilisation, using their numbers and voting strength to secure attention and capture political power, as in UP and Bihar, by forming coalitions with other forces. To be sure, such mobilisation, when it sought politically allocated resources by way of job quotas, generated opposition and violence, as in 1990, but this controversy was small compared to the consequences that awaited Muslims whenever they asserted themselves politically and, even more, in the economic sphere.

Thus the 'economic resurgence' of Muslims in isolated pockets is commonly ascribed to 'Islamic fundamentalism' and the confidence boosted by the flow of petro-dollars from West Asia and the Gulf region in particular. Thus some activity in moving two *madaris* to more spacious grounds in Moradabad, scene of a communal outbreak in 1980, led to the inference that Muslims planned to turn the city into a fortress in order to lay the basis for another Pakistan. A pamphlet was circulated which commented: 'A college built with foreign money [reference to petro-dollars] will be [an] abode of foreign powers; one day this may even place our capital in jeopardy.'[98] In 1990-1 fear and envy of Muslim landed wealth and status, upward mobility and popular power was fomented in the riot-torn city of Khurja.[99]

The *GSC* noted that economic stratification in traditional centres of

[95] *Muslim India* (13), January 1984, p. 3.

[96] See *All India Milli Council*, op. cit., and *A Report on the Mysore session of the All India Milli Council and Council's Activities from Bombay to Mysore* (Bombay: n.d.).

[97] Mann, *Boundaries and Identities*, p. 122.

[98] See Satish Saberwal and Mushirul Hasan, 'Moradabad Riots, 1980: Causes and Meanings' in Engineer (ed.), *Communal Riots in Post-Independence India*, p. 215.

[99] Uma Chakravarti *et al.*, 'Khurja Riots 1990: Understanding the Conjuncture', *EPW*, 2 May 1992.

arts and crafts usually followed the pattern of Hindus being businessmen and Muslims being workers. This relationship began to change in the 1960s, when Muslim artisans and craftsmen started competing with Hindu traders and businessmen for the expanding markets in India and the Gulf states. The competition thus resulted in conflicts which took the form of violent outbursts over the routing of religious processions, cow-slaughter, music before mosques and inter-community marriage.[100] Disputes over such matters had been quite common in British and princely India, but at that time there was no discernible pattern to them. The *GSC* underlined the economic factor and the keen and bitter rivalries over acquiring control or sharing the gains of economic ventures and existing enterprises. According to its findings,

The prolonged nature of violence and the target-oriented destruction of property lends credence to the theory that these are not sporadic expressions of communal anger but pre-planned operations with specific goals and targets in mind ... In our view, therefore, communal conflicts are more the result of the economic competition, which has often resulted in the majority community depriving minorities of their economic gains. Innocent lives were taken in this process to instill a sense of insecurity among the victims and destruction of their properties was aimed at uprooting them economically.[101]

So why were Moradabad, Khurja, Aligarh, Bhagalpur, Ahmedabad, Baroda and Surat specially targeted? In western UP, where growth has been shaped by the commercialisation of agriculture and the rapid expansion of small towns, there appears to be a significant coincidence of rapid socio-economic growth and an increase in communalism.[102] Many towns in the region, as also in other states, are riot-prone because Muslim craftsmen, artisans and weavers reap the rewards of a favourable economic climate, trading relations with Gulf countries and the revival of traditional artisanal and entrepreneurial skills. Noteworthy developments include the changes in Khurja on the Grand Trunk Road where after years of decline the pottery units owned by Muslims picked up business. Then there are the improved fortunes of Muslims in certain areas at Aligarh. Owners of lock-making industries moved into producing building materials and bought property in the civil lines. Residential colonies like Sir Syed Nagar bear testimony to the presence of a substantial middle class and the prosperity that has come to it through trading, business and professional links with the Arab world. Most shops in Amir Nishan and Dodhpur (as opposed to Marris road) have Muslim owners and a predominantly Muslim clientele. Doctors educated at the University's

---

[100] *GSC*, vol. 1, p. 99; see also Ghosh, *Communal Riots in India*, p. 31, and his *Riots Prevention*, p. 58.

[101] Ibid., p. 100.

[102] Zoya Hasan, 'Shifting Grounds', op. cit., p. 185.

Medical College have established clinics and are successful. Some engineers have sought employment in Western countries, principally the United States, and in West Asia; others have set up factories and moved into heavy engineering or electronics.

In Kanpur, another city with a long history of communal conflict, Muslims prospered in the leather industry although most were petty traders, artisans and industrial workers.[103] In Varanasi Muslim weavers have gradually established their hold over the silk saree trade and obtained a financial stake in the industry itself. In Meerut Muslim weavers who have turned to entrepreneurial activities tend to do well in iron foundries, furniture manufacturing, scissor-making and lathe operations. In Moradabad, also in western UP, the traditional methods of producing brassware were reoriented by the Muslims to produce decorative brassware for export to rich Arab states. In Bhagalpur (Bihar) the monopoly of Marwaris in the silk business was broken by some new Muslim exporters. Tension in the city mounted between the loom-owners and traders due to the growth of the latter as an independent force, especially Muslims, who had earlier been dependent on Hindu traders.[104] In Ahmedabad and Bhiwandi, centres of textile manufacturing, Muslims gradually bought up small-scale textile units, which are tempting targets during communal riots. In the Kolagu region of Karnataka the resentment against Mapilla labourers is accentuated by the modest economic success of Muslims as small coffee-planters.[105] Finally, the traditional Hindu mercantile community in the walled city of Delhi resents 'Muslim intrusion' into its commercial enclave. 'Hindus tend to raise their eyebrows', concluded a report on the Delhi riots of May 1987, 'at the assertion of an equal status by a community which they have been used to look down upon as their inferiors in the post-independence era.'[106]

In other words, prosperity bred resentment among those accustomed to Muslim invisibility and deference. Hindu professionals and businessmen expected Muslims to serve them as tailors and bakers. Industrial and office workers seeking jobs, better pay or promotion expect them to stick to their traditional occupations – weaving, gem-cutting, brass tooling. Hindus often respond to Muslim mobility and wealth by challenging the Nehru-style secularism that offers special protection to Muslims.[107]

[103] Stephan Molund, *First We Are People .... The Koris of Kanpur between Caste and Class* (Stockholm Studies in Social Anthropology, 1988); Brass, *Caste, Faction and Party*, p. 282.

[104] *Bhagalpur Riots* (Delhi: People's Union for Democratic Rights [PUDR], April 1990), pp. 3-4.

[105] Janaki Nair, 'Lurching to the Right? Karnataka and the BJP', *EPW*, 31 December 1994, p. 3308.

[106] *Walled City Riots: A Report on the Police and Communal Violence in Delhi, 19-24 May 1987* (Delhi: PUDR, 1987), p. 1.

[107] Rudolphs, 'Modern Hate', op. cit., p. 28.

Sure enough, the 'hewers of wood and drawers of water' theory does not apply to Muslims everywhere. There are regional variations, especially where Muslims, along with Christians, enjoy benefits in the shape of liberal admission to institutions and scholarships, or in Bihar where job opportunities have steadily increased after Urdu earned its rightful status in some districts. Secondly, signs of progress and prosperity were visible in some parts of Rajasthan, Gujarat, Maharashtra, Andhra Pradesh, Tamil Nadu and Kerala.

Much of it, as in Surat or Baroda, is not new. Apart from petty traders and groups of Muslim artisans who have carved out a place for themselves, the Bohra, Khoja and Memon communities continue to play trading and mercantile roles in western India.[108] Ahmedabad is different. Although Gujarat had pockets of Muslim enterprise, including two cotton-spinning mills in Surat started in 1861 and 1874, Ahmedabad had no Muslim mill-owners, and only one industrialist, Munshi Fateh Mohammad Fakir Mohammad, who started a match factory in 1895.[109] The situation improved over the decades because the textile and transport industries expanded, attracting large numbers of Muslim migrants into the city. Though still relatively backward in most sectors of the economy, especially in the professions and in private and government employment, Muslims in Ahmedabad have made their mark in textiles, transport, petty trading and shopkeeping.

The overall progress of the Kerala Muslims is aided by Gulf employment, reservations in education and higher rates of literacy achieved through sustained application. Farook College at Calicut in the Malabar region, from its humble beginnings in 1947-8, generated constructive movements of modernity and progress among the Kerala Muslims: it has been called 'the Aligarh of the south'.[110] Along with other voluntary agencies, the Muslim Educational Society, founded in 1964, promotes primary, secondary and higher education. By 1960, 47.3 per cent of school-age Muslim children were attending school; by 1970, Mapillas accounted for 30 per cent of college students in Malappurram and Calicut districts. At the beginning of 1974, about 700 lower and upper primary schools and thirty-six high schools flourished under Muslim managements. In the state as a whole, there were nine first-grade Muslim colleges and several technical institutions.[111]

---

[108] Douglas E. Haynes, *Rhetoric and Ritual in Colonial India: The Shaping of a Public Culture in Surat City, 1852-1928* (Berkeley, CA: California University Press, 1991), pp. 72-6.

[109] Kenneth L. Gillion, *Ahmedabad: A Study in Indian Urban History* (Berkeley, CA: California University Press, 1968), p. 89.

[110] Mohammad Ali, *The Development of Education among the Mappilas of Malabar*, p. 175. For the impact of the 'Oil Boom' and overseas employment in Hyderabad, see Arifa Kulsoom Javed, *Muslim Society in Transition*, pp. 50-3.

[111] Ibid., pp. 176-8.

The fortunes of the Kerala Muslim migrants to Madras city have improved since the 1940s when they first entered the metropolis. Those from the Malabar region did particularly well in running hotels, biscuit factories, textile concerns and import-export firms. A Muslim timber merchant who came to the city penniless now owns one of the largest timber firms in south India with twenty branches in Madras city.[112] The Malabar Muslim Association has reason to be proud of its achievements. It set up a Medical Relief Centre, primary and secondary schools and colleges.[113] The Islamic Foundation in Madras founded an engineering college in 1984 in the name and style of the 'Saleh Kamel Crescent Engineering College' at Othivakam in Chengalpatlu district. The Al-Ameen Educational Society in Bangalore founded colleges, an evening polytechnic (1977) and a school of pharmacy (1982). In 1984 the society awarded scholarships amounting to Rs 89,745,63.[114]

The picture is much less promising in UP and Bihar. These states have some isolated pockets of affluence, but on the whole 'a rather alarming percentage of the minorities, particularly the poorer sections among the Muslims', live in these states.[115] The country's partition and the sheer scale and magnitude of migration to Pakistan from traditional Muslim centres like Delhi, Aligarh, Farrukhabad, Moradabad, Rampur, Meerut, Muzaffarnagar, Lucknow and Allahabad contributed to the professional classes being skimmed off. The loss has not been made good. Zamindari abolition caused serious hardships to small landowners, zamindars and their dependants. When Hindi was made the sole language of administration and education, the affected sections were the very ones which sought employment at the clerical level, in lower government service or in educational institutions. Indeed, it was difficult for many Muslims whose mother-tongue was Urdu to compete for government posts. This, and the constant fear of discrimination, largely accounts for so few taking the competitive examinations for government posts (Table 8.8).

Widespread illiteracy and a higher drop-out rate at the elementary stage are additional factors (Table 8.9). According to the Planning Commission, the average literacy rate among Muslims was 42 per cent in 1987-8, less than the national average of 52.11 per cent. Muslim women – more than half the total Muslim population – do not receive even school education, let alone higher education. A survey conducted in 1967-8 in Lucknow showed that illiteracy among Hindu women was 32 per cent compared to 50 per cent among Muslim women. None of the

---

[112] Susan Lewandowski, *Migration and Ethnicity in India: Kerala Migrants in the City of Madras, 1870-1970* (Delhi: Manohar, 1980), pp. 169-73.

[113] Ibid., pp. 171-2.

[114] *Muslim India*, August 1984, p. 397.

[115] *GSC*, vol. 1, p. 25.

Table 8.8. REPRESENTATION OF MUSLIMS IN STATE PUBLIC SERVICE COMMISSION EXAMINATIONS
(% of total in brackets)

Examination/state	Persons applied		Appeared		Called for interview		Selected	
	Total	Muslims	Total	Muslims	Total	Muslims	Total	Muslims
Andhra Pradesh								
Group II services	21,532	967 (4.49)	6,857	310 (4.52)	196	26 (13.26)	112	11 (9.82)
Group II (B) services	19,899	950 (4.77)	14,583	639 (4.38)	:	:	664	21 (3.16)
Group I services	5,651	412 (7.29)	1,917	103 (5.37)	85	8 (9.44)	22	1 (4.54)
Dy. executive engineers	1,704	102 (5.98)	593	34 (5.73)	172	4 (2.32)	99	2 (2.02)
Civil assistant surgeons	5,450	166 (3.04)	4,377	131 (2.86)	3,733	103 (2.76)	1,066	25 (2.34)
Total	54,236	2,597 (4.79)	28,527	1,217 (4.27)	4,186	141 (3.37)	1,963	60 (3.06)
Kerala								
Office assistants Gr. II	1,089	123 (11.29)	700	70 (10.00)	552	58 (10.50)	200	20 (10.00)
Block development officers	n.a.	n.a.	6,984	588 (8.42)	143	14 (9.79)	n.a.	n.a.
Total			7,684	658 (8.56)	695	72 (10.36)		
Madhya Pradesh								
Group I and II services	31,885	903 (2.83)	31,221	90 (2.89)	1,356	24 (1.77)	353	6 (1.70)
Maharashtra								
Assistant & sales tax inspectors Class III	8,399	120 (1.43)	5,610	114 (2.03)	712	4 (0.56)	160	:
Forest ranges	2,048	62 (3.03)	1,565	n.a.	189	3 (1.59)	74	:

Assistant Conservators of Forest Class II	2,375	n.a.	2,015	3 (0.15)	164	2 (1.22)	39	1 (2.56)
Total					1,065	9 (0.84)	273	1 (0.37)
Tamil Nadu								
Group III services	2,352	76 (3.27)	..	..	2,097	69 (3.29)	313	9 (2.87)
Group II services	497	12 (2.44)	..	..	470	11 (2.34)	79	3 (3.80)
Assistant surgeons	3,503	162 (4.62)	..	..	3,371	152 (4.51)	1,400	71 (5.07)
Total	6,325	250 (3.95)	..	..	5,938	232 (3.91)	1,792	83 (4.63)
Uttar Pradesh								
Forest rangers	8,086	513 (6.34)	6,149	371 (6.03)	270	11 (4.07)	67	2 (2.98)
Bihar								
Forest rangers	980	22 (2.24)	578	10 (1.12)	110	1 (1.00)	40	1 (2.50)
Total (UP and Bihar)	9,066	535 (5.90)	6,727	381 (5.66)	370	12 (3.24)	107	3 (2.81)
Uttar Pradesh								
Combined State Services	19,557	1,310 (6.70)	12,261	1,037 (8.46)	660	18 (1.21)	244	6 (2.46)
Bihar								
Combined State Services	17,645	709 (4.02)	11,111	504 (4.54)	619	39 (6.36)	233	17 (7.30)
Total	37,202	2,019 (5.40)	23,372	1,541 (6.60)	1,279	47 (3.67)	477	23 (4.82)
Grand total	n.a.			n.a.	14,889	537 (3.61)	4,965	176 (3.54)

Source: Report on Minorities (Delhi: Ministry of Home Affairs, Government of India, 14 June 1983), pp. 34-5.

Table 8.9. URBAN EDUCATION LEVELS
BY HOUSEHOLD RELIGION (%)

Household Religion/ Sex	Not literate	Literate but below primary	Primary	Middle	Secondary	Graduate and above	Not reported
Male							
Hindu	25.3	18.8	16.6	13.9	17.2	7.9	0.3
Muslim	42.4	20.9	16.3	10.0	8.0	2.3	0.1
All	27.7	19.0	16.7	13.3	13.3	7.0	0.3
Female							
Hindu	42.2	17.2	15.0	10.3	10.7	4.2	0.3
Muslim	59.5	18.5	11.4	5.4	4.3	0.8	0.1
All	44.1	17.4	14.5	9.7	10.2	3.8	0.3
Total							
Hindu	33.4	18.1	15.8	12.2	14.1	6.2	0.3
Muslim	50.5	19.8	13.9	7.8	6.2	1.6	0.1
All	35.5	18.3	15.7	11.6	13.2	5.5	0.3

Note: In 1981, of the total population of 665.2 million, the Muslim population stood at 75.6 m., i.e., 11.4%. They accounted for only 9.8% of the rural population, but 16.3% of the urban. Of the total Hindu population (549.7 m.), 78% lived in rural areas and only 22% in urban areas. The corresponding figure for Muslims was 34 and 66% respectively. In the urban areas, as the table indicates, the incidence of illiteracy among Muslims was more than 50% compared with 33% among Hindus.

Source: Sarveksharana, September 1990, quoted in *Frontline*, 12-15 October 1991.

latter who responded had a post-graduate degree. Most of the husbands of the 1,423 women surveyed also had not attended a school. On the other hand, 80 per cent or more of the upper-caste Hindus and Christians had received secondary or higher education.[116] The educational profile of Muslims is much lower in Khurja and Bulandshahr, though they constitute numerically one of the dominant groups along with scheduled castes. The number of Muslims who study in Khurja is about 10 per cent (the corresponding figure for women was 5 per cent) while of Hindus about 75 per cent.[117]

It is not clear whether Muslim children are not sent to schools and colleges because of economic constraints, the absence of religious instruction, the sting of the prevailing bias against Urdu, or because parents in larger arts and crafts centres hardly consider it worthwhile to give their children higher education. What is evident is the lack of concerted effort

---

[116] D.N. Saxena, *Differential Urban Fertility – Lucknow: Report of the Intensive Fertility Survey of Lucknow City* (Lucknow: Demographic Research Centre, 1973), pp. 9-10; and Sushila Jain, *Muslims and Modernisation: A study of their changing role structure and norms in an urban setting* (Jaipur: Rawat, 1986), pp. 225-8.

[117] Uma Chakravarty *et al.*, 'Khurja Riots', op. cit., p. 953.

in UP, though less so in Bihar, to promote literacy or modernise existing educational institutions. Initiatives in Delhi by the Hamdard Foundation or the Crescent School are modest compared to the scale of similar operations in Bihar, and west and south India.[118]

The Dini Talimi (Religious Education) Council of UP had 6,000 small rural schools in which more than 600,000 pupils received religious instruction. Studies by A.R. Sherwani, whose brother was a prominent industrialist in Allahabad, indicate that instruction in such schools seldom goes beyond Class II and that the educational content is confined almost exclusively to Islamic religious texts. Urdu-medium schools, mostly government-run, teach physics, chemistry, mathematics, geography and economics, but Sherwani shows that such institutions fail to maintain the standards of Hindi-medium schools, either in UP or Delhi.[119] Some schools have modified their curriculum, but most have not.

Take Karnataka's largest seminary on the outskirts of Bangalore. More than 400 boys, mainly from south India, are trained to lead prayers, recite the Quran and teach in *makatib* and *madaris*. But the curriculum has not changed, because of the traditions handed down from previous genera-tions: 'There are great spiritual blessings to be had from ancient wisdom which modern education is totally bereft of.' The library is stocked with books, but only on Islam and in Persian, Arabic and Urdu languages. Maulvi Haroon, as a recent graduate, had not heard of liberal and moder-nist authors; they find no place in the institution. The glass doors of the cupboards are covered all over with colourful stickers, all conveying in different ways the same message: 'No to the uniform civil code. [...] In sum, what the students are taught and the fashion in which their tender minds are moulded, time seems to have frozen here many centuries ago.'[120]

The great seminaries at Deoband and Lucknow, which should ideally have given the lead, are sluggish in responding to the winds of change. The few cosmetic changes introduced in their curriculum have not helped to equip their graduates to compete in the wider world of employment, trade or business; many end up as school teachers or prayer-leaders in local mosques. Aligarh and Jamia Millia have attracted some bright students largely through a liberal admission policy, but their numbers are small and with a few notable exceptions their performance has been disappointing.

The *GSC* report found students at Nadwa 'totally devoid of modern secular education which is essential to help them face the realities

---

[118] Marcus F. Franda, 'The Crescent School of Old Delhi', American Field Staff Reports, vol. 3, 1977-8.

[119] Quoted in ibid.

[120] Yoginder Sikand, in *Communalism Combat* (Bombay), January 1995, p. 8.

outside'.[121] The Jamia Millia and Aligarh's Muslim University have not lived up to their reputation. The Jamia, founded in the year of a great political upheaval, is rocked by 'mounting corruption, misguided student agitations, increasing administrative lapses and strained teacher-students relations'.[122] The University at Aligarh seethed with discontent caused by corruption, declining academic standards and inept administration. Other institutions, such as the Shia College in Lucknow, are little better. The Dar al-Mussaniffin, Shibli Nomani's creation, languishes in Azamgarh, and Lucknow's Firangi Mahal, situated in Chowk, is a symbol of the Nawabi city's decline. Declining standards and financial mismanagement plague the once renowned Faiz Aam Inter-College in Meerut.[123]

If so few go to school and college and if so many are inadequately equipped to face the world, it is easy to understand why only 5,336 (2.59 per cent) Muslims competed for the subordinate services commission examinations and so few found employment in the judicial, administrative, police (Table 8.10) and forest services.[124] Figures furnished by the *GSC*

Table 8.10. MUSLIM REPRESENTATION IN THE POLICE

	Total police strength	Muslims	%
Gujarat	63,092	3,897	6.2
Uttar Pradesh	163,485	8,072	4.9
Maharashtra	158,543	6,633	4.2
Delhi	50,798	1,160	2.3

Source: *Towards Secular India* (Bombay), 1, 2, April-June 1991.

report or *Muslim India* need to be updated, although the pattern is likely to remain much the same for many years to come. By and large, Muslims are likely to remain outside the area of state employment and predominantly in the unorganised sector either as workers or as self-employed petty bourgeoisie.

Muslim organisations have not diagnosed the malady, but they need to do so. They must review the performance and functioning of educational institutions, including Aligarh, Deoband, Nadwa and Jamia Millia Islamia, and improve the working of huge numbers of charitable endowments which had once sustained vigorous and creative intellectual life at several urban centres.[125]

[121] *GSC*, vol. 1, p. 26. For a strong plea for reforming Islamic education, see Rasheed Talib in *Times of India*, 11 November 1994. For a different perspective on Nadwa, see Nadwi, *Western Civilization*, pp. 63-6.

[122] 'After 75 years, Jamia stands completely disillusioned'. *Pioneer*, 18 January 1994.

[123] *Qaumi Awaaz* (Lucknow/Delhi: Urdu daily), 2 February 1995.

[124] Syed Shahabuddin and Theodore Wright, Jr., 'India: Muslim Minority Politics and Society' in John L. Esposito (ed.), *Islam in Asia: Religion, Politics and Society* (New York: OUP, 1987).

[125] For a critique of *waqf* administration, see Faridi, *Economic Welfare of Indian Moslems*, pp. 2-3. For recommendations to improve their functioning, see *GSC*, vol. 1, p. 28.

V

'Barq girti hai to bechare Musalmanon par'
[Lightning, after all, only strikes the beleaguered Muslims]

Mohammad Iqbal

Several important conclusions, some spilling over to larger question of minority identity, emerge from the foregoing. The reactions triggered off by the Muslim Convention and the Majlis-i Mushawarat illustrate how the democratic process itself imposed constraints on the articulation of minority grievances and their redressal through formal procedures. Most political activists across the board saw a divide between 'minority' and 'majority' interests, although this divide rested on an undifferentiated view of what constituted a 'majority' or a 'minority'. This made it increasingly difficult after Nehru's death in 1964 to channel the very different aspirations of minority segments through secular formations. The left-wing and democratic forces tried to do so in their limited spheres of influence, countering overt manifestations of Hindu communalism and providing the healing touch in riot-affected areas. But there were limits to what they could achieve. As parliamentary parties they had to tread warily and not identify themselves too closely with minority causes.

The formal and informal channels of articulation created by Nehru had collapsed by the 1970s, and the resulting vacuum was filled by Muslim organisations in UP, Bihar, Andhra Pradesh, Tamil Nadu and Kerala. They had survived on the fringes of Indian politics, but were back in business after Nehru's death. Their agenda was twofold: to create a distinct *Muslim* constituency by dwelling on the Congress failure to assuage their fears and fulfill electoral promises, and to organise and deepen anti-Congress sentiments, in co-operation with regional and local parties. Thus the Muslim Convention, Majlis-i Mushawarat, Ittehadul-Muslimeen and the Muslim League in Tamil Nadu and Kerala raised important issues, but their constituency and their overall reach were limited. They picked up a few seats not through a consolidation of 'Muslim votes' but through a coalition with local or regional forces. In a more general sense they knew that it did not pay to act solely as Muslim parties.

What does one make of 'Muslim identity', an expression widely in vogue but without any clear intellectual underpinnings? It is doubtless true that economic discontent, coupled with escalating violence, lent weight to notions of identity and acted as a catalyst to communitarian strategies. Yet Muslim scholars and activists had recourse to a definition that rested uneasily on the Islamic concept of a unified *millat*, and which will always be problematic. So too is its projection in the political arena.

To identify and locate a set of unified communitarian interests in a mixed and diverse population is politically inexpedient and empirically hard to sustain. Hence the importance of drawing a sharp distinction between political polemics and the actual realities on the ground.

If so, what does one make of the self-image of a minority, religious or otherwise? In a nutshell, the language and vocabulary of communitarian politics, such as those used by the Muslim League or the Majlis-i Mushawarat, need decoding because the dominant priest-politician combination has, for its own reasons, projected a certain image of itself and the 'community' it purports to represent. Thus an outraged Shahabuddin mistakenly assumed that his defeat in the Rajya Sabha biennial election in 1984 'sent shock waves in the Muslim community all over the country'. 'Every Muslim Indian who is politically conscious', he added, 'is bound to draw certain conclusions from this episode and he will not be wrong if he thinks that if the national parties which swear by secularism reject Shahabuddins, Muslim India must find a new strategy.'[126] Wahiduddin Khan rightly regards such reactions as symptomatic of the 'erroneous self-definition *vis-à-vis* the present'.[127]

Finally, we have kept track of the relentless defence of the Muslim Personal Law and the clear and outward signs of conservative and orthodox reactions to modern education, composite and syncretic trends and reformist initiatives.[128] The Jamiyat al-ulama and the Jamaat-i Islami regard modernism as the most dangerous heresy of the day. They have taken the position – indefensible in a liberal dialogue – that changes in Muslim Personal Law are tantamount to an infringement of the 'covenant' of composite nationalism which binds Muslims to India and its Hindu nationals.[129] The intervention of other organisations has deepened support for this viewpoint. Theologians, jurists and public figures gathered in Delhi in April 1989, under the aegis of the Institute of Objective Studies, to explore solutions to contemporary problems 'in the light of and in conformity with the principles of the Shariat'.[130] Maulana Syed Abul Hasan Ali Nadwi and Maulana Minnatullah Rahmani, *Amir-i Shariat* in Bihar and Orissa, were the star performers. The All-India Muslim Milli Council, founded in Bombay on 24 May 1992, set out to 'create collectivity and unity among Muslims on the basis of *Kalimah-Tayyabah* [epitome of the Islamic creed] and 'endeavour to see that Muslims in their

---

126 *Muslim India*, May 1984, p. 196.
127 Wahiduddin Khan, op. cit., p. 41.
128 See chapters 4 and 5.
129 See presidential address by Maulana Syed Asad Madani, Jamiyat al-ulama session held at Bombay on 14-16 January 1983, p. 16; also Nadwi, *Western Civilization*, p. 209.
130 *Islamic Fiqah Academy: Introduction, Aims and Resolutions* (Delhi: n.d.), pp. 3-5.

role of *Khair-i Umma* [welfare of the community] fully discharge their duties.'[131]

These were the loud, clear voices of orthodoxy. Yet there is no reason to conclude that the Jamaat, the Jamiyat or the All-India Milli Council represent some form of a Muslim consensus. At the other end of the ideological spectrum, sections of the Muslim intelligentsia, both before and after independence, attributed different meanings to the 'covenant' with Indian nationalism, and reviewed their past from secular perspectives. They affirmed their faith in a democratic and secular polity, and fashioned their future in relation to the broad nationwide currents of socio-economic transformations. They rejected the world-view of the Jamaat and the Jamiyat on ideological grounds, since they understood the consequences of community-based politics. They were not numerous, and their views were sharply contested during the excitement of the Pakistan movement. But their position was vindicated after partition when India emerged out of the communal cauldron to set its house in order through a democratic and secular regime.

The Babri Masjid-Ramjanmabhumi controversy, followed by the demolition of the mosque, provided yet another historic opportunity to reiterate secular positions, oppose the mixing of religion with politics, and revive long-forgotten internal discussions on the efficacy of reforms and innovation, intellectual regeneration, and developing a secular temper. The nature and outcome of such dialogues, examined in the next chapter, will determine the direction of change and progress among Muslims.

The ebb and flow of Hindu nationalism will remain a vital factor in Indian politics. It will continue to tease and torment religious minorities, but the battle is not lost. The secular ground has been narrowed but it has not disappeared. The critical issue for religious minorities is whether they are adequately equipped and motivated to occupy this territory along with other democratic and secular tendencies. The turf is sticky but surely negotiable.

[131] *All India Milli Council*, p. 23.

9

AYODHYA AND ITS CONSEQUENCES:
REAPPRAISING MINORITY IDENTITY

'... Not only is the welfare of the [Muslim] community itself at stake,
now and for future generations. Also the histories both of India and of
Islam will in part turn on the success or failure of this community in
solving its present problems, on its skill and wisdom in meeting the
challenge of today.'

W.C. Smith (1957), *Islam in Modern History*, p. 260.

This study began with India's partition in August 1947; it concludes with
the demolition of the Babri Masjid on 6 December 1992. These two
significant events left deep scars on the country's fragile polity and
society. Both excited deep religious passions, caused widespread
violence, and deepened fear and anger among large sections of society.
Partition symbolised the triumph of 'Muslim nationalism'; the Babri
Masjid-Ramjanmabhumi affair struck at the roots of the democratic,
secular consensus envisaged by the 'founding fathers' of the constitution.
Mohammad Ali Jinnah manipulated political institutions and processes
adroitly and imaginatively to create a breach in the nationalist struggle;
the BJP, under L.K. Advani's spirited leadership, went on the offensive
with a strategy designed to polarise life in the country along antagonistic
lines.

What lay behind the Ayodhya catastrophe? Does it mark the end of
India's tryst with destiny, a snapping of ties with its secular past? Will the
votaries of Hindutva, a movement for Hindu self-assertion and nationhood, rewrite the nation's agenda, foist a Hindu *Rashtra* upon it, and
reduce religious minorities to the status of second-class citizens? If so,
what is the future for democracy and secularism?

Explanations are sought in the weakening of secular forces, and in the
Congress turning away from its own 'unique institutional and ideological
enterprise'. Some question the wisdom of that enterprise, which they see
as resting on mistaken assumptions and a distorted Western-oriented
version of secularism. Some talk of a 'Hindu backlash' against Muslim
'appeasement', the political nurturing of the minority vote-banks and the

dogged refusal of Muslims to join the 'national mainstream'. In this frame of reference, the Hindutva movement is seen as an expression of 'cultural nationalism' and 'Hindu awakening', which was stifled by 'pseudo-secularists' and the politics of minorityism.

These formulations are of more than academic concern. They have to be confronted by all those who have staked their future in preserving democratic and secular values. As the political scientist Rajni Kothari reminded his readers, it is a daunting task

....to meet the challenges posed by communalism, national chauvinism and religious fundamentalism which constitutes not a mere erosion of democratic and pluralist spaces but a total negation thereof in the name of a declared framework of ideas that seeks to change the very basis of the state.[1]

I

Any number of studies have traced the steady decline of secular values in public life since independence. The delinking of state and religion remains a distant dream; secularisation of state and society an ideal. Inter-community relations – whether Hindu-Muslim, Hindu-Sikh, Hindu-Christian – have steadily soured. Increasingly the political process is communalised and the secular path is strewn with new obstacles and impediments. Centrist and left forces have held their ground in isolated pockets, although their political base has shrunk over the years making them much more vulnerable to divisive ideologies. Socialist and communist parties stole the limelight in spearheading anti-communal campaigns until the 1980s. In recent years, however, they seem to have lost their moral and intellectual fibre. Organisations like 'Sahmat' and 'PMS' (People's Movement for Secularism) in Delhi operate on the fringes of urban life and are sustained by the professional élites. The record of the CPI (Marxist), the senior partner, is marred by a prolonged partnership with different Muslim League factions in Kerala in 1967-9 and from 1974-86. The alliance broke down when the Shah Bano episode persuaded the two wings – The All India Muslim League and the Indian Union Muslim League – to break ranks with the Marxists. The collapse of socialism in eastern Europe and the disintegration of the Soviet Union have proved to be the last straw. With depleted ideological resources and widespread demoralisation in the rank and file, the communist parties are tied to newly-emerging caste formations and dependent on them.

At the other end of the political spectrum, the Hindu parties secured major gains from the mid-1980s onwards. They did not hold the reins of

---

[1] *Pioneer*, 8 January 1993.

power in Delhi but influenced national and regional politics, and during the Masjid-Mandir controversy, enjoyed greater appeal than ever before. The *rath yatra* in early 1991, having released a flood of sublimated 'nationalist' energy, positioned the BJP as the party of Hindu resurgence, as Table 9.1 shows:[2]

Table 9.1. VOTE SHARE OF JANA SANGH/B.J.P. BY STATES, 1952-1991

	1952	1962	1971	1984	1989	1991
Andhra Pradesh	–	1.2	1.6	2.2	2.0	9.6
Assam	3.6	–	2.5	0.4	–	8.6
Bihar	0.4	2.3	12.1	6.9	11.7	16.0
Gujarat	–	1.4	2.2	18.6	30.5	50.4
Haryana	–	–	11.2	7.5	8.3	10.2
Himachal Pradesh	10.7	4.5	10.6	23.3	45.3	42.8
Karnataka	4.2	2.7	1.9	4.7	2.6	28.8
Kerala	–	0.7	1.4	1.8	4.5	4.6
Madhya Pradesh	4.9	19.9	33.6	30.0	39.7	41.9
Maharashtra	–	4.4	5.2	10.1	23.7	20.2
Orissa	–	–	0.2	1.2	1.3	9.5
Punjab	5.6	15.2	4.5	3.4	4.2	16.5*
Rajasthan	3.0	9.3	12.4	23.7	29.6	40.9
Tamil Nadu	–	0.1	0.1	0.1	0.3	1.7
Tripura	6.1	–	0.5	0.8	0.6	3.0
Uttar Pradesh	7.3	17.6	12.3	6.4	7.6	32.8
West Bengal	5.9	1.1	0.9	0.4	1.7	11.7
Delhi	25.9	32.7	29.6	18.8	26.2	40.2

* Election held in 1992.

Note: All figures represent percentage of valid votes secured by the Jana Sangh (1952-71) or BJP (1984-91) in the Lok Sabha election in respective states.

The RSS membership swelled over the years. Before December 1992 it consisted of 16,000 *shakhas*, but a year later the number had risen to 30,000.[3] The BJP made significant inroads in UP, once a Congress

---

[2] See the contributions of Manini Chatterji, Zoya Hasan and Ghanshyam Shah in Bidwai *et al.*, op. cit.; and Swapan Dasgupta, 'BJP Changes Gear: Putting Politics into Rambhakti', *Times of India*, 8 February 1991. For perspectives on the BJP, some from a 'left' standpoint, see the following articles in the *Times of India*: Praful Bidwai, 'Countering Majoritarianism: Another Approach to Ayodhya Dispute' (4 January 1991); Harish Khare, 'BJP's Failure: Relinquishing Its Political Role' (1 December 1992); Anikendra Nath Sen, 'BJP's Predicament' (4 August 1992); Rajdeep Sardesai, 'Not Ayodhya, But Anomie' (18 December 1992). Amulya Ganguli, Arvind N. Das and Dileep Padgaonkar, editor *Times of India*, also wrote excellent articles.

[3] Rajendra Singh, the RSS chief, quoted in *Pioneer*, 11 April 1994.

stronghold, and in Himachal Pradesh, Rajasthan and Madhya Bharat. The Shiv Sena emerged politically strong in Maharashtra, winning the assembly elections in combination with the BJP. A Shiv Sena chief minister assumed power in India's most important commercial and business metropolis, something unthinkable earlier. The Hindutva project, to which the BJP and the Shiv Sena are equally committed, is no longer an abstract article of faith of a handful of determined crusaders on the margins of political life. It is, so we were told by Swapan Dasgupta, on the verge of becoming the new *mantra* of civil society. Its appeal as an alternative pattern of political mobilisation is no longer confined to the northern cow-belt, but cuts across castes and regions.[4] So that the BJP, having led an uneasy life for nearly two decades, picked up a substantial vote in Bengal and occupied a vantage-point in as many as thirty of the 140 seats in Kerala, both states with a history of strong left and democratic movements.

Hindutva's pet project was to pull down the Babri mosque that had stood defiantly since 1528 in the sacred Hindu city. The aim was to erase a hated symbol of Mughal/Muslim rule. Sure enough, what took place on the banks of the Sarju river was nothing short of 'a massive assault on the very foundations of Indian culture and civilisation, its very identity, its *sanskriti* [civilisation], the very tradition and inheritance that the *kar sevaks* and their political leaders thought they were upholding.'[5] The scenes would return, like tormented ghosts, to haunt those who were at the graveside to witness the burial of a secular dream. Except for the diehards in Ayodhya and elsewhere, most people were sickened by the screams of exultation that accompanied each blow of a pickaxe, each thrust of a rod, and the collapse of early sixteenth-century domes.[6]

Yet what happened at Ayodhya did not bring immediate political rewards to the BJP. Nearly a year later, it suffered major electoral reverses in the November 1993 assembly elections in Himachal Pradesh, UP and Madhya Pradesh (Table 9.2). Kalyan Singh, BJP chief minister in UP, had stated that if his party got even one seat less than the 221 it held in the state – 'the cradle of Hindu cultural nationalism' – it would be tantamount to rejection of the *Mandir* movement. In the event, the party lost forty-four seats. Among UP's voters, Harijans are about 21 per cent, Yadavs over 17 per cent and Muslims nearly 19 per cent. Their votes had split in the past, but this time it was different: the Muslim-Dalit-backward castes combination sent the BJP packing.[7]

[4] Swapan Dasgupta, in *Sunday*, 28 February-6 March 1993, and his 'Disaster Averted: Sting has gone out of Mandal', *Times of India*, 29 September 1993.

[5] Rajni Kothari, in *EPW*, 19-26 December 1992, p. 2696.

[6] Dilip Awasthi in Ayodhya, *India Today*, 31 December 1992, p. 27.

[7] See Inderjit Badhwar, ibid., 15 December 1993, pp. 30-1; Sukumar Murlidharan, 'BJP the

Table 9.2. PARTY STANDING IN ELECTIONS
TO STATE ASSEMBLIES, 1993

	Total seats	Congress	BJP	Janata Dal	SP-BSP	Independent and others
Uttar Pradesh	425	28	177	27	176	14
		(46)	(211)	(91)	(42)	(14)
Rajasthan	200	76	95	6	–	22
		(50)	(85)	(54)		(11)
Himachal Pradesh	68	52	8	0	–	8
		(9)	(46)	(11)		(2)
Delhi	70	14	49	4	–	3

Note: Elections were held for 422 seats in UP and 199 seats in Rajasthan. In Madhya Pradesh the Congress won comfortably with 173 seats. Figures in brackets indicate previous party positions.

The physical collapse of the Babri Masjid thus became 'symbolic of the moral collapse of Hindu extremism.'[8] In the political outcome of the fateful event of 6 December 1992, 'the iconography was neither bloody, nor vengeful, nor characterised by any jackbooted march of bigotry. The prevailing images were those of serenity in which a quiet and peaceful transformation took most politicians by surprise.'[9] Middle-class sensibilities were outraged. Rioting in commercial and industrial trading centres halted business, trade and industry. Property worth Rs 3,000 crores was destroyed during the eighteen days following 6 December. Trading losses were estimated at Rs 1,000 crores, the loss of gross value of output of goods and services at Rs 1,250 crores, loss of export Rs 2,000 crores, and loss of tax revenue at Rs 150 crores.[10] The bomb blast in Bombay on 12 March 1993, which killed 317, placed the economic liberalisation agenda in jeopardy, exposing at the same time the volatile mix of class, culture and community that lurked under that city's seeming cosmopolitanism.

The belligerence of Hindu parties alarmed those who, because of their antipathy to the Congress, had hitched their fortunes to the rising BJP-RSS-VHP star.[11] Thus when tension mounted in early January 1993 due to ill-advised moves to 'recover' the Gyanwapi mosque adjoining the Kashi Vishwanath temple, the strong business community in Varanasi

loser: The Verdict from the Heartland', *Frontline*, 17 December 1993; Praful Bidwai, 'Hindutva's march Halted: Why the bubble has burst?', *Times of India*, 4 December 1993.

[8] Wahiduddin Khan, *Indian Muslims: The Need for a Positive Outlook*, p. 11.

[9] Badhwar, op. cit.

[10] Jim Masselos, 'The Bombay Riots of January 1993: The Politics of Urban Conflagration', *South Asia*, special issue, 17, 1994, p. 80.

[11] Dileep Padgaonkar, 'The Morning After: Grim Toll of Voodoo Politics', *Times of India*, 10 December 1992; Ramindar Singh, 'The God That Failed', *Pioneer*, 9 December 1992; Raj Verma, 'Cries for Sanity', *Times of India*, 13 December 1992.

decided that enough was enough. The Kashi Vyapar Mandal had backed the Ram *mandir* movement, but now switched to organising peace marches, and its 500,000 members fell in line.[12] In Surat the city's traditional defences asserted themselves after the January 1993 round of rioting ended. Business interests realised the overriding need for peace and order.[13] In Sidhpur, a communally-sensitive town in Gujarat, Muslim and Hindu leaders pledged to 'shun the path of violence'; the need for peace became clear to the residents after the town was engulfed in a communal frenzy after December 6.[14] Bhiwandi, an industrial township near Bombay, was rocked by Hindu-Muslim riots in 1970, 1974 and 1984, but remained quiet and peaceful in 1992-3. This was because *mohalla* committees brought people from different faiths together every fortnight and impressed on them the virtues of socio-economic interdependence.[15]

Another reason why the BJP failed to reap rich political dividends was that by playing its trump card – the Babri Masjid – with devastating effect, it had deprived its election campaign of some of its fire, energy and enthusiasm. With leaders in jail and the VHP banned from pursuing its activities, it was hard to keep the momentum going or gather additional votes. The anti-Muslim tide had also exhausted itself. More important, the caste-based political alignments in UP, India's most populous state, burst the Hindutva bubble for the time being. Mulayam Singh Yadav of the Samajvadi Party and Kanshi Ram, Bahujan Samaj Party leader, checkmated the Hindu millenarians who had spread the gospel that their brand of 'cultural nationalism' would steamroller caste and regional distinctions. In 1991 the Samajwadi Party and the BSP, with its base of backward castes, Dalits and Muslims, had together won just forty-two seats. Two years later the combine captured 176, just one short of the BJP's tally. In 1991 the vote-winning issues for the BJP were different – the lure of Hindutva, the demonisation of the then UP chief minister Mulayam Singh Yadav (the police had opened fire on the massive gathering in Ayodhya leading to some deaths), and the crusade against the V.P. Singh government for introducing reservations for backward castes in accordance with the Mandal Commission recommendations. In 1992 these issues lost their power. Swapan Dasgupta, the BJP's chief spokesman in the English-language press, conceded that the Hindutva wave had still not acquired 'the necessary degree of universality to emerge as the sole challenger to the post-1947 consensus. Regardless of the fact that the BJP remains the

---

[12] Quoted in Wahiduddin Khan, op. cit., p. 11.
[13] Sudhir Chandra, 'Of communal consciousness and communal violence: Impressions from post-riot Surat', *South Asia*, op. cit., pp. 57-8.
[14] *Times of India*, 18 January 1994.
[15] Rajdeep Sardesai, ibid., 10 December 1992.

potent challenger to the *status quo*, the elections have brought into the open alternative currents of change.'[16]

Finally, the Congress took the wind out of the BJP's sails by subtly appropriating the Ram symbol and turning it into an election plank. The building of a makeshift temple where the mosque had stood in which devotees could worship was permitted, and the prime minister failed to carry out his commitment, announced in the heat of the moment, to rebuild the demolished Babri Masjid. At a rally in Lucknow on 9 October 1993 he obliquely promised that that 'which was destroyed' would be rebuilt, without saying where, when and by whom. The prime ministerial signal was that a new Ram *mandir* would dominate the landscape in Ayodhya. People were left to guess where and by whom it would be built. Would it be by the *shankaracharyas*, high priests of Hinduism, or the *sangh parivar*?

It was comforting that Narasimha Rao placed the *sangh parivar* on the defensive and for the time being asserted his leadership. But in so doing he pitched the Congress into a contest with the BJP which offered a dangerous mix of appeals to religiosity and religious symbols with electoral politics. The ultimate Congress victory in two north Indian states was thus achieved by deploying 'an idiom of political discourse that is deeply conservative, socially illiberal [and] politically retrograde,'[17] Swapan Dasgupta sensed this danger in early 1992. 'If the Congress succeeds in garnishing its stability platform with some placatory gestures to Hindus, the BJP may find that euphoric Ram *bhakti* [devotion] does not substantially translate into a substantial increase in votes.'[18]

In 1994 an ominous trend developed in the BJP's strategy – a move towards aggression and militancy. 'The tiger is not going to change its stripes. Merely add a few more for cosmetic improvement.'[19] That was the message that followed the BJP's electoral slump. On 11-13 March the Akhil Bharatiya Pratinidhi Sabha of the RSS met at Nagpur. The VHP-inspired Dharma Sansad congregated at Hardwar, the holy city on the Ganga river, to renew its pledge to build the Ram temple. On 7-9 April, just three days after the Hardwar conclave, the BJP 'think tank' met at the 'Tiger's Den' in Sariska (Rajasthan) to define *Ram Rajya* and Hindutva in terms of nation-state. Advani made it clear that Ayodhya would remain

---

[16] Swapan Dasgupta, *Times of India*, 5 January 1994.

[17] Praful Bidwai, 'Low-Intensity Democracy: High Cost of Indian Conservatism', ibid., 12 October 1993.

[18] Swapan Dasgupta, 'BJP Changes Gear: Putting Politics into Rambhakti', ibid., 8 February 1991; Harish Khare, 'A Congress-BJP Entente: Yesterday's Heresies, Today's Wisdom', ibid., 6 August 1991.

[19] Yubaraj Ghimre, 'Ram is Still Best', *India Today*, 31 December 1993, p. 36.

the BJP's 'ideological mascot' and that Hindutva, the most distinctive feature of its ideology, was the 'short cut' to cultural nationalism.[20]

Soon after the Sariska gathering, the Hindu holy men (*sants* and *sadhus*) went fishing in troubled waters. Amid the chanting of Vedic hymns and the ringing of temple bells, Swami Muktanda Saraswati, general secretary of Akhil Bharatiya Sant Samiti, threatened to 'liberate' temples at Mathura and Varanasi. The newly-elevated RSS chief, Rajendra Singh, warned that his cadres would not rest until their 'three most sacred places' were returned to them. He endorsed the VHP's Dharam Sansad's organisation of *yatras* and its proposed occupation of the Ayodhya site in November 1994. Around the same time Ashok Singhal, the VHP's general secretary, planned *yatras* and *yagna* to stir the 'Hindu conscience' and stimulate them to grab the sacred land acquired by the central government in Ayodhya.[21]

The extraordinary build-up in March-April 1994 was designed to galvanise demoralised cadres, rescue local and regional politicians from the political wilderness, and renew the otherwise receding prospect of a Hinduised future – as the RSS supremo said with disconcerting candour. The temple agitation, he declared, was as much political as religious, and would therefore be synchronised with the forthcoming elections to ten state assemblies. He had already planned raising the number of RSS *shakhas* from 26,000 to 40,000, to be attended by over one million people. The following newspaper comment was pertinent:

It is almost as if they are seeking a re-enactment of the 1990 developments in Ayodhya in which Mr Mulayam Singh Yadav ordered the police to disperse the crowds of *sadhus*. The resultant violence paid rich dividends to the BJP and the VHP and the attempt now appears to be to recreate a similar situation. This is a dangerous doctrine and it suggests that the Rashtriya Swayamsevak Sangh and its front bodies are prepared to go to any length to convert Ayodhya into a political issue once again. The gloves are off, but it is by no means certain that the agitation will succeed the second time round.[22]

Political commentators wrote the BJP's obituary in 1993 on the strength of certain old-fashioned assumptions, but the party eventually capitalised on factionalism in the Congress and its unpopularity among Muslims to bounce back with major electoral victories in Gujarat and Maharashtra in February-March 1995. Although it performed poorly in Bihar, it was clear that, more than ever before, the BJP-RSS combination commanded the allegiance of millions and exercised, according to its staunch adherents, 'an ideological veto in Indian politics.'[23]

[20] *Pioneer*, 12 April 1994.

[21] Ibid., 14 April 1994. Interview with Ashok Singhal, *The Telegraph*, 4 April 1994; Saroj Negi, 'Sharpening the Hindutva Edge', *Pioneer*, 17 April 1994.

[22] *Pioneer*, 19 April 1994.

The BJP's onward march and the triumph of Hindu nationalism have had differing interpretations.[24] The Ayodhya episode, too, has been analysed in several different perspectives.[25] The debates are rich and illuminating, though sometimes marred by acerbity and polemic. In general, however, the Marxists, modernists, post-modernists and exponents of the subaltern interpretation, with all the shades of difference between them, underline their concern for the erosion of democratic and secular values. They have a line of argument on the state, the decline of institutions and the collapse of the Nehruvian consensus which is unambiguous; it is also contentious. They feel anguished at escalating communal violence, which has brought death and destruction to the Muslims. They have traced the extraordinary upsurge in Hindu nationalist activity and its appeal in certain quarters, although their explanations are often theoretical rather than based on reality. Many facets of Hindu nationalism have been explored, but we are only dimly aware of the energy that pulses behind the concerted endeavour to create a Hindu nation through a cultural and intellectual homogenisation of Hindu society. There is an important lesson to be drawn from Advani's statement in early 1992 that 'we are not a *dharmik sabha* [religious body]. We are primarily a political party'[26] – as from similar statements which make it clear that at the heart of the Hindutva philosophy is the repudiation of the nationalist legacy and the agenda of Hindu-Muslim reconciliation outlined by the 'founding fathers' of the constitution. The chief target is secular discourse, the hallmark of the Nehru era. The planned assault on the Babri Masjid was therefore intended as a big jolt to the secular ideal through a process of 'Hindu reawakening'.

In the ebb and flow of Hindu-Muslim relations, the vandalism at Ayodhya represented a regressive current, in which brazen intimidation was seen to triumph in full view of the state machinery. 'To say that the faith in a professed secular state's capacity and its political will to uphold the constitution is rudely shaken', commented Hasan Suroor of *The Hindu*, 'may be construed as a knee-jerk reaction, but there is no doubt that it would take a long time to restore the sense of confidence not just among the Muslims but the minorities across the board.' The task of liberal Muslims in the circumstances becomes much more difficult, caught, as they are, between their community's intolerance and Hindu

[23] Swapan Dasgupta, 'With Foes Like These', *Times of India*, 1 September 1993.

[24] Sumit Sarkar, 'The Fascism of the Sangh Parivar', *EPW*, 30 January 1993; Jan Breman, 'The Hindu Right; Comparisons with Nazi Germany', *Times of India*, 15 March 1993 and his 'Anti-Muslim Pogrom in Surat', *EPW*, 17 April 1993, pp. 737-41; Achin Vanaik, 'Situating Threat of Hindu Nationalism: Problems with Fascist Paradigm', *EPW*, 9 July 1994.

[25] S. Gopal (ed.), *Anatomy of a Confrontation*, op. cit; *South Asia*, special issue, 17, 1994.

[26] Quoted in Swapan Dasgupta, 'BJP Changes Gear', *Times of India*, 8 February 1991.

communalism. 'Next time around, his plea for reason is likely to carry far less conviction with the Muslim hotheads.' The scenario for every secular Indian was grim. 'As for the fence-sitters they may enjoy the best of both worlds in the short-term but when history does its sums they will have to account a lot for the missing numbers which made it possible for the regressive forces to grow.'[27]

The following sections draw on Hasan Suroor's important observation to underline two specific themes: the lessons drawn by educated Muslims from Hindu mobilisation campaigns in general, and the variety of responses to the demolition of the Ayodhya mosque in particular. The themes overlap, but need separate examination. Our focus, however, is on the liberal and secular discourse and its expression in the aftermath of Ayodhya, an aspect that is important for Muslims not as a religious collectivity but as equal citizens in a plural society. It also has great relevance to the survival of a secular regime in India.

II

'1993 has been a year of meetings for me ... Most of the people I met seemed to have lost their optimism about the way this country is going to develop. But I differ from them. I am still full of hope for India's future ... Have we forgotten, perhaps, that even the blackest of nights is followed by the sunrise? ... In a world ... in which day will quite unfailingly follow night every twenty-four hours ad infinitum, how is it possible that the darkness of despair will not be dispelled by the light of hope?'

— Maulana Wahiduddin Khan (1994)

No doubt this is a comforting thought;[28] however, the Maulana's optimism was misplaced. For most Muslims the initial trauma gave way to a deep sense of betrayal. 'Harassed, humiliated and preyed upon, the post-December Indian Muslim finds himself in a twilight terrain where hope and despair live in uneasy truce.'[29] Scenes of the mosque being pulled down, relayed live on television, offended religious susceptibilities. The post-partition generation had witnessed nothing like it

---

[27] 'A Noble Dream Shattered', *Hindu*, in *From the Press: The Ayodhya Story*, edited by Ali Baquer (Delhi: Media Impact, 1993), p. 128.

[28] The Maulana was, needless to say, sensitive to what happened on December 6. He described the demolition as a 'calamity' and lamented that 'our journey towards progress as a nation had foundered in some impassable quagmire.' Wahiduddin Khan, op. cit., pp. 121, 140.

[29] Mohd. Zeyaul Haq, 'The Muslim Psyche in a Twilight Terrain', *Nation and the World* (Delhi: fortnightly), January 1993, p. 8.

before, nor did they expect to see such a spectacle in secular Bharat. 'The midsummer night's dream that India dreamt 45 years ago clearly lies in tatters. This was certainly not the dawn we had been waiting for.'[30] 'Do you know why the demolition of the Babri Masjid disturbed me?', asked Shabana Azmi, the famous film actress and a key figure in the anti-communal front formed after 6 December. 'Quite apart from all the obvious reasons, I found a large number of people – persons you and I would normally term secular – applauding the event. For the first time the realisation hit me that barely below the surface, prejudice was very deeply ingrained.'[31]

The holocaust in Bombay, Surat and Bhopal proved the hollowness of theories about India's cosmopolitan metropolis, the confluence of cultures and the supposed meeting of minds that takes place through shared work and living. Scores of riot-torn cities reinforced the chilling message that the police and paramilitary forces, with their abysmal record of violence and vandalism in Moradabad, Meerut and Bhagalpur, were not guardians of law and order but perpetrators of crimes against the Muslims. Several moves were afoot, in Bombay, Surat, Ahmedabad and elsewhere, to collect arms and set up vigilance and 'defence' squads. An underground group – Al-Mujahidin – circulated pamphlets in Munger (Bihar) calling on Muslims to take up arms in self-defence. 'From Delhi to Mathura to Ayodhya to Kerala, a section of Muslim youth, inspired by extremist ideology, sees it as a possible cure to the community's problems.'[32] 'Defence Leagues' mushroomed in Aligarh, Meerut and Muzaffarnagar. The defunct Adam Sena, run by the deputy Imam of Delhi's Juma Masjid, was energised. 'What would happen if even 15 lakh out of 15 crore Muslims take up arms and turned terrorist out of frustration?', warned a front-page editorial in the *Azimabad Express*, a Patna-based Urdu daily.[33] This was not the only message from Ayodhya and Bombay. According to a cynical reading,

Muslims must accept the fact of being in a minority refusing to be swayed by the 'radicals' of their own community and provoked by the militants on the other side. This is not the first time that posterity would be paying the price for the actions of its fraternity or ancestors and to go along with the logic of history is not necessarily an act of cowardice. There is a worse option: to do what the ostrich does – refuse to look up and live permanently in the fragile world of illusion.[34]

---

[30] Hasan Suroor, op. cit.

[31] *Communalism Combat*, November-December 1994, p. 2.

[32] *Frontline*, 5 November 1993.

[33] Quoted in *India Today*, 15 February 1993, p. 76.

[34] Hasan Suroor, op. cit.

III

'Qaum kya cheez hai qaumaun ki imamat kya hai
Is ko kya samjhen ye bechare do-rakat ke Imam.'

[What's a nation? How to lead.
Poor mullah! That's beyond his creed.]

What about the religio-political leadership which organised, conducted and led the campaign to defend the Babri Masjid? First, the political base of the Jamiyat al-ulama, the Jamaat-i Islami and the Muslim Personal Law Board is – contrary to several exaggerated assessments – strictly confined to the Urdu-speaking urban Muslims of UP and Bihar, the traditional strongholds of the Muslim League in the 1930s and '40s, and for this reason they have generated little enthusiasm for their pet projects outside north India. Urdu is not spoken by most Muslims across the Vindhyas. The Aligarh Muslim University is a distant institution, not a symbol of their hopes and aspirations. The *ulama* of Deoband's Dar al-ulum and Lucknow's Nadwat al-ulama command respect but are not regarded as the sole arbiters of 'Muslim destiny' to command automatic allegiance. Ayodhya's Babri Masjid carries no emotive appeal or sanctity for people whose history and cultural trajectory have run a different course from the Urdu-speaking élites in the Indo-Gangetic belt. Haider Ali and Tipu Sultan, rather than Balban or Akbar, form part of the cultural and historical legacy of the Karnataka Muslims; mosques in Mysore and Seringapatam and not at Ayodhya have been focal points of their devotion. The Babri Masjid, an otherwise dormant north Indian symbol, only acquired meaning for them after and not before its destruction on December 6.

Anwar Ali Khan, the Prabhani-based convenor of the minorities cell of the Maharashtra Pradesh Congress Committee, concluded in October 1992 that the fracas over Ayodhya was far removed from the mind of the common Muslims. His conclusion was based on discussions with thousands of Muslims from Maharashtra.[35] Life went on as usual at Nagore, a tiny village on the outskirts of Nagapattinam in Madras: when most north Indian states were hotly debating the fate of the Babri Masjid, people there, Hindus and Muslims alike, gathered at the local mosque, which was constructed in memory of a Sufi saint who travelled all the way from Manickapur near Ayodhya to settle at this place.[36] Likewise, Sheikh Chinn Kasim in Karnataka, a devotee of Lord Ram and goddess Saraswati, continued playing the *nadaswaram* musical instrument. 'I do not know anything about secularism and communalism,' he declared. 'All I know

---

[35] Quoted in Javed Anand, 'Raw Deal for Muslims', *Sunday Observer* (Bombay), 7-13 November 1993.

[36] *Asian Age* (Bombay), 27 April 1993.

is that, like my forefathers, I am also dedicated to Lord Rama and Goddess Saraswati. My music is everything to me.'[37]

The *ulama* ignored these trends but were surely aware of them and sensitive to them too. They spoke in different voices, revealing sharp divisions within their ranks. Some insisted on rebuilding the Babri mosque at its original location, called for a boycott of the Republic Day festivities on 26 January 1993, and denounced the prime minister as being hand in glove with the communal forces.[38] But most were seized by a very real sense of fright. Men with pro-Congress leanings, such as Syed Abul Hasan Ali Nadwi and the Jamiyat al-ulama president Maulana Syed Asad Madani, reacted cautiously. The Jamiyat, whose headquarters at New Delhi's Bahadur Shah Zafar Marg wore a forlorn look, took its own time to convene a formal meeting, and when it finally met in early October 1993, it was a quiet affair and there were no calls for strikes and demonstrations. The key actors proposed and adopted mild resolutions, and indeed Asad Madani asked Muslims to vote for secular Congress candidates in the elections to the UP and Madhya Pradesh assemblies in November that year.[39] Syed Abdullah Bukhari, Imam of Delhi's Juma Masjid, kept an unexpectedly low profile. 'Restraint and patience', commented a correspondent in the *Pioneer*, 'are the dominant response of the traditional leadership, and this is evident even from the speeches of the Juma Masjid's Imam in the week following the demolition.' His political advisers had reportedly counselled him against taking a confrontational posture.[40]

The predicament of the Jamiyat, as also the BMAC, was similar to the politically active *ulama* of the early 1920s. The Khilafat bubble was burst by the Turks themselves; the Khalifa-Sultan, a figure of veneration in parts of India, was bundled out unceremoniously from his palace in Istanbul. Having whipped up religious hysteria through sheaves of *fatawa*, the *ulama* were now discredited in the eyes of the common man, who had made such large but futile sacrifices to save a fading symbol of the past. Poor Muslims who undertook the *hijrat* to Afghanistan to defend the honour of Islam were thrown out of the territory by its Muslim ruler, and many died on the trek home. Those who survived discovered that all was not well with the Islamic *umma*. They were comforted by the belief that *dar al-Islam* was no more than an illusion created by theologians.

The 'Save Babri Masjid Campaign', like the Central Khilafat Committee formed in March 1919, ran its course. Religious fervour was roused and promises were made to save the Babri Masjid and hotheads raised the

---

[37] *Times of India*, 18 January 1994.
[38] Ibid., 6 October 1993.
[39] Ibid., 13 November 1993.
[40] Ejaz Ashraf, in *Pioneer*, 20 December 1992.

communal temperature to match the zealotry of the RSS and VHP workers. Muslims turned up in large numbers in small towns to listen to leaders making fiery and intemperate speeches. They cheered and raised slogans, offered money, joined demonstrations, and faced police batons and went to jail for defying orders prohibiting them. The bizarre scenes were reminiscent of the Khilafat days.

The outcome, too, conformed to the familiar picture of a campaign petering out without achieving its target. The energies of the enthusiasts were dissipated. When the dénouement came on that afternoon of 6 December, life almost came to a standstill. Those who flocked to meetings were dumbfounded. The *sherwani*-clad leaders, who had invoked everyone from Imam Husain to Maulana Mohamed Ali to raise the heat of their speeches, were nowhere to be found, and they lost face with their followers. There was not much to look forward to, no great cause to be espoused in mosques and marketplaces. It was the beginning of the end for many publicists who had made their careers out of the Babri Masjid issue.

It was much the same for the tall poppies in the BMAC. They could still gather crowds, adopt benign resolutions and keep up the pretence of negotiating with ruling and opposition parties, but their credibility was at its lowest ebb since independence.[41] The venerable *alim* of Nadwa was snubbed; others were denounced for their many miscalculations and their militancy and belligerence over the last few years.[42] Their appeal for patience and restraint, as Hasan Suroor commented,

....has come a little too late in the day. [It] sounds like the devil preaching the scriptures in a moment of fright and confusion. It is their belligerence which, to some extent, has brought the situation to such a pass. If the community is to move forward, it will have to distance itself from the *mullahs* and the self-serving political operators who have brought it to the brink of self-destruction.[43]

The *ulama*, cool but obstinate, were not prepared to give up and tried to galvanise their followers by insisting that the Babri Masjid be rebuilt. But the move was ill-fated as well as being unpopular. 'This is not the question of application of *Shariat*,' declared Iqbal Masud, the Bombay-based writer. 'This is a question of survival of Muslims.'[44] Saeed Naqvi, a leading columnist, agreed. 'So far tokenism has not stood us in good stead. In fact it has nurtured the monster against which we must wage war.'[45] Saiyid Hamid, Aligarh's former vice-chancellor, gave a stern

---

[41] N.S. Waziri, a High Court lawyer, quoted in *India Today*, 31 October 1993, p. 74.

[42] Ibid., 15 February 1993.

[43] Hasan Suroor, op. cit.

[44] *Pioneer*, 12 April 1993.

[45] Saeed Naqvi in ibid., 20 December 1992. Further references to his writings, unless

warning. Muslims should not be dragged into the debris of a mosque which the Congress government failed to save. If the nation cared for Muslims, 'let it resolve the problems relating to their education and employment.'[46] Imtiaz Ahmad, a sociologist at Delhi's Jawaharlal Nehru University and the moving spirit behind the 'Muslim Intelligentsia Meet', advocated an alternative strategy 'to cut out future losses by wisdom, forbearance and foresight'.[47]

For well over a year after 6 December, the organisations of the *ulama* were battered by their own followers and riven with dissensions. The Muslim Personal Law Board, headed by Maulana Syed Abul Hasan Ali Nadwi, was licking its wounds. The Babri Masjid Movement Coordination Committee, run by Shahabuddin and the Indian Union Muslim League president, Ebrahim Sulaiman Sait, was in disarray. In the following months the League split up and Sulaiman Sait floated his own party.[48] The BMAC – a breakaway group consisting of Salahuddin Owaisi of the Ittehadul-Muslimeen, Zafaryab Jilani (a Lucknow lawyer), and Syed Ahmad Bukhari (the deputy Imam of Delhi's Juma Masjid) – was plagued with differences. The senior Imam, with his penchant for *fatawa*, was marginalised. His deputy's call to boycott the Republic Day celebrations evoked no response. As a journalist reported with exaggerated optimism, it proved 'the losing grip of the old theocracies over the mind' of the Muslim populace and the general distrust among the Muslims of anybody who raises the Babri Masjid issue at this stage'.[49]

The ramshackle coalition they were seeking to build proved unworkable. The BMAC and the Muslim Personal Law Board produced the familiar noises but were not strong enough to operate from a vantage-point in the political spectrum. Despite the initial backing from Rajiv Gandhi and later from V.P. Singh in the Janata Dal, they were not in a suitable position to bargain with the ruling parties or extract concessions from them. With its fate sealed, the collapse of the coalition became imminent. Javed Habib mistakenly believed that the BMAC, of which he was convenor, was earnest in its aim to solve the Babri Masjid issue, but discovered that 'beyond wrangling on minor issues and hair-splitting, the organisation was incapable of doing anything.'[50] Habib did not have a

otherwise indicated, are drawn from his *Reflections of an Indian Muslim* (Delhi: Har-Anand, 1992). This book is a collection of articles published in the Delhi and Lucknow editions of the *Pioneer*.

[46] We have quoted from his collection of essays *Education and Modernisation: Two Wheels of Muslim Regeneration* (Hyderabad: Madina Publications, n.d.), and *Aazmaish ki Ghari* (Delhi: Maktaba Jamia, 1993).

[47] Imtiaz Ahmad, *Times of India*, 24 May 1993.

[48] *Pioneer*, 12 February, 17 April 1994.

[49] 'A Fatal Move', ibid., 12 April 1993.

[50] Quoted in *Frontline*, 5 November 1993, p. 114.

secular image, although post-Ayodhya politics led him to play the tune of a liberal-minded patriot. He was duly rewarded with membership of the Minorities Commission.

In sharp contrast to their muted reaction to the demolition of the Masjid, the *ulama* came into their own in countering the *fatwa* of the *muftis* of the Ahl-i Hadith school, who declared in June 1993 that the popular practice of pronouncing *talaq* thrice in one sitting was un-Islamic.[51] Theologians like Maulana Syed Abul Hasan Ali Nadwi raised a furore: they talked of 'Muslim identity' being endangered, and raised the bogey of an 'imperialist conspiracy' to divide Muslims and to enact and enforce a uniform civil code 'under the pretext of differences among different Islamic schools of thought on the issue of three *talaqs*'.[52] The Jamiyat al-ulama struck a similar note in early October, denouncing the enemies of Islam. The Muslim Personal Law Board rejected any form of interference and insisted on upholding and preserving a 'separate Islamic identity'.[53] The faint stirrings of liberalism in the pronouncements of some Ahl-i Hadith *ulama* were thus scotched by the heavy hand of orthodoxy. Their staunch opposition revealed that the pro-changers 'easily erred on the side of optimism'.[54]

As if this were not enough, at the Muslim Personal Law Board meeting in Jaipur on 9 October 1993 the phalanx of orthodoxy resolved to establish Islamic courts, as was done in parts of Bihar during the Khilafat movement, and dispatch mobile judicial units to rural areas.[55] Such a court surfaced in April 1994 at Okhla in south Delhi, the first in the planned string of courts to be set up across the country to sort out disputes according to the Quran.[56] The clear implication was that by having recourse to such a move, injudicious and ill-timed as it was, sections of the *ulama* were trying to cover up their mistakes in conducting the Babri

---

[51] *Nation of the World* devoted a major part of its 16 August 1993 issue to the controversy. The consensus at the day-long meeting of the 'Muslim Intelligentsia Meet' was that making the threefold divorce pronouncement in one sitting violated Quranic injunctions. The meeting, chaired by Imtiaz Ahmad, called upon the Muslim Personal Law Board to convene a conference of Islamic jurists and intellectuals and provide an authentic 'interpretation on the issue keeping in mind the ground realities'. Organisers of the 'Muslim Intelligentsia Meet' published their own document on the subject.

[52] *Times of India*, 5, 10 September and 6 October 1993; *Pioneer*, 30 September 1993.

[53] *Times of India*, 9, 11 October 1993.

[54] Sakina Yusuf Khan, ibid., 16 July 1993, and her articles on 2 February and 22 August 1993; see also Amulya Ganguli, 'Issue of Fundamentalism: Challenge for the Liberal Muslims', ibid., 12 July 1993.

[55] Ibid., 11 October 1993.

[56] *The Telegraph* (Calcutta), 9 April 1993. I am grateful to Mahesh Rangarajan for this information.

Masjid agitation. In the process they threatened to encroach on secular spaces.

In the long run the decision to establish Islamic courts, defended by legal experts like Tahir Mahmood of the University of Delhi and condemned by others as 'a retrogressive step',[57] was sure to isolate Muslims from the judicial processes and deny their women the limited protection they received from secular courts. Also, it would provide ammunition to Hindu communalists for whipping up fears that minorityism was running amok, flouting restrictions imposed in the interest of normal state functioning.[58] In fact, the conduct of several high-profiled *ulama*, especially those connected with Nadwa and Deoband, gave the unmistakable impression that the real rift after 6 December 1992 was no longer between 'secularists' and 'traditionalists' *per se*, but rather between past-oriented people on both sides. As Javed Anand wrote indignantly in the *Sunday Observer* of Bombay:

If the spirit and message of Islam concerning the status of women were even remotely to approximate to what the *ulama* claim it is, I, a Muslim standing on the threshold of the twenty-first century, would be ashamed of calling myself a Muslim.[59]

IV

With different sorts of pressures mounting after December 1992, the spirit of Islam, the status of women and the future of India's Muslims were among the several different themes being hotly debated in Urdu newspapers, magazines and journals. It was natural that the favourite forum for such discussion should be the Urdu press, which since the last quarter of the nineteenth century has served readers in large tracts of UP and Bihar and in places like Hyderabad, Bangalore and Madras city. Urdu newspapers have mirrored both the intensity of emotions over certain issues and the diversity of intellectual and political trends. In their nascent stage, the leading ones debated and moulded public opinion on wide-ranging issues. The *Tahzib al-Akhlaq* and the *Aligarh Institute Gazette*, for instance, received contributions and comment from those eminent in and learned in political, literary, cultural and theological matters. In general, they reflected their founders' breadth of vision and served as powerful vehicles for promoting Syed Ahmad Khan's passion for secular education, modernism and reform. Admirers read them to be stimulated, and

---

[57] Vinkitesh Ramakrishnan, in *Frontline*, 5 November 1993.

[58] Asghar A. Engineer, *Seminar* (415), January 1994, pp. 66, 67.

[59] Javed Anand, in *Sunday Observer*, 4-10 July 1993.

critics did so to condemn. They were thus widely read on both sides of the divide.

The *Urdu-e Moalla* (Aligarh), *Zamindar* (Lahore), *Al-Hilal* (Calcutta) and *Hamdard* (Delhi) were milestones in the history of Urdu journalism, inheriting Syed Ahmad's intellectual legacy though not his politics of subservience to the raj. They were run by men of extraordinary talent and energy, liberal in outlook and receptive to new ideas. Their editors, some of whom attained prominent positions in public life, were fortified by faith and Islamic conviction, but they were free of religious traditionalism. They departed from their own traditional upbringing and environment, which was often influenced by a rigid interpretation of religious observances, to call for a modified outlook towards existing dogmas and beliefs. They rebuked theologians for their *taqlid*, or unquestioning conformity to scriptures, made readers aware of rationalist and secular currents sweeping across the world, and stressed the need to exercise *ijtehad*. They stressed, just as their mentor Syed Ahmad had done with such remarkable tenacity, that Western education opened up new avenues of progress and advancement without therefore being inimical to Islamic tenets. Thus Abul Kalam Azad rejected *taqlid*, 'the greatest hindrance to human intellectual progress', and insisted that the foundation of belief should be on knowledge and not on *taqlid* and inheritance.[60]

Their writings had an electrifying effect. The *Urdu-e Moalla*, edited by Hasrat Mohani, was compulsory reading at the Aligarh College. The *Zamindar* of Zafar Ali Khan was the staple political diet of the Urdu-reading public of Lahore: its circulation rose from 1,200 in 1910 to 15,000 in 1913. 'Muslims were set on fire' by the passionate writings of Azad. The demand for the *Al-Hilal* was so great that, within three months all the old issues had to be reprinted. At one stage its circulation exceeded 25,000. The English *Comrade* and Urdu *Hamdard*, published by Mohamed Ali, were also successful. 'No paper has so much influence with the students as the *Comrade*, and no individual has the authority over them which is exercised by Mohamed Ali,' the UP government reported. When, at the beginning of his internment in 1915, Mohamed Ali wanted to stop the *Hamdard*, a young journalist begged him not to. 'I do not approve of your decision and I do not think many will... You can't imagine what the loss of *Hamdard* will mean to us – the Musalmans.'[61]

Urdu journalism lost many of its stars to Pakistan. Newspapers lost their readership in Sind and Punjab, and the future of the language itself hung in the balance. Yet Urdu survived on its own strength, and because the language of Mir, Ghalib, Mir Anis, Brij Narain Chakbast, Prem Chand, Iqbal, Firaq and Krishan Chander was spoken not only by the Muslims

---

[60] Douglas, *Abul Kalam Azad: An Intellectual Biography*, p. 76.

[61] Mushirul Hasan, *Nationalism and Communal Politics*, pp. 74-5.

but also by large numbers of Hindus in northern and central India, including the Kashmiri Pandits and the Kayasths. Urdu newspapers did not fare badly (Tables 9.3, 9.4, 9.5), although their non-Muslim readership steadily declined. One could still find people reading the *Qaumi Awaaz* or the *Urdu Blitz* both in bazaars and among the academic and liberal establishments.[62]

Table 9.3. CIRCULATION OF NEWSPAPERS, 1958
(× *1,000*)

Language	Dailies		Weeklies		Fortnightles	
	No. of news-papers	Circulation	No. of news-papers	Circulation	No. of news-papers	Circulation
English	52	9,86	112	9,66	62	3,44
Hindi	73	5,45	233	6,21	60	1,81
Assamese	1	5	3	23	2	2
Bengali	5	1,92	91	1,93	33	1,34
Gujarati	28	2,69	67	3,58	34	46
Kannada	10	1,11	27	80	5	24
Malayalam	21	3,04	18	1,32	6	34
Marathi	34	3,49	86	3,62	9	25
Oriya	4	44	5	9	5	7
Punjabi	9	33	21	32	1	9
Sanskrit	–	–	2	2	–	–
Tamil	17	3,38	34	4,90	29	2,62
Telugu	7	99	38	2,08	23	65
Urdu	44	1,99	1,17	1,95	24	46
Bilingual	12	1,28	76	1,56	18	29
Multilingual	–	–	12	13	6	2
Others	4	4	16	29	4	9
Total	321	36,06	958	38,69	3,21	12,19

Source: Annual Report of the Registrar of Newspapers (Ministry of Information and Broadcasting: Government of India, 1958), p. 33.

The Khilafat movement was the high point in Urdu journalism. Newspapers reached out to large numbers of people and stirred in them nationalist/pan-Islamic sentiments on an unprecedented scale. The post-Ayodhya situation, on the other hand, was somewhat of an anti-climax. The rhetoric of the Khilafat days, having given inspiration to political activism, was a thing of the past. The events of December 1992 demanded sobriety and cool, balanced assessment. Largely, the Urdu-language proprietors and editors met these standards. Readers were allowed to let

[62] *Qaumi Awaaz*, 21, 22 June 1993. For a scathing critique of the Muslim-owned press, see Wahiduddin Khan, op. cit., pp. 69-80.

out their steam. Poems – an effective medium for expressing outraged feelings – were periodically published lamenting the decline of Muslims, along with essays on their dismal future, on the demise of secularism, on police brutalities in Bombay, Surat and Bhopal, on the government's inept handling of the Babri Masjid imbroglio, and on the growing menace of Hindu 'fundamentalism'. Some contributions provoked useful and meaningful exchanges in the correspondence column,[63] although some others wrote in highly emotive and sometimes venomous language. However, most commentators and analysts favoured moderation.[64]

Table 9.4. CIRCULATION PATTERN OF URDU NEWSPAPERS, 1988

Circulation	No.			Circulation (× 1,000)		
	Dailies	*Periodicals*	*Total*	*Dailies*	*Periodicals*	*Total*
75,001 to 99,999	–	1	1	–	88	88
50,001 to 75,000	1	1	2	61	62	123
25,001 to 50,000	3	3	6	95	117	212
15,001 to 25,000	14	7	21	241	119	360
5,001 to 15,000	79	52	131	949	505	1,454
2,001 to 5,000	5	31	36	18	97	115
2,000 and below	8	107	115	14	170	184
Total	110	202	312	1,378	1,158	2,536

Source: Press in India 1989 (Delhi: Publications Division, Ministry of Information and Broadcasting, n.d.), p. 206.

A noteworthy feature was the reflective writings of individuals who tried to set the parameters of an enlightened debate among Muslims.[65]

---

[63] For example, *Karawan* (Delhi), 1-15 June 1993, and Masoom Moradabadi (ed.), *Shaheed Babri Masjid* (Delhi, 1993).

[64] See *Mediawatch on Communalism* (Delhi), pp. 11-13, and Shafey Kidwai, 'Urdu Press: From Crusading Zeal to Rhetoric Invectives', *Pioneer*, 11 April 1994.

[65] There is a long list of people who subscribe to this view. Prominent among them are M.J. Akbar, Nehru's biographer, founder-editor of the *Telegraph* (Calcutta) and currently editor of the *Asian Age*; Asghar A. Engineer, the spirited Bohra reformer, author of numerous books and regular contributor to the *Economic and Political Weekly* and the *Hindu*. A civil engineer turned social activist, he has relentlessly pursued the secular cause. His critique of Muslim obscurantism, based on his reading of religious texts, is pregnant with new ideas; Saiyid Hamid, retired civil servant and founder of the Hamdard Education Society in Delhi; Badruddin Tyabji, retired diplomat and Aligarh University's former vice-chancellor; A.G. Noorani, noted Bombay lawyer, author and contributor to the *Economic and Political Weekly*, the weekly *Frontline* and the daily *Statesman*; and Danial Latifi, senior advocate of the Supreme Court and commentator on matters of religious reforms. The list of journalists is a long one, and includes Faraz Ahmad, Javed Ansari, Javed Anand, Shamsul Islam, Seema Mustafa, Saeed Naqvi, Hasan Suroor and Rasheed Talib.

Table 9.5. NUMBER OF NEWSPAPERS, 1991

Languages	Daily	Tri-weekly, bi-weekly	Weekly	Fortnightly	Monthly	Quarterly	Others	Annual	Total
Hindi	1,381	103	4,969	1,652	2,056	344	109	19	10,633
English	225	18	581	462	2,020	979	556	121	4,962
Assamese	9	2	45	27	38	10	7	1	139
Bengali	71	11	496	359	561	340	112	8	1,958
Gujarati	67	5	263	111	378	47	31	9	911
Kannada	178	5	268	153	361	33	14	2	1,014
Konkani[a]	0	0	0	0	0	0	0	0	0
Kashmiri[a]	0	0	1	0	0	0	0	0	1
Malayalam	174	1	147	131	567	39	15	8	1,082
Marathi	204	15	516	128	388	85	33	81	1,450
Oriya	36	0	70	50	201	71	16	4	448
Punjabi	73	14	261	61	197	24	17	1	648
Sanskrit	3	0	6	1	13	12	3	0	38
Sindhi	8	0	28	9	31	6	2	0	34
Tamil	270	34	287	180	546	20	7	2	1,346
Telugu	71	2	194	125	317	20	5	1	735
Urdu	344	18	903	261	419	42	13	3	2,003
Bilingual	44	12	424	242	369	262	98	26	1,977
Multilingual	13	4	76	41	187	58	24	6	409
Others	58	13	86	33	111	61	14	0	376
Total	3,229	257	9,621	4,026	9,260	2,453	1,076	292	30,214

[a] The virtual nil return, however unlikely it may appear, is based on the information available.

Source: *India 1993* (Delhi: Publications Division, 1994), p. 261.

They did not intervene as an organised entity nor as part of a concerted effort or plan, nor did they claim to speak for or on behalf of the *millat*. Yet one can discern a meeting of minds, consensus on issues facing the nation and the 'community', and agreement that the politics of inter-communal discord were untenable. They attracted notice, not because they wielded influence in public life but because they translated the language of secular modernism into political activism – the first time this had happened since independence. It is easy to dismiss them as 'élitist' or 'psuedo-secularist' and to belittle their loud and clear message of dissent, a favourite pastime of Muslim orthodoxy from the days of Syed Ahmad. Historians desining to record 'success stories' may well find that their voice does not carry as far as the 'man in the street'. In any event, their viewpoint merits serious discussion, whatever cynics might say. They would themselves take the position that well-meaning parties and individuals should consider some basic questions that relate to the very survival of civil society in India. They would want to shift the focus from the traditionalists to the modernists, and to expose the poverty of the intellectual discourse on Muslims by drawing attention to their own reading of social realities, and their own vision of India and the place of minorities in it. They would want to draw on the historical reconstructions of the colonialists, Hindu nationalists and Muslim separatists to chalk out an alternative strategy that would fortify the democratic and secular.

V

'Islam is capable of progress, and possesses sufficient elasticity to enable it to adapt itself to the social and political changes going on around it. The Islam, by which I mean the pure Islam as taught by Mohammad in the Quran, and not that Islam as taught by the Muhammadan Canon Law, was itself a progress and a change for the better. It has the vital principles of rapid development, of progress, and of adaptability to new circumstances.'

Chiragh Ali (1844-95), quoted in J. J. Donohue and J. L. Esposito (eds), *Islam in Transition: Muslim Perspectives* (New York: OUP, 1982)

The 'secular modernists' represent different groups from mixed social and cultural backgrounds. I have drawn on journalists, and others who write for the press, and because of the difficulty of classifying them in neat categories, I describe them as *secular modernists* in recognition of their broadly secular framework of analysis and their commitment to secularism. I also recognise the hazards of placing them in the social ladder or delineating their political predilections with any degree of precision. Sympathisers designate them as 'westernised liberals', and detractors as 'pseudo-secularists', 'carpet-baggers' and 'courtiers'. They offer hope to some, but are an irritant to others. Their counsel, according to Shahabuddin, 'is lost upon the community when they presume to lead them out of the dark forests of orthodoxy into the sunshine of intellectual freedom'.[66]

Among the many concerns of the secular modernists is to come to terms with the collapse of the Nehruvian consensus on secularism and the steady erosion of those liberal, democratic ideals that were at the heart of the Congress ideology and programme till the early 1960s. Their writings reflect their endorsement of Nehru's blueprint for free India, a nostalgia for his liberal and secularised vision.[67] They accept that some of his ideas, rooted in British utilitarian and Fabian thought, were unpopular and therefore gradually repudiated by his own party. They agree that secularism, his favourite project, was not the people's staple diet because – as Girilal Jain, T.N. Madan and Ashis Nandy have reminded us – it rested on certain false assumptions made by an arrogant westernised intelligentsia who were cut off from their *Indian* traditions. At the same time they insist that communalism and Hindu-Muslim strife need not imply the *failure* of the secular experiment. Even if the secular fabric was ripped apart, as indeed happened during the dark days of December 1992, the secular project must be more fully integrated with the nation's agenda. 'The effort has to be to stitch it together ... The need is for a forceful leadership, a state which even now wakes up from its slumber to act decisively and, above all, coherently.'[68] Ideas and movements do not lose their relevance or vitality for all time just because they are under siege at a particular historical juncture.

Seema Mustafa, Hasan Suroor and Saeed Naqvi, all from UP and members of a one-time landed gentry, have explored these themes in their writings. There are specific reasons why they have done so. Seema Mustafa, a freelance journalist whose engaging column in the *Pioneer* was withdrawn in October 1994 by the pro-BJP establishment, is part of the Kidwai clan in Masauli, the home of Rafi Ahmad Kidwai. Her grandmother, Anis Kidwai, was a freedom fighter and social activist. Hasan Suroor's family from Rudauli, a *qasbah* in the Barabanki district, has a similar nationalist past. His father, though serving the raj, took a sympathetic view of Congress-led activities. His mother, Nayyara Khatoon, gave up the *burqa* when the family moved to Ballimaran in the old city of Delhi and headed the Communist party's local unit.

---

[66] *Pioneer*, 14 October 1993.

[67] M.J. Akbar, *Nehru: The Making of India* (London: Viking, 1988), pp. 571, 581.

[68] Seema Mustafa, 'Action without Ideology will hasten disintegration', *Pioneer*, 21 December 1992.

Saeed Naqvi was born in Mustafabad, close to Rae Bareli, in a Shia family of impoverished country gentry, who led a leisured life in the *qasbahs* jealously guarding their small landholdings and their mixed social and cultural inheritance. He too has inherited the family's eclectic, nationalistic and secular legacy, and is wedded to those mixed and often contradictory ideological impulses that moved some of his elders to join the anti-colonial struggle either as Congressmen or as Communists. For years he has been a vocal protagonist of the composite culture in the Indo-Gangetic belt. He has written extensively and with passion and poignancy. Moving from place to place in search of enclaves of inter-community amity and understanding, he has informed readers and television viewers of the great syncretic traditions from Kashmir to Kanyakumari. He has reminded viewers, with great effect, of living examples of cultural fusion – bringing to light the flowering of composite cultures in remote parts of the country, and the interaction that has gone on for centuries, despite past and present misgivings, between Muslims and Hindus. His message is for Advani, as much as for the Juma Masjid's 'burly Imam'. It is simple and straightforward: the communalist onslaught can be blunted by reviving the composite and syncretic character of India's past. His plea to Murli Manohar Joshi, former BJP president and organiser of 'Ekta Yatra', is to

....concentrate on areas that bind us. Passing through Awadh and Brij, examine the literatures of these regions. Visit the ancient 'town of Jais, not far from my own village, and reflect on Malik Mohammad Jaisi's *Padmavat*. Look how the great poet compared Padmavati's eyebrows to the bows of Krishna and Arjun, and come to Vrindavan and let the entire congregation around your *rath* [chariot] chant Raskhan poems on the naughty boy from Gokul. Did they ever know that the real name of this great Krishna *bhakt* [devotee] was Syed Ibrahim? Common folk in Braj may have forgotten Raskhan, but people in Orissa to this day welcome Jagannath with songs written by Salbeg, a Muslim.

And the message to his community is:

I am imploring you to strengthen the hands of your natural allies, those who had the courage to make that film on *sati*, who had the courage to screen it, those who found me the house, the ones who have the sensitivity to understand what Dara Shikoh was all about. These are the people who will one day prompt rational debates on Janambhoomis and the Masjids as well. The alternative is to leave it all to that Imam who, without his knowing it, is in league with the landlord reluctant to rent his house to my daughter.

On another level, secular modernists are beginning to cope with much the same issues that figured on the agendas of Syed Ahmad and the generation that followed him – the steady impoverishment of Muslims, their poor representation in public and private sectors, their educational stagnation, the oppressive state of Muslim women, the stranglehold of traditionalists, and their antipathy to modernising processes. Both as citizens and privileged members of the Muslim élite, they stress the need to marshal their own intellectual resources to review, analyse and comment on how, in the light of post-Ayodhya happenings, their community can, as part of the nation-building process, fortify itself in the economic and educational spheres. 'This cataclysmic event', commented Saiyid Hamid philosophically, 'can still yield something positive. We can take it as a watershed. It can be utilised for heart-searching and stock-taking.' He was beholden – 'in this hour of shock and grief' – to secular parties for the healing touch. But can Muslims 'survive on waves of sympathy'? He bemoaned, much as his intellectual mentor Syed Ahmad did more than a century before, that Muslims have steadfastly refused to 'come to terms with the reality of the present day'. The need of the hour was to change their 'perception, orientation and attitude' so as to advance in the highly competitive world of education, business, trade and commerce. Critical introspection and dissent constituted the first step towards attaining some progress. Seema Mustafa, his niece, insists that the lead must come from Muslim intellectuals.[69]

The question, according to Imtiaz Ahmad, was whether Muslims would continue with the urgent task of asset-building, or exhaust their energies in a struggle to have the Masjid rebuilt. The Ayodhya episode was in that sense 'a turning point in the community's journey towards securing an honourable place in future India'. Now that the mosque was destroyed, it was necessary to enlarge the community's socio-economic and educational resources and assets through promotion of 'ameliorative activities'.[70]

Maulana Wahiduddin Khan, founder of the Islamic Centre in Delhi and editor of *Al-Risala*,[71] emerged as a major exponent of the 'multi-culture model', a model 'truly in consonance with nature'.[72] as against 'cultural

---

[69] Seema Mustafa, 'The narrow, conservative world of Delhi Muslims', *Pioneer*, 4 March 1994.

[70] Imtiaz Ahmad, op. cit.; and Maulana Wahiduddin Khan's comment: 'So far as the Muslims are concerned, their best course would be to close their eyes firmly to the past, and to fix their gaze resolutely upon the future.' *Indian Muslims*, op. cit., p. 12.

[71] Maulana Wahiduddin Khan (b. 1925), published his first book *Naye Ahad ke Darwaze* (On the threshold of a New Era) in 1955. His other work *Mazhab aur Jadid Challenge* (Modern Challenges to Religion) was translated into Arabic and widely read in the Arab world. He edited the *Al-Jamiyat* from 1967 to 1974, established the Islamic Centre in 1976, and launched *Al-Risala* the following month. For his profile and views, see *Nation and the World*, 16 August 1993, pp. 43-7, and his article 'Co-Existence of Religions in India', *Times of India*, 19 August 1993.

[72] Wahiduddin Khan, op. cit., p. 150.

nationalism' or 'uni-culturalism'.[73] The political journey of this man of extraordinary vigour, energy and initiative started with the Jamaat-i Islami before he joined the Jamiyat al-ulama in the 1960s and edited its official organ, *Al-Jamiyat*. He no longer retains links with the Jamaat or the Jamiyat, although he still admires the Tablighi Jamaat, whose head-quarters are adjacent to his own institute in the Muslim-dominated west Nizamuddin locality in south Delhi. He edits *Al-Risala*, travels widely and writes for newspapers and magazines. His eclecticism and unor-thodox ideas, especially on the Babri Masjid issue,[74] cause embarrassment to the religious establishments. He is courted by some, but his heterodoxy does not find favour with the Jamiyat al-ulama or the Muslim Personal Law Board.

At the same time, a scholar of Wahiduddin Khan's background, learning and reputation has a decided advantage over other secular moder-nists. His religious background, deep knowledge of Islam and acknow-ledged status as an Islamic thinker are powerful assets. He can get away with talk of reforms and reinterpretation, and take an unpopular stand on the Babri Masjid without the fear of being ostracised or declared a *kafir*. He can interpret the Quran without incurring the wrath of the *mullahs*. On the other hand, his Western-educated counterparts, who are engaged in similar endeavours, are pitted against a wide array of forces rooted both in history and in contemporary political practices. They are, above all, confronted with entrenched religio-political élites who have zealously maintained that the so-called Muslim issues fall within their exclusive domain. This claim, couched in the political language used when the Muslim League campaign was at its peak in the mid-1940s, has not been contested since that time. The Indian state, on the other hand, has bolstered the religio-political leadership. To swing the 'Muslim vote', ruling and opposition parties pander to their sentiments and readily accommodate them in political structures through nomination, election and appointment. Thus Rajiv Gandhi's government ignored liberal Muslim opinion over the Shah Bano case to negotiate with Muslim priests. On the Masjid-*Mandir* impasse too, men of religion were propped up as the community's sole spokesmen on the assumption that the 'unenlightened hordes' were recep-tive to their *fatawa* and decrees. Liberal and secular-minded Muslims, whose strength and appeal has been neither measured nor assessed, were silenced. Shahabuddin wrote triumphantly: 'No regime shall ever strike a deal with the so-called liberals because they are and shall remain marginal to the situation and peripheral to national politics.'[75] Harsh

---

[73] Wahiduddin Khan, op. cit., pp. 31, 32.

[74] Ibid., p. 28.

[75] *Pioneer*, 20 December 1992.

words, but spoken in the assurance of government and opposition backing and patronage.

Secular modernists were humbled by the weight of orthodoxy and marginalised by a cynical government hoping to win over dwindling Muslim support with the aid of men with flowing beards. But they have since learnt their lesson the hard way and have begun to use the print media and public platforms to disseminate their views and confront their critics through an alternative discourse. This they did during the long-drawn-out controversy at Jamia Millia Islamia, where the pro-vice-chancellor was the victim of a violent agitation because of his remarks on the banning of Salman Rushdie's *The Satanic Verses*.[76] 'If there ever was an irony', reported Hasan Suroor, 'it is being played out these days in Delhi's Jamia Millia Islamia. Under the stony gaze of Mirza Ghalib who used poetic licence to hit at religion, God and other holy cows, a professor is being pilloried for speaking against the culture of book burning.' Behind the ugly display of intolerance

....is a mindset that is in direct opposition to the basic idea of tolerance, and is calculated to encourage fanatical tendencies in other communities.[...] The crux of the issue is simply this: Can a group of people, however aggrieved, set themselves up as censors and muffle even the slightest sign of dissent in the name of the holy cows in the pasture? Is the agenda of the universities going to be set up by ambitious politicians, *mullahs* and their protégés in the students' union and staff associations? Is intellectual debate, traditionally the stuff of the academe, going to be replaced by *fatwa* and religious sermons? And has Big Brother arrived with his return of rabble-rousers, judges and executioners ready to strike down anyone who dares to disagree with them?[77]

Others too rose to the professor's defence.[78] 'Who knows', wrote Saeed Naqvi, 'the liberal Muslim may be coming into his own. This may well be the time for the ruling establishment to give him support and test his reach among a community so far conceded to a leadership that has kept him in the shadow of darkness.'[79] If, on the other hand, he was ousted, as

---

[76] The details of the agitation, starting on 21 April 1992, are outlined in the report of 'Eminent Persons' submitted to the Ministry of Human Resource Development and tabled in Parliament in mid-November 1993. See Ashutosh Varshney, 'Battling the Past, Forging a Future? Ayodhya and Beyond' in Philip Oldenburg (ed.), *India Briefing 1993* (Boulder, CO: Westview Press, 1993), pp. 39-40; Saeed Naqvi, *Reflections of an Indian Muslim*, pp. 182-201, and his *The Last Brahman Prime Minister* (Delhi: Har-Anand, 1996); Arun Shourie, *Indian Controversies: Essays on Religion in Politics*, pp. 363-86; P.C. Chatterji, *Secular Values for Secular India* (Delhi: Manohar, 1995), pp. 85-7.

[77] *Hindu*, 3 and 13 June 1992.

[78] For example, A.A. Engineer, 'Liberal Islam under Challenge', *Hindu*, 9 June 1992; Khalid Hamidi, 'Shaitani Ayaat aur Hamara Amal' (Satanic Verses and our Conduct), *Qaumi Awaaz*, 6 May, 1 and 6 June 1992.

[79] *Pioneer*, 21, 25 June 1992.

was the general clamour in Jamia, the institution 'will cease to be the Jamia of Zakir Husain, an embodiment of the values he stood for. It will come to reflect the personality and values of far smaller men. Not the Muslims alone, India will be by far the poorer for this subversion of the Jamia Millia Islamia university.'[80]

The pro-vice-chancellor did not return to the campus in Okhla. He was assaulted on 4 December 1992, two days before the Babri Masjid was pulled down, but he did not resign. He has stood his ground on the strength of the massive support extended to him by liberal-left groups across the board. Appropriately enough, secular modernists, demoralised after the Shah Bano case, tasted victory under the shadow of Mirza Ghalib's statue on the Jamia campus. The outcome, as expressed by Francis Robinson, a leading historian of South Asian Islam at London University, 'is that communalists on both sides, Hindu and Muslim, have been robbed of a likely issue. After the terrible years of the eighties, in which they endured many defeats at the hands of religious bigotry, those who strive for a secular future for the Indian state feel that they have won a victory.'[81]

For secular modernists there was clearly a much more favourable climate in the post-Ayodhya phase to voice their concerns. They had never been so well placed before. For this reason there was a general flurry of activity under the aegis of a group who call themselves 'Muslim Intelligentsia Meet'. Meetings took place at different places – in Delhi, Aligarh, Kanpur, Lucknow, Allahabad, Varanasi, Surat, Ahmedabad, Bombay – to locate the trauma caused by the Ayodhya episode in the wider context, to seek remedies within a democratic and secular order, to propose composite nationalism as an alternative to emotive religious appeals, and to resolve minority issues outside the communitarian framework. The many people who attended had come to explore alternative approaches and seek new answers to their contemporary dilemma, and they showed in themselves and in the speeches and manifestos a clear sign of rethinking and an urge to take stock of old styles and attitudes. 'If Muslims want a secular, democratic rule of law', said the president of the Lucknow-based UP Muslim Advocates Forum, 'we have to unite with secular, democratic forces and not indulge in sectarian politics.'[82]

The debate centred around issues ranging from social and educational reforms to family planning. There was talk of discrimination in jobs, of

[80] A.G. Noorani, 'Rushdie Revive – II', *Statesman*, June 1992.

[81] Francis Robinson, 'Secularism and *The Satanic Verses*', *BASAS Bulletin*, 18, July 1992. See also Praful Bidwai, 'Of Muslims and Liberals: Jamia stir proves communalists wrong', *Times of India*, 30 May 1993, and his 'Secular Muslims fight back: Lessons of the Jamia Episode', *Times of India*, 7 April 1994; Girilal Jain, 'Muslim Liberals have held their ground', *Pioneer*, 3 June 1992.

[82] Quoted in Sunil Saxena, 'The Insecurity Grows', *Pioneer*, 30 September 1993.

heavy policing during communal riots, of Urdu being denied its rightful status, of *makatib* and *madaris* in towns and villages languishing, of Muslim women in seclusion and victims of inequitable family laws. Some saw a way out in religion-based quotas and 'communal representation', though most repudiated this for fear of a Hindu backlash. Some mooted changes in the traditional system of education, but most favoured schemes to equip Muslims to gain access to professional and technical courses. Some talked of a uniform civil code, but most sought modifications and amendments to family laws. The treatment meted out to Urdu was a common grievance, although it was Maulana Wahiduddin Khan who introduced a discordant note: in his view the pro-Urdu campaign was 'a sign of the desire to remain static'. Whereas learning regional languages was 'a sure sign of progress'.[83]

It is hard to imagine a consensus emerging out of disparate groups working towards different goals, yet the underlying theme of discussions, either at the 'Muslim Intelligentsia Meet' or at other gatherings, was that the *millat* can remain tied to its cherished religio-cultural traditions without spurning ideas of change, progress and social transformation. Islam is not, after all, 'necessarily anti-feminist, a religion of harsh punishments, militancy or *jihad*. It is up to Muslims to interpret Islam anew and put it within the Indian framework.' The *talaq* controversy was not a 'routine criticism or customary innuendo'. Rather, such occasions required cool-headed analyses and wiser responses.[84] The need was to 'situate' the Quran and the *Hadith* in the context of their times: in other words, making them historically specific rather than documents of timeless or eternal value. 'A great responsibility', declared Rasheed Talib, senior journalist and Nehru Fellow, 'falls on the *ulama* of Indian Islam in particular, in the beleaguered state in which their flock find themselves today, to carry forward the tradition established by their forebearers and rethink Islam in the light of modern times.'[85] Hisham Siddiqi, editor of the Lucknow paper *Jadid Markaz*, stated at a meet in Delhi on 20 September 1993 that any purposeful step to stimulate secular politics would bring rewards only if Muslims accept the values of universal education and women's rights.[86] His view was endorsed by Husna Subhani, convenor of the All-India Muslim Women's Association, who also came out strongly against the practice of 'triple divorce' among Muslims.[87]

---

[83] Wahiduddin Khan, op. cit., p. 28.

[84] Ishtiaque Danish, in *Times of India*, 14 October 1993. For a similar perspective, see Iqbal A. Ansari, Zeenat Shaukat Ali and A.A. Engineer in *Seminar*, April 1994.

[85] Rasheed Talib, 'The Problem', *Seminar*, April 1994, p. 15, and his 'Reforming Islamic Education', *Times of India*, 11 November 1994.

[86] Quoted in *Frontline*, 5 November 1993.

[87] Ibid.

There was much to commend in this secularised discourse, including the air of confidence of its protagonists. The secular modernists did not, for a change, carry the banner of Pakistan, nor were they swayed by the fundamentalist rhetoric. Instead they vigorously proclaimed their right to intervene in the existing debates and insisted on making their point of view known. They demanded attention from the government, from political parties, from the media and, above all, from the self-appointed champions of the Muslim 'community'. This spirit was reflected at the first meeting convened by the 'Muslim Intelligentsia Meet' on 24 January 1992.[88]

For the first time since independence, the political and religious leadership were placed in the dock; for the first time their conduct was attacked and their authority questioned. Speaker after speaker urged the predominantly Muslim audience to re-examine existing attitudes, question commonly-held assumptions and confidently seek a better future. It was no good blaming others. Muslims needed to learn from their own mistakes, ask new questions and forge new identities. The door of *ijtehad* was not closed. Everyone was entitled to interpret and apply the Quranic laws anew. India's Muslims, as also their co-religionists in other countries, had done so in the past; why did they have to lag behind in a state of *jumud* (stagnation)? Is it not the Quran which declares 'God changes not what is in a people, until they change what is in themselves'?

The community's salvation did not lie in the hands of the present leaders, who were insensitive to the wider needs and impulses of their own community. The audience nodded in approval. Syed Shahabuddin was listening. The followers of Imam Bukhari were present in full strength. One hopes that they have heeded the warnings, and read the writing on the wall. One hopes that they will read, mark, learn and inwardly digest the message of Hali, delivered nearly a century ago:

Many caravans have long been on the move. Many more are loading up their burdens. Many more are in agitation at the movement all around them. Many are repenting that they themselves are not on the move. You alone amongst them are still sunk in heedless sleep. Take care, lest in your heedlessness you fail to reach the goal.

No longer think your supporters your enemies. No longer think your guides are robbers. Think afterwards of blaming those who give you good counsel, and first look well into your own homes and see: Are your storerooms full, or are they empty. Are your ways of conduct good, or are they bad.[89]

---

[88] The meeting constituted a major point of departure by outlining the basis for a radically different political orientation for the Muslims. The deliberations, chaired by Imtiaz Ahmad, were extensively covered and aroused interest in political and academic circles. See *Times of India*, 25, 26 January; *Hindu*, 25 January; *Economic Times*, 25 January; and *India Today*, 15 February 1993.

[89] Aziz Ahmad and Grunebaum (eds), *Muslim Self-Statement*, p. 96.

DISTRIBUTION OF MUSLIM POPULATION IN INDIA

District/State/Union territory	Muslim population as % of total district population	Rural Muslim population as % of rural population	Urban Muslim population as % of urban population
ANDHRA PRADESH			
Srikakulam	0.24	0.09	1.49
Vizianagar	0.67	0.31	2.56
Vishakapatnam	1.69	0.85	3.53
East Godavari	1.48	0.78	3.94
West Godavari	2.10	1.28	5.23
Krishna	6.09	3.97	10.47
Guntur	10.43	8.08	16.61
Prakasam	6.92	5.68	13.99
Nellore	8.87	6.91	16.35
Chittoor	8.64	7.37	14.91
Cuddapah	14.80	10.90	30.74
Anantapur	11.26	8.96	27.61
Kurnool	16.94	12.71	30.00
Mahbubnagar	8.92	6.60	27.80
Rangareddi	11.26	9.59	16.60
Hyderabad	35.90	–	35.90
Medak	11.15	9.06	26.36
Nizamabad	13.01	8.55	31.76
Adilabad	8.53	5.08	22.93
Karimnagar	5.53	3.20	0.17
Warangal	5.58	3.25	16.80
Khammam	5.88	4.21	14.06
Nalgonda	5.28	3.57	17.40
BIHAR			
Patna	7.45	4.04	13.23
Nalanda	8.33	4.53	32.49

Nawada	11.36	10.40	24.81
Gaya	10.46	9.11	21.60
Aurangabad	9.61	8.59	23.35
Rohtas	9.20	7.77	22.42
Bhojpur	6.46	5.02	18.43
Saran	9.65	9.11	15.48
Siwan	16.57	15.99	28.96
Gopalganj	15.22	15.01	19.23
Paschim Champaran	19.63	19.08	26.47
Pusba Champaran	17.60	17.40	21.83
Sitamarhi	18.44	18.47	18.00
Muzaffarpur	14.26	13.74	20.25
Vaishali	9.07	8.63	15.46
Begusarai	12.06	11.55	16.41
Samastipur	9.73	9.65	11.43
Darbhanga	21.54	21.11	26.02
Madhubani	15.81	15.55	23.92
Saharsa	12.55	12.16	19.00
Purnia	41.59	42.68	28.94
Katihar	36.91	38.74	19.29
Munger	8.52	7.87	12.50
Bhagalpur	13.93	12.35	25.85
Santhal Pargana	16.44	16.45	16.37
Dhanbad	12.17	10.86	13.44
Giridih	15.09	15.05	15.30
Hazaribagh	12.26	11.86	14.80
Palamau	11.13	12.24	44.56
Ranchi	7.77	5.62	15.90
Singhbhum	4.56	1.27	11.52

GUJARAT

Jamnagar	12.29	6.11	22.60
Rajkot	9.67	6.57	14.08
Surendranagar	6.52	4.39	11.80
Bhavnagar	6.48	2.68	14.09
Amreli	5.59	2.99	15.71
Junagadh	9.40	5.25	18.87
Kachchh	18.77	18.76	18.80
Banas Kantha	7.12	5.74	21.77

Sabarkantha	5.36	3.31	23.98
Mahesana	6.36	5.10	11.39
Gandhinagar	2.72	2.00	5.32
Ahmedabad	10.93	3.52	13.83
Kheda	9.42	7.13	18.48
Panch Mahal	4.70	1.48	30.48
Vadodara	7.94	5.55	11.98
Bharuch	16.08	13.73	26.26
Surat	8.55	3.94	14.71
Valsad	4.30	2.73	9.91
The Dangs	1.32	1.32	–
HARYANA			
Ambala	4.77	6.00	1.36
Kurukshetra	0.98	1.05	0.59
Karnal	2.17	2.26	1.91
Jind	1.18	1.29	0.46
Sonepat	1.45	1.47	1.88
Rohtak	0.28	0.29	5.63
Faridabad	11.20	16.51	3.67
Gurgaon	30.79	37.57	3.53
Mahendragarh	0.27	0.29	0.13
Bhiwani	0.55	0.61	0.25
Hisar	0.56	0.62	0.31
Sirsa	0.37	0.36	0.39
HIMACHAL PRADESH			
Chamba	5.75	5.93	3.33
Kangra	0.96	0.97	0.72
Hamirpur	0.66	0.60	1.02
Una	2.08	2.21	0.61
Bilaspur	1.40	1.19	5.74
Mandi	0.71	0.67	1.24
Kullu	0.22	0.20	0.37
Lahulespiti	0.04	0.04	–
Shimla	0.95	0.68	2.44
Solan	1.66	1.46	3.92
Sirmaur	4.83	4.26	10.80
Kinnaur	0.12	0.12	–

JAMMU AND KASHMIR

Anantnag	95.63	96.40	89.25
Pulwana	95.87	95.97	94.89
Srinagar	90.65	98.17	88.82
Badgam	95.94	97.39	87.11
Baramula	96.50	97.54	89.78
Kupwana	97.53	97.82	88.01
Kargil	77.89	77.17	90.70
Ladakh	15.31	12.55	34.23
Doda	57.29	56.84	64.49
Udhampur	26.22	28.43	5.30
Kathua	6.96	7.44	3.19
Jammu	4.27	4.28	4.24
Rajauri	58.28	59.72	32.08
Punch	89.06	93.63	21.28

KARNATAKA

Bangalore	11.61	4.57	15.48
Belgaum	9.62	6.83	19.20
Bellary	12.11	6.22	12.30
Bidar	18.00	15.36	30.17
Bijapur	12.70	9.44	22.99
Chikmagalur	7.95	5.61	18.99
Chitradurga	9.17	4.55	24.21
Dakshinkannad	13.18	12.43	15.52
Dharwad	15.31	10.45	24.24
Gulbarga	16.61	12.08	31.89
Hassan	5.62	3.03	20.73
Kodagu	13.34	9.00	22.10
Kolar	11.41	7.33	25.47
Mandya	4.12	1.82	16.64
Mysore	6.88	2.69	17.97
Raichur	12.28	7.60	31.85
Shimoga	10.80	7.63	18.79
Tumkur	7.23	4.37	25.14
Uttar Kannad	9.71	5.96	20.74

KERALA

Cannanore	25.68	24.16	30.67

Wayanad	24.56	24.56	–
Kozhikode	33.94	32.95	36.60
Malappuram	65.50	65.14	70.01
Palghat	23.12	23.38	20.82
Trichur	14.88	16.41	9.16
Ernakulam	13.40	12.01	15.51
Idukki	6.51	5.63	6.98
Kottayam	4.96	4.65	7.92
Alleppey	7.44	5.57	17.34
Quilon	14.01	12.75	22.35
Trivandrum	12.63	12.49	12.51

MADHYA PRADESH

Morena	3.95	2.49	13.17
Bhind	3.40	2.29	8.82
Gwalior	5.80	3.07	8.03
Datia	3.63	1.77	11.30
Shivpuri	2.74	1.09	13.95
Guna	4.14	2.26	15.61
Tikamgarh	5.57	1.31	14.86
Chhatarpur	3.70	1.80	13.97
Panna	3.30	2.24	15.82
Sagar	4.11	1.52	10.84
Damoh	3.52	2.05	12.22
Satna	2.59	1.17	9.90
Rewa	3.32	1.91	12.76
Shahdol	2.77	1.46	8.81
Sidhi	2.80	2.44	5.70
Mandsaur	8.18	4.85	21.29
Ratlam	10.18	3.36	25.56
Ujjain	11.03	5.36	20.49
Shajapur	9.94	7.18	25.73
Dewas	9.76	7.15	21.10
Jhabua	2.26	0.98	16.37
Dhar	4.89	2.74	19.82
Indore	11.71	7.73	13.76
West Nimar	5.09	2.88	23.31
East Nimar	13.24	6.11	0.32
Rajgarh	5.62	3.47	21.39

Vidisha	9.72	8.10	17.22
Bhopal	23.40	8.86	27.94
Sehore	9.63	7.04	26.54
Raisen	8.84	6.57	29.33
Betul	2.12	0.91	8.95
Hoshangabad	4.45	2.17	11.24
Jabalpur	5.59	1.63	10.43
Narasimhapur	3.16	2.27	8.82
Mandla	1.22	0.79	6.87
Chhindwara	5.21	2.67	13.12
Seoni	5.21	4.18	17.39
Balaghat	2.52	1.62	8.84
Surguja	2.48	1.92	8.39
Bilaspur	1.62	0.88	6.22
Raigarh	0.86	0.55	4.24
Raj Nandgaon	1.68	0.96	0.67
Durg	2.24	0.67	5.60
Raipur	1.86	0.65	7.68
Bastar	0.65	0.34	5.39

MAHARASHTRA

Greater Bombay	14.79	–	14.79
Thane	8.37	5.04	12.55
Raigarh	7.46	6.38	14.00
Ratnagiri	7.21	6.27	17.87
Nasik	9.67	2.40	25.83
Dhule	6.84	3.26	21.61
Jalgaon	10.83	7.97	19.35
Ahmadnagar	6.41	5.11	15.15
Pune	6.00	2.97	9.37
Satara	4.24	2.98	12.61
Sangli	7.37	5.02	15.92
Sholapur	9.47	6.47	16.73
Kolhapur	6.19	4.38	11.66
Aurangabad	15.97	11.90	30.31
Parbhani	11.84	6.78	33.76
Bid	10.92	7.72	28.44
Nanded	11.90	7.85	29.45
Osmanabad	11.10	8.55	25.17

Buldana	10.99	8.23	23.16
Akola	13.12	8.11	28.23
Amravati	10.90	7.01	20.31
Yavatmal	7.51	5.29	20.02
Wardha	4.03	2.61	8.30
Nagpur	6.81	2.23	10.30
Bhandara	2.38	1.65	7.20
Chandrapur	2.922	1.93	21.85
MANIPUR			
Manipur North	0.05	0.02	0.58
Manipur West	0.08	0.08	–
Manipur South	0.76	0.47	2.05
Tengnoupal	1.46	0.07	10.30
Manipur Central	10.46	12.50	6.64
Manipur East	0.10	0.09	0.30
MEGHALAYA			
Jaintia Hills	0.11	0.06	0.62
East Khasi Hills	1.31	0.35	3.05
West Khasi Hills	0.07	0.03	1.64
East Garo Hills	0.80	0.58	7.50
West Garo Hills	9.01	9.71	3.09
NAGALAND			
Kohima	3.70	3.31	4.76
Phek	0.32	0.32	–
Wokha	0.34	0.08	1.90
Zunheboto	0.33	0.15	1.57
Mokokchung	0.79	0.34	2.92
Tuensang	0.32	0.13	2.49
Mon	0.73	0.44	3.74
ORISSA			
Sambalpur	0.69	0.15	3.65
Sundargarh	2.32	0.92	5.51
Kendujhar	0.93	0.56	3.79
Mayurbhanj	0.86	0.68	3.89
Baleswar	3.97	2.39	21.62
Cuttack	3.63	3.04	8.78
Dhenkanal	0.26	0.08	2.40

Phulabani	0.18	0.07	2.09
Balangir	0.29	0.55	1.80
Kalahandi	0.35	0.18	2.98
Koraput	0.40	0.18	2.08
Ganjam	0.20	0.04	1.18
Puri	2.16	1.95	3.36
PUNJAB			
Gurdaspur	0.61	0.65	0.46
Amritsar	0.10	0.08	0.13
Firozpur	0.12	0.10	0.20
Ludhiana	0.51	0.66	0.30
Jalandhar	0.31	0.36	0.22
Kapurthala	0.50	0.56	0.35
Hoshiarpur	0.51	0.57	0.19
Rupnagar	1.06	1.23	0.47
Patiala	1.41	1.74	0.62
Sangrur	6.34	3.84	14.79
Bathinda	0.49	0.54	0.33
Faridkot	0.35	0.49	0.13
RAJASTHAN			
Ganganagar	3.53	2.96	5.72
Bikaner	10.08	7.99	13.29
Churu	9.49	3.56	23.86
Jhunjhunu	9.67	4.96	22.14
Alwar	9.67	10.63	1.09
Bharatpur	8.61	8.90	7.24
Sawai Madhopur	6.75	5.26	16.41
Jaipur	7.28	1.85	16.71
Sikar	10.44	4.65	33.25
Ajmer	8.80	8.35	9.40
Tonk	9.26	3.91	33.06
Jaisalmer	23.19	25.10	2.51
Jodhpur	10.10	6.01	17.78
Nagaur	10.84	6.99	33.42
Pali	4.90	3.22	12.36
Barmer	11.26	11.74	6.34
Jalor	3.50	3.10	8.03
Sirohi	2.72	1.54	1.78

Bhilwara	4.66	1.53	7.53
Udaipur	2.96	1.13	13.24
Chittaurgarh	4.83	2.95	17.18
Dungarpur	2.65	1.06	25.53
Banswara	2.95	1.53	1.58
Bundi	5.49	2.55	19.83
Kota	8.72	4.16	18.44
Jhalawar	6.32	4.15	22.72
SIKKIM			
North	1.02	0.57	3.38
East	0.54	0.44	3.71
South	0.85	0.42	6.61
West	0.45	0.33	5.83
TAMIL NADU			
Madras	15.69	–	15.69
Chengalpattu	3.09	1.91	4.93
North Arcot	6.90	2.39	21.96
South Arcot	3.83	28.80	17.76
Dharmapuri	3.87	2.48	17.27
Salem	2.22	0.89	5.49
Periyar	2.42	0.99	7.48
Coimbatore	4.62	1.35	7.82
Nilgiri	9.30	5.09	13.71
Madurai	4.56	2.41	0.83
Tiruchirapalli	4.71	2.26	11.67
Thanjavur	6.98	5.44	12.13
Pudukkottai	6.58	5.56	13.25
Ramanathapuram	6.83	5.07	11.32
Tirunelveli	6.89	3.45	13.39
Kanyakumari	4.26	3.15	9.38
TRIPURA			
West Tripura	6.71	7.50	2.33
North Tripura	9.14	9.50	4.43
South Tripura	4.37	4.47	3.12
UTTAR PRADESH			
Uttar Kashi	0.38	0.25	2.12
Chamoli	0.42	0.33	1.50

Tehri Garhwal	0.48	0.36	3.19
Dehru Dun	0.31	10.82	5.69
Garhwal	2.11	1.65	6.34
Pithoragarh	0.40	0.23	4.04
Almora	0.57	0.16	6.76
Nanital	12.92	9.01	23.22
Saharanpur	31.56	30.99	32.30
Muzaffarnagar	28.73	27.05	34.79
Bijnor	39.45	30.67	66.06
Meerut	25.30	22.35	31.78
Ghaziabad	21.16	24.53	14.66
Bulandshahr	19.37	16.17	32.70
Moradabad	38.06	31.92	54.70
Rampur	48.06	39.87	67.34
Budaun	19.12	15.13	39.87
Bareilly	27.14	21.05	42.06
Pilibhit	21.11	17.77	38.40
Shahjahanpur	16.55	11.82	36.27
Aligarh	13.16	9.53	25.33
Mathura	6.39	4.87	12.06
Agra	10.97	3.90	22.47
Etah	10.45	7.40	27.10
Mainpuri	5.13	3.67	16.84
Farrukhabad	12.63	10.52	23.71
Etawah	6.34	3.71	20.08
Kanpur	12.48	5.74	20.28
Fathepur	12.86	11.01	31.61
Allahabad	12.77	10.22	22.71
Jalaun	8.21	5.03	20.98
Jhansi	8.39	6.32	11.78
Lalitpur	2.10	1.09	8.66
Hamirpur	6.06	6.21	16.60
Banda	5.50	20.67	12.49
Kheri	10.90	15.84	22.62
Sitapur	17.64	15.37	37.38
Hardoi	10.84	7.99	33.76
Unnao	10.67	8.36	27.80
Lucknow	19.67	10.55	27.89
Rae Bareli	10.17	9.12	23.38

Bahraich	25.01	22.82	53.90
Gonda	22.48	21.41	35.99
Barabanki	20.45	18.47	40.56
Faizabad	12.47	9.85	33.73
Sultanpur	12.95	12.35	30.46
Pratapgarh	10.93	10.41	20.70
Basti	20.39	19.91	29.89
Gorakhpur	10.76	9.62	20.38
Deoria	20.87	21.14	14.64
Azamgarh	13.97	10.86	44.65
Jaunpur	8.33	6.62	32.37
Ballia	5.26	4.42	13.68
Ghazipur	10.07	9.11	21.23
Varanasi	5.46	5.71	23.32
Mirzapur	5.41	4.07	14.32

WEST BENGAL

Koch Bihar	20.78	21.80	7.01
Jalpaiguri	8.74	9.62	3.37
Darjiling	3.64	3.65	3.61
West Dinajpur	35.79	39.76	4.27
Maldah	45.27	48.85	13.82
Murshidabad	58.66	61.83	27.94
Nadia	24.07	29.51	4.36
24 Parganas	23.87	31.70	11.52
Calcutta	15.33	–	15.33
Haora	20.17	22.45	17.39
Hugli	13.76	15.53	9.52
Midiniapur	8.69	8.79	7.70
Bankura	5.64	5.78	3.99
Puruliya	5.45	5.21	7.82
Barddhaman	17.59	19.83	12.23
Birbhum	30.98	32.20	17.45

ANDAMAN & NICOBAR ISLANDS

Andaman	9.66	7.61	14.13
Nicobar	2.94	2.94	–

ARUNACHAL PRADESH

West Kameng	0.61	0.57	1.32

East Kameng	0.28	0.28	–
Lower Subansiri	1.18	0.52	5.75
Upper Subansiri	0.32	0.32	–
West Siang	0.72	0.38	3.54
East Siang	1.27	0.83	4.19
Dibang Valley	1.43	1.43	–
Lohit	1.05	0.71	4.50
Tirap	2.05	2.05	–
CHANDIGARH	2.01	2.13	2.01
DADAR + NAGAR + HAVELI	1.86	1.43	7.79
DELHI	7.74	2.45	8.16
GOA + DAMAN + DIU			
Goa	4.09	1.70	1.64
Daman	10.95	5.80	17.70
Diu	5.99	2.29	4.61
LAKSHADWEEP	94.84	97.45	91.81
MIZORAM			
Aizawal	0.54	0.35	1.01
Lunglei	0.28	0.20	0.61
Chhimptuipui	0.14	0.09	0.61
PONDICHERRY			
Pondicherry	2.56	2.12	2.90
Karaikal	14.25	9.90	21.91
Mahe	27.04	26.60	27.90
Yanam	4.01	–	4.01

Information provided to the author by Professor Aijazuddin Ahmad, Jawaharlal Nehru University, New Delhi.

THE DIVINE LAW

Excerpted from a pamphlet entitled *The Divine Law*, written by Hari Charan Lal of Patna, an influential Arya Samaj leader. The first edition of this widely-circulated pamphlet was published in 1939.

If a man uses his reason he can be saved. Be he an animal or a man if he gives trouble he should be killed. Where the population of the Muhammadans is larger the Hindus are in trouble; where the Hindus command the majority the Muhammadans are happy. The Muhammadans instruct their boys that it is apparent [*sic*] for them to oppress, kill and convert the Hindu *Kafirs* to their religion. Hyderabad has a Muslim government; similar is the case with Bhopal, Decca and other places. The Muhammadans always talk of their good and talk and discuss among themselves. They also purchase guns. The Hindus are sleeping senselessly. After the rule of the British, the Muhammadans would reign; for only that nation can reign which has arms and which is organised. The Hindus do not possess arms and are not organised; the community has been suffering from the bogey of untouchability which stands in the way of organisation. There are some who are wise but they too follow the fools. A servant who has served his Hindu master for 60 years and has been very affectionately treated throughout will kill his master [without a remorse] on the occasion of communal quarrels. Not less than 17 times did Prithwi Raj release Muhammad Ghori who punished Prithwi Raj the 18th time and did not release him. On the occasion of a Hindu-Muslim riot at Calcutta a Muhammadan entered the house of a Hindu *Seth* and requested him to save his life. The *Seth* was moved. He said [when the Hindu rioters arrived there] that he was his own man and a Hindu. When the Hindu [rioters] had departed, that Muhammadan killed the son of the *Seth*. Muhammad Ali or Shaukat Ali, fast friends of Mahatma Gandhi, said: 'Even the most degraded Muhammadan was better than Mahatma Gandhi'. There may be a serious fight, some day between the Hindus and the Muhammadans. Small scuffles on a small scale are happening everywhere. Mr. Jinnah has been fanning the flame of communal fire [lit. inciting]. The Hindus have been fast asleep. If the Hindus live in a *Muhalla* where the Muhammadans are in a majority, they will have to lose their wealth and life. Enmity and animosity is on the increase. Something is sure to happen. If the Hindus take care they will be saved. If not they will have to lose more as compared to the Muhammadans. How can [they] be careful? Only when all – wealth, men and mind – are united as one. The Muhammadans and the Christians do good to their country and their nation. For the good of Turkey the Muhammadans raised a subscription from the Hindus and sent the sum to Turkey. The Christians raised donation from the Hindus in the German war and sent the sum out [of this country]. The Hindus do not give for the help of the Hindus. It is to be greatly regretted. On the occasion of the earthquake the Muhammadans received free gift of money raised from the Hindus. The Hindus remained poor, unemployed, hungry and naked but they did not get any service. Men belonging to other faiths got employment. The Rajas and the Maharajas spend their wealth by inviting prostitutes and others. The Nizam of Hyderabad has been increasing the number of his religious *maulvi* preachers. In the *Tabligh* he spends money in helping the Muhammadans and giving them employment. In Bhopal a very large number of Hindus were converted to the Muhammadan faith; and if the present state of affairs continues the Hindus residing in the Muhammadan kingdoms will be converted to Muhammadanism. The good things of the Muhammadans become known to all of their co-religionists from one to another; but the Hindus do not propagate even their good acts and this is the reason why they are beaten. The Muhammadans do not fear death. The Hindus are afraid of death. The very day the Hindus also do not fear death, the Muhammadans will see their end. They will sleep happily. There is no quarrel with the Christians. The real quarrel is with the Muhammadans. The Christians are wise. They are just waiting for the day when the Hindus would become wise and they would go away after making over the charge to them. They are not going away only because the 25 crores of Hindus are not organised. The Hindus alone are slaves of the Christians as well as of the Muhammadans. The day on which the Hindus would like [to end] their slavery, eighty lakhs of the Christians will go back to their homes; and eight crores of the Muhammadans will die without being killed. The Muhammadan officers help their co-religionists. The Hindus, in service, being afraid of the Government help the Muhammadans alone and suppress their co-religionists. A Muhammadan never cares for his service; he helps his co-religionists. A Hindu cares for his service and does not help his co-religionists. Government notices this foolishness and says that they are not fit even now. They shall be fit only when they would conquer the eight crores of the Muhammadans. Government says that it would go of its own accord and that it only helps the Hindus; because if it had not remained the *teek* [tuft of hair left at the back of the head], the sacred thread, *tilak* [mark on the forehead], temple and the daughters and daughter-in-laws of the Hindus would have become extinct. Have you forgotton the age of Aurangzeb? Look to the Nizam of Hyderabad even today. A Muhammadan rules there even though the population consists of 89 per cent of the Hindus. There is no organisation among you. Even if the selfish 56 lakhs of *sadhus* among you organise themselves, there would be no trace of the eight crores of the Muhammadans. The Brahmans, the *pandas*, and the *pujaris* have shown disunity among you. If they become the reformers there would dawn the age of truth...

There prostitutes, *hakims*, doctors, *vakils*, barristers, officers, nawabs, and kings, all are imbued with the spirit to convert the Hindus to Muhammadanism; by every means, by hook or by crook. When all would become Muhammadans there would be no quarrel. The foolish Hindus say that they are like oceans and that there would be no deficit whatever they lose. These foolish men have never looked to the Census Report. From 33 crores they came down to 22 crores. On account of *Shuddhi* and *Sangathan* their number has now risen up to 25 crores. On account of the oppressions and tyranny of the Muhammadans if the Hindu Arya do not work unitedly their number would further come down from 25 crores...

The Hindus did not treat the Muhammadans badly; while the latter have always treated the former badly. The Hindus should explain their [Muhammadan] bad point in the meetings of their [Hindu] national *panchayats* so that Hindu boys and girls might be careful. They should [neither take from nor give to] the Muhammadans without fight. They would starve. The Muhammadans have become careful; they have begun opening all sorts of shops. Even now if they [do not take from nor give to] still [*sic*] the number of the Hindus including the untouchables is 25 crores. The number of the Muhammadans is 8 crores only. One against every three. They hold consultations in the mosques and kill the Hindus. If the seven crores of untouchables join the Muhammadanism [*sic*] the number of the latter would become 15 crores. If eight crores are taken out from 25 crores, the balance would be only seventeen crores and then all the Hindus would be killed.

The Hindus neither lack strength, nor wealth, nor wisdom, nor number. They lack only organisation. The very day a Hindu will help a Hindu, all will be happy. The high should mix with the low; the low should listen to what the high say and then the high would help them with money and then there would be victory.

> Swami Dayanand came, blew the trumpet of the Vedas
>   and awakened those sleeping.
> God! give me strength, devotion
>   and the skill to reform the country.

RESOLUTIONS OF THE ALL-INDIA JAMIYAT-ULAMA-I ISLAM CONFERENCE, CALCUTTA, 31 OCTOBER 1945*

1. This session ... asserts the fundamental creed of Islam ... that the Islamic *millat* is an independent, separate and distinct nationality which is based entirely on the eternal, universally perfect and comprehensive principles of Islamic religion and the laws of the *Shariat-i Mohammadi*. It is a nationality which under no circumstances can be subject to or part of any other nationality or any other national culture and system of law. Accordingly the basic creed of Islam is that essentially there are two nationalities in the world – the one is the Islamic nationality which is grounded on (*sic*) religion and *Shariat* of laws of Mohammad (Peace be on him) and the other is the non-Muhammadan or non-Islamic nationality, which is based on the denial of the finality, authority, sovereignty, universality and comprehensiveness of the *Shariat* of Mohammad (Peace be on Him) and of Islam...

The All-India Jamiyat-Ulama-i Islam Conference declares that the two-nation theory in origin is the proclamation of the Quran and is not the invention of any man. On this ground this conference declares that the 100 million Muslims in the subcontinent of India are a distinct and independent nationality and a nationality of peculiar constitution which is grounded on the righteous principles of the Islamic *millat* and *Shariat* and not on the basis of race, colour, geography.

....

3. This session ... wholeheartedly supports the demand for Pakistan and the division of India ... Under the present circumstances the only way out for the Musalmans of India and the one and only way to achieve the liberation and deliverance of the Muslim nation and the effective defence and protection of Islamic religion, *Shariat* and culture is that the Muslims should at present concentrate on mobilizing all the forces of Islam for stubbornly opposing all schemes of all India federation and Akhand

* Box no. 56, FMA.

Bharat and achieving Pakistan under the direction of the All-India Muslim League [hereafter AIML].

4. This session ... puts on record its sense of high appreciation and deep gratitude for the monumental services which the AIML under Mr Jinnah's leadership has rendered during the past years for the establishment of the national individuality, integrity (*sic*), and independence of the Muslim nation for raising their status as a nation and an independent party and for launching a struggle for the independence of the *millat* under most disappointing (*sic*) conditions. The services which the Muslim League and its illustrious and patriotic president Mr. Mohammad Ali Jinnah have already rendered for the organisation's defence and independence of the Muslim nation have become historic and will go down to posterity as a proud record of the achievement of faith, courage and perseverance.

This session ... offers the sincerest thanks and deepest gratitude to Mr Jinnah on behalf of the *ulama* and *mashaikh* of Muslim India and assures him of their deep love and sympathy to him and of practical help and whole-hearted support to his noble mission ...

5. This session ... fully recognises the fact that the AIML is the only representative political organisation and spokesman of Muslim India capable of delivering goods on behalf of the Muslim nation. This conference appeals to all brethren in Islam and particularly to the *ulama* and *mashaikh* that they should come forward to mobilise all the forces of Islam in support of the Muslim League and its righteous principles. Thus they should help in making the national voice of Muslim India stronger and irresistible.

6. This session ... appeals to all the Musalmans and to voters in particular that in the coming Assembly and Council elections they should whole-heartedly support candidates set up by the recognised national *Jamaat* (party) of Muslim India, the AIML, and that under no circumstances they should support or help any independent candidate or a candidate set up by any other party. The setting up of candidates against the Muslim League and working for them will be most inimical to the whole solidarity, interest and future of the Islamic *millat* in India which largely depends upon the results of these elections. The issue of Pakistan is also involved in this fight and it is the Islamic duty of Muslim India to achieve cent per cent success for the League in this struggle.

[Resolutions 7 and 8 dealt with matters concerning the *Shariat* and the setting up of Qazi courts, a demand that has recently been renewed in some parts of India. In fact, a number of *Shariat* courts were reportedly set up in parts of UP and Bihar in 1994.]

WHAT DOES SECULARISM MEAN?
(√ one)

☐ Forfeiting the rights of the majority

☐ Appeasement of minorities
at all costs

☐ Inequitable treatment of people
from different faiths

☐ Irresponsible policies and practices
to favour minorities

☐ Fair and reasonable treatment of
people of all faiths

The Constitution of India calls for a secular state with fair and reasonable treatment of people of all faiths.

The BJP upholds this value and views its role as a constructive guardian of national unity and integrity.

The BJP is deeply distressed at the disinformation campaign charging it of inciting communal passions.

The BJP is constrained to point out that it is the government through its various actions that is responsible for alienating the majority community in the country.

It has attempted to systematically forfeit the rights of the majority.

CONSIDER THE FACTS:

Government has donated Rs. 50 lakhs to the Jama Masjid in Delhi.	No concern has been shown and nothing has been done about the dozens of temples demolished in Kashmir.
Prophet Mohammed's birthday has been declared a national holiday on Independence day.	Birthdays of Shri Rama, Lord Krishna and Shivaratri are not national holidays.
Shahi Imam Bukhari is constantly consulted by the Government to formulate policies.	The revered Shankaracharya has been sentenced to jail.
J & K terrorists freed to secure the release of one Rubaiah.	Thousands of devotees of Shri Ram have been detained.
Prompt relief has been provided to the riot victims of Bhagalpur, which was a good cause.	Nothing has been done and no time is available for the Kashmir migrants even in Delhi.
Government has expressed high ideals of respect for the judiciary.	There has been blatant flouting of the Court orders allowing people to offer prayers at Ayodhya.

ARE ALL THESE ACTIONS FAIR AND SECULAR?

Does Secularism merely mean appeasement of the minority?

The BJP is not against any group in the country. The BJP is only appealing for a secular treatment in every sense of the term, and the restoration of fair treatment of all.

The BJP is honestly committed, and will work with all the resources at its command to preserve the unity and integrity of India. And to ensure that this country marches forward to a progressive beat, and to a future of unbridled prosperity, in an atmosphere of permanent friendship among all communities.

Source: Issued by the General Secretary, Bharatiya Janata Party (facsimile).

Myths relating to minorities in India

MYTH: The population of Muslims is increasing rapidly because they are allowed to have four wives and soon Hindus will be a minority in India.

This is a lie easily disproved by census figures.

The Report on the Status of Women in India (1975) shows that the number of polygamous marriages was greater among Hindus than among Muslims. 5.06% of Hindu marriages were polygamous and 4.31% of Muslim marriages (1 out of 25) were polygamous. Besides, it must not be forgotten that there are 25 lakh less Muslim females than Muslim males. This means there is not even one woman per man leave aside four women for every man within the Muslim community.

MYTH: Political parties in the name of secularism appease minority communities.

In fact, political parties have actually appeased fundamentalists of all religions.

● On the 1st of May 1986 the locks of the Babri Masjid were opened, thus accepting the demands of the Hindu fundamentalists BJP/VHP/RSS combine.
● Five days later on the 6th of May 1986, the Congress appeased the Muslim fundamentalists by passing the Muslim Women's bill, overruling the Supreme Court judgement in the Shah Bano case.

This complicity of the Congress with the BJP and Muslim fundamentalists, not only gave fresh lease to the masjid-mandir dispute but also deprived Muslim women of maintenance rights. Hence, IT IS NOT AN APPEASE-

MENT OF MINORITIES BUT IN FACT AN APPEASEMENT OF FUNDAMENTALISTS OF ALL RELIGIONS AND IS NO REAL GAIN FOR THE PEOPLE.

If Muslims, as a community, have indeed been appeased, as claimed by the Sangh Parivar, this should be reflected in their economic and social status. In fact, the incidence of poverty among Muslims is 17% higher than among Hindus. Besides, in proportion to their number they are severely under represented in the bureaucracy, where they are less than 1%, educational institutions, and commerce.

MYTH: The Muslim majority state of Kashmir has special privileges through Article 370

Although Article 370 did envisage a special status for Kashmir because of the circumstances under which it acceded to India, **all the provisions which gave it a greater degree of autonomy than other states ceased to operate in 1954.** Since then Kashmir has been under the direct control of the central government, which has meant the curtailing of democratic rights for everyone living there.

MYTH : Non-Muslims cannot buy land in Kashmir.

The provision is that NON-KASHMIRIS cannot buy land in Kashmir, regardless of religion. This provision was in fact introduced by the Hindu Dogra rulers in 1928 to prevent the alienation of land to outsiders. Such provisions also exist in Hindu majority states like Himachal Pradesh as well as in some North-Eastern states.

MYTH: Hindustan is for Hindus alone.

The idea that Hindustan is for Hindus alone was firmly rejected by our freedom struggle which represented the sentiments of the majority of the people. It is the strength of our civilisation that numerous people belonging to different ethnic groups and communities have contributed to our plural society. In

fact, many people who call themselves Hindus today
had their origins outside of India, such as the Rajputs
who came from central Asia over the 7th and 8th
centuries, while there are many other communities who
have been in India longer, such as the Muslims of
Gujarat and Kerala who came in the 7th c. and the
Christians of Tamil Nadu and Kerala who have been
here since 32 AD.

Not all Muslims are invaders. Many Muslims
emigrated to India as traders, merchants, and artisans
and made India their home. Even those who did come
as invaders adopted this country as their own and
fought further invasions. Let us not forget that it was a
Pathan, Ibrahim Lodhi, himself a Muslim, who fought
against Babar.

**MYTH: All Muslims should go to Pakistan because
they are traitors who caused Partition.**

**All Muslims did not want Partition as is evident
from the fact that the bulk of them chose to stay in
India!** While Muslim zamindars of UP and Bihar, where
Muslims were in a minority, supported the demand for
Pakistan, the Muslim majority Frontier Province rejected
it. **Thus, Partition was a creation of communal
politics played by the elites of both communities
who were abetted by the British in order to divide
the freedom struggle.** The British were helped in their
project by today's self-proclaimed patriots, the RSS and
Hindu Mahasabha, who joined hands with the Muslim
League in boycotting the Quit India Movement in 1942.

The Partition of India took place in a period marked
by sharpening of communal conflict and a series of
communal riots which took the lives of over 2 lakh
people. Today the Sangh Parivar is attempting to create
the same atmosphere of terror and suspicion.

Let us not forget that the Sangh Parivar did not
hesitate to kill a devout Hindu like Gandhi who fought
all his life for a secular India. Today while bringing the

nation to the brink of disintegration, they continue to claim to be patriots.

If the events of the 6th of December were a taste of the Hindu Rashtra which the Sangh Parivar would like to transform India into, then it is clear there would be no room for most Hindus let alone the minority communities.

Source: Sampradayitka Virodhi Andolan (Delhi), December 1992 (facsimile).

SELECT BIBLIOGRAPHY

PRIVATE PAPERS

India Office Library and Records (IOL), London

A.J. Dash Papers
Harry Haig Papers
Harold Mitchell Papers
M.F. Mudie Papers
Linlithgow Papers
Northbrook Papers
Arthur Owen Papers
Major-General Stockley Warren Papers
J.D. Tyson Papers

Nehru Memorial Museum and Library (NMML), New Delhi

M.C. Chagla Papers
Mir Mushtaq Ahmad Papers

Centre for South Asian Studies, Cambridge

E.J. Benthall Papers
M.G. Bell Papers
Patrick Biggie Papers
P. Brendon Papers
H.J. Frampton Papers
H. Ghoshal Papers
H.B. Martin Papers
Ian Stephens Papers

Freedom Movement Archives (FMA), Karachi

Mujtaba Khan Papers
All-India Muslim League Records

Khalid Shamsul Hasan Collection, Karachi

Mohammad Ali Jinnah Papers

OFFICIAL PUBLICATIONS

Census of India, 1921, vol. xv. *Punjab and Delhi*, part I (Lahore, 1923).
Census of India, 1921, Oudh, part I (Allahabad, 1923).
Constituent Assembly Debates (CAD), vols 10-12 (Delhi, 1989 reprint).

352

First Annual Report of the Minorities Commission for the year ending 31 December 1978 (Delhi, 1979).
Gazette of India: Delhi (Delhi, 1978).
Gazetteer of India (Delhi, 1976).
Lok Sabha Debates, August 1953, January-December 1955, December 1957, March 1959, 31 August 1959.
Ministry of Home Affairs, Government of India, 'Contemporary Muslim Attitudes on Their Place in Indian Society', by Gopal Krishna, Centre for the Study of Developing Societies, Delhi, January 1977.
Report of the Committee for the Promotion of Urdu 1975 (Ministry of Education and Social Welfare, Government of India).
Report on Minorities, vol. 2 (Delhi: Ministry of Home Affairs, 14 June 1983).
Sixth Report of the National Police Commission (1981).

NEWSPAPERS, JOURNALS AND MAGAZINES

Asian Survey (California, U.S.A.).
Burhan (Delhi-Urdu).
Economic and Political Weekly (*EPW*) (Bombay).
Frontline (Bangalore – for chapters 8 and 9).
Gagan (Bombay: Urdu), Hindustani Mussalman number, 1975.
Hindustan Times (Delhi).
India Today (Delhi – for chapters 8 and 9).
Indian Economic and Social History Review (Delhi).
Inqilab (Lahore – Urdu, for chapter 2).
Journal of Asian Studies (California, U.S.A.).
Modern Asian Studies (Cambridge, England).
Muslim India (Delhi), 1983-6.
National Herald – for chapter 8
Pioneer (Delhi – for chapters 8 and 9).
Qaumi Awaaz (Delhi – for chapters 8 and 9).
Seminar (Delhi).
Statesman (Delhi).
Sunday (Calcutta – for chapters 8 and 9).

BOOKS AND UNPUBLISHED THESES

Abbas, K.A., *I am not an Island: An Experiment in Autobiography* (Delhi, 1987).
Ahmad, Aijazuddin, *Muslims in India: Bihar*, vol. I (Delhi, 1993), *Muslims in India: Rajasthan*, vol. 2 (1994); and *Muslims in India: Delhi*, vol. 3 (1995).
Ahmad, Aziz, *Islamic Modernism in India and Pakistan 1857-1946* (London, 1967).
——, *An Intellectual History of Islam* (Edinburgh, 1969).
—— and G.E. von Grunebaum (eds), *Muslim Self-Statement in India and Pakistan 1857-1968* (Wiesbaden, 1970).
Ahmad, Imtiaz (ed.), *Caste and Social Stratification Among Muslims* (Delhi, 1973).
—— (ed.), *Family, Kinship and Marriage in Indian Islam* (Delhi, 1976).

Ahmad, Ishtiaq, *The Concept of an Islamic State* (London, 1987).

Ahmad, Mujeeb, *Jamiyyat Ulama-i Pakistan, 1949-1979* (Islamabad, 1993).

Ahmad, Syed Nesar, *Origins of Muslim Consciousness in India: A World-System Perspective* (New York, 1991).

Ahmed, Rafiuddin, *The Bengal Muslims 1871-1906* (Delhi, 1981).

Akbar, M.J., *India: The Siege Within* (Delhi, 1985).

——, *Riot After Riot: Reports on Caste and Communal Violence in India* (Delhi, 1991).

Akhand Bharat or Akhand Pakistan?, Exchange of Population Conference, New Delhi, 28-29 March 1964.

Ali, Ahmed, *Twilight in Delhi* (Delhi, 1991).

Ali, K.T. Mohammad, *The Development of Education among the Mappilas of Malabar, 1800-1965* (Delhi, 1990).

Ali, Sheik, *Zakir Husain: Life and Time* (Delhi, 1991).

All India Milli Council: Perspective, Significance, Aims and Objectives (Delhi: All India Milli Council, n.d.).

Alter, Stephen, and Vimal Dissanayake (eds), *Penguin Book of Modern Indian Short Stories* (Delhi, 1989).

Anderson, Walter & Shridhar D. Damle, *The Brotherhood in Saffron: The Rashtriya Swayamsewak Sangh and Hindu Revivalism* (London, 1987).

Another Lonely Voice: The Life and Works of Saadat Hasan Manto, introduction by Leslie A. Fleming (Lahore, 1985).

Ansari, Sarah F.D., *Sufi Saints and State Power: The Pirs of Sind, 1843-1947* (Cambridge, 1992).

Ayubi, Nazib, *Political Islam: Religion and Politics in the Arab World* (London, 1991).

Baig, M.R.A., *In Different Saddles* (Bombay, 1967).

Baig, Tara Ali, *Portraits of an Era* (Delhi, 1988).

Bannerman, Patrick, *Islam in Perspective: A Guide to Islamic Society, Politics and Law* (London, 1988).

Barlas, Asma, *Democracy, Nationalism and Communalism: The Colonial Legacy in South Asia* (Boulder, CO, 1995).

Basu, Dilip, and Richard Sisson (eds), *Social and Economic Development in India: A Reassessment* (Delhi, 1986).

Basu, Tapan, *et al., Khaki Shorts and Saffron Flags* (Delhi, 1993).

Bayly, C.A., *Rulers, Townsmen and Bazaars: North Indian Society in the Age of British Expansion, 1770-1870* (Cambridge, 1983).

Bayly, Susan, *Saints, Goddesses and Kings: Muslims and Christians in South Indian Society, 1700-1900* (Cambridge, 1990).

Bhagalpur Riots (Delhi [PUDR], April 1990).

Bhalla, Alok, and Sudhir Chandra (eds), *Indian Responses to Colonialism in the 19th Century* (Delhi, 1993).

Bhalla, Alok (ed.), *Stories About the Partition of India*, 3 vols (Delhi, 1994).

Bidwai, Praful, Harbans Mukhia and Achin Vanaik (eds), *Religion, Religiosity and Communalism* (Delhi, 1996).

Binder, Leonard, *Religion and Politics in Pakistan* (Berkeley, CA, 1963).

——, *Islamic Liberalism: A Critique of Development Ideologies* (Chicago, 1988).

Blair, Harry W., *Voting, Caste, Community, Society: Explorations in Aggregate Data Analysis in India and Bangla Desh* (Delhi, 1979).

Brass, Paul R., *Language, Religion and Politics in North India* (Cambridge, 1974).

——, *Caste, Faction and Party in Indian Politics*, vol. 2 (Delhi, 1985).

——, *Factional Politics in an Indian State* (Berkeley, CA, 1965).

Breckenridge, Carol A., and Peter van der Veer (eds), *Orientalism and the Postcolonial Predicament* (Delhi, 1994).

Brohi, A.K., *An Adventure in Self-Expression* (Lahore, 3rd edn, n.d.).

Burger, Angela, *Opposition in a Dominant Party System: A Study of the Jana Sangh, Praja Socialists and Socialist Parties in Uttar Pradesh, India* (Bombay, 1969).

Burki, Shahid Javed, *Pakistan under Bhutto, 1971-1977* (London, 1980).

Butler, Harcourt, *Speeches* (Allahabad, 1921).

——, *India Insistent* (London, 1931).

Carras, Mary C., *Indira Gandhi: In the Crucible of Leadership* (Boston, MA, 1979).

Chagla, M.C., *Roses in December: An Autobiography* (Bombay, 1973).

Chandra, Sudhir., *The Oppressive Present: Literature and Social Consciousness in Colonial India* (Delhi, 1992).

Chatterjee, Joya, *Bengal Divided: Hindu Communalism and Partition* (Cambridge, 1995).

Chatterjee, Partha, *Nationalist Thought and the Colonial World: A Derivative Discourse?* (Delhi, 1986).

Chattopadhyaya, Kamaladevi, *Inner Recesses Outer Spaces* (Delhi, 1986).

Chaudhuri, Nirad C., *The Autobiography of an Unknown Indian* (London, 1951).

——, *Thy Great Hand Anarch! India 1921-1952* (Delhi, 1987).

Chirol, V., *India Old and New* (London, 1921).

Cragg, Kenneth, *The Call of the Minaret* (New York, 1966).

——, *The Pen and the Faith* (Delhi, 1986 reprint).

Crooke, W., *The North-Western Provinces of India: Their History, Ethnology, and Administration* (1897; Delhi, 1975).

Dalmia, Vasudha and H. von Stietencron (eds), *Representing Hinduism: The Construction of Religious Traditions and National Identity* (Delhi, 1995).

Darling, Frank C., *The Westernization of Asia: A Comparative Political Analysis* (Boston, 1979).

Darling, M.L., *At Freedom's Dawn* (London, 1949).

Dalrymple, William, *City of Djinns: A Year in Delhi* (Delhi, 1993).

Das, Veena (ed.), *Communities, Riots and Survivors in South Asia* (Delhi, 1990).

Datta, V.N., *Maulana Azad* (Delhi, 1990).

—— and B.E. Cleghorn (eds), *A Nationalist Muslim and Indian Politics* (Delhi, 1974).

Desai, Anita, *In Custody* (Delhi, 1994).

Douglas, I.H., *Abul Kalam Azad: An Intellectual and Religious Biography*, edited by Gail Minault and C.W. Troll (Delhi, 1988).

Dwivedi, S, *Hindi on Trial* (Delhi, 1981).

Edib, Halide, *Inside India* (London, 1937).

Elliot, C.A., *Laborious Days* (Calcutta, 1892).

Embree, Ainslie T., *Imagining India: Essays on Indian History* (Delhi, 1989).

Engineer, Asghar A. (ed.), *Communal Riots in Post-Independence India* (Hyderabad, 1984).
——, *Lifting the Veil: Communal Violence and Communal Harmony in Contemporary India* (Hyderabad, 1995).
Epstein, T.S., *Economic Development and Social Change in South Asia* (Delhi, 1962).
Faruqi, Ziya-ul-Hasan, *The Deoband School and the Demand for Pakistan* (Bombay, 1963).
Friedmann, Yohanan (ed.), *Islam in Asia*, vol. I: *South Asia* (Jerusalem, 1984).
Fuller, Bampfylde, *The Empire of India* (London, 1913).
——, *Studies of Indian Life and Sentiments* (London, 1910).
Fyzee, A.A.A., *A Modern Approach to Islam* (Bombay, 1963).
Gankovsky, Y.V., and L.R. Gordon-Polonskaya, *A History of Pakistan 1947-58* (Moscow, 1964).
Garrat, G.T., *An Indian Commentary* (London, 1929).
Ghosh, S.K., *Communal Riots in India: Meeting the Challenge Unitedly* (Delhi, 1987).
Gillion, Kenneth L., *Ahmedabad: A Study in Indian Urban History* (California, 1968).
Gilmartin, David, *Empire and Islam: Punjab and the Making of Pakistan* (London, 1988).
Golwalkar, M.S., *Bunch of Thoughts* (Bangalore, 1980).
Gopal, Sarvepalli, *Jawaharlal Nehru A Biography,* vol. 2: *1946-1956* (Delhi, 1979).
——(ed.), *Anatomy of a Confrontation: The Babri Masjid-Ramjanmabhumi Issue* (Delhi, 1991).
Gordon, A.D.D., *Businessmen and Politics: Rising Nationalism and a Modernising Economy in Bombay, 1918-1933* (Delhi, 1978).
Graham, B.D., *Hindu Nationalism and Indian Politics: The Origins and Development of the Bharatiya Jana Sangh* (Cambridge, 1990).
Gupta, Jyotirindra Das, *Language Conflict and National Development: Group Politics and National Language Policy in India* (Berkeley, CA, 1970).
Hamid, Saiyid, *Education and Modernisation: Two Wheels of Muslim Regeneration* (Hyderabad, n.d.).
Haq, Mushir U., *Muslim Politics in Modern India* (Meerut, 1970).
——, *Islam in Secular India* (Simla, 1972).
Hardy, Peter, *The Muslims of British India* (Cambridge, 1972).
——, *Partners in Freedom – and True Muslims: The Political Thought of Muslim Scholars in British India 1912-1947* (Lund, Sweden, 1971).
Hasan, Masudul, *Sayyid Abul A'ala Maududi and his Thought*, vol. 1 (Lahore, n.d.).
Hasan, Mushirul, *Nationalism and Communal Politics in India, 1885-1930* (Delhi, 1991).
——, *A Nationalist Conscience: M.A. Ansari, the Congress and the Raj* (Delhi, 1987).
—— (ed.), *Communal and Pan-Islamic Trends in Colonial India* (Delhi, 1985).
—— (ed.), *India's Partition: Process, Strategy and Mobilization* (Delhi, 1993).
—— (ed.), *India Partitioned: The Other Face of Freedom*, 2 vols (Delhi, 1995).

—— (ed.), *Islam and Indian Nationalism: Reflections on Abul Kalam Azad* (Delhi, 1992).

—— and Narayani Gupta (eds), *India's Colonial Encounter: Essays in Memory of Eric Stokes* (Delhi, 1993).

Hasan, Zoya, *Dominance and Mobilisation: Rural Politics in Western Uttar Pradesh, 1930-1980* (Delhi, 1989).

—— (ed.), *Forging Identities: Gender, Communities and the State* (Delhi, 1994).

Haynes, Douglas E., *Rhetoric and Ritual in Colonial India: The Shaping of a Public Culture in Surat City, 1852-1928* (Berkeley, CA, 1991).

Hosain, Attia, *Sunlight on a Broken Column* (Delhi, 1992).

——, *Phoenix Fled* (Delhi, 1993 edn.).

Hourani, Albert, *Arabic Thought in the Liberal Age, 1798-1939* (Oxford, 1970).

——, *A History of the Arab Peoples* (London, 1991).

Husain, S. Abid, *The National Culture of India* (Delhi, 1956).

——, *The Destiny of Indian Muslims* (Bombay, 1965).

——, *The Way of Gandhi and Nehru* (Bombay, 1959).

——, *Gandhiji and Communal Unity* (Bombay, 1969).

Husain, Intizar, *Basti*, translated from Urdu by Frances W. Pritchett (Delhi, 1995).

Ikramullah, Begum Shaista S., *From Purdah to Parliament* (London, 1963).

——, *Huseyn Shaheed Suhrawardy* (Karachi, 1971).

Imam, Zafar (ed.), *Muslims in India* (Delhi, 1975).

Introducing the Jamaat-e Islami-i Hind (Delhi, 1971).

Islamic Fiqah Academy: Introduction, Aims and Resolutions (Delhi, n.d.).

Jain, Sushila, *Muslims and Modernisation: A Study of their Changing Role Structure and Norms in an Urban Setting* (Jaipur, 1986).

Jalal, Ayesha, *The Sole Spokesman: Jinnah, the Muslim League and the Demand for Pakistan* (Cambridge, 1985).

——, *Democracy and Authoritarianism in South Asia: A Comparative and Historical Perspective* (Cambridge, 1995).

Jalibi, Jameel, *Pakistan: The Identity of Culture* (Delhi, n.d.).

Jamiyat Ulama-i Hind: Objects and Activities in Brief (Delhi, n.d.).

Javed, Arifa K., *Muslim Society in Transition* (Delhi, 1990).

Jayakar, Pupul, *Indira Gandhi: A Biography* (Delhi, 1992).

Jones, K.W., *Arya Dharm: Hindu Consciousness in 19th Century Punjab* (Berkeley, CA, 1976).

Joshi, V.C. (ed.), *Lajpat Rai: Autobiographical Writings* (Delhi, 1965).

Juergensmeyer, Mark, *The New Cold War? Religious Nationalism Confronts the Secular State* (Delhi, 1994).

Kabbani, Rana, *Europe's Myths of Oriental Divide and Rule* (London, 1986).

Kabir, Humayun, *Muslim Politics, 1906-1942* (Calcutta, 1944).

Kandhalwi, Mohammad Zakariya, *Aap Beeti: Autobiography* (Delhi, 1993).

Kettani, M.A., *Muslim Minorities in the World Today* (London, 1986).

Khalidi, Omar, *Indian Muslims Since Independence* (Delhi, 1995).

Khaliquzzaman, C., *Pathway to Pakistan* (Lahore, 1964).

Khan, Major-General Sher Ali, *The Story: Soldiering and Politics in India and Pakistan* (Lahore, 1988).

Khan, Wahiduddin, *Indian Muslims: The Need for a Positive Outlook* (Delhi, 1994).

Khusro, A.M., *Economic and Social Effects of Jagirdari Abolition and Land Reforms in Hyderabad* (Hyderabad, 1958).

Khwaja, Altaf Husain Hali, *Voices of Silence*, English translation of *Majalis-un Nisa* by Gail Minault (Delhi, 1986 edn).

Kiernan, V.G. (ed.), *Poems by Faiz* (London, 1971).

Kirpalani, S.K., *Fifty Years with the British* (Hyderabad, 1993).

Kochanek, Stanley A., *Interest Groups and Development: Business and Politics in Pakistan* (Delhi, 1993).

——, *The Congress Party of India: The Dynamics of One-Party Dominance* (Princeton, 1968).

Kozlowski, G.C., *Muslim Endowments and Society in British India* (Cambridge, 1985).

Kruger, Horst (ed.), *Kunwar Mohammad Ashraf: An Indian Scholar and Revolutionary, 1903-1962* (Berlin, 1966).

Kudaisya, Medha Malik, 'The Public Career of G.D. Birla' (unpublished Ph.D. thesis, University of Cambridge, 1992).

Laird, M.A. (ed.), *Bishop Heber in Northern India: Selection from Heber's 'Journal* (Cambridge, 1971).

Lateef, Shahida, *Muslim Women in India: Political and Private Realities, 1890s-1980s* (Delhi, 1990).

Latif, Bilkees, *Her India: The Fragrance of Forgotten Years* (Delhi, 1984).

Lewandowski, Susan, *Migration and Ethnicity in India: Kerala Migrants in the City of Madras, 1870-1970* (Delhi, 1980).

Liebeskind, Claudi, 'Sufism, Sufi Leadership in South Asia since 1800' (unpubl. Ph.D. thesis, University of London, 1995).

Low, Sidney, *A Vision of India* (London, 1907).

Ludden, David (ed.), *Contesting the Nation: Religion, Community and the Politics of Democracy in India* (Philadelphia, 1996).

Luther, Narendra, *Hyderabad: Memories of a City* (Hyderabad, 1995).

Lytton, Earl of, *Pundits and Elephants: Being the Experiences of Five Years as Governor of an Indian Province* (London, 1942).

Madan, T.N. (ed.), *Muslim Communities of South Asia: Culture, Society and Power* (Delhi, 1995).

Madhok, Balraj, *Dr Syama Prasad Mookerjee: A Biography* (Delhi, 1954).

——, *Hindustan on the Crossroads* (Lahore, 1946).

——, *Indianization* (Delhi, 1980).

Malhotra, Inder, *Indira Gandhi: A Personal and Political Biography* (London, 1989).

Manglori, Tufail Ahmad, *Towards a Common Destiny: A Nationalist Manifesto*, English translation of *Mussalmanon ka Raushan Mustaqbil* by Ali Ashraf (Delhi, 1995).

Mann, E.S., *Boundaries and Identities: Muslims, Work and Status in Aligarh* (Delhi, 1992).

Markovits, Claude, *Indian Business and Nationalist Politics 1931-39: The Indigenous Capitalist Class and the Rise of the Congress Party* (Cambridge, 1985).

Masroor, Mehr Nigar, *Shadow of Time* (Lahore, 1995).

Maududi, A.A., *Nationalism and India* (Lahore, 1947 edn).

——, *The Process of Islamic Revolution* (Lahore, 1955 edn).

Maulana Ikhlaq Husain Qasimi, *Jamaat-e-Islami and Secularism* (Delhi, n.d.).

Metcalf, Barbara Daly, *Islamic Revival in British India: Deoband, 1860-1900* (Princeton, 1982).

Miller, Roland E., *Mapilla Muslims of Kerala: A Study in Islamic Trends* (Delhi, 1992 rev. edn).

Mines, Mattison, *Muslim Merchants: The Economic Behaviour of an Indian Muslim Community* (Delhi, 1972).

Mitra, Asok, *The New India, 1948-1955: Memoirs of an Indian Civil Servant* (Bombay, 1991).

Molund, Stephan, *First We Are People: The Koris of Kanpur between Caste and Class* (Stockholm, 1988).

Muhammad, Shan, *Khaksar Movement in India* (Meerut, 1972).

Mujeeb, M., *Islamic Influences on Indian Society* (Meerut, 1972).

——, *The Indian Muslims* (London, 1967).

——, *Education and Traditional Values* (Delhi, 1965).

——, *Ghalib* (Delhi, 1969).

Mukerjee, Radhakamal, and Baljit Singh, *Social Profiles of a Metropolis: Social and Economic Structure of Lucknow, 1954-56* (Bombay, 1961).

——, *A District Town in Transition: Social and Economic Survey of Gorakhpur* (Bombay, 1965).

Mullick, B.N., *My Years with Nehru, 1948-1964* (Delhi, 1972).

Munshi, K.M., *Sparks from a Governor's Anvil*, vol. 1 (Lucknow, 1956).

——, *The End of an Era: Hyderabad Memoirs* (Bombay, 1957).

Murshid, Tazeen M., *The Sacred and the Secular: Bengal Muslim Discourses, 1871-1977* (Calcutta, 1995).

Naipaul, V.S., *India A Million Mutinies Now* (Delhi, 1991).

——, *Among The Believers: An Islamic Journey* (Suffolk, 1981).

Naqvi, Saeed, *Reflections of an Indian Muslim* (Delhi, 1992).

Nehru, Jawaharlal, *An Autobiography* (London, 1936).

——, *The Discovery of India* (Calcutta, 1946 reprint).

Nomani, Mohammad Manzoor, *Islamic Faith and Practice*, translated from Urdu by Mohammad Asif Kidwai (Lucknow, 1962).

Noon, Firoz Khan, *Scented Dust* (Lahore, 1941).

——, *From Memory* (Lahore, 1966).

Noorani, A.G., *President Zakir Husain: A Quest for Excellence* (Bombay, 1967).

Outram, James, *Memoirs of my Indian Career* (London, 1893).

Pandey, Gyanendra, *The Construction of Communalism in Colonial India* (Delhi, 1990).

—— (ed.), *Hindus and Others: The Question of Identity in India Today* (Delhi, 1993).

Panikkar, K.M., *The Foundations of New India* (London, 1963).

——, *Asia and Western Dominance* (London, 1953).

Panikkar, K.N., *Communalism in India: History, Politics and Culture* (Delhi, 1991).

Philips, C.H and M.D. Wainwright (eds), *The Partition of India: Policies and Perspectives* (London, 1970).

Prakash, I., *Hindu Mahasabha: Its Contribution to India's Politics* (Delhi, 1966).

——, *A Tale of Blunders* (Delhi, 1947).
Qureshi, I.H., *Ulema in Politics* (Karachi, 1974 edn).
——, *From Miraj to Domes* (Karachi, 1983).
Raychaudhuri, T., *Europe Reconsidered: Perceptions of the West in Nineteenth Century World* (Delhi, 1988).
Reeves, P.D., *Landlords and Government in Uttar Pradesh* (Delhi, 1991).
Report on the Mysore session of the All India Milli Council and Council's Activities from Bombay to Mysore (n.d.).
Reza, Rahi Masoom, *The Feuding Families of Village Gangauli*, translated from the Hindi by Gillian Wright (Delhi, 1994).
Rizvi, Abida Riasat, *The Leaves of Gold* (Karachi, 1976).
Rizvi, Gowher, *Linlithgow and India: A Study of British Policy and the Political Impasse in India, 1936-1943* (London, 1978).
Rizvi, S.M., *History of the Dar al-ulum Deoband*, 2 vols (Allahabad, 1980).
Robinson, Francis, *Separatism Among Indian Muslims: The Politics of the United Provinces' Muslims, 1860-1923* (Cambridge, 1974).
Ronaldshay, Earl of, *India: A Bird's-Eye View* (London, 1924).
——, *The India We Served* (London, 1928).
——, *The Heart of Aryavarta: A Study of the Psychology of Indian Unrest* (London, 1925).
Roy, Asim, *The Islamic Syncretistic Tradition in Bengal* (Princeton, 1983).
Roy, M.N. *India in Transition* (Bombay, 1922; 1971 reprint).
——, *The Historical Role of Islam* (Delhi, 1974; 1981 reprint).
Royle, Trevor, *The Last Days of the Raj* (London, 1989).
Russell, Ralph, *The Pursuit of Urdu Literature: A Select History* (Delhi, 1992).
—— and Khurshidul Islam, *Three Mughal Poets: Mir, Mir Sauda, Mir Hasan* (London, 1969).
—— and Khurshidul Islam, *Ghalib: Life and Letters, 1797-1869* (London, 1969).
Ruthven, Malise, *Islam in the World* (New York, 1984).
Saadat Hasan Manto: Kingdom's End and Other Stories, translated from the Urdu by Khalid Hasan (Delhi, 1989).
Sadiq, Muhammad, *Twentieth Century Urdu Literature* (Karachi, 1983).
Sampurnanand, *Memoirs and Reflections* (Delhi, 1962).
Sanyal, Uma, *Devotional Islam and Politics in British India: Ahmad Riza Khan Barelwi and his Movement 1870-1920* (Delhi, 1996).
Savarkar, V.D., *Historic Statement*, edited by S.S. Savarkar and G.M. Joshi (Bombay, 1967).
Save the Country and Millat Movement (Delhi, 1979).
Saxena, D.N., *Different Urban Fertility – Lucknow: Report of the Intensive Fertility Survey of Lucknow City* (Lucknow, 1973).
Sayeed, Khalid b., *Pakistan: The Formative Phase 1857-1948* (London, 1968).
——, *Politics in Pakistan: The Nature and Direction of Change* (New York, 1980).
Schimmel, Annemarie, *Gabriel's Wing: A Study into the Religious Ideas of Sir Muhammad Iqbal* (Leiden, 1963).
——, *Islam in the Indian Subcontinent* (Leiden, 1980).
Seshadari, M.V. (ed.), *R.S.S: A Vision in Action* (Bangalore, 1988).
Shahnawaz, Jahan Ara, *Father and Daughter: A Political Biography* (Lahore, 1971).

Shaikh, Farzana, *Community and Consensus in Islam: Muslim Representation in Colonial India, 1860-1947* (Cambridge, 1989).
Shakir, Moin, *Muslims in Free India* (Bombay, 1972).
——, *Religion, State and Politics in India* (Delhi, 1989).
Shourie, Arun, *Indian Controversies: Essays on Religion in Politics* (Delhi, 1993).
——, *Religion in Politics* (Delhi, 1987).
——, *A Secular Agenda: For Saving Our Country For Welding It* (Delhi, 1993).
Siddiqui, Kalim, *Conflict and War in Pakistan* (London, 1972).
—— (ed.), *Issues in the Islamic Movement 1980-81* (London, n.d.).
—— (ed.), *Issues in the Islamic Movement 1982-83* (London, n.d.).
Siddiqi, M.M., *After Secularism What?* (Rampur, 1952).
Singh, Anita Inder, *The Origins of the Partition of India 1936-1947* (Delhi, 1987).
Sisson, Richard and Stanley Wolpert (eds), *Congress and Indian Nationalism: The Pre-Independence Phase* (Berkeley, CA, 1988).
Smith, D.E. (ed.), *South Asian Politics and Religion* (Princeton, 1966).
——, *India as a Secular State* (Princeton, 1963).
Smith, W.C., *Modern Islam in India* (Lahore, 1943).
——, *Islam in Modern History* (New York, 1959).
Sorenson, R.W., *My Impression of India* (London, 1946).
Srinivasan, Nirmala, *Prisoners of Faith: A View from Within* (Delhi, 1989).
Stepanyants, M.T., *Pakistan: Philosophy and Sociology* (Moscow, 1971).
Stephens, Ian, *Pakistan* (London, 1964 edn.).
Syed Abul Hasan Ali Nadwi, *Muslims in India*, translated from Urdu by M. Asif Kidwai (Lucknow, 1960).
——, *Life and Mission of Maulana Mohammad Ilyas*, translated from Urdu by M. Asif Kidwai (Lucknow, 1983).
——, *Western Civilization – Islam and Muslims*, translated from Urdu by M. Asif Kidwai (Lucknow, 1969).
Talbot, Ian, *Punjab and the Raj, 1849-1947* (Delhi, 1988).
——, *Provincial Politics and the Pakistan Movement: The Growth of the Muslim League in North-West and North-East India 1937-1947* (Delhi, 1988).
——, *Freedom's City: The Popular Dimension in the Pakistan and Partition Experience in North-West India* (Karachi, 1995).
Taleyarkhan, J.H., *They Told Me So* (Bombay, 1947).
Tandon, Prakash, *Punjab Century, 1857-1947* (London, 1961).
——, *Beyond Punjab 1937-1960* (Berkeley, CA, 1971).
Tripathi, Dwijendra (ed.), *Business and Politics in India: A Historical Perspective* (Delhi, 1991).
Tripathi, Kamalapati, *Freedom Movement and Afterwards* (Varanasi, 1969).
Tyabji, Badruddin, *Chaff and Grain* (Calcutta, 1962).
——, *Memoirs of an Egoist*, vol. 1, (Delhi, 1988).
——, *The Self in Secularism* (Delhi, 1971).
Voll, John Obert (ed.), *Islam: Continuity and Change in the Modern World* (Boulder, CO, 1982).
Walled City Riots: A Report on the Police and Communal Violence in Delhi, 19-24 May 1987 (Delhi: PUDR, 1987).
Wolpert, Stanley, *Jinnah of Pakistan* (New York, 1984).
Zaheer, Sajjad, *A Case for Congress-League Unity* (Bombay, 1944).

Zaidi, Ali Jawad, *A History of Urdu Literature* (Delhi, 1993).
Zakaria, Rafiq, *The Widening Divide: An Insight into Hindu-Muslim Relations* (Delhi, 1995).
Zaman, Mukhtar, *Students' Role in the Pakistan Movement* (Karachi, 1978).
Zuberi, Mussarat Husain, *Voyage Through History*, vol. I (Karachi, 1984).

PUBLISHED CORRESPONDENCE AND SPEECHES

Choudhary, Valmiki (ed.), *Dr Rajendra Prasad: Correspondence and Select Documents* (Delhi: in process of publication).
Das, Durga (ed.), *Sardar Patel's Correspondence 1945-50*, vol. 4 (Ahmedabad, 1972).
Gopal, S. (ed.), *Selected Works of Jawaharlal Nehru* (Delhi, in process of publication).
Munshi, K.M., *Indian Constitutional Documents: Pilgrimages to Freedom (1920-1950)* (Bombay, 1967).
Parthasarathi, G. (ed.), *Letters to Chief Ministers, 1947-1949*, 5 vols (Delhi, Jawaharlal Nehru Memorial Fund).
Patel, Vallabhbhai, *For a United India: Speeches of Sardar Patel, 1947-50* (Delhi, 1989).
Pirzada, S. (ed.), *Foundations of Pakistan*, 2 vols, (Karachi, 1970).
The Quaid-e-Azam Papers, 1941-42 (Karachi, 1976).
Speeches of Maulana Azad, 1947-1955 (Delhi, 1956).
Zaidi, Z.H. (ed.), *M.A. Jinnah-Ispahani Correspondence, 1936- 1948* (Karachi, 1976).

TRACTS ON PAKISTAN

Ahmad, Jamiluddin, *Some Aspects of Pakistan*, Pakistan Literature Series (PLS) no. 3 (Lahore, 1946).
Ahmad, Kazi Saiduddin, *The Communal Patterns of India*, PLS no. 2 (Lahore, 1945).
——, *Politico-Regional Division of India*, PLS no. 4 (Lahore, 1945).
——, *Is India Geographically One?*, PLS no. 6 (Lahore: 1945).
Faziel, Ali Ahmad, *Power Resources of Pakistan*, PLS no. 10 (Lahore, 1946).
Mohiuddin, Ghulam, *Hindu Congress ka dawa-i qaum-parasti aur qaum-parast Mussalman* (Publicity and Information Department: Muslim League, n.d.).
Qureshi, I.H., *The Future Development of Islamic Polity*, PLS no. 8 (Lahore, 1946).
——, *National States and National Minorities*, PLS no. 1 (Lahore, 1945).
Zaidi, Syed Azhar Husain, *The New Nazis* (Karachi, n.d.).

ARTICLES AND PAMPHLETS

Agwani, M.S., 'God's Government: Jamaat-i-Islami of India', in Husain Mutalib and Taj ul-Islam (eds), *Islam, Muslims and the Modern State* (London, 1994).
Ahmad, Aziz, 'India and Pakistan' in Ann K.S. Lambton and Bernard Lewis (eds), *The Cambridge History of Islam*, vol. 2A (Cambridge, 1977).

Ahmad, Imtiaz, 'The Muslim Electorate and Election Alternatives in UP', *Religion and Society*, June 1974.

Ahmad, Mumtaz, 'Islamic Fundamentalism in South Asia: The Jamaat-i Islami and the Tablighi Jamaat of South Asia' in Martin E. Marty and R. Scott Appleby (eds), *Fundamentalism and the State: Remaking Polities, Economies and Militance* (Chicago, 1993).

Alavi, Hamza, 'Pakistan and Islam: Ethnicity and Ideology', Fred Halliday and Hamza Alavi (eds), *State and Ideology in the Middle East and Pakistan* (New York, 1987).

Anderson, Michael R., 'Islamic Law and the Colonial Encounter in British India' in Chibli Mallat and Jane Connors (eds), *Islamic Family Law* (London, 1990).

M. Aslam, 'The UP Muslims – 1947, 1967, 1987', in Jim Masselos (ed.), *India: Creating a Modern Nation* (Delhi, 1990).

Baird, Robert D., 'Religion and the Legitimation of Nehru's Concept of the Secular State' in Bardwell L. Smith (ed.), *Religion and the Legitimation of Power in South Asia* (Leiden, 1978).

Bardhan, A.B., *Sangh Parivar's Hindutva versus The Real Hindu Ethos* (Delhi, 1992).

Basu, Amrita, 'When Local Riots Are not Merely Local: Bringing the State Back In, Bijnor 1988-92', *Economic and Political Weekly*, 1 October 1994.

Bilgrami, Akeel, 'What is a Muslim? Fundamental Commitment and Cultural Identity', *Economic and Political Weekly*, 16-23 May 1992.

Brennan, Lance, 'The Illusion of Security: The Background to Muslim Separatism in the United Provinces', *Modern Asian Studies*, 18, 2, 1984.

——, 'The State and Communal Violence in UP, 1947-1992', *South Asia*, special issue, 17, 1994.

Beteille, André, 'Secularism and Intellectuals', *Economic and Political Weekly*, 5 March 1994.

Carroll, Lucy, 'Colonial Perceptions of Indian Society and the Emergence of Caste(s) Associations', *Journal of Asian Studies*, 37, 2, February 1978.

Chakravarti Uma *et al.*, 'Khurja Riots 1900: Understanding the Conjuncture', *Economic and Political Weekly*, 2 May 1992.

Chandra, Sudhir, 'The Lengthening Shadow: Secular and Communal Consciousness' in Bidyut Chakrabarty (ed.), *Secularism and Indian Polity* (Delhi, 1990).

——, 'Of communal consciousness and communal violence: Impressions from post-riot Surat', *South Asia*, special issue, 17, 1994.

Devji, Faisel Fatehali, 'Gender and the Politics of Space: The Movement for Women's Reform in Muslim India, 1857-1900', *South Asia*, 14, 1, 1991.

Dittmer, Kerrin, 'The Hindi-Urdu Controversy and the Constituent Assembly', *Journal of Politics*, 6, 1972.

Facts against Myths (Bombay: Vikas Adhyayan Kendra), August 1993.

Faruqi, Ziya-ul-Hasan, 'The Tablighi Jamaat', S.T. Lokhandwala (ed.), *India and Contemporary Islam* (Simla, 1971).

Franda, Marcus F., 'The Crescent School of Old Delhi', American Field Staff Reports, vol. 3, 1977-78.

——, 'Militant Hindu Opposition to Family Planning in India', American Universities Field Staff Report, South Asia Series, 15, 1981-2.

Freitag, Sandria B., 'The Roots of Muslim Separatism in South Asia: Personal Practice and Public Structures in Kanpur and Bombay', in Edmund Burke III and Ira M. Lapidus (eds), *Islam, Politics and Social Movements* (Berkeley, CA, 1988).

Friedmann, Y., 'The Attitude of the Jamiyyat-i Ulama-i Hind to the Indian National Movement and the Establishment of Pakistan', *Asian and African Studies*, 7, 1971.

Fyzee, A.A.A., 'The Muslim Minority in India', *Quest* (Bombay), 1967.

Gaborieau, Marc, 'Islamic Law, Hindu Law and Caste Customs: A Daughter's Share of Inheritance in the Indian Subcontinent', *Annales Islamologiques*, vol. 27, 1993.

——, 'The Transmission of Islamic Reformist Teachings in Rural South Asia', *Modes de transmission de la culture religieuse en Islam* (Paris, 1993).

Geertz, Clifford, 'Modernization in a Muslim Society: The Indonesian Case' in Robert N. Bellah (ed.), *Religion and Progress in Modern Asia* (New York, 1965).

Gilmartin, David, 'Religious Leadership and the Pakistan Movement', *Modern Asian Studies*, 13, 3, 1979.

Hasan, Mushirul, 'Traditional Rites and Contested Meanings: Sectarian Strife in Colonial Lucknow', *Economic and Political Weekly*, 2 March 1996.

Khan, Mumtaz Ali, 'Mass Conversions of Meenakshipuram: A Sociological Inquiry', G.A. Oddie (ed.), *Religion in South Asia: Religious Conversion and Revival Movements in South Asia in Medieval and Modern Times* (Delhi, 1991).

Khan, Rasheeduddin, 'Muslim Leadership and Electoral Politics in Hyderabad: A Pattern of Minority Articulation', *Economic and Political Weekly*, 10 and 17 April 1971.

——, 'Minority Segments in Indian Polity: Muslim Situation and Plight of Urdu', *Economic and Political Weekly*, 2 September 1978.

Kochanek, S.A., 'Mrs. Gandhi's Pyramid: The New Congress' in H.C. Hart (ed.), *Indira Gandhi's India* (Boulder, CO., 1976).

Krishna, Gopal, 'Electoral Participation and Political Integration', *Economic and Political Weekly*, Annual Number, February 1967.

——, 'Problems of Integration in the Indian Political Community: Muslims and the Political Process' in Dilip Basu and Richard Sisson (eds), *Social and Economic Development in India* (Delhi, 1986).

King, Christopher R., 'Hindu Nationalism in the Nineteenth Century U.P.' in Dhirendra K. Vajpeyi (ed.), *Boeings and Bullock-Carts: Essays in Honour of K. Ishwaran* (Delhi, 1990).

Kishwar, Madhu, 'Codified Hindu Law: Myth and Reality', *Economic and Political Weekly*, 13 August 1994.

Madan, T.N. 'Whither Secularism?', *Modern Asian Studies*, 27, 3, 1993.

——, 'Secularism in its Place', *Journal of Asian Studies*, 46, 4, November 1987.

Manto, Saadat Hasan, 'Not of Blessed Memory', *Annual of Urdu Studies*, 4, 1984.

Marwah, I.S. 'Tabligh Movement among the Meos' in M.S. Rao (ed.), *Social Movements in India* (Delhi, 1979).

Mayer, Peter B., 'Tombs and Dark Houses: Ideology, Intellectuals, and

Proletarians in the Study of Contemporary Indian Islam', *Journal of Asian Studies*, 25, 3, May 1981.

McDonough, Sheila, 'The Spirit of Jamia Millia Islamia as Exemplified in the Writings of Syed Abid Husain' in Robert D. Baird (ed.), *Religion in Modern India* (Delhi, 1981).

McGregor, R.S., 'A Hindu Writer's Views of Social, Political and Language Issues of his Time: Attitude of Harischandra of Banaras (1850-1885)', *Modern Asian Studies*, 25, 1, 1991.

Memon, Muhammad Umar, 'Partition Literature: A Study of Intizar Husain', *Modern Asian Studies*, 14, 3, 1990.

Metcalf, Barbara, 'Nationalist Muslims in British India: The Case of Hakim Ajmal Khan', *Modern Asian Studies*, 19, 1, 1985.

Metcalf, Thomas R., 'Landlords Without Land: The U.P. Zamindars Today', *Pacific Affairs*, Spring/Summer, 1978.

Minault, Gail, 'Sayyid Ahmad Dehlavi and the Delhi Renaissance' in R.E. Frykenberg (ed.), *Delhi Through the Ages: Essays in Urban History, Culture and Society* (Delhi, 1986).

——, 'Hali's Majalis un-Nisa: Purdah and Women Power in Nineteenth Century India' in Milton Israel and N.K. Wagle (eds), *Islamic Society and Culture: Essays in Honour of Professor Aziz Ahmad* (Delhi, 1983).

Mujeeb, Mohammad, 'Social Reform Among Indian Muslims' (Delhi, 1968).

Nandy, Ashis, 'An Anti-Secularist Manifesto', *Seminar*, October 1985.

——, 'The Politics of Secularism and the Recovery of Religious Tolerance', *Alternatives*, April 1988.

——, 'The Political Culture of the Indian State', *Daedalus*, 118, Fall, 1989.

Pandey, Gyanendra, 'The Prose of Otherness' in David Arnold and David Hardiman (eds), *Subaltern Studies VIII: Essays in Honour of Ranajit Guha* (Delhi, 1994).

Qureshi, Zaheer Masood, 'Electoral Strategy of a Minority Pressure: The Muslim Majlis-e-Mushawarat', *Asian Survey*, December 1968.

Reddy, G. Ram, 'Language, Religion and Political Identity – the Case of the Majlis-i Ittehadul-Muslimeen' in David Taylor and Malcolm Yapp (eds), *Political Identity in South Asia* (London, 1979).

——, 'The Politics of Accommodation: Caste, Class and Dominance in Andhra Pradesh' in Francine R. Frankel and M.S.A. Rao (eds), *Dominance and State Power in Modern India: Decline of a Social Order* (Delhi, 1989).

Robinson, Francis, 'Islam and Muslim Society in South Asia', *Contributions to Indian Sociology*, 17, 2, 1983.

——, 'Secularism and the Satanic Verses', *BASAS Bulletin*, no. 18, July 1992.

Rouse, Shahnaz, 'Discourses on Gender in Pakistan: Convergence and Contradiction' in Douglas Allen (ed.), *Religion and Political Conflict in South Asia* (Delhi, 1993).

Roy, Asim, 'The High Politics of India's Partition: The Revisionist Perspective', *Modern Asian Studies*, 24, 2, 1990.

Rudolph, S.H., and L.I. Rudolph, 'Modern Hate', *The New Republic*, 22 March 1993.

Sadowski, Yahya, 'The New Orientalism and the Democracy Debate', *Middle East Report*, July-August 1993.

Saxena, N.C., 'Public Employment and Educational Backwardness Among Muslims in India', *Political Science Review*, April-September 1983.

Schermerhorn, R.A., 'The Locale of Hindu-Muslim Riots', *The Indian Journal of Politics*, January-June 1971.

Serageldin, Ismail, 'Mirrors and Windows: Redefining the Boundaries of the Mind', *American Journal of Islamic Social Sciences*, 2, 1, spring 1994.

Shahabuddin, Syed, and Theodore Wright, Jr. 'India: Muslim Minority Politics and Society', John L. Esposito (ed.), *Islam in Asia: Religion, Politics and Society* (New York, 1987).

Shah, Ghanshyam, 'Communal Riots in Gujarat: Report of a Preliminary Investigation', *Economic and Political Weekly*, Annual Number, 1970.

——, 'Tenth Lok Sabha Elections: BJP's Victory in Gujarat', *Economic and Political Weekly*, 2 December 1991.

——, 'The BJP and Backward Cases in Gujarat', *South Asia Bulletin*, 14, 1, 1994.

Shakir, Moin, 'Congress and the Minority Vote', in Ramashray Roy and Richard Sisson (eds), *Diversity and Dominance in Indian Politics*, vol. 2 (Delhi, 1990).

Shankar, Kirpa, 'Land Transfers in Uttar Pradesh', *Economic and Political Weekly*, 23 July 1988.

Som, Reba, 'Jawaharlal Nehru and the Hindu Code: A Victory of Symbol over Substance?', *Modern Asian Studies*, 28, 1, February 1994.

Spear, Percival, 'The Position of the Muslims, Before and after Partition' in Philip Mason (ed.), *India and Ceylon: Unity and Diversity* (London, 1967).

Sridhar, V., 'Fiction and Fact: The Real Plight of the Minorities', *Frontline*, 12-25 October 1991.

Tambiah, Stanley J., 'Presidential Address: Reflections on Communal Violence in South Asia', *Journal of Asian Studies*, 49, 4, November 1990.

Thapar, Romila, 'Imagined Religious Communities? Asian History and the Modern Search for Hindu Identity', *Modern Asian Studies*, 23, 2 1989.

Troll, C.W., 'Five Letters of Maulana Ilyas' in Troll (ed.), *Islam in India: Studies and Commentaries* (Delhi, 1985).

Vanaik, Achin, 'Reflections on Communalism and Nationalism in India', *New Left Review*, November-December 1992.

Varshney, Ashutosh, 'Battling the Past, Forging a Future? Ayodhya and Beyond' in Philip Oldenburg (ed.), *India Briefing 1993* (Oxford, 1993).

——, 'Contested Meanings: India's National Identity, Hindu Nationalism, and the Politics of Anxiety', *Daedalus*, 122, June 1993.

Whitcombe, Elizabeth, 'Whatever Happened to the Zamindars' in E.J. Hobsbawm (ed.), *Peasants in History: Essays in Honour of Daniel Thorner* (Delhi, 1990).

Willmer, David, 'The Islamic State as *telos*: Mumtaz Shah Nawaz's Narrative of Pakistan and Modernity', *The Indian Economic and Social History Review*, 32, 4, October 1995.

Wright, Theodore P., Jr. 'The Muslim League in South India Since Independence: A Case Study in Minority Group Political Strategies', *American Political Science Review*, September 1966.

——, 'Muslim Legislators in India: Profiles of a Minority Elite', *Journal of Asian Studies*, 23, 4, February 1964.

——, 'National Integration and Modern Judicial Procedure in India: The Dar-us-Salam Case', *Asian Survey*, 6, 12, December 1966.

——, 'Muslims and the 1977 elections: a watershed?', *Asian Survey*, 17, 12, December 1977.

BOOKS IN URDU

Adradi, Asir, *Tarikh Jamiyat al-ulama-i Hind* (Delhi, n.d.).
Mohammad Ali, Choudhry, *Goya Dabistan Khul Gaya* (Lahore, 1956).
Ashraf, K.M., *Hindustani Muslim Siyasat par ek Nazar* (Delhi, 1963).
Basirpuri, Mohammad Akram, *Maududi aur Islam* (Karachi, n.d.).
Congress aur Muslim League ke mutaliq Sharai Faisla (Deoband, n.d.).
Daryabadi, A.M. *Maasireen* (Karachi, n.d.).
——, *Ap Biti* (Lucknow, 1989).
Dar al-ulum Deoband (Deoband, 1994).
Datta, Brahm Narain, *Dal-dal Pat-par* (Lucknow, 1960).
Hamid, Saiyid, *Azmaish ki Ghari* (Delhi, 1993).
——, *Aligarh Tehrik* (Patna, 1989).
Abid Husain, Swaliha, *Mujhe kahna hai kuch apni zaban me: Khwaja Ghulam-us Saiyidain* (Delhi, 1974).
Kashmiri, Shorish, *Boo-i gul Nala-i dil Dud-i Chiragh-i Mehfil* (Lahore, 1972).
——, *Tehrik-i Khatm-i Nabuat* (Lahore, 1980 edn).
——, *Paas-i Diwar-i Zindan* (Lahore, 1971).
Malihabadi, Josh, *Yadon ki Barat* (Delhi, 1992).
Millat-i Islamia aur Jamia Millia Islamia, Delhi (Calcutta, 1941).
Mirza, Jaan Baaz, *Amir-i Shariat* (Lahore, n.d.).
Miyan, Mohammad, *Jamiyat al-ulama-i Hindi: Mazhabi Taleem aur Tarbiat* (Delhi, 1962).
Moradabadi, Masoom, *Shaheed Babri Masjid* (Delhi, 1993).
Mussalmanon ka Shakhsi Qanun, Ulama-i Hind, Muftian-i Karan, Mufasirin wa Muhadisin ka Mutaffiqa Faisla (Delhi, 1985).
Nadwi, Maulana Abul Hasan Ali, *Karawan-i Zindagi* (Lucknow, 1983).
Qureshi, Naseem (ed.), *Aligarh Tehrik: Aghaaz se Anjaam Tak* (Lucknow, 1960).
Rahman, Abdur, *Maimaran-i Pakistan* (Lahore, 1976).
Rahman, Mahmud-ur-, *Jang-i Azadi ke Urdu Shuara* (Islamabad, 1968).
Razi, Maulana, *Mutahida Qaumiyat aur Islam* (Lahore, 1967 edn.).
Rumi, Abdul Quddus, *Maududiat ke ek Aiyane me do Chehre* (Agra, 1979).
——, *Maududiat Benaqab* (Agra, 1984).
Saeed, Ahmad, *Maulana Ashraf Ali Saheb Thanwi aur Tehrik-i Azadi* (Rawalpindi, 1972).
Sherwani, Riazur Rahman, *Mussalmanan-i Hind se Waqt ke Mutalibaat* (Delhi, 1987).
Siddiqi, Asrarul Haq, *Congress Ulama ki Siyasi Karwatain* (Delhi, n.d.).
Sufi, Begum Pasha, *Hamari Zindagi: Khudnawisht Sawana-i Umri* (Karachi, 1973).
Suroor, Ale Ahmad, *Khwab Baqi Hain* (Aligarh, 1991).
Zakariya, Maulana Mohammad, *Fitna-i Maududiat* (Deoband, n.d.).

INDEX